Ninth Edition

Exceptional Lives

Practice, Progress, & Dignity in Today's Schools

Ann Turnbull
University of Kansas, Beach Center on Disability

Rud Turnbull
University of Kansas, Beach Center on Disability

Michael L. Wehmeyer
University of Kansas, Beach Center on Disability

Karrie A. Shogren
University of Kansas, Beach Center on Disability

Director and Publisher: Kevin M. Davis
Content Producer: Janelle Rogers
Executive Development Editor: Linda Bishop
Media Producer: Lauren Carlson
Portfolio Management Assistant: Maria Feliberty
Executive Field Marketing Manager: Krista Clark
Procurement Specialist: Carol Melville
Full Service Project Management: Pearson CSC
Cover Designer: Pearson CSC
Composition: Pearson CSC
Printer/Binder: LSC Communications
Cover Printer: LSC Communications
Text Font: Palatino LT Pro

Cover Photo Credits
Pictured upper left, l. to r. are: Samuel Stuckey, Brianna Stuckey, Dinell Smith, and Marissa Stuckey
Photo credit: Dinell Smith
Pictured upper right: Pablo Garcia
Photo credit: Adie Buchinsky
Pictured lower left: Martae Allen
Photo credit: Christina Perez
Pictured back row: Brant Miller, Nick Valdez; front row: Anna Sabo, Jack Steinberg, Anna Hogsdon, with gratitude to Loyola Marymount University who built Jack's walk-a-bell
Photo credit: Ivey Steinberg

Library of Congress Cataloging-in-Publication Data

Names: Turnbull, Ann P., author.
Title: Exceptional lives : practice, progress, & dignity in today's schools/ Ann Turnbull, University of Kansas, Beach Center on Disability, Rud Turnbull, University of Kansas, Beach Center on Disability Michael L. Wehmeyer, University of Kansas, Beach Center on Disability, Karrie A. Shogren, University of Kansas, Beach Center on Disability.
Description: Ninth Edition. | Hoboken, New Jersey : Pearson, [2020] | Includes bibliographical references and index.
Identifiers: LCCN 2018058024| ISBN 9780134984339 | ISBN 0134984331
Subjects: LCSH: Children with disabilities--Education--United States--Case studies. | Special education--United States--Case studies. | Inclusive education--United States--Case studies.
Classification: LCC LC4031 .E87 2019 | DDC 371.9/0973--dc23
LC record available at https://lccn.loc.gov/2018058024

5 2019

 **Pearson**

ISBN 13: 978-0-13-498433-9
ISBN 10:   0-13-498433-1

Dedications

Ann and Rud Turnbull dedicate this book to their best professor, their son Jay ("J.T.") He was born in 1967 with intellectual disability; by the time he became an adult, he had acquired two more disabilities—autism and serious emotional behavior. Yet, when he died in 2009, he had attained a quality of life and a dignity in his community in Lawrence, Kansas, that few educators had ever thought possible. Those five people (named below) who believed Jay could have the life he and we wanted, and who supported him to have it, are the exception to the "few educators"; they are the exceptional people in Jay's life.

- Dick Schiefelbusch, founder, Schiefelbusch Life Span Institute, University of Kansas
- Steve and Carolyn Schroeder, friends and colleagues, University of North Carolina at Chapel Hill and University of Kansas
- Ed Zamarripa, friend and colleague, University of Kansas
- Mary Morningstar, Jay's teacher and, later, colleague, University of Kansas

Michael Wehmeyer dedicates this book to J.T., who taught him to celebrate each day, and also to his family—Kathy, Geoff, and Graham—who make each day worth celebrating.

Karrie Shogren dedicates this book to J.T. and the lessons he taught her about friendship and to all the advocates who strive every day to make the world a more inclusive place for all.

Jane Wegner and Russell Johnston dedicate their chapter to all the individuals with communication challenges from whom we have learned so much.

Heather Grantham dedicates her chapter to the graduate students in deaf education at Washington University in St. Louis. Heather says, "They humble me every day with their passion and commitment to children who are deaf or hard of hearing. Thanks to them, I have the best job in the world."

Sandy Lewis dedicates her chapter to the students with visual impairments and their families who were my best teachers; the lessons you taught have brought authenticity to what I've taught to the university students with whom I have worked for more than a quarter of a century.

Brief Contents

Contents

Special Features

Nondiscriminatory Evaluation Process

Preface

Welcome to *Exceptional Lives: Practice, Progress, & Dignity in Today's Schools*. This is NOT a typical book introducing you to special education. Not at all. Yes, it explains who the students and professionals in special education are; yes, it describes the research-based practices you should use; and yes, it teaches by letting you meet students, teachers, and families who are like those you will meet wherever you teach.

Two Unique Features

But this edition is unique for two reasons among other books introducing you to special education. First, it rests on an ethical principle and, second, it incorporates seven principles that are the foundations for effective teaching and learning.

The Ethical Principle of Dignity

What distinguishes our book from all other similar books is that we believe, and we teach, that providing specially designed, research-based instruction in inclusive classrooms dignifies students with disabilities and those with exceptional talents and gifts.

Dignity has two aspects. First, it is the value inherent in every person, without regard to the nature or extent of the person's disability. It affirms that, though having a disability, the person is not less worthy. Second, dignity is what you confer by how you teach a student with a disability or extraordinary talent.

When you practice as we teach you to practice, you not only respect the student's inherent dignity, you also enlarge it. Think about your work this way: You carry out two functions. You teach—you are in the education enterprise. And, by teaching, you treat your students and their families with dignity.

Seven Principles of Special Education: The Foundations of the Profession

You will read about dignity in each chapter. There are, however, principles that are the foundations of *special education*. They are

- *respect for your students' diversity and their rights to cultural justice,*
- *education that enables students to make progress,*
- *research-based practices,*
- *inclusion,*
- *self-determination,*
- *partnership with families,* and
- *high expectations.*

So, there are two unique features of this edition. They are the ethical principle of dignity and the seven foundational principles of special education. There's more.

New Features—Ensuring Progress in School

It is timely that this edition aligns with a recent Supreme Court (2017) decision that says special educators must offer their students an education that enables them to make progress in school. When the Court interpreted the federal law of special education, it held that each student's right to an appropriate education is more than a right to an individualized education, preferably in the general curriculum (the curriculum for typically developing students). The Court interpreted "appropriate" education to mean an education that enables your students to make progress in school, year after year. Their education must be appropriately ambitious for them and offer them challenging objectives.

To honor this decision, we have made big changes to this text. They include:

- **A NEW Focus on Educational Progress**. In Chapter 1, we introduce you to Endrew, the young man whose right to an education that ensures his "progress" is the standard for all students receiving special education. Read about the Supreme Court decision and then, in Chapter 4, how that decision affects special education teaching and learning in new and exciting ways.

- **A NEW Chapter on Progress**. In Chapter 4, we describe the procedures for evaluating, offering an appropriate education to, including in the general curriculum, and monitoring student progress in the general curriculum. We describe how those procedures sometimes are the same as but sometimes differ from the procedures educators followed before the Supreme Court decision.

- **A NEW Chapter on School-Wide Supports**. In Chapter 5, we describe powerful school-wide programs that support all teachers in a school to use data-based decision making and teaming, reaching out to every student—not just students with disabilities—to provide the scaffolding required for educational progress and self-determination. This chapter teaches you about the most common and most research-based tiered systems—systems that individualize for all students. There are three of these systems: school-wide positive behavior intervention and supports (SW-PBIS), response to intervention (RTI), and comprehensive, integrated three-tiered systems (Ci3T). Each is useful for implementing school-wide systems and promoting positive academic, social and emotional behavior.

- **A NEW Chapter on Cross-cutting Instructional Approaches**. New Chapter 6 focuses on designing learning environments that promote students' progress. The chapter begins with a discussion on research-based, high-leverage practices that benefit all students—that is, practices that enable inclusion. More than that, this chapter and the ones that follow guide you on how to individualize instruction, services, and assessment to respond to disability-related characteristics. Here, you will learn about the principles of universal design and how to create curriculum that is sufficiently flexible for all students. Alternatively stated, you will learn how to make learning more accessible for all students, reducing the barriers to general education classrooms and curriculum for those with disabilities. Specifically, you will learn about co-teaching arrangements, differentiated instruction, peer mediation, explicit instruction, and embedded instruction. These are the ways and means of universal design. What you learn here will stand you in good stead no matter who your students are. The instructional approaches—all in line with universal design—illustrate the wealth of research-based practices in special education and the promotion of inclusive classrooms.

- **A NEW Chapter on Diversity and Cultural Justice**. New to this edition is in-depth teaching on how you can respond to America's increasingly diverse student populations. Chapter 2 describes the progress of the civil rights movement in education, summarizes research findings about cultural bias related to disability and race, and teaches you about how disability intersects challenges of students from diverse populations. Here, you will learn about bias in classifying students into special education. You will learn how bias and misclassification relates—almost always negatively—to inclusion, bullying, restraint and seclusion, suspension and expulsion, and participation in the juvenile justice system. You will learn how to counteract these negative effects when you read about theories and practices of cultural justice and fairness, especially strategies for teaching restorative practices and being a culturally responsive teacher.

- **NEW Pedagogical Features**. Each chapter now includes two new features to help you apply what you are learning. *Guidelines for Teaching* features provide sequential steps for executing research-based practices, procedures, or processes. *Into Practice Across the Grade Levels* features describe the components of an intervention that are particularly appropriate for some students, even as it describes cross-cutting strategies appropriate for all students. In addition, *Into Practice* features offer multiple, grade-level examples of applied practice.

- **NEW MyLab Education**. One of the most visible changes in the ninth edition, also one of the most significant, is the expansion of the digital learning and assessment resources embedded in the eText and the inclusion of MyLab Education in the text. MyLab Education is an online homework, tutorial, and assessment program designed to work with the text to engage you and improve how you learn and how much you learn. Within MyLab's structured environment, you will find that key concepts are clearly demonstrated through real classroom video footage. More than that, you will have opportunities to practice what you learn, test your understanding, and receive feedback to guide you toward mastery. Designed to bring you more directly into the world of preschool–12 classrooms and to help you see the real and powerful effects of the special education concepts and practices you will read about, the online resources in MyLab Education with the Enhanced eText include:

  ○ **Video Examples**. About 5–7 times per most chapters, an embedded video provides an illustration of a special education principle or concept in action. These video examples most often show students and teachers working in classrooms including teachers and students at CHIME, an inclusive elementary and middle school in Los Angeles. Sometimes, these videos show students or teachers describing their thinking or experiences such as those videos that document the lives of individuals captured by prize-winning filmmaker and cinematographer, Dan Habib.

  ○ **Self-Checks**. In each chapter, self-check quizzes help assess how well you have mastered the content. The self-checks consist of self-grading multiple-choice items that provide not only feedback on whether questions are answered correctly or incorrectly but also rationales for both correct and incorrect answers.

  ○ **Application Exercises**. These exercises give you opportunities to practice applying the content and strategies from the chapters. The questions in these exercises are usually in the form of a constructed response. Once you provide your own answers to the questions, you receive feedback in the form of model answers written by experts.

Three Truths About Special Education—Guidelines for You

It is bold of us to say this, but fortune favors the bold: There are three truths about special education. They are truths because they cannot be disputed successfully. They express what we have learned in our years as teachers and professors, researchers and family members. They also are the guidelines that we hope you will follow when you, your colleagues, and your students and their families undertake the new world—the world of "progress through research-based practice."

People First: Valued Lives and Dignifying Education

Dignity is all about valuing the lives and experiences of people. We value the lives of students with disabilities and see them as individuals first, individuals who laugh and cry, struggle and triumph like everyone else. Some of their struggles are monumental, and some of their triumphs are small; but, if you do your job as we are teaching you to do it, then each student can begin each day with new hope for making progress and achieving goals for greater independence. So can their families. And so can you and your colleagues.

Does this all seem too optimistic, too "frothy" and "light" and "syrupy"? It's not.

As you read earlier in this Preface, the Supreme Court declared that your students have a right to make progress in school. That means you must be appropriately ambitious for them, offer them challenging objectives and have high expectations for them. Your students and their families need to know that you know your business. They will know that if they know you use research-based practices. Those are the practices that also will provide them with hope and confidence for the future. When they have confidence and make progress, you and they will be justified in celebrating their success. So, put aside "frothy" and "light" and "syrupy"—they have no place next to research-based, inclusive practices to promote progress.

Also, bear in mind that your students are likely to make more progress when their families and you have trusting partnerships and collaborate to build on students' strengths, interests, and goals. Earn that trust. The relevance of a student's progress and a family's trust cannot be overstated.

Two features highlight the lives of students with disabilities, their families and their educators.

VIGNETTES.   At or near the beginning of every chapter you will find a vignette—a short but true description of people in special education. For example, Chapter 1 features the student who was the center of the Supreme Court decision we described earlier; and Chapter 4 features a student in a school where inclusion occurs universally. The vignettes convey an important message. Special education is a lively enterprise. It is not an abstract enterprise. It is full of life. It involves real people.

So we begin each chapter by introducing you to a student, family, and teachers. We tell you about them, how they work together, and how their lives and work interact. We thread that story into the chapter so you can see how research-based practices affect and improve the lives of real people.

VIDEOS.   We do more than that. We rely on videos that we commissioned especially for this book. You will come to know students and educators at CHIME, a Los Angeles elementary and middle school. CHIME's classrooms are filled with students of varying abilities and the professional aides and educators who illustrate inclusive teaching practices. Likewise, you will be introduced through videos to wonderful students, families, and educators featured by Dan Habib in award-winning documentaries. You will meet Kelsey, Samuel, Thaysa, and others whose lives have been changed through teaching practices that make a difference.

MyLab Education
Video Example P.1

MyLab Education
Video Example P.2

Inclusive Practices: Equal Educational Opportunities for All

Special education is not separate from general education. No, indeed. It is part of general education. Approximately two thirds of students with disabilities spend 80% of their time in general education classes with the benefit of supplementary aides and services. So, whether you will be a general or a special education teacher, you will need to know about:

- The law governing special education—its requirement that your students' education must give them the opportunity to make progress.
- The differences among your students—differences that require you to use culturally appropriate responsiveness.
- Equal opportunity—the right to equality and equity in education, the chance to have the kind of opportunities that people without disabilities have, both in school and then after they leave school.
- Full inclusion—the right to participate fully in schools and communities, the right to be included, and the right not to be segregated.
- School-wide and classroom-based practices that benefit all students and that occur in typical, ordinary schools and settings.

A revised chapter about procedures to ensure progress (Chapter 4) and new chapters on school-wide systems of supports and cross-cutting instructional strategies (Chapters 5 and 6) teach you how to plan for and practice inclusion for all students. You will learn how to carry out this planning and practice in partnership with families (Chapter 3). Each chapter thereafter then identifies a specific disability or disabilities—the "categorical" chapters. Each describes the disability's characteristics and causes, the specific and appropriate assessments and procedures to qualify students for specially designed instruction, and the individualized supports and services the students should receive. Each offers detailed, state-of-the-art, research-based strategies to illustrate how to educate students with varying abilities and students who are gifted and talented. Each has two special kinds of pedagogical features: *Nondiscriminatory Evaluation Process* and *Inclusion Tips*.

Nondiscriminatory Evaluation Process

Discrepancy Model

To determine the presence of a learning disability, use the following process.

Observation	**Teacher and parents observe:** Student appears frustrated with academic tasks and may have stopped trying.
Screening	**Assessment measures:** **Classroom work products:** Work is inconsistent or generally poor. Teacher feels student is capable of doing better. **Group intelligence tests:** Usually the tests indicate average or above-average intelligence. However, tests may not reveal true ability because of reading requirements. **Vision and hearing screening:** Results do not explain academic difficulties.
Prereferral	**Teacher implements suggestions from school-based team:** The student still experiences frustration and/or academic difficulty despite interventions. Ineffective instruction is eliminated as the cause for academic difficulty.
Referral	**Multidisciplinary team submits referral.**
Nondiscriminatory evaluation procedures and standards	**Assessment measures:** **Individualized intelligence test:** Student has average or above-average intelligence, so intellectual disability is ruled out. Student may also have peaks and valleys in subtests. The multidisciplinary team makes sure the test is culturally fair. **Individualized achievement test:** A significant discrepancy (difference) exists between what the student is capable of learning (as measured by the intelligence test) and what the student has actually learned (as measured by the achievement test). The difference exists in one or more of the following areas: listening, thinking, reading, written language, mathematics. The team makes sure the test is culturally fair. **Curriculum-based assessment:** The student is experiencing difficulty in one or more areas of the curriculum used by the local school district. **Behavior rating scale:** The student's learning problems cannot be explained by the presence of emotional or behavioral problems. **Anecdotal records:** The student's academic problems are not of short duration but have been apparent throughout time in school. **Direct observation:** The student is experiencing difficulty and/or frustration in the classroom. **Ecological assessment:** The student's environment does not cause the learning difficulty. **Portfolio assessment:** The student's work is inconsistent and/or poor in specific subjects.
Determination	The nondiscriminatory multidisciplinary evaluation team determines that the student has a learning disability and needs special education and related services.

Inclusion Tips for Students with ADHD

	Behavior	Social Interactions	Educational Performance	Classroom Attitudes
You Might See	The student is inattentive, withdrawn, forgetful, a daydreamer, and/or lethargic.	The student is constantly late in arriving at school and rarely turns in an assignment when it is due; the student has little conception for time.	The student's work is incomplete and full of errors.	The student's motivation is lacking. The student often lays head on the desk and falls asleep after lunch.
What You Might Be Tempted to Do	Overlook the student.	Have the student miss recess in order to catch up on classwork and previous homework.	Assign failing grades to the student.	Send frequent notes to parents about your disappointment in their child's lack of motivation.
Alternate Teacher Response	Provide Tier 2 and 3 interventions with the student to strengthen academic performance and motivation.	Set up a meeting with the student and parents to develop a time management plan; implement the same accommodations at school and home.	Break the student's larger assignment into smaller parts. Ensure the student understands instructions and adjust the length of the assignment to what is reasonable to complete in a specified time period.	Check out whether sleepiness could be tied to medication side effects by completing a rating scale and talking to the student's parents about the results.
Ways to Include Peers in the Process	Model acceptance and appreciation for the student. Then peers are more likely to do the same.	For projects, pair the student with another student who is conscientious about completing assignments on time.	Seat the student next to other students who are conscientious workers and who provide no distractions.	Be sensitive to any teasing or bullying that might occur from other students about afternoon naps and intervene immediately to curb it.

Educational Progress: Research-Based Approaches Toward Long-Term Outcomes

The title of this new edition clues you to one of its greatly strengthened features. The feature is the research-based practices that ensure your students' *progress*. As we noted above, each categorical chapter (Chapters 7 through 17) describes the most recent research-based practices even as they cite, to a limited degree, the pioneering research. The two pedagogical features in each chapter—*Guidelines for Teaching* and *Into Practice Across the Grade Levels*—teach you how to use research-based strategies toward educational and personal progress.

Guidelines for Teaching

Implementing Peer-mediated Supports

Craft a peer support plan with the educational team:

- Identify opportunities to promote academic, social, and behavioral skills using peer-mediated supports
- Determine what instructional times and activities are appropriate for a peer-mediated support intervention
- Plan what IEP activities and goals can be incorporated into peer-mediated supports for individual students
- Discuss how to recruit peers: volunteer, nomination by teachers, and/or random assignment
- Set goals (jointly with participating students) related to the peer-mediated supports
- Develop data collection methods
- Define roles that teachers, paraprofessionals, family members, and other members of the IEP team can play in facilitating the peer support arrangements
- Plan for ways to create meaningful roles for students with and without exceptionalities in the arrangement (e.g., how can each student serve as the tutor and tutee; what contributions will students with exceptionalities make in peer partner programs?)
- Consider the supports needed by students with exceptionalities to participate
- Consider ways to build in-school and out-of-school relationships and supports in collaboration with families.

Train the educational team:

- Explain the purpose and a rationale for the peer support arrangements
- Describe supporting roles that educators, paraprofessionals, and related service professionals play for peers and students with exceptionalities
- Involve the family in learning about peer support arrangements
- Share peer support plans and explain specific examples for social and academic supports that members of team can facilitate

- Show how to collect data on student progress on outcomes included with the peer support plan
- Plan for regular meetings for problem solving and discussion on progress.

Recruit and train peers:

- Identify peers
- Provide initial training to peers to discuss roles, provide education on various exceptionalities, discuss specific strategies identified in the peer support plan, and adult support that will be available. If paraprofessionals are present in a classroom or during an activity in which a peer support arrangement takes place, include paraprofessionals during the initial meeting as well to clarify their role.
- Provide ongoing support: to update progress, success stories, and concerns. The type and intensity of support and guidance educators provide will depend on the characteristics of the student, the confidence and capabilities of peers, and the context of the class.

Implement the peer-mediated support intervention:

- Create the opportunities for the peer support arrangement to occur during planned activities and instructional times
- Collect data on the impact on students' targeted outcomes
- Share information with members of the team
- Adjust and modify as needed based on data and feedback from students and the team.

SOURCE: Adapted from Biggs, E. E., & Carter, E. W. (2017). Supporting the social lives of students with intellectual disability. In M. L. Wehmeyer & K. A. Shogren (Eds.), *Handbook of research-based practices for educating students with intellectual disability* (pp. 255–273). New York, NY: Routledge; Carter, E. W., Cushing, L. S., Clark, N. M., & Kennedy, C. H. (2005). Effects of peer support interventions on students' access to the general curriculum and social interactions. *Research and Practice for Persons with Severe Disabilities, 30*, 15–25.

Even as you learn those strategies, you will learn how they advance your students' self-determination. Your students will learn to set and pursue their own goals if they have the benefit of instruction in self-determination—knowing how to choose and what to do once they have chosen a course of action. Self-determination dignifies your students.

Together with the research-based practices and inclusion for progress, self-determination ensures that your students will be better able to achieve the nation's four disability outcomes. These are equal opportunity, full participation, independent living, and economic self-sufficiency. Every instructional strategy you use is a means for your students to achieve those outcomes. This edition of *Exceptional Lives* is unique in emphasizing that long-term outcomes, and with them the dignity that your students will have, are the ultimate goals of special education. Take a look at the two features below; you'll see what we mean.

Into Practice Across Grade Levels

Teaching Mindfulness

Physical literacy lesson. Students in the 4th grade learn to breathe like animals. They breathe like dolphins by inhaling as they curve their arms and jump like a dolphin and then exhale when they bring their arms down. They try a crocodile breath by inhaling when they open their arms to mimic a crocodile's jaw and then exhale when they clap their arms together. Students can make up their own breathing patterns for their favorite animals, then write a story about their favorite animals and how they breathe.

Mental literacy lesson. In kindergarten, use different musical instruments to teach students to actively listen. Ask students to mindfully listen to the sound of the instrument for as long as any sound lasts and then to raise their hand at the instant when they no longer can hear the music. As students are able to focus their listening, use longer and longer musical selections to encourage students to extend their listening for a greater period of time.

Emotional literacy lesson. 7th graders practice using their breathing to handle difficult emotions. Have students, one at a time, imagine the following scenarios: being teased by a classmate for a bad grade, having a pop-test in class without having done the assignment, and being reprimanded by the principal and told that they may not attend an overnight field trip because of disruptive behavior. The students are guided to pay attention to where they feel stress in their bodies and to use mindful breathing to release the tension and become relaxed. Then the students imagine the opposite situation. Again, they note carefully their body sensations and the emotions that they experience. The lesson ends when students write in their journal about how emotions feel inside their bodies.

Social literacy lesson. 11th graders with externalizing behavioral disorders meet in a small group with a counselor on a weekly basis. In one session, the counselor invites the students to think of a situation when someone was really nice to them and that made them feel happy. Each student has an opportunity to share that experience with others in the group. They ask each other questions in terms of what emotions they felt; they come up with a number of 1 to 10 in terms of the strength of the emotion. Then the students are encouraged to think of someone whom they think would benefit from having nice things directed to them. They should identify things they could say and do that would bring similar emotions in terms of type and intensity that they had experienced in their own nice interaction. Afterward, all students in the group share what they could do. The counselor encourages the students to try out the nice interaction during the next week.

Global literacy lesson. Students in the 9th grade focus their meditation on elements of the natural world. Ask students to sit in a relaxed position and do breathing for several minutes. Then ask them to imagine the image of a tall pine tree that is strong and towering. With each breath, they should feel the strength and sturdiness of the tree. Then ask them to imagine sitting outside around a fire while feeling the warmth of the fire and the chill of the wind. Finally, they should imagine floating in outer space, enveloped by galaxies. For each of these guided meditations, they should put themselves in nature and experience increasing levels of relaxation.

SOURCE: Adapted from Rechtschaffen, D. (2016). *The mindful education workbook: Lessons for teaching mindfulness to students.* New York, NY: W. W. Norton & Co.

Prologue and Epilogue

This preface is a prologue—words in advance of the main text. It says "hello, here's a preview of your trip with us." A prologue demands an epilogue. It says, "Here's where we have been." Our epilogue features a young woman who struggles with an emotional behavior disorder, a disorder that likely would have kept her from graduating without dedicated educators who did not give up on her. It also features a man with an intellectual disability who now works with faculty at Syracuse University to instruct students such as yourselves. And, it features a young man who grows up before your eyes in this text. Even though he is limited by his various physical disabilities, he has enjoyed the advocacy, support, and inclusive education provided by his family, his educators, and administrators who believed in his worth as a human being and in his abilities to make as much educational progress as his peers.

These vignettes in the Epilogue should confirm what we have been teaching and you have been learning all along: The outcomes of special education are indeed special.

Come with us; be part of a special enterprise that can ensure remarkable results.

Supplementary Materials

This edition of *Exceptional Lives* provides a comprehensive and integrated collection of supplements to assist students and professors in maximizing learning and instruction. The following resources are available for instructors to download from www.pearsonhighered.com/educator. Enter the author, title of the text, or the ISBN number, then select this text, and click on the "Resources" tab. Download the supplement you need. If you require assistance in downloading any resources, contact your Pearson representative.

INSTRUCTOR'S RESOURCE MANUAL The Instructor's Resource Manual includes chapter overviews and outcomes, lists of available PowerPoint® slides, presentation outlines, teaching suggestions for each chapter, and questions for discussion and analysis along with feedback.

POWERPOINT® SLIDES The PowerPoint® slides highlight key concepts and summarize text content. The slides also include questions and problems designed to stimulate discussion, encourage students to elaborate and deepen their understanding of the topics in each chapter, and apply the content of the chapter to both the real world of teaching and their daily lives. The slides are further designed to help instructors structure the content of each chapter to make it as meaningful as possible for students.

TEST BANK The Test Bank provides a comprehensive and flexible assessment package. The Test Bank for this edition has been revised and expanded to make it more applicable to students. To provide complete coverage of the content in each chapter, all multiple-choice and essay items are grouped under the chapters' main headings and are balanced between knowledge/recall items and those that require analysis and application.

Acknowledgments

Ann, Rud, Michael, and Karrie acknowledge their partnerships with the students, families, teachers and other professionals who have contributed to or consented to be featured in this book. Without them, we could not teach effectively what we intend to teach.

We begin by thanking our reviewers. Their wise directives helped guide us on the path we should take for this revision. Thank you Beth Margaret Ackerman, Liberty University; Kagendo Mutua, The University of Alabama; Melinda Pierson, California State University, Fullerton, and Kathleen Puckett, Arizona State University.

We list these partners, beginning with the students themselves, their family members, and the educators who ensure students' progress and dignity. They are:

Chapter 1—Endrew, Joe, and Jennifer

Chapter 2—McKayla Woods, her un-named grandmother, McKayla's teacher Emilio Ortega, and two Oakland United School District staff, David Yusem, director of the Restorative Justice Program, and Cecelia Harrison in Oakland; and Aaron Jabs

Chapter 3—Brianna, Samuel, and Marissa Stuckey and their mother Dinell Smith; Leia Holley and Lesli Girard of Families Together, the Kansas parent information and training center

Chapter 4—Pablo Garcia and his father Sergio and mother Delia; Lori Palen and Tommy

Chapter 5—Kelsey Carroll and her family, and Kelsey's support team at Somersworth High School and the University of New Hampshire, including Jonathan Drake, Kathryn Francouer and JoAnne Molloy

Chapter 6—Jack Steinberg and his parents Ivey and Eric, and Kristina Nowak, Jack's teacher at WISH, his school in Los Angeles and the engineering team at Loyola Marymount University including Anna Hodgson, Brant Miller, Anna Sarno, and Nathan Valdez

Chapter 7—Louise Hastings and her teacher Myra Graham; Susan De La Paz and Cindy Sherman, and the Academy of Orton-Gillingham Practitioners and Educators, especially Peggy Price, Sheila Costello, Christine Elwell, and Melanie Levitt

Chapter 8—Kylie and Joey and their parents Carrie and Paul

Chapter 9—The student whom we anonymize by naming him Anthony, his mother (who wishes not to be named), and his school counselor Amelia Gallagher; Daniel Rechtschaffen, whose videos on DBT were so instructional; Lisa Stinnett; Jim Mazza; Carolyn Webster-Stratton, and Jamila Reid, of Incredible Years® programs; and Dawn Catucci, Monique Johnson, Tara Wright, Michelle Myers, and Victoria Lusk, practitioners of DBT in their schools

Chapter 10—Will Sims and his mother Leigh Ann Schwartz; and Kathleen Kyzar, our former colleague at The University of Kansas, now a professor at Texas Christian University

Chapter 11—Rachel, Jawanda, and John Mast, and Rachel's teacher Audra McClelland

Chapter 12—Thasya Lumingkewas, her mother (who wishes not to be named), and her teacher Holly Prud'homme

Chapter 13—Alana Malfy and her mother Kristina and the teachers at Pembroke Academy and advisors from the University of New Hampshire

Chapter 14—Sam Habib, his father Dan Habib, his mother Betsy McNamara, and his brother Isaiah

Chapter 15—Martae Allen, his mother Erica Baculima, and his home tutor, Christina Perez

Chapter 16—Corbin Thornbury, his mother Lottie, and his teacher, Mickey Damelio

Epilogue—Kelsey Carroll, Micah Feldman, and Samuel Habib

We four authors also acknowledge the superb contributions by authors of three chapters. They, too, were indispensable in describing the most recent research and teaching practices, all the while portraying the students, families, and teachers they describe in the most human of terms. Each was so willing to strive for excellence; each attained it. They are:

- Jane Wegner, professor, and Russell Johnston, doctoral candidate, Department of Speech, Language and Hearing and Schiefelbusch Clinic, The University of Kansas, authors of Chapter 8: Students with Speech and Language Disorders.

- Heather Grantham, Associate Professor and Director of Deaf Education Studies, Program in Audiology and Communication Sciences, Washington University of St. Louis School of Medicine and author of Chapter 15: Students with Hearing Impairments.

- Sandra Lewis, Professor and Coordinator of Vision Disabilities, School of Teacher Education, Florida State University and author of Chapter 16: Students with Visual Impairments.

We happily thank Jennifer Kurth, our former colleague and now Associate Professor of Special Education at the University of Kansas, for bringing her research and teaching talents to bear by writing the MyLab Education Study Plan assessment questions and Application Exercises.

We could not have been able to highlight the way our values are lived out, and how state-of-the-art teaching occurs, were it not for the contributions of the administrators and staff at CHIME school, Los Angeles, California. They are:

- Erin Studer, Executive Director of Charter School Programs for the CHIME Institute

- Rose Beemer, Adie Buchinsky, and Laura Etting, outstanding classroom teachers

- Candace Sullivan, outreach coordinator

Two specialists in videography and their colleagues have enabled us to depict what we write about. They brought images to our written words, allowing us to not only tell but also to show about practice, progress, and dignity in special education. They are:

- Jon Theiss, media producer, resident of Grinnell, Iowa

- Dan Habib, film director and cinematographer, Institute on Disability, University of New Hampshire

Every book is as good as the publishers' staff; these are the people behind the words and pictures who collaborated with us and each other. They are:

- Kevin Davis, Director, Teacher Education and the Helping Professions, who insisted on a revision that would feature practice, link it to students' progress, and reflect our concepts of the ethics and foundational principles of special education. He assembled a superb team at Pearson and was consistently reliable, well informed, and full of good judgment about every aspect of this edition. We are fortunate he will be our editor of our book about parent-professional partnerships, *Families, Professionals, and Exceptionality* (headed into its eighth edition in 2019/20).

- Linda Bishop, our Developmental Editor, who taught us how to organize and display our text, edited our first and last drafts of chapters, contributed to the video features of each chapter, partnered with us and our contributing authors and videographers, navigated the arduous paths of securing permissions from various families and individuals, and maintained her optimistic, goal-focused, cheerful and conscientious habits throughout the entire process. We could not have done this book without her, nor, indeed, the first two editions.

- Janelle Rogers, Content Producer and the development team's favorite. Janelle, who oversaw the entire project, managed budgets and schedules and problem solved when needs arose.

- Kathy Smith, Product Manager, was essential in working with Pearson's Rights & Permissions team to account for every required permission and in providing optional content when permission could not be obtained.

- Joanne Boheme, our copyeditor, ensured that we expressed our ideas clearly and were precise in using punctuation marks and citations.

Among those on whom Ann and Rud relied to assist us as we put words on paper, no one has been so loyal and effective as Lois Weldon, the senior administrative associate at the Beach Center on Disability, which Ann and Rud co-founded (1988) and co-directed for 26 years, until retiring at the end of 2014. Ann and Rud are indebted to her for contributing to not just this edition of our book but also to many previous editions.

Michael Wehmeyer particularly acknowledges the assistance of Juliet Hart Barnett, Ph.D., Liz Mendoza, Rebecca Trillo, and Kathy Puckett in gathering ancillary materials. Michael also acknowledges the ongoing support of his wife Kathy and his sons Geoff and Graham in all his professional activities as well as those of his colleagues in the University of Kansas' Beach Center on Disability and Department of Special Education.

Karrie A. Shogren particularly thanks her colleagues at the Kansas University Center on Developmental Disabilities, especially Kathryn Burke, Mayumi Hagiwara, and Sheida Raley for their ongoing support and efforts to enable research and practice that not only enhances the quality of life but also the self-determination of people with disabilities and their families. Their work informs much of the content of this book.

Heather Grantham (Chapter 15) acknowledges Erika Baculima for being willing to help others learn about hearing loss through telling her son's story.

Sandy Lewis (Chapter 16) acknowledges Mickey Damelio and the Thornbury family for sharing their stories of success and triumph.

Chapter 1
The Purposes, People, and Law of Special Education

Learning Outcomes

1.1 Describe IDEA's four goals of disability policy and the seven core elements of special education; identify the two largest categories of disabilities.

1.2 Define special education, supplementary aids and services, related services, and IDEA's six principles and two requirements of each principle.

1.3 Identify and summarize the basic rules of five other federal laws and describe the principle of dignity, relating it to the *Endrew F.* case.

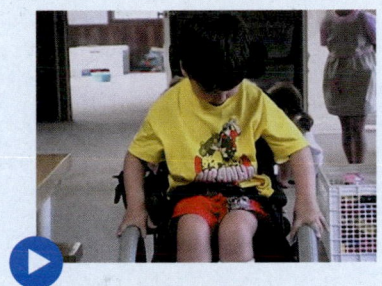

MyLab Education
Video Example 1.1
Meet Samuel. If Samuel were your son, what hopes would you have for his education and adulthood?

Welcome to special education! Welcome to the lives of students with disabilities and the lives of students with remarkable gifts and talents, to their families and educators, to our book, and to the essence of your career in special education.

Goals and Core Elements of Special Education

What exactly is special education? Let's begin with the basics. It is a civil right. A student with a disability who is of school age has the same right to an education as a student who does not have a disability.

Now, let's expand on that basic message. Special education is more than a right. It is specially designed instruction and supports for students with disabilities. Its purpose is to enable them to make progress in school so that they will achieve valued goals and outcomes—goals and outcomes they can attain and enjoy in the same places as students and adults who do not have disabilities. Just what are those goals?

Four Goals of Our Nation's Disability Policy

The federal special education law, **Individuals with Disabilities Education Act (IDEA)**, declares that the nation's goals for students with disabilities are *equal opportunity*, *full participation*, *independent living*, and *economic self-sufficiency* (see Figure 1.1). Here's what these goals mean for each student receiving special education:

- Equal opportunity refers to an equal chance to benefit from and make progress in school.

- Full participation means being in the general curriculum and participating in it.

Figure 1.1 Four National Disability Policy Goals

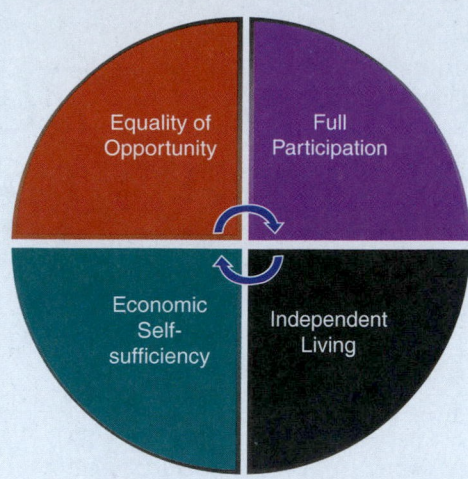

- Independent living refers to having a say about your education and choosing how to live (with whom, where, how).

- Economic self-sufficiency means being able to use your education to get a job, keep it, advance in it, and prove your worth as a productive and contributing person.

A "goal" is "the end toward which effort is directed" (Mish, 1990). So, the nation's policy goals are statements of what you and your colleagues should do, namely, to educate each student in such a way, and with such intensity, that it is likely all of your students will achieve each of these goals, in full or in part, on their own or with support. What you do and how you do it are the core elements of special education. They also are the ultimate lessons of our book.

Seven Core Elements of Special Education

Remember what we said at the very beginning of this chapter: Special education is a civil right. Special education is also, and equally important, a means for teaching so that the right will be realized, not idealized, so that it will be a reality, not a dream, for your students. How can a student expect to participate in that civil right and have equal opportunity, full participation, independent living, and economic self-sufficiency? Seven core elements—elements that you as a teacher will use—work together to meet the goals of special education. They are the following:

- High expectations
- Diversity and cultural justice
- Progress
- Research-based practices
- Inclusion
- Self-determination
- Partnerships with families, based on trust.

The first two elements, high expectations and diversity, relate to hopes and aspirations for all students with disabilities, especially those from unserved or underserved populations. The next five—progress, research-based practices, inclusion, self-determination, and partnerships with families—are the means for achieving the nation's four disability goals; they are the ways, the strategies, you and your colleagues will use. Each element deserves a fuller explanation.

HIGH EXPECTATIONS   How, you might ask, can the goals be achieved if no teacher expects any student to be able to reach them? Low expectations express pessimism. High expectations entail a deep emotional commitment to being the best teacher you can be so your students will be the best they can be in reaching the four goals.

High expectations express hope and confidence that you and your colleagues will do your jobs effectively and that your students and their parents will aspire to become competent, despite a disability, to reach the goals. High expectations should always be your aspiration, a reminder never to give up, never to lose hope, never to abandon your high expectations for low ones. Don't shortchange the parents and students who have high expectations. Those expectations are the foundation on which you can, and should, build. Are you curious about why high expectations matter? If so, read *My Voice: Stel Achieves His Great Expectations*, which details the experiences of Stelios Gragoudas as a student with cerebral palsy in the Boston schools in the 1980s and 1990s and thereafter.

My Voice

Stel Achieves His Great Expectations

Education has always been an important part of my life. My parents always stressed the importance of having the best education you possibly could obtain. It wasn't only learning that excited me; it was also being with other students, playing kickball, and making friends that enriched my educational experience.

I began my school career at the same time that P.L. 94–142 (better known today as IDEA) was passed. Therefore, educating students with disabilities was a new experience for my school district. The faculty did not know how to include students with disabilities into a program for students without disabilities. My teachers did the best they could by including me in all the instances they thought were appropriate. For the subjects that I needed extra help in, I went to a resource room where I could receive the extra assistance I needed. Thinking back, I liked that system. Even though I was out of my homeroom for a couple of hours a week, I still felt as if that room was my base. It was where all my friends were and where I could do exactly what all the other students were doing.

All that changed when I went to middle school and high school. It was as if my education took a 360-degree turn. When a student moves up to middle school, academics are the focal point of the educational experience. Therefore, my educational team had to answer a very important question: Could I keep up with the academic program that was offered at the middle school? My teachers were not too optimistic. They believed that even though I had fared well in elementary school, middle school was going to be too challenging for me. My parents, however, insisted that I be included in the general curriculum as much as possible. So my IEP called for me to be placed in the general curriculum for some of my subjects and in a resource room for the others.

This program was similar to my elementary school experience, with one great distinction. In middle school, my base was not the place where I felt included. It was the place where I felt excluded. That base was my resource room, where I was excluded from most of the students who

were in my academic classes. This did not allow me to form the kinds of friendships that I did in elementary school. I do not have many fond memories of that period of my educational career.

High school was a similar situation. Even though I had good grades in all of my academic classes, my teachers still recommended that academics should not be the focal point of my education and that I should focus on vocational goals. My parents did not agree with this plan. They always believed that I should be pushed to my limit.

The school agreed with hesitation and opted to place me in a collaborative program within the high school. I would be able to participate in the high school classes, and the collaborative program would provide me with a tutor and other supports that I needed to succeed in high school. As I look back, the program was not all that bad. It provided me with additional services that I needed to succeed in my high school, such as speech therapy and adapted gym.

However, the same thing that had happened in middle school was happening all over again. Instead of feeling like a student at my high school, I felt like a guest. Even though I had my classes with students in the high school, when class was over, they would go in one direction and I would go back to the collaborative program. Even though I was free to eat lunch with them, I chose not to because I felt like an outsider who was only a guest in the high school and I felt at home eating lunch with my fellow classmates in the collaborative program.

I always knew that I wanted to go to college. It was what everyone else in my class was thinking about, so I caught the bug as well. Once again, however, I met opposition from my special education teachers. The teachers from my high school classes were more supportive because they knew the work I had done in their classes and felt that I was ready for college-level academics.

The process of applying to school was very exciting. The experience of going to visit schools, meeting students with

(Continued)

disabilities who were already in college, writing essays, and finding out how colleges supported people with disabilities was extremely informative.

It also provided me with a new idea of what it meant to be independent. To that point, independence to me meant going to the mall by myself or going on a trip with my friend instead of my family. In college, independence meant making sure I had all of the supports that I needed to live independently or talking with professors about accommodations that I needed in class. College gave me two things. It gave me the academic background that I needed to begin the career that I am still in today. Equally important, it gave me the skills I needed to live independently and to direct my own future.

I have earned my Ph.D. and am working in higher education in Massachusetts. Sometimes I think it would be amusing to go back to my high school and show some of my old teachers what I have accomplished since I started postsecondary education, but then I think it would be a better idea to focus my attention on improving special education and education as a whole so that every student with a disability can receive the most appropriate education alongside classmates without disabilities.

—Reprinted with permission from Stelios Gragoudas

DIVERSITY AND CULTURAL JUSTICE When you start teaching, you will learn that your students differ from each other. They will differ in abilities and disabilities and, by reason, race, ethnicity, language, and social and economic status. Those are "cultural" differences. And they are the reasons why you will be involved in one civil rights movement—the disability rights movement—and in yet another, the rights movement based on cultural justice.

Indeed, you will learn in Chapter 2 that IDEA arose out of the discrimination that kept students with disabilities out of school or found them to have disabilities or certain kinds of disabilities when they did not. Don't think for a moment that cultural justice is a matter of the past. It is not. As we make clear in Chapter 2, students from diverse backgrounds continue to be those who experience the most discrimination.

What does all that mean? It means that disability itself is a type of diversity. Many students with disabilities have other characteristics: race, ethnicity, language. Broadly conceived, special education is a civil right because it addresses discrimination based on these characteristics. In your work, you will encounter "double diversity," perhaps triple and quadruple diversity. This pile-up of diversity occurs when disability intersects with other minority traits. That intersectionality means you will be engaged in two multiple civil rights causes—one based on disability and others based on additional traits. It also means you will have to master culturally appropriate methods of teaching.

PROGRESS Students have a right to an appropriate education, one that ensures progress toward the four goals. Why do we emphasize "progress?" We do so because the Supreme Court of the United States said, in 2017, that progress is the essence of an appropriate education. That case involved a young man named Endrew. You will "meet" him soon. His education, and the education of all students receiving special education, must ensure progress. Progress toward what? The Court did not say. But IDEA does: progress toward the four national goals.

RESEARCH-BASED PRACTICES If you want your students to attain the four national goals and to make progress toward them in school, you will need to know and use what works. IDEA is clear about that. It declares that the goals of IDEA "have been impeded by . . . an insufficient focus on applying replicable research on proven methods of teaching and learning for students with disabilities." Today, the words "replicable research" are expressed as "research-based practices."

One of IDEA's messages is that you must make sure that what you do, and when and how and where you do it, is based on the research for how to teach effectively so your students will learn. IDEA gives you another message: You should not rest on what you already know; throughout your career, you should pursue professional development to keep learning about what works.

INCLUSION   One of the big four goals of IDEA is "full participation." It should not surprise you that IDEA takes the position that education will be more effective for all students with disabilities when they have specially designed instruction and support that occur in "the general curriculum in the regular classroom."

We are writing and you are learning about rights. So a word or two about language are in order. Lawyers think about "full participation" in terms of integration. Educators like you will use the word "inclusion" to express the right of integration and the goal of full participation.

Let's step back a bit from that last sentence. In it, we reminded you about what we said at the very beginning of this chapter—special education is a civil right. Special education is also, and equally important, a means for teaching so that the right will be realized, not idealized, and so that it will become a reality, not a dream, for your students. How can a student expect to have equal opportunity, full participation, independent living, and economic self-sufficiency without education in the least restrictive, most integrated settings in academic, extracurricular, and other school activities? The short answer is that the student can't. You will find evidence for that statement in each of the chapters beginning in Part III.

SELF-DETERMINATION   Self-determination is about enabling students with disabilities to make things happen in their lives, to set and go after their future goals. These goals can relate to their education or other domains of their lives. In pursuing their goals, students take three important actions. First, they act volitionally; their goals are based on their own choices and preferences and are self-directed. Second, they can develop and implement plans, with appropriate support, to achieve their goals. Third, they learn that a link exists between their actions and the outcomes. This learning leads them to believe they can use their self-awareness and self-knowledge to make progress toward their goals.

Specific skills, beliefs, and attitudes enable students to become self-determined. These include making choices, making decisions, solving problems, planning, setting goals, choosing how to attain the goals, managing oneself, advocating for oneself, and being aware of and knowing oneself. Self-determination links to all four of IDEA's policy goals because it enables students to make progress toward each of those goals.

FAMILIES AS PARTNERS   Families are the foundation for children and youth. No other entity plays such an important role in a student's life as the family. That's why IDEA declares that one way of making the education of students with disabilities "more effective" is to strengthen parents' roles and responsibilities and to ensure that they have "meaningful opportunities to participate in the education of their children at school and at home." Those "meaningful opportunities" are rights, including the right to participate in many decisions related to a student's education. That participation, that partnership between parents/students and professionals/educators, is based on trust. Yes, trust is key, for parent-professional trust, as you will learn in Chapter 3, is the foundation for progress in education.

MyLab Education
Video Example 1.2
What are your perspectives about the appropriateness of inclusion for students with disabilities, and how do you anticipate that this course will impact your perspectives?

Connecting the Four Goals to the Core Elements

It may seem that the four goals and the core elements are only loosely connected to each other. That simply is not so.

Equal opportunity involves the core elements of progress, research-based practices, inclusion, and self-determination. Each of these elements advances a student's right to equal opportunity in school and in life after school.

Full participation involves the same core elements, especially inclusion.

Independent living also involves the same core elements as equal opportunity, especially self-determination.

Economic self-sufficiency involves all of the core elements, as well, but it anticipates the time when the student will work. The phrase "economic self-sufficiency" expresses the idea that special education should be so effective that all students will make progress in school so they will be able to work or otherwise contribute to their communities and families. The key in that sentence is the word "progress."

Progress toward equal opportunity, full participation, and inclusion is the promise of special education; it forms the core of the right to special education; and it is the expression of high expectations for the students and for you, their teachers.

Real Lives and the Dignity of Your Students

We've put a lot of big ideas before you, and you might well think, "How am I going to learn all that?" You will start by learning about the students and professionals with whom you will work. Then you will learn about the law you will follow. In this entire book, you will continue to meet students, families, and educators from whom you will learn.

As you learn from them, you will also learn something you probably do not expect, and that is that special education is not just about teaching and learning. It is much more than that. It is a profession that recognizes students' dignity and then increases it. Yes, you are in the education business. But you also are in the dignity business. Expect to learn about dignity in the last section of this chapter. And then expect to meet those four goals and seven core elements as you read our entire book.

Who will teach you? We will, but so will the students, families, and teachers whom you will meet. The first of these is Endrew.

Meet Endrew, a Winner in the Supreme Court of the United States

"We Won!"

The year is 2017. Who won what? Endrew won his right to an education. An education that will make all the difference for him and for other students with disabilities. Why does that matter to you? It matters because Endrew's victory profoundly affects what educators like you will do for students with disabilities.

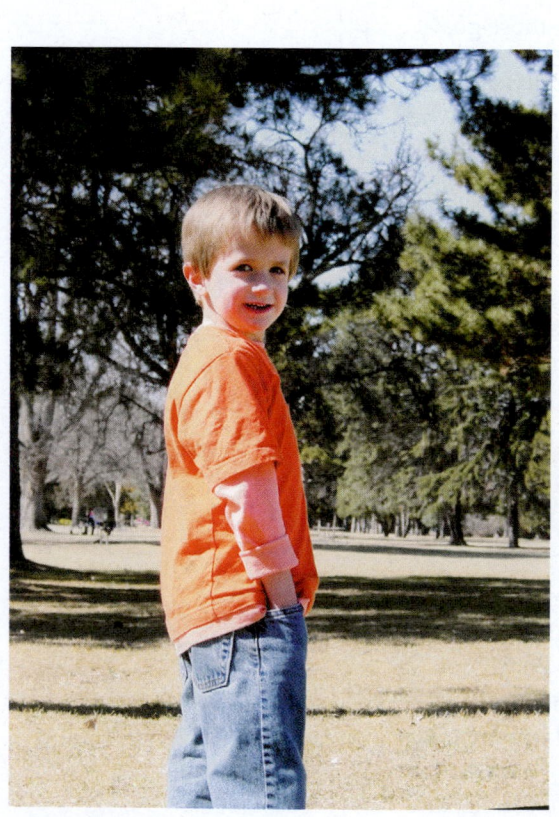

Why, you should ask, does a single student's "win" affect you as an educator? The reason is simple: Ever since 1975, Endrew and all students with disabilities have had a federal right to a free appropriate public education. But for him and many other students with disabilities, his right meant little. Why? It was because many educators had failed to carry out their duty to provide him an appropriate education. Only when educators make a difference to their students is the federal right worthwhile.

So, only when the U.S. Supreme Court interpreted Endrew's right to mean that educators must ensure that he makes progress in school did Endrew's right become real. That's when his parents and lawyer, Jack Robinson, could shout, "We won!"

There was never any question about whether Endrew had a federal right to a free appropriate public education. Never. When he was only 2 years old, he was diagnosed as having autism. Later, he was also diagnosed as having attention-deficit hyperactivity disorder (ADHD). The legal result of both of those conditions is that Endrew had a right under federal law to a free appropriate public education—commonly called FAPE.

But actually having the right and ensuring that it will make a difference in his life was, and still is, much different than having the right as a matter of law. There is a difference between law on the books and law on the streets— between law as written and law as carried out. This chapter is about the role of law in Endrew's life and thereby in the lives of all students with disabilities.

Endrew entered an early intervention program when he was 2 years old, in 2001. He stayed there for 3 years, having rights under federal law to an individualized education program. When he was 6, he entered a kindergarten program and, later, he continued in public school for his 1st- through 4th-grade years. By the time he finished his 4th-grade year, in spring 2010, Endrew's parents

Endrew at age 6.

concluded that his school district had consistently failed to provide him an appropriate education. From fall 2001 through late spring 2010, his academics, speech, and behaviors had changed imperceptibly.

To obtain a meaningful education, Endrew's parents withdrew him from the neighborhood public school and enrolled him in a private school, named Firefly, in Denver, Colorado. He entered the 5th grade in his private school in July 2010 and will remain there until he is 21 years old, when he will "age out" of his rights to a free appropriate public education (FAPE). He has made significant progress there—progress that did not occur throughout his years in public school.

Shortly after enrolling Endrew at Firefly, Endrew's parents exercised their rights against the public school under the federal special education law. They did so by seeking to be reimbursed for the tuition they were paying to the private school. They lost at the first hearing of their case, a hearing before an "administrative judge" in 2012. They lost again when they took their case to a federal trial court in 2014. They appealed and lost again when a federal court of appeal held that a school complies with IDEA if it offers an education that is "merely more than a *de minimis*" education.

Then Endrew's parents took the last step available to them. They appealed to the Supreme Court in a case titled *Endrew F.* They won. So much for *de minimis*, said the Court. Endrew has a right to more than that. How much more? Let's answer that after learning what the lower courts thought he had—only a right to some education, "merely more than *de minimis*."

The term *de minimis* is Latin. It means too trivial or minor to merit consideration; lacking in significance or importance; so minor as to merit disregard. For Endrew himself, a standard of *de minimis* meant that his education was simply so trivial or minor that it consisted of barely any education at all. In his parents' judgment, his education had "stalled."

The Supreme Court agreed. It was clear about its view of the *de minimis* standard: "The IDEA demands more (than a *de minimis* benefit). It requires an educational program reasonably calculated to enable a student to make progress appropriate in light of the student's circumstances."

When the Supreme Court in *Endrew F.* agreed with them that Endrew had a right that ensured his progress, they not only won their case but also changed your role as an educator. This book is about students like Endrew who have a disability, educators such as yourselves, the federal special education law, the meaning of the right to a free appropriate public education, and the Court's essential message that Endrew and all students in special education have a right to an education that ensures progress and thus to an education that signifies they have dignity that no one, especially you as their teacher, can or should try to deny.

Endrew in 4th grade

The name of the case is *Endrew F. v. Douglas County School District RE-1.* We italicize the name of the case and refer to it as "*Endrew F.*" When we write about the student—the Endrew you are meeting now—we do not italicize, and we do not use the initial of his last name.

Students and Professionals

It's time for you to hold on to IDEA's four goals and seven core elements and put alongside of them what you now will learn about the students and professionals in special education.

The Students

IDEA has separate provisions for students. Some provisions relate to their age. Some relate to their different types of disabilities.

THE STUDENTS AND THEIR EDUCATION ACCORDING TO THEIR AGES   You have met only one student in special education—Endrew. There are thousands upon thousands more students who, like him, have rights under IDEA, the fundamental one being a free appropriate public education that ensures they make progress toward the four national goals.

The phrase "free appropriate public education" (FAPE) contains a lot of hidden meaning. One hidden meaning relates to the students and their ages. IDEA recognizes that, for the purposes of special education, there is a significant difference between very young children and youth/young adults. That is why IDEA has separate provisions for students' education according to age. It is best to understand the "separate provisions" by learning about IDEA's four parts.

Part A declares our national policy regarding the education of students with disabilities. Part A declares the four major goals and states what has impeded special education and what can make it more effective in advancing toward the four goals. Part D describes how the federal government will support state and local education agencies to carry out IDEA. Parts B and C describe the ages and rights of the students eligible for IDEA services.

Part B benefits students of ages 3 through 21. For many years, IDEA granted the right to an education to only those students of ages 6 through 21. Over time, however, Congress expanded Part B to also educate children who are between the ages of 3 and 6.

Later, Congress added new provisions, now in Part C, that authorize early intervention services for infants and toddlers from birth to 3 who have a developmental delay or who are at risk for a developmental delay, ages zero through 2. Endrew, the "We Won!" student, entered a Part C program when he was 2 years old; he then entered a Part B program when he was 3 years old. He was in the Part B program when his parents began their long struggle to secure his right to a meaningful—not a *de minimis*—education.

Why should the federal government assist states to educate infants and toddlers who have not yet reached school age (typically, 5 years of age for kindergarten)? It is because early intervention and preschool help prevent later delays and disabilities in the student's development. Does the same reason apply to education for older students? Yes, it definitely does. So, IDEA reflects our nation's concerns with prevention, intervention, and education for children and youth from birth through 21.

In the most current report, 354,081 infants and toddlers, ages birth to 3 (3 percent of the resident population), received early intervention services, and 746,765 preschool students, ages 3 through 5 (6.2 percent), received early childhood services (U.S. Department of Education, 2018). Approximately 6 million students ages 6 through 21 (8.9 percent) received some form of special education. The total number of students, youth, and young adults served by special education was approximately 7 million.

STUDENTS AND THEIR EDUCATION ACCORDING TO DISABILITY CATEGORIES

You now have information about the students' ages and how many students there are. Perhaps you are curious about their disabilities. You should be. You will learn about these students, chapter by chapter, beginning with Chapter 7 and ending with chapter 16. In Chapter 17, you will learn about students with extraordinary gifts and talents. Recall that Endrew has been classified as having autism and ADHD (Chapters 12 and 10, respectively). Figure 1.2 depicts the percentages of students served under each category (U.S. Department of Education, 2017). You should pay particular attention to some aspects of these data.

Not every student who needs supports to learn fits into one or more of the categories. Some students may need simple, basic accommodations, such as a specially assigned seat in class so they will be able to be closer to their teacher and pay better attention. Others will need specially designed instruction and supports to enable them to access and progress in the general education curriculum. So, IDEA adds one other qualifier to the definition: The student's disability must create a need for special education and related services. The law adopts a "functional" definition of disability. The functional approach takes into account how the students function in school. In doing so, it addresses the unique learning needs of students, considering their disability, and what you, a teacher, must do to educate them. Over half of all students with disabilities are classified into two disability categories: specific learning disabilities (35 percent) and speech or language impairments (20 percent).

Figure 1.2 Percentage Distribution of Students Ages 3–21 Served Under the Individuals with Disabilities Education Act (IDEA), Part B, by Disability Type: School Year 2015–16

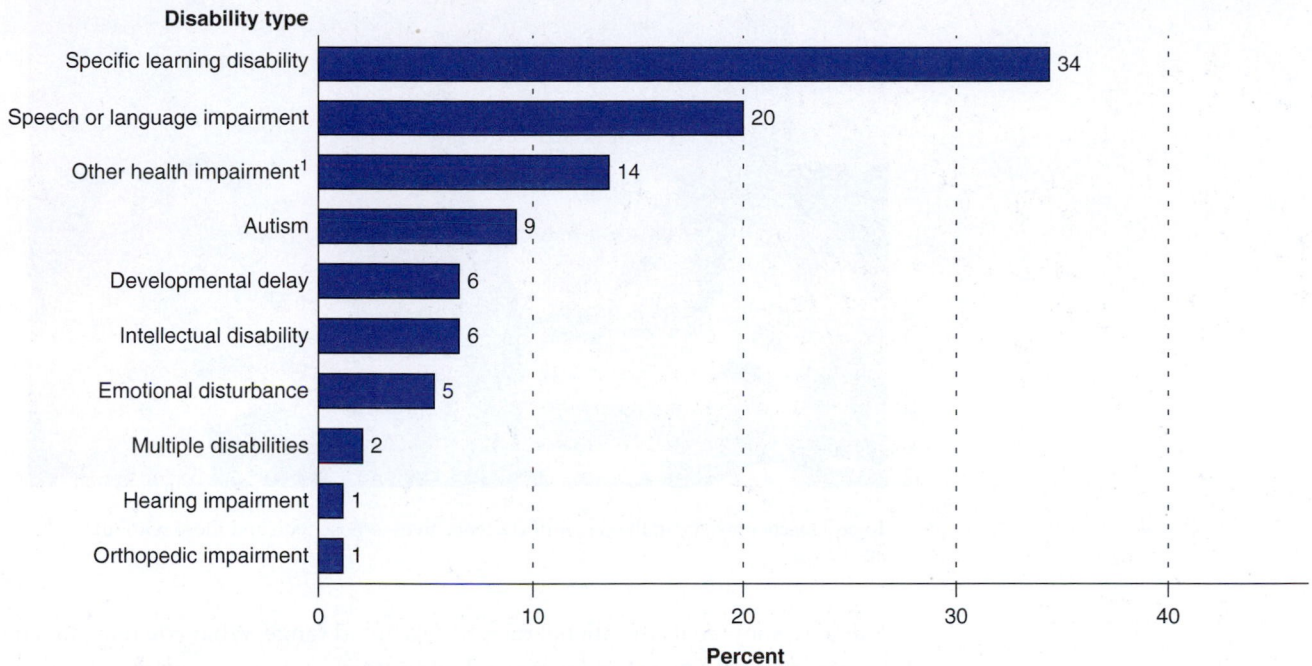

[1]Other health impairments include having limited strength, vitality, or alertness due to chronic or acute health problems such as a heart condition, tuberculosis, rheumatic fever, nephritis, asthma, sickle cell anemia, hemophilia, epilepsy, lead poisoning, leukemia, or diabetes.

NOTE: Deaf-blindness, traumatic brain injury, and visual impairment are not shown because they each account for less than 0.5 percent of students served under IDEA. Due to categories not shown, detail does not sum to 100 percent. Although rounded numbers are displayed, the figures are based on unrounded estimates.

SOURCE: U.S. Department of Education. (2017). *39th Annual Report to Congress on the Implementation of the Individuals with Disabilities Education Act.* Retrieved from: https://www2.ed.gov/about/reports/annual/osep/2017/parts-b-c/39th-arc-for-idea.pdf/. See *Digest of Education Statistics 2017,* table 204.30.

GIFTED STUDENTS   The federal special education law, IDEA, applies only to those students with disabilities whom we have described above. What about gifted and talented students? Aren't they also "exceptional?" Yes, they are indeed. But a separate federal law, the **Jacob K. Javits Gifted and Talented Students Education Act**, provides federal support for gifted and talented students, including a focus on identifying and serving students who over time have been underrepresented in gifted and talented education. The underrepresented group includes students who are diverse in terms of disability and race/ethnicity, as well as those learning English. Gifted education is governed by state law. The National Center for Education Statistics reports that 6.4 percent of public school students are participating in gifted education programs—a total of 3.2 million students (Snyder, de Brey, & Dillow, 2016). Female students slightly outnumber male students.

Professionals

Now that you know about the students, what about the educators? The teachers include general and special educators. They have earned the right to teach by satisfying state "teacher certification" standards.

In addition, some students receive direct support from paraprofessionals. Paraprofessionals usually do not have teaching certificates. But that does not mean they are insignificant. They assist teachers, usually by working directly and more intensively with one or more students. They thereby enable the teachers to use their abilities and knowledge more effectively. Paraprofessionals serve under teachers' direction and supervision. They may help a student with academic skills; more likely, they assist the student in self-help (for example, cleanliness and behavior). Approximately the same number of special education teachers and paraprofessionals serve students with disabilities throughout the United States.

Zurijeta/Shutterstock

To be a teacher is to be in the center of students' lives—those with and those without disabilities.

You Tube

▶

MyLab Education
Video Example 1.3
In the video titled "Teach Special Education," consider points made about the profession of special education that particularly resonate with you.
http://www.youtube.com/watch?v=2XsaK3pWyII

You now know that educational roles have a broad range. What you may not know is how rewarding it can be to educate students with exceptional needs.

The most recent data indicate that 339,833 special education teachers were employed to teach students ages 6 through 21 (U.S. Department of Education, 2018). If you are considering a career in special education, your job prospects are good. To understand your opportunities completely, you should know that a study of supply and demand for 62 education fields identified 14 as having a considerable shortage, 9 of which were in areas related to special education (American Association for Employment in Education, 2008). The four areas with the most critical shortages were teachers trained to support students with emotional or behavioral disorders, visual impairments, and severe disabilities, as well as those who specialize in early childhood. The regions of the country with the most severe shortages were the Northwest and the Southeast. It is encouraging that the number of new teachers hired in public schools is projected to increase by 28 percent from 2010 to 2021 (Hussar & Bailey, 2013). This 28 percent increase refers to general and special education teachers; separate data were not provided for special education teachers alone.

MyLab Education Self-Check 1.1

MyLab Education Application Exercise 1.1: Is Molly Eligible for Special Education Services?

The Law of Special Education: Individuals with Disabilities Education Act (IDEA)

We have already emphasized that special education is a right. It's your duty as an educator to make that right a "real right"—the kind of right Endrew did not have until his parents sued to enforce it. The question you may ask is this: Why is it a right? The answer lies in a shameful part of our nation's recent history. During the early and middle decades of the 20th century, schools generally discriminated against students

E.D. Torial/Alamy Stock Photo

IDEA's purpose is to ensure that every student with a disability, such as the young boy here, benefits from an education, no matter what the student's age or type of disability.

with disabilities in two ways. First, they totally excluded some students from school or did not provide an appropriate education when they did allow these students to attend school. Second, they often classified students as having a disability when in fact the students did not, or they classified them as having a particular type of disability when, in fact, they did not.

In Chapter 2, you will learn more about the history of discrimination, which students experienced it more than others, and how discrimination in special education eventually met the powerful counterforce of the federal courts and Congress. Now, however, it's time to learn about the right to education and the law that grants that right, Individuals with Disabilities Education Act (IDEA).

Defining Special Education

We've put a lot of ideas in front of you—the nation's four goals and the seven core elements of our book. We even briefly defined special education and told you that you are in the dignity business. At this point in the chapter, you may well seek some very concrete information, and you may ask: "What exactly is special education?"

The answer lies in the *Individual Disabilities and Education Act (IDEA)*. IDEA defines "special education" as specially designed instruction, at no cost to a student's parents, that meets the student's unique needs in school. Two phrases are key: "specially designed instruction" and "unique needs." Congress said that special education is a service for students rather than a place to which they are sent. Endrew's specially designed instruction supports him to achieve goals related to speech and language, reading, and behavior. Those are his major unique needs, and they are areas in which he has made progress in his private school.

IDEA also provides that special education includes more than "specially designed instruction." It consists of **related services** and **supplementary aids and services**.

RELATED SERVICES Because special education is individualized to meet each student's unique needs, it is often necessary to provide more than specialized instruction. Professionals, in addition to educators, do this by supplementing instruction with what are known as *related services*. These are services that are necessary to assist the student in benefiting from special education. Figure 1.3 identifies and defines related services.

Figure 1.3 Related Services as Required and Defined by IDEA

1. *Audiology:* identifying students with hearing loss; determining the range, nature, and degree of hearing loss; referring for medical or other professional attention; providing habilitative activities; operating programs for treatment and prevention of hearing loss; counseling and guiding students, parents, and teachers regarding hearing loss

2. *Counseling services:* counseling by social workers, psychologists, guidance counselors, or other qualified professionals

3. *Early identification and assessment:* implementing a formal plan for identifying a disability as early as possible in a student's life

4. *Interpreting services:* providing means for communication by and with students who are deaf or hard of hearing, or who are deaf-blind, including by oral transliteration, cued language transliteration, sign language transliteration and interpreting services, and transcription services (CART, C-Print, and TypeWell)

5. *Medical services:* providing services by a licensed physician to determine a student's medically related disability that results in the student's need for special education and related services

6. *Occupational therapy:* improving, developing, or restoring functions impaired or lost through illness, injury, or deprivation; improving independent functioning; and preventing through early intervention initial or further impairment or loss of function

7. *Orientation and mobility services:* assisting a student who is blind or has a visual impairment to attain systematic orientation to and safe movement within school, home, and community environments, including by teaching spatial and environmental concepts, use of cane or service animal, and use of low-vision aids

8. *Parent counseling and training:* assisting parents to understand their student's special needs, providing them with information about student development, and helping them to acquire the necessary skills that will allow them to support the implementation of their student's IEP or IFSP

9. *Physical therapy:* providing services by a physical therapist

10. *Psychological services:* administering and interpreting psychological and educational tests and other assessment procedures; obtaining, integrating, and interpreting information about student behavior and conditions related to learning; planning and managing a program of psychological services, including psychological counseling for students and parents; and assisting in developing positive behavioral intervention strategies

11. *Recreation and therapeutic recreation:* assessing leisure function; operating recreation programs in schools and community agencies, and providing leisure education

12. *Rehabilitative counseling services:* planning for career development, employment preparation, achieving independence, and integration in the workplace and community; offering vocational rehabilitation services

13. *School health services and school nurse services:* enabling a student to receive a free appropriate public education per the student's IEP; includes services provided by a school nurse or other qualified person

14. *Social work services in schools:* preparing a social or developmental history on a student; operating counseling groups and counseling for individuals; working with parents and others on those problems in a student's living situation (home, school, community) that affect the student's adjustment in school; mobilizing school and community resources; and assisting in developing positive behavioral intervention strategies

15. *Speech pathology and speech-language pathology:* identifying students with speech or language impairments; diagnosing specific speech or language impairments; referring for medical or other professional attention; providing speech and language services; and counseling parents, students, and teachers regarding speech and language impairments

16. *Transportation:* providing travel to and from schools and between schools, travel in and around school buildings, and specialized equipment (e.g., special or adapted buses, lifts, and ramps)

SUPPLEMENTARY AIDS AND SERVICES Because both special and general educators provide services to students with disabilities and because they often provide those services in general education settings, IDEA acknowledges that these teachers and related service professionals may need extra support to do their work. Accordingly, it authorizes schools to provide "supplementary aids and services." These are "aids, services, and other supports . . . provided in regular education classes or other education-related settings to enable students with disabilities to be educated with nondisabled students."

Note that "supplementary aids and services" are to be provided in general education classes and in "other" education-related settings (that is, other than classes such as in extracurricular activities) and, importantly, are for the purpose of promoting education of students with and without disabilities together. Why, you may ask, is that "together" important? You'll find the answer later in this chapter. You see, IDEA is not just about supporting students; it is also about supporting educators—all of them, general and special alike.

It is not enough for IDEA simply to identify the eligible students and to specify that they have a right to specialized instruction, related services, and supplementary aids and services. Doing that much is just a start. That is why IDEA also establishes

Figure 1.4 IDEA's Six Principles

- *Zero reject*: a rule against excluding any student.
- *Nondiscriminatory evaluation*: a rule requiring schools to evaluate students fairly to determine if they have a disability and, if so, what kind and how extensive.
- *Appropriate education*: a rule requiring schools to provide individually tailored education for each student based on evaluation and augmented by related services and supplementary aids and services.
- *Least restrictive environment*: a rule requiring schools to educate students with disabilities alongside students without disabilities to the maximum extent appropriate for the students with disabilities.
- *Procedural due process*: a rule providing safeguards for students against schools' actions, including a right to sue schools in court.
- *Parent and student participation*: a rule requiring schools to collaborate with parents and adolescent students in designing and carrying out special education programs.

six principles that govern students' education (Turnbull, Stowe, & Huerta, 2007)—*zero reject, nondiscriminatory evaluation, appropriate education, least restrictive environment, procedural due process,* and *parent and student participation.* Figure 1.4 describes those six principles.

Zero Reject: All Means All

What do you understand about the word "zero"? What do you understand about the word "all"? Those are good questions to ask before you learn about the zero-reject principle, the first of IDEA's six principles.

The zero-reject principle prohibits schools from excluding **any** student with a disability (as defined by IDEA) from a free appropriate public education. Its purpose is to ensure that *all* children and youth (ages 3 through 21), no matter how severe their disabilities, will receive a free appropriate public education—four words captured simply as FAPE. Like Endrew, **every** student with a disability has a right to an IDEA-based education.

Accordingly, the principle applies to the state and all of its school districts and schools, including charter schools and other state-operated programs. Those include schools for students with visual or hearing impairments, psychiatric and other hospitals, and residential institutions for people with various disabilities. As you will learn later, the zero-reject principle also applies to some students in private schools.

EDUCABILITY AND CONTAGIOUS DISEASES To carry out the zero-reject rule, courts have ordered state and local education agencies to provide services to students who traditionally (but unjustly) have been regarded as not able to learn because of the significant extent of their disabilities (educability). Similarly, courts have ordered these agencies to use health precautions (to safeguard educators and other students) so that they may comply with IDEA and provide services to students who have contagious diseases such as tuberculosis or human immunodeficiency virus/acquired immunodeficiency syndrome (HIV/AIDS). The courts say that "all" means "all."

DISCIPLINE To ensure that all students with a disability receive an appropriate education and that the schools are safe places for teaching and learning, IDEA regulates how schools may discipline students who qualify for IDEA's protections. IDEA's protections are especially important for students from racially/ethnically diverse backgrounds, as you will learn in Chapter 2; that is so because schools' discipline related to suspensions and expulsions have been applied to them substantially more often than to other students. The principles of the IDEA discipline amendments are simple, but their details are complex. You can learn about these principles in *Guidelines for Teaching: Implementing IDEA's Discipline Requirements.*

MyLab Education

Video Example 1.4
Before reading about the six principles of IDEA, link to this video. In it, Rud Turnbull, a co-author of this book, talks about "Embracing IDEA." If you make an outline of Rud's major points, you will find that outline aligns very closely with this section of your textbook. https://www. youtube.com/watch?v=QVEt7HX 5tpg&feature=youtu.be

Guidelines for Teaching

Implementing IDEA's Discipline Requirements

In these Guidelines, we state only IDEA's general rules governing student discipline. The rules are complex, and you should confer with your school administrators about the rules and how to implement them.

Bear in mind these fundamental propositions.
- School safety is a major concern for all students and educators.
- School safety sometimes requires educators to discipline special education students.
- When disciplining their special education students, educators may not, as a general rule, discipline them differently than students who do not have disabilities. This is a rule of equal treatment. There are exceptions; the exceptions take into account students' disabilities and their IDEA right to a free appropriate public education. We explain the exceptions immediately below, beginning with "Apply short-term . . . "

Apply short-term discipline for violation of school code of conduct.
- Short-term discipline is for a period of not more than 10 consecutive school days or for 10 days altogether.
- The discipline may consist of in-school suspension, out-of-school suspension, or change of placement.
- During the short-term period of discipline, educators may—but are not required to—provide services to the student.

Apply long-term discipline for other behavior or when there is a pattern of short-term discipline.
- Long-term discipline occurs when the discipline is for more than 10 consecutive school days.
- Long-term discipline also occurs when educators impose short-term discipline that constitutes a pattern of discipline for the same behavior for more than 10 school days altogether. The "pattern" exists because the educators impose short-term discipline, for exactly or substantially the same behavior, for more than 10 school days. In effect, the educators "tack" one short-term discipline to another; they attach one to another. So, long-term discipline occurs when the short-term discipline cumulates into more than 10 days.
- Long-term discipline is not limited to violations of school codes of conduct.
- Discipline becomes long-term on the 11th day of the discipline.

Take action to change the student's behavior.
- Address the behavior by conducting a **functional behavioral assessment** (FBA). The FBA identifies why the student behaved as they did and what interventions and services the student should receive so the behavior is likely not to recur.
- The services are set out in a **behavior intervention plan** (BIP).

Determine if the student's conduct is a manifestation of the student's disability.
- Remember the first rule about discipline: Educators may not discipline a student with a disability in any way or for any reason that is not the same as—equal to—how they discipline a student who does not have a disability. This is the rule of equal treatment. But it has an exception.
- To determine whether they may treat the student with a disability the same as a student who does not have a disability, educators must determine whether the student's behavior is a manifestation of the student's disability. If the student's behavior is a manifestation of disability, the equal treatment rule does not apply; educators should not punish a student because of the student's disability. If the student's behavior is not a manifestation of disability, then the equal treatment rule does apply; educators may punish a student as they may punish a student who does not have a disability because the student's disability basically is irrelevant to the student's behavior.
- To determine manifestation, educators must conduct an FBA and then develop a BIP.
- When developing a BIP, educators must consider using **positive behavior support**.
- A manifestation exists if the student's behavior is caused by the student's disability or by educators' failure to implement the student's IEP.
- If the behavior is a manifestation of disability, educators may place the student into an alternate educational setting, but there, they must continue to educate the student consistent with the student's IEP. This is how students with disabilities are treated differently than students without a disability; they continue to receive their education during the time they are have long-term discipline.
- If the behavior is NOT a manifestation, educators may discipline the student in the same way they would discipline students who do not have disabilities for the same behavior.

Discipline immediately for weapons, drugs, and serious bodily injury.
- Educators may immediately remove a student with a disability from the student's current educational placement and put the student into an alternate educational setting if the student violates the weapons/drugs/injury rules.
- The rules are that no student may bring weapons to school, may not possess any drugs (other than those prescribed for the student), and may not cause serious bodily injury to any person while at school.

Comply with the rules about notice.
- Educators must notify the student's parents about any discipline and about their rights to appeal.

Nondiscriminatory Evaluation

The effect of the zero-reject rule is to guarantee all students with a disability access to an appropriate education—it opens the school doors. That is not enough, however; mere access never is. To ensure an appropriate education, IDEA requires educators to conduct a **nondiscriminatory evaluation** of the student.

TWO PURPOSES   The nondiscriminatory evaluation has two purposes. The first is to determine whether a student has a disability as defined by IDEA. If the student does not have a disability, then the student has no right to receive special education under IDEA or any further evaluation related to special education under IDEA.

If, however, the evaluation reveals that the student has a disability, the evaluation process must then accomplish its second purpose: to define whether the student needs special education and related services. That information is necessary to plan an appropriate education for the student and determine where the student will be educated—the "what," "by whom," and "where" of individualized education. In Endrew's case, the "what" is the specific educational program he receives; the "by whom" is the professionals who educate him; and the "where" is the general and special education setting in which he receives it, whether in the public school that Endrew once attended or in the private school that he now attends.

NONDISCRIMINATORY EVALUATION REQUIREMENTS   Because evaluation has such a significant effect on students and their families, IDEA surrounds the evaluation process with evaluation safeguards. Figure 1.5 highlights IDEA's evaluation safeguards and its additional provisions. Those additional provisions relate to the right of parents to consent or not consent to the evaluation.

Once the evaluation team has determined that a student has a disability and has identified the special education and related services that the student needs, then educators must provide the student with that kind of education and those services, describing them in the student's individualized education program (IEP), as you will learn in the next section. In short, the nondiscriminatory evaluation leads to, and is the very foundation of, the student's appropriate education.

Figure 1.5 Nondiscriminatory Evaluation Safeguards

Assessment Procedures

- They use a variety of assessment tools and strategies to gather relevant functional, developmental, and academic information, including information provided by the student's parent that may enable the team to determine if the student has a disability and the nature of specially designed instruction needed.
- They should include more than one assessment because no single procedure may be used as the sole basis of evaluation.
- They may be requested by a parent, the state education agency, another state agency, or the local education agency (initial evaluations).
- They are selected and administered so as to not be discriminatory on a racial or cultural basis.
- They are administered in the language and form most likely to produce accurate information about the student's current levels of academic, developmental, and functional performance.
- They must be used for the purposes for which the assessments are valid and reliable.
- They are administered by trained and knowledgeable personnel and in conformance with instructions by the producer of the tests or material.

Parental Notice and Consent

- Inform the parents fully and secure their written consent before the initial evaluation and each reevaluation.
- If the parents do not consent to the initial evaluation, the school may use dispute resolution (due process) procedures to secure approval to proceed with the evaluation or reevaluation.
- Obtain parents' consent before any reevaluation unless the school can demonstrate that it has taken reasonable measures to obtain their consent and parents have failed to respond.
- Provide to the parents a full explanation of all due process rights, a description of what the school proposes or refuses to do, a description of each evaluation procedure that was used, a statement of how the parents may obtain a copy of their procedural safeguards and sources that they can contact to obtain assistance in understanding the provisions of the notice, a description of any other options considered, and an explanation of any other factors that influenced the educators' decisions.
- Do not treat the parents' consent for evaluation as their consent for placement into or withdrawal from a special education program; secure separate parental consent for these changes.

IDEA does not specify who the members of the evaluation team must be. It simply says that a local educational agency must ensure that qualified personnel and the student's parents are part of the evaluation team. But because one of the members of the team that develops the student's IEP must be a person qualified to interpret the evaluation results, usually at least one member of the evaluation team will be a member of the IEP team. To the greatest extent possible, it is helpful to have overlap between members of the evaluation team and members of the IEP team. Regardless of the precise team membership, however, the result is the same: The evaluation leads to IEP decisions about program (appropriate education) and placement (least restrictive environment).

Appropriate Education

IDEA defines "appropriate education" in two different but mutually compatible ways. First, IDEA defines "appropriate education" according to how educators, a student's parents, and sometimes the student plan what services the student has a right to receive and where the services will be provided. Second, IDEA defines "appropriate education" according to the results the process will achieve; those results are the "standards" the educators must meet.

PROCESS DEFINITION OF APPROPRIATE EDUCATION   Even by enrolling students (zero reject) and evaluating their strengths and needs (nondiscriminatory evaluation), schools still do not ensure that each student's education will be appropriate for that student. That is why IDEA guarantees the right to FAPE—a free "appropriate" public education. Remember that special education consists of specially designed instruction to meet a student's unique needs; it also may consist of related services and supplementary aids and services, depending on the student's needs.

How might a school ensure those rights for each student? IDEA answers the question by requiring professionals to follow a detailed process for deciding what is appropriate for the student. This approach is the process approach. Why, you may ask, does IDEA focus on process? That is a good question.

It is a maxim of law that fair procedures tend to produce fair and acceptable results. IDEA exemplifies that maxim. It does so by specifying exactly who will develop a student's IEP, what they must put into the IEP, the timelines they must meet, the types of meetings they must hold to develop the IEP, and the action they must take to measure a student's progress.

As we have already noted, the key to an appropriate special education is *individualization*, such as tailoring a student's education to build on strengths and meet learning needs. Educators individualize by developing an **individualized education program (IEP)** for each student ages 3 through 21. Similarly, children from birth through age 2 and their families receive an **individualized family services plan (IFSP)**.

Each student's IEP/IFSP is based on the student's evaluation and is planned to improve the student's educational outcomes; that is, it is outcome-oriented.

The IEP is the foundation for the student's appropriate education; it is the assurance that a student will benefit from special education and make progress in school—essentially, that the student will have real access to education that aligns with the four goals of equality of opportunity, full participation, independent living, and economic self-sufficiency.

IEP Team Participants.   You have already learned that the IEP team must include at least one person who can link the evaluation to the student's nondiscriminatory evaluation. But the team must include others as well:

- The student's parents
- At least one general education teacher with expertise related to the student's educational level
- At least one special education teacher

- A representative of the school system who is qualified to provide or supervise special education and is also knowledgeable about the general education curriculum and the availability of school resources
- An individual who can interpret the evaluation results
- At the discretion of the parent or agency, other individuals with expertise regarding the student's educational needs, including related service personnel
- The student, when appropriate, and especially when the student has reached the age of majority, usually 18 (the age is set by state law).

Other people may be included in the IEP meeting. For example, a parent might wish to bring another family member or a friend who knows about the special education process.

Components of the IEP.   IDEA requires the IEP to include eight components, shown in Figure 1.6. To comply with IDEA and ensure that the student will benefit from special education, a student's IEP team *must* include every component in each IEP.

Five Special Factors.   In addition to addressing each of these eight required components, the IEP team must also carefully consider five special factors when developing a student's IEP.

- If the student's behavior impedes learning, including that of other students, the IEP team must consider whether to use positive behavioral interventions and supports or other strategies to address the student's behavior.
- If the student has limited English proficiency, the IEP team must consider language needs in the IEP.
- If the student is blind or visually impaired, the IEP team must provide (not merely consider providing) instruction in braille and the use of braille. The team may determine that such instruction is not appropriate for the student, but only after it evaluates the student's reading and writing skills, needs, and appropriate reading and writing media, including an evaluation of future needs for instruction in braille or the use of braille.
- For every student, the IEP must consider the student's communication needs. If the student is deaf or hard of hearing, the team must consider language and communication needs, opportunities for direct communication with peers and professional personnel in the appropriate language and communication mode, academic level, and full range of needs, including opportunities for direct instruction in language and communication mode.
- Also, for every student, the IEP team must consider the need for assistive technology devices and services.

Timelines.   IDEA requires an IEP to be in effect at the beginning of each school year. Educators and parents may make changes in the IEP either through a team meeting or by developing a written document that amends or changes the current IEP. Also, the team must review and, if appropriate, revise the student's IEP at least once a year.

The purpose of the required IEP review meeting is to determine whether the student is making progress toward achieving annual goals. Accordingly, IDEA requires the IEP team to review the student's IEP and revise it as appropriate to secure that kind of progress. A review may cause a re-evaluation and even a change of placement.

Ages Birth to 3: IFSP Considerations.   As you know, Congress amended IDEA by adding Part C, providing services for infants and toddlers (birth to 3) and their families. In doing so, Congress transported the IEP requirements (for children and youth ages 3 through 21) into Part C and renamed the IEP as the "individualized

Figure 1.6 Required Components of Every IEP

The IEP is a written statement for each student ages three through twenty-one. Whenever it is developed or revised, it must contain the following statements:

1. The student's present levels of academic achievement and functional performance, including
   - How the student's disability affects the student's involvement and progress in the general curriculum (for students ages six through twenty-one)
   - How a preschooler's disability affects the child's participation in appropriate activities (for children ages three through five)
   - A description of the benchmarks or short-term objectives for students who take alternate assessments that are aligned to alternate achievement standards

2. Measurable annual goals, including academic and functional goals, designed to
   - Meet each of the student's needs resulting from the disability in order to enable the student to be involved in and make progress in the general curriculum
   - Meet each of the student's other educational needs that result from the disability

3. How the student's progress toward annual goals will be measured and when periodic reports on the student's progress and meeting annual goals will be provided

4. The special education and related services and supplementary aids and services, based on peer reviewed research, to the extent practicable that will be provided to the student or on the student's behalf and the program modifications or supports for school personnel that will be provided for the student to
   - Advance appropriately toward attaining the annual goals
   - Be involved in and make progress in the general curriculum and participate in extracurricular and other nonacademic activities
   - Be educated and participate in those three types of activities with other students with disabilities and with students who do not have disabilities

5. An explanation of the extent, if any, to which the student will not participate with students who do not have disabilities in the regular classroom and in extracurricular and other nonacademic activities

6. Any individual appropriate accommodations that are necessary to measure the student's academic and functional performance on state- and district-wide assessments; if the IEP team determines that the student will not participate in a regular state- or district-wide assessment or any part of an assessment, an explanation of why the student cannot participate and the particular alternate assessment that the team selects as appropriate for the student

7. The projected date for beginning the special education, related services, supplemental aids and services, and modifications, as well as the anticipated frequency, location, and duration of each

8. Beginning no later than the first IEP that will be in effect after the student turns sixteen, and then updated annually, a transition plan that must include
   - Measurable postsecondary goals based on transition assessments related to training, education, employment, and, where appropriate, independent living skills
   - A statement of transition services, including courses of study, needed to assist the student to reach those postsecondary goals
   - Beginning no later than one year before the student reaches the age of majority under state law (usually age eighteen), a statement that the student has been informed of those rights under IDEA that will transfer to the student from the parents when the student comes of age

family services plan"—the IFSP—to reflect the central role of the family in the lives of young children.

The IFSP describes the services that both the infant (or toddler) and the family will receive. Like the IEP, the IFSP is based on the student's development and needs; it specifies outcomes for the student. Unlike the IEP, however, the IFSP also provides the option for families to identify their resources, priorities, and concerns related to enhancing their student's development. Furthermore, the IFSP must include outcomes and services for the student's family if the family wants to achieve specific outcomes related to the student's development.

SUBSTANTIVE DEFINITION OF APPROPRIATE   It was not until the Supreme Court took one case, and then a second one, that the process definition was expanded to include a substantive definition of appropriate education. A substantive definition tells what students have a right to receive; the definition relates to the content of a student's curriculum. By contrast, the "process" definition tells how a student's IEP team and teachers satisfy the substantive right. As you learn about these cases, imagine that you are the student with a disability; your right to an appropriate education depends on how the Court values you and your right under IDEA.

Case Example: "Benefit"—The Case of Amy Rowley.   The first case, *Board of Education v. Rowley* (1982), involved a student, Amy Rowley, who had significant hearing loss. Her school provided her with a special tutor, hearing aids, and speech therapy, complying, it thought, with IDEA. Her parents, who also were deaf, asked the school to provide her with an interpreter, a related service. The school refused to provide the interpreter and Amy's parents sued. The Court upheld the school's decision; Amy did not have a right to the interpreter. Why?

Amy did not qualify for an interpreter because, as the Court interpreted IDEA, Congress intended the law to provide nothing more than "equal access" to education and that such access must be "sufficient to confer some educational benefit" on Amy and other students covered by IDEA. Because Amy was fully included in the general education curriculum and classroom, was already receiving three different services, was earning passing grades, and was being promoted from grade to grade, she was receiving precisely the "access" that Congress intended. Indeed, she was making progress, as IDEA intended. The Supreme Court determined that she had no right to the interpreter.

Case Example: "Progress" —The Case of Endrew F.   The *Rowley* decision prevailed as the law of appropriate education until, 35 years later, in early 2017, the Court decided *Endrew F.* The facts in that case were substantially different from those in *Rowley*, and the Court's interpretation of IDEA's appropriate education principle was, predictably, different.

As you read earlier in the chapter, Endrew was diagnosed with autism when he was 2 years old. He enrolled in public school for the 1st grade but, with IEPs that were substantially the same during his 1st through 4th grades, his academic and functional progress "essentially stalled."

If, however, you have had the privilege of visiting Endrew at his home and having dinner with his parents, as we have had, you would hear more about Endrew's education. That "more" was scattered throughout our dinner conversation with his parents. We summarize it here, with his parents' approval.

> Endrew's behaviors became so difficult for his teachers to handle. They escalated during his 3rd- and 4th-grade years, so much so that his teachers often called me (his mother) for assistance or to take him home from school. They baby-sat him, treating him as if he were a 2-year old student. It seemed they didn't know what to do for him or lacked the resources to do what he needed. Sometimes they blamed us for his behaviors. They offered the same IEP over and over again, year after year, with only five or so words changed from one IEP to another. They basically had the attitude that "we are the experts," and were interested only in checking the boxes on their IEP form. They were combative when we met with them, laid down the rules, talked down to us, and interrupted us when we offered ideas or made comments.

You already know that Endrew won his case in the Supreme Court. Now, let's learn exactly what he won and why. In *Endrew F.*, Chief Justice Roberts, writing for a unanimous Court (that is, on behalf of all of the Justices on the Court), rejected the lower courts' interpretation of IDEA. Under that interpretation, a school complies with IDEA if it offers an education that is "merely more than a *de minimis*" education.

To meet the "make progress" standard, the Court ruled that a school must abide by IDEA's premise that the "focus on the particular student is at the core of IDEA" and that "the IEP is the centerpiece of the statute's delivery system." Accordingly, "Crafting an appropriate education" is a "fact-intensive exercise" that results in a "plan" focused on "student progress."

In creating the student's IEP, the Court said that the IEP team must give "careful consideration" to the student's "potential for growth" and thereby the student's capacity for progress. "A substantive standard (of appropriate education) not focused on student progress would do little to remedy the pervasive and tragic stagnation that prompted Congress to act" when it created the law in 1975.

If, said the Court, earning passing grades that justify grade-to-grade advancement "is not a reasonable prospect for a student, his IEP need not aim for grade-to-grade advancement. But his educational program must be appropriately ambitious in light of his circumstances, just as advancement from grade to grade is appropriately ambitious for most students in the regular classroom."

The Court then continued to justify its "progress" standard:

> It cannot be the case that (IDEA) typically aims for grade level advancement for students with disabilities who cannot be educated in the regular classroom but is satisfied with barely more than *de minimis* for those who cannot. When all is said and done, a student offered an educational program providing 'merely more than *de minimis*' progress from year to year cannot be said to have been offered an education at all. For students with disabilities, receiving instruction that aims so low would be tantamount to "sitting idly . . . awaiting the time when they were old enough to 'drop out.'"

Next, the Court added that "all" students with disabilities "should have the chance to meet challenging objectives." The Court's "all" applies without regard to where the student receives special instruction and supports. The Court is more concerned with "what" the student receives than with where the student receives services and supports. That is a proper concern. Why?

It is proper because modification of the content of a curriculum typically can occur without regard to where the student receives instruction and supports. As you will learn, IDEA prefers the student to be in the general education curriculum, to be integrated and included. But not all students are integrated and included, as you will learn later in this chapter. Their placement, however, does not make a difference with respect to "challenging objectives." What does matter is that the student—wherever placed—has challenging objectives, and those are possible by modifying the content of the curriculum, especially the curriculum in general education.

In a nutshell, *Endrew F.*

- converts the Rowley standard of "benefit" to "progress" and states that the IEP must be reasonably calculated to ensure progress
- requires the IEP team to take into account the student's circumstances, including, importantly, the "potential for growth"
- requires an "appropriately ambitious" program for students who, unlike Amy Rowley, are not progressing from grade to grade
- declares that every student should have the chance to meet "challenging objectives"
- considers the student's "circumstances," including those related to his "educational needs" in school, including his needs for related services.

The challenge for you, as a general or special educator, is to have the competence, including that based on research of how students learn and how teachers should educate them, and the attitude, to meet the Court's *Endrew F.* standard. If you pay close attention to each of the following chapters in this book, you will have the necessary competence.

What about Endrew? What's his future, now that the Court has defined his right to an appropriate education? The answer lies in what his parents have told us, for they speak for him and themselves.

One of their goals, and his, is "to be happy, before anything else." That goal reflects the fact that Endrew obviously was not happy in the public school programs, but he could be. Indeed, the Supreme Court quoted his teachers as saying that he has a "sweet

MyLab Education
Video Example 1.5
Keith Jones, an advocate for Special Education, worked hard to be "educated" in public schools. How might the *Endrew* decision benefit students like Keith attending school now?

disposition" and "show(ed) concern" for friends. Yet his teachers said he still "exhibited multiple behaviors that inhibited his ability to access learning in the classroom." In particular, he would, in the Court's words, "scream in class, climb over furniture and other students, and occasionally run away from school."

For Endrew, progress, both before and after the Court's decision, has consisted of extinguishing those behaviors and restoring his sweet disposition. Those two goals have been largely accomplished. That is one reason why Endrew has continued to learn to read and speak clearly, but only one reason. Another is that he has had intensive instruction in reading and speaking. All of this amounts to one result: Endrew, in his parents' words, will be a "productive member of society."

Endrew at age 16

They acknowledge he will need support, probably for a lifetime. But they foresee various possibilities. He might choose one or more of several options about the work he will do. He might want to work in a restaurant or in an office filing documents and doing other clerical work, or he could own his own company, supporting other businesses by shredding documents, servicing vending machines, or providing janitorial services. He might choose to work as an assistant to a veterinarian, for there are horses on ranches near his home; or to work as a paraprofessional in a student-care center or in a school.

Whatever he does, his parents are keen for him to be happy, and that means he should choose what makes him happy. For them, having the "fantastic" support of family and friends during their years of dispute with the public schools was an essential part of the past and is a key to Endrew's future. Yes, specialized instruction and support make a great difference for him, and always will. But support—whether "formal" support from various professionals or "informal" support from family and friends—will always be necessary and available.

Is it realistic to think that Endrew might choose what he wants to do? Might he choose the kind of support he gets, and from whom? Yes. He's already shown he has plenty of self-determination and wants to make his own choices, with support.

The next question is whether the choices that lie ahead are simply too unrealistic. Are they far beyond the "high expectations" that IDEA promotes? No, not at all. The expectations are quite realistic. People with significant disabilities can and do lead productive lives and contribute to society.

Indeed, Endrew's parents have already taken action to make those expectations a reality, having bought a condo suitable for him to live in, by himself or with support, or to use as an office if he operates his own business. As much as any family in America, Endrew's family has taken IDEA's opening paragraph to heart: Endrew has a right, and they sued to enforce it; and his right is the means by which he will be the productive member of society that IDEA expects.

Least Restrictive Environment

Once the schools have enrolled a student (zero-reject principle), fairly evaluated the student (nondiscriminatory evaluation principle), and provided an IEP/IFSP (appropriate education principle), they must contribute one more element to the student's education—namely, education alongside students who do not have disabilities. This is the fourth IDEA principle—the principle of the **least restrictive environment (LRE)**.

Robin Sachs/PhotoEdit, Inc.

IDEA provides that students with disabilities will be in classes, extracurricular activities, and other school events with students who do not have disabilities, like the children in this classroom.

You will hear that phrase when you teach; you also will hear another, with a similar meaning. That phrase is "inclusion." Educators use this term when speaking about the place in which students ages 3 through 21 receive some of their services. They also use the term to refer to the fact that the student will participate with other students in that place. Thus, "inclusion" is about both place and participation. In early intervention (ages birth through 2), however, IDEA prefers services in the student's "natural environment," which can be home or an out-of-home student-care or education center. Without regard to a student's age, "inclusion" refers to place and participation.

A few more comments are in order about the phrase "least restrictive environment." Lawyers have used the word "integration" when talking about students from racially/ethnically diverse backgrounds being educated in the same place as students not from those same backgrounds. "Integration" comes from the civil rights movements, and, as you will learn in Chapter 2, disability rights as a movement emerged from the civil right movements; indeed, disability rights is a civil rights movement of its own. So, you may use "least restrictive environment" (as IDEA does) or "inclusion" or "integration," as many educators and lawyers do, or, for infants and toddlers, "natural environment," as IDEA and many early-childhood educators do. Whatever word or phrase you use, you will be correct if you mean, broadly, IDEA's goal of "full participation."

THE RULE: A PREFERENCE FOR INCLUSION   IDEA prefers that students with disabilities be educated with those who do not have disabilities. It does this by requiring that (1) a school must educate a student with a disability with students who do not have disabilities to the maximum extent appropriate for the student and (2) a school may not remove the student from the regular education environment unless, because of the nature or severity of the student's disability, he or she cannot be educated there successfully (appropriately, in the sense that the student will benefit and make progress), even after the school provides supplementary aids and services for the student.

SETTING ASIDE THE PREFERENCE   The school may set aside this preference of inclusion only if the student cannot benefit from being educated with students who do not have disabilities and only after the school has provided the student with supplementary aids and services in general education settings. In that event, the IEP team may place the student in a less typical, more specialized, less inclusive program. Generally, the most typical and inclusive setting is general education, followed by resource rooms, special classes, special schools, homebound services, and hospitals and institutions (also called residential or long-term-care facilities). You will learn more about these different settings in Chapter 4.

ACCESS TO GENERAL EDUCATION CURRICULUM   IDEA defines the general curriculum as not only the academic curriculum but also the extracurricular and other school activities. Accordingly, schools have to ensure that students with disabilities may participate in extracurricular (athletics, special interest groups or clubs) and other nonacademic activities (recess periods, school dances, school field trips). In short, when providing academic, extracurricular, and other nonacademic activities to students who do not have disabilities, schools must include students with disabilities in all those activities to the maximum extent appropriate for each student with a disability.

Figure 1.7 Mix and Match

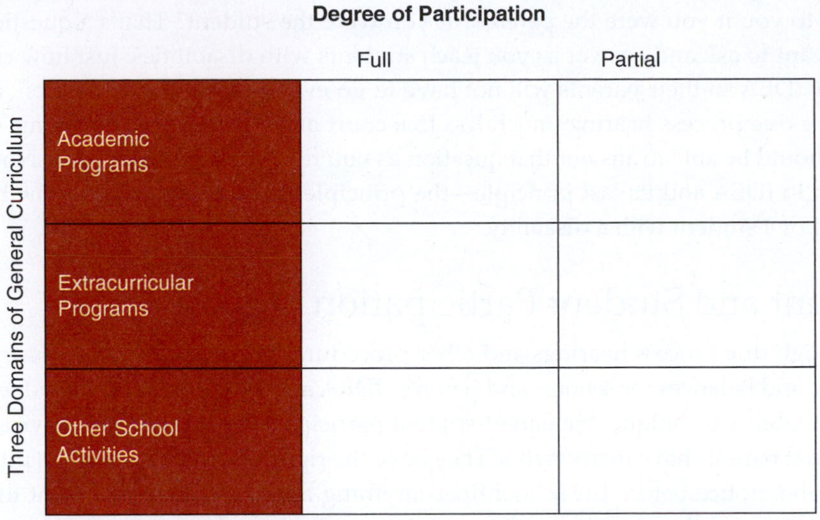

Degree of Participation

	Full	Partial
Academic Programs		
Extracurricular Programs		
Other School Activities		

Three Domains of General Curriculum

SOURCE: Turnbull, H. R., Stowe, M. J., & Huerta, N. E. (2007). *Free appropriate public education: The law and children with disabilities* (7th ed.). Denver, CO: Love Publishing, p. 216. Used with permission.

THE "MIX AND MATCH" RULE   By stating its preference for inclusion, identifying the three components of the general curriculum, and requiring that the student's IEP must specify the extent, if any, to which the student will NOT be with students who do not have disabilities in each of those components, IDEA creates a "mix and match" rule. In a nutshell, IDEA requires the IEP team to specify whether the student will be included full-time or part-time in each of the three components of the general curriculum. Figure 1.7 illustrates the "mix and match" rule.

Procedural Due Process

RULE OF FAIRNESS   Schools do not always carry out IDEA's first four principles: zero reject, nondiscriminatory evaluation, appropriate education, and least restrictive environment. What's a parent to do? That was the question facing the parents of Amy Rowley and Endrew, too. Or what if a school believes that one type of special education is appropriate, but a parent disagrees and believes that the proposed placement will not benefit the student? The answer lies in the **procedural due process** principle, which basically seeks to make schools and parents accountable to each other for carrying out the student's IDEA rights.

PROCEDURES FOR RESOLVING DIFFERENCES   When parents and educators disagree, IDEA provides each with three different ways to resolve their disagreements.

- First, they may meet face-to-face in a **resolution session**. There, they try to hammer out their differences, without any "external" person helping them or ruling in favor of one or the other of them.

- Second, they may resort to **mediation**. Mediation occurs when the parents and school agree to submit their dispute to an independent, disinterested, trained person. That person listens to both the school personnel and parents and tries to find common ground on which they will agree and resolve their dispute. IDEA does not require mediation, and it may not be used to deny or delay the right to a due process hearing (see below). But IDEA strongly encourages mediation.

- Third, if the parties still cannot resolve their disagreements, each has a right to a **due process hearing** (a mini-trial) before an impartial hearing officer. The due process hearing is similar to a regular courtroom trial. At the hearing, the parents and schools are entitled to be represented by lawyers, present evidence, and cross-examine each other's witnesses. If the school or the parent is dissatisfied with the decision of the hearing officer, either may appeal to state or federal courts.

What would you have done if you had been Endrew's parents and had no idea how the Supreme Court would decide your case? Just how much would "appropriate" mean to you if you were the parents? If you were the student? That's a question you will want to ask and answer as you teach students with disabilities: Just how can you satisfy IDEA so their parents will not have to go even to a resolution session, mediation, or due process hearing, much less to a court and especially the Supreme Court? You should be able to answer that question as you read the rest of our book. Now, let's return to IDEA and its last principle—the principle that asks you to imagine being a parent of a student with a disability.

Parent and Student Participation

Although due process hearings and other procedural safeguards provide a system of checks and balances for schools and parents, IDEA also offers another, less adversarial accountability technique: the parent-student participation principle. You have already read that parents have many rights. They have the right to be members of the IEP team, to receive notice before the school does anything about the student's right to a free appropriate public education, and to use three techniques for resolving disputes (due process). In addition, parents have the right to receive notices, provide consent, review their child's records, control who has access to personally identifiable information on their student and family, and serve on advisory committees, as highlighted in *Guidelines for Teaching: Implementing IDEA's Parent Participation Requirements.*

Guidelines for Teaching
Implementing IDEA's Parent Participation Requirements

Give written notice to parents.

- Educators must provide written notice to parents before proposing or refusing to initiate or change the student's identification, evaluation, placement, and/or provision of services.
- The notices must contain
  - The action being proposed or refused
  - The reason for the action
  - A description of the due process safeguards available to parents.

Obtain written parental consent.

- Educators must fully inform the student's parents in the parents' native language or other communication mode unless it is clearly not feasible to do so.
- Parents must be able to understand the proposal and agree or not in writing.
- Parents must understand that their consent is voluntary and that they may revoke it at any time.
- Parents must provide their consent
  - Before an evaluation or re-evaluation of their child
  - Before educators provide special education and related services
  - Before educators disclose personally identifiable information.

Provide parental access to records.

- Parents have the right to inspect and review all educational records about their student and family.
- Parents have the right to request educators to explain the records and to receive a response to their request.
- Parents who believe that the information is inaccurate or violates their privacy or other rights may request educators to amend the information.
- If educators refuse to honor the parents' requests, they must advise the parents of their right to initiate a due process hearing.

Protect student and family personally identifiable information.

- Educators must ensure that procedures are in place to protect the confidentiality of the students' and parents' personally identifiable information.
- Educators must obtain parents' written consent before disclosing personally identifiable information to anyone other than authorized representatives, officials, or employees of agencies participating in the student's education.

Serve on special education advisory committees.

- All local and state special education advisory committees should have parent representatives to ensure that parents' perspectives are considered.

Finally, one year before a student reaches the age of majority (usually age 18), the school must advise him or her that all of the IDEA rights that belonged to parents will transfer to the student when he or she attains the age of majority. The only exception to this transfer-of-rights rule is that the parents' rights will not transfer to the student if the student has been determined, under state law, to be incompetent.

A state court determines whether or not the student is competent. If the court determines that the student is not competent, then the student's rights, even as an adult, transfer to the student's legally appointed guardian, usually one or both parents.

We caution you: Please do not urge parents to seek to be their student's guardian. You may tell them, if they ask, that you are not qualified to give that advice because you are not a lawyer. You may say that you are available to provide facts about the student's abilities. But resist any pressure you might feel from your school administrators to push the parents toward guardianship, as many alternatives are available that enable the student to take on adult roles and responsibilities, with the support of their parents or other people.

Bringing the Six Principles Together

How do the six principles ensure an appropriate education for students with disabilities? Figure 1.8 illustrates and describes the fact that the first four principles—zero reject, nondiscriminatory evaluation, appropriate education, and least restrictive environment—are the *inputs* into a student's education. The other two principles, procedural due process and parent–student participation, are *accountability techniques*, ways to make sure that the other four principles are implemented correctly.

Figure 1.8 Relationship Among IDEA's Six Principles

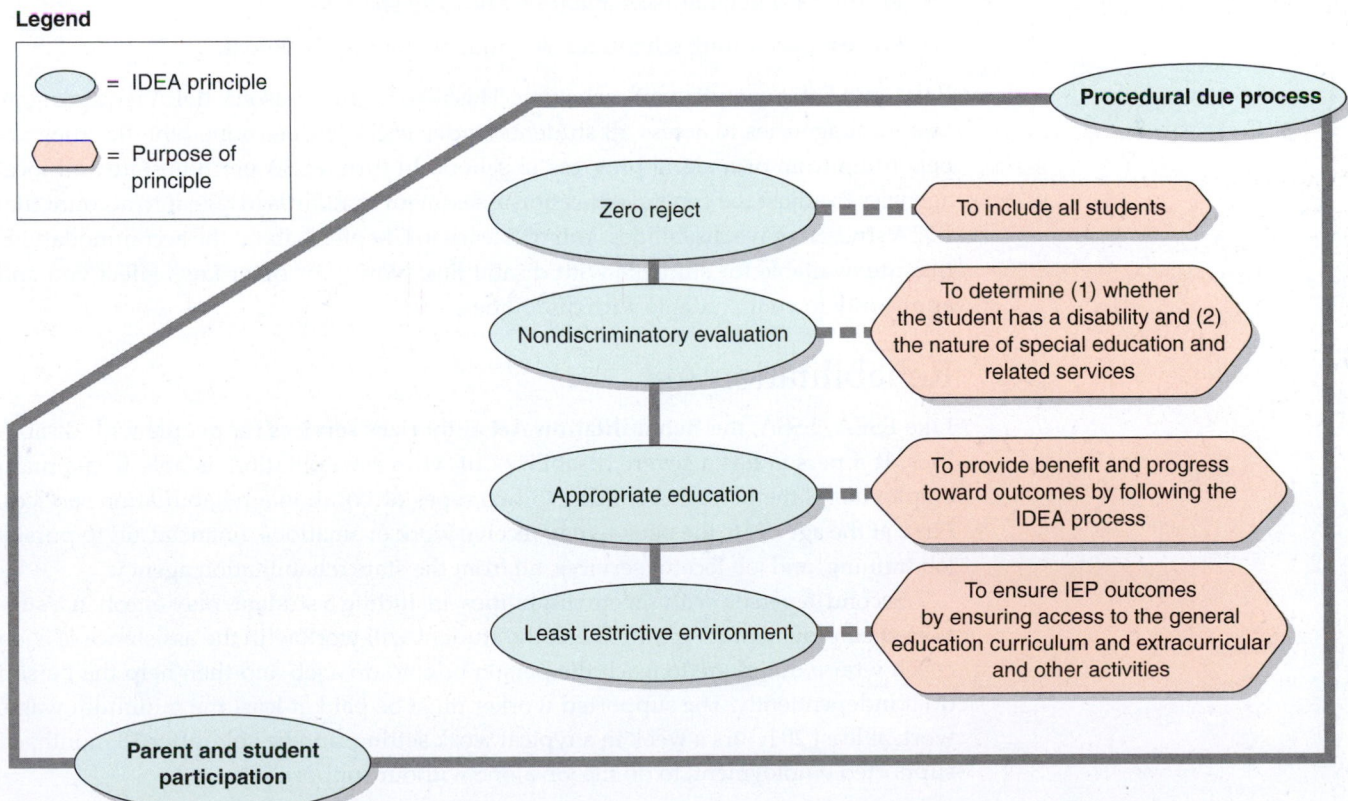

Legend

= IDEA principle

= Purpose of principle

Procedural due process

Zero reject ---- To include all students

Nondiscriminatory evaluation --- To determine (1) whether the student has a disability and (2) the nature of special education and related services

Appropriate education --- To provide benefit and progress toward outcomes by following the IDEA process

Least restrictive environment --- To ensure IEP outcomes by ensuring access to the general education curriculum and extracurricular and other activities

Parent and student participation

MyLab Education **Self-Check 1.2**

MyLab Education **Application Exercise 1.2:** Molly Has Dyslexia

Other Federal Laws

Up to now, you have been learning about IDEA. However, other laws affect you and your students. One of them relates to the education of students who do not have disabilities. Think of it as a combined general and special education law. By contrast, IDEA is a special education law only.

In addition, four federal laws benefit only students with disabilities. Two of them authorize services for the students. By contrast, two protect students and adults with disabilities against discrimination based solely on their disability.

A Combined General and Special Education Law: The Elementary and Secondary Education Act and Every Student Succeeds Act

The principal federal law affecting both general and special education is the **Elementary and Secondary Education Act (ESEA)**. Congress enacted it in 1965 as part of President Johnson's "War on Poverty." ESEA authorizes federal funding for states to operate elementary and secondary education programs, especially those that benefit students from low-income families. ESEA also applies to students with disabilities, including those who receive IDEA services.

In 2015, Congress amended ESEA by enacting the **Every Student Succeeds Act (ESSA)**. (Figure 1.9 highlights ESSA's major requirements.) ESSA's key provisions intend to improve the results of all education programs, special and general alike. They do so by requirements to ensure that:

- All students are held to high standards
- Results of statewide assessments are broadly shared
- Lowest-performing schools are accountable for improvement.

IDEA and ESSA complement each other. This is so for two reasons. IDEA requires state and local agencies to assess all students under ESSA to determine whether they are benefiting from or making progress in school. In turn, ESSA permits state and local agencies to adjust the general education assessment standards to take into account that IDEA students have disabilities. You will learn in Chapter 4 about the accommodations that are available for students with disabilities. Now, four other laws affect you and apply only to your students with disabilities.

Rehabilitation Act

Like ESEA/ESSA, the **Rehabilitation Act** authorizes services for people with disabilities. If a person has a severe disability but, with rehabilitation, is able to maintain employment, the person is entitled to two types of vocational rehabilitation services. First, at the age of 16, the person may receive work evaluations, financial aid to pursue job training, and job locator services, all from the state rehabilitation agency.

Second, a person with severe disabilities, including a student, may enroll in a supported employment program. There, the student will work with the assistance of a job coach whose duties are to teach the person how to do a job and then help the person do it independently. The supported worker must be paid at least the minimum wage, work at least 20 hours a week in a typical work setting, and be able, after 18 months of supported employment, to do the job alone without support.

Tech Act

The **Technology-Related Assistance to Individuals with Disabilities Act**, often called the Tech Act, grants federal funds to the states so that they can help create

Figure 1.9 Key Requirements of Every Student Succeeds Act (ESSA)

ASSESSMENTS. States must continue to test all students on statewide assessments.

- **Areas**. Reading/language arts and math, every year in grades 3-8 and once in high school; and science once in each grade span (3-5, 6-9, and 10-12).
- **Alignments**. These assessments must be aligned to the state's challenging academic standards.

ALTERNATE STANDARDS. States must use the same challenging academic content for all students except that a state may use **alternate achievement standards for students with the most significant cognitive disabilities**.

- **Standards**. These alternate standards must be aligned with existing standards, promote access to the general education curriculum, and ensure the student remains on track to pursue postsecondary education or employment.
- **States may not include more than 1 percent** of all students in alternate achievement standards.
- **Parent notifications**. States must notify parents how their child's achievement is being measured against alternate achievement standards. The IEP team determines when/if a child takes part in alternate assessments.

UNIVERSAL DESIGN FOR LEARNING and ACCOMMODATIONS. States must use the principles of **Universal Design for Learning** when developing assessments.

States must provide appropriate **accommodations** for students with disabilities. Because students have had accommodations in their learning, they should receive them during assessments. Using new accommodations has a negative impact on student performance.

GOALS AND MEASURES OF INTERIM PROGRESS. States must establish ambitious long-term **goals**, with measures of **interim progress**, for all students and separately for each subgroup, including students with disabilities. The long-term goals include improved academic achievement in the aggregate and improved high school graduation rates.

STATE-DEFINED ALTERNATE DIPLOMA. States may choose to award a state-defined alternate diploma to students with the most significant cognitive disabilities who are assessed using alternate achievement standards. States may count the diplomas only if the requirements for the diploma are standards-based, aligned with state requirements for a standard diploma, and obtained within the time period for which the state ensures the availability of a free appropriate public education.

TEACHER AND LEADER QUALITY. States may use ESEA funds to train and recruit high quality teachers and support staff, including principals and other school leaders.

IMPROVING CONDITIONS FOR LEARNING AND TEACHING. SEAs must develop plans on how they will support LEAs to **improve conditions for learning and teaching**.

- **Bullying and harassment**. States may undertake to reduce bullying and harassment.
- **Overuse of discipline**.
- States may undertake to reduce discipline practices such as suspensions and expulsions and to decrease the use of aversive behavioral interventions such as restraints and seclusions — all issues that disproportionately affect students with disabilities.

---

statewide systems for delivering assistive technology devices and services to people with disabilities, including students with disabilities. The Tech Act creates a statewide capacity to serve people with disabilities. Instead of directly benefiting the people themselves, it helps the states meet the people's needs. In Chapters 5 through 16, we describe how technology benefits students.

Two Antidiscrimination Laws—Section 504 and Americans with Disabilities Act

Education and rehabilitation are, of course, necessary to address the need for support created by a student's disability. But they are not sufficient by themselves. IDEA, for example, does not prohibit public or private agencies from discriminating against the student on the basis of the student's disability. Yes, a student such as Endrew may receive special education, but that service might not create opportunities for him to use the skills in the workplace that he has acquired through special education. Prejudice against people with disabilities may still limit opportunities

Students with disabilities can greatly benefit from assistive technology. IDEA requires that assistive technology be considered when developing the IEP for all students with disabilities.

for students to show that, although they have a disability, they are nonetheless still able to work.

How can society attack the prejudice? One answer is to use antidiscrimination laws such as those that prohibit discrimination based on race or gender. The first such law, enacted in 1975 as an amendment to the Rehabilitation Act, is known as **Section 504**. The second, enacted in 1990, is the **Americans with Disabilities Act (ADA)**. These are similar laws. They provide that no otherwise qualified individual with a disability shall, solely by reason of the disability, be discriminated against in certain realms of American life.

Section 504 applies to any program or activity receiving federal financial assistance. Because state and local education agencies receive federal funds, they may not discriminate against students or other persons with disabilities on the basis of their disabilities. Figure 1.10 highlights Section 504 requirements that are important for you to know in your teaching role.

Clearly, Section 504 is limited in scope. What if a student attends a private school that receives absolutely no federal funds? What if an individual seeks employment from a company that does not receive any federal funds, wants to participate in state and local government programs that are not federally aided, or wishes to have access to telecommunications systems such as closed captioning for people with hearing impairments? In none of those cases will the person receive any protection from Section 504. Here, ADA comes to the person's rescue.

ADA extends civil rights/nondiscrimination protection to people with disabilities in the following sectors of American life: private-sector employment, transportation, state and local government activities and programs, privately operated businesses that are open to the public ("public accommodations"), and telecommunications. When Endrew leaves school and goes to work, ADA will protect him against discrimination in employment and allow access to those elements of life that people without disabilities take for granted.

Basically, IDEA and the Rehabilitation Act authorize federal, state, and local educational agencies to undertake programs in education and employment, respectively. Both laws provide funds for state and local agencies to pay for those programs. By contrast, Section 504 and ADA prohibit discrimination solely on the basis of disability in education, employment, and other sectors of American life. But these two laws do not provide federal aid.

Together, these five laws—the one combined general and special education law, two service-provision laws, and two antidiscrimination civil rights laws—support students' transition from school to post-school activities, including work. That is why the transition components of a student's IEP anticipate outcomes largely consistent with those that any student, with or without a disability, typically will want: equal opportunity in all aspects of life, full participation in their communities, independent living in the sense of choosing how to live, and economic self-sufficiency in the sense of having an unbiased opportunity to work. Those results cannot be achieved so long

Figure 1.10 Section 504 Requirements Pertaining to the Education of Students with Disabilities

Two Elements of Disability

The term "disability" has two elements:

- It is a physical or mental impairment.
- It must substantially limit a major life activity, including learning.

A physical or mental impairment is

- A physiological disorder or condition,
- Cosmetic disfigurement,
- Anatomical loss affecting one or more of the following body systems such as neurological or respiratory, or
- Mental or psychological disorder such as an emotional disorder or specific learning disabilities.

Major Life Activity

The major life activities include:

- Caring for oneself
- Performing manual tasks
- Walking
- Seeing
- Hearing
- Speaking
- Breathing
- Learning
- Working.

Age Irrelevant

Sec. 504 applies to services across the lifespan; if a "covered" public agency provides services for people without a disability (for example, a local government agency providing services for elderly/aged people), it may not discriminate against people with disabilities of the same age. Likewise, if a state or local education agency or institution of higher education provides services to students who do not have a disability, it may not discriminate against students who have a disability.

Prohibited School Actions

Sec. 504 prohibits a state or local education agency (basically, a school district or state-operated school) from discriminating solely on the basis of the student's disability. The agency may not

- Deny the student the opportunity to participate in or benefit from its services
- Afford the student an opportunity to participate that is not equal to that which it affords to students without disabilities
- Provide the student an aid, benefit, or service that is not as effective as that which it provides to students without disabilities
- Deny the student the opportunity to be a member of a planning or advisory board
- Otherwise limit the student's enjoyment of any right, privilege, advantage, or opportunity enjoyed by students without disabilities.

Disability in School: Sec. 504 and IDEA

Sec. 504 does not authorize special education. Instead, it prohibits discrimination. In effect, however, the regulations under Sec. 504 and IDEA are nearly identical; the Sec. 504 regulations ensure against discrimination in evaluation, basically create a right to an appropriate education, and guarantee a right to education in the least restrictive environment.

Distinguishing Sec. 504 and IDEA Students

Given Sec. 504's prohibitions and required opportunities, it may seem that there is no distinction between students who are protected by Sec. 504 and students who qualify for IDEA benefits. That is not so. There is a distinction between these two types of students. The distinction lies in IDEA's definition of "special education." IDEA defines special education as specially designed instruction to meet the unique needs of a student with a disability.

By definition, not every student who has Sec. 504 rights needs specially designed instruction. For example, if a student has asthma that limits the student's participation in school activities during asthma attacks but does not require specially designed instruction (the student can learn the same curriculum as other students without disabilities), then the student is covered by Sec. 504 but not IDEA.

as discrimination exists. And that is the message the Court gives in *Endrew F.* and that his parents give:

> *We could not believe that the law was that Endrew had a right to nothing more than a de minimis education. We did not want to be in the national spotlight. It made us sick to our stomachs to know that the school thinks we are in this fight for the money (tuition reimbursement). We're not. We are in it so the next family won't have to go through all this that we endured. It was the right thing to do—to sue for Endrew's education. It was so humbling to be the guests of the Supreme Court and to hear the arguments in our son's case. It was a surreal experience. We were confident even though we had lost in other courts. The cost and emotional stress were worth it. Parenting is hard.*

The Core Principle of Dignity

In the very first pages of this chapter, before you met Endrew, we identified and explained the four goals of IDEA and the seven core elements of special education. We also wrote that these seven elements connect with the essence of our book and the work you do in special education. That essence is expressed by the word *dignity*. Whatever you do that is consistent with any of the four goals and seven core elements, you will acknowledge and enlarge the dignity of your students; in doing that, you will honor an ethical principle of education.

Remember what Endrew's parents said about the lawsuit they brought: "It was the right thing to do." Why? It was done in part to secure his rights under IDEA; in part to convince the Supreme Court that he had rights to something more than a *de minimis* education; in part to put Endrew onto a road to full participation, independent living, and economic self-sufficiency; in part to set a precedent for other parents; and in part to persuade the Court to see Endrew as inherently worthy of a right beyond *de minimis*, to regard him as having inherent worth, and then to ascribe to him a right larger than the lower courts gave him and thereby to give him greater dignity than the lower courts gave him.

The Principle of Dignity

Dignity is the state of being worthy, honored, or esteemed (Mish, 1990). Let's put those words into your work as an educator.

- "Worthy" refers to the worth your students have—their worthiness to be educated. Their worth lies within them; it is inherent; it belongs to them from birth.

- "Honored" and "esteemed" refers to how you respect them by treating them as having not just a right to an education but also having your respect for their willingness to learn, their desire to overcome the challenges their strengths and needs present, and their achievements, however modest or robust they may be.

We not only are special education professors but also were the parents of a son with several disabilities. His name was Jay. And they and he are now in the past tense—"were" and "was"—because Jay died suddenly, unexpectedly, and, painlessly when he was 41 years old. These facts relate to the principle of dignity, not just because Rud and Ann have written about dignity but most of all because they tried—and succeeded, against many odds—to be sure that Jay had a life of dignity. He was in the first cohort of students who benefitted from IDEA; he entered school at the age of 8, in 1976. He did not have an inclusive education, much less an *Endrew F.* appropriately ambitious one, until he was in his last year of school, at age 21. He did not have a life of dignity until Ann and Rud, with their friends and colleagues, created it for him, in their hometown of Lawrence, Kansas.

They wanted that kind of life for him. He wanted it for himself. Like them, he—instinctively, because his mental capacity was limited indeed— "knew" he was worthy: "I am a man, not a boy," he often said; "I have a home, not a house; I have a job; I have friends; I go to church; I ride the bus; I make choices about my life."

So, too, did the other two authors of this book want Jay to have a dignified life. Mike Wehmeyer and Karrie Shogren became his friends when they started their work at The University of Kansas. They went to lunch with him; they made sure he had accommodations at work; they came to his parties; they supported him to prosper in his job and community.

Jay insisted on being worthy, even though he was more than a bit unable in many ways. Ann, Rud, Mike, and Karrie were equally insistent. All five knew that, for students with disabilities, less able is not less worthy. And for students who are exceptionally gifted and talented, more able does not mean more worthy. That is the point Mike made as he eulogized Jay.

MyLab Education
Video Example 1.6
Link to the video of Mike providing the eulogy at Jay's memorial service. What do you understand about Mike's reference to the "business of dignity?"
https://www.youtube.com/watch?v=H8N7uVOQTDU&feature=youtu.be

IDEA and the Principle of Dignity

By adhering to the seven core elements of special education and the instructional strategies you will learn in our book, you will be prepared to demonstrate respect for and to your students. You will do something about them—respect *for* them—and you will do something they will recognize—respect *to* them. You will implicitly acknowledge that they deserve your respect, not just your skills. By respecting them, you will affirm that they have dignity no one can take away from them. It's a dignity you can enhance; it's one you must try to ensure.

Why does dignity relate to special education? It is because of what Congress said at the very beginning of IDEA:

> Disability is natural part of the human experience and in no way diminishes the right of individuals to participate in or contribute to society.

Think about the words "natural part." They mean that there is nothing unnatural about disability. Think about the words "human experience." They refer to the basic fact of being part of humankind.

Now, let's "translate" those words. Let's understand them to say, "We who are educators welcome you who have disabilities into our schools and profession. The fact that you have a disability is simply a natural part of your experience as a human being—indeed, it's a natural part of our experience, too, as we are all human beings together." Let's say, in unity, to students with disabilities, "Welcome to our schools." "Welcome to the general education settings of our schools."

There's more to IDEA's very first sentence. After proclaiming the "natural part of the human experience," IDEA says that disability "in no way diminishes the right of individuals to participate in or contribute to society." So, you should understand this much, already: Dignity, rights, and especially rights to education go hand in hand.

The Supreme Court and *Endrew F.*

You know that the Supreme Court interpreted IDEA's "appropriate education" requirement, in *Endrew F.*, by holding that his right is one to progress. In doing so, the Court told us something about dignity.

> *When all is said and done, a student offered an educational program providing "merely more than de minimis" progress from year to year can hardly be said to have been offered an education at all. For students with disabilities, receiving instruction that aims so low would be tantamount to "sitting idly . . . awaiting the time when they were old enough to 'drop out.'" . . . The IDEA demands more: It requires an educational program reasonably calculated to enable a student to make progress appropriate in light of the student's circumstances.*

With this decision comes no more barely minimum education, no more "sitting idly" and waiting to "drop out" or become 21 and "age out" of IDEA. Now, progress in education is the key. "Appropriately ambitious," "challenging objectives," and "potential for growth" consistent with the student's "circumstances" are the ingredients of your students' education.

Now, take IDEA's "natural consequence of the human experience." Add to it the Court's language in *Endrew F.* Then consider the meaning of dignity as encompassing students' inherent worth and educators' respectful work on their behalf. Do you get the sense that Congress and the Court are going beyond "rights" and their meaning? You should. There really is no other way of understanding the deeper meaning of IDEA as interpreted by the Supreme Court.

We are going beyond "rights," but to what? We are now saying that these students with disabilities—your students—have inherent worth: Less able is not less worthy. And it is your duty to affirm their worth in all you do for and with them and their families.

Professional Principles as Sources

You might say, "Well, I'm not likely to be held to account at law for whether I treat my students respectfully. All I have to do is teach effectively." You may be right. You personally may never have to defend, in court, what you do as a teacher; the odds are against that.

But as a professional, you also will be expected to comply with the Code of Ethics of the Council for Exceptional Children, the nation's special education professional association. Look at Figure 1.11, the CEC Code of Ethics. CEC's very first statement of "Special Education Professional Ethical Principles" commands special educators to "maintain challenging expectations" for their students to "develop the highest possible learning outcomes and quality of life potential in ways that respect

Figure 1.11 Council for Exceptional Children Special Education Professional Ethical Principles

Professional special educators are guided by the Council for Exceptional Children (CEC) professional ethical principles, practice standards, and professional policies in ways that respect the diverse characteristics and needs of individuals with exceptionalities and their families.

They are committed to upholding and advancing the following principles:

1. Maintaining challenging expectations for individuals with exceptionalities to develop the highest possible learning outcomes and quality of life potential in ways that respect their dignity, culture, language, and background.
2. Maintaining a high level of professional competence and integrity and exercising professional judgment to benefit individuals with exceptionalities and their families.
3. Promoting meaningful and inclusive participation of individuals with exceptionalities in their schools and communities.
4. Practicing collegially with others who are providing services to individuals with exceptionalities.
5. Developing relationships with families based on mutual respect and actively involving families and individuals with exceptionalities in educational decision making.
6. Using evidence, instructional data, research, and professional knowledge to inform practice.
7. Protecting and supporting the physical and psychological safety of individuals with exceptionalities.
8. Neither engaging in nor tolerating any practice that harms individuals with exceptionalities.
9. Practicing within the professional ethics, standards, and policies of CEC; upholding laws, regulations, and policies that influence professional practice; and advocating improvements in the laws, regulations, and policies.
10. Advocating for professional conditions and resources that will improve learning outcomes of individuals with exceptionalities.
11. Engaging in the improvement of the profession through active participation in professional organizations.
12. Participating in the growth and dissemination of professional knowledge and skills.

Approved, January 2010

their dignity, culture, language, and background." There it is again—the connection between dignity and outcomes.

We acknowledge that seven core elements and the principle of dignity are a lot to grasp. How do they apply to your students? The answer lies in how they apply to Endrew. Here is what his parents told us as we had dinner with them and Endrew, in their home, 6 months after the Supreme Court decided in their favor:

> *There was no guaranteed outcome. We were right. We knew it. It was worth it to fight for what we believed in.*

This was a matter of Endrew's parents being right all along, through 7 years of losing before finally being able to say, "We Won!" That kind of being right was not just about the law. It was a different kind of "right." It was a "rightness" that proclaimed "Our son is worthy." The word "dignity" captures that kind of worthiness. Just as the Court dignified Endrew, so, too, did his parents, from the moment he was born. Will you join them and the Court?

MyLab Education Self-Check 1.3

MyLab Education Application Exercise 1.3: Molly's IEP Meeting

---

Summary

Goals and Core Elements of Special Education

National disability policy has four goals: equal opportunity, full participation, independent living, and economic self-sufficiency. Also, special education has seven core elements: high expectations, diversity and cultural justice, progress, research-based practice, inclusion, self-determination, and partnerships based on trust.

Students and Professionals

Approximately 13 percent of the nation's entire school population has a disability. By contrast, students who are gifted and talented represent 6.7 percent of the nation's school population. Approximately two thirds of students with disabilities have learning disabilities or language impairments. The professionals are general educators, special educators, paraprofessionals, and the professionals who deliver related services and supplementary aids and services.

The Law of Special Education: Individuals with Disability Education Act (IDEA)

There are six principles of IDEA. The first four principles are inputs into a student's education. The last two are accountability techniques. The principles are as follows:

- Zero reject, a rule against exclusion
- Nondiscriminatory evaluation, a rule of fair assessments
- Appropriate education, a rule of individualized benefit
- Least restrictive placement, a rule of presuming placement in general education programs
- Procedural due process, a rule of fair dealing and accountability
- Parent and student participation, a rule of shared decision making.

Other Federal Laws

Other federal laws affect students' education. The Educating Students for Success Act seeks to improve the education of all students (general and special alike) by requiring states to be accountable for the education they offer. The Rehabilitation Act addresses the employment needs of students and adults with disabilities. The Tech Act supports states to make assistive technology available to students with disabilities. Section 504 and the Americans with Disabilities Act protect students and adults with disabilities from discrimination based solely on their disability.

The Core Principle of Dignity

Less able is not less worthy (Turnbull, 1976). What about students with special gifts and talents? Let's reverse our thinking and say, "Being exceptionally gifted and talented, being so much more able does not make a person more worthy."

We have said that dignity is the state of being worthy, honored, or esteemed. So, dignity has two aspects: It is inherent in your students and it is a matter of how you regard them, of what "worth" you attribute to them.

The word "inherent" refers to that which is in the constitution or essential character of something or someone (Mish, 1990). A synonym of "inherent" is "intrinsic," meaning "belonging to the essential nature or constitution of a thing or person" (Mish, 1990).

Worthiness comes from the simple fact that the person is human, possessing capacities—and needs for supports—for thinking and feeling. "People have dignity because the essence of who they are cannot be replaced (Evans & Vaandering, 2016, p. 32).

If "worthy" refers to inherent humanness, then "honored" or "esteemed" refers to how some individuals regard a person. You may say, for example, that you are honored to be admitted to a certain college or university or that you have been esteemed by colleagues who chose you for a leadership position. Dignity, then, is a matter of "standing" among others; a student who has a disability and who receives a varsity letter for playing or being a manager of a varsity sport is "honored" and "esteemed" by his colleagues; he has been dignified by them (Turnbull, 2011).

Addressing the Professional Standards

In Chapter 1, The Purposes, People, and Law of Special Education, we have covered the following Council for Exceptional Children (CEC) Initial Level Special Educator Preparation Standards: Chapter 1—2.0, 4.0, 4.3, 4.4, 5.1, 5.2, 5.5, 6.0, 6.1, 6.2, 6.3, 6.4, 6.5, 7.0, 7.3. Refer to the Appendix for a full listing of the CEC Standards with description and supporting explanations.

Chapter 2
Disability and Cultural Justice

 ## Learning Outcomes

2.1 Distinguish between macrocultures and microcultures; describe the progress of the disability rights movement in education; and explain the current outcomes of education for students with disabilities.

2.2 Summarize research findings about cultural bias related to disability and race, and characterize the themes of intersectionality and disproportionality across six key educational considerations.

2.3 Describe implementation of the Watch, Think, and Act process and identify three of the five strategies for teaching restorative practices and three examples of culturally responsive teaching.

Meet McKyla and Mr. Ortega—Restoring Justice to a School and a Community, One Circle at a Time

Students' progress in special education can occur because of a Supreme Court decision, as you learned when reading Chapter 1. Students' progress also can occur because entire systems of education apply research-based practices in their programs, as you will learn in Chapters 4, 5, and 6.

There is, however, a system-wide change that rests explicitly on justice. It is the change that is occurring within the Oakland, California, Unified School District (OUSD)—not just there, but elsewhere as well. That change derives from a research-based practice called restorative justice.

Meet McKyla Woods, a student at Oakland's Madison Park Business and Art Academy, who receives special education support, and Emilio Ortega, the school's Restorative Practice Facilitator/Leader. Then read about the significance of restorative justice as it occurs in their school and in Oakland at large.

Like so many other students in schools across America, McKyla uses social media. She's also a victim of it. She texts her friends and receives texts from them. She also gets texts from peers who are not her friends, texts that tease and bully her. It's not just social media that offend her—it's face-to-face comments from her peers (those in upper and lower grades alike), rumors about her, verbal attacks about her mother, and sometimes teachers' comments to her.

Agnes Marcelo

McKyla admits she has a hard time keeping "cool," especially when she believes that her peers or teachers misunderstand or misinterpret what she has intended to say. Of course, her angry responses don't cool down a situation; they escalate it. What should she and Mr. Ortega do to avoid school discipline, head off confrontations that can get out of hand, and satisfy her deep need to find a place of her own? How can they find a place that is safe for her, her peers, and her teachers?

The answer is to use the restorative practice program that operates throughout the Oakland, California, school district. Mr. Ortega directs the program at McKyla's school. He's also McKyla's one-on-one confidant and supporter.

To engage in restorative practice—to learn how to relate, repair, and restore their relationships—Mr. Ortega convenes the students or faculty with whom McKyla has issues; they sit in a circle and commit to listening to each other with no interruptions. Mr. Ortega's insistence on that commitment is not just a matter of teaching good manners for life; it's also the way he, McKyla, and her peers and teachers have of being able to say, with or without emotion, what they want to say, what they need to explain, in their own words, and with respect for the process and each other. McKyla puts it this way: "I have a 100 percent chance to speak my mind. No one shuts me up or cuts me off. I can talk about anything with Mr. Ortega, he keeps confidential what I say, but he also encourages me to speak my mind in the circle."

As the circlers speak their minds, they begin to apologize for offending each other. They learn how to resolve conflict without fights or other violence. Mr. Ortega emphasizes that restorative practices are an integral part of school discipline. That is so because the practice incorporates positive activities that use conflict and harm as a way to build positive relationships while also helping to "correct" and transform students' behavior.

He also makes another important point: Restorative practices are alternatives to the harmful punishment that students inflict on each other by fighting, aggression, and verbal abuse. The practices also are alternatives to the punishment that teachers impose on students by suspending them from school or removing them from classes.

In a nutshell, the students are learning two curricula at Madison Park Academy. One is the state-prescribed curriculum. The other is the civic virtue of being members of the same community, whether it is Madison Park Academy or greater Oakland. Justice comes to Madison Park, one student at a time, one circle at a time, slowly and deliberately. Civic virtue—too often lost—is being restored; justice is returning to a place where it had vanished.

As of 2018, Oakland's population of 410,000 is multiethnic. Public notices are printed in English, Spanish, Chinese, and Vietnamese. The city is a hub for education: Early education, adult education, and postgraduate education occur city-wide. Activities for older adults are widespread; accessibility and accommodations for persons with disabilities are, too. Centers for the arts and culture flourish. Affordable housing exists. Minority-owned businesses benefit from targeted public initiatives. Minimum wage increases have been approved by voters. But the city council's Number 1 priority is public safety. *Forbes* Magazine has rated Oakland as having the third-highest crime rate among all American cities. Remember these two facts: priorities and rate. Each relates to the Oakland schools and to its program on restorative justice.

As of the 2017–2018 school year, the Oakland system served just over 50,000 students in 87 district-operated and 35 charter schools—a total of 122 schools. Within the district-operated schools (excluding charter schools), the majority of the 50,000 students are either Black or Hispanic; the percentage of Black students is declining as the percentage of Hispanic and White students is increasing.

Also within the 87 schools, only 3.6 percent of all students are suspended (out of school) for more than 1 day—a rate lower than the average of 29 percent for students with disabilities and 14 percent for students without disabilities (Lipscomb, 2017b). Leaders in the Oakland school district credit the restorative justice program with contributing to the low suspension rate.

To connect justice with students' progress in school, the Oakland district operates a program titled "Restorative Justice." Pay attention to both words, but start with "justice." That's a word whose meaning and application are the subjects of thousands of treatises and court decisions, all beyond the scope of this book. But, for you and us, here and now, the word has a particular meaning.

Within the Oakland school system as a whole, "justice"—a sense of fairness and a commitment to equal opportunity and equity—relates to a commitment to be a "full-service" district, to serve the "whole child," to "eliminating inequity," and to "providing each child with excellent teachers, every day." The district's teachers and students "will find joy in their academic experience" and graduate with the skills to be "caring" and prepared for college, career, and community success.

Within the special education program in particular, the district affirms that each student "deserves recognition, attention, and respect" and "rigorous academic programs" that support "high achievement." In common with students who do not need special education, those who do need it will "thrive."

What about that word "restorative"? It refers to a process whereby students, faculty, or community members who have been offended, injured, or hurt by a student, faculty member, or staff do not prosecute or sue for redress. Instead, they form a circle in which the offender accepts responsibility for the offense and those who have been offended decide, with the offender, what to do to restore not just the condition before the offense but, much more importantly, how to restore or create a relationship among the offender and the offended. "I can really speak my mind," says McKyla. "I make the circle a safe place for everyone," says Mr. Ortega.

David Yusem is the coordinator of the school district's restorative justice program. He emphasizes that the program is not about punishment or exclusionary discipline; it's about relationships and consensual decisions.

He describes the restorative justice program as a systems-change initiative that gives priority to discovering what a student needs and wants and thereby knowing what services the student should have in the school system or in the community's public health, mental health, antidrug, recreation, or other education programs. It is a means to open the community inside and outside the school system to the student.

Everyone in the circle has a voice; no one person may dominate the discussion, all voices are valued, and the circle—the community, not a person—decides how to restore a damaged relationship. The many-voice approach allows cultural differences to "speak." Inclusion is honored; empowerment emerges, not just the power of a single or a few people, but the power of all to be in community with each other.

In a city rated as the third most dangerous, the search for justice exists: not merely justice in the sense of "fault or punishment" but justice as a commitment to relationships. There is less discipline than restoration; the pipeline from school to prison is breaking.

School systems do change. Sometimes it takes a Supreme Court decision to initiate a change. Sometimes it takes research-based practice to solidify a change. And sometimes it takes the diligent pursuit of justice for a community to make all the difference for its students, its schools, and itself.

Culture and Disability
Macroculture and Microculture

Assume we ask you, "What is your culture? What is your cultural heritage?" How would you answer? Would you wonder what we mean by "culture"? You probably would wonder about this because the word is used in so many contexts that it often loses its meaning. **Culture** refers to the "customary beliefs, social forms, and material traits of a racial, religious, or social group; also, the characteristic features of everyday existence . . . shared by people in a place and time" (*Merriam-Webster's Collegiate Dictionary*, 2003).

It may be debatable whether those of us who live in the United States have customary beliefs, social forms, and material traits, that is, whether we share characteristics of everyday existence. Perhaps we do. If so, then we collectively represent a **macroculture**, a dominant societal culture. It seems hard to deny that the American macroculture includes at least democracy and capitalism. It may include more; it may, but maybe not. That is so because here—especially here, given our history and the many demographic groups in America—there are **microcultures**. That term refers to specific characteristics of those of us in America, and to the specific beliefs, forms, and traits that some of us share with others but not with all of us. Look at Figure 2.1 to see how race/ethnicity, language, socioeconomic status, disability, and other characteristics are microcultures. As you will soon learn, students' microcultures make a difference in terms of their school success.

Which of those microcultures represent your cultural identity? What are the three microcultures with which you most strongly identify? As you consider those microcultures, think of the people with whom you experience a sense of "we-ness"—a sense of alignment of beliefs, social forms, and material traits, as well as their values, behaviors, communication styles, interests, and/or traditions. Now think of the people with whom you experience a sense of "other-ness"—a sense of distance from their beliefs, social forms, and material traits. Which microcultures do your "we-ness" and "other-ness" relationships represent?

We have one last question for you: Is your particular set of beliefs, code of conduct, and lifestyle so "part" of you, so engrained, that it is a "personal cultural measuring stick" of your comfort level with others who do not share them? Be honest. And then consider whether disability itself is a particular culture and whether you share that culture with others, with the students you will teach. If your answer is "no," then it is perhaps because you have not been in, or even known about, the disability rights movement.

Figure 2.1 Microcultural Identity

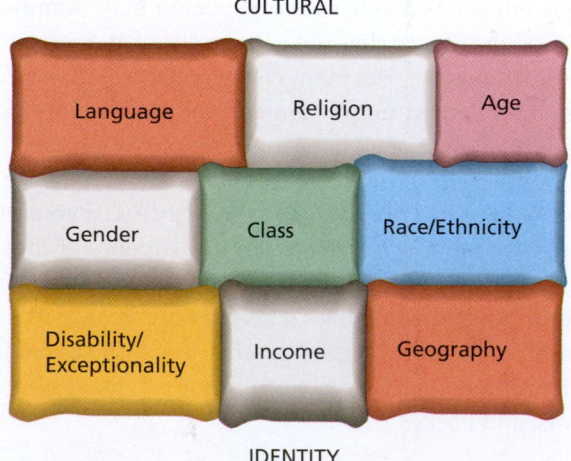

CULTURAL

Language	Religion	Age
Gender	Class	Race/Ethnicity
Disability/Exceptionality	Income	Geography

IDENTITY

Disability Rights Movement in Special Education

You learned in Chapter 1 that special education is a civil right. The question you may ask is this: Why is it a right? The answer lies in a shameful part of our nation's recent history.

TWO TYPES OF DISCRIMINATION   During the early and middle decades of the 20th century, schools discriminated against students with disabilities in two significant ways (Turnbull, Stowe, & Huerta, 2007). First, they often completely excluded many students with disabilities. If any students with disabilities were admitted, they were not provided with an effective or appropriate education. So, there were two kinds of exclusion: "pure" exclusion consisted of never granting any access to education, and "functional" exclusion consisted of granting access but not conferring any benefit for the students once they had access to school.

Second, schools often classified students without disabilities as having disabilities. Other schools often classified students as having one type of disability (for example, intellectual disability) when, in fact, they had another (for example, a learning disability or emotional-behavioral challenges). Taken together, these practices are known as misclassification. Frequently, these misclassified students were members of diverse microcultures.

PARENT ADVOCACY   The disability rights movement in special education began in the early 1950s; it began with the efforts of parents of children and adults with disabilities. First, they started parent advocacy organizations at the local and state levels to garner strength in asserting that their children were entitled to an education. As local and state groups swelled with members, soon parents came together to form national organizations. Two of the first were the National Association for Retarded Children (now called The Arc of the United States) and United Cerebral Palsy. Today, hundreds of similar organizations are committed to the rights of people with various disabilities. Second, parents and the organizations they created started providing educational programs for children and youth in community buildings and church basements, with parents and other family members serving as volunteer teachers. Third, parents were relentless advocates and worked closely with professional leaders primarily from the Council for Exceptional Children (the oldest and largest special education professional association) to create what is now the Individuals with Disabilities Education Act (IDEA). No doubt, these parents and their organizations were the "leading force" (Kirk, 1984, p. 41) in the right-to-education movement.

COURT CASES   Beginning in the early 1970s, parents were joined by professional advocacy organizations and civil rights lawyers. These powerful advocates began to sue state and local school officials, claiming that exclusion and misclassification violated students' rights to an equal education opportunity under the U.S. Constitution (Turnbull, Shogren, & Turnbull, 2011). Relying on the Supreme Court's decision in the school race-desegregation case *Brown v. Board of Education* (1954), they argued that because the Court held that schools may not segregate by race, schools also may not segregate or otherwise discriminate by ability and disability. Their argument was the essence of simplicity: Students are students, regardless of their race.

The advocates for students with disabilities were successful. They argued that students are students, regardless of their disability. In 1972, federal courts ordered the Commonwealth of Pennsylvania and the District of Columbia to (1) provide a free appropriate public education to all students with disabilities, (2) educate students with disabilities in the same schools and basically the same programs as students without disabilities, and (3) put into place certain procedural safeguards so that parents of students with disabilities could challenge schools that did not live up to the courts' orders (*Pennsylvania Association for Retarded Children (PARC) v. Commonwealth of Pennsylvania*, 1971, 1972; *Mills v. D.C. Board of Education*; Turnbull et al., 2007).

MyLab Education
Video Example 2.1
Learn about the broad disability rights movement from the amazing leaders who were instrumental in establishing rights for people with disabilities across the lifespan. https://www.youtube.com/watch?v=OrM5hZX0hNc

A resource you can use for teaching about the disability rights movement to 4th through 6th graders is titled *Disability Rights Movement (Civic Participation: Working for Civil Rights)* by Amy Hayes.

CONGRESS' ACTION   These two cases prompted Congress to act. In 1975, it enacted IDEA (then called the Education for All Handicapped Students Act, enacted as Public Law 94–142). At that time Congress intended to open up the schools to all students with disabilities who are of school age and make sure that those students had the chance to benefit from education. The law was concerned principally with access and benefit. Over time, those goals remained but new ones arose.

Congress amended the law several times later, and in 1990 renamed it Individuals with Disabilities Education Act, known as IDEA. Congress amended IDEA most recently in 2004. You learned about IDEA in Chapter 1, so now you have the history behind it. You also know from Chapter 1 that Endrew was the student around whom the Supreme Court strengthened IDEA in 2017. Endrew is not a member of a racial minority. But like students with disabilities, no matter what their race/ethnicity or native language may be, Endrew is a member of another minority—the disability minority.

MICROCULTURE OF DISABILITY   The early court cases and the enactment of the federal law were the points of the spear that advocates used to solidify a microculture comprising people with disabilities, parents, educators, other professionals, and committed citizens. Don't think that disability rights have just focused on special education. They haven't; indeed, the disability rights movement addresses nearly every aspect of American life. That's the scope of the Americans with Disabilities Act (Chapter 1). It exempts religious organizations and small private companies, but it extends to state and local governments and to private-sector employment, transportation, communication, and technology (Fleischer & Zames, 2011).

What are the implications of this disability microculture for you? As you become a teacher in special education and/or general education, we hope you will affiliate with disability advocates in your community to implement IDEA fully. It is one thing to have law on the books; the next step is to ensure that all educators and all schools commit to implementation, especially since the *Endrew F.* decision sets new standards for special education. That's law on the streets. As you will learn in this chapter, significant challenges exist for all students with disabilities, especially ones from diverse microcultures. One of the challenges involves the words you and others use.

USING LABELS AND LANGUAGE   One consequence of the disability rights movement is that many people with disabilities, their families, and the educators and other professionals who support them are acutely sensitive to the labels and language they and others use to refer to students and adults with disabilities. They have good reasons to be sensitive. The answer begins with a lesson about classifying a student as having a disability and thus being eligible for IDEA services and Section 504 protection.

There is no consensus about the benefits and drawbacks of identifying students as having a particular disability and then assigning a label to the disability and the student (Gold & Richards, 2012). IDEA requires that a student be identified as having a disability, and it lists the disabilities of the students it covers. On the one hand, then, the students have rights to fair evaluations, progress in education (including their potential for growth and access to ambitiously appropriate goals and challenging objectives, as you learned in the vignette about Endrew himself), and protection against discipline of more than 10 days (as you will learn later in this chapter). So, there are benefits of having a label.

On the other hand, labeling can lead educators to make biased decisions about a student's strengths and needs. In one study, researchers gave preservice teacher educators videos of students and asked them to identify students' behavior as "on task" or "off task" (Allday, Duhon, Blackburn-Ellis, & Van Dycke, 2011). The researchers told some of the preservice teacher educators that the students had oppositional defiant disorder (a type of emotional or behavioral disorder); they told others that the students had attention-deficit hyperactivity disorder (ADHD); and they told still others that students were gifted and talented. The students' labels made a difference: Teachers were less likely to rate the behavior of students who were gifted and talented as "off task." Labels can lead to predictions that can influence whether a student or groups of students are educated in one way—to their advantage or their disadvantage. Labels can also be stigmatizing for students and a focus of bullying.

The second issue has to do with the language you and other educators will use to describe your students and others with disabilities. Does the language identify the person first and the disability next, or vice versa? This issue is known as "person-first" or "identity-first" language. Person-first language puts the person before the disability. For example, instead of using a phrase such as "autistic students" or "the autistics," say "students with autism." Over the past several decades, person-first language has been promoted as a way to extend dignity to people with disabilities by recognizing their whole personhood first ("identity first") and then, and only then, identifying the person as having a disability.

Figure 2.2 provides guidance on traditionally respectful language pertaining to disability terminology—language that is still endorsed largely within the field of special education. Additionally, these guidelines are currently sanctioned by dozens of national organizations within the broad disability field.

Figure 2.2 Your Words, Our Image

You are in a unique position to shape the public image of people with disabilities. By putting the person first and using these suggested words, you can convey a positive, objective view of an individual instead of a negative, insensitive image.

Do say	Don't say
Disability	Differently abled, challenged
People with disabilities	The disabled, handicapped
Person with spinal cord injury	Cripple
Person with autism, on the autism spectrum	Autistic
Person with Down syndrome	Mongoloid
Person of short stature	Midget, dwarf
Uses a wheelchair, wheelchair user	Confined to a wheelchair, wheelchair-bound
Has a learning disability	Slow learner
Has chemical or environmental sensitivities	Chemophobic
Has a brain injury	Brain damaged
Blind, low vision	Visually handicapped, blind as a bat
Deaf, hard of hearing	Deaf-mute, deaf and dumb
Intellectual disability	Retarded, mental retardation
Amputee, has limb loss	Gimp, lame
Congenital disability	Birth defect
Burn survivor	Burn victim
Post-polio syndrome	Suffers from polio
Service animal or dog	Seeing eye dog
Psychiatric disability, mental illness	Crazy, psycho, schizo
How should I describe you or your disability?	What happened to you?
Accessible parking or restroom	Handicapped parking, disabled restroom

Want more information?
Download our brochure *Guidelines: How to Write and Report About People with Disabilities* at *www.rtcil.org/guidelines.*

Research and Training Center on Independent Living
The University of Kansas
4089 Dole Center, 1000 Sunnyside Ave.
Lawrence, KS 66045-7561
E-mail: rtcil@ku.edu
Phone: 785-864-4095
TTY: 785-864-0706
Web: www.rtcil.org

©2013 Eighth Edition

Your Words, Our Image

KU
RESEARCH
& TRAINING CENTER
ON INDEPENDENT LIVING
Life Span Institute

During the last decade of the 20th century, many disability activists began to abandon person-first language in favor of identity-first language (Brueggemann, 2014). Many "adults with disability" (person-first) have expressed that they perceive their disability to be an inherent part of who they are and they are proud of themselves as they are and connect with other "disabled adults" (identity-first). The Deaf community has a long and rich history of celebrating cultural solidarity within the Deaf culture. Identity-first language has also been endorsed by the National Federation of the Blind and the Autistic Self-Advocacy Network.

So, what language should you use? We recommend that you be sensitive to both perspectives and recognize that language preferences exist along a continuum from strong person-first to strong identity-first (Dunn & Andrews, 2015). Our best advice is easy to follow: Refer to students by their names. Don't use labels; use names. And as you or other educators use labels for compliance with IDEA or for other valid reasons, such as to secure services for students, avoid those that demean and stigmatize (as highlighted in Figure 2.2). We encourage you to be sensitive to the fact that labels and language too often separate and devalue people, both inside and outside school (van Swet, Wichers-Bots, & Brown, 2011). They often tend not to dignify a person but, instead, to demean a person, given societal stigma. It's a dignity issue.

Outcomes of Education for Students with Disabilities

In Chapter 1 (Figure 1.1), you learned that IDEA and the Americans with Disabilities Act (ADA) have the following four national disability policy goals for students with disabilities:

- Equality of opportunity
- Full participation
- Independent living
- Economic self-sufficiency.

Just how close have Americans with disabilities come to attaining those goals? They have come not nearly close enough. That's clear from various indicators—markers of proof that educators need to do a better job.

The first indicator is the extent to which students with disabilities are receiving a high school diploma. Based on the 2013–2014 school year, the national rate of students receiving a high school diploma is 82 percent, whereas the rate for students with disabilities is 66 percent (National Clearinghouse for Educational Statistics, 2017a; 2017b). The graduation rates are highest for students with visual impairments and speech or language impairments (82 percent for both) and lowest for students with intellectual disabilities (42 percent) and multiple disabilities (50 percent) (U.S. Department of Education, 2018). The good news is that the overall rate of 70 percent graduation for students with disabilities improved by 13 percent over a 10-year period. The bad news is that still approximately one third of students with disabilities are not graduating with a diploma. Why?

You may recall that the Supreme Court, in *Endrew F.*, was determined to set a standard of appropriate education that was higher than "merely *de minimis*." Its standard is now about progress and potential for growth. That is so because the Court itself was concerned about students "sitting idly" and just waiting to "drop out." Law and drop-out interact powerfully.

That's not just a lesson from the Court. There are data—distressing data. The rate is 6.5 percent for students without disabilities, but it is almost 3 times higher, 18.5 percent, for students with disabilities (National Clearinghouse for Educational Statistics, 2017a; 2017b). Indeed, the drop-out rate has decreased by 10 percent over a 10-year period. At least three factors lead to drop-out among students with disabilities relative to students who do not have disabilities: (1) they are retained in grades (they do not advance in grades); (2) they have lower than average grades; and (3) they are disciplined more often by suspensions and expulsions (Zablocki & Krezmien, 2012).

Students who have been suspended or expelled were 3 times more likely to drop out than students who did not have these experiences. By contrast, students who had emotional engagement—enjoyed school, got along with teachers and peers, felt that adults cared about youth—were significantly less likely to drop out. Receiving a diploma or a general educational development (GED) certificate has been linked to a number of positive outcomes, including substantially higher income, better employment, increased health, and decreased likelihood of being in prison (U.S. Department of Education, 2010). In a word, the less often students are suspended or expelled, the more likely they will not drop out and instead will make progress, being productive and contributing to society, as IDEA anticipates. As you read in the opening vignette, the suspension rate in the Oakland system is substantially less than the national suspension rate.

The second indicator relates to employment and income. Adults without disabilities have an employment rate over twice that of adults with disabilities (76 percent vs. 35 percent), (b) incomes approximately one-third higher, and (c) a poverty rate more than 2 times lower (Institute of Disability, 2016). The employment gap between these two groups has increased by 2.5 percentage points over the past 8 years.

The third and final indicator focuses on overall satisfaction with life. Approximately two thirds of individuals without disabilities report they are very satisfied with life in general; by contrast, approximately one third of individuals with disabilities report the same satisfaction. The following trends contribute to general life satisfaction (National Organization on Disability, 2010):

- Slightly more than half of adults with disabilities report that they are struggling financially (living paycheck to paycheck, going into debt) compared with one third of people without disabilities (58 percent versus 34 percent).

- Approximately one fifth of adults with disabilities report going without needed health care compared with one tenth of people without disabilities (19 percent versus 10 percent).

- Adults with disabilities are approximately twice as likely to have inadequate transportation as compared to people without disabilities (34 percent versus 16 percent).

- Slightly more than half of adults with disabilities report accessing the Internet compared with the vast majority of adults without disabilities (54 percent versus 85 percent).

You may remember from Chapter 1 that three federal laws authorize services to students with disabilities (IDEA, the Vocational Rehabilitation Act, and the Tech Act) and two other laws prohibit discrimination based on disability (Section 504 of the Vocational Rehabilitation Act and Americans with Disabilities Act). Why is it that outcomes have not shown more substantial improvement since IDEA was passed in 1975—over 40 years ago? What can you do as a teacher to improve outcomes?

MyLab Education Self-Check 2.1
MyLab Education Application Exercise 2.1: Disability Rights Movement

---

Cultural Bias and Students with Disabilities

Cultural bias occurs when we—any one of us, we authors or you readers, really anyone—use our "personal cultural measuring stick" to judge categories of people according to our own code of conduct and lifestyle (Thiederman, 2015).

Cultural bias happens explicitly and implicitly. **Explicit bias** represents our attitudes on a conscious level that we readily express and consistently apply when we are with people who do or do not share our cultural identity. People vary in the extent to which they are comfortable expressing beliefs that others consider undesirable because they represent injustice or bigotry. The "others consider . . . undesirable" expresses a concept called "social desirability." Social desirability can influence our willingness to be open about our explicit bias; we may be biased, but we hide our bias because it is socially undesirable to have that bias.

By contrast, our **implicit bias** operates on an unconscious level; we have a bias, it influences our attitudes about other people, but we are not even aware of our bias. An applicable metaphor from medieval times focuses on small rooms in castles and homes that were used for baking bread. These rooms became so full of the remains of yeast over decades and even centuries of baking that it became unnecessary to add yeast to bread dough. The yeast "culture" simply permeated the air in the room and made the bread rise. Similarly, the culture with which we identify comprises invisible values, behaviors, sentences, images, joys, fears, stories, and so on, about what constitutes "good/bad" and "right/wrong." It is easy to lose track of how pervasively we are predisposed as we "breathe the air of invisible 'messages'" (Vohs, 1993).

Are you honest enough with yourself to admit your explicit biases? Have you thought about whether you have implicit biases? Are you interested in the answers? If so, we encourage you to take the Implicit Association Test (Greenwald & Nosek, 2001). It measures how closely and quickly our brains link concepts such as gay or straight with words such as "appealing" or "disgusting." Its basic premise is that linkages form more quickly when aligned with unconscious beliefs. Here's a link to the test about implicit biases related to disability and race.

We also encourage you to reflect on your results on implicit bias and to consider how they align and do not align with your explicit cultural beliefs or biases. If your scores surprise you by indicating that you have unconscious bias, you may feel embarrassed or defensive. Don't fret, not yet. The fact of the matter is that everyone has biases because everyone "breathes the air of invisible 'messages'." As a teacher, you will want to act without bias toward any of your students. You will want to purge your biases. Within the context of this chapter, we will particularly focus on students with disabilities, including their multiple microcultures.

CULTURAL BIAS RELATED TO DISABILITY   A review of 18 studies using the Implicit Association Test directed toward individuals with physical, hearing, vision, and intellectual disabilities revealed the following results (Wilson & Scior, 2014):

- Moderate-to-strong negative implicit bias existed across all studies for people with those four types of disabilities.

- Increased contact between the person taking the test (the "respondent") and people with disabilities contributed to slight increases in positive responses in a couple of studies.

- Paid caregivers of individuals with intellectual disability were mostly negative.

- Child protection workers were more likely to anticipate future risk of child neglect for parents with mild intellectual disability, as compared to parents with typical intelligence.

CULTURAL BIAS RELATED TO RACE   More research studies have been done about racial bias than disability bias. Some have focused on teachers' decisions about a student's education. The first study investigated preschool educators' implicit bias (Gilliam, Maupin, Reyes, Accavitti, & Shic, 2016). In this study, preschool educators watched a video of preschoolers (with equal numbers of boys/girls and Black/White preschoolers) after being told to expect challenging behavior by students; in fact, no

Link here to read a description of the Implicit Association Test: https://implicit.harvard.edu/implicit/iatdetails.html

Then link here to take the Implicit Association Test once for disability and a second time for race: https://implicit.harvard.edu/implicit/takeatest.html

such behavior was present. The researchers tracked the educators' eye gazes while they watched the video.

What are your hunches about the results? How did the educators use their "personal cultural measuring stick" to evaluate the preschoolers' anticipated challenging behavior? When educators were advised to expect challenging behavior in the videos, they more closely focused their eye gaze on Black preschoolers, especially Black boys. Their close attention to Black boys indicated that they expected these boys to misbehave. Remember, none of the preschoolers were misbehaving. None! These educators also reported explicit perspectives that boys, especially Black boys, require the most attention.

A second research study involved kindergarten through 12th-grade teachers who were asked to imagine themselves as a middle school teacher (Okonofua & Eberhardt, 2015). The teachers reviewed a school record for a student with two behavioral infractions (major infraction—insubordination; minor infraction—class disturbance). The student's race was interchanged between Black and White throughout the experiment. What, do you think, the results showed? They demonstrated that the teachers had an implicit bias that Black students, not White students, (1) were troublemakers, (2) had consistent multiple infractions, and (3) warranted future suspensions.

What are the "take-away" lessons from the research about cultural bias and the microcultures of disability and race? They are that explicit bias and implicit bias affect our behaviors, leading us to make decisions that that fail to dignify students.

Disability, Intersectionality, and Disproportionality

You have learned that disability itself is a microculture; that race is, too; and that an interaction exists between the disability microculture and some of the other microcultures depicted in Figure 2.1. Now it's time for you to learn about a concept called "intersectionality." Generally speaking, it describes how disability, race, and other microcultures intersect with each other and thereby affect some students more negatively than others, causing disproportionate discrimination in special education.

The term **intersectionality** was introduced by Crenshaw (1989), a legal scholar who is a Black woman. She avowed that being Black and a woman constituted "double-discrimination—the combined effects of practices which discriminate on the basis of race, as well as on the basis of sex" (p. 149). Race and sex intersect so that, in any individual, "the whole is greater than the sum of the parts." That's also true with respect to disability and other microcultures.

Disproportionality in special education refers to the overrepresentation or underrepresentation of students with disabilities who also are from various microcultures. Simply stated, students who have a disability and are from racially/ethnically diverse backgrounds are—relative to students with disabilities who are not from those populations—classified more often as having a disability, experience less inclusion, are bullied more often, undergo more restraint and seclusion, are suspended and expelled more frequently, and are placed more usually into the "pipeline" from special education to the juvenile justice system.

In this section, you will learn about the alignment of intersectionality and disproportionality related to six key educational considerations—classification as having a disability, extent of inclusion, bullying, restraint and seclusion, suspension and expulsion, and participation in the juvenile justice system. What are your predictions about how disability, race, gender, LGBTQ, and English learning align with these six considerations? What microculture combinations put students most at risk?

Classification as Having a Disability

OVERALL DISABILITY On average, across the states, 13 percent of all children and youth ages 3 to 21 receive IDEA (National Center for Education Statistics, 2017a).

RACE Compare that average with the data below. Two groups exceed the national average, while two groups are just 1 percent under it and only one group is significantly under it (National Center for Education Statistics, 2017a). You will easily see the disproportionality:

- American Indian/Alaska Native—17 percent
- Black—15 percent
- White—13 percent
- Two or more races—13 percent
- Hispanic—12 percent
- Pacific Islander—12 percent
- Asian—7 percent

GENDER Although male and female students are enrolled in general education in equal proportion, approximately two thirds of students receiving special education services are male (U.S. Department of Education, 2011). (We note here that national reporting does not address transgender.)

STUDENTS LEARNING ENGLISH Fourteen percent of the students learning English are identified as having a disability, even though students learning English make up only 10 percent of the school population (National Center for Educational Statistics, 2017b).

INTERSECTIONALITY AND DISPROPORTIONALITY We summarize: If the student is male, belongs to the American Indian/Alaska Native or Black race, and is learning English, the student has an increased chance to be classified as having a disability. The intersection is clear; thus, the intersectionality is high.

Extent of Inclusion

OVERALL DISABILITY The overall rate of inclusion for students with disabilities is 63 percent for spending 80 percent or more time in general education settings and 5 percent for being placed in entirely separate settings (U.S. Department of Education, 2018—reference for all data in this section, unless otherwise specified). Students who are least likely to spend 80 percent or more time in general education classes are classified as having multiple disabilities (13 percent) and intellectual disabilities (17 percent). Students who are most likely to be placed entirely in segregated settings are those with multiple disabilities (24 percent) and those with emotional and behavioral disorders (17 percent).

RACE Figure 2.3 sets out the demographics regarding the extent of inclusion of students with disabilities by race. As you consider all the bars of the graph, what trends do you find for racial groups that have the lowest percentages of 80 percent or more of their time in the general education class? You are correct if you identified Native Hawaiian/Other Pacific Islanders, Asian, and Black. Next, what trends do you see for the highest percentage of placement in separate educational environments? The three groups having the highest percentage include Black, Asian, and White students.

STUDENTS LEARNING ENGLISH Fifty-seven percent of students who are learning English are in the general education classroom for more than 80 percent of the school day, which aligns with the racial groups having the lowest representation of general education placement. Two percent are in segregated settings, which is half of the students in the microcultures of disability and race.

Figure 2.3 Percentage of Students Ages 6 Through 21 Served Under IDEA Within Racial/Ethnic Groups by Educational Environment

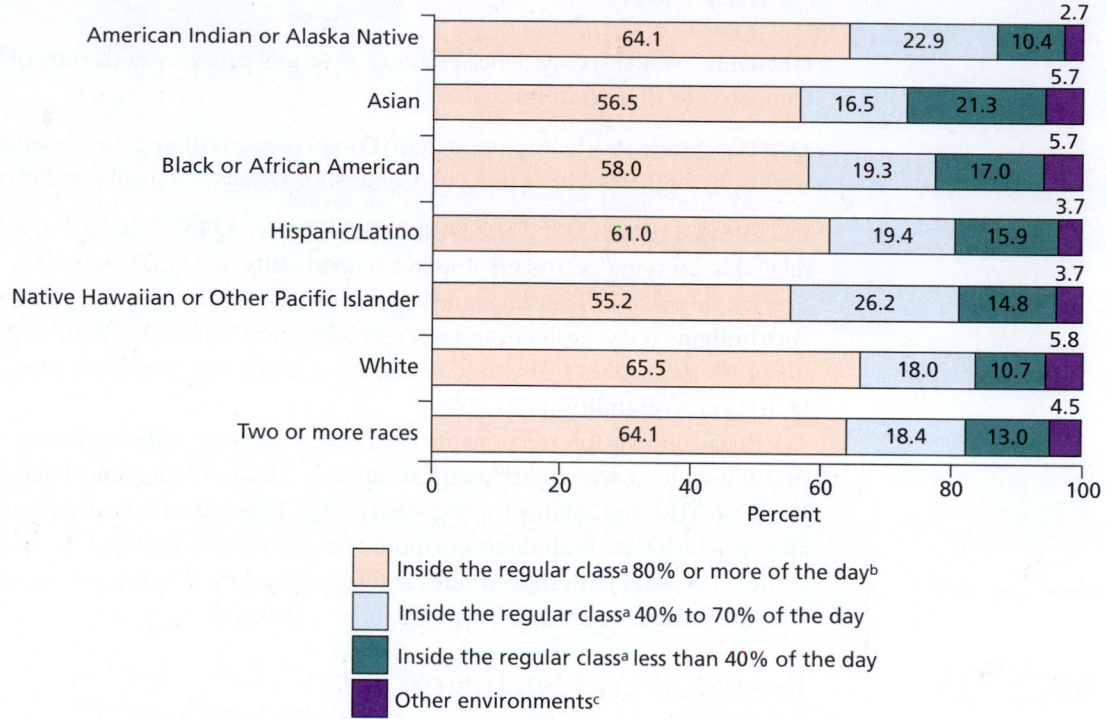

aPercentage of day spent inside the regular class is defined as the number of hours the student spends each day inside the regular classroom, divided by the total number of hours in the school day (including lunch, recess, and study periods), multiplied by 100.
bStudents who received special education and related services outside the regular classroom for less than 21 percent of the school day were classified in the *inside the regular class 80% or more of the day* category.
c"Other environments" includes *separate school, residential facility, homebound/hospital* environment, *correctional facilities*, and *parentally placed in private schools*.
NOTE: Percentage was calculated by dividing the number of students ages 6 through 21 served under *IDEA*, Part B, in the racial/ethnic group and educational environment by the total number of students ages 6 through 21 served under *IDEA*, Part B, in the racial/ethnic group and all the educational environments, then multiplying the result by 100. The sum of bar percentages may not total 100 because of rounding.

SOURCE: U.S. Department of Education, ED*Facts* Data Warehouse (EDW), OMB #1975-0240: "*IDEA* Part B Child Count and Educational Environments Collection," 2015. These data are for the 50 states, DC, BIE schools, PR, the four outlying areas, and the three freely associated states. Data were accessed Fall 2016. For actual *IDEA* data used, go to https://www2.ed.gov/programs/osepidea/618-data/state-level-data-files/index.html.

INTERSECTIONALITY AND DISPROPORTIONALITY Once again, we see an intersection of disability and race (Asian and Black). A student at that intersection is more likely than any other student not to be in general education classrooms. We are unable to locate data on gender and inclusive placements. Based on other data (some of which we have described), it is fair to assume that, again, male students—especially those who are Black—have the lowest rate of placement in general education classrooms and the highest rate of placements in separate educational environments.

Bullying

OVERALL DISABILITY The national average of students who experience bullying on school property is 21 percent (National Center for Education Statistics, 2016—reference for all data in this section, unless otherwise specified). The trend across 30 studies indicates that students with disabilities are, at a minimum, approximately twice as likely to be victims of bullying than students without disabilities (Rose, Monda-Amaya, & Eselage, 2011).

RACE The national averages of bullying according to race include:

- American Indian/Alaska Native and Pacific Islander—26 percent
- Black—25 percent

- White—22 percent
- Hispanic—17 percent
- Asian—16 percent

GENDER Females experience bullying on school property at the rate of 23 percent, as compared to 19 percent for males.

LGBTQ Students identifying as LGBTQ experience bullying on school property at the frightfully high level of 34 percent (Centers for Disease Control and Prevention, 2017).

INTERSECTIONALITY AND DISPROPORTIONALITY The strongest intersection related to bullying occurs for students who identify as LGBTQ who also have disabilities; it is 48 percent. Translated, nearly half of LGBTQ students with disabilities experience bullying (Gay, Lesbian, and Straight Education Network [GLSEN], 2016). We were unable to locate data that would enable us to factor race as a triple consideration with LGBTQ and disability status.

Regarding the intersectionality of disability, gender, and race, female students with disabilities who are either American Indian/Alaska Native and Pacific Islanders or Black have the highest disproportionality rates. This is the first category of intersectionality in which female students are more often represented than male students. The disability and racial pattern continues in terms of highest disproportionality for students who are American/Indian/Pacific Islander and Black.

Restraint and Seclusion

Restraint and seclusion are regarded as forms of aversive intervention for students who engage in highly problematic behavior. Restraint is divided into two categories—mechanical and physical (U.S. Department of Education Office for Civil Rights, 2016—reference for all data in this section). **Mechanical restraint** refers to any "device or equipment [used] to restrict a student's freedom or movement (p. 6)"; examples include handcuffs, tape, weights, and ropes. **Physical restraint** refers to "a personal restriction that immobilizes or reduces the ability of a student to move his or her torso, arms, legs, or head freely (p. 6)"; it includes holding a student in a way that the student is unable to move. **Seclusion** refers to the involuntary confinement of a student alone in a room or area from which the student is physically prevented from leaving. It does not include a timeout, which is a behavior management technique implemented as part of an approved program, involving the monitored separation of the student in a nonlocked setting, and is implemented for the purpose of calming (p. 7).

OVERALL DISABILITY Although students with disabilities make up approximately 13 percent of the public school population, they receive 67 percent of all restraints or seclusions. That rate is 5.5 times the rate at which they are in school. "More than 100,000 students were placed in seclusion or involuntary confinement or were physically restrained at school to immobilize them or reduce their ability to move freely—including 69,000 students with disabilities served by IDEA" (p. 5).

RACE/ETHNICITY AND GENDER The highest rates of restraint and seclusion were for American Indian/Alaska Native and Black males—approximately 2.5 times their population rate. We were unable to locate data that report race/ethnicity and gender standing alone rather than in combination.

INTERSECTIONALITY AND DISPROPORTIONALITY The intersectionality pattern continues: Students in the racial groups of American Indian/Alaska Native and Black, are, if male, more likely to be subjected to restraint and seclusion than any other group of students with disabilities. Further, restraint and seclusion are rare in most school districts; however, in a small proportion they are "relatively common" (p. 8).

MyLab Education

Video Example 2.2
Jino was repeatedly restrained and secluded in public school with dreadful long-term physical and emotional impact In standing in Jino's shoes, what impact do you think experiencing restraint and seclusion would have on you? https://www.youtube.com/watch?v=mrn1fXaXfeA&feature=youtu.be

Suspensions and Expulsions

OVERALL DISABILITY Twenty-nine percent of students with disabilities receive suspensions; that rate is slightly over twice as many as students without disabilities (29 percent) (Lipscomb et al., 2017). Does that rate surprise you? It should, given that you learned in Chapter 1 that IDEA requires IEP teams to consider the research-based intervention known as **positive behavior support** if the behavior of students impedes their own learning or that of others. You also learned in Chapter 1 that students with disabilities may not be suspended for more than 10 consecutive or cumulative days (when a pattern exists) without their educators conducting a **functional behavior assessment** and, once again, considering **positive behavior support**. Thus, even with those protections against ongoing suspensions, the rate of suspensions is still twice as high for students with disabilities than for their peers without disabilities.

Students who are Black—especially male Black students—are disproportionally placed in special rather than general education classes.

The four top disability categories (in order of priority) for suspension rate are emotional and behavioral disorders, other health impaired (primarily ADHD), specific learning disabilities, and intellectual disability (Losen, Ee, Hodson, & Martinez, 2015). The suspension rate for students with emotional and behavioral disorders is approximately 2.25 times greater than for students with other health impaired (primarily ADHD) and approximately 8 times higher than the category with the lowest suspension rate, speech or language impairment.

RACE/ETHNICITY Black/African American and American Indian/Native American students have the highest rates of suspensions and expulsions. American Indian/Alaska Native students represent 0.5 percent of the school population, but their rate of multiple out-of-school suspensions is 4 times higher (2 percent) and their rate of expulsions is 6 times higher (3 percent) than any other group of students (U.S. Department of Education Office for Civil Rights, 2014—reference for all data in this section, unless otherwise specified). Black students represent 16 percent of the school population, but their rate of multiple out-of-school suspensions is approximately 2.5 times higher (42 percent) and their rate of expulsions is slightly more than 2 times higher (34 percent). Alarmingly, the suspension rate for Black/African American students at the preschool level is slightly higher than at the elementary/secondary level. Asian and White students both have an especially low rate of suspensions.

GENDER Male students receive approximately three fourths of suspensions and expulsions. By contrast, female students receive approximately one fourth.

STUDENTS LEARNING ENGLISH Students learning English represent 10 percent of the school population but only 7 percent of suspensions.

LGBTQ We were unable to locate data on students who are LGBTQ in terms of multiple out-of-school suspensions, but their rate of at least one in-school or out-of-school suspension is 15 percent (Gay, Lesbian, and Straight Education Network [GLSEN], 2016).

INTERSECTIONALITY AND DISPROPORTIONALITY Figure 2.4 depicts the weighty effect of the intersection of race, disability, and gender, especially for students who are Black/African American (Losen, Ee, Hodson, & Martinez, 2015). We have been unable to locate a similar disaggregation for students who are Native American/Alaska Native, but we suspect, based on data previously reported, that the disproportionality would be similarly problematic. These data on suspensions are especially troublesome given

MyLab Education

Video Example 2.3
In this video, a Black principal speaks candidly about discipline and race. What is your perspective on this principal's conclusion about White teachers responding to the behavior of Black/African American boys?

David Grossman/Alamy Stock Photo

Figure 2.4 Intersectionality of Race, Disability, and Gender Regarding Suspensions

Racial Group	%R	%R-D	%R-D-G
Black	17	24	27
White	5	9	11

R = Race

D = Disabilities

G = Gender

that students who are suspended have—as you learned earlier in this chapter—highly significant rates for school drop-out and involvement with the justice system (Balfanz, Byrnes, & Fox, 2015; Shollenberger, 2015).

Participation in Juvenile Justice System

OVERALL DISABILITY   The rate of students with disabilities enrolled in the juvenile justice system is almost double their rate of representation in public high schools (23 percent vs. 12 percent) (U.S. Department of Education Office for Civil Rights, 2016—reference for all data in this section, unless otherwise specified).

RACE/ETHNICITY   Students in three racial groups—Native Hawaiian/Other Pacific Islander, American Indian/Alaska Native, and Black—have about a double or slightly higher percentage of enrollment in juvenile justice educational programs as contrasted with their public high school representation. Of the student enrollment in juvenile justice facilities, Black students constitute the largest percentage at 42 percent.

GENDER   Boys represent 86 percent of the population in juvenile justice educational programs but only about 50 percent of the total public school enrollment.

STUDENTS LEARNING ENGLISH   Students learning English have a 1 percent greater representation in juvenile justice educational programs than in public high schools (6 percent vs. 5 percent).

INTERSECTIONALITY AND DISPROPORTIONALITY   The intersectionality of high rates of juvenile justice participation related to disability, race (Native American/Other Pacific Islander, American Indian/Alaska Native, and Black), and gender (male) leads to disturbing disproportionality.

MyLab Education Self-Check 2.2

MyLab Education Application Exercise 2.2: Cultural Bias

Educational Approaches for Enhancing Dignity

You may remember we said in Chapter 1 that there are seven core elements of our book. One is diversity and cultural justice. And you also may remember that dignity is the overriding principle. It's time to consider both, starting with a question.

Are you ready to learn how you can infuse cultural justice—fairness in the provision of education to students representing all microcultures—and dignity into your teaching, especially as you teach students from microcultures characterized by intersectionality and disproportionality? We assume you are. And we assume you will want to learn from teachers such as you will be.

Let's start with a lesson from a teacher, Mike Lamb; he attended private schools in Chicago and had just graduated from a highly selective, largely white private university before taking his first job. It was at an elementary school in inner-city Chicago. Almost all of the students were African American; the school itself had long been classified as underperforming. Neither of those facts inhibited Mike; both, however, influenced how he taught. As you read *My Voice: The Four-R Approach*, seek especially to discover how Mike learned to infuse his teaching with cultural dignity.

My Voice

The Four-R Approach

"Mr. Lamb, why do I gotta raise my hand?"

"I ain't no little kid!"

"You not my daddy!"

As a first-year reading teacher on Chicago's South Side, I often heard these comments. On good days, I faced skepticism; on bad, defiance.

To my students, I had no depth. Why, I asked myself, can't they detect my good intentions? Why don't they give me the benefit of the doubt? How can I reach and convince them?

I was shocked when my assistant principal told me in my second month at the school, "I think you've lost them for the year. You'll just have to try to find some way to make the best of it." Was this how my teaching career would go: Was I a white liberal with good intentions who would ultimately fail? I intended to make the opposite result happen.

Critical self-reflection forced me to realize that I had no context for my students. Half of the staff left the school each year, and students had no idea why I would stay, let alone genuinely care about them. I had been operating on assumptions about myself and my students, but to communicate with them, I had to ask myself: Why am I here? Is it about me or about them? Who am I and where did I come from? What do I bring to them? What strengths do they bring to the table? I found that the most important tools were concepts any teacher can use.

I needed to make my respect for my students, their families, and their lives clear. No matter who I was, what decisions I had made in my own life, or what my values were, I had to show them that I respected their essential humanity, their innate goodness.

Nor could I let their misbehavior cause me to think that they were flawed. Equally, I could not judge them by their test scores alone. I had to affirm that each could become a better reader, regardless of his or her scores.

Now I started to connect with my students. However, it was not until I brought my mother to school for Thanksgiving that relationships began to form. I knew about the importance of relationships, but I was not sure exactly how to build them.

I had determined that my students' parents were essential for both me and their children's education. I called all of them the first day of school, seeking their trust. At the first parent-teacher conference, I said I was all about power and opportunity for our students. From then on, they were major resources for me. I do not remember one interaction that ended negatively that year. But I couldn't get my students to buy in.

I thought about relationships and differences and realized I needed to find roots with my students. Could they and I transcend the power-over relationship in which I was dominant and they were acquiescent? I believed so; now, my duty would be to reach out and learn about my students.

To reach out meant giving them the benefit of the doubt and teaching them to give the same to me. We had to find ways to create relationships. With a relationship, we could understand; with understanding, we could give each the benefit of any doubts. We could begin to trust, to solve our problems together.

When I brought my mother to class before Thanksgiving, my students saw me as not just their teacher but as a man with a visible origin and palpable values. They asked her, "What was he like as a kid?" They asked me, "What was your most embarrassing moment?" We began to see each other as people; the common humanity became manifest. Now my students saw me as a more whole person; they also could get some dirt on me. My mother was now "Grandma," making me "School Daddy." They were still skeptical, but less so; still angry, but less so.

Late in the fall term, I asked my assistant principal for guidance. She turned the question back on me, asking what I had learned at my high school and what I thought my students deserved to know. That was a turning point: thereafter, I built rigor into my curriculum. We would become critical thinkers together, whether reading Shakespeare's *Much Ado About Nothing* or Bradbury's *Fahrenheit 451*.

I knew I could not control whether my students liked me or thought I was cool. But I could control my academic

(Continued)

expectations of them. I knew hard work in school gave me power to make my own decisions about the opportunities that came to me because of that work.

I was determined to give my students this same sense of control over their own futures by insisting on hard work and academic rigor. At the start of the school year, only 12 percent of my eighth-grade students met standards on the Illinois Test of Basic Skills (ITBS) reading test; at the end, 71 percent met national standards on the state test. The next year I began a two-year loop with my new homeroom. After the seventh- and eighth-grade years, these students had the same success: from only 12 percent achieving standards, 67 percent did. Three of them who had started below the thirty-sixth percentile ended up scoring in the ninety-fourth during their eighth-grade year.

Expecting hard work also caused the students to feel more respected. When low expectations exist, students feel unchallenged; they believe their teachers are condescending.

When challenges arise, resilience is essential. My students usually would get into trouble or fail academically because they let little issues spiral out of control; they were uncertain of forgiveness and lacked strategies to resolve routine problems. When called to account for minor matters, they would escalate their reactions; they did not expect understanding and forgiveness.

Challenged by test questions or difficult reading passages, they would make the problem appear to be a question of their behavior instead of their intelligence.

But I talked about overcoming obstacles. And they began to open themselves up to conflict- and problem-resolution strategies, whether they were interacting with other students or reading a difficult passage. Simply shifting their mindset to one that left them open to solutions and resolution was a major accomplishment for them.

For us as teachers, the question is this: What respect, relationships, rigor, and resilience have we helped put into place to provide our students with opportunities to respond with better versions of themselves? Arguments about each other's mommas and their struggles to comprehend Shakespeare or Bradbury will happen. But who will students become as a result of these challenges?

—Reprinted with permission from Michael Lamb.

We hope you will incorporate Mike's Four R's:

- Respect—how you regard students (remember what we said in Chapter 1: how you regard a student is to attribute dignity to the student or, conversely, to demean the student)

- Relationships—how you bond with students

- Rigor—how you ensure high expectation for students, including the *Endrew* standard of having appropriately ambitious programs and challenging objectives

- Resilience—how you support students to overcome challenges.

The bottom line is that Mike's Four-R approach rested on his belief that his students have their own internal, intrinsic dignity and that he should behave toward them and their families in a way that acknowledges that fact and treats them with the dignity they inherently deserve. What he believed and how he acted relate directly to the general matter of cultural bias and, indeed, to the matter of your own biases.

We encourage you to take special note of the vast improvement the students made on meeting standards on the state assessment test in reading—from 12 percent to 71 percent one year and from 12 percent to 67 percent another year. That is amazing progress!

Link here to read about Mike's current position as the Executive Director of Turnaround Children, a national organization based in Washington, D.C., focusing on using research-based tools to enhance cultural justice for students from diverse backgrounds. https://www.turnaroundusa.org/team/michael-lamb/

Addressing Your Own Cultural Biases

If you took the bias-assessment tests we presented earlier in this chapter, you have learned something about your own implicit bias with respect to disability and race. You also now know about the powerful impact of intersectionality and disproportionality. What do intersectionality and disproportionality tell us about implicit and explicit bias? The answer matters, especially because biases proclaim that those students who are subject to single, double, or triple bias are more likely than not to be treated in a demeaning way, that is, in a way that is the opposite of a dignifying way. That conclusion rests on the data we have presented.

The conclusion is troubling because biases, especially implicit ones, are difficult to eradicate (Forscher et al., 2017)—difficult, though not impossible, to reduce, even erase, over a long term (Devine, Forscher, Austin, & Cox, 2012). Why wait? Why not start now to address bias?

Guidelines for Teaching

Watch, Think, and Act to Eliminate Implicit Bias

<u>Watch</u> out for personal attitudes, beliefs, opinions, comfort/discomfort around others, and actions for indications of implicit bias.

- When you notice one of your negative perceptions, consider whether you apply that negative perception to everyone who shares similar characteristics and/or microcultures.
- For at least a couple of weeks, keep notes about interactions and experiences in which you have positive and negative judgments that relate to microcultures or other person-related categories.
- Review your notes and look for themes related to how you use your "personal cultural measuring stick" to form positive and negative judgments about others.
- Consider the extent to which you practiced empathy for the people you encountered in your notes and identify the people/categories of people around which you did not practice empathy.
- Maintain openness and non-defensiveness as you begin to have more awareness and insight about your implicit biases.

<u>Think</u> about the negative biases with which you have become aware through attending to your own attitudes and behavior. Then consider how you would want to be treated if you were in the circumstances of people against whom you hold negative biases. Reflecting on your values, consider how you differentially treat people in light of your learned positive and negative biases.

- Start with the bias that you think will be the easiest to eliminate. Identify all of the people whom you know (at least as an acquaintance) who align with the unfavorable view that you hold.
- For these people, seek to "take the shoes test" by standing in their shoes and thinking about what it feels like to be them. If you were in their shoes and it were your life rather than theirs, how would you want to be regarded by others? Would you want to be treated with dignity?

- Reflect on your values in terms of your own belief about treating others with dignity.
- Identify the people in your life whom you almost always treat with dignity and those whom you almost never treat with dignity. Think of the positive and negative biases that are in play.

<u>Act</u> to others in opposition to your negative biases—as if they do not exist.

- Consider your bias (the one easiest to change) that you identified above and what you learned from taking the "shoes test" with the people you know that align with this first bias.
- Identify specific steps you will take to treat them with the "dignity golden rule"—to treat them with the dignity with which you want others to treat you.
- Again, take notes on the extent to which you implement the specific steps.
  o Identify the circumstances in which you were successful and unsuccessful.
- Identify themes across successful and unsuccessful implementation; work to eliminate the circumstances around unsuccessful implementation and expand on the circumstances around successful implementation.
- Reach out to one or two people against whom you have this bias (again, start with the easiest) and seek to spend time with them and, perhaps, even develop a friendship.
- Concentrate on their positive attributes.

<u>Now</u> that you have worked through your "easiest bias," start the process again with another bias and continue to do so until you work through all of your implicit biases. Then continue to be on guard for avoiding the incorporation of new implicit biases.

SOURCE: Based on Thiederman, S. (2015). *3 keys to defeating unconscious bias: Watch, think, act.* San Diego, CA: Cross-Cultural Communications.

Guidelines for Teaching: Watch, Think, and Act to Eliminate Implicit Bias sets out guidelines you can follow for watching, thinking, and acting in order to eliminate any biases you may have with respect to other people, in general, and your future students, in particular—especially those who have a disability, are male, and are Black and American Indian/Alaska Native. This feature does more than that; it guides you as you seek to infuse dignity into your teaching. In encouraging you to follow the guidelines, we are not "accusing" you of having biases but rather we are recognizing that we all "breathe the air of invisible 'messages'"; we are all prone to biases, especially implicit biases of which we may not be aware.

Restorative Justice

At the beginning of this chapter, you "met" McKyla Woods and her teacher, Emilio Ortega, and you learned about restorative justice in their school and its role within

Oakland schools and Oakland itself. It's now time for you to learn what restorative justice is and how you can implement this practice.

Restorative justice is communal; it evokes traditions of the Maori in New Zealand, Native American, Latin American, and African-descended people and their determination to create or hold fast to the ties that bind them, to their relationships with each other. Thus, it is not hierarchical, with school administrators or judges deciding who did what to whom and what the consequences must be. Furthermore, it is inclusive: No offender and no offended persons are exempt, whether they be students or faculty and administrators.

Howard Zehr (2015), the "father of restorative justice" in the United States, characterizes restorative justice as follows:

> Restorative justice requires, at minimum, that we address the harms and needs of those harmed, hold those causing harm accountable to "put right" those harms, and involve both of these parties as well as relevant communities in this process (p. 35) . . . (The outcomes) are responsibility, reparation, and healing for all. (p. 43)

School shootings, especially at Columbine, Colorado, in 1999, were the catalysts that eventually impelled educators to use restorative justice (Evans & Vaandering, 2016). They did not use it immediately. Instead, they obeyed federal and state policy requiring them to adopt zero-tolerance policies. These policies required suspensions and expulsions that negatively affected the academic performance of all students, especially those from ethnic and cultural minorities. Those policies still exist, but starting in the early 2000s, a new approach to school harms arose, especially in Oakland and then elsewhere. This new approach—referred to as restorative justice or restorative practice—responded to harm and issues about discipline, but it did more than that: It also "spoke" to the students' dignity. Let's consider the dignity matter before we consider how to practice restorative justice.

Restorative justice closely aligns with cultural dignity because it affirms that "human beings are *worthy*" (p. 31) and that "people have dignity because the essence of who they are cannot be replaced" (Evans & Vaandering, 2016, p. 32). Those affirmations apply to any student or faculty member who is involved in a conflict at any school. The affirmations would, however, be no more than words unless practices advanced them. Restorative justice is such a practice. In the Oakland schools, it is a significant program of the education of all students.

Restorative practice has three core components (Evans & Vaandering, 2016):

- Creating learning environments characterized by justice and equity
- Nurturing relationships through authentic connection, belonging, and trust
- Repairing harm and transforming conflict when dignity is violated.

These components are manifest when students and faculty, such as McKyla and Mr. Ortega, form into a restorative justice circle

- seeking to learn, together, how to shift their attention from broken rules to why rules were broken,
- from who is to blame to who has been harmed, and
- from what punishment will be determined to how harm can be repaired and community among teachers and students can be restored or, if not lost, then created (Zehr, 2002).

A broad range of approaches to restorative practices helps members of a restorative-justice circle activate the three core components and three shifts of emphasis and focus. Figure 2.5 identifies five types of restorative practices; they range from informal to formal (Wachtel, 2016). Each rests on a single foundation: the expression of feelings and the search for empathy.

Figure 2.5 Foundation and Continuum of Restorative Practice from Informality to Formality

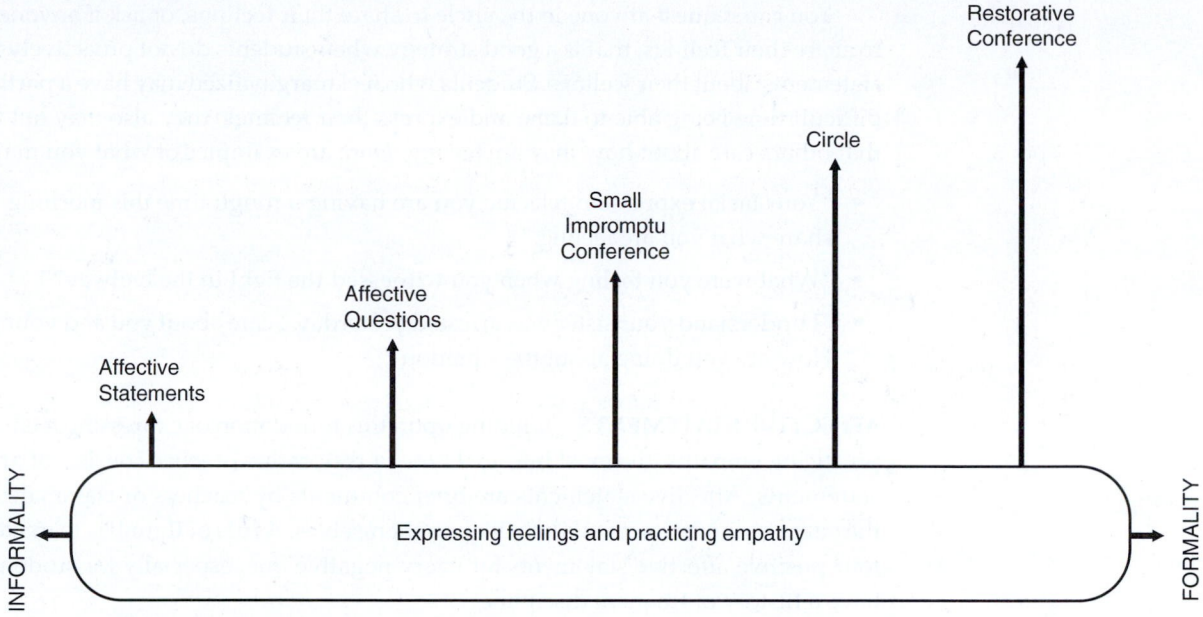

SOURCE: Based on: Wachtel, T. (2013). Defining restorative. Retrieved from: www.iirp.edu/pdf/Defining-Restorative.pdf.

FOUNDATION OF EXPRESSING FEELINGS AND EMPATHY   The foundation of restorative justice is the act of expressing feelings regarding the positive or negative action of oneself and others. You can model the use of "I statements" to express a broad range of feelings while encouraging students to do likewise. A framework for simplifying the hundreds of possible feelings is to think about feelings through six major categories (Turnbull et al., 2013):

Happy   Sad   Angry   Worried   Scared   Okay

Each category has a range of intensity from mild to moderate to intense. You and your students can work together to create examples of mild, moderate, and intense feeling, such as this example for feeling sad:

- Mild—unsure, mixed up, confused
- Moderate—distressed, hurt, empty, drained
- Intense—crushed, despairing, miserable, hopeless

When one person expresses a feeling, others must respond. Otherwise, there is no "common" ground, no "community" that can be created. As your students express their feelings, you can coach them to practice empathy. Empathy involves seeking to understand the feelings from the speaker's perspective by (1) trying to "walk a mile" in the speaker's shoes, (2) listening in order to understand rather than to plan what you will say next, and (2) expressing care in words and actions (Ciramicoli & Ketcham, 2000). For example, you could say something like the following:

- "I hear you are feeling anxious about the upcoming assessments. I understand that taking assessments is way down your priority list. Would you help me plan something special we can do as a class to celebrate doing our best with the questions and getting the whole thing behind us?"

- "I hear your excitement that your parents came to the play last night. I saw them clapping for you. They were obviously very proud of you."

Within restorative justice practices, the expression of feelings and an empathetic response to those statements build the foundation for strengthening emotional bonds, leading to trusting relationships among students and between students and educators.

You can request anyone in the circle to share their feelings, or ask if anyone wants to share their feelings; that is a good strategy when students do not proactively initiate statements about their feelings. Students who feel marginalized may have a particularly difficult time being able to name and express their feelings; they also may not believe that others care about how they are feeling. Here are examples of what you may say:

- "Your facial expression tells me you are having a rough time this morning. Please share what you are feeling."
- "What were you feeling when you witnessed the fight in the hallway?"
- "I understand your sister was arrested yesterday. I care about you and your family. How are you doing about the situation?"

AFFECTIVE STATEMENTS Building upon this foundation of expressing feelings and practicing empathy, the most informal type of restorative practice consists of **affective statements**. Affective statements are brief comments by teachers or classmates about the effect of another person's behavior on themselves. A rule of thumb is to make about four positive affective statements for every negative one, especially for students who have a history of frequent discipline.

- "It made me happy throughout the whole science class that you stayed in your seat and completed your work."
- "Wow—your performance in the class debate blew me away. Have you considered going to law school?"
- "Last quarter you were absent 7 days, and this quarter you have had perfect attendance. I am giving you a thumbs up."
- "When you use your phone in class, I feel disappointed that you are not paying attention and worried that you are missing important learning."

AFFECTIVE QUESTIONS Affective questions build on affective statements by asking the student involved in wrongdoing the following questions:

- "What were you thinking when this incident happened?"
- "Who was affected by what you did and how were they affected?"
- "What do you think are the next steps in making things right?"

As students answer these questions, you may want to express your own feelings and empathy, modeling what you want your students to do.

SMALL, IMPROMPTU CONFERENCE In behavioral incidents that involve a few people and occur on a sporadic basis, a small, impromptu conference is an option for bringing together the involved parties for group problem solving. The same affective questions that you use for a single individual are appropriate for everyone in the conference.

CIRCLE The circle extends restorative practices to larger groups where students such as McKyla and teachers such as Mr. Ortega can share their feelings, offer solutions to problems, and find their common ground and means for peace. *Guidelines for Teaching: Implementing Circles as a Restorative Practice* outlines what some leaders in restorative practice describe as the 10 essential elements of circles and tips for how to implement each element (Boyes-Watson & Pranis, 2015). The goal is to infuse these 10 elements with culturally responsive practices in order to support the active participation of all students and especially those whose "intersectionalities" put them at high risk for disproportionate discipline sanctions such as suspension, expulsion, restraint, seclusion, and juvenile justice involvement. McKyla is not at risk now; the circle deters those consequences.

Guidelines for Teaching

Implementing Circles as a Restorative Practice

Sit in a circle as a symbol of equality and connectivity.

- Ensure that students hear and see each other (when students are blind, orient them to their place in the circle).

Begin with mindfulness as a way to invite students to be present.

- Have a moment of silence with several deep breaths.
- Consider using a short music clip for students to listen for last tone and raise their hands accordingly.

Open the circle in a way to focus on the issue to be addressed.

- Use an opening to match the purpose of the discussion such as a quote, short reading (maybe in unison), song, etc.

Embed a centerpiece as a focal point.

- Use a centerpiece to align with the students' microcultures, such as a Mexican woven fabric.
- Vary centerpieces to represent the broad range of students' microcultures.
- Invite students to bring a rock, flower, or other object from their home to create a centerpiece.

Use a talking piece to structure and equalize dialogue.

- Identify an object as a talking piece that, like the centerpiece, aligns with students' microcultures.
- Teach the students that they can only talk when holding the talking piece; thus no interruptions are allowed and they can fully listen without planning what they will immediately say in response.
- Hold the talking piece yourself, as the circle keeper, when you speak; only talk without the talking piece when you need to for maintaining circle guidelines.
- Pass the talking piece from person to person.

Identify values, in the beginning of using circles, as a basis for guidelines.

- Invite students to write a value on a paper plate based on the values they want to use in the circle.
- Encourage a classmate to (a) sit beside a student with a disability who needs prompting to think of a value and/or (b) assistance in writing the value.

- Invite each student to share the value and place the paper plate in the middle of the circle as the talking piece is passed.

Create circle guidelines, in the beginning of using circles, aligned with values.

- Consider having the students generate circle guidelines that will enable them to experience circle safely and trust.
- Consider the alternative of sharing draft guidelines and inviting students to make desired changes for the final guidelines.

  - "Respect the talking piece;
  - Speak from the heart;
  - Listen from the heart;
  - Personal information shared in the circle is confidential except where safety is at risk;
  - Remain in the circle." (p. 31)

Ask guiding questions to strengthen relationships, explore issues, and generate an action plan.

- Provide questions, as the circle keeper, or encourage one or more students to provide questions, as experience in the circle builds in order to:
  - Boost students' confidence in sharing their own life experiences and stories
  - Encourage sharing feelings and practicing empathy
  - Move from describing the problem to coming up with solutions.

Make agreements when the circle needs to take action.

- Use consensus to make decisions.
- Record decisions if needed.
- Ask all students to commit to implementing agreements.
- Express hope that implementation will occur.

Close the ceremony to affirm contributions and connectedness.

- Use similar options as in opening the circle, such as deep breathing and readings.
- Guide students in transitioning to their next activity.

SOURCE: Based on Boyes-Watson, C., & Pranis, K. (2015). *Circle forward: Building a restorative school community.* St. Paul, MN: Living Justice Press.

The educator can implement circles in several ways (Boyes-Watson & Pranis, 2015; Riestenberg, 2012):

- Academics, such as by sharing writing and overcoming homework obstacles
- Social and emotional learning, such as by discussing what self-respect means and how to de-escalate anger
- Building relationships, such as by establishing personal boundaries and eliminating bullying
- Addressing cultural taboos, such as by abolishing the "R-word" and other hate speech and eradicating sexual harassment.

You may convene circles at the start or end of your day (assuming you are a homeroom teacher), or, if you are a restorative justice facilitator such as Mr. Ortega, you may convene them on an as-needed basis, particularly when teasing or bullying provokes a student.

RESTORATIVE CONFERENCE   A restorative conference is the most formal option in Figure 2.5. It occurs when one or more students have engaged in behavior that warrants suspension or expulsion. The restorative conference is an alternative to these exclusionary forms of discipline. That is so because it addresses the consequences of the students' behavior and holds them accountable in a particular way. When schools use it instead of suspension or expulsion, they—and you—address the problem of disproportionality.

Mr. Ortega is one of many restorative justice facilitators in Oakland Unified School District. Another is Cecilia Harrison. They and other school staff have received professional development in how to address particular situations. They convene the appropriate people—the students (offenders and victims), their parents or primary caregivers, educators (teachers and administrators), and others as appropriate (for example, school psychologists or other mental health professionals). The conference can occur in a circle; the key is to include all of the participants comfortably and effectively. The more that restorative justice characterizes the school's culture and the offenders and victims involved have had many opportunities to rehearse restorative practices characterized by less formality, the more readily they will be able to incorporate foundational skills (expressing feeling and practicing empathy), full disclosure, and problem solving into their contributions. The general script for offenders poses these questions (Watchel, 2016, p. 7):

- "What happened?"
- "What were you thinking of at the time?"
- "What have you thought about since?"
- "Who has been affected by what you have done?"
- "What do you think you need to do to make things right?"

In turn, the victims may respond to these questions (Watchel, 2016, p. 7):

- "What did you think when you realized what happened?"
- "What impact has this incident had on you and others?"
- "What has been the hardest thing for you?"
- "What do you think needs to happen to make things right?"

After everyone has had a chance to ask and answer questions and express feelings, the person who has been most injured—in the vignette, McKyla—shares her feelings and sense of what should happen after the circle dissolves. Others offer their opinions about how to restore or repair relationships, and about who should do what, when, why, and how. The ultimate decision usually is collective but may require a school administrator's agreement to carry out a decision that extends beyond the members of the circle.

You can link here for a practical and comprehensive resource for implementing a wide range of circles across all grade levels: http://www.livingjusticepress.org/vertical/sites/%7B4A259EDB-E3E8-47CD-8728-0553C080A1B0%7D/uploads/Circle_Forward_Front_Matter.pdf/.

You can find helpful adaptations for students with disabilities in this resource: https://www.jkp.com/usa/restorative-practice-and-special-needs.html/

MyLab Education
Video Example 2.4
What are three examples of how the student re-entering school from incarceration is treated with dignity in the restorative conference? https://www.youtube.com/watch?v=uSJ2GPiptvc

In *Guidelines for Teaching: Including Students with Disabilities in Restorative Justice Activities*, Cecilia Harrison highlights accommodations she makes for students with disabilities; you may rely on her suggestions—she is an experienced restorative justice practitioner and a faculty member in the Oakland school district.

Guidelines for Teaching
Including Students with Disabilities in Restorative Justice Activities

Individualization.

- "I get to know and develop meaningful relationships with all of my students."
- "When students have limited expressive language and do not want to talk, I work with them individually, creating a cue card with words or phrases they and I think they may need to sit in the circle. Not all will join in, but some do."
- "Because the questions and activities are geared toward whatever grade level or classroom I have, even my wiggliest students—those with ADHD—enjoy participating. They get to prepare questions to ask the group and the activity we will use. I also incorporate a lot of movement, offer coloring pages or manipulatives, and do small circles so there is not too much stationary time."

Empathy.

- "Those closest to my heart are vulnerable because they are easily put on a fast track to the school-to-prison pipeline. They are underestimated on their capacity to teach us so much when we allow ourselves to view the world from their point of view."

Accessibility.

- "I work closely with my students' other teachers to ensure that any activity is accessible to them, to make sure their aide comes with them, and to work with them individually."
- "I have a son who has mobility issues, so I am hyper-aware of needs like his and plan to make my room and myself (my location in the room) as accessible as possible."

Collaboration.

- "I rely on proxies or other people to help my students who need a trusted helper."

Universal Design for Learning.

- "When working with text, I have a template of what I am teaching or moderating that I project onto a big screen while each student has a hard copy. I read aloud. I highlight what I am reading. I check for their understanding, with an aide. I ask them to write on their templates, and I type words they cannot spell in big letters on my on-screen template."

Media.

- "I teach in a community severely impacted by poverty, violence, and other situations triggered by the poverty. We have quite a few students in general ed who have not been identified as having intellectual disability. I approach all students as if each of them needed an IEP. I also ask them to watch "Inside Out" (a Disney PixarWikia) to start a conversation about feelings and emotions. I include an activity in which they create their Islands of Personality (a Disney PixarWikia) so they can recognize how their bodies and brains do/feel like when they are happy, sad, scared, disgusted, and angry. Making a "Me" poster with their name at the top and a list of things they can do helps them open up. Watching *Shrek the Musical* with pauses for them to reflect and discuss prejudice and stereotyping also helps."
- "When I have students who are in conflict with each other a lot, I use a reward system whereby they get points if they make a positive choice even when they get upset with each other, and I will often have them change seats during a circle (even though the circle is very brief), and I give kind reminders to help them re-enter the circle's activities."

SOURCE: Used with permission of Cecelia Harrison, East Oakland Pride Elementary School, Oakland Unified School District.

You might wonder if restorative justice practices are uniquely aligned with the Oakland district and if they will work in other cultural contexts such as on American Indian reservations, given your understanding of the intersectionalities impacting American Indian students. Restorative conferences vary in many ways in terms of their implementation and follow-up. In *My Voice: Aaron Jabs—From Big Brother to Teaching How to Live in the World*, a principal at the Ponemah School (elementary and middle) on the Red Lake Reservation in Ponemah, Minnesota, describes a restorative conference in which he co-facilitates.

My Voice

Aaron Jabs—From Big Brother to Teaching How to Live in the World

I serve as principal at Ponemah School, which is a Pre-K to 8th grade elementary school serving students in the Red Lake Indian Reservation in northern Minnesota. One hundred percent of our student population is Native American. Our district has a deep respect for the Native culture, especially in terms of beliefs about the Creator and native traditions such as all movement being clockwise. We use the Seven Grandfather Teachings as our core school values (see Figure 2.6).

Before implementing restorative practices at our school, my days were consumed with managing hallway misbehavior and suspensions. We would have students using the F-word at least 10 times a day. We had a rule that saying the F-word would be punished by suspension. We were sending them home every day. They would go home, come back 1 to 5 days later, and they hadn't learned any other ways to handle their frustration. They would have a brief period of good minutes of behavior, and then the F-word returned. It was a never-ending process of excluding them from instruction.

After using restorative practice, the F-word is not an automatic suspension. It is not a slam dunk that we are going to suspend you. We just don't hear it anymore. It's funny that you stop punishing for it and take a more comprehensive approach in terms of getting into feelings, and it stops. We now hear the F-word maybe 5 to 10 times per year rather than at least 10 times a day.

One component of restorative practice is called a restorative circle. My major involvement in circles at the present time is with a group of six 7th- and 8th-grade girls who are divided into two factions. Unfortunately, many of these girls live with extended family because their parents are using drugs, in prison, or dead. Not only have these girls hated each other, but it has been multigenerational—the families have been in arguments and fights for decades. Before starting the circle, these two factions were getting into daily fights inside and outside school. We were getting multiple daily calls from family members telling me about how their children were being mistreated. We told them that the district can't make them stop, but we can use restorative practices to teach them to treat others with respect.

We convened a series of restorative conferences using a circle approach. We were in a room surrounded by the Seven Grandfather Teachings of our school. These teachings come directly from the girls' American Indian culture, which is the culture. When we started the circle, we first asked them surface questions about themselves to help them get used to being in a room together without insulting each other, using the F-word, or hurling a chair, which are all behaviors they had exhibited before. We asked them to describe their favorite thing and to characterize their mood by a type of weather. It wasn't surprising that they described thunder and lightning. Next, we asked them to write a value that they would like for the circle to use on the back of a paper plate and then to share the value and what it means with the group. They placed the plates in the middle of the circle so we could always relate back to them. Other activities involved having the students write on a card what they were thankful for and then to share what they wrote with everyone. It was interesting to me that every single girl was most thankful for a teacher. The Dean of Students asked their former teachers to recall positive things about them and then prepared a strip of paper with each statement and the corresponding girl's name. The girls took turns choosing a strip from a basket and then reading it out loud. This gave them a chance to say positive things about each other with no hurtful language.

We met during the last 20 minutes of the school day when the classes are wrapping up, so the girls are not losing instructional time. We started off meeting every day for a couple of weeks, and then we moved to several times a week. We have been meeting for 6 weeks, and we expect that we will meet for another 2 or 3 and get down to once a week. It's amazing to watch how the interaction is shifting into alignment with our Seven Grandfather Teachings. We are spending a lot of time over 6 weeks teaching these students to get along and show respect. At the end of it all, every minute will be worth it. I suspect we will need to reconvene a circle about every 7 to 9 weeks throughout the rest of the school year. The great thing is that we will not need to send them home to miss out on needed academic instruction.

In terms of background in moving from punishment to restorative practices, we sent our staff to restorative practice workshops over a 2-year period. They each received about 60 hours of training. The staff went in several different cohorts so we could have everyone on the same page. In some of our classes, teachers have their students circle up each morning as a way to check in with each other and get the day started on a positive note. Sometimes, when one or more students in the class are misbehaving, the teacher will have the students circle up right at that moment and ask questions such as "What did you notice today that is different?' "What do you expect of yourselves?" It is amazing how the students misbehaving want to be respected by their classmates.

For my principal role, the change from punishment to restorative practices has been huge. I don't have to be Big Brother anymore, and I have a chance to teach students the invaluable skills of how to get along in the world.

—Reprinted with permission of Aaron Jabs.

Figure 2.6 Seven Grandfather Teachings

Ponemah's school-wide expectations are explained through our teaching and modeling Ojibwe Teachings. These expectations need to be taught across settings. Teachers model, students practice, and teachers reinforce expectations that are consistently applied by every adult. Teach and reteach all expectations.

Wisdom

To have wisdom is to know the difference between good and bad, and to know the result of your actions.

Love

Unconditional love to know that when people are weak they need your love the most, that your love is given freely, and you cannot put conditions on it or your love is not true.

Respect

Respect others, the environment, and respect yourself. If you cannot show respect, you cannot expect respect to be given.

Honesty

To achieve honesty within yourself, to recognize who and what you are. Do this and you can be honest with all others.

Humility

Humble yourself and recognize that no matter how much you think you know, you know very little of all the universe.

Truth

To learn truth, to live with truth, to walk with truth, and to speak truth.

Bravery

To be brave is to do something right, even if you know it's going to hurt you.

3 School-Wide Expectations

The staff chose *Wisdom, Love*, and *Respect* to encompass all of the teachings and create the school-wide expectations.

SOURCE: *Ponemah School Pride: Behavior Manual*. Ponemah Elementary School, Red Lake Public School District, Ponemah, MN.

You may well ask, "What does the research tell us about restorative justice?" You may also want to know about the practices and the issue of intersectionality. Two groups of researchers have studied how restorative practices work in two large high schools comprising a diverse student body; their research focused on the effect of the practice relative to gender, racial disproportionality, and discipline (Gregory, Clawson, Davis, & Gerewitz, 2016; Gregory & Clawson, 2016). The results documented that:

- greater restorative practice implementation is associated with stronger student-teacher relationships across racial/ethnic groups (as reported by students and teachers' use of exclusionary discipline)

- a reduction of 21 percent occurred in referring students for office discipline sanctions based on misconduct and defiant behavior

- teachers who used more affective statements (the most informal restorative practice strategy) made fewer discipline office referrals of African American and Hispanic male and female students, as compared to teachers who used fewer affective statements.

What does all this mean for you? Among other things, it means that, if you want to reduce the amount of discipline your students may experience, then you should express your own emotional responses to your students and encourage them to do likewise to you and their classmates. But be forewarned: Change does not come quickly. When change does occur, the demeaning results of the intersection of disability and other diverse traits are likely to diminish. In their place, the dignifying results of education, not discipline that removes opportunities for education, should increase.

Cultural Responsiveness Teaching

In addition to enhancing your students' emotional and social development, as well as avoiding exclusionary discipline, how else can you promote cultural justice while extending dignity to students? There is an answer. It's called "culturally responsive teaching."

MyLab Education
Video Example 2.5
What are two points you take from this video about culturally responsive teaching?

Culturally responsive teaching uses the experiences, perspectives, family and social networks, strengths, and needs of diverse students as a resource to ensure learning and positive outcomes (Gay, 2013). You have learned that male American Indian/Alaskan Native students with disabilities are at disproportional risk for negative educational experiences and outcomes. The intersection of their disability and microcultures does not bode well for them. As their teacher, you will not be educating them in a vacuum that seals them from their culture. Consider this fact in light of the highly disappointing results from the most current national survey of American Indian/Alaska Native 8th graders (National Assessment of Educational Progress, 2017):

- Only 7 percent of teachers attended professional development or community programs on developing culturally responsive practices 3 times or more during the previous 2 years.

- Only 15 percent of teachers implemented culturally responsive practices to a moderate or large extent during the previous 2 years.

- Only 19 percent of students had reading teachers who gave them assignments to read about or discuss current issues of concern in their cultural community.

- Only 7 percent of students had math teachers who required them to participate in activities that integrate math with cultural themes.

- Only 22 percent of students had administrators who reported that a culturally relevant community member was involved 3 or more times in a typical school year to share traditions and culture with students and staff.

What do these data mean for you? They mean you can improve these dismal data by implementing the culturally responsive practices in the feature *Into Practice Across Grade Levels: Culturally Responsive Practices.*

Monkey Business Images/Shutterstock

Encouraging students from different microcultures to work together on a shared class project is a way to provide culturally responsive teaching

It's time to come to the end of this chapter, but not to the end of your concerns about cultural justice and dignity and not to the end of your learning how to support all students. Keep on learning by studying the feature *Inclusion Tips for Diverse Classrooms.* And then ask yourself: "What difference might I see in one of my students if I use those tips?" You'd be surprised what a difference you might make. You might see more inclusion; you might inculcate higher expectations into your students and even into their peers and other teachers; you might contribute even just a bit to changing the distressing data; and you, your students, and their families might develop some ideas about appropriately ambitious education and progress toward outcomes. Whatever you do, you will make your students understand that you respect them—and doing that, you dignify them.

Into Practice Across Grade Levels

Culturally Responsive Practices

Integrate books by diverse authors. A **6th-grade** project includes searching the website of the Society of Children's Book Writers and Illustrators to review their list of award-winning books by diverse authors and illustrators. All students chose a book, read it, prepared a poster presentation highlighting their most significant cultural learning, and participated in a poster session in sharing their learning with their classmates.

Gather first-person accounts of the civil rights movement. In cooperative learning groups composed of students with and without a disability, an **11th-grade** social studies class studied a unit on the disability rights movement. As part of this unit, the students developed oral histories by interviewing disability leaders at the local and state level to learn from them about the disability rights movement over the past 50 years.

Confront marginalization of diverse groups. In advance of Columbus Day, **9th-graders** study an indigenous perspective on the discovery of America. Their capstone activity is to write and perform a play for middle school students to align with the Columbus Day holiday.

Enable students to delve into their microcultures. A **3rd-grade** class has a unit on microcultures. As students determine the microcultures with which they most strongly identify, all students have an opportunity to be a "class mentor" for their chosen microculture. These mentors are co-leaders with the teacher in guiding a music or art activity to teach about their self-identified microculture.

Teach diverse languages. In a **kindergarten** class, teach students key words in sign language and Spanish so that they can begin to communicate with classmates who use sign as their primary communication and classmates who are learning English and whose primary language is Spanish.

Inclusion Tips for Diverse Classrooms

	Behavior	Social Interactions	Educational Performance	Classroom Attitudes
What You Might See	A middle school youth with an intellectual disability makes an obscene gesture to the teacher.	A student who is learning English rarely communicates with classmates.	A 5th-grade American Indian boy is reading on the 2nd-grade level. When a book report was assigned, he had chronic absences.	An undercurrent starts in class of some students making fun of classmates when they make mistakes.
What You Might Be Tempted to Do	Send the student to the office to receive a discipline sanction.	Excuse her from interaction with classmates and class discussions due to her limited English.	Assume the reason the student is absent is due to sickness and make no contact with him.	Scold the students and punish them by taking away recess and class privileges.
Alternate Teacher Response	Engage the student and his foster parent in a restorative conference.	Invite her to bring artifacts from home to share her Mexican culture with the class and to teach her classmates Spanish words for the artifacts.	Find a book that has cultural relevance for the student and is aligned with one of his priority interests. Call him to tell him you miss him and are excited to share a book that you think he will especially enjoy.	Convene a circle and ask affective questions of the students who are making fun of others and of the victims, to probe the harm being done and determine what corrective actions are needed.
Ways to Include Peers in the Process	Because the student has communication challenges, encourage him to bring a friend to assist him with communicating.	Pair her with a classmate who speaks Spanish but who is fluent in English. Encourage them to plan together which Spanish vocabulary to teach.	If he enjoys the book and is interested in doing so, encourage him to read it to younger students who attend the after-school program.	Involve the entire class in the circle, including the students who have been the "bystanders."

MyLab Education Self-Check 2.3

MyLab Education Application Exercise 2.3: Culturally Responsive Practice

Summary

Disability as a Microculture

Microcultures include race/ethnicity, language, socioeconomic status, disability, and other characteristics. Disability is a microculture composed of children and youth with disabilities, their families, and adults with disabilities. The disability rights movement in special education started with parents who advocated for their children and helped persuade Congress to enact our federal special education law, now called IDEA. One part of disability rights is being respectful regarding the use of labels and language, both of which can convey dignity or stigma. Another part is recognizing that the long-term educational results for people with disabilities regarding achievement scores, high school graduation/drop-out, employment, income, and life satisfaction do not yet fulfill our country's four national disability policy goals—equality of opportunity, full participation, independent living, and economic self-sufficiency.

Cultural Bias and Students with Disabilities

Cultural bias occurs when we use our "personal cultural measuring stick" to judge others according to our own cultural norms. Cultural bias happens explicitly and implicitly. You had an opportunity to take the Implicit Association Test to understand any implicit bias you might have about the microcultures of disability and race. You also learned about the research on implicit bias toward people with disabilities and research documenting that teachers tend to anticipate problem behavior more from Black male students than from White students.

Disability, Intersectionality, and Disproportionality

Within the field of special education, there is over- and underrepresentation of students from the microcultures of race, gender, and language. Six factors are key in the intersection of disability and race: classification as having a disability, extent of inclusion, bullying, restraint and seclusion, suspensions and expulsions, and placement in juvenile justice facilities. The greatest risk for unfavorable outcomes occurs when a combination of three key microcultures is present—disability plus race (Black, American Indian) plus gender (male).

Educational Approaches for Enhancing Cultural Dignity

The Four R's for enhancing cultural dignity include respect, relationships, rigor, and resilience. Recognizing that we all have cultural biases and that implicit bias is especially difficult to eradicate, you can use the Watch, Think, and Act strategy to replace your bias with dignifying perspectives. This strategy enables you to gain insight about your implicit bias; develop ways to make re-interpretations to see positives rather than negatives; and change your behavior so that you form trusting and dignifying relationships with people against whom you have held a bias in the past.

Restorative practices provide a broad array of ways to engage with students to repair harm and take positive action. These practices start informally with affective statements and affective questions and move toward more formality with short, impromptu conferences, circles, and restorative conferences as the most formal practice. All of these practices are undergirded by expressing feelings and practicing empathy. Restorative practices in many schools are an alternative to suspensions and expulsions.

Culturally responsive teaching uses the experiences, perspectives, family and social networks, strengths, and needs of diverse students as a resource to ensure learning and positive outcomes.

Addressing the Professional Standards

In Chapter 2, Disability and Cultural Justice, we have covered the following Council for Exceptional Children (CEC) Initial Level Special Educator Preparation Standards:

Chapter 2—1.1, 2.0, 2.1, 2.2, 2.3, 5.1, 5.7, 6.0, 6.1, 6.2, 6.3, 6.5, 7.0, 7.3. Refer to the Appendix for a full listing of the CEC Standards with descriptions and supporting explanations.

Chapter 3
Today's Families and Their Partnerships with Professionals

∨ Learning Outcomes

3.1 Define family, parent (according to IDEA), family quality of life, and the five domains of family quality of life, and then identify two indicators for each domain.

3.2 Identify the six *partnership principles* and two indicators for each and then describe the six *partnership types* and two subtypes for each.

3.3 Summarize two actions to give parents emotional and informational support, prepare them to be partners in IEP meetings, and assist their son or daughter with homework.

Meet the Stuckey Family—A Mother and a Trio of Exceptional Children

Let us introduce you to the Stuckey family. As you meet them, ask yourself three questions: How are they similar to and different from your family?

Brianna. Brianna is the oldest child, age 15. She has cerebral palsy, with muscle contractions, and uses braces; she also has partial hearing loss and blindness. Her immune system is weak, and she takes prescription drugs. She has often required hospitalization. Brianna is intelligent and earns passing grades in the general education academic curriculum. Extracurricular activities include being a cheerleader.

Samuel. Samuel is the middle child, age 14. In 4th grade, he tested into the gifted and talented program. In addition to being a Boy Scout, he has musical talent in piano and percussion; is a Lego maniac and mathematics whiz; and has a fascination with science, especially astronomy and aerospace physics. Although it is very challenging for him, he loves to read and write. Samuel is a procrastinator who gets by on natural talent and good manners.

Merissa. At age 11, Merissa is the youngest child. She has hearing loss and uses a hearing aid. She skipped kindergarten and was admitted early to 1st grade. In 4th grade, she was bored; she tested into the gifted and talented program and received a more challenging curriculum. Problematically, she developed asthma and was sick most of that year. Merissa is always the youngest student in her class. She plays piano, flute, and handbells. Activities include participation in student council and Girl Scouts. She is also a gymnast.

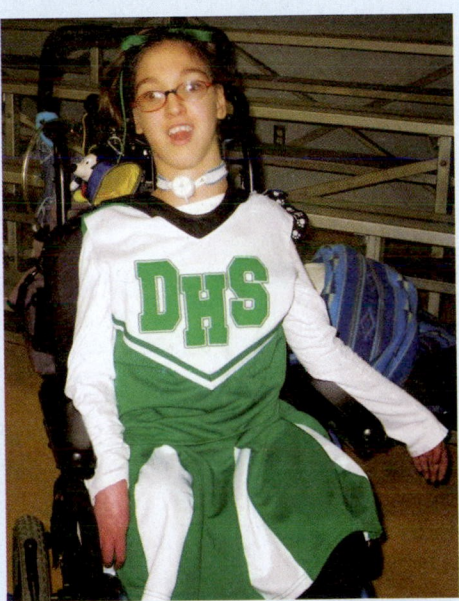

Dinell Smith

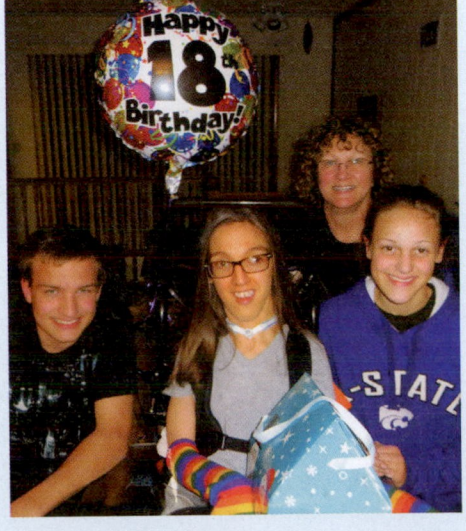

H. R. Turnbull

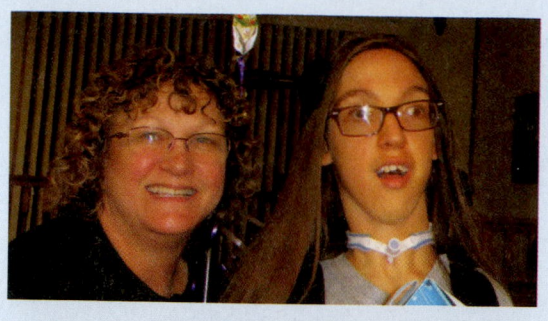

H. R. Turnbull

H. R. Turnbull

Mother. The mother, Dinell, is the daughter of a teacher. "Raised poor" in Arkansas, she was taught by her family to be independent and self-reliant. She is a musician and won scholarships and beauty contests in college. She was a teacher and still regards herself as one, believing herself the equal of any of her children's teachers. Having taught herself about assistive technology, she serves on state and regional assistive technology councils and is a key player in the state's deaf-blind technical assistance consortium. Dinell believes in partnership but is willing to confront others when her children's educators are unwilling or unable to provide an appropriate education. How similar are Dinell's views on partnership with those of your primary caretaker when you were in elementary and secondary school?

Father. Michael, an aerospace engineer, is recently divorced from Dinell. He works overtime daily. He shares Dinell's belief that Brianna's purpose in life is to teach the world about people with disabilities. He asserts that Samuel and Merissa are more mature, compassionate, and empathetic because of Brianna. Michael believes in his children and their futures.

Understanding Today's Families
Defining Family

Who is in your family? Before answering, define the word *family* as it applies to you. Does it include only your blood relatives, people who have married into your blood family, or others who carry out family roles but who are not related by blood or marriage? How nuclear or extended is your family? Does your family have same-sex or different-sex parents?

The U.S. Census Bureau (2010) defines *family* as a group of two or more people related by birth, marriage, or adoption who reside together. The Stuckey family does not match the standard definition: Although its members are all related by blood or marriage, Michael, divorced from Dinell, does not reside with her and the children. Do you see a problem with the Census definition?

Try out a different definition of "family." Consider this one: A **family** consists of two or more people who regard themselves to be a family and who carry out the functions that families typically perform. This definition means that people who do not reside together are still considered family, such as when one of the parents is on military duty stationed away from home for extended periods. It also means that people who are not related by birth, marriage, or adoption qualify as family, such as when two adult partners are not married but are living together as a couple. In our definition of family, the key criterion is whether each person regards the others as family members and if, together, they carry out some of the various family functions. The Stuckey family fits this functional definition because Michael carries out some of the family functions from his separate residence.

According to the Individuals with Disabilities Education Act (IDEA), the term *parent* means:

- A natural, biological, or adoptive parent of a child; a foster parent, unless state law prohibits a foster parent from acting as a parent
- A guardian except in the case when a court or state agency is acting in the place of a family
- An individual acting in the place of a biological or adoptive parent, such as a grandparent, stepparent, or other relative

- An individual who is legally responsible for the child's welfare
- A surrogate parent (as referred to in IDEA) who acts as an **educational advocate** for children when the state holds legal custody (some states prohibit foster parents from representing the child in educational decision making, as with the individualized education program (IEP); in these cases the agency with legal authority in the state must appoint the surrogate parent/educational advocate).

You will find that some of your students have families whose composition is surprisingly varied. To make this point, we highlight the composition of 13 families in a research study (Harry, Klingner, & Hart, 2005). Only one family was nuclear, with two biological parents living in the home and working full time. Three families were headed by fathers only, one by a grandmother, five by mothers, two by a mother and a stepfather, and one by an uncle. Two families had a parent with mental illness. In two families, an absent parent was living abroad.

This description illustrates the vast diversity of families you are likely to encounter in your work as an educator. You should not expect to communicate primarily with mothers of children and youth with and without disabilities and to have only mothers involved in parent-teacher meetings, progress reporting, and school activities. There may well be other family members—even *many* other family members—who are able and even eager to be educational partners. That results from the varied demographics of families. We encourage you to ask families which members are available to support your student in achieving school success and then consider how you can reach out to those family members in establishing a trusting partnership.

Demographics of Today's Families

Demographics is defined as the statistical comparison of populations (Mish, 1990). Demographics are about numbers. But numbers do not tell enough about families. So before we introduce you to the demographics of today's families, let's return to the Stuckey family and consider some of their characteristics.

They have moved from place to place: from the state where Dinell and Michael were married to the state where Dinell lives with the three children. They have had job changes: Dinell no longer is employed as a teacher, and Michael's former employer has sold the company for which he worked, but he continues to do the same work for his new employer. They have faced health challenges with Brianna, and her life has been in jeopardy many times since. They have been confronted by Brianna's numerous illnesses and disabilities and by challenges to meeting the needs of their two gifted children, Stephen and Merissa. They have had financial challenges because, for some years, they lacked any public support for the services and technologies Brianna needed. You have already learned that Dinell and Michael have divorced each other. Dinell now uses her maiden name, not her married name. Is Michael still a member of the family? We don't know enough to say. Does he still have rights under IDEA with respect to Brianna? The answer may depend on the terms of any divorce decree from a court or the terms

Families vary tremendously in the number of members and even the number of generations within the same household.

Jonathan Nourok/Photo Edit, Inc.

of a divorce settlement between Dinell and Michael. You may need to know what role, if any, Michael retains in making decisions about his children's education, so you may need to ask Dinell or him.

Dinell acknowledges that she may never be an empty-nest parent unless she can find a residential option for Brianna, when she reaches adulthood, that would provide her opportunities for community inclusion and dignity, in contrast to long-term care in a hospital or nursing home. After all, Brianna needs a tremendous amount of support just to breathe, much less communicate and participate in her school and community. Here's the point: As a teacher, you will have to consider families' needs and long-term visions as much as family demographics. But you should be aware of the demographics of families as you enter your profession.

As you learned in Chapter 2, children and youth with disabilities, as a group, are disproportionately from racially diverse populations; their families generally align with this same racial distribution. For example, 14 percent of youth with an IEP are White, as compared to 19 percent of youth who are African American—a 5 percentage point difference (Lipscomb et al., 2017).

Family demographics differ for youth with and without disabilities (Lipscomb et al., 2017):

- Parent has a college degree or higher, 26 percent versus 37 percent (students with and without disabilities).

- Parent has a job, 80 percent versus 87 percent (with and without disabilities).

- Parent is married or in a marriage-like relationship, 63 percent versus 72 percent (with or without disabilities).

Demographics can make a difference in the capacity of families to provide school-related support. Throughout this chapter, you will learn how you can support families who experience a broad range of demographic circumstances.

Understanding Family Quality of Life and Your Role as an Educator

For nearly 50 years, researchers have been documenting the effect of children with disabilities on their families. What they have found is what we know about the Stuckey family: There are more caregiving responsibilities and occasional or even frequent higher stress levels for families who have children with disabilities than for families in the general population (Wang & Singer, 2016). Indeed, a comprehensive analysis of many research studies related to maternal depression concluded that approximately one third of mothers of children with disabilities experienced depression; by contrast, approximately 18 percent of mothers who have children without disabilities experience depression (Singer, 2006). Alternately stated, approximately two thirds of mothers of children with disabilities do not experience depression.

However, research has also documented positive impacts within families of children with disabilities in areas such as resilience, empowerment, social networks, and problem solving (Carroll, 2013). No doubt exists about Dinell's resilience and empowerment: She has mastered knowledge about Brianna's medical needs and opportunities for communication and participation through assistive technology, and she regularly must teach Brianna's teachers and nurses how to provide for her daughter's physical, communication, and socialization needs.

Nor are Dinell's social networks constrained because of Brianna. Dinell serves on state and regional assistive technology and deaf-blind consortia and for many years was a paid consultant on assistive technology in Brianna's schools. As for problem solving, Dinell is an expert, having designed much of Brianna's assistive technology and programmed books for her to read by using homemade and specially designed

MyLab Education
Video Example 3.1
Despite the challenges Samuel and his family need to manage, consider the positive contributions that Samuel has brought to his family. Which three positive contributions most stand out to you?

technologies that keep her alive and enable her to learn. So what is there to know about the quality of life of families such as the Stuckeys who are affected by disabilities?

We and our colleagues at the Beach Center on Disability at the University of Kansas have investigated what quality of life means to families who have children with and without disabilities (Chiu et al., 2013). Using the families' descriptions, we have concluded that **family quality of life** refers to the extent to which (1) the families' needs are met, (2) family members enjoy their life together, and (3) family members have a chance to do the things important to them. According to these criteria, you are on solid ground in concluding that the Stuckey family has a good quality of life. The academic and social needs of their three children are well met, and Brianna's health needs are also met by professionals at the school. Brianna's teachers consult with and take lessons from Dinell about how to use the many technologies on which Brianna depends, especially those that allow her to speak and give her mobility. Dinell and her children enjoy their life together, as do Michael and the children when they visit him. And they have a chance to do what they want: Dinell as an assistive technology expert, Michael as an engineer, Brianna as the child who joyfully rides with her brother and sister to their many after-school activities, and Stephen and Merissa as outstanding participants in school and community activities. But as you have learned, a "good" quality of life does not equal a "perfect" one. Challenges, real ones, occur in every domain of their life. Let's consider those family-quality-of-life domains.

Through open-ended interviews with families as well as national surveys, we identified five **domains of family quality of life**: emotional well-being, parenting, family interaction, physical/material well-being, and disability-related support

Figure 3.1 Family Quality of Life: Domains and Indicators

Emotional well-being: the feelings or affective considerations within the family. Indicators for family members include the following:

- Have friends or others who provide support
- Have support needed to relieve stress
- Have some time to pursue individual interests
- Have outside help available to take care of the special needs of all family members.

Parenting: those activities that adult family members do to help children grow and develop. Indicators for family members include the following:

- Know how to help their child learn to be independent
- Know how to help their child with school work and activities
- Know how to teach their child to get along with others
- Know how to have time to take care of the individual needs of every child.

Family interaction: the relationships among family members. Indicators for family members include the following:

- Enjoy spending time together
- Talk openly with each other
- Solve problems together
- Show they love and care for each other.

Physical/material well-being: the resources available to the family to meet its members' needs. Indicators for family members include the following:

- Have transportation to get to the places they need to be
- Have a way to take care of expenses
- Feel safe at home, work, school, and in their neighborhood
- Get medical and dental help when needed.

Disability-related support: support from family members and others to benefit the family member with a disability. Indicators for family members include the following:

- Achieve goals at school or work
- Make progress at home
- Make friends
- Have a good relationship with the service providers who work with our family member with a disability.

Jose Carrillo/PhotoEdit, Inc.

Families enjoying their time together is an important indicator of family quality of life.

(Hoffman, Marquis, Poston, Summers, & Turnbull, 2006; Summers et al., 2005). Figure 3.1 briefly defines each domain and highlights some of the indicators associated with each. As you carefully review Figure 3.1 in terms of the specific domains and indicators, reflect on what you can do as an educator (1) to do no harm to the family quality of life of your students and (2) to improve their family quality of life.

In the domain of physical/material well-being, for example, one of the indicators is "Feels safe at home, work, school, and in their neighborhood." When students with disabilities are bullied at school by their peers and/or harshly criticized by their teachers, it is likely they will not feel safe. This lack of safety—indeed, fear—on the part of students reverberates through the family, often creating stress for all family members in their worry and concern about the family member with a disability. So, when you help to create a school culture of dignity for all students, you are contributing to the quality of life of the student with a disability, as well as the quality of life of the student's family.

Let's apply these family quality of life domains to the Stuckeys. Despite the divorce, it seems as though Dinell, Michael, and the children are doing well in the domain of emotional well-being, especially related to having friends who provide support. Because of Brianna's chronic life-threatening conditions and need for constant support, however, Dinell and Michael are justifiably anxious about whether they will have the financial resources to keep nurses and caretakers available for Brianna throughout her life. Their greatest uncertainty concerns disability-related support. Brianna has a good deal of intelligence. But her deaf-blindness, her inability to communicate without assistive technology, her lack of mobility, and her teachers' inexperience are troublesome. Dinell wonders what more she can do to partner with Brianna's teachers. She recognizes that partnership is a necessary means to an end—namely, that Brianna can have a job; participate actively, not as a passive observer, in her small hometown where nearly everyone knows her and her family; and make her own decisions about how to live her life. Brianna must have an appropriately ambitious education to achieve these goals—an education that supports her self-determination in crafting her own life. The question, then, is what kinds of partnerships do Brianna, Dinell, and the school staff need to advance these IDEA outcomes?

Samuel's parents are not alone in appreciating the positive contributions that Samuel has brought to the family. Indeed, research has consistently documented that families of children with a broad range of disabilities report enhancements in areas such as family love, strength, unity, spirituality, purpose, and close friendships (Carroll, 2013).

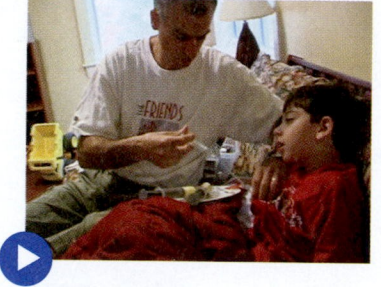

MyLab Education

Video Example 3.2

Refer to Figure 3.1. Then, summarize the ways the indicators that Samuel's intensive support needs affect his family's quality of life, both positively and, if at all, not positively.

MyLab Education Self-Check 3.1
MyLab Education Application Exercise 3.1: Who Is a Family?

Understanding Partnerships

Defining Partnerships and Their Policy Foundation

Partnership refers to a relationship involving joint responsibilities and close cooperation (Mish, 1990). **Family-professional partnerships** are relationships in which families and professionals collaborate, capitalizing on each other's judgments and expertise to increase the benefits of education for students, as well as the benefits of support for families and professionals (Turnbull, Turnbull, Erwin, Soodak, & Shogren, 2015).

In Chapter 1, you learned that family-professional partnership is one of IDEA's six principles. It is also embedded in all of the other IDEA principles.

- Zero reject—Parents have the assurance that their child with a disability may not be suspended for more than 10 days in a school year without receiving a **functional behavior assessment** and a **behavior intervention plan**.

- Nondiscriminatory evaluation—Parents have the right to consent to their child's initial and subsequent nondiscriminatory evaluation, and to receive a copy of the evaluation.

- Individualized education program—Parents have a right to attend the IEP meeting, which must be scheduled at a time that makes it possible for them to attend.

- Least restrictive environment—Parents have a right to consent to their child's placement, which must be in the least restrictive environment appropriate for their child.

- Due process—Parents have a right to object to professional decisions through a **dispute resolution session**, **mediation**, and/or **due process hearing.**

- Parent participation—Parents have a right to access to all educational records on their child and to restrict educators from releasing personally identifiable information about the child without parental consent.

Taken as a whole, these reciprocal rights of parents and responsibilities of educators mean that families and professionals should become partners in making decisions about the education of students with disabilities.

However, no federal law grants parents of children who are gifted the right to make decisions in partnership with teachers. In a national survey, slightly less than half of the states indicated that there are state or local requirements related to the participation of parents of children who are gifted in educational decision making (National Association for Gifted Children, 2015). Whether required by federal or state policy or not, it is sound educational practice to form partnerships with families of all of your students. To that point, bear in mind that Dinell has more rights and responsibilities for partnerships with Brianna's teachers than she has with respect to Stephen's and Merissa's teachers in the gifted program.

Importance of Partnerships

Schools that foster partnerships among administrators, faculty, families, and students are more likely to have high levels of trust and higher student outcomes than schools in which partnerships are fragile or nonexistent. A comprehensive review of school characteristics that lead to improvements in student achievement found that teachers' trust of parents and students strongly predicts higher reading and math scores (Hoy, 2012). This finding is particularly compelling because for many years the major predictor of school achievement was found to be the student's socioeconomic status and racial/ethnicity affiliation.

This teacher is required to work with students' parents as well as the students themselves. Parent-professional partnerships can strengthen students' progress.

Tyler Olson/Fotolia

One research team reported that schools with higher trust levels are 3 times more likely to be identified as having reading and math improvement (Bryk & Schneider, 2002).

A national longitudinal study of family involvement in the education of secondary students with disabilities also reported a strong relationship between family-professional partnerships and positive student outcomes (Newman, 2005). As compared to youth with less involved families in their school, youth with more involved families:

- Were less behind grade level in reading and tended to receive better grades
- Had higher rates of involvement in organized groups and more individual friendships
- Were more likely to have had regular paid jobs after high school.

Consider Figure 3.1 and the domain titled disability-related support. One of the indicators is that the family members "have a good relationship with the service providers who work with our family member with a disability." You should not be surprised to learn that research has documented that families who experience positive family-professional partnerships are more likely to report higher levels of family quality of life (Kyzar et al., 2015, in press; Eskow et al., 2015). In *My Voice: Lori Palen—Breathing Easy at Last*, a parent tells about a partnership that has affected her son, Tommy, a kindergartener who has multiple disabilities.

My Voice

Lori Palen: Breathing Easy at Last

When our son, Tommy, was in his first year of preschool, my husband and I initiated a due process hearing against the school district where Tommy was attending school. This wasn't something we'd expected or wanted to do, but we felt that it was necessary.

Before telling you about the result of that process, I'd like to tell you more about the challenges that Tommy faces. He has a rare genetic syndrome called Rubinstein-Taybi syndrome (RTS). RTS is associated with developmental delays and a variety of health issues. Tommy has learning difficulties; he struggles with attention and imitation and following directions, and he does not yet talk, read, or write. Although he walks, Tommy needs support to travel long distances and navigate obstacles like stairs and curbs. Tommy's biggest medical issue is lung disease; he uses an oxygen tank and his blood oxygen levels must be monitored throughout the day. He also has feeding issues that require a feeding tube and medication, and he has glaucoma that has harmed his vision. Tommy needs help from a variety of support professionals, including a special education teacher; a nurse; physical, speech, and occupational therapists; a vision teacher; and an orientation and mobility specialist. We anticipate that Tommy will need most, if not all, of these supports for the remainder of his school career.

Our family won our due process case and won when the school district appealed to the State Review Hearing Officer. The school district decided not to appeal again, and our relationship has been positive and productive since then.

Tommy attends our neighborhood elementary school and is included in a regular education classroom for part of each day. He also spends lunch, recess, and snack time

Thomas Yellin

with his regular education peers, and he goes with them to "specials" classes (art, music, PE, technology, media center), assemblies, and field trips. To us, Tommy's inclusion is an affirmation of his dignity, a demonstration that he is a full member of the school community.

Tommy's teachers and therapists are deliberate, caring, and collaborative in meeting Tommy's needs. Consistent with the *Endrew F.* decision, they are setting ambitious outcomes and challenging objectives. They are collecting good data and using it to drive recommendations. His principal is an active member of our team. The tone of our meetings is friendly and solution-focused. My husband and I feel like our opinions are heard and valued.

Tommy is making friends and making progress. Many students and staff greet Tommy when we drop him off at school, and I hear that he's quite popular on the playground! Tommy seems motivated to do what the other kids do . . . to communicate, to attend to and participate in learning tasks, to walk around the school independently, to feed himself at lunch and snack. He is using more sign language, making progress with a picture exchange system, sitting longer during circle time, successfully using scissors and writing tools, sorting objects for the first time, and navigating physical obstacles in his environment.

We are optimistic that this inclusive placement will benefit not only Tommy, but also his classmates who will encounter people with diverse strengths and challenges over their entire lives. We also hope that Tommy's experience is reinforcing the idea that inclusion is both feasible and beneficial, and that this will make it easier for school and district staff to advocate for inclusion for other students.

Personal feature written by Lori Palen about Tommy used with permission.

Families who experience stronger partnerships with educators experience less family stress than families who do not have solid partnerships (Burke & Hodapp, 2014; 2016). Think about the findings in these terms: You can very likely boost families' quality of life by being a trusted partner with them in educating their children. They are more likely to reciprocate the trust, and your quality of life as a teacher is likely to be better as a result.

Creating and Sustaining Partnerships

You now have the definition of partnerships and are grounded in federal policies regarding parents' rights and responsibilities. You next need to understand how to put that definition to work. Start by having a framework—Figure 3.2—that illustrates *partnership principles* and *partnership types*.

Figure 3.2 Sunshine Framework for Trusting Family-Professional Partnerships

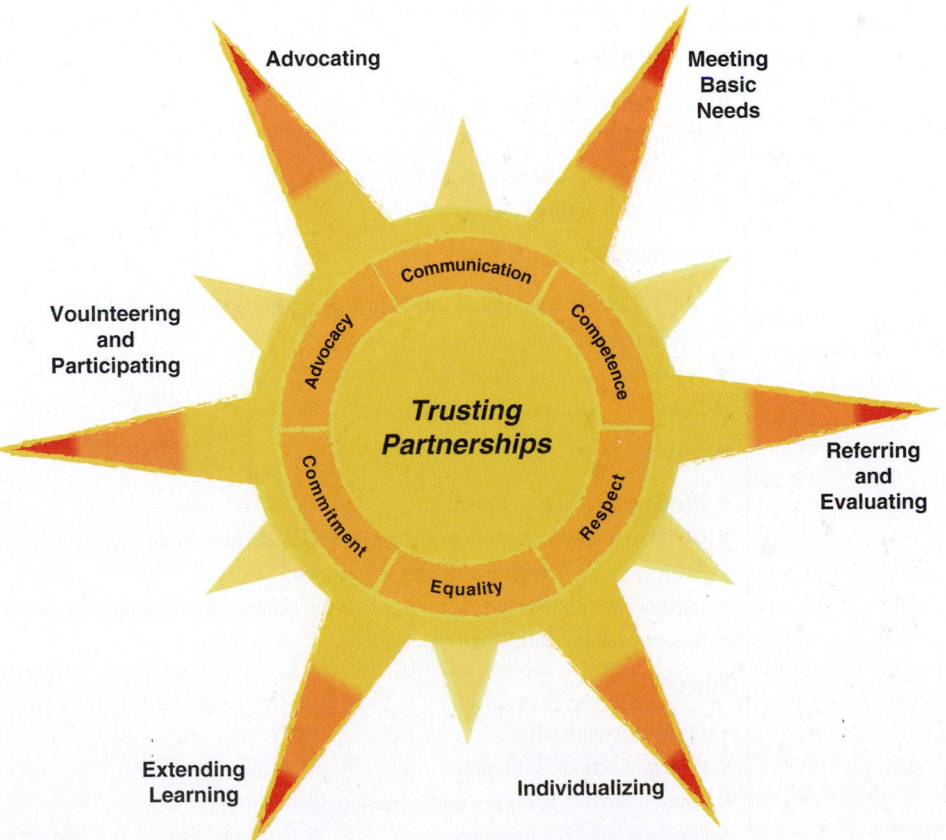

MyLab Education

Video Example 3.3
In "Trusting Partnerships in Inclusive Education," Ann Turnbull, co-author of this book, describes the seven partnership principles and how she and her family experienced the six partnership principles leading to trust. Consider what you can do to form trusting partnerships with families to put students on the inclusive road to adulthood. http://youtu.be/GuOcwJbTtpc

Figure 3.2 uses the sun as the graphic metaphor for partnerships. Trusting partnerships are the core of the sun. Circling around the trusting partnerships are six *principles* essential for trust. They are communication, competence, commitment, advocacy, respect, and equality. (Blue-Banning, Summers, Frankland, Nelson, & Beegle, 2004; Turnbull et al., 2015). Figure 3.3 briefly defines each *partnership principle* and highlights key indicators associated with each one.

Turn your attention back to Figure 3.2. There, we depict *partnership types* in each of the sunrays. These partnerships types include:

- Meeting families' basic needs
- Referring and evaluating for special education
- Individualizing through the development and implementation of the IEP
- Extending learning to home and community

Figure 3.3 Principles of Partnerships

Communication

- Be friendly.
- Be clear.
- Share good news.
- Be honest, even with bad news.
- Listen.
- Empathize.

Professional Competence

- Set high expectations for students and partnership teams.
- Continue to learn, especially when faced with new challenges.
- Search out successful solutions from professionals, families, and individuals with disabilities.
- Search out research-based practices.

Commitment

- Be available for communication.
- Be flexible.
- Be willing to try new approaches.
- Go "above and beyond."

Advocacy

- Build alliances with others with similar and dissimilar viewpoints.
- Communicate your viewpoints on key issues.
- Create win-win-win solutions.
- Speak up for students and partners.

Respect

- Build on a person's strengths.
- Communicate to partners that their perspectives and recommendations are helpful.
- Seek to "walk a mile in your partner's shoes."
- Partner with cultural guides to increase the likelihood of culturally responsive practice.
- Ensure cultural justice and dignity.

Equality

- Apply the golden rule.
- Highlight others' strengths.
- Avoid intimidating and/or embarrassing others.
- Create a level playing field.
- Point out commonalities.

- Volunteering and participating at school
- Advocating for systems enhancement.

Trust radiates from the sun's center and invigorates each type of partnership. Figure 3.4 includes the sub-types of *partnership types*.

Figure 3.4 Partnership Types and Sub-types

Meeting Basic Needs

- Providing emotional support
- Providing informational support
- Promoting social connections
- Addressing health
- Addressing safety
- Addressing financial subsistence
- Connecting with community resources to address needs

Referring to and Evaluating for Services and Supports

- Advocating for student, family, and teacher rights in the referral and evaluation process
- Taking advantage of resources from the state's Parent Training and Information Center and Community Parent Resource Center, if available
- Initiating and reviewing student referral
- Collecting and summarizing evaluation information on student
- Explaining and discussing evaluation results

Individualizing Services and Supports

- Partnering with families in IEP meetings
- Advocating for student and family in the IEP process
- Taking advantage of resources from the state's Parent Training and Information Center and Community Parent Resource Center, if available
- Addressing how to monitor and enhance the student's progress in the general curriculum
- Ensuring an appropriately ambitious program with challenging objectives
- Planning for transitions to next educational level or to employment

Extending Learning in Home and Community

- Guiding families in helping with homework
- Addressing behavioral challenges in home and community settings
- Helping to build friendships with neighborhood and community peers
- Supporting students and families to be included in community recreational activities
- Supporting students and families to attend community venues and events
- Building community partnerships to address school, student, and family needs

Participating and Volunteering with School

- Creating family-friendly school environments and program
- Encouraging families to attend program/school/community events and meetings related to students' development and progress
- Guiding families in being a classroom volunteer to assist with a student's progress
- Guiding families in how to contribute to other school-related tasks and activities
- Guiding families in whether and how to volunteer in community events that have school, student, and family benefits

Advocating for Systems Improvement

- Taking advantage of resources from Parent Training and Information Centers
- Participating in advocacy and leadership training
- Mentoring families and being mentored by families in advocacy activities
- Participating in program and community advocacy events and encouraging partners to consider participating in them
- Ensuring substantial parent membership on local and state advisory council

The U.S. Department of Education often refers to these partnership types and subtypes in terms of opportunities for family engagement. **Family engagement** refers to developing a trusting partnership between families and educators in which they share responsibility for student achievement and school improvement (SEDL, 2013; U.S. Department of Health and Human Services and U.S. Department of Education, 2016). As you will note in this definition, trusting partnerships are the essence of family engagement.

The alignment between the concept of family engagement and trusting family-professional partnerships is clearly evident in the vision of the U.S. Secretary of Education during the Obama administration:

> My vision for family engagement is ambitious . . . I want to have too many parents demanding excellence in their schools. I want all parents to be real partners in education with their children's teachers, from cradle to career. In this partnership, students and parents should feel connected—and teachers should feel supported. When parents demand change and better options for their children, they become the real accountability backstop for the educational system. (Arne Duncan, U.S. Secretary of Education, May 3, 2010; cited in SEDL, 2013, p. 3)

In the remainder of this chapter, you will learn how to establish trusting partnerships with families around three of the six *partnership types*. We refer you to a book that several of us have co-authored on trusting family partnerships to learn about the remaining three partnership types (Turnbull, Turnbull, Erwin, Soodak, & Shogren, 2015).

MyLab Education Self-Check 3.2

MyLab Education Application Exercise 3.2: Understanding Family Partnerships

---

Strategies to Form Trusting Partnerships with Families

Meeting Basic Needs: Providing Emotional and Informational Support

Meeting basic needs entails using school, community, and state and federal resources to support students and families in terms of emotional, informational, health, financial, and other basic needs. You might think that this is not the role of the school and that your job is to teach and not be concerned about these other mitigating factors. You would not be correct.

The reason why you and other educators must be sensitive to this issue is that basic needs must be met for students and families in order to allow them significant energy and time to make educational progress. You learned earlier in the chapter that families who have children with disabilities are more financially strapped than those who have children without disabilities. Whether students have a disability or not, coming to school hungry, sick, without adequate rest (e.g., having eight or more family members sleeping in a one- or two-room dwelling), or without appropriate clothing for the weather puts students at a vast disadvantage when it comes to being engaged with their school work.

Lest you think these factors do not relate to your students, we call your attention to the **related services** that IDEA requires and that you learned about in Chapter 1. Children and youth with disabilities have the right to receive related services that will enable them to benefit from special education. Three of the related services particularly tied to meeting basic needs include **counseling services**, **school health services**, and **social work services**. As a teacher, you are not alone in addressing basic needs; instead, you have a team of professionals who can be your trusted partners in providing the types and sub-types of supports highlighted in the meeting basic needs category of Figure 3.4.

In addition to school-based professionals, networks of national, state, and local programs support families who have members with disabilities and the professionals who serve those families. You may—indeed, you often should—refer families to these programs, as well as take advantage of these programs' opportunities to expand your own competence in supporting families.

PARENT-TO-PARENT PROGRAMS Parent-to-Parent (P2P) programs are national and state resources that are particularly effective in meeting two needs of families. Those needs are for emotional support and information. P2P programs provide those supports to families who have children and youth with a full range of disabilities (Singer et al., 1999) or who are gifted (McGee, 2012) or who, like the Stuckey family, have children in both categories.

P2P programs are staffed mostly by parents of individuals with disabilities who focus on establishing one-to-one matches between a veteran parent who has successfully resolved a challenge and a referred parent who is facing the challenge for the first time. The staff of parent leaders provide initial training and ongoing support to veteran parents in how they can be effective in giving emotional and informational support to referred parents.

P2P staff typically use six factors in determining the appropriate match of a veteran parent and a referred parent. These are (1) similar disability, (2) similar challenge, (3) veteran parents who can respond within 24 hours, (4) children with disabilities who are close to the same age, (5) families in the same geographical area, and (6) families with a similar family structure (e.g., single parent).

P2P consists of approximately 34 statewide programs and hundreds of local programs, with at least one in every state (K. Brill, personal communication, February 25, 2014). Each year, P2P programs match approximately 155,000 parents who are seeking support with more than 7000 trained support parents.

> To find out about programs in your state, link to http://www. p2pusa.org/ and then link to the "For Parents" box at the top of the page. You will find a U.S. map with links to P2P websites in states that have programs.

If you are in one of the states that has a P2P program, you can encourage families to contact it if they would like to talk to another family in a similar situation. If your state does not have a P2P program, you can encourage families to contact a neighboring state to seek a match.

Compared with other family-directed networks, P2P has been the most thoroughly researched in terms of its particular outcomes for families (Shilling et al., 2013). In the first experimental study conducted on P2P, more than 80 percent of parents reported finding P2P to be helpful in making them feel more prepared to deal positively with their child and family situation, view their circumstances in a more positive light, and make progress on priority goals (Singer et al., 1999). A perspective from a parent who has participated in P2P highlights the value of this type of support:

> *When our son with Down syndrome was born three years ago, my husband and I were shocked and devastated . . . . The couple that our Parent to Parent program sent us were such warm, optimistic, "normal" people, they gave us hope. About a year later, my husband and I were trained by our program to be support parents. The Parent to Parent office has many requests for visits from both father and mother. My husband was one of very few men willing to go through formal training. I have also found that support for non-English-speaking families is hard to come by. It has been satisfying to me to be able to serve the Spanish-speaking community. (Beach Center, undated)*

P2P is also a resource for professionals. A school administrator said that he was certain the program would help families but "didn't realize until later that it would also be helpful to our staff. As professionals, we often feel inadequate because we cannot understand what families are going through because we haven't actually experienced what they have.

Our staff was aware that the Parent to Parent program could fulfill a need for families that we could not" (Santelli, Markey, Johnson, Turnbull, & Turnbull, 2001, p. 66). When parents of students you teach could benefit from being matched with a veteran parent "who has walked a mile in their shoes," you can share information about this valuable resource.

PARENT TRAINING AND INFORMATION CENTERS   Parent Training and Information Centers (PTIs) are authorized by IDEA and funded by the U.S. Department of Education. The majority of PTI staff and board members are parents of children with disabilities. The mission of PTIs is to assist families in ensuring that their children have an appropriate education. They help families (1) understand the nature of disabilities, (2) communicate with educators, (3) know their rights and responsibilities, (4) obtain appropriate educational services, and (5) link with other community resources. PTIs serve families of children with all disabilities, from birth to age 26. They offer workshops, publications, newsletters, websites, one-to-one support, as well as a variety of other resources (Burke, 2015).

You can be helpful to families by letting them know about the availability of the PTI in their locality, and you personally can also benefit by receiving newsletters and attending meetings to gain more information about developing trusting partnerships with families. Dinell has relied on the PTI in her home state to teach her the fundamentals of special education law that you learned about in Chapter 1—namely, IDEA, Section 504, and Americans with Disabilities Act (ADA); to give her examples of how other students with severe multiple disabilities have gained access to and participated in the general curriculum with appropriately ambitious IEPs; and to bolster her expectations for Brianna's life after high school. She also learned about the state's Deaf-Blind Technical Assistance Consortium through PTI contacts and now is a member of its governing board and contributes ideas and strategies to Brianna's school district, ensuring Brianna's progress as well as that of other students.

COMMUNITY PARENT RESOURCE CENTERS   Community Parent Resource Centers (CPRCs) operate in traditionally underserved communities to provide support to families who experience cultural and linguistic diversity. Unlike PTIs, which have a state or regional focus, CPRCs are funded at the community level and provide in-depth supports and services to families who are challenged by poverty, lower education levels, and language differences.

CPRCs are similar to PTIs in their funding source (U.S. Department of Education), mission (preparing families to ensure that their children have an appropriate education), and staffing (mostly parents on staff and as board members). The primary difference is that CPRCs specialize in providing culturally responsive support at the community level, whereas PTIs provide support at the state level to majority and diverse families alike.

There are approximately 30 CPRCs. Most are located in large cities in which a high concentration of poverty and disability exists among ethnically, linguistically, and culturally diverse populations (for example, Hispanic populations in New York City and African American populations in Houston and New Orleans). As you reflect on what you learned about cultural injustice and disproportional challenges of students in Chapter 2, you can have a keen appreciation for family organizations that are particularly geared to provide needed support to families with a pile-up of challenges.

CENTER FOR PARENT EDUCATION AND RESOURCES   Each PTI and CPRC receives technical assistance and other support from a national program—Center for Parent Education and Resources. Located in Newark, New Jersey, it is affiliated with six regional centers, and each of these centers provides a hub of resources for the PTIs and CPRCs. Each regional program has a rich website of helpful resources.

On a disconcerting note, a national survey documented that the average reading grade level of documents prepared by state and local education agencies to explain IDEA and state-based rights and responsibilities to parents is grade 16. Based on the national survey, only a few parent documents scored in the high school range (6 percent), slightly

MyLab Education
Video Example 3.4
In this video, Rud Turnbull interviews leaders from a Community Parent Resource Center, United We Stand of New York, about services they provide to meet families' basic needs related to housing. Envision how students' families might benefit from having support from United We Stand and how stable housing can affect the students' readiness to learn in your class, as well as students' dignity. https://www.youtube.com/watch?v=stcU5jOIQz8&feature=youtu.be

Locate your state's PTI, as well as CPRC (if one is available in your state), by linking to http://www.parentcenterhub.org/, which is the National Center for Parent Information and Resources. On the homepage, link to "Parent Centers" in the top navigation bar and then to "Find Your Parent Center." Each parent center is identified as either a PTI or a CPRC.

over half scored in the college range (55 percent), and slightly over one-third (39 percent) scored in the graduate or professional range (Mandic, Rudd, Hehir, & Acevedo-Garcia, 2012). Clearly, when the reading level is this high, the majority of parents will have a hard time gaining solid knowledge and skill from relying solely on a written document. It is estimated that the average adult reads at about the 9th-grade level and that most popular novels are written at the 7th-grade level. The PTIs and CPRCs are uniquely qualified to address and overcome this readability gap for parents of children with disabilities.

Annually, PTIs and CPRCs reach 1.1 million parents, professionals, and families in providing direct assistance through telephone calls, meetings, home visits, letters, and e-mails. In additional to direct assistance, another approximately 25 million parents and professionals receive indirect assistance through newsletters, websites, media activities, and other modes of information dissemination. A national report of PTIs and CPRCs indicated that 90 percent or more of parents stated they have received relevant information enabling them to make more informed decisions, have shared information they received with other families, and have found the information they received to be useful (National Parent Technical Assistance Center, 2013).

FAMILY-TO-FAMILY HEALTH INFORMATION CENTERS   A valuable resource in supporting families to address their children's health needs is Family-to-Family Health Information Centers (F2Fs). The mission of F2Fs is to provide support and advocacy for parents of children and youth with special health care needs and the professionals, such as yourself, who serve them. The U.S. Department of Health and Human Services funds a center in every state and the District of Columbia.

Link to http://www.fv-ncfpp.org and click on the map to find a Family-to-Family Health Center program in your state.

The F2Fs are mostly staffed by parents of children with health-related needs. These staff members support other families by advising on how to navigate health care systems; providing information on insurance; highlighting community, state, and federal resources to cover medical expenses; and supporting parents to receive school-based related services regarding health, such as medical services, school health services, and school nurse services. In 2015, F2Fs served approximately 1 million families and 350,000 professionals.

Given that health care needs are greater among families from diverse racial/ethnic backgrounds, a strength of F2Fs is that they have strong cultural responsiveness to families whose language is other than English and to families who live in underserved communities. You can benefit from F2F support in terms of expanding your own knowledge about the health care needs of families from diverse backgrounds. You can do this by attending their meetings and community events, reading newsletters and other printed material, and following them on social media (Family Voices, 2016).

We hope you have concluded that many resources have been developed specifically for families. *Into Practice Across Grade Levels: How Families Have Benefited from Family-Directed Resources* highlights how parents have benefited from these different organizational resources. In fact, however, many families do not know about these resources. Be their partner by giving them information about the programs; indeed, be a better partner by taking advantage of what you can learn from them.

Into Practice Across Grade Levels

How Families Have Benefited from Family-Directed Resources

Four family-directed family-support activities occur under the auspices of a single agency, Families Together of Kansas. Those activities are the following:

- The Parent Training and Information Center (PTI)
- Parent to Parent (P2P)
- Family to Family Health Information Center (F2FHIC)
- Education Advocate (EA).

Funded by federal, state, and private funds and assisted by The University of Kansas's Beach Center on Disability, Families Together supports families of children ages birth through 26, offers its training weekends in both English and Spanish, and operates special training weekends for Spanish-speaking Kansans.

Two of its long-time staff, Leia Holley, the mother of a grown son, Sean, who has autism, and Lesli Girard, who also

(Continued)

has a son with a disability, describe below how they supported families.

The families' needs varied; Families Together's responses were individualized and often carried out in collaboration with state and local government agencies, including local education agencies. Families Together is a resource for families and professionals alike. What a family learns can become an activity that the child does or a service that the child benefits from having. In turn, the child's teachers or related service providers or other professionals are able to execute their duties to the child and family more effectively. Collaboration leads to progress. Inclusion occurs. A person flourishes and becomes respected.

Early Childhood (ages birth through 5)—The Case of the Overwhelmed Parent Who Received Three Services from a Single Agency: One-Stop Support

Parent to Parent

The parent felt isolated. She was in tears because no one understood what it was like to have a child with cerebral palsy. She was overwhelmed and didn't feel that she could help her **2-year-old** daughter. She was a single mom living paycheck to paycheck.

Through our P2P program we were able to match her with another mother whose child was 4 years old. The mother soon became hugely satisfied with the support and insight provided by the supporting parent.

PTI—Our PTI staff connected the mother with the local interagency coordinating council (specializing in securing services for young children and supporting their parents). Through our guidance, her daughter began receiving services and the mother had someone who could help her learn how to take care of her daughter.

F2F—The child was receiving Medicaid. Our F2F staff were able to assist the mother as she navigated services, therapies, and other supports available through the state's early periodic screening, detection, and treatment (EPSDT) program, "KanBe Healthy" (the state's Medicaid program).

Grades 1–3 (ages 6 through 8)—The Case of the Lonely Boy: No More Isolating Education

PTI—The mother was concerned that her child in **2nd grade**, who had an emotional and behavioral disorder (obsessive-compulsive disorder, Chapter 9) and ADHD (Chapter 10), did not have any friends. Our PTI staff helped the mother understand how to work with the school to create a **circle of friends**. Her son became friends with another student who lived with his dad. The dad was a single father who was struggling with raising three boys. The friendship between the two boys provided opportunities for both boys to enjoy activities they would otherwise not be able to participate in because they were excluded on account of their behaviors.

PTI—The mother was concerned that her son was in a self-contained "autism classroom" all day. She believed he needed to be with his peers to learn appropriate communication and social skills. Our PTI staff helped the mother understand her son's rights with regard to the IDEA principle of the

least restrictive environment (Chapter 1—LRE/inclusion) and how to work with her son's IEP team to ensure her son was able to participate in the general education classroom with peers who do not have disabilities.

Grades 4–6 (ages 9 through 11)—The Case of the Deployed Soldier and the Waiting Mother: Comrades in Arms

P2P—A military family was transferred to a new duty station at Ft. Riley, in central Kansas. The mother had no family and friends, and the dad was deployed often. Through our P2P program, the mother was matched with another military parent who had been stationed at Ft. Riley and who also had a child with autism. The mother now had support and was able to find resources. She also had someone who understood how it felt to live with a child who has autism. The supporting parent helped the mom find a support group. The child was in **5th grade**.

PTI—The same family also needed help understanding their child's IDEA rights. They were struggling to get the school to implement the IEP as written. The mother learned what her rights are and what they mean to her son (Chapter 1) and learned what words to say—magic words, as it were—to persuade the school to comply with IDEA.

Grades 7–9 (ages 12 through 14)—The Case of the Isolated Grandmother and Troubled Grandson: Avoiding the Gangs and Entering Therapy

PTI—A grandmother who was raising her **9th-grade** grandson needed help. Her grandson was being suspended as well as placed in seclusion in his school. Our PTI staff helped the grandmother understand the process of creating a behavior intervention plan (BIP, Chapters 4 and 5). The grandmother was also concerned that her grandson was being influenced by other students. They live in an area where gangs are prevalent. Her grandson had no acceptable male role models, and his self-esteem was low. Our PTI staff suggested the grandmother work with the school to connect her grandson with one of the teachers so that he could help the teacher and use a **check-in/check-out process** (Chapter 5) to be able to voice his concerns to his teacher.

Our staff also connected the grandmother with the local mental health center. Her grandson began Medicaid-supported services. These services provided him with therapy as well as with a youth support worker who could help him work through his anger. The grandmother was able to use a case manager to help her navigate the health and education systems as well as to have a better understanding of how to help her grandson.

P2P—The grandmother was matched with a parent whose child had similar challenges. The grandmother now had support and was able to brainstorm about how to help her grandson with someone who understood the behaviors.

Grades 10–12 and Transition from School to Postschool Activities (ages 15 through 21)—The Case of Segregation: Having High Expectations and Getting Real Work

PTI—The parents were told that their son in **12th grade**, who has significant support needs, would have to work in a sheltered workshop. The parents believed he could be a greeter at the local farm store. The family lived in a rural area with limited job opportunities (according to the school). After brainstorming about the student's strengths and needs as well as possible postsecondary goals with our PTI staff, the mother became excited about her son's employment possibilities. Her son loved to be with people as well as to be outside. Her son is now a trail guide at a local nature center. He uses his communication device to describe the various areas along the trail. The trail is wheelchair accessible.

MERGING PARTNERSHIP PRINCIPLES INTO THE PROVISION OF EMOTIONAL AND INFORMATIONAL SUPPORT   You have learned about valuable local, state, and national services available for families of students with disabilities. Remember that as a teacher you yourself can be competent in supporting families and learning about their emotional needs by using the resources of these programs. Here's how you can infuse each of the six partnership principles into your interactions with families concerning these resources.

- Communication—Gather information on the P2P, PTI, CPRC, and F2F programs in your area and develop a handout for families with a program description, website URL, and contact information.

- Competence—Scan the websites and attend meetings, workshops, and other events to develop greater knowledge and skill about how to support families.

- Commitment—Print newsletters and other helpful resources from the website and share them with families who do not have e-mail access. Consider how to get these materials translated into the native language of the families or how to acquire the materials in a form that families with adults with disabilities can use them.

- Advocacy—For parents unable to attend workshops not in their immediate geographical area, invite a staff member from one of the programs to meet with the parents of students you teach at a convenient location, distributing information or even conducting a workshop.

- Respect—Be especially attuned to the needs, strengths, and preferences of families from culturally diverse backgrounds who may feel intimidated when making contact with organizations whose staff are largely from the majority culture.

- Equality—Encourage families who have never attended a workshop to give it a try by orienting them on what to expect and seeking to find one or more parents who frequently attend workshops to accompany them.

Individualizing Services and Supports: Partnering with Families in IEP Meetings

As you learned in Chapter 1, IDEA requires children ages birth to 3 to have an individualized family service plan (IFSP) and children and youth ages 3 to 21 to have an individualized education program (IEP). You learned about the requirements for the content of the IEP document and the people who must attend, including especially the student's parents (as defined—see the definition in the early pages of this chapter). To understand the original

Teachers, such as the one pictured here, need to know how to be partners with the families of children of different races and sexes.

purpose of parent participation, consider what a sponsor of the original federal law (now IDEA) said, in 1975:

> One of the greatest benefits that can come to the handicapped child is to have the parents brought into the meetings . . . this was one of the reasons the idea of the mandatory meeting was developed, to make sure the parent is part of the education of the child. (Williams, 1975, p. 19489)

We point out to you the word *handicapped* in the first line of this quote. That was the preferred language in 1975; now, however, the preferred language is *child with a disability*.

> A few years later, the Department of Education clarified parents' expected roles: The IEP meetings serves as a communication vehicle between parents and school personnel and enables them as equal participants to jointly decide what the child's needs are, what services will be provided to meet those needs, and what the anticipated outcomes will be. (*Federal Register*, 1981, p. 5462)

The term *equal participants* means only one thing: IDEA's expectation is for parents and professionals to be partners in the IEP process.

The 1975 and 1981 explanations still hold true. In response to the *Endrew F.* decision, the Department of Education issued yet another guideline about communication with parents concerning their child's progress.

> Public agencies may find it useful to examine current practices for engaging and communicating with parents throughout the school year as IEP goals are evaluated and the IEP Team determines whether the child is making progress toward IEP goals . . . Parents and other IEP Team members should collaborate and partner to track progress appropriate to the child's circumstances. (U.S. Department of Education, 2017)

Given these policy expectations, what do you predict that research has found about parent attendance and participation in IEP meetings? Do you anticipate that the norm has been for parents to be equal participants? Don't anticipate that.

A national profile of attendance and satisfaction revealed the following (Wagner, Newman, Cameto, Javitz, & Valdes, 2012):

- Approximately 90 percent of parents reported attending the meeting.
- Parents who had higher levels of participation in supporting their child's learning at school and home and who belonged to parent support groups were significantly more likely to attend the IEP meeting.
- Parents of students from diverse races and parents of students with incomes below $25,000 were less likely to attend meetings and were less satisfied with their participation.
- Parents of European American children had higher rates of participation and satisfaction than parents in the other racial/ethnic groups.
- Parents with higher incomes and parents from two-parent families were more likely to be satisfied with their participation.
- Parents were more satisfied with their IEP involvement when their children were younger; however, their attendance did not differ significantly across elementary and secondary years.
- Parents whose child had been suspended or expelled were less likely to be satisfied with their participation in the IEP meeting.

Other relevant research results are also highly troublesome. A 16-year review of research showed a clear trend that the majority of parents attended meetings but had a passive role, with the discussion and decision making dominated by teachers and administrators (Blackwell & Rossetti, 2014). The study found that educators experienced significant challenges in developing IEPs that enabled students with disabilities to participate effectively in the general curriculum within general education classes. The authors concluded that ". . . the federal intention of parents and guardians being equal partners in collaborating with schools to develop IEPs is not being realized" (Blackwell & Rossetti, 2014, p. 11).

Many parental complaints, involving those that proceed through due process hearings, are related to the IEP. Approximately one quarter of due process hearings across 14 states focused on the IEP and program appropriateness, and another one quarter focused on placement decisions, which are typically made during the IEP meeting (Mueller & Carranza, 2011). Similarly, complaints filed by parents of children with autism over 6 years in midwestern states indicated that IEP content and implementation was the most commonly cited complaint, constituting almost three quarters of all complaints (White, 2013).

Typically, only one family member (the mother) attends, whereas three or more professionals—sometimes as many as 8 or 10—attend. Parents often have not had opportunities to learn about their IDEA-based rights and responsibilities or to understand the meaning of the terms the educators use. Sadly, the whole IEP process can bewilder many families. What can you do to avoid having an IEP meeting that confuses parents? The research teaches what you should practice, even though the research on infusing partnership principles into IEP meetings is limited.

Of the six studies identified in one national review, only one documented a significant enhancement in family participation (Goldman & Burke, 2015). In the successful study, parents of preschoolers had opportunities to complete developmental assessments of their child's functioning at home, and then they were able to attend a meeting with a school liaison at their child's school to receive an overview of what would happen at the IEP meeting. Families who received this upfront information and support made an increased number of contributions at the IEP meeting as compared to a group of parents who received only a handout describing the IEP meeting.

Another study conducted shortly after IDEA was implemented compared the meetings of students when a professional member of the IEP team was designated to welcome and introduce parents, direct questions to them during the meeting, clarify jargon, make statements affirming the value of the parental contributions, summarize at the end of the meeting, highlight next steps, and thank parents for their attendance. These easy-to-implement steps resulted in significantly greater parental contribution as compared to IEP meetings when no one was designated to provide support to parents (Goldstein & Turnbull, 1982).

So, you should ask, "What should I do?" First and foremost, you can help families prepare for the IEP meeting by encouraging them to take advantage of the information and training from the organizations that you learned about in the previous section. All of these organizations can be helpful, but note especially that the particular mission of the Parent Training and Information Centers and the Community Parent Resource Centers is to prepare families to be a trusted partner in educational decision making, including the very important IEP meetings. Because these programs are staffed by experienced parents, they can be exceedingly helpful in guiding families to know their rights and learn how to be active participants in the IEP meeting. In some situations, these programs might even have a staff member who will accompany parents to IEP meetings and support them in expressing their suggestions about each IEP component.

Second, you can also advocate within your school by encouraging administrators, other educators, and related service providers to structure IEP meetings according to the *Guidelines for Teaching: Tips for Partnering with Families in Developing Appropriately Ambitious IEPs*, which focuses on IEP partnership tips.

Guidelines for Teaching

Tips for Partnering with Parents in Developing Appropriately Ambitious IEPs

Prepare in Advance.

- Appoint an IEP coordinator to organize and facilitate the meeting.
- Ask the family about their preferences regarding the meeting (e.g., time, location) and encourage them to invite others who can be helpful partners at the meeting.
- Arrange for an interpreter to attend the meeting if the parents need one.
- Decide who should attend the meeting and include the student if appropriate and if the family agrees. Discuss preferences about attending with the student and encourage the student's self-determination.
- Arrange a convenient time and location for the meeting, based on family preferences.
- Partner with the school social worker to assist the family with logistical needs such as transportation and child care.
- Inform the family and students who are at least 16 years of age orally and/or in writing about the following:

  –Purpose of the meeting
  –Time and location of the meeting
  –Names and roles of participants
  –Option to invite people with special expertise

- Exchange information in advance by giving the family and student the information they want before the meeting.
- Encourage and arrange for the student, family members, and their advocates to visit optional future educational placements for the student before the meeting.
- Review the student's previous IEP and document the extent of the student's progress for each goal and identify facilitating and impeding factors related to progress.
- Request an informal meeting with any teachers or related service providers who will not attend the meeting. Document and report their perspectives at the meeting.
- Consider whether providing snacks is appropriate and possible and make arrangements accordingly.
- Make sure the evaluation report is complete and has clearly synthesized results.
- Consider convening a meeting with parents to share evaluation results if it is the initial evaluation or the 3-year re-evaluation. (Parents will be more prepared to plan the IEP if they have had an advance opportunity to understand and reflect on the evaluation results.)
- If the team has developed a draft IEP, send a copy to parents in advance.
- Provide written information on IDEA rights and responsibilities before the meeting and ask the parents if it would be helpful to them to have a pre-discussion of these rights and responsibilities. Encourage them to contact the Parent Training and Information Center and the Community Parent Resource Center (if available in their area) to gain relevant information.

Connect and Start.

- Greet the student, family, and their advocates.
- Share informal conversation in a comfortable and relaxed way.
- Serve snacks if available.
- Share an experience about the student that was particularly positive or one that reflects the student's best work.
- Provide a list of all participants or use name tags if there are several people who have not met before.
- Introduce each participant, briefly describing the participant's role in the meeting.
- State the meeting's purpose, review its agenda, and ask if additional issues need to be covered.
- Ask participants how long they can stay, discuss the meeting time frame, and, if needed to complete the agenda, offer to schedule a follow-up meeting.
- Ask if family members want you to clarify their legal rights and do so upon their request.

Review the Student's Formal Evaluation and Current Levels of Performance.

- Give family members written copies of all evaluation reports.
- Avoid educational jargon and clarify terms that puzzle the family, student, or their advocates.
- If a separate evaluation meeting has not been scheduled, discuss evaluation procedures and tests and the results and implications of each.
- Highlight the student's strengths as well as needs.
- Invite families and other meeting participants to agree or disagree with evaluation results and to state their reasons.
- Review the student's developmental progress and current levels of performance in each subject area or developmental area.
- Ask families if they agree or disagree with the student's current performance levels; ask why.
- Strive to resolve disagreements among participants using *partnership principles*.
- Proceed with the IEP only after all participants agree about the student's current levels of performance and potential for progress.

Share Future Visions and High Expectations.

- Encourage the student and family members to share their future visions and high expectations for the future as well as the student's strengths, gifts, and interests; and encourage professionals to do likewise.
- Express enthusiasm about the future visions and high expectations and about commitment to goals and outcomes that will be planned at the meeting.

Translate Priorities into Appropriately Ambitious Written Goals.

- Discuss and prioritize the student's needs in light of the student's and family's future visions, high expectations, strengths, interests, and preferences.
- Generate appropriately ambitious goals for all academic and functional areas that require specially designed instruction.
- Determine the evaluation criteria, procedures, and schedules for documenting progress to ensure that appropriate progress is being made.
- Determine how parents will be regularly informed of progress.

Determine the Nature of Supports and Services to Ensure Progress.

- Identify placement options that reflect the least restrictive environment.
- Consider characteristics of placement options (e.g., building characteristics, staff and student characteristics).
- Specify supplementary aids/services and related services the student will receive to ensure progress in the general curriculum, as well as in extracurricular and other nonacademic activities.
- Explain the extent to which the child will not participate in the general education program.
- Document and record the timeline for providing supplementary aids/services and related services.
- Discuss benefits and drawbacks of types, schedules, and modes of providing related services the student needs.
- Consider the five special factors identified in IDEA (positive behavior support, limited English proficiency, use of braille, language and communication modes for people

who are deaf or hard of hearing, and assistive technology), and make plans as needed for the student.
- Specify dates for initiating supplementary aids/services and related services, frequency, and anticipated duration.
- Share names and qualifications of all personnel who will provide instruction, supplementary aids/services, and related services.

Determine Modifications in Assessments.

- Determine necessary modifications for the student to participate in state- or districtwide assessments of student achievement.
- If the student is not able to participate in state or district assessment, provide a rationale and specify how the student will be assessed.

Conclude the Meeting.

- Assign follow-up responsibility for any task requiring attention.
- Summarize orally and on paper the major decisions and follow-up responsibilities of all participants.
- Set a tentative date for reviewing IEP implementation.
- Identify preferred options for ongoing communication among all participants.
- Reach a consensus decision with parents on how they will be regularly informed of the student's progress toward the annual goals and the extent to which that progress is appropriate in achieving the goals of the appropriately ambitious programs.
- Express appreciation to all team members for their collaborative decision making.
- Affirm the value of partnership, and cite specific examples of how having a trusting atmosphere enhances the quality of decision making.

SOURCE: Turnbull, A. P., Turnbull, H. R., Erwin, E., Soodak, L., & Shogren, K. (2015). *Families, professionals, and exceptionality: Positive outcomes through partnerships and trust* (7th ed.). Boston, MA: Merrill/Prentice Hall.

Third, you may use one of the most beneficial approaches to IEP partnerships—the process known as IEP meeting facilitation. Pay attention to the word "facilitation." A facilitated IEP meeting seeks to prevent or minimize whatever conflict and disagreement between parents on the one hand and educators on the other might occur. In that kind of meeting, a trained facilitator, who is not a member of the IEP team, guides constructive and respectful communication during the IEP meeting toward consensus building (CADRE, 2017; Mueller & Vick, 2017). The facilitator's primary goal is to ensure that the IEP team members address all issues fully, ensure that all members have their voices heard, avoid pitfalls that often lead to conflict, and use decision-making techniques that tend to lead to agreement rather than disagreement. An analysis of the perspectives of 32 parents and professionals who participated in facilitated IEP meetings identified five key procedures:

- Having a premeeting with families
- Creating and following a meeting agenda
- Having norms established and displayed on chart paper about expected partnership behavior (e.g., listening to others, not interrupting, not making critical remarks)

Go to www.key2ed.com and navigate to Resources. Click on Facilitated Meeting with a Neutral Facilitator to learn about different parts of a facilitated IEP meeting. Can you identify three ways in which the facilitator encourages participation?

Go to www.key2ed.com to learn more about IEP facilitation and training opportunities from Key2Ed for workshops provided throughout the United States.

- Utilizing a "parking lot" for important issues that need to be addressed at a later time but would divert attention at the present time
- Taking notes about key ideas and decisions and displaying them visually so everyone can remember and refer to them.

Facilitated IEP meetings are endorsed in 27 state education agencies as recommended practice, indicating that facilitated IEPs are helpful in avoiding formal due process procedures (Government Accountability Office, 2014). We encourage you to seek opportunities to participate in facilitated IEP training.

MERGING PARTNERSHIP PRINCIPLES INTO PARTNERING WITH PARENTS IN IEP MEETINGS   Again, you can incorporate all of the partnership principles identified in the Sunshine Framework for Trusting Family-Professional Partnership in your ongoing participation in IEP meetings. Let's return to the partnership principles so you will understand how they are infused into all aspects of partnering with families during the IEP process:

- Communication—During the meeting, ask parents questions about their perspectives on their child's progress and invite their suggestions for each of the IEP components.
- Competence—Continue your own education about being the strongest IEP partner possible by joining the Council for Exceptional Children and regularly reading its top-rated journals about research-based practices for developing and implementing IEPs.
- Commitment—Meet with parents in advance to orient them to the IEP meeting agenda and to identify the topics that will be discussed.
- Advocacy—Speak up with your professional team about ways that not only you but also everyone on the team can be more welcoming and supportive of families before, during, and after IEP meetings.
- Respect—Ask parents if they would prefer to be called by their first name or family name and avoid what often happens in meetings, which is to not use their name but to say "the family."

SolStock/E+/Getty Images

Parents of children with disabilities often spend significant time in the evenings and on weekends helping their child with homework.

- Equality—Let parents know in advance who will be attending the meeting and encourage them to bring other family members, friends, or parent advocates if they would feel more secure in terms of having a roughly equal number of professionals and family representatives.

Extending Learning in Home and Community: Guiding Families in Helping with Homework

What was your experience with homework? Did your parents or other family members help you? How? If they didn't, why? Was their help an overall positive or negative experience for you and them? Or was it both? A review of homework research studies reported the following negative and positive experiences concerning parents who helped their children without disabilities with their homework (Van Voorhis, 2011):

- Positive—Students often improved their homework performance; children were in a better mood and more attentive; the home environment had increased structure that promoted concentration.

- Negative—Parents had higher rates of frustration and embarrassment when they were not confident and competent with skills that were the focus of homework; parents tended to help their children finish more quickly rather than take the time to teach the content; parents and children had increased stress and tension in their relationship.

Parents of students with disabilities may face special hurdles in helping their children do homework. Their children may need more time to do the homework; that time may intrude on other activities of other family members. A family's quality of life most likely will be affected. A mother of a middle school student with learning disabilities and attention-deficit hyperactivity disorder (ADHD) describes the impact of her son's extensive need for homework assistance on family quality of life on weeknights and weekends.

> I sometimes dread getting home from work, because I always know that I am going back to 7th grade all over again. We rush through dinner at home so that I can sit with Jason and guide him, step-by-step through hard and long assignments. We try to be done by 10:00, but often we are not and have to start over before breakfast the next morning. Our family life too often revolves around his homework. I hardly get a chance to even know what my other two children, who do not need so much assistance, are doing in their school work. Because it takes Jason so much more time than his classmates, I wish he could have 10 math problems rather than 30.

Despite the pros and cons, research has documented that the amount of homework students do is positively related to their academic achievement (Cooper, Robinson, & Patall, 2006). Compared with average students in classes that did not have homework, average students in classes that required homework scored 26 percentile points higher on tests. The link between homework and higher achievement gets stronger as students move from elementary to secondary schools. In implementing the findings of the *Endrew F.* decision, it is likely that appropriately ambitious educational programs that have challenging objectives will have significant homework expectations.

In Figure 3.1, you learned about the five domains of family quality of life and indicators for each one. In the domain of parenting, one of the indicators is "Know how to help their child with school work and activities." This is especially important because students with disabilities rely on their parents for help with homework more than their classmates without disabilities do.

- Compared to 54 percent of parents of students without IEPs, 62 percent of parents of youth at the secondary level with IEPs report helping with homework at least once per week (Lipscomb et al., 2017).

- Black (71 percent) and Hispanic (63 percent) parents report more frequently helping with homework than do parents who are White, Asian, or other races (59 percent).

- Approximately 20 percent of secondary students with disabilities receive homework assistance from families 5 or more times per week (Newman, 2005).

- Students with disabilities are 5 times as likely as their classmates without disabilities to get frequent homework assistance from their family (Newman, 2005).

The IEP meeting is an appropriate time to discuss with families what is possible for them in terms of assisting with homework. You should inquire how long it typically takes for their child to complete homework and what they suggest to maximize the benefit and minimize the strain of homework. Be sensitive to the fact that many parents are not able to provide their children with assistance because they themselves may not be educated sufficiently or may have other limitations. Furthermore, parents who work outside the home, particularly those who have more than one job and/or who are single, simply may not have the time or energy to help their child do homework. Indeed, families vary in having access to educational resources, computers, and reference materials.

One way to form trusting partnerships around homework is assign homework that aligns with the following five characteristics (Vatterott, 2010):

- Purposeful—Homework should be linked to specific IEP goals and other appropriately ambitious learning outcomes.

- Efficiency—Homework should require a reasonable amount of time; one policy is 10 minutes starting with 1st graders and then the addition of 10 minutes for each rising grade level. Remember that many students with disabilities will require more time to complete each assignment than their classmates without disabilities.

- Ownership—Homework should be relevant to the students.

- Competence—Homework should cover content that has already been taught to the students.

- Aesthetic appeal—Homework is more likely to be completed when it is visually attractive and uncluttered.

Guidelines for Teaching: Tips for Partnering with Students and Parents for Homework Success provides tips on how you can partner with students and parents around homework. We encourage you to especially incorporate the partnership principle of communication at the beginning of the school year, during the IEP meeting, and periodically throughout the year about homework expectations, completion, and grading, as well as about the effect of homework on a family's quality of life.

Because homework can have a detrimental effect on families' quality of life, educators such as yourself and your colleagues can sponsor after-school programs whose purpose is to support students in completing their homework. These programs benefit students both with and without disabilities (Merriman, Codding, Tryon, & Minami, 2016). Effective after-school programs have the following characteristics (Huang & Cho, 2009):

- They are staffed by volunteer adults and paid instructors and use peer-to-peer tutoring.

- They instruct in study skills including time management, organizational skills, using reference sources to conduct research, test-taking skills, and notetaking.

- They create a positive and nonthreatening atmosphere that is more informal and less structured than classes during the school day.

- They ensure regular communication between the school and after-school teachers to share homework assignments and progress.

Guidelines for Teaching

Tips for Partnering with Students and Parents for Homework Success

Provide guidance to parents.

- Provide them with teachers' names and preferred times and methods for being contacted with questions about homework.
- Discuss homework expectations with them during meetings and seek to identify strategies that will work best for each family.
- Use regular communication (notes, progress reports, phone calls, e-mail messages) to communicate about homework, especially when challenges exist.
- Provide guidance about homework, including directions, an exemplary model, an evaluation rubric, and the link between homework and general curriculum standards.
- Encourage parents to set up a consistent homework routine in terms of schedule and location.

Teach students to strengthen their homework efficiency.

- Provide a checklist that students use at school and at home with the steps they need to follow organizationally to complete their homework successfully (e.g., using a book bag and school binder, recording homework assignments, breaking projects and test preparation down into small steps, and planning an afternoon and evening schedule to ensure homework time allocation).
- Teach students self-management strategies for homework, including how to listen to and correctly write down the assignment, estimate the time it will require for completion, identify materials needed to take home, recruit assistance when needed, monitor progress, and self-reward homework completion.
- Ask students to evaluate the time required and accuracy of their homework when they complete it while watching television, listening to the radio, or working in a quiet setting. Encourage them to reflect on the most effective setting as well as on their personal preferences.
- Teach students to graph homework completion and then explain the graphs to their parents in parent-student-teacher meetings.
- Teach students to use a tape recorder with a beep-tape set at 10-minute intervals or less and have them log whether or not they were engaging in on-task homework behavior at the time of the beep.

Provide appropriate accommodations.

- Ensure that homework is the appropriate length, especially for students who require more time for completion or who have lower levels of energy.
- Allow students with writing and spelling challenges to do their homework on a computer to have the benefits of spell-check and grammar-check.
- Guide students in breaking large assignments into successive and manageable steps.
- Provide reinforcement, such as extra resource time or special treats for homework completion. You can give reinforcement to students on an individual basis or to students based on a class average. Another option is to choose a randomly selected student and provide a reward to the entire class based on that student's performance.
- Use cooperative homework teams in which three or four students work together to submit assignments to one team member, who is assigned to be the checker and who then grades the papers and gives them to the teacher. Students work together on corrections.
- Seek feedback from students at periodic intervals in terms of the appropriateness of the accommodations.
- Provide homework that links the classroom with real life, such as learning to tell time by developing a schedule of favorite television shows.

SOURCE: Based on Bembenutty, H. (2011). The first word: Homework's theory, research, and practice. *Journal of Advanced Academics, 22*(2), 185–192; Carr, N. S. (2013). Increasing the effectiveness of homework for all learners in the inclusive classroom. *School Community Journal, 23*(1), 169–182; Hampshire, P. K., Butera, G. D., & Hourcade, J. J. (2014). Homework plans: A tool for promoting independence. *TEACHING Exceptional Children, 46*(6), 158–168; Stockwall, N. (2017). Designing homework to mediate executive functioning deficits in students with disabilities. *Intervention in School and Clinic, 53*(1), 3–11; Langberg, J. M., Epstein, J. N., Becker, S. P., Girio-Herrera, E., & Vaughn, A. J. (2012). Evaluation of the Homework, Organization, and Planning Skills (HOPS) intervention for middle school students with attention deficit hyperactivity disorder as implemented by school mental health providers. *School Psychology Review, 41*, 342–364; Turnbull, A. P., Turnbull, H. R., Erwin, E., Soodak, L., & Shogren, K. (2015). *Families, professionals, and exceptionality: Positive outcomes through partnerships and trust* (7th ed.). Boston, MA: Merrill/Prentice Hall.

MERGING PARTNERSHIP PRINCIPLES INTO SUPPORT FOR PARENTS IN PROVIDING HOMEWORK ASSISTANCE As you have learned about the two *partnership types* that we have addressed, part of your responsibility in implementing *partnership types* is to ensure that you embed *partnership principles*. Here are examples for you to follow:

- Communication—Support students in developing a written log of homework assignments so that they can clearly communicate to their parents what you expect from homework.

- Competence—Seek opportunities to learn how to diversify your homework assignments so they align with your students' preferred learning styles.
- Commitment—Be available to parents who feel overwhelmed by the amount of homework assistance they are providing and brainstorm about how to accommodate for them.
- Advocacy—If you believe that the inordinate homework assignments given by other teachers are interfering with the students' time and attention needed to complete the homework for your subject, have a conversation with the other teachers to achieve mutually reasonable expectations.
- Respect—When parents are unable to assist with homework for a variety of reasons, rather than judgmentally criticizing them, seek opportunities for the student to have homework assistance in other ways, such as through an after-school program.
- Equality—When homework problems occur, invite parents to share their perspectives and thus learn what you may not have already considered.

Trust and Dignity

You may ask, "OK, where is that word trust and what does it and the six principles have to do with dignity?" Good question.

First, as we taught you in the early pages of this chapter, trust is what results when the other elements of partnerships exist. Trust culminates from the practices we have described.

Next, dignity is like the aura—the light—that emanates from the sun's rays, those practices we have described. Each practice signifies to a family member and to the student that you value them. Remember what we have said in Chapter 1. It was this: To value is to dignify. We put it this way: "Less able does not mean less worthy, and more able does not mean more worthy."

MyLab Education Self-Check 3.3

MyLab Education Application Exercise 3.3: Creating Family Partnerships

---

Summary

Understanding Today's Families

Families consist of two or more people who regard themselves to be a family and carry out the functions that families typically perform. Compared with the families of children without disabilities, a greater proportion of families of children with disabilities have parents who are less likely to have a college degree or further training, to have a job, and to be married or be in a marriage-like relationship.

Understanding Family Quality of Life and Your Role as an Educator

Family quality of life refers to the extent to which (1) the families' needs are met, (2) family members enjoy their life together, and (3) family members have a chance to do the things important to them. The five domains of family quality of life are emotional well-being, parenting, family interaction, physical/material well-being, and disability-related support.

Understanding Partnerships

Family-professional partnerships are relationships in which families and professionals collaborate with each other and capitalize on each other's judgment and expertise to increase benefits for students, families, and professionals alike. Family-professional partnerships are important because (1) schools with strong partnerships are more likely to have high levels of trust, (2) partnerships result in more positive student outcomes, and (3) positive family quality of life is more likely when families experience positive partnerships with professionals. The Trusting Partnerships Sunshine Framework consists of six *partnership principles* (communication, competence, commitment, advocacy, respect, and equality) that fuse to create trust between families and professionals. Each sunray represents *partnership types* (meeting basic needs, referring and evaluating, individualizing, extending learning, volunteering and participating, and advocating). The *partnership principles* are infused into each of the sunrays representing *partnership types* to create trust.

Strategies to Form Trusting Partnerships with Families

In the *partnership type* of meeting basic needs, you can provide additional emotional and informational support through the Parent-to-Parent Program, Parent Training and Information Center, Community Parent Resource Center (if available in your community), Center for Parent Education and Resources, and Family-to-Family Health Information Center. These programs are staffed primarily by families who have children with disabilities, and they offer practical assistance to families and professionals.

The *partnership type* of individualizing services and supports can occur through the *partnership subtype* of enhancing family participation in IEP meetings. Although IDEA calls for parents and professionals to be joint educational decision makers, the trend of parent participation over the past 40 years indicates that parents typically attend meetings but have low rates of participation. Parents characterized by racial/ethnic diversity and low income typically attend meetings at a lower rate and are less satisfied. You can encourage and facilitate families to take advantage of the resources of Parent Training and Information Centers, and Community Parent Resource Centers can provide families with needed information and advocacy skills. These programs are staffed primarily by parents of sons and daughters with disabilities; these parents have firsthand experiences and vast knowledge to pass along to parents who take advantage of their services. You can link to the websites of each of these programs and find state and community resources.

For the *partnership type* of extending learning in home and community, you can support parents to provide assistance with their child's homework. Keep in mind that students with disabilities often have greater challenges with homework, placing more responsibility on their parents for assistance. You can contribute to enhancing family quality of life by ensuring that you provide guidance to parents, teach students to be more efficient in doing homework, and provide appropriate accommodations. Students with disabilities and their families can greatly benefit from after-school programs focused on homework assistance that ultimately "lightens the families' load" in providing homework assistance.

Addressing the Professional Standards

In Chapter 3, Today's Families and Their Partnerships with Professionals, we have covered the following Council for Exceptional Children (CEC) Initial Level Special Educator Preparation Standards: Chapter 3—1.1, 2.0, 2.1, 4.3, 5.1, 5.5, 6.0, 6.2, 6.3, 6.5, 7.0, 7.1, 7.2, 7.3. Refer to the Appendix for a full listing of the CEC Standards with descriptions and supporting explanations.

Chapter 4
Ensuring Educational Progress

4.1 Discuss the relationship of the nondiscriminatory evaluation to the IEP and its components about student progress and identify how the NDE contributes to understanding students' potential for growth.

4.2 Describe how to determine a student's present levels of performance and identify how that and the design of supplementary aids and services are used to determine a student's IEP.

4.3 Define inclusion and compare and contrast the argument for inclusion with historic models of special education, considering IDEA's least restrictive environment and placement decision requirements.

Meet Pablo Garcia—Making Progress in an Inclusive School

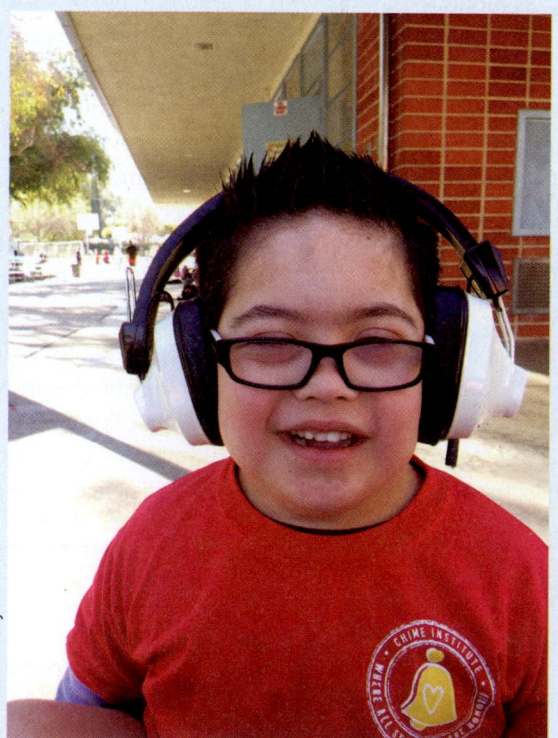

Adie Buchinsky

What criteria should educators, families, and students apply when evaluating a school? What should you apply when seeking your ideal teaching job? We'll give you two choices.

The first choice consists of the "Three A" criteria: Academic success, Artistic superiority, and Athletic championships.

The second choice consists of the "Three C" criteria: Character and culture, Commitment and the diligent pursuit of excellence, and Competence and the attainment of excellence.

We must make a disclosure: We created a false choice. In fact, you could have made the second choice—the "Three C" criteria—and still have chosen the "Academic success" portion of the first choice if you had known about CHIME school, a K through 8 charter school in Los Angeles.

Visit CHIME and you will find that the Three C standard guides that school. Indeed, because CHIME emphasizes character, commitment, and competence, it is precisely the school where 11-year-old Pablo Garcia can make the progress that the Supreme Court, in *Endrew F.*, said is the standard of an appropriate education under the Individuals with Disabilities Education Act (IDEA).

CHIME is a K through 8 charter school. That's the simplest way to describe it. A more expansive description is that its culture is completely inclusive: It educates students from nearly 50 different communities in Los Angeles County, representing upwards of a half-dozen different ethnicities and races, and including 150 students with disabilities (including 60 with "low incidence" disabilities) who, collectively, represent nearly 20 percent of the total student body of 770 students. Yes, students with and without disabilities learn together. That is why we feature CHIME in this chapter about progress in the general education curriculum. We also feature it throughout the book, not just in this chapter. It is a model from which you can learn much about progress and inclusion—about appropriate education and the principle of the least restrictive environment (inclusion).

One of the students at CHIME is Pablo Garcia. You might assume, correctly, from his name that he is Hispanic; his at-home language is both English and Spanish, but his at-school language is English—"spoken," however, not as you might expect.

You should know what you cannot assume: Pablo has intellectual disability. He is a young man with Down syndrome (Chapter 11). Pablo's father and mother, Sergio and Delia, and his teachers, Rose Beemer, Laura Etting, and Adie Buchinsky, agree that Pablo's greatest challenge is to communicate effectively. They also agree that, as his communication ability grows, his academic progress does, too. Progress in an inclusive school, in the general education curriculum, suits not only Pablo but all students. CHIME's character, its culture, is inclusive. Students with disabilities attend classes with students who do not have disabilities, and teachers certified as regular educators conduct classes along with teachers certified as special educators.

Having learned about CHIME's culture, you are right to ask: What about its commitment? Its commitment is unrelenting, diligent pursuit of excellence. What about the administrators' and teachers' competence? They co-teach—general and special educators alike modify their curriculum to include Pablo and other students with disabilities in the general education curriculum.

MyLab Education
Vignette Video 4.1
Why did Pablo's teachers and CHIME school administrator focus on Pablo's communication skills?

There's more to CHIME than character, commitment, and competence, more to its way of ensuring that Pablo makes the progress in inclusive education that IDEA and the Supreme Court say is his right. Pablo also makes progress because his nondiscriminatory evaluation is the basis for his individualized education program (IEP): His need to learn to communicate (a need his evaluation revealed) results in an education that ensures his progress.

By providing the related service of speech-language therapy and an augmentative alternative communication device, and by carefully tracking his communication progress over several years, Adie, Rose, and Laura, together, have ensured that Pablo can be included academically and socially with other students and can express his choices and become more self-determined. More than that, Pablo has paraprofessionals with him throughout the day, receives related services from occupational therapists and speech-language specialists, and benefits from a functional behavioral assessment and positive behavior support program that makes his behavior less challenging.

You need to know one more fact about Pablo and CHIME. Pablo's teachers care so much about him. What's not to care about Pablo? He is courteous; he is empathetic; he is well liked and supported; and he received a standing ovation from the entire student body when he won the "Good Character" award as a 5th grader, in 2018. Who were the electors, those who chose him? They were his classmates. Why did they choose him to receive the award? He won because, in their judgment, he was the student who most exemplified the character trait of the month, namely, "kindness."

A combination of factors—character and culture, commitment, and competence—coalesce at CHIME, making it an excellent site for you to learn how superb educators evaluate students fairly and then use research-based practices to ensure students' progress. The fact is that Pablo makes progress in the general education curriculum and in an inclusive school because the school's leadership and teachers, and his peers, are in a school where character and culture, commitment to evidence-based education, and competence shared across disciplines are valued. Pablo is in a model school. You would be fully justified in saying that Pablo and his peers attend a school whose members, faculty and students alike, value and dignify each other.

Learning Standards and the General Education Curriculum: What All Students Should Learn

You have already learned that progress is one of the core elements of our book. You also learned that both the Individuals with Disabilities Education Act (IDEA) and the Supreme Court's decision in *Endrew F.* (2017) require that students receiving special education services make progress. In fact, it was Endrew's lack of progress that compelled his parents to move him to a private school and to seek reimbursement from the school district. How do you, as a teacher, ensure that students with disabilities make progress? Progress in what?

These are good questions. Fortunately, standards, policies, and practices are in place that can guide you in answering those questions. You will learn how to evaluate a student and plan for an educational program that, as described in *Endrew F.*, recognizes the student's potential for growth and capacity for progress.

In *Endrew F.*, the Supreme Court cut to the core of special education under IDEA:

> A focus on the particular child is at the core of the IDEA. The instruction offered must be "*specially* designed" to meet the child's "*unique* needs" through an "*individualized*" education program. An IEP is not a form document. It is constructed only after careful consideration of the child's present levels of achievement, disability, and potential for growth (p. 12).

Careful consideration of a student's present levels of performance, disability, and potential for growth begins with understanding what all students are expected to learn because that is what students with disabilities are now expected to learn as well. Indeed, ever since 1997, IDEA has required that the IEPs of all students receiving special education services state how the student will be involved with and progress in the general education curriculum, how the student's progress will be assessed, and how state and district-wide assessments will be modified (as appropriate) for the student. Congress, in IDEA, explained why this requirement is justified:

> Almost 30 years of research and experience has demonstrated that the education of children with disabilities can be made more effective by having high expectations for such children and ensuring their access to the general education curriculum in the regular classroom, to the maximum extent possible.

The general education curriculum is the same curriculum as that which drives instruction for students without disabilities, which in turn, is a curriculum based on a state's academic content standards. The "high expectations" are what CHIME has for Pablo and all students—namely, that all will make progress in the general education curriculum so that, in turn, they may achieve IDEA's "big four" policy goals: equal opportunity, full participation, independent living, and economic self-sufficiency.

Challenging Academic Content Standards

One way that IDEA defines a free appropriate public education (FAPE) is as special education and related services that meet the standards of the state educational agency. Standards define the general education curriculum for students in any state. The federal Every Student Succeeds Act (ESSA, Chapter 1) requires that each state adopt challenging academic content standards. Academic content standards define the knowledge, skills, and understanding that students should attain in academic subjects. In essence, the standards describe what our society thinks all students should know—what Pablo should know, too, so that he may attain IDEA's policy goals.

The standards must be uniform across the state, and states must, at a minimum, establish academic standards and procedures for assessing students' progress in three core areas—mathematics, reading or language arts, and science. State standards must, in general, be aligned with entrance requirements for postsecondary education (college, university, community college, and vocational/technical schools). In addition, states may develop standards and assessments for any other subjects. All standards and assessments must be uniform across the state, must be aligned with the challenging academic content standards set by the state, and must be administered in each of grades 3 through 8 and at least once in grades 9 through 12 (for mathematics and reading or language arts) or (for science) at least once during grades 3 through 5, 6 through 9, and 10 through 12.

ESSA requires that all students participate in state assessments. Some students with disabilities may be able to participate in the state assessments, with accommodations. **Accommodations** are changes to the presentation of instructional content or test or assessment administration that support a student's participation in the learning activity or assessment, but that do not in any way modify the content or assessment. Examples of accommodations include extra time, a calculator, oral or signed administration of assessment items, and other such supports. *Into Practice Across Grade Levels: Testing Accommodations* provides more information about testing accommodations. Whether a student receives accommodations and, if so, the types of accommodations the student receives, are decisions made by the student's IEP team. In addition, a small percentage of students with disabilities may not be able to participate in state assessments even with accommodations. In these cases, states may administer alternate assessments that you will learn about later in this chapter.

Pablo takes the alternate assessment, consistent with his evaluation and IEP. Because he gets a bad case of nerves when he thinks he is being tested, his teachers take him to a separate room (out of his classroom), tell him he is "practicing" taking a test, and then let him take the actual test. Are they being deceptive? No. They are accommodating him so that he will demonstrate exactly what he has learned and so that they will monitor his progress accurately and respond accordingly.

Into Practice Across Grade Levels

Testing Accommodations

What are testing accommodations?

Testing accommodations refer to any change in standardized testing materials or procedures that allows a student with a disability or English language learners to provide evidence of their knowledge or skills. Accommodations do not change what is assessed; they only change how it is assessed. Testing accommodations enable students with disabilities or English language learners to have equal opportunity to express and demonstrate what they know.

Example: A district assessment in **4th-grade** math requires that students solve word problems. A student with intellectual disability may be able to solve the problems if given accommodations to support reading the word problem, adding and subtracting (not the primary focus of the assessment), and recording the answer. The content of the assessment remains the same, but the student is provided oral presentation of the word problem, the use of a calculator, and a scribe.

When are testing accommodations required for students with disabilities?

IDEA requires that the IEP contain a statement of any individual appropriate accommodations that are necessary to measure the academic achievement and functional performance of the student on state and district-wide assessments and, if the student cannot participate in the regular assessment, that appropriate accommodations and modifications in administration of State or district-wide assessments must be provided if necessary to ensure the participation of students with disabilities in those assessments.

Example: The IEP team of an **8th-grade** student with autism examines data from the nondiscriminatory evaluation process and determines that the student may be able to participate in the state reading assessment if there are accommodations for the student's distractibility and limited reading skills. The IEP team recommended that the student be provided a setting for taking the test that reduced distractions

(Continued)

and that directions would be repeated for the student as requested and any explanation of directions that is needed will be provided.

Who decides if testing accommodations are required?
IDEA indicates that it is the IEP team that is responsible for determining whether a student with a disability requires testing accommodations. It is best to think about this in another manner—not so much whether accommodations are needed, but instead what it will take for the student to participate equitably in state and district-wide assessments. For some students, that may mean the provision of testing accommodations. For other students, the IEP team may decide that the student needs to be involved in the alternate assessment.

Example: The IEP team is considering the best option for participation for a **5th-grade** student with a reading-related learning disability. The special educator is aware that a widely established testing accommodation, read-aloud administration, has been shown to enable students with learning disabilities to participate in state and district-wide testing. After a discussion of the benefits and potential drawbacks (stigma associated with having items read aloud), the team decided that the best option for ensuring equal participation was to include read-aloud accommodations in the IEP.

Who decides what testing accommodations to use?
Deciding on testing accommodations or the need for them is the role of the IEP team. If the IEP team determines that a student needs testing accommodations—to have an equal opportunity to show what the student knows—the student's IEP must include a statement of any such modifications.

Example: The IEP team is trying to determine if a **3rd-grade** student with multiple disabilities can participate in the state assessment for science or if the student needs to participate in the alternate assessment. The student has

been included in the general education curriculum in science for the year, working with peers without disabilities on projects and performing well with adaptations to the lesson objectives. Rather than remove the student from the regular assessment, the IEP team decides that if the student can use an AAC communication device and provide answers from that assessment, the student may be able to successfully complete the regular assessment.

What options are available for testing accommodations?
Many testing accommodations have been shown to be effective. The National Center on Educational Outcomes, which is a U.S. Department of Education–funded technical assistance center for assessment and accommodations, identifies accommodations in assessment presentation (braille, use of a dictionary, interpreter for instructions, large print, read aloud, sign language administration, simplified language, visual cues), presentation modality (through audio files, through computer, via DVD), student response (using a calculator, dictating responses to someone else, recording responses on a digital recorder, using a spell-checker, using a word processing software program), scheduling (extended time, breaks during the testing period), and setting, as CHIME uses for Pablo (student alone or in a small group, a specialized setting).

Example: A **10th-grade** student with visual impairments uses multiple accommodations to successfully participate with her peers who do not have disabilities in the state mathematics assessment. Rather than have questions read aloud, she has opted to have them digitally recorded so she can listen to them through headphones. The sheet on which she marks her answers has large print, and she uses a hand-held magnifying glass to read through the items as she listens to them. She uses the magnifying glass to assist her in recording her work and answers on the sheet.

ESSA does not specify what standards must be adopted, only that states must adopt challenging academic content standards in, at least, the content areas of mathematics, reading or language arts, and science. But a majority of states have adopted college and career readiness standards developed by the Common Core State Standards initiative. California, where CHIME operates, is one of those states.

COLLEGE AND CAREER READINESS STANDARDS   The Common Core State Standards (CCSS) initiative originated with state governors and education leaders in 48 states, the District of Columbia, and two U.S. territories through the National Governors Association in collaboration with the Council of Chief State School Officers. The standards intend to provide real-world learning goals (what students should know and be able to do at each grade level) to ensure that K through 12 students across the United States graduate from high school ready for colleges and careers. Teachers contributed to developing the CCSS, serving on work groups and providing feedback and input. Currently, 42 states, the District of Columbia, and four territories have adopted the college and career readiness standards in mathematics and English language arts or literacy. Some of the 5th Grade CCSS literacy, writing, math, and science standards adopted by California are shown in Figure 4.1. They apply to all CHIME students, including Pablo. That's one form of inclusion.

You can find information on all of the CCSS college and career readiness standards at http://www. corestandards.org/

Figure 4.1 Examples of Common Core State Standards Adopted in California

Grade 5 English Language Arts & Literacy
Reading Standards for Literature: Quote accurately from a text when explaining what the text says explicitly and when drawing inferences from the text.
Reading Standards for Literature: Determine a theme of a story, drama, or poem from details in the text, including how characters in a story or drama respond to challenges or how the speaker in a poem reflects upon a topic; summarize the text.
Reading Standards for Informational Text: Explain the relationships or interactions between two or more individuals, events, ideas, or concepts in a historical, scientific, or technical text based on specific information in the text.
Reading Standards for Foundational Skills: Know and apply grade-level phonics and word analysis skills in decoding words.
Reading Standards for Foundational Skills: Read with sufficient accuracy and fluency to support comprehension.
Grade 5 Writing
Write opinion pieces on topics or texts, supporting a point of view with reasons and information.
Write informative/explanatory texts to examine a topic and convey ideas and information clearly.
Grade 5 Mathematics
Operations and Algebraic Thinking: Write and interpret numerical expressions.
Number and Operations—Fractions: Use equivalent fractions as a strategy to add and subtract fractions.
Number and Operations—Fractions: Apply and extend previous understandings of multiplication and division to multiply and divide fractions.
Measurement and Data: Convert like measurement units within a given measurement system.
Geometry: Graph points on the coordinate plane to solve real-world and mathematical problems.
Geometry: Classify two-dimensional figures into categories based on their properties.
Grade 5 Science
Physical Sciences: Design and build simple series and parallel circuits by using components such as wires, batteries, and bulbs.
Physical Sciences: Know the role of electromagnets in the construction of electric motors, electric generators, and simple devices, such as doorbells and earphones.
Life Sciences: Know decomposers, including many fungi, insects, and microorganisms, which recycle matter from dead plants and animals.
Life Sciences: Know ecosystems can be characterized by their living and nonliving components.
Earth Sciences: Differentiate among igneous, sedimentary, and metamorphic rocks by referring to their properties and methods of formation (the rock cycle).
Earth Sciences: Know some changes in the earth are due to slow processes, such as erosion, and some changes are due to rapid processes, such as landslides, volcanic eruptions, and earthquakes.
Investigation and Experimentation: Conduct multiple trials to test a prediction and draw conclusions about the relationships between predictions and results.
Investigation and Experimentation: Differentiate observation from inference (interpretation) and know scientists' explanations come partly from what they observe and partly from how they interpret their observations.

SOURCE: Reprinted with permission of California Department of Education, https://www.cde.ca.gov/RE/cc/

An additional collaboration of state education leaders and science educators (including the National Science Teachers Association) developed the Next Generation Science Standards, which (as of 2018) have been adopted by 18 states.

Information on Next Generation Science Standards is available at https://www.nextgenscience.org/

An Appropriately Ambitious Educational Program

In *Endrew F.* the Supreme Court interpreted IDEA's appropriate education principle to mean that each student receiving IDEA services has a right to an appropriately ambitious educational program. Specifically, IDEA requires that the IEP of students with disabilities include a statement of measurable annual goals designed to meet the student's needs that result from the student's disability to enable the student to be *involved with and make progress in the general education curriculum*, and to meet each of the student's *other educational needs* that result from the student's disability. You can see from Figure 4.2 that Pablo's IEP contains information about his *progress* toward his communication goals. You'll learn much more about creating an appropriately ambitious educational program later in this chapter. For now, however, let's look more closely at IDEA's requirements.

Figure 4.2 Pablo's Progress Toward Current Communication Goal

Goal	Given a core word vocabulary on his speech-generating device, Pablo will use 10 core vocabulary words (e.g., look, stop, like) to create novel sentences with varied meaning (e.g., "you stop," "stop it") in 4 out of 5 opportunities, with minimal prompting.	Goal Not Met	Requires moderate prompting
Objective 1	As above, for 3 core words.	Goal Met	Core words: here, there, have, it
Objective 2	As above, for 7 core words.	Goal Not Met	

GENERAL EDUCATION CURRICULUM   The Department of Education regulations implementing IDEA define the general education curriculum as, simply, the same curriculum that states make available to students without disabilities. As you know, that curriculum constitutes the academic content standards that describe the knowledge, skills, and understanding that all students should know. All means all, and in the context of ESSA and IDEA, the clear expectation is that all students with disabilities should be involved with and progress in challenging academic achievement standards. Such an educational program begins with ensuring that those students are involved with and progress in the general education curriculum. Under the "all means all" theory, that seems right, but is it? The answer is "yes," but with an understanding about what "yes" means.

Alternate Academic Achievement Standards.   Both *Endrew F.* and IDEA recognize that there are some students who, even with high-quality supports, will have difficulty meeting some academic content standards. To address this, ESSA permits states to establish **alternate academic achievement standards** for **students with the most significant cognitive disabilities**. Because, as you learned earlier, ESSA connects standards with assessments, ESSA allows states to develop **alternate assessments based on alternate academic achievement standards** but it restricts states from using the alternate assessments for more than 1 percent of the total number of all students in the state. Thus, students with the most significant cognitive disabilities constitute the 1 percent of students who educators predict will not be successful in the state assessments, with or without accommodations.

The state alternate academic achievement standards established for students with the most significant cognitive disabilities must do the following:

- Be aligned with the challenging academic content standards set for all students
- Promote access to the general education curriculum, consistent with IDEA's principle of least restrictive environment (inclusion)
- Be described in each student's IEP
- Ensure that the student is on track to pursue postsecondary education or employment.

Some of the alternate academic achievement standards that apply to CHIME and Pablo are in Figure 4.3. Some are a direct match to their CCSS equivalents, and others are not.

OTHER EDUCATIONAL NEEDS   The general education curriculum is not the only educational domain in which you should work to ensure student progress. In addition to the statement concerning measurable goals and supports to enable students with disabilities to be involved with and progress in the general education curriculum, IDEA also requires that the IEP include measurable annual goals designed to meet a student's other educational needs that result from the disability. Those needs are best thought of as whatever a student needs to learn to be successful in life that is not reflected in the general education curriculum. These are learning goals that may be unique to the student, such as Pablo's need to wash his hands thoroughly after going to the bathroom and before meals. It's now appropriate for you to learn how to identify those unique learning needs.

Figure 4.3 Alternate Academic Achievement Standards from California

Grade 5 English Language Arts & Literacy	Core Content Connectors
Reading Standards for Literature: Quote accurately from a text when explaining what the text says explicitly and when drawing inferences from the text.	Refer to details and examples in a text when explaining what the text says explicitly.
Reading Standards for Literature: Determine a theme of a story, drama, or poem from details in the text, including how characters in a story or drama respond to challenges or how the speaker in a poem reflects upon a topic; summarize the text.	Summarize a text from beginning to end in a few sentences.
Reading Standards for Informational Text: Explain the relationships or interactions between two or more individuals, events, ideas, or concepts in a historical, scientific, or technical text based on specific information in the text.	Determine the main idea, and identify key details to support the main idea.
Reading Standards for Foundational Skills: Know and apply grade-level phonics and word analysis skills in decoding words.	Identify grade-level words with accuracy and on successive attempts.
Reading Standards for Foundational Skills: Read with sufficient accuracy and fluency to support comprehension.	Identify grade-level words with accuracy.
Grade 5 Mathematics	
Operations and Algebraic Thinking: Write and interpret numerical expressions.	Generate or select a comparison between two graphs from a similar situation.
Number and Operations—Fractions: Use equivalent fractions as a strategy to add and subtract fractions.	Identify what to do with the parts when given the key word (using the fractional parts).
Number and Operations—Fractions: Apply and extend previous understandings of multiplication and division to multiply and divide fractions.	Limit to whole numbers and 1 or more; show what happens to set when have one of these (1x) versus some other number (e.g., 2x).
Measurement and Data: Convert like measurement units within a given measurement system.	Measure an object or quantity using 2 different units to show they mean the same thing (e.g., 12 inches and 1 foot). If larger unit, there are less; smaller units, you need more.
Geometry: Graph points on the coordinate plane to solve real-world and mathematical problems.	Identify the *x*- and *y*-axis; or concept of intersection.

SOURCE: Reprinted with permission of California Department of Education/California Alternate Assessment, https://www.cde.ca.gov/ta/tg/ca/altassessment.asp

Nondiscriminatory Evaluation: Evaluating for Disability, Levels of Achievement, and Potential for Growth

As you read in Chapter 1, IDEA requires educators to conduct a nondiscriminatory evaluation (NDE) for each student. Obviously, planning for progress requires evaluation and assessment information. The NDE has two purposes. The first is to determine whether a student has a disability. If the determination is that the student does have a disability, then the second purpose of the NDE is to determine the nature and extent of special education and related services the student needs to progress. In *Endrew F.*, the Supreme Court interpreted IDEA to require an IEP that is *constructed only after careful consideration of the child's present levels of achievement, disability, and potential for growth*. To teach you how to connect the NDE with the IEP, we discuss the three factors you must take into account in evaluating a student:

- The nature of the student's disability (from both NDE and *Endrew F.*)
- The student's present levels of achievement (from both NDE and *Endrew F.*)
- The student's potential for growth (from *Endrew F.*).

Evaluation to Determine the Nature of Disability

You may think of eligibility determination as a diagnostic and possibly even a medical process. Certainly, information about the type and **etiology** (cause) of a student's disability is important to know. It is equally important, however, to remember that eligibility for special education is determined on the basis of the student's educational need and not strictly on diagnostic categories or medical conditions. IDEA defines a child with a disability as a child who (1) meets the diagnostic criteria for one of the disability categories (see Figure 1.2) and (2) needs special education and related services. Pablo's evaluation shows he meets both criteria.

So, eligibility determination is not just about the diagnosis of a disability (and, in some states, giftedness); it is also about the need for specially designed instruction. Fundamentally, as IDEA and *Endrew F.* make clear, it is about student progress. The two functions of NDE (determining eligibility and identifying special education and related service needs) have the same intent: to ensure that students have the supports and services they need to progress in school.

As you learned in Chapter 2, however, disproportionate representation of students from diverse backgrounds—their overplacement into special education—is a matter of cultural justice. Is it odd to discuss the role of nondiscriminatory evaluation in planning for progress and also talk about the role of this process as contributing to overrepresentation? No, not at all.

The issues are with the role of nondiscriminatory evaluation and decisions about where students receive special education services. In Chapter 1, you learned about the IDEA least restrictive environment (LRE) mandate and the law's preference for inclusion. Specifically, IDEA states that *to the maximum extent appropriate, children with disabilities . . . are educated with children who are not disabled, and special classes, separate schooling, or other removal of children with disabilities from the regular educational environment occurs only when the nature or severity of the disability of a child is such that education in regular classes with the use of supplementary aids and services cannot be achieved satisfactorily.*

The data we presented in Chapter 2 show that students from diverse backgrounds, particularly Black and American Indian/Pacific Islander students, are disproportionally served in segregated settings outside general education classrooms. An education for students with disabilities that emphasizes progress is one in which students (1) are provided challenging objectives that in turn arise in and through the general education curriculum and (2) have the specially designed instruction, supplementary aids and services, and related services needed to promote students' involvement with and progress in the general education curriculum.

Students with disabilities are significantly more likely to receive an educational program comprising these elements—challenging objectives and specially designed instruction with supports—if they are in the general education setting (Wehmeyer et al., 2016). That's why CHIME school provides related services—speech-language and occupational therapy, and a communication device—to educate Pablo in the general education curriculum: He will make more progress there than elsewhere.

You'll learn more about planning for progress with each of these elements in a moment. For now, just keep in mind that if planning for an appropriately ambitious education consisting of challenging objectives begins with the nondiscriminatory evaluation, so, too, does the tyranny of low expectations and a *de minimis* education. You know what we are about to say, but we will say it anyhow: IDEA imposes the duty on all members of a student's evaluation team to take the "high" approach and avoid the *de minimis* approach in doing the evaluation. Yes, *Endrew F.* did not speak about the evaluation, but it did speak about the "appropriate" education and the student's IEP. Because an IEP rests on the evaluation, the same "high" must influence the evaluators, just as it influences the professionals who developed Pablo's evaluation.

A number of assessment tools and processes are used to determine the nature of a child's disability. Consistent with the fact that assessment to determine disability can also become assessment to determine a student's needs for special education and related services, you will learn more about common assessments and assessment processes used to determine disability (e.g., achievement tests, curriculum-based assessments, ecological assessments, behavioral rating scales, and adaptive behavior scales) in a subsequent section. For now, however, there are some processes and tools that are more specific to the disability determination process that you should know about. These are screening and pre-referral processes and intelligence testing.

SCREENING AND PRE-REFERRAL PROCESSES A source of data comes from the fact that some students may have received **pre-referral interventions** to address difficulty in academic content areas or **screening** (assessing for a condition or situation in the absence of symptoms) tools to identify students at risk for difficulty because of emotional and behavioral issues. Pre-referral interventions involve one or more of three actions:

- The delivery of more intense instruction
- Instruction for a longer duration
- Different types of instruction provided to a student who is having difficulty, to address that student's performance before "referring" the student for evaluation for eligibility for special education services.

Again, data from these actions can and should affect decisions about a student's present levels of academic achievement. But educators supplement the data from those actions by using different kinds of screening tools, most frequently vision and behavioral screening tools. Screening tools involve some form of assessment or evaluation delivered to all students in a school to "screen" for the potential for later difficulties.

For example, most states require students entering school for the first time to be screened for vision problems. The screening detects vision problems that should be corrected before they arise once the student is already in classes. The same strategy applies to screening for behavioral and attention-related issues. The idea is to use validated screening tools to identify students who are at risk for later school problems because of behavioral or attention-related issues. The Student Risk Screening Scale (SRSS; Drummond, 1994) is a widely used screening tool shown to be useful across age and grade levels (Lane, Menzies, Oakes, & Kalberg, 2012; Lane et al., 2013). You can download the SRSS for free and use it to find students who might need supports related to their behavior.

You can download the SRSS for free at the U.S. Department of Education's technical assistance site on Positive Behavior Interventions and Supports at https://www.pbis.org/resource/1128/student-risk-screening-scale-%E2%80%93-internalizing-and-externalizing-srss-ie

INTELLIGENCE TESTS The nondiscriminatory evaluation process usually assesses the student's intelligence, using a number of common intelligence tests, including the Wechsler Intelligence Scale for Children (WISC; Lindstrom & Sayeski, 2013). Intelligence tests measure a sample of a student's performance on tasks related to reasoning, memory, learning comprehension, and ability to learn academic skills. They infer the student's intellectual capacity based on the student's performance, usually represented as an intelligence quotient, or IQ, score.

The bell-shaped curve in Figure 4.4 shows below-average, average, and above-average ranges of intelligence on the WISC (this graph is from the WISC-IV; the latest edition is the WISC-V, 2014). Note that 50 percent of students at any particular age average an IQ below 100, and 50 percent average an IQ above 100. Most states identify students with IQs at or above 130 as gifted (Chapter 17) and students with IQs at or below 70 as having intellectual disability if they also meet other criteria (Chapter 11).

You can find more information about the WISC-V at https://www.pearsonclinical.com/psychology/products/100000771/wechsler-intelligence-scale-for-childrensupsupfifth-edition--wisc-v.html.

The WISC is appropriate for use with students from ages 6 to 16 years, 11 months. It provides scores related to the following four indexes: verbal comprehension, perceptual reasoning, processing speed, and working memory. Diagnosticians compare and contrast index scores in discerning patterns of relative strengths and weaknesses. Sixteen subtests measure the four index areas.

Figure 4.4 Ranges of Intelligence

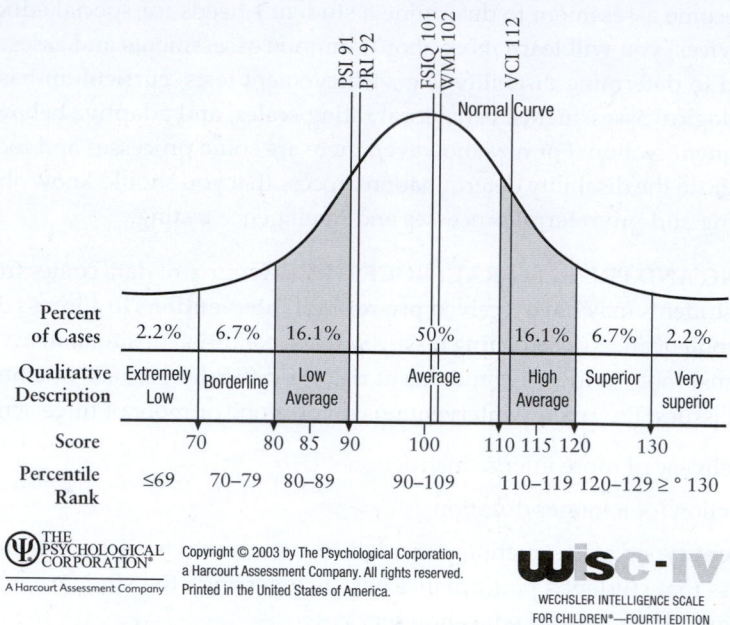

Intelligence tests like the WISC-V are important tools for diagnostic purposes, but they provide relatively limited information for planning of special education services. They also require specific training and expertise to administer, so as a teacher, you will partner with a school psychologist to understand the implication of intelligence testing for the students you teach.

Evaluation to Determine Present Levels of Achievement

The general rule under IDEA is that, in conducting an evaluation, the evaluation team must use a variety of assessment tools and strategies to gather relevant functional, developmental, and academic information about the student. The information assists educators in both determining the nature of the student's disability and the student's present levels of achievement and performance. Specifically, IDEA requires that the team collect data to determine the student's present levels of academic achievement and related developmental needs. Further, IDEA requires that the IEP must include a statement of the student's present levels of academic achievement and functional performance.

Unlike evaluation to determine the presence of the disability, these *present levels* assessments enable IEP teams to determine how the student's disability affects the student's participation and progress in the general education curriculum (and, for preschool children, how the disability affects the child's participation in appropriate activities). You should know about some of the tools you and other educators usually will use to obtain data about the student's present levels of achievement and how they relate to the assessments a state requires to determine a student's progress. You might find it odd that IDEA does not specifically define either academic achievement or functional performance, but we can generally approach these as obtaining information about a student's current strengths and areas of instructional need to progress in the general education curriculum (academic achievement) and to meet goals related to other educational needs (functional performance).

PRESENT LEVELS OF ACADEMIC ACHIEVEMENT The saying that you can't know where you're going until you know where you've been certainly holds true for education. You can't know how to plan for progress if you don't know what students already know! Determining academic achievement involves assessing a student's present levels of performance in the three areas of core content—mathematics, reading, or language arts. One obvious source of information is the student's history of learning content linked to academic achievement standards or, for some students (those in the 1 percent cohort), information about performance on alternate academic achievement standards, such as those Pablo's IEP team would consider (and you learned about in Figure 4.3).

In addition to information about the student's performance on state assessments or alternate assessments, educators will seek information about student work pertaining to (1) achievement tests, (2) curriculum-based measurement, (3) ecological assessments or inventories, (4) functional behavioral assessment and behavioral rating scales, and (5) adaptive behavior scales.

Achievement Tests. Achievement tests reveal much about a student's present level of academic achievement. They do so by measuring the student's knowledge, skills, or accomplishments in specific content areas. The most commonly used achievement tests are standardized; they are **criterion-referenced assessments** or **norm-referenced assessments**. Criterion-referenced assessments measure student performance compared to an existing or predetermined standard. Such assessments provide information on whether a student has skills or knowledge linked to certain standards (grade, age, etc.). They compare student results with some established level of proficiency. Technically speaking, state assessments are criterion-referenced achievement assessments. Other commonly used criterion-referenced achievement tests include the *Woodcock Johnson Tests of Achievement*, the *Peabody Individual Achievement Test*, and the *Wechsler Individualized Achievement Test*, Second Edition (WIAT-II). Pablo's team used the Kaufman Tests of Academic Achievement (Third Edition) to assess areas of academic needs.

Another form of achievement test is the norm-referenced achievement test. Norm-referenced assessments provide information about a student's percent ranking compared to the population with whom the measure was normed. They compare a student's score with other students' scores. These achievement tests allow educators to compare district or state performance, but frequently the test scores become part of the student's records. Commonly used norm-referenced achievement assessments include the *Iowa Assessments* (previously *Iowa Test of Basic Skills*), the *Metropolitan Achievement Test*, and the *California Achievement Test*.

> You can find more information about the WIAT-II at https://www.pearsonclinical.com/psychology/products/100000664/wechsler-individual-achievement-test-second-edition-wiat-ii.html

> The University of Iowa College of Education provides more information on the Iowa Assessments at https://itp.education.uiowa.edu/ia/default.aspx

Curriculum-based Measurement. Another source of information for present levels of academic achievement involves the use of **curriculum-based measurement** (CBM). CBM involves directly assessing a student's skills in the content of the curriculum. Under standardized conditions, the teacher gives the student brief timed samples or probes based on the student's course content. The teacher then scores the student's performance for speed, fluency, and accuracy. Because CBM probes are quick to administer and simple to score, they can be given repeatedly. In fact, research on the use of CBM in reading achievement suggests that CBM oral reading measures were highly related to scores on standardized assessments of reading achievement (Reschly, Busch, Betts, Deno, & Long, 2009).

The types of probes vary according to content. Reading probes typically involve two measures: a maze task, in which a student reads a passage (aloud or silently) with words deleted and then selects words to replace the missing words; and reading aloud for a specified duration while a teacher counts the correct number of words read (oral reading fluency). CBM of spelling requires students to write words dictated to them for a specified time; the teacher counts the correct letter sequences. When CBM is applied to math, students answer computational questions for a set time period; the teacher then counts the number of correct answers. You'll learn more about using CBM in math in Chapter 7.

MyLab Education

Video Example 4.1

In this IEP meeting, Dani shares the functional goals that she strongly prefers . . . making ice cream! Dani's teacher, Ms. Priest, talks about Dani's goals related to sequencing and diet/nutrition that are related to cooking and, of course, making ice cream. Would you think to include these goals on an IEP?

PRESENT LEVELS OF FUNCTIONAL PERFORMANCE The next part of the *present levels* process involves assessing student present levels of performance in so-called "functional" domains. The IDEA regulations don't define functional explicitly, stating that they are widely understood to refer to skills associated with activities of everyday living. In Pablo's IEP, the present levels section addressed the importance for speech and communication skills training, adaptive physical education, and early vocational skills.

If you think about the tasks and activities that make up your daily routines (e.g., making purchases, using public transportation, managing time), you'll understand immediately that the number and types of such activities are myriad! These are the *other educational needs* referred to in IDEA and are as unique as each student. Functional skills differ by students' age; for young students, motor skills might be an important focus for functional performance, while for an adolescent, community living skills may be most important. They also differ by students' ability levels.

The breadth and diversity of such skills lead to an obvious challenge: How do you assess to determine a student's functional performance over such a wide array of areas and domains? You'll learn about a couple of ways to narrow the field of possible skills to a more manageable few in a moment. For now, let's talk broadly about processes to use in determining functional performance levels.

With a few exceptions, standardized assessments are less useful in determining present levels of functional performance than they are in determining academic achievement levels. For very young children, various assessments of motor skills and development may provide information on functional performance. Teachers should work closely with occupational therapists and other developmental specialists to understand and administer those assessments. At the other end of the age spectrum, standardized ways of assessing transition planning needs can provide valuable information about student functional performance levels. You'll learn about one of these, the *Transition Planning Inventory*, in Chapter 11.

In most cases, assessment to determine functional performance begins when you talk with a student's parents and, if the student is older, the student as well. For the student with more extensive support needs, curricular materials are available that can help structure those conversations, such as the *Choosing Outcomes and Accommodations for Children* (COACH) process (Giangreco, Cloninger, & Iverson, 2011). The conversations and interviews can establish priorities for the student's functional goals based on student and family preferences and interests; in turn, the conversations and interviews assist you to identify potential areas of needed instruction, both of which help you narrow down the possible population of functional skills you need to assess. For example, Pablo's parents were important sources of information about his communication needs.

Having gathered this initial information, you will use a number of processes and procedures to obtain the information you want. These include:

- Observations and situational assessments in the home or community
- Reports from others familiar with the student's performance in a particular functional area
- Environmental assessments
- Records reviews and portfolios
- Adaptive, behavioral, or functional skill inventories, social histories
- Employability, independent living, and personal-social skills rating scales
- Technology or vocational education skills assessments.

Of course, what you do to determine functional performance levels will vary by student. Very few, if any, students will require the entire battery listed above. The point is that a wide array of means can help you assess functional performance.

Ecological Assessments or Inventories. One way to narrow the potential number of skills a student with more extensive support needs might have to work on, and to gather data to determine levels of functional performance, involves the use of ecological assessments or inventories. The ecological inventory process begins by observing a student in one or more functional domains (vocational, recreational/leisure, independent living, etc.) to determine what current environments the student and family access across a typical week or two.

That process results in knowledge about what environments within these domains students might need to learn something about, and what skills and activities within these naturally occurring environments might be areas for instruction. Working with families and other stakeholders, you can use this information to identify the highest priority instruction among the skills and activities identified for possible IEP goals. You will learn more about conducting ecological inventories in Chapter 11.

Functional Behavioral Assessment and Behavioral Rating Scales. Some functional performance levels are affected by a student's patterns of problem or antisocial behavior. In Chapter 1, you learned that IDEA requires a functional behavioral assessment (FBA) when students have been suspended for more than 10 days. An FBA is a process for systematically gathering information you and others can use to determine why a student engages in problem behaviors and how you can influence events and circumstances to change these behaviors.

There are three basic steps for conducting an FBA. The first is to complete the analysis (FBA); then develop a behavior intervention plan (BIP); and finally incorporate that plan into the student's IEP, thereby addressing the student's behavior and enabling the student to interact with peers and teachers in the general education classroom. In Chapter 12 you will learn more about how to perform an FBA, and you'll see an example of a plan from that process in *Guidelines for Teaching: Functional Behavioral Assessment*.

Behavioral rating scales and screening tools have the same purpose: to assess potential issues. Screening tools (for example, vision screening) are given to every student as a means to catch possible problems early. By contrast, behavioral rating scales are used with individual students (and not the entire school) when a behavioral or attention issue has already arisen. They are more time intensive than screening because they rely on interviews to identify attention disorders (Vaughn & Hoza, 2013). Pablo's IEP team used a behavioral rating scale to determine that many of his behaviors were typical, but that he had areas of instructional need in attention, social skills, and communication related to social and emotional behavior.

The Behavioral and Emotional Rating Scale—Second Edition (BERS-2) assesses strengths in interpersonal capacity, family involvement, intrapersonal competence, school functioning, and affective ability (Buckley, Ryser, Reid, & Epstein, 2006; Epstein, 2004). You will learn more about the BERS-2 in Chapter 9. The scale is highly reliable and valid; that is to say, it has strong psychometric properties and measures students' emotional and behavioral strengths (Benner, Beaudoin, Mooney, Uhing, & Pierce, 2008; Epstein, 2004). Assessment information is collected from three perspectives: student (Youth Rating Scale), teacher (Teacher Rating Scale), and parent (Parent Rating Scale). A Spanish version is also available (Sharkey, You, Morrison, & Griffiths, 2009).

Adaptive Behavior Scales. Another assessment of functional performance involves measures of adaptive behavior. Adaptive behavior refers simply to skills that reflect what it takes for a person to function successfully (that is, adaptively!) in society. Although clear relationships exist between IQ scores and adaptive behavior scores, research shows that these are distinct and different constructs (Tasse, Luckasson, & Schalock, 2016).

Adaptive behavior scales provide a measure of a person's typical performance across three areas associated with functioning successfully in everyday life (Schalock et al., 2010).

- Conceptual skills refer to language; reading and writing; and money, time, and number concept skills.

- Social skills are those skills that enable a person to engage in and sustain relationships, interact socially, and solve social problems, among others.

- Practical skills are those skills that are performed day in and day out: personal and grooming skills, safety skills, cooking and cleaning skills, health care skills, clothing care, and so on.

Educators such as yourself or other professionals such as school psychologists or social workers interview people—a parent, friend, family member—who knows the student well. To "know well" means that the person giving information about the student should be reliable and familiar with the student, particularly with respect to the student's conceptual skills, social skills, and practical skills. A student's teacher may know a lot about conceptual skills but next to nothing about practical skills. That is so because the student is more likely to perform conceptual skills at school and practical skills at home.

Also, there is a difference between not being able to perform a skill and never having the opportunity to do so. That is why you and other professionals need to be certain that the student you are assessing actually has had chances to perform the skills being assessed. In Chapter 11, you'll learn more about a specific measure of adaptive behavior, the *Diagnostic Adaptive Behavior Scale*.

Evaluation to Determine Potential for Growth

Let's return to the *Endrew F.* decision. There, the Court required that schools offer an IEP that is reasonably calculated to enable a child to make progress appropriate in light of the child's circumstances. The Court added that every child should have the chance to meet challenging objectives.

Reasonable calculations begin with the evaluation process. The information from the evaluation is the foundation for the IEP. In turn, the IEP describes a program that enables a child to make progress appropriate in light of the child's circumstances.

What does *in light of the child's circumstances* mean? A recent "frequently asked questions (FAQ)" from the U.S. Department of Education's Office of Special Education Programs helps us dissect this statement. As you know, the student's IEP must enable the student to make progress. Further, IDEA requires that students with disabilities be involved with and progress in the general education curriculum as well as achieve goals to address their other, unique educational needs. Accordingly, the FAQ provided: "The essential function of an IEP is to provide meaningful opportunities for appropriate academic and functional advancement, and to enable the child to make progress." The Court did not elaborate on the meaning of the term "in light of the child's unique circumstances." But the FAQ provides that the phrase "unique circumstances" reflects the focus on the individualized needs of students with disabilities that are intended to be met by specially designed instruction, supplementary aids and services, and related services. Because Pablo has communication challenges, he has related services from a speech-language specialist and an augmentative alternative communication (AAC) device.

Determining present levels of academic achievement and functional performance has been a part of the process of planning for IEPs in one form or another for many years. What is new is the fact that *Endrew F.* emphasized that the IEP must be *reasonably calculated* to ensure progress by carefully considering the student's present levels of achievement and performance *and* potential for growth. The FAQ states that "[t]he 'reasonably calculated' standard recognizes that developing an appropriate IEP requires that . . . school personnel will make decisions that are informed by their own expertise, the progress of the child, the child's potential for growth, and the views of the child's parents." Note the emphasis on "calculation"—the insistence that those who develop the IEP engage in a reasoned process—a calculation about progress and potential for growth.

MyLab Education
Video Example 4.2
Pablo has benefitted from his use of an augmentative communication device that allows him to communicate with teachers and peers. What data does Pablo's team collect that help them ensure the AAC device meets Pablo's needs?

So, how do you determine the student's potential for growth? Certainly, determining present levels of performance is one step in determining potential for growth, but what if that current performance was based on low expectations? Perhaps a student could have achieved more if provided with the chance to meet challenging objectives, as the *Endrew F.* decision requires. It is clear that Endrew himself would not have performed as well had he remained in his original school district. So, current levels of performance are just one indicator of potential for growth.

As with measuring levels of performance, how you assess potential for growth will vary according to the student's age and disability. Determining potential for growth in motor skills will be very different from determining potential for growth in reading or mathematics. However, one factor will remain critical, independent of the student's age or type of disability: high expectations! Students learn what adults expect them to learn. The point of the focus on potential for growth is, itself, a statement that we believe all students can learn and all students can progress. So, taking for granted your high expectations for your students, several ways of collecting information enable you to see each student's potential for growth. Pablo's IEP reflects challenging objectives related to literacy (letter sounds and upper and lower case letters, answering who, what, and where questions), math (identifying numbers up to 60, adding and subtracting), and, of course, communication skills.

PROGRESS MONITORING   One way to predict future growth is to monitor progress across time. In Chapter 7, you will learn about the response to intervention (RTI) process for determining the presence of a learning disability based on the student's performance in instruction. The notion of progress monitoring is critical to the RTI process, and involves assessing student progress in areas in which universal screening determined that students were at risk for academic difficulties. Within RTI, progress monitoring involves frequent and repeated (usually at least monthly) assessments of student learning and performance that, when charted or graphed, provide information about progress. The intent of progress monitoring is to assess progress in content knowledge (typically academic) over time and to determine the student's rate of progress, both for its own sake and to determine the efficacy of the instruction being provided (e.g., response to intervention). Frequently, curriculum-based measurement, which you learned about earlier in this chapter, is used to provide probes to monitor progress (Jenkins, Schulze, Marti, & Harbaugh, 2017). Progress monitoring involves the use of multiple tools or processes to gain information about student progress, and a myriad of tools have been developed to use in the progress monitoring process.

Progress monitoring provides a useful framework within which to assess potential for growth. That is, progress monitoring focuses on frequent points of data collection intended to identify what students have learned in discrete areas. Unlike achievement tests and similar tests of academic achievement, which are intended to provide a broader picture, assessment to determine potential for growth will involve monitoring progress across domains. So, whether assessing for reading fluency or specific job skills, collecting data using multiple tools or processes frequently across time will provide valuable information to reasonably calculate a student's potential for growth.

FORMATIVE ASSESSMENT   Another means of determining potential for progress involves the use of formative assessment processes. Formative assessment, like progress monitoring, involves frequent assessments of student progress. Usually contrasted with **summative assessment**, which is used to assess educational outcomes (like results on state tests in core content areas), formative assessment involves a wider array of strategies across time to check for student understanding and learning.

One element of formative assessment is that teachers and students interact and, in many cases, students self-assess their knowledge and understanding. Examples of frequently used formative assessment processes include the following:

- Student summaries and reflections are read by teachers and evaluated to assess understanding and learning.

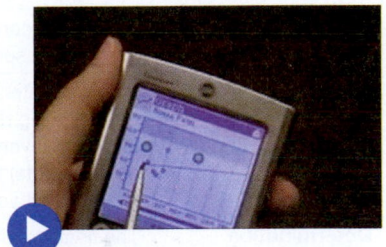

MyLab Education
Video Example 4.3
In this video the classroom teacher talks about her use of DIBELS (Dynamic Indicators of Basic Early Literacy Skills) to monitor student progress of early literacy skills, including phonemic awareness, fluency, and comprehension. She is using a hand-held technology device to accomplish this task. How does tracking reading fluency contribute to progress monitoring?

Figure 4.5 Nondiscriminatory Evaluation Process

Determining the Presence of a Disability

Observation	Across the disability category chapters, you will learn about issues that you, as a teacher, may observe or have reported to you by a parent or by another professional, such as a speech therapist, that may be a first indication of a student's need for special education services in that disability category. These range from observing specific student behaviors (student appears frustrated, distracted), difficulty in reaching typical developmental milestones in language or social interactions, problems with classwork, or changes in the student's mood or affect. All of these can provide indications of the need for screening, pre-referral interventions, or more intensive instruction.
Screening	For some students, screening tools may provide an indication of the need for special education services. Such tools may include classwork, group intelligence tests, vision or hearing screening tools, behavior screening tools, and other means to assess, across the school population, students who are at risk for school difficulty. In each disability category chapter, you'll learn about relevant screening tools (if any) that might be used with students.
Pre-referral or more intensive instruction	Observation information and universal screening information may lead to increases in the intensity, type, or duration of interventions. In some states and for some students, this may take the form of pre-referral interventions meant to minimize the need for special education. In districts implementing Multi-Tiered Systems of Supports, this may result in Tier 2 interventions that ramp up the amount of time students receive instruction, change instructional strategies, or use the same strategy over more trials. In the following disability category chapters, you'll get information about when pre-referral strategies and tiered strategies may be a next step in the process.
Referral	If students continue to have difficulty learning, they may be referred for evaluation for eligibility for special education and related services.
Nondiscriminatory evaluation procedures and standards	In this chapter, you have learned about the requirements for and process of the nondiscriminatory evaluation. In the following disability category chapters, you will learn about specific standardized assessments (e.g., intelligence tests, achievement tests, etc.), rating scales, and other processes (curriculum-based assessment, ecological assessments) that are pertinent to students with that disability. You learned about many of these tools in this chapter, but you will learn more specific information in each of the category chapters.
Determination	The final step in the process is the determination of a student's need for special education and related services.

- Teacher feedback on draft versions of products can provide information on student understanding.
- Graphic organizers can be used by students to depict relationships between ideas and constructs and, thus, provide information about student understanding.
- Teachers can interview students to gain information about their understanding.
- Observation of group and classwork is another means to get information about student understanding.

CHARTING, GRAPHING, AND PLOTTING DATA   Educators display the data they have collected by bar charts, line graphs, or scatter plots. These displays make it easier for educators to see progress and thus chart growth. More than that, they make it easy for the student's parents and the student to understand that the student is making progress; that understanding in turn prompts the student to be more invested in learning.

Nondiscriminatory Evaluation Process

In each of the chapters in this text focused on a particular disability category, there will be a figure depicting the nondiscriminatory evaluation process specific to students in that disability category. Figure 4.5 provides a general frame for the NDE process, taking into account the discussion in this section.

MyLab Education **Self-Check 4.1**

MyLab Education **Application Exercise 4.1:** Educational Planning for Katie

Developing an Individualized Education Program to Ensure Progress

You learned in Chapter 1 that IDEA requires that every student receiving special education services have an individualized education program (IEP) that details the components of the student's educational program. You also learned that IDEA requires educators to include students' parents as members of the team that develops an IEP. So when Pablo's IEP was revised most recently, his parents, Serio and Delia Garcia, were on the team. So, too, were Rose Beemer (special education teacher), Deanne Torvinen (school psychologist, presenting the NDE information), Ada Harrington (speech-language pathologist), Lauren Etting (general education teacher), and Erin Studer (CHIME's executive director/principal).

In Figure 1.6 in Chapter 1, you learned about the required components of the IEP. In this chapter, you'll learn more about how to develop an IEP to provide an *appropriately ambitious* education program that, first, enables every student to have the chance to meet *challenging objectives* and to be involved with and progress in the general education curriculum, and, next, takes into account the information you are learning about students' achievement and performance and their *potential for growth*.

Components of Appropriate Ambitious Individualized Education Programs

At the onset, you should think about what the IEP is intended to achieve. Obviously, the IEP describes a student's individualized education program. *Individualized* means that the education program should be specific to the student's learning needs. After *Endrew F.*, however, we have to think about individualized a bit more broadly. As you've learned, the Supreme Court said the IEP must be reasonably calculated to enable a child to make progress that is appropriate in light of the child's unique circumstances. Too often in the past, the IEP has been an alternative curriculum; that is, it was made up of a series of mainly functional goals that were separate from the general education curriculum and that constituted the student's own curriculum based, too often, on the student's disability label and the severity of that disability.

Pablo's IEP Team meets to discuss Pablo's educational program.

Instead of developing an alternative or separate curriculum with the IEP, your task now, under *Endrew F.*, is to design an IEP that is appropriately ambitious with challenging objectives based on high expectations for your student's potential for growth that ensure progress. Remember that the IEP must be aligned with content standards reflecting the general education curriculum. The important elements of the IEP involve the types of specially designed instruction (special education), supplementary aids and services, and related services that a student will require to progress.

PRESENT LEVELS OF ACADEMIC ACHIEVEMENT AND FUNCTIONAL PERFORMANCE You've learned about how to assess to determine a student's present levels of academic achievement and functional performance. IDEA requires that the IEP include a statement of the student's present levels of academic achievement and functional performance, including:

1. How the student's disability affects the child's involvement and progress in the general education curriculum
2. For preschool children, as appropriate, how the disability affects the child's participation in appropriate activities
3. For students with disabilities who take alternate assessments aligned to alternate achievement standards, a description of benchmarks or short-term objectives.

The statement of <u>P</u>resent <u>L</u>evel of <u>A</u>cademic <u>A</u>chievement and <u>F</u>unctional <u>P</u>erformance (which goes by the somewhat ungainly acronym PLAAFP!) involves a summary of the information gathered while determining present levels during the nondiscriminatory evaluation. The statement describes the effect of the student's disability on performance in the general education curriculum and in relation to the student's other educational needs.

This statement of present levels therefore has to take into account the student's academic strengths and areas of instructional need and the student's areas of functional need. All of this information must be linked to data from the nondiscriminatory evaluation and other data collection efforts; the information should, in turn, inform the IEP team when making decisions about specially designed instruction, supplementary aids and services, and related services that the student needs to make progress in the general education curriculum and to achieve identified functional goals. Pablo's *present levels* statements address a wide array of issues, from academics, to behavior, to functional skills, as should most IEPs.

Now, you should exercise caution regarding the statement about a student's present levels of achievement. Why? Because that statement can become overly negative. That is, the language pertaining to how the student's disability affects involvement with and progress in the general education curriculum can lead to an overemphasis on the disability and academic and functional deficits. If it does, the statement about present levels becomes a litany of what the student cannot do.

That is not the intent, however. It is a simple fact that a student is eligible for special education services because (1) that student has a disability and (2) as a function of that disability, the student is in need of specially designed instruction. The present levels statement must address instructional needs, but it should do so in the context of strengths-based approaches. As much emphasis should be on the student's strengths, interests, and abilities as is put on a student's limitations. Each performance area on Pablo's IEP includes a summary of his strengths—from his effort and capacity in matching, his skills with sight words, to his addition and subtraction skills.

This is important for a number of reasons. First, an overly negative PLAAFP statement can create an uncomfortable atmosphere during the IEP meeting and put parents and family members (as well as students as they get older) on edge. No individuals like to have their limitations, or those of their child, emphasized. A child with a disability is a child first and foremost. The PLAAFP must communicate what that child is good at and emphasize that child's potential for growth. Second, when the PLAAFP emphasizes strengths, abilities, and interests, the goals that are linked to the PLAAFP will more likely be appropriately ambitious and constitute challenging objectives, as required by *Endrew F.*

MEASURABLE ANNUAL GOALS The PLAAFP provides a prologue, if you will, for the goals set through the IEP process. That is so because IDEA requires the IEP of every student receiving special education services to contain a statement of measurable annual goals, including academic and functional goals, designed to:

1. Meet the student's needs that result from the student's disability to enable the student to be involved in and make progress in the general education curriculum

2. Meet each of the student's other educational needs that result from the student's disability.

The decision-making process to determine measurable annual goals must begin with the general education curriculum. As you've learned, too often in the past, this was not the case, with IEP teams generating IEP goals that were outside the general education curriculum that became, in essence, an alternative curriculum. It is clear from IDEA, however, that the IEP should be a plan to identify goals, modifications, and strategies needed to enhance, not replace, the general education curriculum. The "guts" of this statement lie in IDEA's principle of education in the least restrictive environment—the core element of inclusion.

Your determination of present level of academic achievement across multiple core content areas will logically lead to goals that enable students to further their level of academic achievement. The decision-making process to determine such goals should begin with the general education curriculum. Consider students who are in the same grade as the student for whom the IEP is being developed. What are these students learning? What standards are driving their educational tasks and activities? Those are the tasks and activities that the student with the disability should be involved with.

The IEP team can then ask what types, levels, and intensity of specially designed instruction, supplementary aids and services, and related services will support the student's progress in these tasks and activities linked to the general education curriculum. You'll learn more about those in a moment. Just keep in mind for now that goals in the IEP that pertain to academic achievement should be linked to the general education curriculum and reflect high expectations through challenging objectives. One of Pablo's goals in reading comprehension is to "answer concrete wh- questions (who, what, where) about a reading passage at his current reading level by pointing at the correct word or picture with 80 percent accuracy." The first objective is to focus on "who" questions. The second objective applies the same mastery criteria to "what" and "where" questions.

Another set of goals will identify the student's "other educational needs." These goals pertain to a student's functional performance, as assessed in the PLAAFP. Through that process, you will have identified areas of priority to the family and student, areas of student strengths, and areas of student instructional needs. For Pablo, these other educational needs include early vocational instruction and sight word safety vocabulary instruction.

Whether pertaining to academic or functional content, IEP goals meet various "usability" standards. They should be easily understandable by all stakeholders, including (as they get older) students, and should be worded to reflect what the students will do upon completion of the goal, rather than what they will not do. IEP goals should be measurable and observable, and should clearly describe how the student will demonstrate mastery of the goal. Goals are accompanied by objectives that break the attainment of the goal into discrete steps that allow all stakeholders to observe progress.

HOW PROGRESS IS MEASURED AND WHEN REPORTS ARE PROVIDED IDEA requires that the IEP include a description of how the student's progress toward meeting annual goals will be measured, and how frequently progress reports will be provided to parents. There are obvious linkages between the attainment of IEP goals and the description of progress. Well-written goals provide information about performance and progress. The information goes beyond simply reporting a student's progress on IEP goals, however. The intent is broader, reflecting IDEA's intent that students receiving special education services should progress in the general education curriculum and in areas of functional performance; these two elements—progress in the general education curriculum and in areas of functional performance—are consistent with the *Endrew F.* criteria of growth and capacity for progress.

Accordingly, the description of how progress will be measured, often referred to as the evaluation criterion, will include information reflected in IEP goals as well as other sources of information that might indicate mastery of content and progress in the general education curriculum or in functional performance. Student classwork, performance on tests or assessments, or information given by re-administration of achievement tests or other sources of information that informed the present levels assessment might all contribute to a broader understanding of the student's progress.

IDEA does not specify any intervals or timing for reports on student progress (as determined by evaluation criterion) to parents and other members of the IEP team. The clear intent of the "reporting" language is to ensure that if a student is not making adequate progress in the general education curriculum, the IEP team should revisit the IEP goals, services, and statements. So the frequency for reporting must connect to the purpose of reporting.

This idea is consistent with the intent of progress monitoring and other processes we've discussed already. What is important here is not the student's lack of progress in and of itself, but the response to that lack of progress in the form of changes to instruction and supports. Like any goals, one can set the right goal, but have the wrong action plan! If my goal were to improve my cardiovascular performance, an action plan of going to the gym every other week will likely not enable me to make progress. But if I'm carefully tracking my heart rate at rest and at maximum performance, over time I can determine that my progress is not adequate and adjust my action plan. The special education and related services and supplementary aids and services constitute the action plan for special education.

SPECIAL EDUCATION AND RELATED SERVICES, SUPPLEMENTARY AIDS AND SERVICES The heart of special education lies in the provision of specially designed instruction, supplementary aids and services, and related services. The IEP should be as much about describing these modifications to instruction and context as it is about describing curricular content (which is determined, as you now know, by the general education curriculum and other educational needs). Further, IDEA emphasizes both participation in the general education curriculum and participation in extracurricular and other nonacademic activities. The IEP needs to address these as well as academic content modifications. Each of these three elements (specially designed instruction, supplementary aids and services, and related services) is important, so let's take some time to describe what IDEA intends with regard to each.

Special Education. IDEA requires that states identify, locate, and evaluate students with disabilities who are in need of special education and related services. As you learned in Chapter 1, special education, as defined in IDEA, refers to specially designed instruction, at no cost to the parents, to meet the unique needs of a child with a disability. The Department of Education regulations define specially designed instruction as *adapting, as appropriate to the needs of an eligible child under this part, the content, methodology or delivery of instruction (i) to address the unique needs of the child that result from the child's disability; and (ii) to ensure access of the child to the general education curriculum, so that the child can meet the educational standards within the jurisdiction of the public agency that apply to all children.*

You will learn about different types of specially designed instruction as you read this book, so we won't go through many in this section. But, there are some aspects of what is meant by specially designed instruction that you need to know.

First, think about how people use the term "special education." Does it seem that they often use it to refer to a place ("he's in special education, a special education classroom") or, sometimes, a student ("he is a special education student")? Though widely used in these ways, special education is neither a place nor a person; it is, simply, specially designed instruction. Second, specially designed instruction does not replace high-quality instruction provided to all students; it is intended to supplement that instruction. Third, specially designed instruction should be customized to fit the need of the student. Fourth, to the degree possible, specially designed instruction should be research-based.

When Congress enacted the most recent version of IDEA, in 2004, it stated that IDEA has been impeded by "an insufficient focus on applying replicable research on proven methods of teaching and learning." "Research-based practice"—the term we use in this book— refers to the fact that a practice (intervention) has been evaluated in typical settings with scientific designs and found to have statistically significant effects.

Again, you will learn about many interventions that have been shown to be effective and meet these standards; we will teach you to "use what works." The U.S. Department of Education maintains the What Works Clearinghouse to assist teachers in identifying the evidence for students in various academic and instructional areas.

You can find a list and description of evidence for educational practices at the What Works Clearinghouse website at https://ies.ed.gov/ncee/wwc/

But, you may ask, what am I to do if there are not any interventions or practices that meet the standard of research-based? That's a fair question because not every educational practice with students with disabilities has been subject to the same level of rigorous research. Indeed, for some students with disabilities, research using large group designs is exceedingly difficult, if not impossible, due to the low incidence of the disability or ethical issues with regard to withholding services to one group of students and not another. The answer to what you should do is that you should use practices that have the best available research evidence, even if the amount of research is scant. Further, just because a rigorous study showed that an intervention worked, that does not mean it will work with every individual student. So, if you are collecting data based on the evaluation criterion we have discussed previously, you will be providing your own evidence of the intervention's impact with your student, and you may change interventions, alter the intensity of the intervention, or do whatever you need to ensure that your student progresses.

Related Services. You learned in Chapter 1 that related services are those necessary to assist the student in benefiting from special education. Figure 1.3 listed related services as required and defined by IDEA. Pablo receives two related services —speech-language therapy for his communication and occupational therapy for his handwriting.

The standard for *benefiting from special education* has changed in light of *Endrew F.* What the IEP team now must do is design an educational program that is appropriately ambitious and that enables the student to have the chance to meet challenging objectives that are based on the student's potential for growth and that ensures progress. In *Endrew F.*, benefit is equated with progress and growth. As at CHIME and for Pablo, educators need to partner with related service professionals in designing an appropriately ambitious educational program.

Supplementary Aids and Services. IDEA defines supplementary aids and services as "aids, services, and other supports that are provided in regular education classes, other education-related settings, and in extracurricular and nonacademic settings, to enable children with disabilities to be educated with nondisabled children to the maximum extent appropriate."

These services and aids supplement the student's specially designed instruction and related services and, like that instruction and those related services, ensure that a

Figure 4.6 Supplementary Aids and Services

Domain	Definition	Examples
Universal design for learning	Modifications to how curriculum is presented or represented or to the ways in which students respond to the curriculum	Digital Talking Book formats, advance organizers, video or audio input/output
Access	Modifications to the community, campus building, or classroom to ensure physical and cognitive access	Curb cuts, wide doors, clear aisles, nonprint signs
Classroom ecology	Modifications to and arrangements of features of the classroom environment that impact learning	Seating arrangement, types of seating, acoustics, lighting
Educational and assistive technology	Technology that reduces the impact of impairment on a student's capacity	Calculator, augmentative communication device, computer
Assessment and task modifications	Modifications to time or task requirements (but not content or material) to assist in participation in assessment or educational task	Extended time, scribe, note taker, oral presentation
Teacher, paraprofessional, or peer support	Support from another person to participate in instructional activities	Peer buddy, paraeducator, teacher

student receives an appropriate education, especially to ensure participation and progress in the general education curriculum and to ensure an appropriately ambitious educational program with challenging objectives. Figure 4.6 provides a table that illustrates types of supplementary aids and services that might be implemented.

Supplementary aids and services are modifications and supports to promote student participation and progress in the general education curriculum. As Figure 4.6 shows, they include modifications to ensure physical and cognitive access to the environment, classroom ecological variables such as seating arrangements and classroom acoustics, educational and assistive technology, assessment and task modifications, and support from other persons. We will discuss these supplementary aids and services throughout the book. For now, what is important to know is that the IEP team must identify supplementary aids and services that enable students with disabilities *to be educated with their non-disabled peers* to the maximum extent appropriate. We'll return to this issue when we discuss the IEP team's role in "placement" decisions. *Into Practice Across Grade Levels: Designing Supplementary Aids and Services* provides ideas for designing supplementary aids and services for students with disabilities across age and grade levels. Pablo's IEP includes the use of assistive technology as a need, the use of a paraeducator, and co-teaching, all of which are forms of supplementary aids and services.

Into Practice Across Grade Levels

Designing Supplementary Aids and Services

Map the curriculum to know when and where to teach content and identify needed supplementary aids and services. Although not necessarily a supplementary aid and service in and of itself, the curriculum mapping process helps educators implement these supports and ensures high-quality planning. When members of a student's IEP team engage in curriculum mapping, they use the school calendar as an organizer because it is a statement of what must occur and when. The IEP team members then collect information about each teacher's curriculum. The information includes descriptions of the content to be taught during the year, the processes and skills emphasized, and the student assessments used. After discussing the curriculum with each of the student's teachers, they often develop a curriculum map for the school, identifying gaps or repetitions in the curriculum content. At that point, they can determine how to support students to access the curriculum framework, performance objectives, and other standards at the appropriate grade or course. So, for example, as a result of a curriculum map, an IEP team knows that the best place for a **3rd-grade** student to receive more intensive instruction in reading comprehension is in the fourth period, during which all 3rd graders are receiving instruction in the district-adopted reading curriculum and the reading specialist has time to provide more individualized supports in the general education setting.

Identify assistive and educational technology that can provide supports to students to be educated with their peers who do not have disabilities. Assistive technology (AT) includes any piece of equipment, commercial or handmade, that assists an individual to perform various functions, such as communication. One form of AT is an augmentative and alternative communication (AAC) system. AAC supports students who have difficulty communicating verbally to communicate more effectively. Other forms of assistive technology include print-to-speech devices or electronic braille devices for students with visual impairments, mobility devices for students with physical disabilities, and hearing aids and devices for students with hearing impairments. Other educational technologies that can provide support for students include digital talking books, laptop or computer-based instructional programs, calculators, tablet PCs and iPads, smartphones, and even 3D printers. All of these may provide needed supports for learning. For example, a **7th-grade** student with visual impairments can read along with her peers in her Communication Arts class as they read *Moby Dick* by using a digital talking book version.

Consider the role of teachers, paraprofessionals, and other adults in supporting students to be successful in the general education classroom. Adults and the role of adults in the classroom constitute an important consideration for supplementary aids and services. You'll learn about teaching and the roles of special educators and general educators across the text. It's important, however, to remember that paraprofessionals are critical to student success as well. Appropriate roles for paraprofessionals include providing individualized instruction to groups of students with and without disabilities, facilitating friendships among students with and without disabilities, supporting peer tutors, using state-of-the-art technology, teaching in community settings, and assisting students with personal care (e.g., bathroom care and feeding). Most paraprofessionals provide 1:1 instruction for students with intellectual disability in general education classroom settings. That role certainly can help students progress in the general curriculum. It also enables general educators and special educators to concentrate on other students—with and without disabilities—and on their progress in the general education curriculum. It can also serve to isolate the student, however, if it is not done well. A **7th-grade**

student with intellectual disability who is taking Algebra 1, for example, might benefit from ongoing supports provided by a paraprofessional, but it might be best if that support was provided with a group of students, rather than in isolation.

Consider the role of peers in supporting students with disabilities in the general education classroom. Peers can play an important role in supporting students with disabilities in academic, behavioral, and social areas. Using peer learning models provides one means to differentiate instruction. Peers can provide tutoring supports, can model appropriate responses, and can actually provide direct instruction. It's important not to disrupt the education of students without disabilities, but plenty of evidence indicates that through peer mentoring, peer tutoring, or service learning models, students with and without disabilities can benefit from working together. Class-wide peer tutoring is an example of a peer-learning model. Wexler, Reed, Pyle, Mitchell, & Barton (2015) showed that students with disabilities in elementary grades (**3rd, 4th, and 5th grades**) improved math and reading skills as a result of class-wide peer tutoring.

Configure the classroom to ensure student success. Consider modifying aspects of the classroom environment when designing supplementary aids and services. Such modifications may include student seating arrangements, classroom furniture arrangement, and lighting and auditory features. Students with hearing impairments, for example, need to be seated where the classroom acoustics allow them to hear lectures or instructions. Similarly, students with visual impairments may need to be seated nearer to media (smartboards, screens, etc.). Fluorescent lights produce a flicker that may be a problem for students at risk for seizures, so other lighting options might be considered. Students with attention and hyperactivity difficulties and some students with autism may not be able to sit in traditional classroom desks all day, so a more open classroom in which students can move around may be of benefit. A **9th-grade** student with attention-deficit hyperactivity disorder (ADHD), for example, may have difficulty concentrating if the desk faces the windows and there are a lot of people outside, so arranging the classroom to minimize such distractions would be a form of supplementary aid and services.

Consider task and test modifications that enable students to be successful. Many students with disabilities can benefit from test and task modifications. Task modifications involve changes to some aspect of the activity or the student's response to an activity that allows the student to be successful while still showing evidence of learning. Task modifications are not the same as alternative tasks; they are modifications that allow students to succeed. Some involve the types or forms of responses, such as responding orally rather than in written format for students who have difficulty writing. Others involve offering a range of lesson and unit objectives that vary by complexity and level of understanding so that all students can master content related to the "big ideas" of a lesson. And other types of task modifications involve how students receive information. So, an

(Continued)

11th-grade student with a learning disability related to writing might benefit from someone designated to take notes in a classroom.

Consider modifications to the scope or sequence of instructional content. Sometimes students benefit from changes to the scope or sequence of instruction. Like task modifications, such changes do not alter the curriculum, but may sequence it differently, accelerate the content, or condense content. Acceleration is when students move through education programs faster than their peers. For example, an **8th grader** who is gifted may go from middle school to the high school each morning to take honors geometry at the 9th-grade level, then return to middle school for the remainder of the day. Other gifted students may benefit from delivering content they are likely to master quickly in a condensed timeline, much like units, so that they can move through content more quickly or they can expand content to learn more about a topic than their classmates might be learning.

Additional Components of the IEP

The IEP team must make decisions about a number of other factors that will affect the student's educational program. At first, you may think these don't seem to be related to planning for progress. You'd be wrong to think that: Each one contributes to the overall possibility for growth and progress.

RATIONALE OF THE EXTENT, IF ANY, THE STUDENT DOES NOT PARTICIPATE IN THE REGULAR CLASSROOM, EXTRACURRICULAR ACTIVITIES, AND OTHER SCHOOL ACTIVITIES We will talk more about the IEP team's role in the student's participation in the regular education classroom and other activities that are typical for students without disabilities shortly. If, however, the team decides that a student should receive education somewhere other than the regular education classroom or should not fully participate in other activities, including extracurricular activities, then the team must state why it has reached that conclusion; it must provide a rationale against inclusion.

Let's state that point in different terms. In essence, the presumption of IDEA in favor of placement in the least restrictive environment, bolstered by *Endrew F.*, is that, to ensure growth and progress, every student should be educated in the general education classroom and participate in the life of the school through extracurricular activities and other school activities. A decision to do otherwise must be explained on the IEP. For CHIME and Pablo, inclusion in the general education curriculum is the rule.

ACCOMMODATIONS FOR TESTING OR ALTERNATE ASSESSMENT DECISIONS You read about the role of state assessments in progress in an earlier section of this chapter, and you learned that some students may be eligible to take tests using modifications. You also learned that approximately 1 percent of the student population can take alternate assessments. As for Pablo and other students, the IEP determines whether a student takes the state test with modifications (and determines what modifications are required) or alternate assessment. The team should base its decision on student performance indicators identified during the nondiscriminatory evaluation and the level of present performance assessments, and not simply on a student's type of disability or level of impairment. If, however, students need modifications or need to take the alternate assessment, those decisions can improve the chances for student progress.

DOCUMENTATION OF FREQUENCY, LOCATION, AND DURATION OF SERVICES AND MODIFICATIONS The IEP must include information about when, where, and for how long the services described in the IEP will be provided, including when special education and related services will begin to be provided, how frequently such services will be provided, and for how long. Different special education and related services may be provided at different frequencies and duration, so the statement needs to be specific regarding what the modification (e.g., special education, related services) is intended to achieve. This statement must also include information about where each modification will occur; that is, will it be in all locations, only in the general education classroom, in a separate classroom, in the community, or elsewhere? Of course, the intent of all modifications is to ensure student growth and progress, so in making frequency, location, and duration decisions, the IEP team should ask what will most likely ensure growth and progress. Pablo's IEP describes frequency, total minutes, and type of instruction, including 30 minutes of adaptive PE a week and 1200 minutes of language and speech therapy.

TRANSITION SERVICES   Beginning no later than the first IEP after the student turns 16, or earlier if deemed necessary by the IEP team or mandated by the state, the IEP team must consider what transition services are needed for a student to successfully transition from school to adulthood. Transition services are defined in IDEA as *a coordinated set of activities that promote movement from school to such post-school activities as post-secondary education, vocational training, employment, adult services, independent living and community participation. They must be based on the individual student's needs, taking into account his or her preferences and interests. Transition services must include instruction, community experiences, and development of employment and other post-school adult living objectives. If appropriate, daily living skills and functional vocational evaluation may also be included.*

The IEP for students for whom transition services are considered must contain goals focused on these school and postschool outcomes and must contain a statement of transition services, including courses of study.

SPECIAL FACTORS   In Chapter 1, you learned that the IEP team must consider a set of "special factors" when planning for a student's educational program. The fact that IDEA identifies these factors as "special" indicates that they are critical for the student's progress and, if not specifically requiring attention, might be overlooked by IEP teams.

Many of these are self-explanatory with regard to their effect on planning for progress. The first special factor involves positive behavioral interventions and supports (PBIS) or other strategies to address a student's problem behavior. A lack of PBIS was Endrew's parents' initial concern that led to their due process hearing and ultimately to the Supreme Court. A recent study showed that implementation of PBIS over a 9-year period resulted in significantly improved academic achievement (Madigan, Cross, Smolkowski, & Strycker, 2016). You will learn about PBIS in Chapter 5 and more about how to implement it in Chapter 9.

Also, ensuring a student's language needs if the student has limited English language proficiency, ensuring alternative materials (braille) if the student is blind or has a visual impairment, or ensuring that a student who is deaf or hard of hearing has appropriate supports and accommodations are, similarly, obvious issues to ensure student progress.

The role of technology is another critical feature of ensuring progress; whether it is considering the need for assistive technology, as required in the special factors section, or whether it is the role of technology as a supplementary aid and service. Technology can both ensure stronger academic performance and enhance motivation and student engagement in learning (Rashid & Asghar, 2016). Pablo's augmentative and alternative communication device is an example of technology that ensures progress.

These "other" requirements that the IEP team must consider are, of course, important aspects of designing an educational program that is challenging and addresses the student's unique learning needs. A final element of the IEP team requirements involves decisions pertaining to where students learn what is in the general education curriculum or what is on the IEP.

MyLab Education
Video Example 4.4
In this video, a student is using an Alphasmart NEO, an inexpensive device that allows students to type and print their work. How does this device contribute to the student's inclusion in this science activity?

The Least Restrictive Environment and Educational Placement

One of the more difficult and, often, controversial decisions for which you and other IEP team members, including students' parents, are responsible relates to where and with whom students will receive their education. The decision is about the meaning—for each student—of the IDEA principle of education in the **least restrictive environment** (LRE). You learned about that principle in Chapter 1. Another name for the principle is "inclusion", one of the core elements of our book. You know much about it because you know about Pablo. But it's important to learn more about it now.

> IDEA requires state and local education agencies (SEAs and LEAs) to ensure that:
>
> (i) To the maximum extent appropriate, children with disabilities, including children in public or private institutions or other care facilities, are educated with children who are nondisabled; and
>
> (ii) Special classes, separate schooling, or other removal of children with disabilities from the regular educational environment occurs only if the nature or severity of the disability is such that education in regular classes with the use of supplementary aids and services cannot be achieved satisfactorily.

What, exactly, does "maximum extent appropriate" mean? IDEA does not say maximum extent *possible*, which would be an unambiguous statement of the primacy of the general education classroom as the starting placement option for all students. No, the notion of the maximum extent *appropriate* leaves some discretion to the IEP team, including parents, to judge or determine how much a student with a disability is educated in the general education setting, with their peers who do not have disabilities.

The problem is that far too often, IEP teams make placement decisions based on their perceptions about types and severity of disability and what is common practice in the district. For example, a student with intellectual disability may be "placed" in a self-contained classroom (we'll discuss alternative placement options in a moment) because that is where educators historically have "placed" students with that label and where the services the student needs are located. Note that at CHIME, the presumption in favor of inclusion/LRE works for Pablo and all other students with disabilities.

You also learned in Chapter 1 that IDEA defines special education as specially designed instruction, not as a place. IDEA is clear that the services required by a student are not specific to a location, but to a student's educational need. Here, the law and research call into question the practice of placement by disability category or severity (Quirk, Ryndak, & Taub, 2017; Ryndak, Hughes, Alper, & McDonnell, 2012). That and earlier research justify IDEA's stating that schools need to have high expectations for students with disabilities and ensure their access in the general education curriculum to the maximum extent appropriate. Other research has shown that the *place* in which students with disabilities gain such access to the general education curriculum is in the general education classroom (Ryndak et al., 2014). No doubt, CHIME follows the research evidence.

So, in interpreting the notion of educating students with disabilities alongside their peers without disabilities to the maximum extent appropriate, we can again turn to *Endrew F.* for guidance, which requires that schools provide an educational program that is appropriately ambitious while taking into account the child's circumstances, namely, the child's need for special education and related services. Because of IDEA itself and because of the "circumstances" language in *Endrew F.*, it is indisputable that you and other members of a student's IEP team must presume in favor of educating students with disabilities in the general education classroom.

The second part of the LRE statement both provides clarity and is a source of some confusion about the intent of the LRE requirements. This part of the statement requires that the *removal of children with disabilities from the regular educational environment occurs only if the nature or severity of the disability is such that education in regular classes with the use of supplementary aids and services cannot be achieved satisfactorily*. Too often, the focus of this statement is on the nature or severity of the student's disability and promotes placement as a function of the type or severity of a student's disability. But, that phrase is only one part of the requirement. Look a little more closely at the language that describes least restrictive environment.

MyLab Education
Video Example 4.5
Dr. Erin Studer, the Executive Director for the CHIME Charter Institute, discusses the redesigning of education to benefit students versus adults. How does his vision and administrative leadership align with the definition of least restrictive environment?

First, note that the statement indicates that removal from the regular education environment should only occur under certain circumstances. Again, the presumption is that the student should be educated in the general education classroom. Second, the statement indicates that such removal occurs only if the nature or severity of the disability is such that education in regular classes with the use of supplementary aids and services cannot be achieved satisfactorily. If one takes this statement at face value, it suggests that students must have received education in the regular class with supplementary aids and services and only if that is not successful should they be removed. Taking anything at face value is risky, as you are about to learn.

While, historically, the emphasis in this statement has been placed on the nature and severity of the student's disability (Hyatt & Filler, 2011; Sauer & Jorgensen, 2016), it should be, instead, on the implementation of supplementary aids and services in the regular class. In essence, the LRE statement presumes that a student has received education in the regular class and has received the full range of special education and related services and supplementary aids and services and only if that has happened and the student is not successful should you and the IEP team consider an alternative placement. As you observe current practice in schools, you should ask yourself if the IEP team is observing that standard, which reflects high expectations and quality services. Is research-based evidence being met, or are decisions being made solely on the basis of the student's disability? At CHIME, inclusion is the rule; there are no exceptions. Wherever Pablo can be included, he is. That's also true of the many other students with disabilities—some 19 percent of the entire student body.

Continuum of Alternative Placements

Given the above discussion concerning the emphasis on inclusion in IDEA, IDEA requires SEAs and LEAs to ensure that a continuum of alternative placements is available to meet the needs of students with disabilities for special education and related services and that such alternative placements must make provisions for supplementary aids and services to be provided in conjunction with regular class placement.

The language pertaining to a continuum of placements is part of IDEA's definition of special education, namely, specially designed instruction at no cost to the family to meet the unique needs of the child, including instruction in regular classes, special classes, special schools, home instruction, and instruction in hospitals and institutions. We will discuss each of these as we consider current trends in student placements.

Trends in Student Placements

The U.S. Department of Education tracks the placement of students with disabilities as a function of percentage of time spent in the regular setting. That information is provided in Figure 4.7. Figure 4.7 provides the most recent data on placement trends by all students receiving special education services (U.S. Department of Education, 2018).

There is good news to celebrate in these data. The IDEA report (U.S. Department of Education, 2018) shows that 95 percent of students with disabilities receive some proportion of their education in a regular classroom setting and, as you can see from Figure 4.8, over 60 percent of students receive that education in the regular education classroom for 80 percent of their day or more.

Be aware, however, that these data also hide issues of concern. You will find the data for placement by disability category in each of the chapters about a specific disability. When you look at some of those data, you will learn why they should concern you. For example, consider the following:

- Only 16.5 percent of students with intellectual disability and 13.3 percent of students with multiple disabilities are educated in the general education setting 80 percent of the day or more.

Figure 4.7 Placement Categories Designated by the U.S. Department of Education

Time spent inside regular class

80 to 100 percent of a student's time

40 to 79 percent of a student's time

Less than 39 percent of a student's time

Time spend in separate settings

Settings include separate school, residential facility, parental placement in a private school, correctional facility, and home or hospital. Although each is a separate placement category, the "separate setting" in Figure 4.8 includes all of them.

Figure 4.8 Educational Environments for Students Ages 6 Through 21 Served Under IDEA

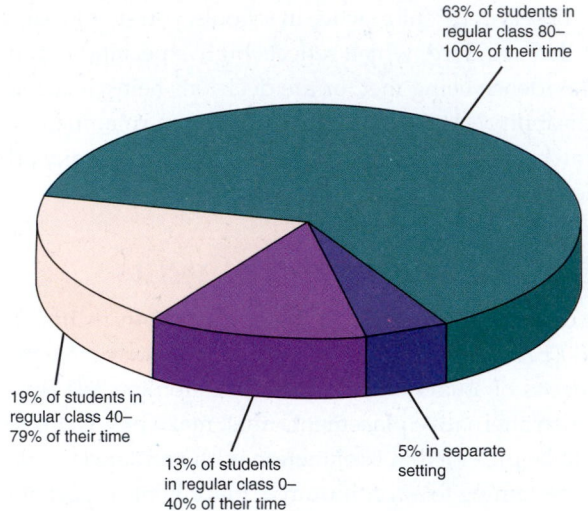

63% of students in regular class 80–100% of their time

19% of students in regular class 40–79% of their time

13% of students in regular class 0–40% of their time

5% in separate setting

SOURCE: U.S. Department of Education. (2018). *39th annual report to Congress on the implementation of the Individuals with Disabilities Education Act.* Retrieved from https://www2.ed.gov/about/reports/annual/osep/2017/parts-b-c/39th-arc-for-idea.pdf/

- Almost half of students with intellectual disability and 46 percent of students with multiple disabilities are educated in the regular class 40 percent of the day or less.

- Seventeen percent of students with emotional disturbance and 24 percent of students with multiple disabilities are educated in a separate school or an environment wholly outside the general education setting.

- One third of students with autism spend 40 percent or less of their day in general education settings.

- Thirty-six percent of students who are deaf-blind are educated less than 40 percent of the day in the regular education setting, while almost 29 percent of these students are educated in separate schools and settings outside the regular education setting.

A particularly troubling trend is that, over the past 10 years, placement of students with disabilities for 80 percent of the day or more increased only 7.5 percent, and the placement in separate settings has remained stable (U.S. Department of Education, 2018).

Not surprisingly, the percentage of students with disabilities in the different placement categories varies according to the age of students and their type of disability. More elementary students than secondary students are served in typical schools with peers who do not have disabilities. Students with less intensive support needs (for example, speech or language impairments and learning disabilities) are more likely to be in general education classrooms for the largest percentage of time compared with students with more intensive support needs (for example, students with intellectual disability or multiple disabilities). In Chapter 2, you learned that placement category also varies based on students' racial or ethnic background (Perzigian, Afacan, Justin, & Wilkerson, 2017).

These data suggest that for some students the presumption of inclusion in the regular education setting is not being implemented. It's important that you consider, before discussing the benefits of education in regular classrooms and inclusion, the potential barriers to progress imposed by placement in settings outside the general education classroom.

Issues in Residential, Home, and Hospital Placements

Settings that have a residential component—special boarding schools, hospitals, and students' homes—are generally regarded as the most restrictive placements. Students who attend residential schools sometimes do so because their local schools have not developed the capacity to provide special education services for them. Sometimes, however, they attend special schools to acquire the capacity to learn in more typical settings, as, for example, when they are relearning after a traumatic brain injury (Chapter 13). That distinction means that you, and IEP team members, must distinguish those situations in which a student needs a more restrictive environment from those in which schools need to expand their capacity to serve all students.

As compared with other students with disabilities, students with hearing impairments, visual impairments, and deaf-blindness are most likely to attend residential schools (U.S. Department of Education, 2018). Similarly, students with multiple disabilities, physical disabilities, and traumatic brain injury are most likely to be educated in a hospital or their homes (U.S. Department of Education, 2018).

What issues concerning students' progress are raised by placement in residential, home, and hospital settings? We have to say that we don't really know because there simply is no research asking these questions, in large measure because of the low percentage of students placed in these settings. Overall, only 0.3 percent of students are placed in a residential facility and 0.4 percent in a homebound or hospital program. As you will learn when reading about special school placements, however, it is clear that instruction on challenging academic content occurs at higher rates in general education settings than in segregated settings; accordingly, one can presume this will be an issue within residential, home, or hospital settings.

Issues in Special School Placements

Separate schools typically congregate students from a specific disability category and provide services specifically related to the educational characteristics of that disability. As compared with other students with disabilities, students with multiple disabilities are those most likely to be educated in special schools; the next most likely are students with deaf-blindness and emotional and behavioral disorders (U.S. Department of Education, 2018). Students, particularly students with emotional disorders, are frequently placed in special schools because of problem behavior that many teachers do not know how to address.

What are the issues pertaining to placement in a separate or special school for progress? Again, it is an issue of involvement in the general education curriculum. In a study of the effects on academic progress of schooling in a separate school versus regular classes, de Graaf, van Hove, and Haveman (2017) compared the educational experiences of Dutch students with Down syndrome educated in regular schools or separate schools. Students educated in regular schools received significantly higher amounts of instruction in academic content areas and had better gains in academic progress, particularly reading. This is a theme you will find repeated in issues pertaining to segregated or self-contained classrooms.

Issues in Specialized-Settings Placements Within Typical Schools

Specialized settings in many schools include resource rooms and self-contained classes. Students who are in regular classes for 40 to 79 percent of their education are often served in resource rooms. Resource rooms are staffed by special education teachers who work with students with disabilities for as little as one period or as many as several periods during the school day, depending on the students' needs for specially designed instruction. Students with learning disabilities are most likely to be served in resource rooms (U.S. Department of Education, 2018).

There is no consensus in the field with regard to the relative harms or benefits associated with resource room models. On the one hand, advocates of inclusive practices argue that pulling students out of regular classes increases stigma and that strategies used in resource rooms could be delivered in the regular class just as effectively. On the other hand, advocates for resource room models argue that students with learning disabilities benefit from more intense instruction in the resource room (Kauffman, Nelson, Simpson, & Ward, 2017).

So, resource rooms are the first type of specialized setting within typical schools. The second type are self-contained classrooms. Self-contained classrooms usually are settings in which students with more intense support needs than those students served in resource rooms are placed. Students with intellectual disability, autism, multiple disabilities, and emotional disorders are most likely to be served in self-contained classrooms (U.S. Department of Education, 2018).

What are the issues pertaining to placement in specialized settings within typical schools, and particularly in self-contained classrooms, with regard to progress? Traditionally, students who are placed in self-contained settings spend proportionally more time working on functional skills and less time (compared to regular class settings) on academic core content. Wehmeyer and Shogren (2017) reviewed the literature showing that the location in which students are involved with the general education curriculum is the general education classroom.

Race, Ethnicity, Placement, and Special Education

You learned about the provocative issues surrounding cultural diversity and special education when you read Chapter 2. It is important to return to the issues pertaining to race, ethnicity, and placement. The fact is, students from some racial and ethnic populations are identified to receive special education at higher rates than students from other racial and ethnic groups, and also to be placed in more restrictive environments at higher rates.

The U.S. Department of Education tracks this using a *risk ratio* statistic. This statistic is calculated as a ratio of children in a particular racial/ethnic group as a function of all children receiving special education. A risk ratio of 1.0 means that children in that racial/ethnic category are equally likely to receive special education services as children in all other racial/ethnic groups. A risk ratio of 2.0 means that children in that racial/ethnic category are twice as likely to receive special education services as are all other racial/ethnic groups.

The most recent report on children ages 6 through 21 from the U.S. Department of Education (2018) indicates that American Indian or Alaska Native children have a risk ratio of 1.7, Black or African American children have a risk ratio of 1.4, and Native Hawaiian or Other Pacific Islander children have a risk ratio of 1.5. White (0.9) and Asian (0.5) children were the only groups with risk ratios under 1.0, indicating they are less likely than all other racial/ethnic groups to receive special education services.

If you bear in mind the risk ratio for children ages 6 to 21 within racial/ethnic groups by disability category, you will note that these disproportionate trends continue. African American children are twice as likely as all other racial/ethnic groups to be categorized as having an emotional or behavioral disability and more than twice as likely (risk ratio 2.2) to be identified as having intellectual disability. American Indian or Alaska Native children also had high risk ratios for being labeled as having intellectual disability (1.6) or emotional or behavioral disability (1.7), as did Native Hawaiian or Other Pacific Island children (1.7 or 1.3, respectively).

The U.S. Department of Education does not report risk ratio data by race/ethnicity and placement, but that does not thwart your learning. Go back to what you learned from the section about placement trends. Children with intellectual disability or children with emotional or behavioral disabilities are at the greatest risk for being placed in the most segregated settings. Thus, overidentification within certain disability categories will result in overrepresentation in highly restrictive educational placements. In *Guidelines for Teaching: Preventing Discrimination in Special Education*, you can learn about ideas to prevent discrimination based on race, ethnicity, and English language ability.

Guidelines for Teaching

Preventing Discrimination in Special Education

Ensure nondiscrimination in referral practices

What not to do: A 3rd-grade teacher had a class of 11 Black students and 14 White students. She referred 5 of the Black students for an evaluation for special education based on "aggressive behavior" and referred 4 White students for Tier 2 behavioral interventions based on numerous behavioral infractions. The parents of one of the Black students filed a complaint with the U.S. Office of Civil Rights (OCR) based on a claim of discrimination against the Black students on the basis of race.

OCR's response: OCR found evidence that the teacher relied on racial stereotypes in determining whether to refer for more intensive instruction or for special education.

What are appropriate practices?

- Provide training to teachers focusing on racial bias in special education referrals.
- Establish measurable special education criteria to consider for making a referral.
- Provide training in culturally responsive teaching practices.
- Provide training on positive behavioral interventions and supports.

Ensure nondiscriminatory evaluation

What not to do: Two 6th-grade students, one Latino and one American Indian, were referred for a nondiscriminatory evaluation due to their low performance in math and reading. For the Latino student, the team reviewed her academic records, considered teacher and parent input, administered appropriate assessments, and observed her in a couple of classes before determining that she did not have a disability. For the American Indian student, the team determined that she had a learning disability based on an IQ test. The parents of the American Indian student filed an OCR complaint alleging discrimination.

OCR's response: OCR inquired about whether there was a prudent reason for providing such different treatment of two students with similar educational challenges. Furthermore, both Section 504 and IDEA require information for more than one measure to determine that the student has a disability.

What are appropriate practices?

- The special services team at school should have a list of required criteria for every evaluation and should always ensure that those criteria are addressed.
- Ensure students who are similarly situated in terms of educational needs have an evaluation process that follows the same general protocol.

Ensure individualized decisions in referring students to more segregated settings

What not do to: The secondary options in a school district include six high schools and one alternative school for students with emotional and behavioral disorders (EBD). The principal of the alternative school has concerns that the majority of referrals come from a single high school.

(Continued)

An inquiry into this situation revealed the fact that the principal at this high school automatically refers any student identified as having EBD who has received three office referrals for behavioral infractions. Half of the alternative-school students come from this high school alone.

OCR's response: Because of the high school's uniform policy of referral after three behavioral infractions, OCR would consider it a violation of IDEA and Section 504 to disregard the need for individualized consideration of the placement requirements of students with disabilities.

What are appropriate practices?

- IEP teams must consider supplementary aids and services that might enable students with EBD to be educated with their peers who do not have disabilities.
- Provide training ensuring that administrators understand that students with disabilities must receive specially designed instruction, supplementary aids and services, and related services that maximize the student's participation in the general education classroom.
- Review policies to make sure that "one-size-fits-all" standards are not in violation of the need to provide individualized student supports.

Prevent race-based underidentification of students with disabilities

What not do to: A kindergarten teacher is concerned that two of her students, a Black student and a White student, have difficulty following instruction, staying still during classwork, and refraining from verbal outbursts. She suspects that the White student may have ADHD, so she refers him for an evaluation. She perceives that the Black student is not motivated in class to pay attention, and does not understand appropriate social interaction due to not having suitable guidance from his parents. She meets with the student's mother to encourage the mother to help her son comply with kindergarten expectations for classroom behavior.

OCR's response: The two students had very similar educational needs, yet the White student was referred for an evaluation to inquire about the need for special education and/or related services, while the Black student's educational needs were considered to result from lack of parental guidance. OCR determined that similarly situated students of different races should be treated in the same way unless there is a valid, nondiscriminatory rationale for treating them differently.

What are appropriate practices?

- Provide training to teachers focusing on racial bias in special education referrals.
- Provide training in culturally responsive teaching practices.
- Provide training on positive ways to work with parents of all children.

Avoid letting limited English proficiency delay special education services

What not do to: A middle school teacher suspects that a Spanish-speaking student with limited English proficiency has a learning disability; however, he delays referring the student for an evaluation until the student has become more proficient in English.

OCR's response: OCR would find evidence for a Section 504 and Title VI violation if a student is suspected of having a disability and the school district delays evaluation. Rather, the student must be evaluated, if parental consent is obtained, in an appropriate language and in a timely manner.

What are appropriate practices?

- Ensure that the district meets expectations for nondiscriminatory evaluation in the student's native language.
- Ensure that appropriate English language learner (ELL) services are provided to students who need such supports.

MyLab Education Self-Check 4.2

MyLab Education Application Exercise 4.2: Katie's Present Levels of Performance

---

Inclusion and Ensuring Educational Progress

Defining Inclusion

As you have learned in previous sections, students in particular disability categories are more likely to be served outside the general education classroom. It is important, though, that you understand that a disability label is not destiny when it comes to placement. There are examples of successful inclusion across age and disability categories, and it is IDEA's presumption that students with disabilities, independent of category, be educated alongside their peers without disabilities. So what exactly is meant by inclusion? As we have explained, IDEA has a presumption in favor of students with disabilities being educated with their peers who do not have disabilities. That's what inclusion is all about. It is, after all, one of the four national policy goals of IDEA: full participation. And it is one of IDEA's six principles. That's what you learned in Chapter 1.

Inclusion refers to the participation of students with disabilities alongside their peers without disabilities in academic settings and in extracurricular and other school activities. Inclusion is what happens at CHIME for students such as Pablo—students who have disabilities. The provision of supplementary aids and services is important to IDEA's emphasis. As you learned previously in this chapter, supplementary aids and services are aids, services, and other supports that are provided in general education classes, in other education-related settings, and in extracurricular and nonacademic settings, to enable students with disabilities to be educated with students who do not have disabilities, to the maximum extent appropriate.

It is true enough that IDEA allows placements other than the general education classroom, but it is equally true that IDEA presumes that the setting of choice for students is the general education classroom and that students will not be removed from that setting unless inclusion in the general education classroom cannot be achieved satisfactorily with the use of supplementary aids and services and specially designed instruction.

The IEP team is responsible for making placement decisions. Although IDEA allows placement across several settings, it presumes, as you must, that students will be educated in the general education classroom and will participate in extracurricular and other school activities with their nondisabled peers.

MyLab Education
Video Example 4.6
In this video, the IEP team is discussing the means to and benefit from inclusion for Nikki. How does Nikki's mother seem to feel about her daughter being included?

CHARACTERISTICS OF INCLUSION   Inclusion has four key characteristics: home-school placement, the principle of natural proportions, restructuring teaching and learning, and age- and grade-appropriate placements.

Home-School Placement.   Within an inclusive model, students attend the same school they would have attended if they did not have a disability. This is the same school other students in the neighborhood attend.

Principle of Natural Proportions.   The principle of natural proportions holds that students with exceptionalities should be placed in schools and classrooms in natural proportion to the occurrence of exceptionality within the general population (Brown et al., 1991). If, for example, 10 percent of students in a school district receive special education services, the principle of natural proportions holds that, if a classroom has thirty students, not more than three should have a disability.

Restructuring Teaching and Learning.   Inclusion through restructuring requires general and special educators to work in partnership with related service providers, families, and students to provide supplementary aids and services and special education and related services (Sailor, McCart, & Choi, 2018). Tremendous variability exists in how teachers provide special education services within general education classrooms. But in inclusive schools, pooling the strengths and talents of educators who have different types of professional development and capacities enables all students to be successful in the general education classroom.

MyLab Education
Video Example 4.7
Pablo's teachers talk about how important inclusion is to them. What strikes you as important from what they describe?

Age- and Grade-Appropriate Placements.   Finally, inclusion favors educating all students in age- and grade-appropriate placements so that students with disabilities go to school with their same-aged peers.

Two major issues are at the heart of the inclusion debate: (1) eliminating the continuum of placements and (2) increasing the amount of time students spend in the general education classroom.

Eliminating the Continuum of Placements.   The concept of a continuum of services has been part of special education since Congress enacted IDEA in 1975. As you've learned, the continuum refers to services that range from the most typical and most inclusive settings to the most atypical and most segregated settings. There was a time when accommodating students with disabilities in general education classrooms through supplementary aids and services was not considered an option. That limited perspective caused Taylor (1988) to observe that students with disabilities were caught in the continuum of services. Unfortunately, once students were placed in more restrictive settings, few ever left them for general education classrooms.

The inclusion movement has tried to limit the need for more restrictive settings by creating a new partnership between special and general educators. This partnership seeks to provide individualized instruction to students in general education classrooms through a universally designed general education curriculum (Ryndak et al., 2014). The priority for inclusion in the general education classroom now rests on the premises that it is not often appropriate or even necessary to remove some students from the general education classroom and place them in a more specialized and restrictive setting to provide individualized and appropriate education; that in order to gain access to the general education curriculum, students must be in the general education classroom; and that there is sufficient evidence to support inclusion as a research-based practice (Ryndak et al., 2014; Jackson, Ryndak, and Wehmeyer, 2010).

Increasing the Amount of Time in General Education Classrooms.   Research confirms that students with disabilities can be successfully educated in the general education classroom, given adequate support and instruction (Jackson et al., 2010), and IDEA expresses a preference for inclusion. So how can teachers increase the amount of time students with disabilities are served in the general education classroom? In Chapters 5 through 15, you will learn about strategies to promote progress, and ways to support students with disabilities in inclusive settings. In the next section, you will learn why it's important to increase student inclusion.

Student Outcomes Associated with Inclusion

By now, most stakeholders in the education of students with disabilities have accepted the importance of including students. For many parents of younger children with disabilities, inclusion is an expectation (Khetani, Cohn, Orsmond, Law, & Coster, 2013). So what benefits accrue when students are included?

First, there is almost universal agreement that students with disabilities gain social and communication benefits from their involvement in inclusive settings (Jackson et al., 2010; Wehmeyer et al., 2016). Second, and particularly important in light of current trends in standards-based reform, research shows that students with disabilities can and do benefit academically from involvement in the general education classroom. For example, students with learning disabilities or emotional and behavioral disorders who were educated in more inclusive settings enrolled in postsecondary education at more than twice the rate of their peers who were not included (Rojewski, Lee, & Gregg, 2013). Similarly, students without disabilities educated in inclusive classrooms made significantly greater academic progress in mathematics and reading than did students without disabilities who did not have students with disabilities in their classroom (Cole, Waldron, & Maid, 2004). Why? This resulted because the additional supports provided in the general education classroom that are intended to support the students with disabilities benefit all students. An analysis of the Pre-Elementary Education Longitudinal Study (PEELS, a Department of Education dataset, following children across disability categories through preschool and into early elementary) found a strong, positive relationship between the number of hours students with disabilities spent in general education classrooms and their achievement in math and reading (Cosier, Causton-Theoharis, & Theoharis, 2013).

In particular, research shows that students with disabilities receiving their education in the general education classroom are significantly more likely to have access to the general education curriculum. Students being educated in the general education curriculum are more likely to be working on activities linked to grade-level standards in the general education classroom. Clearly, inclusion with support (through specially designed instruction, related services, supplementary aids, and services) is feasible and important. You will learn more about the positive outcomes of inclusion in Chapters 5 through 15 and be provided with tips for inclusive practices for students from that categorical area. *Inclusion Tips Across All Disabilities* provides ideas to include students across disability categories.

Inclusion Tips Across All Disabilities

	Behavior	Social Interactions	Educational Performance	Classroom Attitudes
What You Might See	The student shows an apparently poor attitude toward other students and does not easily cooperate with them during instructional activities.	The student has few friends and doesn't appear to want any.	The student's work is acceptable, but needs constant supervision.	The student never volunteers answers and is reluctant to participate in class activities.
What You Might Be Tempted to Do	Discipline the student for his poor behavior and separate the student from the rest of the class.	Encourage the student to take the initiative toward others but also allow the student to be alone whenever the student chooses.	Assign an aide to work with the student and allow unfinished work to be completed at home.	Carefully choose activities that allow the student to work alone.
Alternate Responses	Identify the student's strengths and work together on a list of positive things the student can say when responding to other students during instructional activities.	Collaborate with the school counselor to plan ways to teach the student specific social skills.	Collaborate with the special education teacher to create step-by-step assignments that the student can do independently. Set up a reward system for each step successfully completed without supervision.	Together with the special education teacher, work with the student ahead of time on content to be covered and plan specific things for which the student can successfully contribute.
Ways to Include Peers in the Process	Ask the student to identify peers the student would like to work with. Then work with this small group to practice verbal responses that would be helpful.	Work with identified peers to practice specific social skills with the student in and out of the classroom.	Encourage the student to work with peers to monitor assignments. Ask peers to work with the student to construct a tracking system for class assignments.	Plan with peers positive contributions that each can make to upcoming class activities.

INCLUSION AND PROGRESS   Until this past decade, the inclusion movement consisted of two generations of different practices. The first generation focused on moving students with disabilities from segregated settings into the general education classroom. The second focused on developing and evaluating practices to support the presence of students with disabilities in the general education classroom. Both phases focused primarily on the place in which students were educated.

Now, however, ESSA's standards-based reforms and IDEA's command for access to the general education curriculum have created conditions for a third generation of inclusive practices. (Remember, from Chapter 1, that ESSA refers to the Every Student Succeeds Act, the general education law that also applies to special education.). What's the significance of ESSA?

Today, the focus is no longer exclusively on where a student is taught. It also includes (1) "what"—curriculum mastery, or what a student is taught and learns—and (2) "how"—the methods and pedagogy that teachers use. Nothing about the first two generations of inclusive practices is obsolete or unimportant. In fact, as we describe in Chapters 5 through 17, efforts to achieve outcomes associated with first- and second-generation inclusive practices (inclusion in the general education classroom and implementation of high-quality instructional strategies to support students in the general education classroom) continue but with new emphasis on "what" and "how." What and how are two cornerstones of a dignifying education.

MyLab Education Self-Check 4.3
MyLab Education Application Exercise 4.3: Where Will Katie Receive Educational Services?

Summary

Learning Standards and the General Education Curriculum: What All Students Should Learn

ESSA—the Every Student Succeeds Act—requires that all students be provided an education based on challenging academic content standards. IDEA requires that students receiving special education be involved with and progress in the general education curriculum, and participate in state and district-wide assessments, with or without accommodations, or in alternate assessments. The Supreme Court, in *Endrew F.* (2017), interpreted IDEA's doctrine of appropriate education and its IDEA provisions to mean that students with disabilities should receive an appropriately ambitious educational program. These three policy initiatives intend to ensure that students with disabilities are held to high expectations and gain access to challenging academic content. Finally, IDEA requires that the IEPs of students with disabilities include goals pertaining to other educational needs (e.g., those not in the general education curriculum).

Nondiscriminatory Evaluation: Evaluating for Disability, Levels of Achievement, and Potential for Growth

IDEA and *Endrew F.* require the nondiscriminatory evaluation (NDE) process to include consideration of evaluation to determine the nature of a child's disability, consideration of evaluation to determine the child's present levels of

achievement, and consideration of evaluation to determine the child's potential for growth. The disability determination process is important for both ascertaining eligibility for special education services and identifying the student's need for special education and related services. Common assessments and assessment processes used to determine disability include screening and pre-referral processes and intelligence tests. IDEA also requires that these myriad of assessment tools be used to determine the student's present levels of academic achievement and functional performance. Common tools for determining present levels include achievement tests, curriculum-based measurement, ecological assessments, behavioral rating scales, and adaptive behavior scales.

Endrew F. emphasized the need to evaluate to determine a student's potential for growth. Data collected through progress monitoring, **mastery assessment**, formative assessment, and other forms of collecting data can, in combination with knowledge gained by the present levels information, contribute to understanding a student's potential for growth.

Developing an Individualized Education Program to Ensure Progress

An appropriately ambitious IEP is one that emphasizes the student's potential for growth, provides challenging objectives, and ensures that students are involved with and progress in the general education curriculum and satisfy other educational needs. The NDE data provide the information needed to write the present levels of academic achievement and functional performance section. This should emphasize student strengths and not simply be a statement of deficits. The IEP must contain measurable annual goals that ensure students can be involved in and progress in the general education curriculum and meet other educational needs, and must identify modifications and accommodations to enable the student to participate in state and district-wide testing and to progress in the general education curriculum. Determining student progress becomes an important feature of IEPs in light of *Endrew F.* and can be done through processes like progress monitoring and curriculum-based measurement.

The IEP also must describe the special education and related services and supplementary aids and services that enable students to be successful. Of particular importance for educating learners in the general education setting are supplementary aids and services that provide supports through classroom, assessment, and task modification; utilizing teachers, paraprofessionals, and peers; and implementing assistive and educational technology, among other strategies.

The Least Restrictive Environment and Educational Placement

The IEP team is also responsible for placement decisions. IDEA has a strong preference for educating students with disabilities alongside their peers without disabilities through the use of specially designed instruction and supplementary aids and services, and students should only be educated outside the general education setting if implementation of such strategies and supports has proven not to be successful. Although there has been progress in educating learners with disabilities in the general education setting, too many students are placed outside the regular class due to a disability label or racial/ethnic/linguistic characteristics.

Inclusion and Ensuring Educational Progress

Historically, students with disabilities were too often educated outside the regular education curriculum. Inclusion refers to the participation of students with disabilities alongside their peers without disabilities in academic settings and in extracurricular and other school activities. IDEA allows placements other than the general education classroom, but it presumes that the setting of choice for students is the general education classroom and that students will not be removed from that setting unless inclusion in the general education classroom cannot be achieved satisfactorily with the use of supplementary aids and services and specially designed instruction. There are documented benefits in academic and social outcomes for students with disabilities when they are educated with their peers who do not have disabilities.

Addressing The Professional Standards

In Chapter 4, Ensuring Educational Progress, we have covered the following Council for Exceptional Children (CEC) Initial Level Special Educator Preparation Standards: Chapter 2—1.0, 1.2, 2.1, 4.3, 4.4, 5.1, 6.1, 6.5, 6.6, 7.1. Refer to the Appendix for a full listing of the CEC Standards with descriptions and supporting explanations.

Chapter 5
School-wide Systems of Supports

⌄ Learning Outcomes

5.1 Summarize the characteristics of school-wide systems of supports and how those systems use tiered supports, screening and progress monitoring, and data-based decision making and teaming to benefit all students, including those with disabilities.

5.2 Identify key considerations in the implementation of school-wide positive behavior interventions and supports (SW-PBIS) and the role of tiered supports within SW-PBIS.

5.3 Identify key considerations in the implementation of response to intervention (RTI) to address students' academic needs and the role of tiered supports within RTI.

5.4 Describe the characteristics of comprehensive, integrated three-tiered systems (Ci3T) to simultaneously address students' behavioral, academic, and social and emotional needs.

MyLab Education

Vignette Video 5.1

What are your first impressions of Kelsey?

MyLab Education

Vignette Video 5.2

What is it about Kelsey's family that might affect her at school?

Meet Kelsey, the "Yes . . . but" Student

We bet you will recognize Kelsey. She's the one about whom you may say, "Yes, she's got a lot going for her," before you add, "but she's got issues." You may have been in school with various "Kelseys." Or at some point you may have been like a "Kelsey." Here is one more bet: You will want to find out about those issues, and then about what turned her around and how you might be able to renew and support students such as Kelsey in your work as an educator.

Kelsey grew up with her mother, but not in a strife-free home. She had a boyfriend but frequently argued with him. She worked during high school as a cashier and bag-checker at a local grocery store but knew that the job was not a career for her. Instead, she wanted to be a police officer, a firefighter, or a nurse. Yes . . . but.

Kelsey was "goth" in her sophomore year in high school and had to repeat that year because her academic performance was unsatisfactory, but she moved through her junior year with success. In her senior year, however, she once more was in danger of failing courses and was at risk for not graduating and having to repeat a grade, yet again. But she knew she was smart enough to make progress and, with the support of a group of teachers and counselors from the school and the nearby University of New Hampshire, she ultimately did. Yes, she had academic talent, but she needed the right supports to use her strengths and achieve her goals. Yes . . . but.

During Kelsey's sophomore year, she had gotten in trouble for selling drugs. This was one of the reasons the year was so hard for her. During her senior year she began to use prescription drugs. She understood why she needed to take the medications and believed they helped, but she sometimes tossed the drugs into a toilet because she did not always like the way they made her feel. Drugs and defiance seemed to be twins— "relatives" who were hard to abandon. Yes . . . but.

She opposed certain teachers and, at times, cursed at them and at school administrators. She could listen to her teachers' requests when they made sense to her, but these requests often did not, and Kelsey accumulated an unusual number of office referrals because of her behavior. Even with these issues, however, she had a way of endearing herself to teachers when she was able to show her strengths and gifts. Similarly, she fought at times with her peers, but she was also the captain of the cheerleading squad for 2 years. Yes . . . but.

Kelsey did not have an individualized education program (IEP) or special education services. Instead, she received accommodations specific to her attention-deficit hyperactivity disorder (ADHD; Chapter 10). Her ADHD did not so significantly affect her learning that she needed special education services and supports. (You learned in Chapter 1 that special education services are available to only those students who need additional support for learning the general education curriculum.) She qualified for those accommodations for ADHD under Section 504 of the Rehabilitation Act (Chapter 1).

Kelsey knew she did not have a disability, but she understood that she needed medication and academic and emotional supports during her senior year. She described herself quite simply: "A little bit of caring takes me a long way." But she sometimes acted out when support was offered. Yes . . . but.

During her senior year, these supports consisted of additional attention from her teachers, tutoring from some of her peers, and counseling from a university staff member. Because Kelsey was determined to graduate and because she received the accommodations and supports she needed, she did graduate. Yes . . . with "but" no longer added on.

The supports go by the name school-wide positive behavior interventions (SW-PBIS). They turned her around, renewed her, and brought her back to her essential nature, her true self. They did so by building on her strengths and supporting her so she could communicate how she felt and what she wanted in ways that were not perceived as defiant by her teachers. They found the "yes" behind the "but"—the competent Kelsey behind the defiant Kelsey.

In this chapter, you will learn about SW-PBIS and other school-wide systems that focus on promoting valued academic, behavior, and social and emotional outcomes for all students—repeat: all students, those who, like Kelsey, have 504 accommodation plans and those who receive special education services and have IEPs.

MyLab Education
Vignette Video 5.3
What about Kelsey might endear her to her teachers?

Characteristics of School-wide Systems

In Chapter 1, you learned about special education law, the Individual with Disabilities Education Act (IDEA), and the importance of supporting students to make progress toward goals that lead to valued long-term outcomes, including equality of opportunity, full participation, independent living, and economic self-sufficiency. In Chapter 2, you learned about issues related to the diverse populations of students receiving special education. In Chapter 3, you discovered that it is necessary for professionals and parents to have trusting partnerships for the sake of the students' education. In Chapter 4, you came to understand how and why individualized evaluation, programs, and placement enable students to make progress in the general education curriculum and attain their individualized learning goals.

MyLab Education

Video Example 5.1

CHIME is an inclusive charter school in California. What does "all means all" mean in an inclusive school like CHIME that focuses on supporting *all* students?

In this chapter you are going to take a step back from these particulars about special education and focus instead on the general education curriculum and how it is delivered in today's schools. Why? To support students with disabilities in accessing and progressing in the general education curriculum, you first need to understand the general education curriculum. This is especially true because, as you learned in Chapter 1, IDEA's least restrictive environment (LRE) principle holds that students with disabilities are first and foremost members of the broader, general education school community and that all students, including Kelsey, have a right to effective educational supports in the general education classroom and curriculum to achieve their goals.

Increasingly, schools are adopting school-wide systems to organize the instruction and supports for learning that are provided to all students, including those with disabilities (Jimerson, Burns, & VanDerHeyden, 2016; McIntosh & Goodman, 2015). So, what is it about school-wide systems that makes them school-wide? In part, it is because school-wide systems are a general education initiative, designed to benefit all students, including those with disabilities. It is also because these systems borrow many practices from special education and such practices work for all students. The interface of general and special education is clear, yet school-wide means exactly that: all students, school-wide, whether they have or do not have disabilities or, like Kelsey, have other education needs.

School-wide systems do not focus only on students, however. The concept of "school-wide" encompasses all people in the school building. Essentially, all members of a school's staff participate in school-wide systems, thereby promoting consistency in teaching and learning for everyone. In such systems, administrators, general and special education teachers, related service providers (e.g., speech, occupational, and physical therapists), support staff, custodial staff, security/resource officers, volunteers, and, really, anyone else in the school building support students to learn (Filter, Sytsma, & McIntosh, 2016).

In the sections that follow, we will introduce you to three core features of school-wide systems that benefit all students. The first feature is **tiered supports**. The second is **screening and progress monitoring**. The third involves **data-based decision making and teaming**. These are the big ideas that drive school-wide systems.

We will then introduce you to three exemplary school-wide systems. They are:

- *School-wide positive behavioral interventions and supports* (SW-PBIS) (Horner & Sugai, 2015; Lewis, Mitchell, Bruntmeyer, & Sugai, 2016)

- *Response to intervention* (RTI) (Jimerson et al., 2016)

- *Comprehensive, Integrated, Three-tiered* (Ci3T) model of prevention (Lane, Oakes, Cantwell, & Royer, 2016).

In learning about these features of school-wide systems, you will learn how educators practice school-wide system–based education and why the practice is so powerful.

But before we introduce the core features of school-wide systems and the three systems—SW-PBIS, RTI, and Ci3T—that exemplify those features, we emphasize that there is no single, universally agreed upon framework for implementing these systems. This is so because school-wide systems are relatively new and many advances are occurring in the field right now, even as we write this book (Jimerson et al., 2016). That fact is exciting if only because it means that new ways are emerging to support all students. But it also means that you may become confused because there is not always clarity in language or in implementation. Keep this in mind as you read this chapter and as you learn more in other chapters that follow. Pay careful attention to the terms themselves. We will define them; we will include them in the glossary. Also, regard this chapter as a blueprint for understanding the key features of school-wide systems. This chapter, this blueprint, offers a foundation on which you can build your knowledge about educating students with exceptionalities.

Three Key Features of School-wide Systems

What makes systems school-wide? You know one answer already: They involve everyone at a school. They do more than that, however. They give priority to *preventing* problems in learning before they occur (McIntosh & Goodman, 2015). To prevent problems, school-wide systems provide *high-quality, universal instruction and supports* for all students, with *increasingly intensive instruction and supports* (sometimes called "tiers" of support) for students who need them (L. S. Fuchs, Fuchs, & Malone, 2018).

Pay special attention to the following words: "increasingly intensive instruction and support." They teach you that some students will receive more support than others. You may be thinking, How do educators know who needs more support than others? The short answer consists of three parts. First, educators use a tiered approach to teaching; increasingly intense instruction and support tends to prevent later problems in school. Second, they screen students and monitor their progress; the data from screening and monitoring progress are the essential foundations on which educators make decisions. Third, no single educator makes a decision about a student's needs for support; team-based decision making is equally essential. Let's now consider these three parts of the short answer.

TIERED INTERVENTIONS AND SUPPORTS: PROVIDING INCREASINGLY INTENSIVE INSTRUCTION AND SUPPORTS AND EMPHASIZING PREVENTION   As you just learned, the purpose of school-wide approaches is to prevent problems in learning by providing high-quality instruction and supports for all students, with *increasingly intensive instruction and supports* for students who need it. The premise of school-wide systems is that if all students receive high-quality instruction and supports, then more students will progress and even excel. However, when students continue to struggle even after receiving high-quality instruction and supports, they need a more intensive approach. To make it easier for educators to understand why and how to provide more intensive instruction and supports, school-wide systems adopt the language of "tiers" —tiers in which educators group students according to the students' needs and then deliver increasingly intensive instruction and supports to them.

Accordingly, Tier 1 refers to the high-quality instruction and supports provided to *all*—repeat: *all*—students to promote their progress. Tier 1 provides *universal* instruction and supports (L. S. Fuchs et al., 2018). Tier 2 refers to supports provided to students who need more intensive instruction and support to learn at Tier 1. This instruction is usually for small groups of students and is provided at low intensity (as you will learn later in the chapter) in the general education classroom or in other locations in the school building (Lane, Oakes, Cantwell, & Royer, 2016). Tier 3 refers to even more intensive supports for an even smaller number of students who need supports beyond those provided at Tier 2. Tier 3 supports are usually one-to-one, occur more frequently, and include instructional trials (i.e., the number of times a student practices a skill) (Shogren, Wehmeyer, Lane, & Quirk, 2017). Figure 5.1 shows how the three tiers interact, with successively smaller numbers of students receiving Tier 2 and Tier 3 supports. But remember this principle about tiered instruction: Tier 1 instruction and supports form the basis of Tier 2 and Tier 3 instruction; *all* students receive this universal instruction and support.

In the chapters about particular disabilities, we will give you examples of instruction in Tiers 1, 2, and 3. For now, remember what we just taught you: School-wide systems focus on providing more intensive instruction and supports for students who need it to make progress in school. Also remember that receiving Tier 2 supports does not mean that students will no longer receive Tier 1 supports; likewise, receiving Tier 3 supports does not mean that students will no longer receive Tier 1 and 2 supports. Instead, the focus shifts to using the Tier 2 and 3 supports to enable students to engage more successfully in the Tier 1 curriculum. Tiers 1, 2, and 3 complement each other; they are integrated, not separate (Shogren et al., 2017). The idea behind tiered supports is that students move fluidly between the supports they need. This is what distinguishes school-wide systems—students get what they need, when they need it.

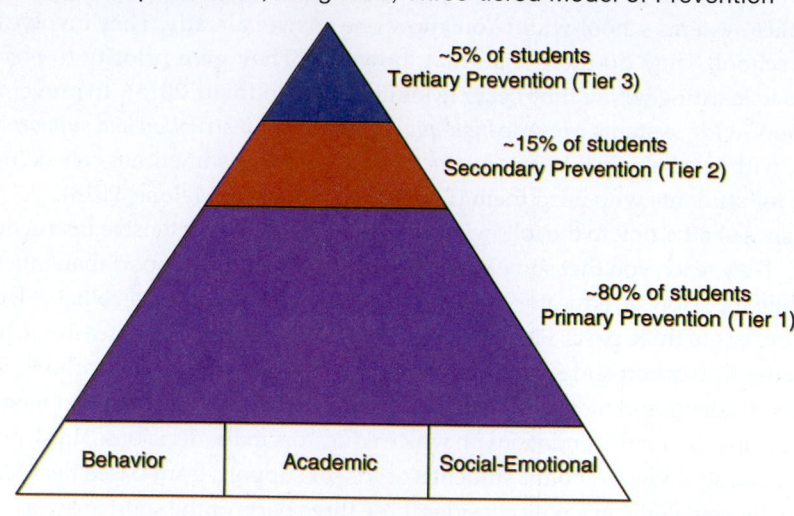

Figure 5.1 Comprehensive, Integrated, Three-tiered Model of Prevention

~5% of students
Tertiary Prevention (Tier 3)

~15% of students
Secondary Prevention (Tier 2)

~80% of students
Primary Prevention (Tier 1)

Behavior   Academic   Social-Emotional

SOURCE: Based on Lane, K. L., Kalberg, J. R., & Menzies, H. M. (2009). *Developing schoolwide programs to prevent and manage problem behaviors: A step-by-step approach.* New York: Guilford Press.

COLLECTING AND USING DATA: SCREENING AND PROGRESS MONITORING   You may well ask, "How will I know which students need what kinds of more intensive support and why and when they need it?" Part of the answer lies in the second of the three features of school-wide systems: Educators collect data through the two processes of, first, screening all students and, second, monitoring students' progress. Your decisions rest on data; it's as simple as that.

Note, however, that there is a difference between the data that educators collect. As we just wrote, two types of data are screening data and progress monitoring data (Riley-Tillman & Johnson, 2017). These types of data differ in two major respects: timing and purpose.

Screening occurs before instruction because screening tools have a narrow but important purpose: to obtain data for use in identifying factors likely to predict whether a student will make progress in school without support or whether the student may need additional support (Lane, Oakes, Cantwell, Schatschneider, et al., 2016). Typically, universal screening occurs for all students in a school; it is predictive in that it identifies students who need additional instruction and support immediately.

By contrast, progress monitoring—you learned about it in Chapter 4—occurs after screening and has a different purpose: to secure data that enable you to know whether a student is making progress in attaining IEP goals and objectives or, as for Kelsey, whether she is making progress in school because she is receiving accommodations. Unlike screening data, progress monitoring is not predictive; it is explanatory. And it relates to students who have already been screened and are now receiving instruction, to investigate the extent to which they are benefiting from the instruction.

For example, screening may examine school readiness indicators as young children begin school, leading educators to target instruction and supports to promote the students' progress as they begin school. Screening of middle and high school students can identify those who may be at risk of struggling for various reasons, leading to more intensive instruction being provided early to prevent problems (Oakes, Lane, Cantwell, & Royer, 2017; Stormont, Thompson, Herman, & Reinke, 2016). Return to the important point we made earlier: Screening is a vital part of prevention. Screening data alert the educator to whether a student such as Kelsey needs support to prevent failure and ensure progress.

Progress monitoring, in contrast, yields data about how well or poorly a student is mastering a curriculum. The data tell you about the student's progress in any of the three tiers. The data then allow you to decide whether a student should move between tiers. Kelsey may have had the benefit of screening; we do not know. We do know, however, that she benefited from progress monitoring. She received support at Tier 1 and Tier 2; the decision to support her at Tier 2 was based on the data that monitored her lack of progress in Tier 1.

DATA-BASED DECISION MAKING AND TEAMING   Collecting data involves assembling the information that you and your colleagues will use to decide whether a student might need, or demonstrably does need, intensified—higher tiered—instruction and supports. Of course, someone has to use the data to guide decision making. In school-wide systems, teams frequently work together to make data-based decisions about a student's movement between tiers. As we noted earlier, a student's movement between tiers is a fluid process. So, the third feature of school-wide systems, data-based decision making and teaming, provides the structure for using the screening and progress monitoring data to decide whether a student needs to move from one tier to another, either "up" or "down" the tiers of support.

The specific types of teams will vary according to the framework that a school, district, or state has adopted to implement school-wide systems of supports. Regardless of the framework, such systems of support require teams that make decisions based on data. We can differentiate three types of teams in terms of emphasis. First, teams can focus on a single student, such as the teams that supported Kelsey. Second, teams can attend to the needs of all or most students in a particular academic area, as in subject-area teams (mathematics or reading) or grade-level teams. Third, school-level teams can pay particular attention to all students' behavioral, academic, and/or social-emotional issues and adjust school-wide supports.

These types of teams can be school-based, operating in a particular school. This is a building-based team. There also may be district leadership teams (Eagle, Dowd-Eagle, Snyder, & Holtzman, 2015; McIntosh & Goodman, 2016). So, teams can occur at two levels: at a school itself or at the district within which the school operates.

Effective teams have a shared mission, clear purpose, and specific roles for each member (Algozzine et al., 2016; Crone et al., 2016). Their members also need to know how to interpret and understand the data collected through screening and progress monitoring tools. Specific methods and strategies enable teams to use the data and decide which students will make greater progress if they receive more intensive support in a higher tier (Todd et al., 2011). They also identify students who no longer need the additional instruction and supports at Tier 2 or 3.

 This IRIS instructional module will teach you more about data-based individualization to intensify instruction. These strategies apply across content areas and grade levels to make data-based decisions to promote student outcomes. https://iris.peabody.vanderbilt.edu/module/dbi1/

The Three Foci of School-wide Systems: Behavioral, Academic, and Social and Emotional Needs

At this point in the chapter, you have learned about the key features of school-wide systems—tiered supports, collecting and using data from screening and progress monitoring, and data-based decision making and teaming. What you have not yet learned enough about is how school-wide systems focus on three different areas of students' development and learning. These are behavioral needs; academic needs; and social-emotional needs.

With respect to behavior, *school-wide positive behavioral interventions and supports* (SW-PBIS) is one of the mostly widely known and utilized school-wide systems (Horner et al., 2013; Lewis, McIntosh, Simonsen, Mitchell, & Hatton, 2017). It focuses on teaching and supporting all students to develop prosocial behaviors that lead to positive outcomes. You encountered this kind of system when you read

School-based teams and effective problem solving that address student and school needs are a critical part of school-wide and tiered systems of supports.

about Kelsey. At Kelsey's school, SW-PBIS was used to promote positive behavior and prevent drop-out, and she strongly benefited from this approach.

With respect to academics, start by thinking about the usual academic areas—English/language arts and math. Each of these areas of the curriculum (and other areas as well) can be targeted through one type of school-wide system that you will learn about soon. That system is known as *response to intervention* (RTI) (Jimerson et al., 2016). The purpose of RTI is to provide high-quality academic instruction and support for all students, with more intensive supports and instruction for students who struggle academically. It is concerned with preventing academic problems.

Yet another type of school-wide system—*multi-tiered systems of supports* (MTSS)—integrates academics and behavioral supports. It targets students' academic and behavior domains simultaneously (McIntosh & Goodman, 2016). Increasingly, education leaders are recognizing the interconnectedness of academic and behavior skills. Think about it—if a student is struggling behaviorally, as Kelsey was, it will likely be much harder for the student to achieve academic goals. The reverse is also true: If a student struggles academically, the student might be more likely to act out or socially withdraw. That certainly seemed to be the case for Kelsey. Academics and behavior interacted and affected her negatively in both domains of her development. In schools such as hers, where combined academic and behavior supports exist, fewer students require additional (Tiers 2 and 3) supports than would be expected (McIntosh, Chard, Boland, & Horner, 2006). So, this combination is working.

Some educators, researchers, and administrators propose adding another area to MTSS: social-emotional learning (Greenber, Domitrovich, Weissberg, & Durlak, 2017). Later in this chapter, you will learn about the Comprehensive, Integrated, Three-tiered (Ci3T) model of prevention; uniquely, it integrates academic (RTI), behavior (PBIS), and social-emotional learning supports (Lane, Oakes, Cantwell, & Royer, 2016).

Now, for the sake of review and clarity, take a look at Figure 5.1 again. You may have noticed that the base of the triangle identifies behavioral, academic, and social-emotional areas of learning. In doing so, Figure 5.1 depicts that all students need instruction and supports in all three areas. Ci3T responds to that need, and it does so by using the tier approach. It is, then, is a multi-tiered system of support; indeed, it is a framework for MTSS.

Almost every state has an initiative related to the use of school-wide systems (Horner & Sugai, 2015; Jimerson et al., 2016; McIntosh & Goodman, 2015). But, in each of these states and the schools in the states, educators make decisions about the best approach to school-wide systems, given the data that reveal specific needs of the states, schools, and students. The overall purpose does not change: to prevent problems and then to give students the instruction and supports they need.

In the sections that follow, we will teach you more about the three school-wide systems just named—PBIS for behavior, RTI for academics, and MTSS/Ci3T for behavior, academics, and social-emotional learning. You will learn how these three school-wide systems work, how the tiers operate within each. But remember that these are just examples of the implementation of school-wide systems. When you begin your teaching career, you will want to learn about the school-wide system that is in place, as participating in school-wide systems helps you keep your promise to support all students, including those with disabilities.

MyLab Education **Self-Check 5.1**

MyLab Education **Application Exercise 5.1:** A School-wide System of Supports

How to Implement School-wide Systems—Positive Behavior Interventions and Supports

Having read about the key features of school-wide systems, you are now prepared to learn about specific examples of school-wide systems of support. Remember reading about Kelsey's experiences at the beginning of the chapter? She benefited from a widely adopted and research-based school-wide system whose name you already know: SW-PBIS, school-wide positive behavior interventions and supports (sometimes also abbreviated as SWPBS, without a hyphen). And, it's not just Kelsey who benefits from SW-PBIS; over 20,000 schools across the United States are using SW-PBIS (Lewis et al., 2017).

Supporting students to be successful is not just about teaching academic skills. It is also about teaching and supporting students to develop and use nonacademic skills that are crucial to academic and life success. Given the issues surrounding discipline that you learned about in Chapter 2, you should not be surprised to know that educators increasingly focus on students' behavior. Academic progress depends in large part on prosocial behaviors. Both academic and behavior skills make it possible for a student to be included in the general curriculum, consistent with IDEA's principle of education in the least restrictive environment and with a focus on promoting dignity that comes with progress in any curriculum or environment. Kelsey is a prime example of that fact; the more her behaviors received attention, the better her academics became. She progressed to graduation, although, at various times through her senior year, she was at risk of not graduating.

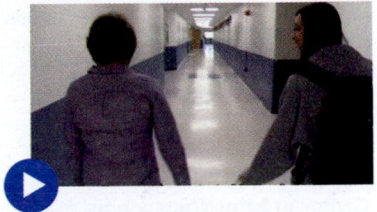

MyLab Education
Video Example 5.2
Pay attention to the factors that induce Kelsey to be involved in a SW-PBIS program that focuses on achieving in school and graduating. What supports are in place to help her be successful?

What Is SW-PBIS?

SW-PBIS has two focal points. First, it establishes school-wide expectations and practices at Tier 1; and, second, it supports groups of (Tier 2) and individual (Tier 3) students who need more intensive support to learn and use prosocial behaviors (Horner & Sugai, 2015). You should not be surprised to know that SW-PBIS uses both types of data that you learned about before—screening data and progress monitoring data—and team-based decision making to determine what and when students need additional supports. Indeed, SW-PBIS is a perfect example of a school-wide system of support. And, it has a long research pedigree.

SW-PBIS: THE EMERGENCE OF A RESEARCH-BASED APPROACH   SW-PBIS emerged from research beginning in the mid-1980s on individualized supports for students with the most significant behavioral support needs, including those with intellectual disability and autism spectrum disorders (Chapters 11 and 12, respectively). Individual PBIS focused on addressing behavior and communication challenges. Because it was data-driven, vigorously implemented, and carefully researched, the approach proved highly successful (Carr et al., 2002; Sugai et al., 2000).

To determine just how effective individual PBIS was, a team of researchers reviewed over 100 articles published between 1985 and 1996; each article reported research on individual PBIS. Collectively, the articles measured 366 different behavioral outcomes across grade levels and disability categories. This analysis concluded that individual PBIS caused an 80 percent reduction in problem behavior for approximately two thirds of the 366 behavioral outcomes (Carr et al., 1999). The analysis also concluded that the reduction in problem behavior was more likely than not when PBIS interventions were based on a functional behavioral assessment (FBA)—a process that enables educators to understand why students are engaging in the behaviors of concern so that they then may develop interventions based on that understanding. (You will learn more about these processes in Chapter 12.)

MyLab Education
Video Example 5.3
Learn more about how teachers set up PBIS systems in their classroom. How did the teacher set expectations for students and reinforce them for meeting them?

Learn more about SW-PBIS from the PBIS Technical Assistance Center at https://www.pbis.org/. Bookmark the site in your browser; it is the top website nationally and internationally on both individual PBIS and SW-PBIS.

Not surprisingly, as researchers and educators implemented individual PBIS, they learned they needed to pay attention to how students' behavior and environments interact. They discovered that changing environments was sometimes more effective than focusing on changing individual students. This understanding—that students' behaviors arose in part from the way schools operated and how teachers were prepared to teach appropriate behavior in a proactive and preventative way—caused the researchers to focus on school-wide interventions and supports.

School-wide PBIS still focuses on individual students, but it also creates supports for all students by redesigning school environments, particularly by making sure that all students will understand and meet clearly stated behavioral expectations (Horner et al., 2013). Consistent with the tiers approach in school-wide systems, SW-PBIS starts at the bottom of the triangle (look again at Figure 5.1), with a focus on behavior, providing high-quality instruction and supports for all students and offering more intensive interventions and supports for students who need it.

Given the results of individualized PBIS and the emergence of SW-PBIS, the U.S. Department of Education funded a technical assistance center in 1997 to develop and provide resources for teachers and schools. This center has been instrumental in transforming PBIS from a research-based individual approach to a research-based school-wide system. SW-PBIS is now about the whole school and is being used by schools across the country (Horner & Sugai, 2015; Sugai et al., 2000).

There is more to this transition from individual to school-wide support. The "more" is that SW-PBIS complies with IDEA. In Chapters 1 and 4, you learned that one of the five factors that an IEP team must consider is whether a student's behavior impedes the learning of that student or of others. If it does, the IEP team must then consider whether to use "positive behavioral interventions and supports" (the IDEA term) or other strategies to address the student's behavior. SW-PBIS is the research-based way of meeting this requirement for all students in a school, including those with an IEP or 504 plan. Kelsey, for example, benefited significantly from SW-PBIS at her school. You will read more about Kelsey later in this section and the role that SW-PBIS played in her success and that of other students in her school. Her school reduced its drop-out rate and increased its graduation rate, as we will make clear.

Implementing SW-PBIS

So, how, exactly, did SW-PBIS support Kelsey, and how does it support other students across the nation and world? When Kelsey started high school, there was a lack of clear expectations and reinforcement of positive behavior. Instead, the school responded to problems as they came up. Students were disciplined far more than their peers in other districts for a range of offenses, including dealing drugs, coming to class drunk, and failing to demonstrate competencies on statewide examinations. The school had shockingly low rates of graduation. Kelsey was on an all-too-typical path: discipline, failure, and drop-out without a diploma. What made the difference for her and her school? It was how the school shifted to a prevention approach by using SW-PBIS.

TIER 1 INTERVENTIONS AND SUPPORTS As you now know, Tier 1 SW-PBIS instruction and supports are universal—they are available to all students in a school. In a nutshell, they are a form of primary prevention: preventing behavioral issues before they occur. Tier 1 SW-PBIS instruction and supports make clear to all students what the school expects from them (Horner et al., 2013; Horner & Sugai, 2015). For example, when implementing SW-PBIS, a team, in concert with input from school personnel, families, and students, identifies three to five behavioral expectations for all students and—this is important—all faculty and administrators. Whoever interacts with Kelsey and any other student has the same set of expectations that they communicate in similar ways. By insisting on universal expectations for students' behavior and by reinforcing students for meeting these expectations, the administrators, faculty, and students support each other; they renew their commitment to a common code of behavior. The expectations are simple to understand, positively stated, and regularly reinforced. Here are four examples:

- Respect Yourself
- Respect Others
- Be Safe
- Be Responsible.

Having identified a small number of behavioral expectations, such as those listed above, the school community then takes action to put the expectations into effect, school-wide (universally). Here are some steps that school communities take (Bohanon et al., 2006; Horner & Sugai, 2015; Lane, Menzies, Ennis, & Oakes, 2015):

- *Clearly define behavioral expectations.* The definitions should be simple, positive, and succinct and available to all members of the school.

- *Teach behavioral expectations.* Educators and all members of the school community should teach each expectation explicitly across environments (e.g., classrooms, lunchrooms, and hallways), so all students know exactly what is expected of them everywhere in the school.

- *Frequently acknowledge appropriate behaviors.* A rule of thumb is to have at least four times as many positive affirmations as negative interactions for students' behavior; the strategy seeks a 4:1 ratio. For example, in the "ticket" system used at Kelsey's school, a student such as Kelsey received a "ticket" (like a traffic ticket) when she was "caught being good." She then could exchange the ticket for various positive reinforcers, such as school supplies. The ticket system has two important functions: (1) it makes explicit the school-wide expectations and (2) it recognizes the students who conform to the expectation because, unlike other students, they now have a "ticket" they can exchange for some particular and unusual benefit.

- *Use screening data to identify students who might need immediate, more intensive support.* For example, educators may screen students for indicators of depression or frequent issues with attendance, indicating a need for more intensive supports to address these issues and promote engagement in Tier 1 supports.

- *Use progress monitoring to document students' behavioral performance.* Educators will collect data on how many tickets they distribute and on how many students have discipline referrals or other behavioral issues that need more attention. They then will use these data to inform the school-wide behavior support team about what adjustments might need to happen to promote greater student engagement (see the next bulleted step). You soon will learn more about how to monitor progress and engage in data-based decision making in SW-PBIS.

- *Evaluate problems and adapt on an ongoing basis through a team approach.* A school-based team should routinely review data on school-wide discipline referral patterns as well as attendance and suspension rates. The team must focus on trends in where and when various types of behavior occur more frequently than other behavior throughout the school as a whole. Teams should also determine whether certain groups of students (e.g., those based on classes, race/ethnicity, gender, and disability) are disproportionately having problems (Chapter 2 described the issue of disproportionality.) The team can use the data to identify groups of or individual students who need more intense supports that will enable them to benefit from *universal, school-wide support.* After identifying the areas and students of need, the team will make decisions about providing Tier 2 supports to groups of students in specific environments in the school. The team will also analyze the environmental factors (e.g., classroom management practices or teacher attitudes) that may affect the groups of students with higher-than-average discipline referrals.

TIER 2 INTERVENTIONS AND SUPPORTS After implementing universal, Tier 1 supports in SW-PBIS, researchers found that approximately 15 to 20 percent of students needed more intensive support (Tier 2). In Tier 2, students receive support for "can't do" problems (e.g., students need to learn a skill) or "won't do" problems (e.g., students need supports to use a skill they already have) (Mitchell, Bruhn, & Lewis, 2016; Riffel & Mitchiner, 2015).

A widely used and thus good example of Tier 2 intervention is the check-in/check-out (CICO) intervention (Hawken & Breen, 2017). CICO emphasizes daily interactions between the student and school staff to promote the student's appropriate behavior. Although variations of CICO exist, the student usually meets twice daily with an adult mentor, once in the morning and once at the end of the day. In the morning, the student and mentor review the behavioral expectations for the day, which are specified on a daily progress report, and set a daily behavioral goal. The student receives feedback from teachers throughout the day, documents it on the Daily Progress Report, and then shares this information with the mentor at the end of the day. The student and mentor note successes, and the mentor delivers the reinforcer if the student has achieved the daily goal. The student can share the daily progress report with family members. A large majority of students who receive Tier 2 supports never require Tier 3 supports (Cheney, Flower, & Templeton, 2008).

At Kelsey's school, comprehensive Tier 2 supports were in place (Malloy, Bohanon, & Francoeur, 2018). Students who received Tier 2 supports, such as check-in/check-out, had better school attendance and behavioral outcomes, and their academic performance improved, too, because they were not dropping out as much as before and were more engaged in their learning. *Guidelines for Teaching*: *Key Interventions at Tiers 1 and 2* offers an overview of how Kelsey's school provided Tier 1 and Tier 2 interventions.

MyLab Education

Video Example 5.4

Kelsey has a team of people who help keep her on track. Why does regular checking in with faculty support Kelsey to progress in school?

Guidelines for Teaching

Key Interventions for Tiers 1 and 2

Tier 1

- Establish a Tier 1 leadership team and team leader with clear roles and responsibilities.
- Establish school-wide behavioral expectations.
- Provide staff-wide training on positive approaches to discipline and include guidelines and tools for implementation.
- Implement and provide training on the School-wide Information System (SWIS) to enable data-based decision making for early identification and problem solving (Sugai & Horner, 2010).
- Implement a "respect" intervention with (a) skits performed by teachers and students and (b) election of "respect student of the week" from each class and include a drawing for a prize.
- Implement additional interventions based on progress monitoring.

Tier 2

- Establish a Tier 2 team and coach to develop, implement, and monitor Tier 2 interventions.

- Conduct brief functional behavioral assessments of students receiving Tier 2 services and develop brief behavior support plans based on assessment results.

  - Implement check-in/check-out as a group-based intervention (Hawken & Breen, 2017)
  - Provide training
  - Establish a coordinator to oversee implementation and monitoring
  - Provide training to all faculty
  - Implement as a group-based intervention
  - Have students check in at the start of the day with a coordinator to review behavioral expectations and goals
  - Have teachers use a checklist to indicate the extent to which the student met the goals in each class
  - Have the student meet with the coordinator at the end of the day to review the score card with teacher feedback.

SOURCE: Based on Malloy, J. M., Bohanon, H., & Francoeur, K. (2018). Positive behavioral interventions and supports in high schools: A case study from New Hampshire. *Journal of Educational and Psychological Consultation*, 1–29. doi: 10.1080/10474412.2017.1385398

TIER 3 INTERVENTIONS AND SUPPORTS   Tier 3 interventions are for students who continue to struggle academically and behaviorally even during or after the time they received Tier 1 and 2 research-based interventions and supports (Mitchell et al., 2016). In Tier 3, as in Tier 2, educators use different interventions and supports to promote student outcomes. As we taught you earlier, SW-PBIS is individualized to each school and/or district, so each school will develop the best framework for implementing SW-PBIS for its particular situation, including the interventions and supports within Tiers 1, 2, and 3.

Commonly, Tier 3 supports might include a functional behavioral assessment (FBA). You read earlier that the purpose of an FBA is to determine *why* students are engaging in behaviors so educators can develop solutions tailored to the *why*. Cause and response go hand-in-hand. The educators then integrate cause and response into an individualized, behavior intervention plan (BIP) (O'Neill, Albin, Storey, Horner, & Sprague, 2015). Kelsey benefited from Tier 2 supports, but the data suggested she still was struggling with attendance, acting out in class, and making progress on her goals. At Kelsey's school, students who did not respond to Tier 2 interventions after 6 weeks or who had six or more discipline referrals in a 4-week period then received Tier 3 supports. The Tier 2 interventions are in *Guidelines for Teaching*: *Key Interventions at Tiers 1 and 2*.

The first step in providing those Tier 3 supports for Kelsey was for the behavior support team to conduct an FBA and learn (1) what triggered her behavioral challenges (her frustration at not being able to do the work she was assigned and at having to wait for her teacher to respond to her request for help) and (2) where her behavioral challenges occurred most often (in math class). The behavioral support team at her school (the principal, counselor, one or two of Kelsey's teachers, and Kelsey) then developed a plan for preventing her behavior (frequent and, when possible, immediate or quick responses to her) by teaching her new strategies to request help and wait for that help to occur.

Kelsey's team also decided that she would benefit from additional individualized supports offered through Project RENEW—Rehabilitation for Empowerment, Natural supports, Education, and Work. Project RENEW was developed by researchers at the University of New Hampshire's Institute for Disability Studies. The focus of this Tier 3 intervention was to equip Kelsey with skills that would help her with the transition to adulthood, developing the prosocial skills that would be needed in environments she wanted to work and learn in as an adult.

Project RENEW has four phases: (1) engagement and personal futures planning, (2) team development and planning, (3) implementation and monitoring, and (4) transition to less intensive supports. *Guidelines for Teaching*: *Four Phases of RENEW—A Tier 3 Intervention* includes the steps taken by RENEW's leaders in implementing the four phases.

The RENEW program has impressive successful outcomes (Malloy et al., 2018). Why? As we said, it is because RENEW is comprehensive and provides supports for students who, based on data about them, need intensive, individualized supports. The school team that participates in RENEW includes school staff, family, and community members. Also, all students have a written action plan. Each student's action plan generates high school academic credits and includes independent study, internships, and community learning experiences.

In one evaluation of RENEW, only 1 of the 25 students receiving support dropped out before graduating; except for the 5 who moved out of New Hampshire, all of the other students, including Kelsey, brought their grades up enough to graduate with a regular diploma or general equivalency diploma (GED) (Malloy et al., 2017).

Now, we bet you could have guessed that Kelsey graduated from high school. But, we bet you could not have predicted this about Kelsey: After graduating, she became a RENEW consultant, teaching students and faculty in schools inside and outside New Hampshire about RENEW.

MyLab Education
Video Example 5.5
Kelsey's action plans for the future involve employment and community college. What other goals does Kelsey have that surprise you?

The Institute for Disability Studies at the University of New Hampshire offers all of its RENEW resources for free on its website. Go to https://iod.unh.edu/ and enter Project RENEW in the search function. The institute also provides professional development related to RENEW for facilitators who implement RENEW, coaches who mentor new facilitators, and trainers who provide training to new facilitators and coaches.

Guidelines for Teaching

Four Phases of RENEW—A Tier 3 Intervention

Phase 1: Engage in futures planning.

- Identify students and invite their participation
- Conduct futures planning

  - Identify the student's dreams, goals, strengths, preferences, challenges, and sources of support
  - Support students to prioritize goals in order to pick one for immediate attention

Phase 2: Engage in initial planning and develop team.
Facilitator and student . . .

- Develop an action plan
  - Focus on initial goal by brainstorming action steps to accomplish the goal
  - Identify resource people within the student's family and social network
- Invite people to join the team to support the student

- Plan and implement team meetings
- Support the student to conduct the meeting
- Support the student to select what actions to pursue

Phase 3: Implement and monitor the plan.
Student and team . . .

- Arrange for team to have regular meetings to plan actions to accomplish goals
  - Work on one goal at a time
  - Track progress
  - Problem solve when obstacles are encountered and readjust as needed
- When the first goal has been implemented successfully, circle back to phase 2 and iteratively go through the process

Phase 4: Transition to less intensive supports.
Student and facilitator . . .

- Implement one goal after another
- Transition out of RENEW once goals have been accomplished and the student has mastered the skills of problem solving

SOURCE: Based on Drake, J., & Malloy, J. (2015). A practice guide to implementing RENEW in high schools. Retrieved from https://iod.unh.edu/sites/default/files/renew_implementation_in_high_schools_rdq_practice_guide_0.pdf

SWIS: A TOOL FOR DATA-BASED DECISION MAKING AND TEAMING   In the previous sections about the three tiers of instruction and support in SW-PBIS, you learned about the differing intensities of supports that are available across the three tiers. You also learned that educators collect and use data to make decisions and solve problems when students face various challenges.

Schools using SW-PBIS collect and use screening and progress monitoring data in different ways. A widely used tool is the School-Wide Information System (SWIS) (May et al., 2000). SWIS enables educators to collect and organize data at the student, classroom, and school levels. For example, they might collect data on indicators such as attendance and discipline referrals. Remember how Kelsey's team used these data? The team used the data to address the interaction between academic achievement and behavioral challenges. Similarly, SWIS generates graphs and reports that can enable teams to:

- Understand more thoroughly what is happening in the school as a whole
- Monitor and evaluate the frequency and types of discipline referrals
- Track whether students are meeting behavioral goals
- Document the effect of Tier 2 and Tier 3 supports.

Remember that Kelsey's team looked at data on her class attendance, her acting out in class, and progress on her goals. These data, collected via SWIS, enabled her team to decide what support Kelsey needed in her current or next tier.

Educators can use SWIS to understand not just one student's experiences, but also trends in school-wide discipline referrals and other indicators that might prompt changes at Tier 1. For example, SWIS data enable educators to determine whether students need more instruction on behavioral expectations. The same data-change process can happen at Tier 2. For example, if students are participating in check-in/check-out, data collected through SWIS on a student's check-ins and progress toward goals will affect the nature or extent of the support a student receives. Overall, the graphs of the various sources of data entered into SWIS over time, across settings, and for individual and groups of students help the team make data-based decisions to support students as they move between tiers, ensuring the students' progress (Tobin, Lewis-Palmer, & Sugai, 2002).

After entering data into SWIS or another system like it, teams need a systematic process for evaluating the data and graphs that a system like SWIS can produce. One such system is the Team-Initiated Problem-Solving (TIPS) process (Newton, Todd, Algozzine, Horner, & Algozzine, 2009; Newton, Horner, Todd, Algozzine, & Algozzine, 2012). The Team-Initiated Problem-Solving process guides teams through five steps:

- Identifying problems
- Developing hypotheses
- Identifying solutions
- Implementing an action plan
- Evaluating and revising the action plan.

These sound like the steps you take when solving a problem, right? Using data to figure out the best way to support students in SW-PBIS is essentially like solving a problem. You can engage in this process individually or with a team. Working with a team gives you the opportunity to bounce ideas off each other. To work as a team to solve a problem, behavior support teams typically take the following steps:

- Collect data (using a system like SWIS) and organize the data in ways that are understandable to all members of the team.
- Convene team members regularly so they may interpret the data and generate solutions to problems that are identified for the school, for groups of students, or for individual students.
- Use the data to identify problem areas, generate potential solutions, and implement and test those solutions.
- Bear in mind that the process is iterative—data should be used to identify changes in students' needs over time and then to determine whether one or more students move to or from Tiers 1, 2, or 3.
- The problem-solving process can promote greater understanding of what does or does not work across all tiers. Assume, for example, that all students are struggling at Tier 1 and that the rate of absenteeism and suspensions is still high. It is fair to conclude that Tier 1 needs to change. Educators might need to revisit their behavioral expectations or how they teach them. They might find it useful to talk with students and their families to make sure the expectations are congruent with the values of all members of the school community.
- Problem solving must stay goal-oriented (improving outcomes for all students) and continue until there is data-based evidence of improvement.

Ultimately, data are a necessary part of problem solving, and "effective problem solving requires access to the right data, in the right form, at the right time" (Algozzine et al., 2015, p. 213).

When engaging all members of the school community in identifying expectations and using data-based decision making, educators should take into account the perspectives of all such members: the senior and mid-level administrators, teachers, school psychologists, related service professionals, students, and families (Eagle et al., 2015; McIntosh, Kelm, & Canizal Delabra, 2016). It can be particularly useful to engage families in SW-PBIS. Families can be part of the SW-PBIS leadership team, and ensuring they have an equal voice in the data-based decision-making process is critical to

Visit https://www.pbisapps.org/ to find examples of SWIS and how it is applied in schools. Can you find videos that show you how the SWIS Suite works?

Visit www.pbis.org and search for TIPS. See what you can learn about how the TIPS meeting works as presented in the Team Meeting Videos.

MyLab Education

Video Example 5.6

How do teachers apply the idea of *all means all* to behavioral expectations for students with and without disabilities?

success (Garbacz et al., 2016). Including them can promote better family-professional partnerships to implement SW-PBIS across home and school, enhancing home-school communication and shared expectations (Chapter 3).

Research Outcomes

Remember, Kelsey is the "yes . . . but" student: Yes, she's had problems; but with the right instruction and supports, she was able to build on her strengths and succeed. SW-PBIS was a part of those "right" supports for her.

It is the same for other students, too; the general rule is that SW-PBIS works (Nese & McIntosh, 2016). Data from high schools in 37 states that implemented SW-PBIS showed SW-PBIS plays an important role in reducing problem behaviors and improving school attendance, graduation, and climate in hundreds of elementary, middle, and high schools (Freeman et al., 2016). Likewise, a relationship exists between changes in the behavior outcomes targeted through SW-PBIS and academic changes. In over 2000 elementary schools in Florida in which SW-PBIS has been implemented for over 10 years, researchers observed small, positive effects of SW-PBIS on academic outcomes in reading and math (Gage, Leite, Childs, & Kincaid, 2017).

Researchers are investigating how to use SW-PBIS to reduce disparities in discipline referrals for children and youth from diverse backgrounds using practices you learned about in Chapter 2. You will recall that in Chapter 2 you read about the Grandfather Teachings at the Ponemah Elementary School on the Red Lake Indian Reservation. These Grandfather Teachings were the school-wide expectations for the SW-PBIS program. They exemplify how culturally responsive approaches can be part of SW-PBIS. Overall, teams implementing SW-PBIS can benefit from using (1) cultural knowledge and self-awareness, (2) a commitment to culturally relevant practices, and (3) culturally valid decision-making skills to promote equitable outcomes for all students (Vincent, Randall, Cartledge, Tobin, & Swain-Bradway, 2011).

SW-PBIS is one of the most promising school-wide system reform initiatives available to promote positive, prosocial behavior. It is not, however, the only reform initiative. Other school-wide systems target other important areas, such as academic learning, as you will learn next.

MyLab Education Self-Check 5.2

MyLab Education Application Exercise 5.2: School-wide Positive Behavior Intervention Supports

---

How to Implement School-wide Systems—Response to Intervention

You have just learned about how the key features of school-wide systems are implemented in SW-PBIS, focusing on students' behavior. You also discovered that SW-PBIS can affect academic outcomes. So, imagine the effect that school-wide systems can have when they target academic learning and progress. Don't just imagine it; learn about it. It's called "RTI."

What Is RTI?

Response to intervention (RTI) is a framework that uses the key features of school-wide systems to promote effective instruction and supports for learning. Like SW-PBIS, RTI focuses on using tiered supports and data-based decision making to benefit all students, not with respect to their behavior but rather with respect to their learning of essential academic content (Jimerson et al., 2016; McIntosh & Goodman, 2016). It applies research-based instructional practices to teach academic content and ensure that students have early access to effective instruction (Jimerson et al., 2016).

RTI: PROMOTING ACADEMIC PROGRESS FOR ALL STUDENTS RTI received attention in general and special education in the early 1990s as a means of reforming how instruction was delivered for all students, particularly reading instruction for young children (Gersten, Jayanthi, & Dimino, 2017). In its early iteration, RTI's purpose was to intervene early to *prevent* ongoing problems; note the emphasis on prevention. It centered on early screening for problems, high-quality instruction for all students, and the use of data to identify students who needed intensive intervention in order to make academic progress.

Soon RTI became a strategy for identifying students who might have specific learning disabilities (Chapter 7). Indeed, in 2004, Congress reauthorized IDEA and permitted state and local education agencies the option of using RTI as a means of identifying students with those disabilities. The basic idea was that if RTI was being implemented and all students were receiving high-quality instruction and supports for academic learning and progress, it would be easier to determine if a student's academic needs were the result of a learning disability or ineffective instruction (D. Fuchs & Fuchs, 2017; Miciak, Fletcher, & Stuebing, 2016).

It appears from recent data that at least 45 states recommend RTI for educators to organize instruction and supports for all students (Hudson & McKenzie, 2016), and between 16 and 20 states require educators to either partially or completely implement RTI to identify students with learning disabilities (Zirkel, 2017). RTI is not just about special education and identifying students with learning disabilities, even though it was included in IDEA in that regard. It is also about general education and focusing on all students and instructional staff; RTI is a school-wide intervention. Further, it aligns with the Every Student Succeeds Act (ESSA; Chapter 1) because it uses research-based practices to support academic learning and progress (Gersten et al., 2017).

Frameworks for RTI have even been extended to the delivery of intervention to students with gifts and talents (Johnsen, Parker, & Farah, 2015). Indeed, nine states have adopted statutes with specific attention to gifted students in their RTI or tiered systems of supports frameworks (National Association for Gifted Children & the Council of State Directors of Programs for the Gifted, 2015). The short summary is that RTI benefits typical students and two types of exceptional students—those with disabilities and those who have unusual gifts and talents (Chapter 17). The National Center on Response to Intervention is a hub for information about RTI for state and local education agencies, families, teachers, and students such as yourself.

> The National Center on RTI provides freely accessible webinars, modules, and other resources for administrators, educators, and families. Go to https://www.rti4success.org/ to access RTI resources.

We told you at the beginning of this chapter that there is no single model for implementing school-wide systems and that many advances are occurring even as you are reading this book. This holds especially true for RTI. It is a relatively new strategy, and the means for implementing it effectively are still emerging. The curriculum areas to which it primarily applies are literacy (especially reading) and math.

It appears that "virtually all educators are familiar with RTI" but there are "many models and variations of models that compete with one another across the country" (D. Fuchs & Fuchs, 2017, p. 255). Nonetheless, all RTI models should include the key features of school-wide systems that you have already learned about. In the sections that follow, you will find examples of how tiered supports, screening and progress monitoring, and data-based decision making and teaming are relevant across grades and content areas to organize instruction and supports using an RTI framework. Whatever RTI model educators use, its ultimate goal is to provide a research-based framework that will enable all students to learn and progress in the general education curriculum.

Implementing RTI

That being the goal, and because RTI is a school-wide model, RTI uses screening data to identify students who may struggle with only Tier 1 instruction; these data permit educators to know what instruction they should intensify through Tier 2 and 3 supports. Similarly, RTI relies on progress monitoring to determine how and when students need to move across the tiers.

In the sections that follow, we will give examples of some interventions and supports that educators might consider at Tiers 1, 2, and 3. Let's start with the key concepts. Look at Figure 5.2. This figure highlights key aspects of Tiers 1, 2, and 3 for reading instruction. Even though the figure relates to reading instruction, its principles generalize to math, as you will soon learn. For example, you can see the differences between the focus and types of instruction delivered across the tiers. The figure is consistent with the focus on tiered supports and intensifying instruction. As you might expect from what you learned about SW-PBIS, the groupings and the amount of instructional time at Tiers 2 and 3 are increasingly more intensive than at Tier 1.

 This IRIS instructional module will teach you more about RTI and how it can be implemented in schools. This specific module is the first of five modules in a series that provide information on and examples of RTI. https://iris.peabody.vanderbilt.edu/module/rti01/

TIER 1 INSTRUCTION AND SUPPORTS You know that prevention is a key part of school-wide systems like RTI. In Tier 1 of RTI, prevention occurs by ensuring that all students have access to instruction that is guided by a research-based scope and sequence of knowledge and skills (Foorman & Wanzek, 2016). You might be wondering, what exactly is a research-based scope and sequence of knowledge and skills? Let's think about reading and how Tier 1 was defined in Figure 5.2, implementing Tiers 1, 2, and 3 for reading instruction.

Figure 5.2 Implementing Tiers 1, 2, and 3 for Reading Instruction

	Tier 1	Tier 2	Tier 3
Definitions	Implement reading instruction and programs and administer screening assessments.	Use instructional intervention in small groups to supplement, enhance, and support Tier 1.	Extend individualized reading instruction in groups of 1–3 students beyond the time allocated for Tier 1.
Focus	Include all students.	Identify students with reading difficulties who have not responded to Tier 1 efforts.	Identify students with marked difficulties in reading or with reading difficulties who have not responded adequately to Tier 1 and Tier 2 efforts.
Program	Provide scientifically based reading instruction and curriculum, emphasizing the critical elements.	Provide specialized, scientifically based reading instruction and curriculum emphasizing the critical elements.	Provide sustained, intensive, scientifically based reading instruction and curriculum highly responsive to students' needs.
Instruction	Provide sufficient opportunities to practice throughout the school day.	Provide additional attention, focus, and support.	Provide carefully designed and implemented, explicit, systematic instruction.
Interventionist	Provide instruction through general education teacher.	Provide instruction through personnel determined by the school (e.g., classroom teacher, specialized reading teacher, other trained personnel).	Provide instruction through personnel determined by the school (e.g., specialized reading teacher, special education teacher).
Setting	Provide instruction in a general education classroom.	Provide instruction in an appropriate setting designated by the school.	Provide instruction in an appropriate setting designated by the school.
Grouping	Provide instruction through flexible grouping.	Provide instruction through homogeneous small group instruction (e.g., 1:4, 1:5).	Provide instruction through homogeneous instruction in smaller groups (e.g., 1:2, 1:3).
Time	Provide instruction for minimum of 90 minutes per day.	Provide instruction for 20–30 minutes per day in addition to Tier 1.	Provide instruction for 50-minute sessions (or longer) per day depending upon appropriateness of Tier 1 and Tier 2.
Assessment	Administer screening assessments at beginning, middle, and end of academic year.	Administer progress monitoring twice a month on target skill to ensure adequate progress and learning.	Administer progress monitoring at least twice a month on target skill to ensure adequate progress and learning.

SOURCES: Adapted from Vaughn Gross Center for Reading and Language Arts at The University of Texas at Austin. (2005). *Implementing the 3-tier reading model: Reducing reading difficulties for kindergarten through third grade students* (2nd ed.). Austin, TX: Author; Vaughn, S., & Roberts, G. (2007). Secondary interventions in reading: Providing additional instruction for students at risk. *TEACHING Exceptional Children, 39*, 40–46; Klinger, J. K., Vaughn, S., & Boardman, A. (2015). *Teaching reading comprehension to students with learning difficulties* (2nd ed.). New York: Guilford Press.

For example, under "program" in Figure 5.2, it says to "provide scientifically based reading instruction and curriculum emphasizing the critical elements." So the first step in determining a research-based scope and sequence of knowledge and skills is figuring out what the critical elements are. This is what schools do when they are determining the Tier 1 instruction and supports they want to provide for reading (or any other content area).

A large amount of research has been done over the past three decades to identify key skills associated with reading. For example, strong readers know phonological structures and alphabetic principles. Understanding phonological structure involves understanding how individual sounds combine to make words. Understanding alphabetic principles involves understanding how symbols in words connect with speech (American Educational Research Association, 2009; Foorman & Wanzek, 2016).

In addition to grasping phonological structures and alphabetic principles, strong readers also need to develop fluency in these skills, building reading comprehension as they learn to map letters to sounds, and sounds to words, while reading longer and more complex texts. So, both the skills associated with reading and having multiple opportunities to build comprehension and fluency are important (Jimerson et al., 2016; Klinger, Vaughn, & Boardman, 2015).

In RTI you are not limited to one specific curriculum or set of instructional practices to use; instead, you can focus on selecting research-based curricula and instruction practices that most affect student learning outcomes and are consistent with the school context.

Many schools have adopted reading programs that are commercially available and provide instructional materials with a research-based scope and sequence of knowledge and skills. Two examples of such curricula are *Reading Street* and *Imagine It* (Cuticelli, Collier-Meek, & Coyne, 2016). Each teaches core reading skills. Each also focuses on engaging students and getting them excited about reading. Increasing students' motivation and engagement can lead to better learning outcomes (Wexler, Vaughn, & Swanson, 2016). Also, noncommercial curricula and strategies teach early literature skills (Solari, Denton, & Haring, 2017; Spear-Swerling, in press).

Explore the Reading Street curriculum at https://www.pearsonschool.com/index.cfm?locator=PS1gC9. Can you understand how the lesson aligns with Tier 1 instruction?

So far, we've focused on how educators apply RTI to teaching reading skills. RTI is also being applied to other domains of learning. As in reading, instruction in mathematics consists of a core set of critical skills and specific instructional practices. The research-based scope and sequence of knowledge and critical skills include:

- Teaching whole numbers in elementary school and rational numbers (i.e., a number that can be expressed as an integer or quotient) in middle school
- Providing explicit and systematic instruction (e.g., teach students models or strategies to solve problems and verbalize thought processes)
- Teaching word problem–solving skills
- Including visual representations
- Providing a range of examples (Gersten et al., 2009; Jitendra & Dupuis, 2016).

Specific instructional practices exist to teach these skills. For example, when teaching word problem–solving skills, you may use schema-based instruction. This type of instruction focuses on teaching your students to understand the structure of word problems and then to identify similar problems and transfer skills among problems. You teach by

- Changing problems (the problem calls for an increase or decrease in the quantity)
- Grouping problems (the problem calls for combining groups to form a larger group)
- Comparing (the problem calls for identifying similarities and differences between sets).

Students then learn a systematic process to understand the problem structure, use a visual representation to depict the problem structure, learn the steps to solve the different types of problems, and apply those steps (Jitendra & Dupuis, 2016).

At this point, it is not important that you understand the specifics of teaching reading and math concepts at the Tier 1 level, given the availability of entire courses

MyLab Education

Video Example 5.7

Tier 1 instruction is for all students in the class. In what ways did the teacher enable the class to identify key steps in solving story problems?

and professional development resources to which you will be exposed in much more detail in your ongoing education. What is important for you to understand is that Tier 1 instruction identifies the research-based scope and sequence of knowledge and skills and uses research-based curricula and instructional practices to teach these skills. Only by providing research-based instruction and supports can all students have the opportunity to learn and progress in the general curriculum.

TIER 2 INSTRUCTION AND SUPPORTS In RTI, just as in SW-PBIS, Tier 2 instruction and supports are for students who struggle with achieving the Tier 1 learning outcomes. Students typically receive Tier 2 supports if educators who have monitored their progress have concluded they need more intensive intervention. Tier 2 supports are designated to occur over a limited amount of time, in small groups, and with an embedded progress monitoring system to evaluate the effectiveness of the intervention with regard to the targeted skill. The key features in Tier 2 interventions are as follows:

- Supplemental to Tier 1 (e.g., provided additional and more intensive content in key skills)
- Research-based
- Clear, with an implementation manual that includes all materials needed by teachers
- Delivered by a skilled teacher with small groups of students (L. S. Fuchs et al., 2018).

Guidelines for Teaching: Intensifying Instruction at Tier 2 provides more details on specific areas to think about when implementing Tier 2 interventions across content areas.

Guidelines for Teaching

Intensifying Instruction at Tier 2

Review the guidelines below. For case examples and more information on how RTI has been used for students with disabilities at Tiers 2 and 3, visit: http://images.pearsonclinical.com/images/ca/rti/rti_scenarios.htm

Intensifying Instruction to Support Cognitive Processing.

- Students need to develop strategies that help them engage with learning, often called self-regulation skills.
- Teaching students to set goals for their learning, to learn strategies to remember important skills related to learning (e.g., parts of a paragraph, ways to solve an equation), and to organize their learning can be beneficial.
- These strategies can promote greater empowerment and motivation in learning activities.

Intensifying Instructional Delivery.

- When more intense instruction at Tier 2 is provided, it is important to make it systematic and explicit instruction.
- The steps in learning tasks should be broken down and communicated in multiple and concrete ways.
- Learning tasks should be broken down into manageable chunks.
- Peers and educators can model the completion of learning activities.

- Students should also have multiple opportunities to respond and develop confidence in their understanding.

Intensifying Learning Time.

- Tier 2 instruction provides more opportunities for instruction, practice, and feedback.
- This can be accomplished by providing more frequent instruction, by providing longer units of instruction, or by increasing the length of the intervention.
- Overall, there is no clear evidence for the "right" increase in learning time, particularly for older students. However, in elementary school, evidence suggests that 20 weeks of intervention might be most useful at Tier 2. With other students, more time may be needed, given longer learning histories.

Intensifying Instruction by Reducing Instructional Group Size.

- Consider smaller learning groups (Tier 2) and one-on-one instruction (Tier 3).
- At Tier 2 for reading instruction, providing instruction to 3 to 4 students has been shown to be effective. There is mixed evidence for one-to-one instruction. It appears that students might benefit from learning with peers.

SOURCE: Based on Vaughn, S., Wanzek, J., Murray, C. S., & Roberts, G. (2012). *Intensive interventions for students struggling in reading and mathematics: A practice guide*. Portsmouth, NH: RMC Research Corporation, Center on Instruction.

The What Works Clearinghouse contains a research-based practice guide that describes Tier 2 supports across content areas. The guide for reading is titled "Assisting Students Struggling with Reading: Response to Intervention (RtI) and Multi-Tier Intervention in the Primary Grades." It recommends

- Focusing on up to three foundational reading skills (e.g., letter sounds, fluency, vocabulary, comprehension) during instruction
- Providing instruction in small groups of three to four students who score below the benchmark (i.e., a score that suggests the student needs more instruction in skills critical to the Tier 1 curriculum)
- Delivering instruction 3 and 5 times a week for 20 to 40 minutes (Gersten et al., 2008).

You can access the entire guide at https://ies.ed.gov/ncee/wwc/PracticeGuide/3

When providing Tier 2 interventions in math, educators create more opportunities for:

- Systematic, explicit instruction
- Procedural strategies
- Cumulative review
- Motivators to promote positive behavior (L. S. Fuchs, Fuchs, & Malone, 2016).

You'll learn more about some of these specific instruction practices in Chapter 6 and in the exceptionality-specific chapters that follow, but an example of Tier 2 math instruction that addresses these areas is Pirate Math Secondary Prevention (L. S. Fuchs, Powell, Schumacher, Seethaler, & Fuchs, 2017).

This approach to instruction focuses on teaching students to solve word problems at the 2nd-grade level. The curriculum includes 39 lessons, so students receive instruction for 13 weeks, with 3 sessions per week for 30 minutes (in addition to the core curriculum or Tier 1 instruction—there is also a Pirate Math Whole Class Instructional Program for Tier 1). Pirate Math Secondary Prevention focuses on providing more intensive instruction involving single- and double-digit word problems. It includes scripts for teachers and activities to promote students' motivation and engagement (e.g., students can earn points during the lesson and then use points for rewards in the "treasure chest"). Students who are taught with Pirate Math at Tier 2 have shown greater gains in computation and word problem solving than students who struggled with word problems but did not receive the Pirate Math intervention (L. S. Fuchs et al., 2016).

Explore the Pirate Math curriculum at https://vkc.mc.vanderbilt.edu/fuchs-dev/pirate-math/. Can you understand how the curriculum could help build math skills?

TIER 3 INSTRUCTION AND SUPPORTS   If progress monitoring data continue to suggest that students struggle even as they access Tier 2 interventions and supports, intervention and supports are further intensified by adding Tier 3 supports. The What Works Clearinghouse, in its practice guide "Assisting Students Struggling with Reading: Response to Intervention (RtI) and Multi-Tier Intervention in the Primary Grades" suggests that, when students continue to struggle with Tier 2 supports, Tier 3 supports should focus on:

- Targeting a smaller number of the highest priority reading skills
- Providing multiple and extended instructional sessions
- Providing these instructional sessions one-on-one or in small groups
- Providing frequent feedback based on responses
- Teaching to mastery
- Individualizing (Gersten et al., 2008).

Because of the importance of Tier 3 intensive intervention, the U.S. Department of Education

Rawpixel/123RF

Tier 2 interventions are delivered with small groups of students and promote explicit instruction that teaches students critical skills to access the curriculum.

Visit and bookmark https://intensiveintervention.org/. This will be a key website for your professional practice.

funded a National Center, the National Center on Intensive Intervention (NCII), that provides resources for state and local education agencies to deliver more intensive interventions in an individualized, research-based way.

The National Center on Intensive Intervention states that:

> Intensive intervention helps students with severe and persistent learning and behavioral needs, including students with disabilities. It is a process, not a specific program or product. The process is driven by data, characterized by increased intensity and individualization, and considers the academic and behavioral needs of the student. In some schools, intensive intervention may be known as "Tier 3 intervention."

The NCII has a list of various formal and informal assessments: https://intensiveintervention.org/resource/informal-academic-diagnostic-assessment-using-data-guide-intensive-instruction-dbi. What assessments might be useful to learn more about?

To effectively deliver Tier 3 intervention, NCII recommends "data-based individualization." Data-based individualization refers to the process of identifying students who do not respond to Tier 2 interventions and supports and then collecting data on possible causes of their non-response. That is the same approach that SW-PBIS uses with respect to behavior; the functional behavioral assessment (FBA) determines the cause of non-response in SW-PBIS. In RTI, you analyze a student's reading or math performance to identify specific patterns of errors. Your analysis then is the basis of your recommendation for Tier 3 interventions.

The Taxonomy of Intervention Intensity (L. S. Fuchs et al., 2018) is helpful in devising individualized instruction. *Into Practice Across Grade Levels*: *Applying the Taxonomy of Intervention Intensity* provides more details on the seven elements of the taxonomy and how to implement them. Specifically, it highlights that ongoing data should be collected to determine the impact of Tier 3 interventions. If students continue to not show progress, then ongoing assessment of the potential causes of non-response as well as adaptation of the interventions and supports being utilized is necessary.

Into Practice Across Grade Levels

Applying the Taxonomy of Intervention Intensity

Strength. The research findings on how powerful the intervention is for the targeted outcome. *Example*: A teacher can go to the What Works Clearinghouse to identify the evidence for a particular intervention.

Dosage. The frequency with which the student is exposed to instruction and receives feedback from the teacher. *Example*: Recommendations for how frequently the intervention is delivered and how the teacher delivers feedback are followed—for instance, if the instruction should be delivered 4 times a week for 35 minutes, with feedback, provided this occurs. And, if there are supposed to be 20 opportunities for a student to respond and receive feedback during each instructional session, the teacher tracks the data to make sure this happens.

Alignment. The degree to which there is a focus on priority academic skills that are linked to success in Tier 1 and Tier 2 skills, e.g., grade-level and general curriculum content. *Example*: Assessment information on the highest priority skills is used to select instructional targets. For instance, if the highest priority skill is reading comprehension, research-based practices for grade-level reading comprehension skills will be targeted.

Attention to Transfer. The degree to which generalization to other contexts and formats is emphasized. *Example*: A plan is in place for making sure students recognize the connections between what they have learned and other skills they have mastered. If a student is learning vocabulary, for instance, a plan is in place to make sure they can recognize the word and use it in different instructional contexts.

Comprehensiveness. The degree to which explicit instruction is incorporated into instructional sessions. *Example*: The instruction is delivered using principles of explicit instruction, including use of simple and direct language, modeling strategies, ensuring background knowledge, fading support, and providing practice.

Behavioral and Academic Support. Principles to promote engagement in academic learning are present. *Example*: Students are taught self-regulation skills so they can more effectively engage in their own learning. Effective behavior supports are in place to promote greater engagement in academic learning.

Individualization. Ongoing data are collected to adjust intervention based on learning needs. *Example*: Progress monitoring data are used to make adjustments to Tier 3 supports.

SOURCE: Adapted from Fuchs, L. S., Fuchs, D., & Malone, A. S. (2018). The taxonomy of intervention intensity. *TEACHING Exceptional Children, 50*(4), 194–202. doi:10.1177/0040059918758166; National Center on Intensive Intervention (n.d.), Validated intervention program. Retrieved from: https://intensiveintervention.org/intensive-intervention/validated-intervention-program

Team-Based Decision Making Across Tiers

You've already read about the role of data, both screening and progress monitoring data, across the three tiers as implemented in RTI. But, you have not yet learned about specific data systems. Commonly used screening tools include academic screeners such as AIMSweb (Pearson Education, 2008) and the Dynamic Indicators of Basic Early Literacy Skills (DIBELS; Good et al., 2004). AIMSweb includes screening and progress monitoring tools for reading and math for students in grades K through 8. These tools are aligned with key skills that are aligned with success in these domains, as we have described in the Tier 1 sections. These screening tools can be completed quickly—most only take between 1 and 4 minutes. Then these data can guide instruction and enable data-based decision making.

Visit https://www.aimsweb.com/ to learn more about AIMSweb and how it can be used for academic screening, progress monitoring, and data-based decision making in schools.

You also already learned, in the Tier 3 Instruction and Supports section, about how to engage in data-based individualization. Whether focused on Tier 3 data-based individualization or evaluation of the efficacy of Tier 1 supports for all students, or Tier 2 supports for smaller groups of students, team-based decision making is a critical component of the process of interpreting academic screening and progress monitoring data.

As you found out earlier in the chapter, the types of teams used in RTI can vary. Teams can operate at the classroom level, when general and special educators and paraprofessionals work together to review student data and determine the need for more intensive instruction (Abbott, Beecher, Petersen, Greenwood, & Atwater, 2017). Teams can also operate at the grade level, when all teachers who interact with students in, for example, grade 3, work together to identify students who are struggling or may need further instructional supports, and review the screening and progress monitoring data to make decisions about providing targeted instruction at Tier 2 for small groups of students with similar learning needs. Or, in later grades it may be that content teams are used, when all members of the Math or English department, for example, will meet along with a specialized math or reading interventionist and special education teachers to identify areas of need specific to the content area being targeted (McIntosh & Goodman, 2015).

While meeting, team members need a structure for quantifying the following:

- Student rates of responsiveness to instruction to identify those who need more intensive interventions (e.g., which students are struggling at Tiers 1 and 2)

- Instructional effectiveness when intervention is intensified (e.g., do Tier 2 and 3 supports work to address the learning problems encountered by a student or group of students)

- Next steps for determining more intensive interventions, as needed (e.g., using the data-based individualization process to develop individualized interventions) (National Center on Response to Intervention, 2010).

By following these steps, team members can make data-based recommendations (Crone et al., 2016). That is so because these decision rules provide a framework for determining the expected progress in learning (e.g., learn 10 vocabulary words) and then determining the student's actual progress (e.g., the target student has learned 1 word).

Graphing conventions (which are available in some data systems) can enable decisions to be made by a teacher or a team about needed changes in instruction intensity (Deno, 2016). To see examples of graphs, and examples of how teams use data to make decisions with regard to reading and mathematics, visit the RTI Action Network, which includes articles written by implementers of RTI on how data are used.

The RTI Action Network http://www.rtinetwork.org/ includes great resources on team-based decision making. Visit the Connect with Others section to discover how educators are using RTI across the country.

Research Outcomes

A wide body of research exists about the positive effect of RTI on academic outcomes. Researchers analyzed 37 studies (published between 2000 and 2015) about RTI and academic success. They found that positive effects occurred for students in grades 4 through 12 when effective Tier 1 reading instruction was delivered. Students who were "at risk" for reading problems showed greater growth than their peers who did not receive Tier 1 interventions (Swanson et al., 2017).

Even when students continue to need more intensive supports, there are effective interventions for teaching critical skills for success in reading and math. For example, researchers examined the effect of Tier 2 mathematics interventions; in one study, a curriculum called ROOTS that provides a 50-lesson curriculum for kindergarten math intervention focused on number and operations was examined. In comparing classrooms that used ROOTS with those that did not use ROOTS, researchers found that students gained more math skills and the achievement gap between students receiving Tier 2 supports and those not receiving them was reduced (Clarke et al., 2016; Doabler et al., 2016).

Researchers also conducted meta-analyses, reviewing all studies conducted in an area of inquiry to determine the effect of interventions. Those meta-analyses concluded that Tier 2 (Wanzek et al., 2016) and Tier 3 (Wanzek et al., 2013) reading interventions can have a positive effect on foundational reading skills such as fluency and decoding. Researchers caution that it is important to account for how long students need intensive instruction and use data as a guide. For example, the impact of intensive reading instruction on reading fluency was higher when students received intensive intervention over 2 years, rather than over only 1 (Miciak et al., 2018).

Some questions still remain about the consequences of implementing RTI as a comprehensive framework to ensure learning outcomes. A recent national evaluation of the implementation of RTI used data collected from 146 schools that had more than 3 years of experience in implementing RTI, to determine the results of reading outcomes among elementary school students. Over 20,000 students contributed data to the analysis. Contrary to expectations, the data suggested that there were no significant differences in reading scores for at-risk students in grades 2 and 3 that could be linked to the use of RTI. But, as you will learn, research findings can be interpreted in multiple ways. And sometimes the findings reveal more about what needs to happen in future research and implementation.

For example, one area that must be considered in interpreting the study relates to "fidelity of implementation." Fidelity of implementation consists of determining whether teachers implemented RTI and its interventions consistently: Do they regularly follow implementation guidelines such as using screening data effectively to identify those at risk, delivering the curriculum for x number of sessions over x number of weeks?

Fidelity will determine whether RTI is successful as practiced. To promote fidelity, all teaching staff at a school should know how to implement the interventions, especially more intensive interventions. Fidelity also requires educators to align interventions at Tiers 2 and 3 with Tier 1 instruction and content. Not only does alignment of tiers promote access to the general education curriculum; it also supports more opportunities for learning (Gersten et al., 2017).

Assessing a school's readiness (essentially screening for schools, not just students) should be a part of planning for using RTI. Ongoing high-quality professional development for teachers must also occur. Fidelity data should drive data-based decision making at the school and classroom level (essentially progress monitoring for schools, not just students!). Finally, students with disabilities should be included and have access to all parts of the RTI system, as their inclusion will lead to greater collaboration among general and special educators and to a culture of inclusion (Arden, Gandhi, Zumeta Edmonds, & Danielson, 2017).

When each component is in place, RTI provides a useful, research-based framework for preventing challenges and promoting academic learning and progress for all students. Research-based practice and implementation through partnerships among educators, families, and students (including those with disabilities and those with exceptional gifts and talents) constitute gold-standard approaches in implementing RTI in today's schools.

> **MyLab Education** Self-Check 5.3
>
> **MyLab Education** Application Exercise 5.3: Response to Intervention

How to Implement School-wide Systems—Integrating Behavior, Academics, and Social-Emotional Learning

In the two previous sections you learned about two school-wide systems, SW-PBIS and RTI. Each of these systems focused on one area of learning: SW-PBIS on behavior and RTI on academics. You may have sensed some overlap in the outcomes of these systems, as when you learned that SW-PBIS led not only to increases in prosocial behaviors but also to slight increases in academic learning and progress. Not surprisingly, some researchers and practitioners have asked this question: Why not combine these systems and determine what outcomes derive when educators target both academics *and* behavior simultaneously? The question has prompted a response.

The response is known as the multi-tiered system of support—MTSS. This approach integrates school-wide systems of supports for behavior (SW-PBIS) and academics (RTI). Other approaches, like the *Comprehensive, Integrated, Three-tiered (Ci3T) model of prevention*, also integrated supports for social-emotional learning (Lane, Oakes, Cantwell, & Royer, 2017). Other models, like *SWIFT* (McCart, Sailor, Bezdek, & Satter, 2014), also focus on integrating inclusive practices for students with disabilities through MTSS. Upon learning about Ci3T and SWIFT and how it includes students with disabilities into school-wide systems, you will discover other means for promoting progress.

Multi-tiered Systems of Support—MTSS

MTSS brings together high-quality, tiered supports for behavioral and academic outcomes. MTSS integrates all the practices discussed in the SW-PBIS and RTI sections, so you already know a lot about MTSS. What you may not know is the unique feature of MTSS: MTSS aligns academic and behavioral instruction and supports delivered through SW-PBIS and RTI school-wide; it links the overlapping and unique elements of both approaches. This overlap can support educators to use resources more effectively, engage in joint training, and collectively use data-based decision making. Ultimately, the goal is that more and more students make gains in prosocial behaviors as well as academic learning and progress.

You may have noticed how SW-PBIS and RTI apply the key features of school-wide models. The main difference is in the area of learning within which these approaches are applied. For example, the screening and progress monitoring tools for identifying students' needs in behavioral and academic domains will be different, but screening and progress monitoring are the foundation for data-based decisions for both SW-PBIS and RTI. Research-based curriculum and instructional practices used to teach specific behavioral or academic skills will also be different, but both SW-PBIS and RTI use a

Figure 5.3 Features of MTSS

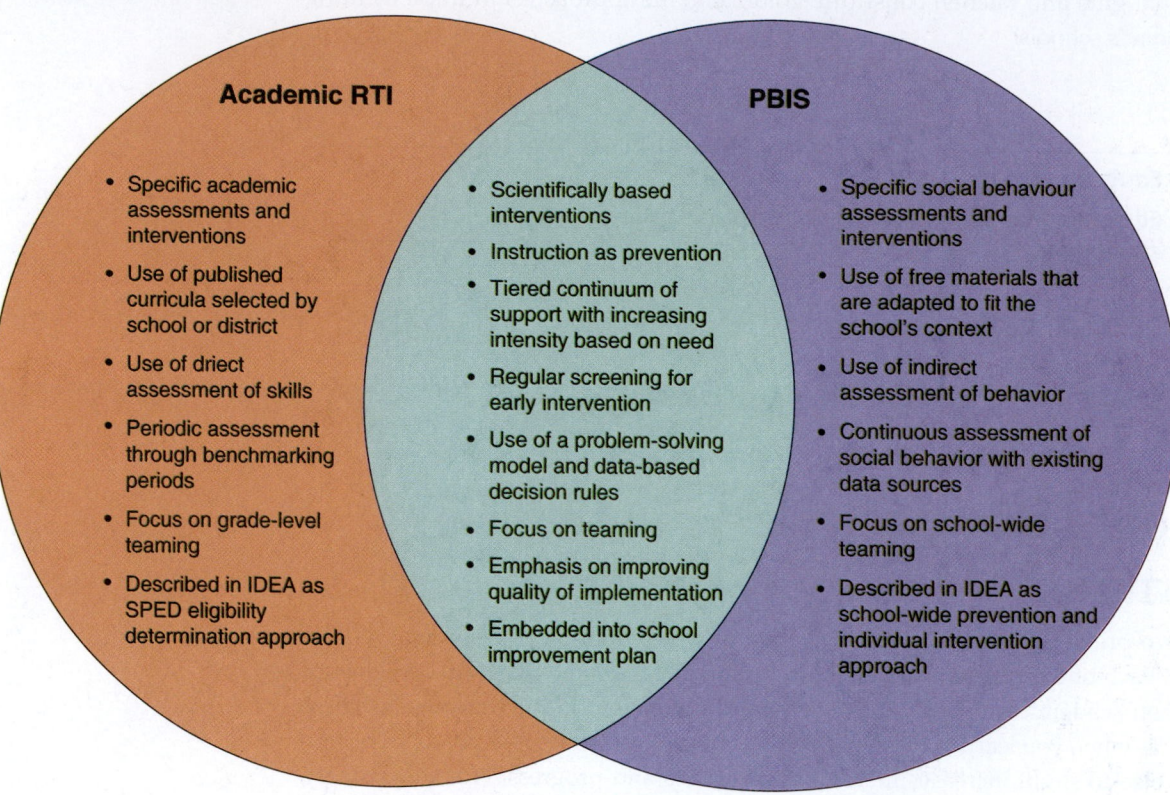

Academic RTI

- Specific academic assessments and interventions
- Use of published curricula selected by school or district
- Use of driect assessment of skills
- Periodic assessment through benchmarking periods
- Focus on grade-level teaming
- Described in IDEA as SPED eligibility determination approach

- Scientifically based interventions
- Instruction as prevention
- Tiered continuum of support with increasing intensity based on need
- Regular screening for early intervention
- Use of a problem-solving model and data-based decision rules
- Focus on teaming
- Emphasis on improving quality of implementation
- Embedded into school improvement plan

PBIS

- Specific social behaviour assessments and interventions
- Use of free materials that are adapted to fit the school's context
- Use of indirect assessment of behavior
- Continuous assessment of social behavior with existing data sources
- Focus on school-wide teaming
- Described in IDEA as school-wide prevention and individual intervention approach

SOURCE: McIntosh, K., & Goodman, S. (2015). *Integrating multi-tiered systems of support: Blending RTI and PBIS*. New York, NY: Guilford Press. Used with permission.

tiered approach. Look at the features of MTSS in Figure 5.3; this figure was created by leaders who are working to merge SW-PBIS and RTI. It highlights the areas of difference between RTI and SW-PBIS as well as the areas of overlap.

BREAKING DOWN SILOS In MTSS, schools systematically plan to fully integrate the key elements of SW-PBIS and RTI, giving students exposure to interventions and supports for both academics and behavior. To that end, MTSS attacks the silos that educators erect (McIntosh & Goodman, 2015), breaking down the barriers between the systems that focus on academics and the systems that focus on behavior and then bringing practice to bear on both, simultaneously. For example, Kelsey learned better when she had support in all of her academic classes to use prosocial behaviors, and she was more likely to use prosocial behaviors when she was engaged in academic learning aligned with her needs. Simple words summarize the point: join behavior and academics—break down the silos that separate them, and combine them.

Combination is occurring and having positive outcomes. For example, in schools that implement combined behavioral and academic supports, fewer students required additional (Tier 2 and 3) supports than would be expected (McIntosh et al., 2006). And many states are increasingly emphasizing the coordination of the SW-PBIS and RTI initiatives under the auspices of MTSS frameworks (Zirkel, 2017). In fact, you'll see the terminology of MTSS being used more and more frequently when states describe the efforts they are undertaking to use the key features of school-wide systems (although part of the confusion is that sometimes people will use MTSS when they are referring to just RTI or SW-PBIS, but increasingly leaders are emphasizing that MTSS should include both). So, over time, you are going to see more and more examples of ways to systematically integrate academic and behavioral supports under MTSS frameworks.

COMPREHENSIVE, INTEGRATED, THREE-TIERED (CI3T) MODEL A framework for combining behavior and academics and for adding another domain of learning has emerged. It is the Comprehensive, Integrated, Three-tiered (Ci3T) model of prevention. Note the emphasis on prevention, a familiar theme of this chapter.

Ci3T expands beyond MTSS to establish a single unified system to meet students' behavioral, academic, and social-emotional needs comprehensively. Like MTSS, Ci3T also focuses on breaking down silos. It eliminates separate teams and associated structures (e.g., a team for reading, a team for behavior, a team for social-emotional learning) and creates a single team—the Ci3T team—that plans for all domains simultaneously (Lane et al., 2015; McIntosh et al., 2006). Now instruction and supports for behavior, academics, and social-emotional learning are unified into one system (Lane, Oakes, Lusk, Cantwell, & Schatschneider, in press).

Moreover, all students—those typically developing and those with an IEP or 504 plan—participate in three different but unified efforts to prevent each of three challenges to students' progress: (a) behavior: a school-wide PBIS framework; (b) academics: instruction in core academic curriculum according to state and district standards using an RTI framework; and (c) social-emotional learning: instruction in social skills using a validated curriculum to address district-identified goals (Lane, Menzies, Oakes, & Kalberg, 2012).

Social-emotional learning (SEL) is defined as "implementing practices and policies that help students and adults acquire and apply knowledge, skills, and attitudes that enhance personal development, social relationships, ethical behavior, and effective, productive work" (Taylor, Oberle, Durlak, & Weissberg, 2017, p. 1157). The question is this: Does teaching a social-emotional curriculum benefit students? The answer is yes. A recent meta-analysis of SEL included 82 social-emotional learning interventions as used with almost 100,000 students across the United States and internationally (Taylor et al., 2017). The analysis suggested that students who received social-emotional instruction and supports had better social-emotional skills and well-being outcomes. Explicit frameworks for teaching social-emotional skills are emerging as parallels to frameworks for behavior and academics.

IMPLEMENTING CI3T: BREAKING DOWN SILOS   Ci3T has established a robust implementation framework. Specifically, the Ci3T leadership team (the group that oversees work in all three areas: behavior, academics, and social-emotional learning) works with input from faculty and staff to build a Ci3T Blueprint to define roles and responsibilities for key stakeholders (students, faculty and staff, families, and administrators) in each of the three domains. You can see what a Ci3T Blueprint might look like for a given school in Figure 5.4. The academic domain sets out roles and responsibilities to ensure that core curricula are implemented with integrity and accessed by all students through the use of research-based strategies to facilitate their engagement and progress.

The behavioral domain includes a PBIS framework—not a curriculum—that involves an instructional approach to behavior. Using a data-informed approach, faculty and staff collaborate to establish school-wide expectations (e.g., Be Respectful, Be Responsible, Be Ready to Learn) for each common area in the school (e.g., classrooms, hallways, lunch room), just as you learned in the SW-PBIS section. Expectations are taught explicitly through the school year, with opportunities for students to practice and be acknowledged for meeting expectations. Efforts are also coordinated across home and school. By having universal expectations and a universal reinforcement system (e.g., PBIS tickets) that involves all faculty and staff, students receive feedback and reinforcement from multiple sources. Finally, the school team adopts and implements a research-based social skills curriculum, paying attention to issues of effectiveness and feasibility to address the priorities of the school itself or of the school district or state (e.g., self-determination skills, bullying prevention, character education; Lane et al., 2012). You will learn more about some of these priorities in the chapters that follow. The primary goal of the Blueprint is to describe clear roles for students, faculty and staff, and family members, as well as responsibilities to be met—that is, to define how the Ci3T framework will be implemented in the school.

Figure 5.4 Sample Ci3T High School Blueprint

Sample High School Ci3T Primary (Tier 1) Plan	
Mission Statement	Our district and school mission is to educate and prepare all students for postsecondary options of continued education and employment and to increase experiences leading to students becoming responsible global citizens and life-long learners.
Purpose Statement	The purpose of our Ci3T plan is to bring our community, administrators, faculty, staff, parents, and students together with common language as we work to meet the academic, behavior, and social needs of ALL students, enabling them to become self-determined, self-regulated learners at school and beyond.
School-wide Expectations	1. Be Respectful 2. Be Responsible 3. Be Ready to Learn

Academic Domain Roles and Responsibilities (sample items)	Behavior Domain Roles and Responsibilities (sample items)	Social Domain Roles and Responsibilities (sample items)
Students will: • Do all work with best effort • Be prepared with completed homework and all necessary materials.	Students will: • Take responsibility for own actions • Participate in SW-PBIS program.	Students will: • Actively engage in social skills curricula • Apply lessons from social skills instruction to daily interactions.
Faculty and Staff will: • Differentiate instruction • Embed literacy strategies in ALL subjects taught.	Faculty and Staff will: • Create clear routines in the classrooms • Complete a behavior screener (e.g., SRSS-IE) 3 times a year.	Faculty and Staff will: • Model social skills taught through curricula • Communicate with families for successes and concerns.
Families will: • Encourage students to be on time daily • Provide a regular, appropriate study time and place.	Families will: • Review, support, reinforce expectations • Communicate any home or school behavior concerns.	Families will: • Learn the social skills that are being taught • Support, model, and reinforce social skills when demonstrated at home.
Administrators will: • Review data on academic interventions with staff • Support identification of professional learning needs.	Administrators will: • Share school-wide, aggregated data with staff 3–4 times per year • Reinforce staff who implement Ci3T plan.	Administrators will: • Monitor implementation of social skills program to ensure fidelity • Provide social skills professional learning opportunities.

SOURCE: Adapted from Lane, K. L., Oakes, W. P., Cantwell, E. D., & Royer, D. J. (2016). *Building and installing comprehensive, integrated, three-tiered (Ci3T) models of prevention: A practical guide to supporting school success.* Phoenix, AZ: KOI Education.

After the overall framework and roles and responsibilities are established, teams identify the specific Tier 1, 2, and 3 interventions and supports they will use in an integrated way to support behavioral, academic, and social-emotional learning. Teams use a tool called Intervention Grids, which document the interventions and supports that will be utilized. Bear in mind that Ci3T, like all school-wide models, is a framework within which teams individualize Tier 1, 2, and 3 supports. Figure 5.5, which describes academic, behavioral, and social support across three tiers, gives examples of what this might look like in a given school.

The interventions and supports in Figure 5.5 include research-based strategies, practices, and programs. Some are aligned with SW-PBIS and RTI, as you already know. The unique element of Ci3T, however, is that it focuses on integrating across the learning domains. For example, Tier 2 supports might link behavior supports (e.g., a program like check-in/check-out) with academic supports (e.g., small-group reading interventions, such as those you learned about in the RTI section). The link becomes transparent and accessible to all staff in the school when the team names the support, describes the opportunity (e.g., who is doing what to whom, and under what conditions), explains how students can receive this extra support (inclusion criteria), collects data to monitor

Figure 5.5 Academic, Behavioral, and Social Supports Across Three Tiers

	Academic	Behavior	Social

Tier 1	• **Teach district-approved programs with fidelity**
	
	  • Differentiate instruction
	  • Use proactive, evidence-based strategies to support active engagement (e.g., instructional choice)
	  • Create and teach lesson plans, following using effective practices (e.g., modeling, guided practice)
	
	• **Provide meaningful and appropriate practice opportunities**
	
	• **Use multiple data sources to determine if students need Tier 2 or Tier 3 supports**
		• **Implement SW-PBIS with fidelity**
		
		  • Teach, model, and reinforce behavioral expectations (e.g., Show Respect, Give Best Effort)
		  • Provide behavior-specific praise paired with PBIS tickets when students meet behavioral expectations
		
		• **Use multiple data sources to determine if students need Tier 2 or Tier 3 supports**
			• **Teach evidence-based, school-wide social skills curricula with fidelity**
			• **Foster and model positive social interactions among teachers, students, and families**
			
			  • Maintain communication with families
			  • Seek ways to engage families as partners in school program
			
			• **Provide behavior-specific praise when students demonstrate expected social skills**

Tier 2		• **Provide targeted, low-intensity strategies, practices, and programs designed to support students who need more than Tier 1 supports**	
	Examples (implemented in isolation or in combination):		
	• Math Small Group Support • Self-Regulation Strategy Development (SRSD) for Writing • Repeated Readings	• Check-in/check-out or Behavior Education Program (BEP) • Behavior contracts • Self-monitoring interventions	• Small group counseling • *Positive Action*® Counselor's Kit Lessons (e.g., Healthy Minds and Bodies, Getting Along with Others)
Tier 3	• **Provide more intensive intervention efforts for students who have significant support needs**		
	Examples (implemented in isolation or in combination):		
	• Lindamood Phoneme Sequencing® (LiPS) • Individualized Math Support • One-on-one reading interventions	• Functional Assessment–based Intervention (FABI) • Individualized De-escalation Plan	• Individualized counseling • Mental health supports from community agencies

progress, and states the exit criteria (either because the intervention is concluded successfully or because more intensive intervention is needed).

In the Ci3T model, the term "all staff in the school" refers to general and special education teachers, instructional coaches, counselors, administrators, and other professionals who collaborate with each other and families to support students' progress. They have defined roles and responsibilities. So do families and students. The Ci3T Blueprint supports transparency and clarity as to what is available for all (Tier 1), some (Tier 2), and a few (Tier 3) students (Lane, Oakes, Jenkins, Menzies, & Kalberg, 2014).

SWIFT   The School-wide Integrated Framework for Transformation (SWIFT) is another example of how schools combine the features of school-wide systems to target multiple, interrelated areas related to learning and progress in the general education curriculum, particularly for the benefit of students with disabilities. SWIFT focuses on integrating MTSS (defined by the use of SW-PBIS and RTI that you learned about earlier) with other effective practices, such as promoting family partnerships (Chapter 3); building administrative leadership (this chapter's section on RTI); and the inclusion of students with disabilities, including those with the most significant support needs (Chapter 13). Research has begun to demonstrate the benefits for students, both with and without disabilities, in regard to academic and behavioral outcomes, suggesting all students (not just students with disabilities, but all students) achieve at higher levels when an inclusive model is used (Choi, Meisenheimer, McCart, & Sailor, 2017). SWIFT is focusing on the most effective ways to include students with disabilities across tiers, an especially important consideration given that some RTI models have not had this focus (Arden et al., 2017).

Go to http://www.ci3t.org/ for more information on Ci3T, including implementation resources that are freely available for teachers and Ci3T leadership teams.

We repeat this important point: SWIFT is innovating to ensure that students with disabilities can access all tiers of instruction and supports and that special education is recognized as a source of support for students with disabilities to engage and progress in behavioral, academic, and social-emotional learning across the tiers. Those who implement RTI and MTSS should recognize a core lesson from SWIFT: Special education is not a tier but instead is a means of enabling students to access and progress in teaching and learning undertaken through the SW-PBIS, RTI, MTSS/Ci3T, and SWIFT frameworks.

Including Students with Disabilities in School-wide Systems

School-wide systems of supports have implications for supporting students with and without disabilities. Also, promoting the involvement of students with disabilities in school-wide systems fulfills the LRE requirement of IDEA. It creates the opportunity for students with disabilities to learn skills that promote access to and progress in the general education curriculum. To engage students with disabilities, bear in mind these points:

- The Tier 1 strategies support all students in the school.
- Screening and progress monitoring systems determine when and how all students will receive Tier 2 and Tier 3 supports.
- The Tier 2 and 3 instruction and supports provide more intensive instruction to enable all students to access the Tier 1 curriculum.
- Special education services and supports enable students with disabilities to access all of the school-wide activities highlighted in the three preceding bulleted statements.

The challenge for you and your colleagues will be to incorporate research-based instructional practices that you will learn throughout all remaining chapters into school-wide approaches to ensure the progress of all students, including those with disabilities. By embedding system-wide supports that incorporate special education supports and services for all students across all tiers, educators such as yourself profoundly influence the education and life outcomes of students with disabilities. You ensure that they progress in school; that they do so in inclusive environments; that they benefit from partnerships among all educators and other professionals; and that, in sum, they receive an education that dignifies them for what they are and can do rather than an education that devalues them by pointing out what they are not and cannot do. Kelsey once was the "yes . . . but" student. Now, as a professional with a family and career of her own, she is simply the "yes" student.

Visit http://www.swiftschools.org/ and navigate to the Resource Shelf. If you go to Films & Videos, you can link to a video called *Together: A SWIFT film on Integrated Educational Framework* to understand how SWIFT is being implemented in schools across the country.

MyLab Education Self-Check 5.4

MyLab Education Application Exercise 5.4: A Comprehensive, Integrated Three-tier Model

Summary

Characteristics of School-wide Systems

Tiered systems of supports are a general education initiative that focuses on improving outcomes for all students by using a prevention framework. Core features include an emphasis on tiered supports that are typically organized into universal or Tier 1 supports, with more intensive supports provided as needed by students (Tiers 2 and 3). Other core features include the use of screening and progress monitoring data, data-based decision making, and teaming and collaborative problem solving.

How to Implement School-wide Systems— Positive Behavior Interventions and Supports

School-wide PBIS creates supports for all students by redesigning school environments, particularly making sure that all students will understand and meet clearly stated behavioral expectations. SW-PBIS uses a three-tiered model combined with data-based decision making to enhance student behavioral outcomes by detecting and intervening to address behavioral challenges early and providing increasingly intensive behavioral supports as needed. There is a strong research base for SW-PBIS.

How to Implement School-wide Systems— Response to Intervention

RTI uses the key features of school-wide systems to promote effective instruction and supports for learning. RTI focuses on using tiered supports and data-based decision making to benefit all students in learning essential academic content. RTI also uses screening and progress monitoring data, as well as team-based problem solving, to identify students' academic needs across the tiers. At least 45 states recommend RTI for educators to organize instruction and supports for all students.

How to Implement School-wide Systems— Integrating Behavior, Academics, and Social-Emotional Learning

School-wide systems focus on one domain of learning, and multi-tiered systems of supports integrate multiple domains of learning. However, both frameworks share the same core features. Integrating multiple domains of learning into tiered frameworks is important to consider given data that suggest the interrelatedness of behavioral, academic, and social-emotional learning and outcomes. Students with disabilities can be included across all tiers, and special education supports and services should be structured to enable student participation and progress in school-wide and multi-tiered frameworks. Ongoing research and development is under way to understand the best ways to include students with a range of disabilities in these initiatives.

Addressing the Professional Standards

In Chapter 5, School-wide Systems of Supports, we have covered the following Council for Exceptional Children (CEC) Initial Level Special Educator Preparation Standards: Chapter 5—1.2, 2.1, 3.2, 3.3, 4.1, 4.2, 5.6, 6.2, 7.1, 7.3. Refer to the Appendix for a full listing of the CEC Standards with descriptions and supporting explanations.

Chapter 6
Cross-cutting Instructional Approaches

⌄ Learning Outcomes

6.1 Describe high-leverage practices related to collaboration, assessment, social/emotional/behavioral support, and instruction that can be used to enable students with disabilities to make progress toward outcomes.

6.2 Summarize how educators design learning environments and identify examples of specially designed instruction and supports that ensure progress toward outcomes.

Meet Jack Steinberg—Progressing by Persevering

Leave it to the Supreme Court to define "appropriate education" as education that involves "making progress." This was the essence of the *Endrew F.* decision.

Leave it to students, families, and teachers to exemplify the Court's definition.

Jack Steinberg, his parents Ivey and Eric, and his teachers at WISH Academy, in Los Angeles, do just that. They refine "making progress" to include "persevering." To progress, a student, the family, and the educators must persevere. The dictionary tells us that persevering means persisting in an enterprise—here, Jack's education—in spite of counter-influences, opposition, or discouragement.

That's exactly what they did, and, in spite of a significant counter-influence, Jack's disability, Jack is on his way to college—but not until he graduates from WISH Academy, in 2021.

Why is Jack's disability a significant counter-influence? It's because his disability leads to the need for support to talk and walk and eat and bathe or clean himself. He talks slowly, but people can understand him as long as they are patient; he's very good about repeating what he says if they don't understand him. He walks with the support of a person or a device. He needs supports to cut his food into chewable pieces and to take care of his bodily needs by himself. He has limited vision. In a nutshell, Jack needs a great deal of support from others to do any of those acts that most Americans take for granted—after all, they don't have disabilities.

But Jack is also remarkably able. He earns As and Bs in all but two of his academic subjects in the common core curriculum for California high-schoolers. He takes the same courses that his peers who do not have disabilities take to prepare for 4-year colleges. He has 15 faithful lunchroom buddies who do not

Ivey Steinberg

have disabilities, and he names each of them, laboriously but well enough that a person not familiar with his speech can understand them. He participates in a ju-jitsu class and uses the same exercise device, the Alter-G, that the Los Angeles Clippers pro-basketball players and Stanford University football players use.

And he names—again, slowly and deliberately—the entire starting roster of the 1955 Brooklyn Dodgers, the team that beat the perennial champions, the New York Yankees, to win that year's World Series, the only one the Dodgers won while in Brooklyn. Year after year the Dodgers came close; in Brooklyn and beyond, the perennial October cry arose: "Wait until next year!" Next year came in 1955.

Jack, Ivey, Eric, and the teachers at WISH are pretty much like those Dodgers of '55. Year after year, Jack, Ivey, Eric, and the teachers at WISH persevere in spite of the obstacles of obtaining a charter for and then successfully operating an elementary and middle school. They persevered and succeeded. But they also knew that, based on the success they had achieved so far, they needed to create WISH as a secondary school. A huge obstacle loomed, however, namely, that the authorities responsible for recommending for or against another charter secondary school opposed chartering the WISH as a school for grades 9 through 12. In large part because Ivey and other parents lobbied the school board and mobilized the press to cover the board's vote on chartering WISH, the board voted to grant the charter. Victory!

Another obstacle was that WISH Academy was to co-locate with a large non-charter public high school. That school was not accessible to students with disabilities; such ramps as were in place did not comply with the standards of the Americans with Disabilities Act (ADA), and there were no bathrooms for students who needed changing rooms or accessible toilets. Leave it to Ivey to persuade the head of the facilities division of the Los Angeles Unified School District (LAUSD) to retrofit the school to accommodate Jack and other students at the Academy, to do it in a matter of weeks to make sure it was ready for the first day of school, and to use funds from a budget initiative that the voters passed years before but that were sitting idly, largely because LAUSD did not hire anyone to allocate them until a year before Jack was to go to high school.

Two major obstacles were overcome. One was political: opposition to a charter school. The other was structural: a non-accessible site.

What obstacles remained? You might think they relate to Jack's disability. You'd be wrong. No doubt, Jack has significant disabilities. But he has comparable strength and determination, as well as a roster of teammates that makes for annual championships. They persevere for progress. How?

Engineering students at Loyola Marymount University have worked with Ivey and Eric to design a device that enables Jack to stay upright in school so that he can participate and progress in his education (not being able to do this would be an obstacle!). With the device—one at school and one at home—he can stretch his heel tendons, stay in an upright posture so his gastrointestinal system will function more normally, lock into a desk on which he puts his touch-screen computer and textbooks, and move from place to place. The entire device breaks down into three units that he, Eric, and Ivey can carry onto an airplane. Talk about mobility!

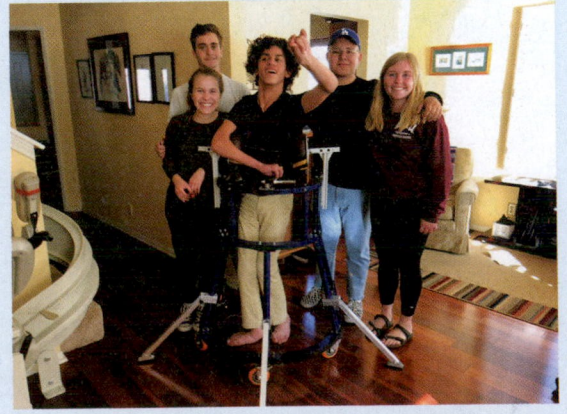

What about academics? Academics are no problem at WISH Academy. He uses his own voice to ask and answer questions. Are you surprised to know that Jack's favorite class is public speaking? Don't be. Just consider who Jack is and what drives Ivey and Eric: Jack's inclusive education and progress to college. Are you surprised that he takes other general education courses, including the one Christina Nowak, his education specialist, teaches, which preps students to pass the state's required examination in core subjects? Don't be. Jack and WISH Academy are into the exceptional, big time.

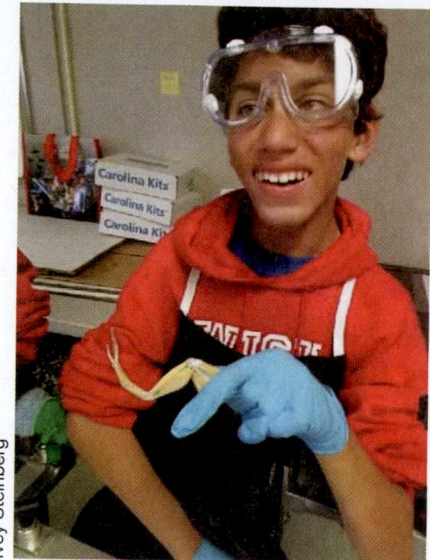

Ivey Steinberg

His computer has a large-print screen; all written materials his teachers give him are in large-print type. They "chunk" the text he has to read, putting short portions of it on each page. They substitute true-false or multiple-choice tests for long- or short-essay examinations. They give him more time to finish his examinations and allow him to use his computer to answer the questions. They abbreviate his homework so it covers the essence of the work they expect from his peers who do not have disabilities.

Two paraprofessionals, Patrick and Leo, on a rotating schedule take notes for Jack, but only in his physics class, and assist him in taking care of his personal needs. They avoid hovering over him; Jack needs space to be himself and practice in being as independent as possible.

Eric and Ivey hire tutors to work with Jack at home two afternoons a week and for 5 hours on weekends. They are not unlike other parents who hire tutors for their children who do not have disabilities.

Importantly, all these curriculum accommodations occur because WISH Academy administrators and teachers acknowledge that, if Jack doesn't "get it" in class, it's not because of Jack. It's because they have not yet learned how to find a better way to teach him. WISH Academy, like the WISH Elementary School and Middle School that Jack attended, deliberately embraces differences. The mindset at these two schools is to meet the challenges of disability headlong and then overcome them.

Given that Jack believes in himself, that is, no "wait until next year" but instead "watch me now"; given that Ivey and Eric and Jack's schoolmates and teachers believe in him; given that motivation and persistence surround him at home and school—given all that, you should not be surprised that Jack, Ivey and Eric, and Jack's teachers are prepping him to attend one of the nation's 15 or so colleges that hold themselves out to be especially accessible to people with disabilities. One of them is nearby: California State University at Fullerton. Look out, CSUF: Jack's on his way.

You'll know when he arrives. He's the guy with the Dodgers hat and a pennant with three words: Progressing by Persevering.

Using High-Leverage Practices to Support Student Learning

Individualization is a key principle of special education services. It's what the Individuals with Disabilities Education Act (IDEA) requires; it's also what the Supreme Court in *Endrew F.* insisted is the core of a student's appropriate education. To individualize,

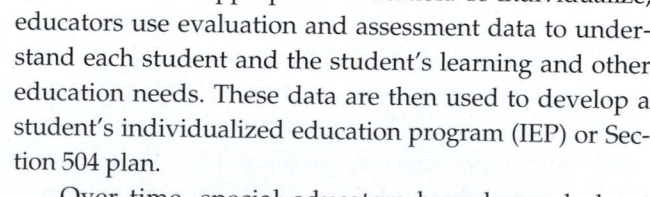

Rawpixel.com/Shutterstock

educators use evaluation and assessment data to understand each student and the student's learning and other education needs. These data are then used to develop a student's individualized education program (IEP) or Section 504 plan.

Over time, special educators have learned about practices that work across learning environments and curricular areas and for all students. In this section, you will learn about these "high-leverage practices." These are need-to-know practices that you can use with all students, in diverse learning environments, to enhance their progress and support a variety of learning outcomes, especially the four that you learned about in Chapter 1—equal opportunity, full inclusion, independent living, and economic self-sufficiency.

Teachers use strategies to promote active engagement of students.

As you learned in Chapter 1, the Council for Exceptional Children (CEC) is a major professional organization for educators who support students with exceptionalities. It develops materials and holds conferences and training to support educators to stay up-to-date on research-based practices. You can learn more about the resources CEC provides by going to its website.

Go to https://www.cec.sped.org/ for more information about CEC and the resources they offer to special educators.

Recently, CEC partnered with the CEEDAR (Collaboration for Effective Educator Development, Accountability, and Reform) Center to undertake a comprehensive effort to identify "high-leverage practices in special education." You and all educators can "leverage" these practices across multiple settings, ages, and students with exceptionalities. High-leverage practices:

- Affect instruction
- Occur with high frequency
- Are research-based
- Are usable across content and settings
- Are fundamental to effective teaching (McLeskey et al., 2017).

These practices are about the *delivery* of special education services and supports; they are a "starting point for selecting, designing, and implementing effective specially designed instruction" (Riccomini, Moron, & Hughes, 2017, pp. 21–22). We'll teach you more about specially designed instruction and how it differs from high-leverage practices in later sections, but for now, let's focus on the high-leverage practices and how they shape your work.

There are four domains of high-leverage practices:

- Collaboration
- Assessment
- Social/emotional/behavioral
- Instruction (McLeskey et al., 2017).

These four domains should be familiar to you. You've learned a bit about each of them in previous chapters and will learn more about what these practices mean for students with specific exceptionalities in later chapters. Note especially that CEC and CEEDAR have affirmed these domains are highly "intertwined" (McLeskey et al., 2017).

Figure 6.1 lists 22 high-leverage practices organized into the four domains. We'll tell you more about each domain in the sections that follow. Each domain has detailed exemplars of effective practices.

Go to https://highleveragepractices.org/ and learn more about high-leverage practices in special education and their use by classroom teachers.

Collaboration

You already know from the first five chapters and from the vignette about Jack Steinberg that collaboration—or partnership, which is the term we use in Chapter 3—among professionals and families is vital for supporting students with disabilities to make progress and achieve valued outcomes. Ivey and Eric, Jack's parents, work with his teachers, especially Christina Nowak. At the start of Jack's first high school year at WISH Academy, Ivey, Eric, and Christina met weekly to discuss Jack's education; these were "formal," regularly scheduled meetings. After the 10th week of the 1st semester, they met twice a month; Jack's progress no longer required meeting more frequently. Nor were additional meetings necessary; Ivey and Christina talked daily. In Christina's words, "Ivey is the expert about Jack. I respect her; I regard her as my equal in Jack's education. I don't make decisions without consulting with her. Our conversations are candid, civil, and constructive. We trust each other."

Figure 6.1 High-Leverage Practices Identified by CEC and CEEDAR

Collaboration

1. Collaborate with professionals to increase student success.
2. Organize and facilitate effective meetings with professionals and families.
3. Collaborate with families to support student learning and secure needed services.

Assessment

4. Use multiple sources of information to develop a comprehensive understanding of a student's strengths and needs.
5. Interpret and communicate assessment information with stakeholders to collaboratively design and implement educational programs.
6. Use student assessment data, analyze instructional practices, and make necessary adjustments that improve student outcomes.

Social/Emotional/Behavioral Practices

7. Establish a consistent, organized, and respectful learning environment.
8. Provide positive and constructive feedback to guide students' learning and behavior.
9. Teach social behaviors.
10. Conduct functional behavioral assessments to develop individual student behavior support plans.

Instruction

11. Identify and prioritize long- and short-term learning goals.
12. Systematically design instruction toward specific learning goals.
13. Adapt curriculum tasks and materials for specific learning goals.
14. Teach cognitive and metacognitive strategies to support learning and independence.
15. Provide scaffolded supports.
16. Use explicit instruction.
17. Use flexible grouping.
18. Use strategies to promote active student engagement.
19. Use assistive and instructional technologies.
20. Provide intensive instruction.
21. Teach students to maintain and generalize new learning across time and settings.
22. Provide positive and constructive feedback to guide students' learning and behavior.

SOURCE: Based on McLeskey, J., Barringer, M.-D., Billingsley, B., Brownell, M., Jackson, D., Kennedy, M., . . . Ziegler, D. (2017). *High-leverage practices in special education*. Arlington, VA: Council for Exceptional Children & CEEDAR Center.

Educators also must collaborate with each other. In Chapter 5 you learned about school-wide systems and practices. These require general and special educators to collaborate in using specially designed instructional practices across Tier 1, 2, and 3 supports for academics, behavior, and social-emotional learning. Nuances are associated with collaboration. Consider the matter of "titles."

You may think that educators' titles are relatively unimportant. They are not. At WISH Academy, Christina does not have the label "special educator," even though she prepared as one in college. Instead, she is titled "education specialist" and co-teaches every one of Jack's courses, planning and delivering instruction to all of the students in the classes, not just to Jack. This benefits Jack's education in the general curriculum, the courses required for him and all students who do not have disabilities to earn their diplomas: English, history, mathematics, and science. Christina is a specialist in education, not a special educator. Her title does not set her aside; it signifies that she is regarded as an indispensable member of the entire faculty and of Jack's team, a collaborator with all of his other teachers.

As students move into high school and begin to prepare for the transition to adult life, you will need to apply research-based strategies to build collaborations and partnerships with other professionals outside the school system, including disability professionals who support adults with disabilities in the community to find jobs and continue their education (Flowers et al., 2018).

Assessment

You have already learned about the importance of assessment in special education. In Chapter 4 you read about how information needs to be collected from various people and assessments to evaluate a student and then determine if the student needs special education services and supports, and, if so, what types of services and supports best align with the student's learning goals. To make those determinations, educators need data.

That is why, for example, Christina monitors Jack's progress informally on a daily basis. To assess his progress, she also uses the same tests she and other teachers administer to Jack's peers. Because Jack has test anxiety (didn't you?), Christina and he go to a separate room to "take the test." There, Christina tells Jack that he is just "practicing" to take a test; by characterizing "real" testing as "practice" testing, she alleviates Jack's anxiety, enabling him to demonstrate exactly what he has learned. It's a simple change but an effective one for assessing Jack.

Whether assessing to determine if a student needs special education services and supports or collecting screening or progress monitoring data in the context of school-wide systems (Chapter 5), you and your colleagues should always use the high-leverage practices of collecting multiple sources of information, sharing information with each other to inform the process by which you make decisions, and using data as the basis of your decisions (Filderman & Toste, 2018). As your students enter high school, you should also always consider how to involve them in their IEP meetings; that involvement advances their self-determination.

High-leverage practices are intertwined and collaborative. That's the conclusion of a report by the What Works Clearinghouse (Hamilton et al., 2009):

- Data must be a part of an "ongoing cycle of instructional improvement" (p. 8)—teachers must have time and supports for using data and making data-based instructional decisions.
- Students should be involved in understanding and using data; students can be collaborators as well—here's where self-determination comes into play.
- Data should be used school-wide, necessitating professional collaboration.
- Supports should be provided, such as having all members of a student's team know how to interpret data and use it for the student's benefit and for the teachers, as well.

Social/Emotional/Behavioral

High-leverage practices acknowledge that academic learning and instruction are not the only important curriculum for students with exceptionalities. Indeed, teaching social, emotional, and behavioral skills is essential. That kind of teaching enables students to engage more effectively in academic learning and prepares students for college and career readiness (Morningstar, Lombardi, Fowler, & Test, 2017); it supports them to make progress. The high-leverage practices align well with school-wide positive behavior interventions and supports—SW-PBIS (Chapter 5). You may recall from that chapter that SW-PBIS expects all students to learn about a school's expectations. SW-PBIS also supports students who struggle to understand and integrate the behavioral expectations into their behavior at school.

MyLab Education

Video Example 6.1

Moving from elementary to middle school is also a big transition for students. How do CHIME teachers Lauren and Rose emphasize the importance of collaboration when planning for this transition?

Alternatively stated, high-leverage practices emphasize creating a positive learning environment, providing positive feedback, explicitly teaching social behaviors, and conducting assessments to understand why students might be struggling behaviorally. Think about Jack. He has a circle of friends, his lunch buddies. They gather daily at lunch; they also gather twice a week, as a school-sponsored "club" that Christina directs, to just hang out and, in doing so, they learn how to improve their social and emotional/behavioral capacities. Jack's education, as well as theirs, is not only about academics; it's also about developing the attitudes and skills of students to be in and of their communities, whether at school or elsewhere.

Instruction

Instruction is the final domain of high-leverage practices. That makes sense. Collaboration, assessment, and social-emotional-behavioral support together form the foundations for effective instruction.

There are 12 high-leverage instruction practices; you will find them listed in Figure 6.1. You can use each across content areas, across grade levels, and as required to meet student needs. These high-leverage practices provide a starting point for thinking about specially designed instruction that will be individualized for each student who needs special education. And, you can use them whether you are a general educator or, like Christina at WISH, a special educator titled as an "education specialist" to remove any stigma that may attach to Jack and her when they work together.

Did any of the Figure 6.1 practices benefit you as a student? Did you learn better when you were engaged? How might you build student engagement in learning, across instructional areas? That's not much of a challenge for Christina because, in her words, "Jack wants to go to college. He is very motivated by positive reinforcement; he loves to be told he's done a good job in any of his work. Ivey, Eric, and I agree: Reinforce Jack and amazing results occur."

Look at some of the other high-leverage practices. High-leverage practice No. 11 focuses on identifying and prioritizing short- and long-term goals. This practice emphasizes the need to center on short-term outcomes, such as learning vocabulary words, as well as long-term outcomes, such as being a literate reader who can interact with materials in college and career environments. This practice reminds us to think about how short- and long-term goals must relate to each other to promote outcomes.

Also look at high-leverage practice No. 14. It focuses on teaching cognitive or meta-cognitive strategies to support learning or independence. Cognitive and meta-cognitive strategies include decision-making and problem-solving skills. Think about how important it is in your day-to-day life to be able to generate and try solutions to problems you encounter. It simply makes sense, for a student's long-term outcomes regarding full participation and independent living, to teach strategies for solving problems as part of the student's academic learning. When a student can identify multiple pathways to achieve a goal, such as earning an A in a class or learning a strategy to solve fractions, the student is more likely to make progress in school and develop self-determination.

When you had specific goals for learning, when you had opportunities to have materials that were accessible to you and your learning needs, and when you received positive and constructive feedback, did you learn better? The answer most likely is yes. The same will be true for your students with exceptionalities. That's why it's important to understand and integrate high-leverage practices into your work as an educator. These practices provide a starting point for how to deliver special education services and supports.

MyLab Education Self-Check 6.1

MyLab Education Application Exercise 6.1: High-leverage Instructional Practices

Designing Learning Environments to Enhance Student Outcomes

To apply high-leverage practices in specific learning environments, you must know which practices work and where they are needed—that is, you must know who your students are, what they need in order to learn, and what their school environments are. For the moment, let's focus on school environments.

The most common learning environment is the classroom. Promoting access to and progress in the general education curriculum, however, includes providing experiences not only in the classroom but also in other environments, such as the lunch room, playground, study hall, and gym, as well as in any extracurricular and school activities (e.g., student council or sports). Remember that Jack has a circle of friends who convene at lunch and as a club outside lunch; he also participates in gym and various extracurricular activities that he enjoys. To create effective learning environments, focusing on the design of the classroom and other school environments can have very great impact (Lippman, 2010). You do not need to do that work alone. Jack's mother, Ivey, had a major role in designing the physical features of WISH Academy to meet Jack's needs and thereby make life easier for all students. Often, what is designed to help one student ends up helping all.

Designing effective school and classroom environments includes three different but related aspects of students' learning environments: the physical set-up, the culture that characterizes the learning environment, and the ways that professionals interact in the learning environment. Take a simple example. Do you learn better in a loud environment with many distractions or a quieter environment that allows you to focus? The same idea—environment affects learning—applies to the design of the classroom and the instruction in it. The good news is that several relevant research-based practices are available. These practices take into account how educators use physical spaces, how they deliver instruction, how they ensure that their students engage with instructional materials, and how they collaborate with other educators. It's time for you to learn about two of these: universal design for learning and collaborative teaching.

Universal Design for Learning

One approach for designing learning environments, curricula, and instructional methods and materials is known as **universal design for learning—UDL** (Hall, Meyer, & Rose, 2012). Originally, UDL served as a framework to make learning more accessible to students with disabilities by reducing barriers to accessing the general education curriculum. Now, however, UDL is a research-based framework for designing classrooms, curricula, and instruction to be accessible to all students, including those with and without disabilities (Ralabate & Nelson, 2017). UDL has become more universal.

Uniquely, UDL brings together the fields of education and neuroscience, using information about how the brain works in order to understand more fully how to design learning environments and instruction (Nelson & Johnson, 2017). UDL acknowledges that different students need different supports for accessing information and demonstrating knowledge. Accordingly, UDL provides a framework that takes into account students' variability (Salend & Whittaker, 2017).

The universal design framework is organized around three main principles:

- Provide multiple means of engagement
- Provide multiple means of representation
- Provide multiple means of action and expression.

You and your colleagues can use multiple options and "checkpoints" to promote these three principles across learning environments (CAST, 2018).

MyLab Education
Video Example 6.2
Universal design creates multiple pathways for learning. How do students benefit from universal design?

Explore the UDL Guidelines website at http://udlguidelines.cast. org/ The Universal Design for Learning Guidelines (as shown in the CAST website) is a graphic organizer that details the options and checkpoints and can be used to implement UDL. It's worth bookmarking because it makes specific recommendations about how to implement UDL in the classroom.

MyLab Education

Video Example 6.3

Students in Ms. Etting's class have classroom responsibilities. How are students supported to determine roles and ways that they will engage in the classroom?

Go to https://abledata.acl.gov/ and search for Dynavox. What did you learn about the different features of a Dynavox communication system?

MULTIPLE MEANS OF ENGAGEMENT—THE FIRST PRINCIPLE   When focusing on multiple means of engagement, your goal is to design learning environments, curricula and curricular goals, and instructional materials and methods so that all students can engage with their learning in multiple ways, becoming purposeful and motivated to learn. The UDL framework provides options for promoting student interest, sustaining student effort and persistence, and promoting student self-regulation. For example, if you are working on a reading lesson, you might allow your students to choose the stories they will read so they can make selections that align with their interests and backgrounds. You should also make sure that students know their learning goals. Here's the basic proposition behind those two strategies, stated as a rhetorical question: Are you more motivated when you set your own goals or when others set them for you?

Jack answers the questions when he tells you he wants to go to college. Ivey supports Jack in reaching his goal by identifying the 15 colleges and universities that are most accessible to students with disabilities. Christina also makes sure that Jack takes the course "Academic College Enhancement," in which she emphasizes how to set goals, remember what they are, and organize activities to attain them. Jack sets his own goals, he and his team remember them, and his team then supports him to make progress toward those goals.

MULTIPLE MEANS OF REPRESENTATION—THE SECOND PRINCIPLE   When designing learning environments and instruction to enable multiple means of representation, your goal is to create various options for students to interact with the information you present to them. Creating these options requires you to select options for perception, language, symbols, and comprehension. For example, when books are available in a digital format (like this one can be), a screen reader can "read" the text aloud. Other technologies enlarge the font, change the color scheme, and otherwise encourage students to engage with the content. You can provide links to outside sources so that your students will have access to multiple sources of information and engage with the information and its sources in different ways.

Christina uses several approaches for Jack that take into account Jack's limited vision. She tells him what he needs to know—the verbal approach. She also scans written instructions into his computer, which has a program, KAMI, that enlarges the print and allows him to highlight it—the technological approach.

Christina and Jack exemplify the accessibility-engagement-choice cycle. They "chunk" material Jack needs to learn. To do that, Christina and her co-teachers decide what Jack "needs to know," not what is "easy" for him to learn. To arrive at the essence of a lesson, they break down the lesson into different parts. They begin by simplifying the directions he needs to follow. They then delete nonessential words in a text; not every word is as important as every other, and Jack needs to absorb the key ideas, not every ancillary or tangential one. For Jack, it's all a matter of adding "simplification" to the accessibility-engagement-choice cycle. It's not at all a matter of "dumbing down" the curriculum; instead, it's a matter of using multiple means to present it so Jack gets the essence of all of it.

When working with students with disabilities, you, like Christina, will find various ways to provide content. For example, a free electronic platform called Book Builder lets teachers create e-texts that can include pictures, graphics, and even avatars that coach students as they navigate text. The texts available in Book Builder (in 12 languages) can benefit students by developing their vocabulary and comprehension; the texts

Teachers provide various options for students to interact with the information presented to them.

are especially effective for students with autism and other disabilities (Knight, Wood, Spooner, Browder, & O'Brien, 2015).

MULTIPLE MEANS OF ACTION AND EXPRESSION—THE THIRD PRINCIPLE The final principle entails multiple means of action and expression. That is, it focuses on how students demonstrate their learning and the options your students have for physical action, expression and communication, and executive functioning. Let's simplify that thought. Answer this question: Is completing a written test the only way to show what you have learned, that you have achieved the goals of your learning? What other options enable you to demonstrate what you have learned? If you were able to list other options, you are already on the path to using UDL.

Educators are always setting learning goals for their students (Nelson, 2014; Nelson & Johnson, 2017). How might a student demonstrate mastery of a goal? Consider this example of a goal in an elementary level social studies class, a goal related to geography:

- Students will draw the important features of a map.

Does this meet the guidelines for UDL? Does it provide multiple means of action or expression? Why or why not?

Now consider this goal, nearly identical to the previously stated goal but expressed in different terms:

- Students will demonstrate an understanding of features on a map (title, symbols, scale, compass, etc.).

What's the difference? In the second goal, students can demonstrate their learning in multiple ways. They can verbalize their understanding, they can use technology to highlight aspects of a map, or they can work with a peer to draw features. "Demonstrate" is much broader than "draw," so it provides more options for action and engagement. Options are at the heart of UDL.

To provide Jack options, other than writing, for expressing what he knows, Christina converts a teacher-created document into a Google.doc version so that Jack can type his responses directly into the document—the technological approach, again. She also enables him to use his computer to answer questions, using KAMI, and she substitutes true-false and multiple-choice answers for short-essay answers that other students must provide—the combination of technology and reformatting.

IMPLEMENTING UDL It bears repeating that, in a nutshell, UDL is all about how you set up learning environments, curriculum and curricular goals, and instruction and instructional materials. UDL is a framework that enables your students to become motivated, resourceful, and strategic.

UDL does more than benefit your students. It also benefits you and your colleagues; it's as good for teachers as it is for students. Why? UDL makes you and your colleagues more intentional in designing schools and classrooms and the instruction that occurs there. It makes you and them focus more on creating inclusive environments and promoting access for students with exceptionalities. As one teacher said, students "really just blossom and really thrive and kind of regain their confidence in my class because they know they can show me what they know and show me in different ways, not just paper and pencil" (Lowrey, Hollingshead, & Howery, 2017, p. 20).

Here are the steps UDL leaders suggest you take as you begin to implement UDL in your classroom (Salend & Whittaker, 2017). These steps should take place while reviewing and considering the checkpoints in that leaders in the UDL field have developed for implementing the three principles of UDL. Remember, UDL will be individualized

Go to http://bookbuilder.cast.org/ to find examples of books that have been created and shared by teachers across the country.

to different learning environments and student learning needs, but these checkpoints offer ideas as you are working through the steps that follow:

1. Work to understand student learning needs. What is the best way for you to represent materials for students? Would students benefit from the information being displayed in different ways?

2. Identify relevant education and learning goals. What are the short- and long-term learning goals of the curriculum? Would students benefit from having choices in their goals?

3. Examine the learning environment. What aspects of the classroom could be more universally designed, allowing you to present information in several different ways?

4. Identify barriers in the current environment and curricula. Do the goals allow students only one option for their response? Could you consider providing different ways for students to express themselves through words, actions, and expressions?

5. Identify universally designed solutions. As you work to identify universally designed solutions, one of the critical steps is to anticipate students' needs and then build multiple means of representation, expression, and engagement into the curriculum from the start. The best way to do this is to use backwards design, or starting with the end goal in mind and planning lessons from there.

6. Evaluate how you implement the solutions and adjust them as needed. Are you seeing changes in students' attainment of their goals?

We mentioned in Step 5 the importance of backwards design. Figure 6.2 provides an overview of the UDL Instructional Planning Process. It provides you with concrete ideas about how to engage in backwards planning, and more specifically how to use the UDL Guidelines and checkpoints to establish outcomes of your instruction, anticipate learner needs, and deliver instruction aligned with UDL guidelines for representation, expression and action, and engagement. This backwards planning process concludes with reflection, during which you use what you have learned from trying the UDL guidelines to come up with new ideas regarding your future instruction. UDL promotes opportunities not only for student growth but also for your growth as an educator.

Teaching Arrangements

Another aspect of designing the learning environment requires educators to collaborate with each other to deliver high-quality instruction. Do you recall how several teachers supported Jack and how they collaborated to make sure he was successful in the general education classroom? Remember that Christina is the "education specialist" who co-teaches with Jack's classroom teachers in his four core academic classes. Co-teaching exemplifies collaboration between general and special educators.

This IRIS instructional module will teach you more about UDL with great examples of how it can be used to develop learning goals, instructional materials, instructional methods, and assessments. https://iris.peabody.vanderbilt.edu/module/udl/

CO-TEACHING   The concept of co-teaching is quite simple: A general education and special education teacher work together as equal partners in the classroom. Each is responsible for all students, and each takes an active role in the classroom (Villa & Thousand, 2016). Each addresses the needs of students with and without exceptionalities in the classroom and is knowledgeable about students' IEPs or Section 504 goals and accommodations.

Co-teaching thereby gives students an opportunity to learn from two professionals, each with different expertise. Co-teaching arrangements are particularly beneficial as today's schools implement inclusive practices with an increasingly diverse student body (Scruggs & Mastropieri, 2017).

The success of co-teaching depends on a number of factors, but effective collaboration is a necessity. Think about the high-leverage practices you learned about earlier and the

Figure 6.2 UDL Instructional Planning Process

As a framework, UDL requires educators to think proactively about the variability of all learners. In consideration of the UDL Critical Elements, educators implementing UDL should use a backwards design instructional process that incorporates the following five steps.

STEP 1: ESTABLISH CLEAR OUTCOMES

Establish a clear understanding of the goal(s) of the lesson and specific learner outcomes related to:

- The desired outcomes and essential student understandings and performance for every learner. (What will learning look like? What will students be able to do or demonstrate?)
- The desired big ideas and their alignment to the established standards within the program of study that learners should understand.
- The potential misunderstandings, misconceptions and areas where learners may meet barriers to learning.
- How goals will be clearly communicated to the learners, in ways that are understandable to all learners.

STEP 2: ANTICIPATE LEARNER VARIABILITY

- Curriculum barriers (e.g., physical, social, cultural or ability-level) that could limit the accessibility to instruction and instructional materials.
- Learner strengths and weaknesses specific to lesson/unit goals.
- Learner background knowledge for scaffolding new learning.
- Learner preferences for representation, expression and engagement.
- Learner language preferences.
- Cultural relevance and understanding.

STEP 3: MEASURABLE OUTCOMES AND ASSESSMENT PLAN

Prior to planning the instructional experience, establish how learning is going to be measured. Considerations should include:

- Previously established lesson goals and learner needs.
- Embedding checkpoints to ensure all learners are successfully meeting their desired outcomes.
- Providing learners multiple ways and options to authentically engage in the process, take action and demonstrate understanding.
- Supporting higher-order skills and encouraging a deeper connection with the content.

STEP 4: INSTRUCTIONAL EXPERIENCE

Establish the instructional sequence of events. At minimum plans should include:

- Intentional and proactive ways to address the established goals, learner variability and the assessment plan.
- Establish a plan for how instructional materials and strategies will be used to overcome barriers and support learner understanding.
- A plan that ensures high expectations for all learners and the needs of the learners in the margins (i.e., struggling and advanced), anticipating that a broader range of learners will benefit.
- Integrate an assessment plan to provide necessary data.

  Considerations should be made for how to support multiple means of . . .

  - **Engagement:** A variety of methods are used to engage students (e.g., provide choice and address student interest) and promote their ability to monitor their own learning (e.g., goal setting, self-assessment and reflection).
  - **Representation:** Teacher purposefully uses a variety of strategies, instructional tools and methods to present information and content to anticipate student needs and preferences.
  - **Expression & Action:** Student uses a variety of strategies, instructional tools and methods to demonstrate new understandings.

STEP 5: REFLECTION AND NEW UNDERSTANDINGS

Establish checkpoints for teacher reflection and new understandings. Considerations should include:

- Whether the learners obtained the big ideas and obtained the desired outcomes. (What data support your inference?)
- What instructional strategies worked well?
- How can instructional strategies be improved?
- What tools worked well?
- How could the use of tools be improved?
- What strategies and tools provided for multiple means of representation, action/expression and engagement?
- What additional tools would have been beneficial to have access to and why?
- Overall, how might you improve this lesson?

SOURCE: The "UDL Instructional Planning Process" was created by the UDL Implementation and Research Network, Inc. (UDL-IRN) and is licensed under an international Creative Commons License – CC BY-ND.

importance of collaboration for supporting students. When general and special educators regard each other as partners, they are more effective co-teachers (Gebhardt, Schwab, Krammer, & Gegenfurtner, 2015). And, not surprisingly, teachers who have more frequent communication and interaction with their co-teachers (and a smaller number of co-teachers) find that co-teaching is more beneficial for students (Pancsofar & Petroff, 2016).

CO-TEACHING ARRANGEMENTS   So, how does co-teaching work? One common technique involves one teacher designing and delivering instruction while the other teacher is providing individualized support to students (Pancsofar & Petroff, 2016). This approach is referred to as "one teach, one assist" (Friend & Cook, 2010). The technique draws on the skills of the general educator in terms of the content of instruction and on the skills of the special educator in individualizing based on student needs. But, this also can be a less collaborative approach when the two teachers do not jointly plan what they will teach and who will have what role. Having time to plan is highly important to successful co-teaching (Pancsofar & Petroff, 2016).

An alternative to "one teach, one assist" is a "teaming" approach. Here, both educators take responsibility for class content and jointly plan for and deliver instructional content. Teaming tends to lead to more feelings of partnership among teachers and a greater sense of shared responsibility for all students. The *Into Practice Across Grade Levels: Different Types of Co-teaching Arrangements in a Science Class* feature provides examples of "one teach, one assist," "teaming," and other types of co-teaching arrangements: parallel teaching, alternative teaching, station teaching, and one teach, one observe. The guidelines give you some ideas of how co-teaching may occur in an inclusive 8th-grade science class, co-taught by Ms. Sweeney, a general education science teacher, and Mr. Corgan, a special education teacher.

MyLab Education
Video Example 6.4
Teaming can be a collaborative effort within a classroom but it can also involve communicating across grade levels. How can teachers effectively plan for collaboration to make the curriculum accessible to all students?

Into Practice Across Grade Levels
Different Types of Co-teaching Arrangements in a Science Class

Teaming.

Teachers work together to lead the class, both using their areas of expertise to benefit all students. *Example:* Ms. Sweeney and Mr. Corgan lead the class together in a lecture on rivers and streams as dynamic systems impacting topography. Ms. Sweeney uses her extensive knowledge of science to develop the content and Mr. Corgan utilizes his knowledge of universal deisgn for learning to create multiple ways for students to engage with the content.

One teach, one assist.

One teacher delivers content, and the other provides support to individual or groups of students as needed. *Example:* As Ms. Sweeney (general educator) teaches a lesson on water systems and habitats, Mr. Corgan (special educator) circulates and supports students individually as needed.

Parallel teaching.

The teachers divide the time that they are responsible for instruction. *Example:* Ms. Sweeney and Mr. Corgan each lead half the class in a lesson on Earth's surface, with instructional differentiation as needed provided by both teachers during their teaching time.

Alternative teaching.

The teachers teach different content, with the special education teacher responsible for more intensive instruction with smaller groups. *Example:* Ms. Sweeney leads most students through a critical thinking activity on topography, while Mr. Corgan reviews essential prior content knowledge with a small group in need of support.

Station teaching.

Teachers take responsibility for different learning stations in the classroom. *Example:* Mr. Corgan leads a station reviewing the weathering of rock and soil, Ms. Sweeney leads a station introducing the effects of rivers and streams, and students work through the textbook together as peer tutors at a third station.

One teach, one observe.

One teacher teaches content and the other observes and collects data. *Example:* Ms. Sweeney leads the class in a lesson about Earth's surface, while Mr. Corgan observes and collects data on student participation.

SOURCE: Developed by Kathryn Burke, University of Kansas, former special education teacher, adapted from Friend, M., & Cook, L. (2010). *Interactions: Collaboration skills for school professionals* (6th ed.). Columbus, OH: Merrill.

CO-PLANNING   We've mentioned how important collaboration is in the context of co-teaching. A critical aspect of co-teaching, then, is effective co-planning (Wilson, 2016). The logistics of coordinating time to co-plan can often be the most challenging element of co-teaching. Here is how you can undertake co-planning:

- Use the unique expertise of both teachers
- Share the classroom and instructional workload
- Break down content and steps for co-planning, at the unit, weekly, and daily level
- Plan for long-term goals and objectives, but also communicate frequently about daily preparation and instructional adjustments (Pratt, Imbody, Wolf, & Patterson, 2017).

Whatever co-teaching arrangement you use, the general education teacher typically serves as the content expert, particularly related to curriculum competencies, lesson pacing, and general classroom management (Friend, Cook, Hurley-Chamberlain, & Shamberger, 2010). The special education teacher also possesses content knowledge but brings additional expertise on individualized instruction to meet the support needs of all students, particularly those with exceptionalities (Pratt et al., 2017).

Hero Images/Getty Images

In a co-teaching arrangement, the general educator generally is the content expert; the special educator shares expertise on individualizing instruction.

After reading this, you are probably wondering, how do teachers do this? And, what are the benefits for them and for their students? The feature *My Voice: Angela and Kelsey—A Teaching Partnership* reveals how Angela, a general education science teacher, and Kelsey, a special education teacher, do it and how their collaboration benefits them and their students.

My Voice

Angela and Kelsey—A Teaching Partnership

Angela Dieker and Kelsey Stolt are middle school teachers—Angela teaches general education science classes, and Kelsey supports students with disabilities in a variety of subjects. Together, they co-teach a 7th-grade science class. As Angela has noted, "Teaching students with moderate to severe disabilities is a collaborative effort that involves many different people."

Angela has observed the shift in inclusive education during her time in the field. "I was an education student in the years just after the passage of IDEA in 1975 and in my beginning years of teaching I saw the special education classroom move from an annex building that was a full city block down the street from the main school building. I remember hearing at the time that "by law" the special education program could no longer remain in a separate building. Unfortunately, though, the special program only moved into a self-contained classroom in the basement of the main building. The students with disabilities, during the eight years that I spent at that school, were never included in the general education classes."

Regarding the promotion of inclusion as a part of co-teaching efforts, Kelsey, a newer teacher who has spent 3½ years in the classroom, talked about things as straightforward as modifying the physical environment of a classroom to better fit a student's needs: "When I am in a classroom with a student, I always feel strange moving around seating arrangements or asking the teacher if she would mind turning off a set of lights. I need to remember that these are simple ways that I can make the environment more accessible for the students I am working with."

Angela and Kelsey have built a partnership in which they can communicate about small or large changes to meet the needs of all their students. Angela said, "Although the physical space [in my classroom] is limited and the lab stations are in fixed locations within the room, there are some items which I can move or change in an attempt to minimize distractions and make the space more conducive to learning."

Managing paraprofessionals as members of the teaching team has been another area of focus for Angela and Kelsey.

(Continued)

While traditionally paraprofessionals are given guidance on working with students from special education teachers, Angela has learned to take on that role as well. "Too much adult assistance given to students with moderate to severe disabilities is a common practice. I have a paraprofessional who accompanies a student with a low incidence disability to my science class. This adult asked, with good intentions, that I move a student without a disability to a different seat in the classroom so that she, the para-educator, could sit at the table in the group beside the student she accompanies to the class. I explained to her that I had given a great deal of thought to the seating arrangement and groupings in the classroom and that I would prefer she pull a chair up to the table when the student needs assistance, to scribe for example, but that I would like for the students at the table to interact with the student."

While Kelsey also reported challenges such as coordinating times for team members to meet and managing paraprofessionals, she also said, "It is clear that full inclusion is best practice for students with severe disabilities, and I should continue my efforts to fully include all of my students . . . It is nice to have research backing my thoughts."

SOURCE: Written by Kathryn Burke, University of Kansas. Quotations printed with permission from Angela Dieker and Kelsey Stolt, Lawrence, Kansas.

Specially Designed Instruction and Supports for Students with Disabilities

You may remember that instruction was one domain of the high-leverage practices that you learned about at the beginning of this chapter, and Figure 6.1 identified several instructional practices that should be considered across grade levels, content areas, and abilities to deliver effective special education supports and services. You may also remember we said that these high-leverage practices provide a starting point for thinking about specially designed instruction that will be individualized for each student who needs special education services and supports. So, high-leverage practices for instruction provide guidance on effective strategies that you can consider as you develop individualized, specially designed instruction for each student you support (Riccomini et al., 2017).

Because of the importance of instruction, in this section we will provide you with more information on a few specific instructional practices and supports that can particularly benefit students with disabilities. High-leverage practices can help ensure you are providing specially designed instruction for individual students, based on a particular student's learning needs. You'll learn even more in the chapters that follow about specially designed instruction for students with particular exceptionality-related needs. Start now, however, by learning about general strategies that, being research-based, can ensure that your students will make progress in the general education curriculum and achieve their individualized learning goals.

To begin, let's review what you learned in Chapter 4 about specially designed instruction, as IDEA defines that term: *Specially designed instruction* means adapting, as appropriate to the needs of an eligible child . . . the content, methodology, or delivery of instruction—(i) to address the unique needs of the child that result from the child's disability; and (ii) to ensure access of the child to the general curriculum, so that the child can meet the educational standards within the jurisdiction of the public agency that apply to all children.

Specially designed instruction, then, is used to ensure that each student makes progress in the general education curriculum and achieves individualized learning goals (Taub, McCord, & Ryndak, 2017). Being inherently individualized, specially designed instruction should vary for each student but is always based on the student's individualized learning needs, determined through the high-leverage practice of meaningful assessment (Yell & Bateman, 2017).

Specially designed instruction is a necessity, for sure. However, it is not always sufficient to ensure progress. It can help to ensure progress, but by itself it may not be enough. What complements it is the array of supports that enable students to engage with specially designed instruction and the general education curriculum.

The array includes the **related services** in a student's IEP. These services encompass those delivered by physical therapists, occupational therapists, speech-language pathologists, psychologists, social workers, and other related service professionals. For example, a physical therapist might work with a student with a physical disability to ensure the best positioning for participation in activities in the general education classroom (see Chapter 14). At WISH Academy, Jack receives three related services. Through occupational therapy (OT) he is learning to use American Sign Language to communicate. Through physical therapy, he is learning how to walk on his own. Through speech therapy, he is learning how to be more articulate.

The array also includes **supplementary aids and services** specified in a student's IEP. Supplementary aids and services encompass aids, services, and other supports that are provided to a student to enable education in the general education classroom and curriculum. Supplementary aids and services can include extended time on testing, different pacing for classroom learning, and support from peers or a paraprofessional in the classroom.

Taken together, specially designed instruction, related services, and supplementary aids and services support students to access and progress in the curriculum, achieving their individually valued outcomes, as well as IDEA's four goals of equal opportunity, independent living, full participation, and economic self-sufficiency. To support students with disabilities to engage and progress in the general curriculum, you will need to understand the general education curriculum standards adopted by a school (Chapter 4) as well as the school-wide systems and their use of tiered systems (Chapter 5). The general education curriculum and academic, behavioral, and social and emotional skills are your starting points as you identify the specially designed instruction and supports your students need to engage in that curriculum.

At this point, you may wonder, "When will I learn about how to teach students with particular types of disability or special gifts and talents?" The answer is, "Soon enough." For example, you'll learn about communication and social interaction for those with communication disorders (Chapter 8), about how supports for those interactions are especially useful for students with autism spectrum disorders (Chapter 12), and about orientation and mobility skills for students who are vision impaired or blind (Chapter 15). The good news—the general point for now—is that there are a wide array of specially designed instruction practices, some of which are high-leverage practices that are likely to benefit all students without regard to the nature or type of their learning abilities or needs, their ages, or the curriculum they must learn. Others, however, will be more specialized to the individualized needs of students, some of which will be related to the characteristics of their disability.

As you are trying to identify research-based practices for teaching specific skills or supporting students of a specific age or with a specific exceptionality to access the general education curriculum or achieve individualized learning goals, you will have access to great web-based resources. Earlier in this chapter, you learned about the CEC and High-Leverage Practices websites and the resources they provide. An additional resource is the What Works Clearinghouse. The U.S. Department of Education and Institute of Education Sciences developed the Clearinghouse; it is a definitive resource of research-based practices. Its information is searchable and is presented in an educator-friendly format.

When you visit the website, you'll notice a section on Children and Youth with Disabilities. If you navigate to this section, you'll find a number of different curricula or instructional strategies that have been reviewed. For example, you'll discover Peer Assisted Learning Strategies (PALS; D. Fuchs, Fuchs, Mathes, & Simmons, 1997), a peer-mediated support intervention (you'll learn more about these later) in which peers tutor and coach each other to learn. PALS promotes student reading and literacy outcomes.

Go to https://ies.ed.gov/ncee/ wwc/ and review the synthesis of research to better understand what works in education.

And research has shown it benefits students with learning disabilities, young children, adolescents, and English language learners. The What Works Clearinghouse, then, is a rich source of resources for you now and later.

Instructional Practices for Students with Disabilities

It bears repeating that specially designed instruction is individualized and enables students with disabilities and gifts and talents to engage with the curriculum and achieve their individualized learning goals. Many research-based practices are available, but in this section we will highlight two that warrant your particular attention—explicit instruction and embedded instruction.

EXPLICIT INSTRUCTION Explicit instruction is a high-leverage practice that can impact the learning of students with disabilities. This practice requires you to make it crystal-clear to your students exactly what they will learn or the intended outcome of your instruction (Woods, Geller, & Basaraba, 2018). For example, you might start a lesson by saying, "Today we will explore a strategy for multiplying fractions." You then will model the targeted skills or concept (a strategy for multiplying fractions), step-by-step, using clear, succinct language. For instance, you might state, "The first thing I do when I compare fractions is make sure the denominators are the same." And, you will explicitly define the term "denominators." Then, after explicitly stating the concept of why and how to multiply fractions, you provide your students opportunities to practice doing just that.

This approach—teaching a logical sequence of objectives (Archer & Hughes, 2011) by identifying the critical content of the curriculum and showing your students how to proceed (Smith, Sáez, & Doabler, 2018)—is sometimes called the "I do, you do, we do" model. It promotes your students' engagement by reducing any ambiguity that might creep into your teaching and their learning.

You can use several instructional strategies to effectively implement explicit instruction (Archer & Hughes, 2011). It is important to use these strategies:

1. Before instruction
2. During instruction
3. During student practice.

The *Into Practice Across Grade Levels: Implementing Explicit Instruction* provides you with examples of you how can integrate explicit instruction before and during instruction as well as during student practice.

Into Practice Across Grade Levels

Implementing Explicit Instruction

Before Instruction.

- Prioritize content based on age-appropriate curriculum and student strengths and needs.
- Sequence introduction of skills by level of difficulty, importance, and content-related factors. *Example: Plan to support students learning to write narratives by first allowing them to orally dictate their content. As they make progress, encourage them to write their ideas in bullet points, then full sentences.*

- Break down skills and strategies into smaller instructional units. *Example: When planning to teach students how to solve word problems, plan for breaking them down into weekly units that address comprehending the text, choosing operations, writing and solving equations, and writing answers in word form.*
- Create organized and focused lessons.
- Plan for the use of techniques that organize content knowledge. *Example: When planning to introduce a*

social studies unit on tribal communities in North America, incorporate several instructional topics you've already covered that are linked, such as U.S. geography and landforms.

During Instruction.

- State learning goals and expectations clearly.
- Review prior knowledge and skills. *Example: Create a K-W-L (What do I know? What do I want to know? What have I learned) and ask students to share what they know about the topic already as you add it to the chart.*
- Model instructions step-by-step. *Example: To model instructions, step-by step, say something like, "Right now, I'm scanning the text looking for key words to help complete this section of our story map."*
- Use clear, concise, and consistent language.
- Provide sufficient examples and nonexamples. *Example: Create a clearly labeled anchor chart with an example of a sentence with appropriate capitalization and punctuation (e.g., starts with a capital letter, ends with a period) and a nonexample (e.g., random capitalization, no punctuation at the end).*

- Ask for student responses frequently.
- Teach the lesson at a reasonable pace.

During Student Practice.

- Provide opportunities for guided and supported practice. *Example: "Now that I've shown you how to do addition with regrouping, let's try one together. Who can tell me the first step?"*
- Monitor student performance.
- Ask for student responses frequently. *Example: "Now, it's your turn. Skim the text and underline information you can use for the 'character' section of the story map."*
- Offer instantaneous affirmative and corrective feedback. *Example: "Hannah, the information you underlined is about the plot. Here's an example about a character (points in text). What details can you find about this character?*
- Ensure student practice is distributed and cumulative.

SOURCE: Adapted by Kathryn Burke, former special education teacher, University of Kansas, from Archer, A. L., & Hughes, C. A. (2011). *Explicit instruction: Effective and efficient teaching.* New York, NY: Guilford Press.

When beginning to use explicit instruction, focus on a level at which your students are already proficient. Start the lesson by reviewing prerequisite skills; when you do that, you refresh your students' memory, enabling them to be successful and building their confidence to attack new curricula (Doabler et al., 2016). During the lesson, make simple and concise word choices. Focus on foundational vocabulary to enable your students to connect to related words and concepts (Santoro, Baker, Flen, Smith, & Chard, 2016)—for example, define "denominator." That helps students understand and recall core concepts. As they practice the skill(s), provide feedback, evaluate their progress, and determine whether they are understanding. As needed, repeat your instruction.

As you might expect from reading about explicit instruction, teachers and students interact frequently. During your interactions with students, focus on these practices to implement explicit instruction:

- Clearly and concisely model concepts
- Provide regular opportunities for students to practice what you modeled
- Provide immediate feedback on student performance.

The "I do, you do, we do" model that characterizes explicit instruction has been shown to benefit students with and without disabilities. For example, when explicit instruction is used to teach elementary math concepts, kindergarteners who receive instruction using a curriculum that integrates explicit instruction show greater gains in numerical sense and skills than students who do not receive explicit instruction (Clarke et al., 2016). Similar effects are noted when explicit instruction is used to teach social studies content to upper elementary students with learning disabilities (Ciullo, Falcomata, & Vaughn, 2015) and reading skills to elementary students with autism spectrum disorders. For example, 45 elementary students with autism spectrum disorders showed more progress in vocabulary, main idea identification, and text structure when their teachers used explicit instruction versus typical instruction (Roux, Dion, Barrette, Dupéré, & Fuchs, 2015). Likewise, explicit instruction is highly effective in teaching math concepts to older students with learning disabilities (Leach, 2016). This is why explicit instruction is an important strategy to understand and integrate into your teaching: It benefits a wide range of students with disabilities.

EMBEDDED INSTRUCTION Embedded instruction also supports students in making progress while engaging with the general education classroom and curriculum. Embedded instruction differs from explicit instruction in that it focuses on "embedding" additional opportunities for learning for students with exceptionalities in the general education curriculum, instruction, and activities. In embedded instruction, you insert additional learning opportunities within the natural context and flow of the school day (Jimenez & Kamei, 2015). For example, during the transition between science stations in a science class, you might have students with disabilities focus on building skills related to transitioning effectively between tasks (which may be an IEP goal for some students). During the transition time, students could practice skills they are learning about communicating with peers, with prompts from you, the teacher, during this time. You'll learn more about how embedded instruction can support the learning of students with intellectual disability, with a focus on enabling progress and participation in general education environments in Chapter 11.

However, embedded instruction can be effective for a wide range of students, across the ages, and in different content areas. In fact, embedded instruction can also focus on advanced or more in-depth opportunities to practice skills related to the curriculum. For example, during independent work activities, you might have some students practice additional and more advanced science vocabulary (which may be a goal for students who are gifted) or give extra time to practice identifying key social studies vocabulary words that the class is learning (which may be a goal for students with disabilities who might need more time to practice key content). Embedded instruction also works with young children; as early as preschool, for example, educators can use embedded instruction to target skills (e.g., social skills, communication skills) during natural routines in the classroom, such as playtime or transition time.

When using embedded instruction in the classroom, you start by identifying the target student's priority learning goals. Remember that embedded instruction, as a form of specially designed instruction, is individualized to the particular student and the skills targeted to that student. After identifying priority learning goals, you can plan instruction to take advantage of natural opportunities in the general education environment.

Key considerations in implementing embedded instruction include:

- The targeted learning goals for students in the general education class are based on the students' IEP goals and objectives and are aligned with the general education curriculum.

- The delivery of embedded instruction is planned for and scheduled within the natural flow of typical instruction and activities in the general education classroom.

- The instruction is integrated into class activities and transitions between activities so that students do not miss important class content.

- Embedded instruction is implemented using effective instructional practices (perhaps even explicit instruction), and generalization to other learning environments and goals is planned for.

- Student progress and performance data are regularly recorded and reviewed to make instructional decisions on the effectiveness of the embedded instruction (McDonnell, Jameson, Riesen, & Polychronis, 2014; McDonnell, Johnson, & McQuivey, 2008).

Figure 6.3 provides examples of how teachers start to plan for and collaborate to implement embedded instruction.

When using embedded instruction in the general education classroom, you will find it useful to develop a plan that facilitates conversation between general and special educators and guides implementation. Figure 6.4, which shows an embedded

Go to https://embeddedinstruction. net/ for examples of how embedded instruction is used to support teachers working with preschoolers. You can learn about projects in the United States and around the world. (Yes, embedded instruction is being used in New Zealand, Australia, Turkey, and Portugal, to support young children with disabilities!)

Figure 6.3 Implementing Embedded Instruction

- **Who can embed instruction?**

  - General education teachers, special education teachers, paraprofessionals, and peers

- **What are appropriate grade levels for embedded instruction?**

  - Any grade levels: elementary, middle, and high schools

- **What skills can be embedded during general education instruction?**

  - Embedded instruction can be used to teach a variety of skills (e.g., vocabulary words, time telling, content-specific words/terms). However, identifying and selecting skills aligned with the general education curriculum that are meaningful and relevant to students' specific learning goals should be the focus.

- **What content areas are appropriate for embedded instruction?**

  - Any subjects (e.g., language arts, science, math, social science, art, music) in which students with exceptionalities have individualized learning goals.

- **In what contexts can instruction be embedded?**

  - Any time during the lesson or instructional period when there are natural breaks
  - During opening and closing activities
  - During transitions, breaks, and independent seat work
  - At any other naturally occurring opportunities during the lesson or lab

- **What are possible barriers for implementing embedded instruction?**

  - Finding the right balance between the natural flow and pace of the general education classroom and embedded instruction
  - Ensuring that students also have opportunities for breaks and engaging informally with peers

- **What preparation needs to take place before implementing embedded instruction?**

  - Establish collaboration between general education and special education teachers to plan for embedded instruction within general education curriculum and standards
  - Select students' IEP goal(s) and objective(s) to be embedded for instruction
  - Establish the student's baseline performance by conducting a baseline assessment on a target skill
  - Develop an individualized embedded instruction plan that identifies what skill(s) will be targeted, during what activity, and by whom
  - Implement the embedded instruction plan

SOURCES: Adapted by Mayumi Hagiwara, University of Kansas, former special education teacher, from: Jimenez, B. A., & Kamei, A. (2015). Embedded instruction: an evaluation of evidence to inform inclusive practice. *Inclusion, 3*, 132–144. doi:10.1352/2326-6988-3.3.132; McDonnell, J., Jameson, M. J., Riesen, T., & Polychronis, S. (2014). Embedded instruction in inclusive settings. In D. Browder & F. Spooner (Eds.), *More language arts, math, and science for students with severe disabilities* (pp. 19–25). Baltimore, MD: Brookes; and Ruppar, A. L., Afacan, K., & Pickett, K. J. (2017). Embedded shared reading to increase literacy in an inclusive English/language arts class: Preliminary efficacy and ecological validity. *Education and Training in Autism and Developmental Disabilities, 52*, 51–63.

instruction plan in an elementary school, provides an example. This format is adaptable across ages and exceptionality-related needs and learning goals.

When incorporating embedded instruction into natural activities, routines, and transitions, students have improved performance both on individualized learning goals and in the general education curriculum (McDonnell, 2014). For example, embedded instruction in the general education classroom has shown as much effectiveness as small-group instruction in a separate classroom for teaching vocabulary words to middle school students with disabilities, suggesting that additional, embedded instruction can be provided while students are included in the general education classroom (McDonnell et al., 2006). Similar outcomes have been found for junior high students (McDonnell, Johnson, Polychronis, & Riesen, 2002). And, embedded instruction has been combined with other evidence-based practices to teach literacy skills to high school students in general education English/language arts classes. (Ruppar, Afacan, Yang, & Pickett, 2017). A variety of professionals can effectively use embedded instruction, including early childhood and special education teachers (Bishop, Snyder, & Crow, 2015), paraprofessionals (McDonnell et al., 2002), and general education

Figure 6.4 Embedded Instruction Plan in an Elementary School

Student Name: <u>Mary</u>   **Instructors:** <u>Ms. Santos (special education teacher) and Ms. Smith (general education teacher)</u>

Peer(s)' Name: <u>Juan & Diane</u>   **Class:** <u>3rd-grade science</u>

Goal: When presented with written and visual vocabulary cards, Mary will match corresponding written and visual images with 100% accuracy on 3 consecutive instructional days.

Instructional activities distribution schedule: Instruction will occur during the transition time between science stations and at the end of small-group activities in the general education science class.

Peer engagement/Peer prompts:

Juan and Diane, with support from Ms. Santos, will spread four written and visual cards linked to the science lesson related to weather during each trial on the table in front of Mary, within her physical reach.

3-second delay—"Mary, match the words with their pictures."

Reinforcement:

Provide verbal praise to Mary, such as "Good job matching the words and pictures!"

Error correction:

- Say, "Let's try it again" and spread the cards out again.
- If Mary makes correct pairings and incorrect pairings, point to which ones are correct and which ones are incorrect.

Generalization: When changing the weather cards (a classroom activity that all students engage in during morning routine), Ms. Smith will ask Mary to name a card that corresponds with one of the visual vocabulary cards.

SOURCE: Adapted by Mayumi Hagiwara, University of Kansas, former special education teacher, from McDonnell, J., Jameson, M. J., Riesen, T., & Polychronis, S. (2014). Embedded instruction in inclusive settings. In D. Browder & F. Spooner (Eds.), *More language arts, math, and science for students with severe disabilities* (pp. 19–25). Baltimore, MD: Brookes.

teachers (Polychronis, McDonnell, Johnson, Riesen, & Jameson, 2004). In fact, teachers and caregivers in early intervention home visits can even work together in learning to embed interventions (Salisbury et al., 2018), showing the wide range of ages that can be targeted with embedded instruction.

Instructional Supports for Students with Disabilities

Instructional supports provide students with tools or resources that enable them to engage with the general education curriculum to achieve their individualized learning goals. Because they are individualized and rest on assessments and collaboration, a student's related services and supplementary aids and services are vital instructional supports. In the chapters that follow, you will learn exactly how to support students who have specific disability-related needs. Now, however, you will learn about two supports that benefit nearly all students. They are assistive technology and peer support.

ASSISTIVE TECHNOLOGY   Technology is essential to our lives; it is especially so to promote access, inclusion, and progress for students with exceptionalities. When we discussed Book Builder earlier in this chapter, we introduced you to instructional technologies in the context of UDL. Assistive technology (AT), however, differs slightly from instructional technology, although there is increasing overlap in our modern world (Shepley, Lane, Ayres, & Douglas, 2017). What defines assistive technology is that it focuses on enabling a student to have *access* to the general education classroom and curriculum (and all other important activities in school and outside school); by contrast, instructional technology focuses on building a student's skills to *learn* the general education curriculum. Access is necessary for learning, and learning makes access meaningful.

In determining a student's needs for assistive technology, as IDEA requires IEP team members to do, you and your partners on a student's IEP team should:

- Assess aspects of participation that are difficult for the student in the general education classroom and curriculum.

- Determine if there are assistive technologies that could address these participation barriers.

- Collect information about possible assistive technology options in collaboration with the student, family, and related service professionals.

- Experiment with different assistive technologies to determine the best fit for the student and the student's needs.

- After identifying most appropriate assistive technologies, develop a plan for supporting the use of the technology in the classroom and collect data on impact on outcomes related to the student's access.

- Develop a plan to maintain devices, how a student will use assistive technology across home and school, and how to respond to a student's changing preferences and needs.

To determine if a student could benefit from assistive technology and when and if changes are needed over time, use the high-leverage practices related to assessment, particularly collecting multiple sources of assessment information and collecting ongoing data on intended outcomes. Collaboration by IEP team members can help to identify the most appropriate low- and/or high-tech solutions to enable student participation. This team approach is critical and should involve the entire IEP team

Collaboration and effective assessment practices are critical because of the range of possible AT-related supports, and the different domains of participation that can be targeted through AT. For example, AT might address needs related to:

- Environmental access (e.g., automatic door openers, a switch that a student can use to turn on lights or to indicate a desire to respond to a question)

- Mobility (e.g., motorized or manual wheelchairs, crutches, adapted equipment such as bicycles for participation in sporting activities)

- Positioning (e.g., adjustable tables that students can lean on, standers that students can use to stand upright during activities, wedges that enable students to sit up during circle time)

- Communication (e.g., picture symbols, voice-output devices)

- Learning (e.g., screen reading programs that read text aloud, amplifiers so students can more clearly hear instruction that a teacher is delivering, large-print books or magnifiers).

This is just a starting point. Assistive technology can address a wide range of access-related needs—which is why it is so important to individualize and plan collaboratively with students and families. In fact, one of the major findings of a synthesis of over 60 studies on assistive technology published over a 15-year period was that families and students need to be involved in identifying, selecting, and maintaining AT for it to impact student outcomes (Alper & Raharinirina, 2006).

As a teacher, it is critical for you to consider AT and its potential to affect access and progress for students you support. Recently, it has been suggested that there is significant underutilization of AT to support students with disabilities across grade levels (Quinn et al., 2009) and especially at the high school level (Bouck, 2016). This is particularly true for assistive technologies that might promote access to learning opportunities and general education environments for students with learning disabilities, emotional-behavior disorders, mild intellectual disability, speech-language impairments, and other health impairments, such as attention-deficit hyperactivity disorder (Bouck, 2016). This is troubling given data that suggest when students receive

MyLab Education
Video Example 6.5
In this video, Elle and her mother share her story using Dynavox. How did Elle's IEP team help find the best assistive technology for Elle? https://www.youtube.com/watch?v=g95TO20hnmo

appropriate AT services and supports while they are in school, they are more likely to have positive postschool outcomes in the areas of employment, postsecondary education, and independent living (Bouck & Flanagan, 2016).

Ensuring access to needed technologies to enable communication, mobility, and participation is also critical. While students with multiple disabilities, physical disabilities, and sensory impairments may be more likely to access needed AT for communication and mobility, there are ongoing limitations to how effectively plans are developed for students to be able to use their AT across environments and across home and school (Quinn et al., 2009). Again, this is why collaboration and assessment are important.

So, you might be wondering, given the range of assistive technologies, the differing domains that assistive technology can target, and the differing needs of students with disabilities, how can AT be individualized to the needs of each student? How can you figure this out as an educator? This is a reasonable question, as teachers tend to report low knowledge of specific AT devices and how to individualize based on students' needs (Okolo & Diedrich, 2014).

The good news is that resources are available that you can use as an educator. For example, each state has an Assistive Technology Program (ATP). It is an important resource for learning about and acquiring (or learning where to acquire) assistive technologies. ATPs are funded by the federal government to provide various services, including assistive technology demonstration and loan programs. Students, families, and teachers can use these loan programs to get individualized advice and test out possible AT devices. Visit the Association of Assistive Technology Act Programs website to learn more and search for the available state programs where you are now or will be in the future.

> Go to https://www.at3center.net/stateprogram to learn more assistive technology resources in your state. Select the AT Program and then enter your state to find out more about where you can get additional information on AT.

Many states have also developed additional resources specifically for teachers, to provide ideas and examples for how to identify needs for assistive technology and determine the best types of assistive technologies for specific needs. For example, the Georgia Project for Assistive Technology offers guidance for educators on possible assistive technologies that can support students in many of the domains identified previously; comprehensive lists of high- and low-tech solutions are available.

> Go to http://www.gpat.org/ and select Assistive Technology devices. From here, you can explore to find examples of technologies that are effective in promoting access to learning and communication for students.

One final resource that can be highly useful is AbleData, a website funded by the federal government to provide a database of assistive technologies for people with disabilities and those who support them. For example, remember the video about Elle and how her team selected a Dynavox? There is information on AbleData about different types of Dynavox systems, descriptions of the differences, and ratings from users of this assistive technology. So, this website can be a very useful resource, as you can search it for any assistive technology you are considering or for ideas based on a specific area or need for which you are seeking solutions.

PEER-MEDIATED SUPPORTS   When you were an elementary school student, you might have been paired with a classmate to read a story together or do a classroom activity. You may have enjoyed the activity as well as engaging with your peer, perhaps even developing a friendship over time. Or maybe when you were a high school student you asked a friend (not your math teacher) for help with your math homework. Were there other occasions when you received support from or gave support to your classmates? Was one or more of those occasions important to your learning and building friendships? If so, you benefited from peer-mediated support. So it should not surprise you to learn that students with and without disabilities benefit both socially and academically from peer-mediated supports (Brock & Huber, 2017; Carter, Sisco, Chung, & Stanton-Chapman, 2010; Schaefer, Cannella-Malone, & Carter, 2016).

Having peers deliver instruction and supports can also be as effective in some circumstances as using teachers or paraprofessionals (Biggs & Carter, 2017). Peer-mediated supports promote social interactions, access to a wider range of social supports, increased academic engagement, decreased use of paraprofessionals, and greater achievement of learning goals in students with disabilities (Brock, Biggs, Carter, Cattey, & Raley, 2016; Brock & Huber, 2017). Further, peers without exceptionalities who participate in peer-mediated interventions maintain or even improve their own academic achievement while serving as a peer support (Schaefer et al., 2016). That is true across a wide range of grade levels, including elementary school, middle school, and high school levels. Peer-mediated supports can even be used to teach skills across a wide range of areas including academic behaviors, communication initiations/responses, and interactions (Schaefer et al., 2016).

Peer supports can promote social interactions.

To implement peer-mediated interventions, you need to design a classroom environment to promote collaboration, full participation, and belonging among all students—those with and those without exceptionalities (Biggs & Carter, 2017). Each of the following examples of peer-mediated interventions involves students with and without disabilities.

- **Peer Support Arrangements.** Increase opportunities for social interactions and shared learning by arranging one or more peers to provide ongoing academic and social support for a student with disabilities in a general education classroom.

- **Peer Networks.** Promote peer interactions and social connections by establishing structured social groups outside the classroom instruction/activities and during non-instructional times of the day. For instance, peer network activities can happen during lunch, during recess, or after school. These non-instructional times still are times when learning occurs and relationships develop; these times and occasions are of the general curriculum. Jack Steinberg's progress in school has always involved peer networks; his lunch buddies and circle of friends club exemplify peer networking.

- **Peer Partner Programs.** Create a more inclusive school climate by developing structured opportunities for interactions during and beyond the school day, such as regular-basis activities focused on social and/or service learning.

- **Peer Tutoring Programs.** Ask peers to tutor each other as they learn specific academic content. Peer tutoring typically involves each student taking on a tutor as well as a tutee role, promoting self-regulated learning. Earlier in this chapter you read about one peer tutoring program—Peer Assisted Learning Strategies (PALS)—and the research base.

Peer-mediated supports require collaboration not only among peers with and without exceptionalities but also among general and special educators, paraprofessionals who are supporting students with exceptionalities, and other members of a student's IEP team, including families. *Guidelines for Teaching: Implementing Peer-mediated Supports* provides guidance on steps to take in beginning to use peer-mediated supports.

MyLab Education
Video Example 6.6
Peer-mediated support requires collaboration. What training might this peer have gotten to support another student's learning?

Guidelines for Teaching

Implementing Peer-mediated Supports

Craft a peer support plan with the educational team:

- Identify opportunities to promote academic, social, and behavioral skills using peer-mediated supports
- Determine what instructional times and activities are appropriate for a peer-mediated support intervention
- Plan what IEP activities and goals can be incorporated into peer-mediated supports for individual students
- Discuss how to recruit peers: volunteer, nomination by teachers, and/or random assignment
- Set goals (jointly with participating students) related to the peer-mediated supports
- Develop data collection methods
- Define roles that teachers, paraprofessionals, family members, and other members of the IEP team can play in facilitating the peer support arrangements
- Plan for ways to create meaningful roles for students with and without exceptionalities in the arrangement (e.g., how can each student serve as the tutor and tutee; what contributions will students with exceptionalities make in peer partner programs?)
- Consider the supports needed by students with exceptionalities to participate
- Consider ways to build in-school and out-of-school relationships and supports in collaboration with families.

Train the educational team:

- Explain the purpose and a rationale for the peer support arrangements
- Describe supporting roles that educators, paraprofessionals, and related service professionals play for peers and students with exceptionalities
- Involve the family in learning about peer support arrangements
- Share peer support plans and explain specific examples for social and academic supports that members of team can facilitate

- Show how to collect data on student progress on outcomes included with the peer support plan
- Plan for regular meetings for problem solving and discussion on progress.

Recruit and train peers:

- Identify peers
- Provide initial training to peers to discuss roles, provide education on various exceptionalities, discuss specific strategies identified in the peer support plan, and adult support that will be available. If paraprofessionals are present in a classroom or during an activity in which a peer support arrangement takes place, include paraprofessionals during the initial meeting as well to clarify their role.
- Provide ongoing support: to update progress, success stories, and concerns. The type and intensity of support and guidance educators provide will depend on the characteristics of the student, the confidence and capabilities of peers, and the context of the class.

Implement the peer-mediated support intervention:

- Create the opportunities for the peer support arrangement to occur during planned activities and instructional times
- Collect data on the impact on students' targeted outcomes
- Share information with members of the team
- Adjust and modify as needed based on data and feedback from students and the team.

SOURCE: Adapted from Biggs, E. E., & Carter, E. W. (2017). Supporting the social lives of students with intellectual disability. In M. L. Wehmeyer & K. A. Shogren (Eds.), *Handbook of research-based practices for educating students with intellectual disability* (pp. 255–273). New York, NY: Routledge; Carter, E. W., Cushing, L. S., Clark, N. M., & Kennedy, C. H. (2005). Effects of peer support interventions on students' access to the general curriculum and social interactions. *Research and Practice for Persons with Severe Disabilities, 30*, 15–25.

Selecting Instructional Strategies

To ensure your students' progress toward the goals of disability policy and special education you learned about in Chapter 1, you will have to select and implement effective instructional practices. You have learned about high-leverage practices that should be used across ranges of students, ages, and content. You know that, within these practices, a student has a right to an individualized education, documented in the IEP that is guided by individualized, specially designed instruction and supports with related services and supplementary aids and services. For this reason, you must understand the (1) environment, (2) the student, and (3) the interaction between the two (Thompson, Hughes, Walker, & DeSpain, 2017).

This is a "person-environment fit" model of understanding and instructing students (Thompson, Shogren, & Wehmeyer, 2017). So, in selecting instructional practices, take the following into account:

1. Understand each student.

2. Find out how the student's exceptionality affects learning and what the student needs in order to learn.

3. Study the curriculum that all students are learning.

4. Review the student's individualized learning goals.

5. Think about instructional (i.e., classroom) and non-instructional environments and how your student does or can learn in each environment.

6. Appraise each of these previous points, in combination with the IEP team or in light of the student's Section 504 plan, to identify instruction and supports and then to implement and evaluate them, using data to determine if they lead toward the targeted outcomes in the short- and long-term.

Implementing Appropriate Strategies Across Settings

In addition to the person-environment fit, you need to take into account one other factor. It is **generalization**, namely, promoting the transfer of learning to new environments and activities (Alberto & Troutman, 2013). Learn about generalization by reviewing Figure 6.4, which shows an embedded instruction plan in an elementary school; pay attention to the bottom of the plan and the focus on "generalization." That section of the plan reads:

> Generalization: When changing the weather cards (a classroom activity that all students engage in during morning routine), Ms. Smith will ask Mary to name a card that corresponds with one of the visual vocabulary cards.

Generalization refers to the act of taking something learned in one activity and applying it in another setting (Alberto & Troutman, 2013). Generalization ensures that your students will learn they can use the same skill in different activities and settings. Limited use of a skill is just that: limited, because the skill is not useful in other situations. Generalization tends to guarantee that what is limited becomes less so.

In the embedded instruction plan (Figure 6.4), Ms. Smith is making sure that Mary takes what she learned in the embedded instruction sessions about matching words to pictures to a different activity in which the pictures are presented during a class activity. The goal of the embedded instruction was not just that Mary learned to match the words and cards during the instructional sessions, but also that she could use her understanding of the words and pictures in different contexts. Think about all the different ways that you generalize skills you have learned. Your ability is what you want your students to have.

Evaluating Fit of Strategies over Time

Finally, never forget the importance of keeping in mind the long-term outcomes that IDEA desires (Chapter 1). The ultimate goal of special education is to promote a lifetime of equality of opportunity, full participation, independent living, and economic self-sufficiency.

If you and the IEP team "plan with the end in mind" as you are selecting instruction and supports, you will take into account not only a student's short-term goal (e.g., learning to match words and pictures) but also the student's long-term goal (e.g., having the literacy skills needed to engage in ongoing education, employment, and community participation). In fact, planning for the transition from school to adult life should start in elementary school (Papay, Unger, Williams-Diehm, & Mitchell, 2015). What you do in preschool and elementary school, as well as in middle and high school, will affect postschool outcomes; you are teaching so your student will be able to endure the marathon of life. That consideration will inform your decisions and priorities for instruction and curriculum. It entails evaluating how the strategies you use to teach a particular student or group of students fits with their needs and goals over time.

Just as Jack Steinberg wants to go to college, and his parents Ivey and Eric concur, so, too, does his teacher Christina support him, and her teaching, toward that outcome. They share his high expectations, and they dignify him by doing just that and by teaching him with instructional strategies that research proves are effective. This instruction all occurs in inclusive settings. To do less is to let Jack "sit idly, waiting for the time to drop out"—a result that the Supreme Court, in *Endrew F.*, condemned as inconsistent with IDEA. Jack's perseverance, that of his parents, and that of his educational team have all contributed to enhancing his self-determination and to ongoing progress in accomplishing short-term and long-term goals.

> **MyLab Education Self-Check 6.2**
> **MyLab Education Application Exercise 6.2:**
> Universal Design for Learning

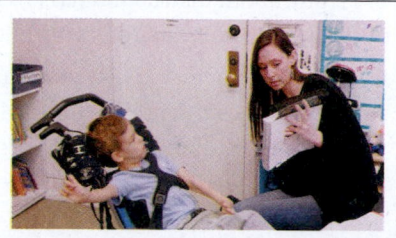

Summary

Using High-Leverage Practices to Support Student Learning

High-leverage practices can be effective across learning environments, curricular areas, and learners; for these reasons, they are important for educators to know and understand. High-leverage practices can be grouped into four categories: collaboration, assessment, social/emotional/behavioral, and instruction.

Designing Learning Environments to Enhance Student Outcomes

Designing environments involves thinking carefully about how to promote student learning and engagement through the layout of the physical space and the design and delivery of the curriculum and instruction. UDL provides one framework that focuses on offering multiple ways for students to engage, take action and expression, and see content represented. How educators work together also affects the educational environment; indeed, co-teaching provides ways for general education and special education teachers to work together to support all students in the classroom.

Specially Designed Instruction and Supports for Students with Disabilities

Specially designed instruction and supports are individualized based on a student's needs, to enable the student to learn and engage with the general education curriculum and individual learning goals. Examples of specially designed instruction include explicit instruction and embedded instruction. Examples of specially designed supports include assistive technology and peer support arrangements.

Selecting Instructional Strategies

It is important to understand the student and the student's learning environments and then to identify the instruction that will maximize the "fit" between the person and the environment. This is called a person-environment fit model. When selecting and implementing instructional practices, it is also important to plan for generalization and maintain a focus on long-term outcomes, no matter the age of students you are working with.

Addressing the Professional Standards

In Chapter 6, Cross-cutting Instructional Approaches, we have covered the following Council for Exceptional Children (CEC) Initial Level Special Educator Preparation Standards: Chapter 6—2.1, 3.1, 3.2, 3.3, 4.3, 5.1, 5.3, 5.4, 6.2, 6.4, 7.1, 7.3. Refer to the Appendix for a full listing of the CEC Standards with descriptions and supporting explanations.

Chapter 7
Students with Learning Disabilities

Learning Outcomes

7.1 Define learning disabilities, their common characteristics, their causes and at least one specific challenge related to students' academic achievement, memory, and emotions.

7.2 Describe how to identify and evaluate students, and describe the differences between the discrepancy and RTI models for identifying learning disabilities.

7.3 Summarize data on student placements and describe the key components of strategies for educating students in math, reading, and writing, identifying two commonalities across strategies.

Meet Louise Hastings, the Peacemaker and Problem Solver

There is a special place in this world for the peacemakers. However much we might worship the victorious warrior, we value still more the person who offers the olive branch and induces opposing parties to accept it. That is one reason why Louise Hastings is so well respected at her middle school. She's the one who, in her words, tells her classmates to "calm down, sit down, chill out, and leave it alone" when they get "really hyper" or start crying or fighting. She's the one who, in the words of one of her teachers, Myra Graham, is a candidate for the school-designated role of peer mediator.

There is a special place, too, for the problem solvers. However much we admire a person who acts passionately about issues, we look to the analyst to figure out what the problem is, why something is a problem, what the possible solutions are, and how to evaluate whether the solutions are working once they are applied. That is another reason why Louise is so important in school. She brings her analytical ability to bear as a member of a clique of White and African American girls who are the school's leaders.

Louise dignifies herself and is dignified by her teachers because of her character and behavior. Special education is not all about learning; it's also about who you are and who you can become.

As a new middle school student, Louise takes courses in math, English, science, social studies, fine arts, gym, music, and technology (using computers). If you were to visit her school, you would find her in class among students who have no disabilities and those who do. You might find her working in a small group with other students in receiving

Jupiterimages/Stockbyte/Getty Images

Jupiterimages/Stockbyte/Getty Images

Tier 2 reading instruction and receiving Tier 3 math instruction from her teacher, Myra. Additionally, Louise serves as a peer model on social skills for a small group of her peers. But you would find her using strategies similar to those that all 8th graders use to understand the curriculum in science and social studies, although it is helpful for her to have instruction from Myra on new vocabulary. The research-based strategy of differentiated instruction promotes her inclusion in the general curriculum.

Louise's reliable allies—not only Myra but also her parents, Harry and Elizabeth—agree that Louise brings something extra to her education and her school. That "something extra" underlies her peacemaking and her happy personality and perhaps explains both. It's a sense that Louise can do whatever she chooses if she puts her mind to it, learns the strategies for doing it, and applies her problem-solving skills to make her choices come true, whether on her own or with help. Louise puts it this way: What she most likes about school is "learning new things." Elizabeth describes that sense of great expectations somewhat differently: "I tell Louise that there is nothing she can't accomplish." And Myra explains why Louise's future seems bright. It's because there are "so many positives" in Louise's life: her leadership capacities, her ability to advocate for herself and others, her willingness to work, her diligent use of the strategies she is learning for mastering her coursework, her friends, and her family's support.

Defining Learning Disabilities

The Individuals with Disabilities Education Act (IDEA) defines the term **specific learning disability** as a "disorder in one or more of the basic psychological processes involved in understanding or in using language, spoken or written" (IDEA, 2004). IDEA provides that the "disorder may manifest itself in an imperfect ability to listen, think, speak, read, write, spell, or do mathematical calculations." (In the rest of this chapter, we will use the term "learning disabilities" and not include the word "specific" in front of that term. Why? We do so because educators generally do not use the word "specific" to modify "learning disabilities.")

A student's nondiscriminatory evaluation team may determine that the student has a learning disability only under two circumstances. One is inclusionary and the other is exclusionary; both must exist.

- The student's disorder may include "such conditions as perceptual disabilities, brain injury, minimal brain dysfunction, dyslexia, and developmental aphasia." This is the **inclusionary standard**; it identifies what conditions are included.

- A student may *not* be classified as having a learning disorder if the student has "a learning problem that is primarily the result of visual, hearing, or motor disabilities, of intellectual disability, of emotional disturbance, or of environment, cultural, or economic disadvantage." This is the **exclusionary standard**; it says that these causal conditions are excluded.

Learning disabilities continue to be the most prevalent of all disabilities. Thirty-five percent of all students with disabilities served under IDEA have specific learning disabilities, for a total of 2,310,000 students (National Center for Educational Statistics, 2017). Two thirds of students with learning disabilities are male; Asian students are underrepresented, while Black and Hispanic students are overrepresented in the category of learning disabilities (Cortiella, 2011).

Describing the Characteristics and Causes

Characteristics

ACADEMIC ACHIEVEMENT   There is no such thing as a typical student with learning disabilities. One student may exhibit strengths in math and nonverbal reasoning but weaknesses in receptive and expressive language skills. Another student may be strong in motor skills, reading, and receptive language but show weaknesses in math, as Louise does. Students classified with learning disabilities have average or above-average intelligence. That is so because IDEA sets out an exclusionary criterion: The student may not have an intellectual disability. Nevertheless, students with learning disabilities almost always demonstrate low academic achievement in one or more areas and experience challenges in how they learn and process new information (Pullen, Lane, Ashworth, & Lovelace, 2017). Only about 20 percent of students with learning disabilities have academic weaknesses in both reading and math (Compton, Fuchs, Fuchs, Lambert, & Hamlett, 2012). Louise, for example, has powerful social skills, satisfactory language skills, and slightly delayed reading skills; math, however, challenges her greatly. Her social skills are why she's a peacemaker and problem solver, and a leader. Her learning disability does not blunt her other abilities. That's why she has high expectations for herself; certainly, her teacher Myra Graham and her mother expect much from her.

Overall academic achievement is a typical major challenge for students with learning disabilities. Approximately two-thirds of those students have failed one or more courses at the secondary level; by contrast, almost half of students in the general population have failed one or more courses at the secondary level (Cortiella & Horowitz, 2014). Approximately two thirds of students with learning disabilities graduate from high school with a regular diploma, but 12 percent graduate with a certificate and 19 percent drop out. In the *Endrew F.* case (Chapter 1), the Supreme Court showed concern about dropping out; that's why it added "appropriately ambitious" and "challenging objectives" to the "progress" element in IDEA's meaning of "appropriate education."

READING DISABILITIES/DYSLEXIA   Two different terms are often used to describe reading disabilities. They are reading disability and dyslexia. The two terms are generally considered synonymous, so we we will use them interchangeably.

Approximately 80 percent of students with learning disabilities experience reading challenges (Mercer, Mercer, & Pullen, 2011). That fact is especially troublesome because reading is so important to performance in most academic domains and to adjustment to most school activities. Students with a reading disability typically experience challenges related to the following types of reading tasks:

- *Phonemic analysis*: demonstrating sound-simple awareness that leads to being able to break down words into their basic phonemic parts
- *Word identification*: decoding words that do not follow phonemic guidelines

Teachers, parents, and students can work together to improve the student's reading

Digital Vision/Photodisc/Getty Images

MyLab Education
Video Example 7.1
In this video, Elizabeth describes her math, reading, and writing challenges. Why do you think she has such a vivid memory of her flash card instruction?

- *Reading fluency*: reading in an automatic fashion with appropriate speed and smoothness

- *Reading comprehension*: accurately interpreting the meaning of reading passages and drawing appropriate conclusions.

In early elementary school, students with reading disabilities often struggle with phonemic analysis, word identification, and reading fluency. Comprehension becomes a greater challenge for students with reading disabilities as they progress through higher grade levels; that is so because the higher the grade level, the more comprehension is essential.

MATHEMATICS DISABILITIES Students' mathematical difficulties can range from mild to severe; it is likely that Louise's are moderate to severe. Students' difficulties with math primarily include the following two issues (Geary, 2013):

- *Procedural problems*: frequent errors in understanding math concepts, computing simple and complex math problems, and sequencing the steps of complex problems

- *Fact retrieval*: difficulty memorizing math facts and retrieving facts when needed.

Approximately 7 percent of all elementary and secondary students experience a math disability (Geary, 2013). A major contributor to procedural and fact retrieval problems is working memory.

MEMORY Many students with learning disabilities have difficulty with short-term, long-term, and working memory. **Short-term memory** challenges cause difficulty in recalling information shortly after it is presented. **Long-term memory** challenges involve difficulty in storing information permanently for later recall. **Working memory** refers to how students process information in order to remember it.

For example, consider the steps involved in a math word problem. It is necessary for students to focus on some information, ignore other information, and do computations while still being able to focus on the key elements of the word problem. An ability to preserve some information while processing other information is the essence of working memory. Focusing specifically on improving working memory can show improved outcomes for working memory; however, these outcomes do not then translate to improvements in reading and math performance (Swanson, 2016). When, however, teachers provide training directly on an academic task, such as word problems in math, students improve in both math calculation and word memory.

EMOTIONAL CHARACTERISTICS
Students with learning disabilities often experience emotional challenges, frequently as a by-product of their academic challenges. For example, students with learning disabilities are more likely to experience depression and anxiety than their peers who do not have these disabilities (Nelson & Harwood, 2011). Sometimes, teachers might overlook their students' emotional needs while vigorously addressing their academic needs. One can hardly say that Louise has any of the emotional and social characteristics that sometimes affect individuals with learning disabilities. Although students with learning disabilities have a higher incidence of emotional challenges than students without disabilities, the majority of

Ron Nickel/Design Pics Inc/Alamy Stock Photo

Computer games using math facts can be a motivational way for students to advance their math and working memory skills.

students with learning disabilities do not experience mental health problems (Snowling & Hulme, 2008).

Given the academic characteristics of students with learning disabilities, and taking into account that Louise resembles many of them, you should not be surprised to learn that students with learning disabilities should be held to high academic and extracurricular expectations (consistent with IDEA and Every Student Succeeds Act [ESSA]). Receiving the proper supports in school and after they leave school contributes to their well-being across the life span.

Causes

NEUROLOGICAL MECHANISMS   Learning disabilities are linked to neurological problems and structural brain differences (Ashkenazi, Black, Abrams, Hoeft, & Menon, 2013). Neuroimaging technologies have enhanced scientists' ability to assess brain activity accurately, pinpointing the areas of the brain that are associated with reading and math deficits. For example, the neural wiring of brain regions in the left hemisphere has been precisely located in relation to impairments in reading. By contrast, the right hemisphere is associated with math disabilities. Increasingly, however, evidence has revealed that individuals with math disabilities have deficits in distributed brain regions.

GENETICS   Specific types of learning disabilities seem to be linked to specific genes. In elementary students from kindergarten through 4th grade, individual differences in reading and spelling are primarily due to genetic influences (Christopher et al., 2013). A study of twins from 8 to 20 years of age suggested that genetic influences accounted for two thirds of reading deficits (Astrom, Wadsworth, Olson, Willcutt, & Defries, 2012).

ENVIRONMENTAL CAUSES   Environmental factors that enhance or impede development can contribute directly to learning disabilities and can indirectly affect the extent to which neurological abnormalities and genetic factors impact learning. The negative effects of low socioeconomic status and poverty, as well as ineffective teaching practices, not only affect students' achievement levels when entering kindergarten but also contribute to their slower rate of growth over time (Judge & Watson, 2011). There is no evidence of any environmental causes of Louise's disability.

MyLab Education
Video Example 7.2
What are two ways that the information you learn in this video will influence how you provide instruction and accommodations to students in your future classes who experience dyslexia? https://www.youtube.com/watch?v=zafiGBrFkRM

MyLab Education   **Self-Check 7.1**
MyLab Education   **Application Exercise 7.1:** Helping Ms. Williams Understand Her Class

---

Evaluating Students with Learning Disabilities

As you learned earlier in the chapter, a student must have a disorder that manifests itself as an imperfect ability to listen, think, speak, read, write, spell, or do mathematical calculations. The question facing state and local education agencies is how to operationalize that definition. Just how much of an impairment must a student demonstrate?

Determining the Presence of a Learning Disability

To answer that question, IDEA regulations had long authorized education agencies to apply a discrepancy standard, that is, a "severe discrepancy" between the student's intellectual ability and achievement. During the 1970s and 1980s, states almost always used the discrepancy standard for identifying students with a learning disability. But some members of the learning disabilities professional community began to have serious concerns about the discrepancy standard and to explore other options for identifying learning disabilities. Their concerns and initiatives have caused Congress to amend IDEA.

IDEA now authorizes three options for identifying students with learning disabilities. First, it provides that a state or local educational agency *may* take into consideration whether a student has a severe discrepancy between intellectual ability and achievement in oral expression, listening comprehension, written expression, basic reading skill, reading comprehension, mathematical calculation, or mathematical reasoning. An agency *may* use the discrepancy standard, but it is not required to do so under federal law. Second, an agency may now use a process to determine if the student responds to scientific, research-based intervention. This is called the response to intervention (RTI) approach. Third, the regulations for implementing IDEA state that the identification of students as having a learning disability "may permit the use of other alternative research-based procedures for determining whether a child has a specific learning disability."

Given these three options for determining the presence of a learning disability, state and local education agencies have much leeway in adopting an approach for identifying students with learning disabilities. Because the third option is not now often used, we will focus on the two primary ways to identify students with learning disabilities—the ability-achievement discrepancy model and the RTI model (which you learned something about in Chapter 5).

Nondiscriminatory Evaluation Process

Discrepancy Model

To determine the presence of a learning disability, use the following process.

Observation	**Teacher and parents observe:** Student appears frustrated with academic tasks and may have stopped trying.
Screening	**Assessment measures:** **Classroom work products:** Work is inconsistent or generally poor. Teacher feels student is capable of doing better. **Group intelligence tests:** Usually the tests indicate average or above-average intelligence. However, tests may not reveal true ability because of reading requirements. **Vision and hearing screening:** Results do not explain academic difficulties.
Prereferral	**Teacher implements suggestions from school-based team:** The student still experiences frustration and/or academic difficulty despite interventions. Ineffective instruction is eliminated as the cause for academic difficulty.
Referral	**Multidisciplinary team submits referral.**
Nondiscriminatory evaluation procedures and standards	**Assessment measures:** **Individualized intelligence test:** Student has average or above-average intelligence, so intellectual disability is ruled out. Student may also have peaks and valleys in subtests. The multidisciplinary team makes sure the test is culturally fair. **Individualized achievement test:** A significant discrepancy (difference) exists between what the student is capable of learning (as measured by the intelligence test) and what the student has actually learned (as measured by the achievement test). The difference exists in one or more of the following areas: listening, thinking, reading, written language, mathematics. The team makes sure the test is culturally fair. **Curriculum-based assessment:** The student is experiencing difficulty in one or more areas of the curriculum used by the local school district. **Behavior rating scale:** The student's learning problems cannot be explained by the presence of emotional or behavioral problems. **Anecdotal records:** The student's academic problems are not of short duration but have been apparent throughout time in school. **Direct observation:** The student is experiencing difficulty and/or frustration in the classroom. **Ecological assessment:** The student's environment does not cause the learning difficulty. **Portfolio assessment:** The student's work is inconsistent and/or poor in specific subjects.
Determination	The nondiscriminatory multidisciplinary evaluation team determines that the student has a learning disability and needs special education and related services.

DISCREPANCY MODEL The *Nondiscriminatory Evaluation Process: Discrepancy Model* feature highlights the nondiscriminatory process for identifying students with learning disabilities by using the ability-achievement discrepancy model. As we already have noted, this is the traditional procedure. Generally, students are referred for evaluation because, even after systematic instructional intervention, they seem to have more ability than is indicated by their academic performance in one or more subject areas. The discrepancy model rests on the premise that students do not achieve at their expected level of ability. Thus, measurement compares and contrasts what a student is expected to achieve based on intelligence quotient (IQ) and what a student actually achieves based on achievement test scores. Accordingly, a nondiscriminatory evaluation commonly establishes a discrepancy between the student's intellectual ability, as measured by an IQ test, and the student's achievement, as measured by a standardized achievement test. You learned about IQ and standardized achievement tests in Chapter 4.

Completing individualized evaluation measures, often with an adult whom the student does not know, can be an intimidating experience for a student who may already be self-conscious about educational performance.

Approximately two thirds of states allow local education agencies to use the discrepancy model, one fifth of states prevent its use, and 13 percent do not specify whether or not it may be used (Maki, Floyd, & Roberson, 2015). Approximately 14 states that allow for the ability-achievement discrepancy model do not specify how discrepancies must be determined in order to identify a student as having a learning disability. One state may use 1 standard deviation (15 points), another may use 1.5 standard deviations (22 to 23 points), and another may use 2 standard deviations (30 points).

The discrepancy model is not free from concerns. They include difficulty in differentiating learning disabilities from low achievement, wide variation in ways to calculate the discrepancy, and delay of identification while waiting for the student to experience failure (Hosp, Huddle, Ford, & Hensley, 2016). Because of these concerns, the discrepancy model increasingly is in disfavor in the professional literature, yet it continues to be allowed in two thirds of state guidelines (Maki et al., 2015). Only 20 percent of states disallow its use, and 13 percent do not have related guidelines. There is variation across states that allow the discrepancy model in terms of the magnitude of the discrepancy, but the most common magnitude is 15 to 20 standard score points or 1.5 standard deviations.

RESPONSE TO INTERVENTION MODEL When Congress reauthorized IDEA in 2004, it took into account the criticisms of the IQ–achievement discrepancy approach. It did so by providing that schools not be required to document a severe discrepancy between intellectual functioning and achievement and that they may use alternative processes. A local educational agency may now use a process that determines whether a student responds to "scientific, research-based intervention." This process is known as response to intervention (RTI).

In Chapter 5, you learned about RTI as a problem-solving approach that involves multiple tiers of research-based interventions matched to each student's needs. Each of the tiers within the RTI model (there are typically three) involves increasing degrees of intensive instruction. Although RTI is a model for instruction, it also is used to identify students with learning disabilities, with an emphasis on discovering optimal levels of intensive instruction for these students to make academic progress (Hosp et al., 2016). It is one of the major research-based practices available to students who may have learning disabilities. There are others, as you will learn later in this chapter.

Because of the option that IDEA offered, 16 percent of states have required the RTI approach as the only procedure for determining the presence of a learning disability, and 17 percent of states provide that RTI may be used in combination with other identification methods (Maki et al., 2015). The remaining approximately two thirds of states permit the use of RTI. Ninety percent of states provide guidance for how RTI should be used to identify whether a student has a learning disability. However, this guidance has wide variability related to factors such as the length of time a student spends at each tier, the type of data that must be collected, and indicators for determining that a student is not making adequate progress.

The *Nondiscriminatory Evaluation Process: RTI Model* feature provides a general overview of the steps of the RTI process. IDEA provides the option for RTI, but it does not provide specific guidance. Thus, the decision is left up to state and local education agencies.

Nondiscriminatory Evaluation Process

RTI Model

To use RTI as an evaluation method to determine the presence of a learning disability, schools must make sound decisions addressing the following six components:

1. **Specify the number of prevention tiers.**
   - Three key tiers in RTI programs include primary prevention, secondary prevention, and tertiary prevention.
   - Primary prevention is generally considered to be the general education program with the core curriculum and instruction associated with grade-level norms.
   - Secondary prevention consists of small-group tutoring in core academic subjects, especially reading and math.
   - Tertiary prevention consists of an individualized program characterized by systematic instruction and ongoing progress monitoring.

2. **Identify students for prevention.**
   - Provide quality instruction in the general curriculum (Tier 1).
   - Conduct universal screening of all students in the school at the beginning of the school year to identify students who are not successful with core instruction.

3. **Provide intervention.**
   - Implement two intervention models including problem solving and standard protocols (Tier 2).
     Problem solving involves defining the problem related to learning, analyzing the factors contributing to the problem, developing and implementing a plan to address the problem, and evaluating the effectiveness of systematic instruction.
     Standard protocols involve implementing instructional programs whose effectiveness has been verified through experimental research.
   - Implement intervention for a period of time, approximately 3–4 times per week for 10–20 weeks.

4. **Classify response.**
   - Identify criteria for determining when a student's response is adequate and when the student needs to receive more systematic instruction.
   - Consider the student's rate of improvement and actual achievement compared with classmates whose learning is progressing at the Tier 1 level.

5. **Conduct multidisciplinary evaluation.**
   - For students unable to respond adequately to Tier 2 prevention, design a multidisciplinary evaluation to address the questions and issues that are problematic for the student (Tier 3).
   - Implement the multidisciplinary evaluation to pinpoint learning challenges around which Tier 3 intervention should be designed.
   - Rule out the presence of other disabilities, especially an intellectual disability.

6. **Provide special education.**
   - Implement intervention characterized by instruction that is highly explicit, intensive, and supportive (Tier 3).
   - Ensure lower student-teacher ratios and extended instructional time.

SOURCE: Based on information from Fuchs, G., & Fuchs L. (2007). A model for implementing responsiveness to intervention. *TEACHING Exceptional Children, 38*(5), 14–20.

Proponents of the RTI model as a method for identifying learning disabilities emphasize that screening and monitoring of all students should begin at the earliest elementary years and should be accompanied by evidence-based instruction. As students progress through the tiered system, identification of learning disabilities is based on three criteria: response to evidence-based instruction in terms of progress rates and performance levels, assessment of achievement compared with peers, and determination that the learning problems are not caused by another disability or by environmental or cultural factors (exclusionary standard) (Fletcher & Vaughn, 2009).

Determining the Nature of Specifically Designed Instruction and Services

Although the discrepancy model has largely relied on general achievement tests for evaluating a student, scores from achievement tests, such as grade-equivalent scores—a student is reported to be reading at the 3rd-grade, 1-month level—do not provide explicit guidance for instruction. For example, a grade-equivalent score for reading does not offer adequate guidance in developing an individualized education program (IEP).

An alternative, at least with respect to reading, is to focus on fundamental skills necessary for reading proficiency. These include **phonological processing**, which is the capacity to use the sound system of language to process oral and written information (Morris, 2011; Wagner & Torgesen, 2009). Using this sound system involves skills related to phonological awareness, phonological memory, rapid naming of letters, and oral vocabulary. Phonological processing at the kindergarten level predicts reading achievement through the primary grades up to 8th grade (Adlof, Catts, & Lee, 2010).

The Comprehensive Test of Phonological Processing, Second Edition (CTOPP-2) is a standardized way to evaluate a student's current level of performance related to the critical reading skills of phonemic awareness, memory, and rapid naming (Wagner, Torgesen, Rashotte, & Pearson, 2013). CTOPP-2 is particularly useful at Tiers 2 and 3 for identifying students whose phonological achievement indicates a need for more intensive instruction. It also identifies a student's strengths and weaknesses and is useful for monitoring a student's progress based on intervention. It is appropriate to use for individuals ranging in age from 4 to 24. The test requires about 40 minutes to administer.

For a photo and more information about the CTOPP-2, go to http://www.pearsonclinica.com/language/products/100000737/comprehensive-test-of-phonological-processing/

MyLab Education Self-Check 7.2

MyLab Education Application Exercise 7.2 Discrepancy Models and Response to Intervention

---

Including Students with Learning Disabilities

Myra is the inclusion facilitator who works with Louise and Louise's 6th-grade teacher. Myra is a "Jill of all trades." Sometimes she collaborates with a general educator to teach math, language arts, and reading; sometimes she provides consultation for the general educators who teach science or social studies. In these roles, she focuses on differentiated instruction and co-teaching. You would always find Myra among the educators who convene as a student's IEP team; you would find her advocating for Louise to have some extra time to take the math section of the statewide assessments of student proficiency; and you would always find her following up on what Louise is learning, how she is learning, and how her teachers are instructing her. Myra is a collaborator,

Figure 7.1 Extent of Inclusion for Students with Learning Disabilities

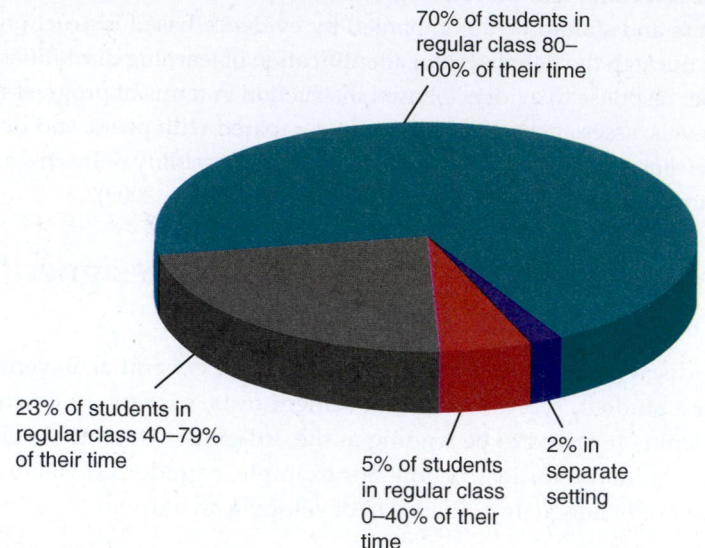

70% of students in regular class 80–100% of their time

23% of students in regular class 40–79% of their time

5% of students in regular class 0–40% of their time

2% in separate setting

SOURCE: U.S. Department of Education. (2017). *39th Annual Report to Congress on the Implementation of the Individuals with Disabilities Education Act*. Retrieved from: https://www2.ed.gov/about/reports/annual/osep/2017/parts-b-c/39th-arc-for-idea.pdf/

For multiple ways to assist students with learning disabilities in reading, vocabulary, spelling, and language arts, go to Reading Rockets, a national multimedia resource for finding research-based instructional strategies for reading. The web address is http://www.readingrockets.org. On the website, find Helping Struggling Readers. Once there, select Best Practices in Planning Interventions for Students with Reading Problems.

a specialist, an advocate, and a monitor on behalf of Louise and the school as a whole. She's also a person who encourages Louise to advocate for herself because Myra knows that a self-determined student ultimately becomes a more effective adult. Whatever her work, Myra acts as a partner to her peers and to Louise.

As Figure 7.1 shows, 70 percent of students with learning disabilities spend 80 percent or more time in the general education classroom. This is the second highest rate of inclusion as contrasted to other disabilities, exceeded only by students with communication disorders. You have already learned high-quality instructional strategies in Chapter 6 that are effective in inclusive settings for students with learning disabilities, including differentiated instruction, access to repeated independent practice, and effective progress monitoring (McLeskey & Waldron, 2011). *Inclusion Tips for Students with Learning Disabilities* provides basic suggestions to consider.

Inclusion Tips for Students with Learning Disabilities

	Behavior	Social Interactions	Educational Performance	Classroom Attitudes
What You Might See	The student continually disrupts other students when the student needs to be working independently on assignments.	The student misinterprets social cues, misinterpreting facial gestures and/or verbal inflections.	The student's work is inconsistent or generally poor.	The student easily gives up in areas of weakness to get out of doing work.
What You Might Be Tempted to Do	Move the student's desk away from peers or send the student to the principal's office.	Point out the misinterpretation and tell the student how to do it "right."	Lower the student's grade for poor or incomplete work.	Excuse the student from some assignments or reprimand the student for an unwillingness to try.
Alternate Teacher Response	Use tips/advanced organizers to guide the students' learning on independent assignments.	Include the student in the IEP conference to collaboratively address the student's priorities for improving his social skills.	Use differentiated instruction to ensure that the student's learning strengths and needs are addressed.	Use curriculum-based measurement to enhance the student's awareness of the progress the student is making.
Ways to Include Peers in the Process	Match the student with a peer tutor of whom the student can ask questions when the student is not sure what is supposed to be done.	Establish a peer partnership in which the peer can practice specific and priority social cues with the student.	Include the student in cooperative learning groups with classmates strong in academics and social skills.	Give the student opportunities to tutor others (peers or younger students) in areas of the student's strengths.

A Canadian study compared the achievement of students with learning disabilities during early elementary years who received their education in inclusive classrooms (with co-teaching) and in special education classes (Tremblay, 2013). The study also included a group of students without disabilities. Although the human resources were deemed similar for each of the three groups of students, during grade 2 the students in the inclusive classrooms made significantly more progress than their counterparts in special classes, and the gap between their achievement and that of students with no disabilities decreased. A problematic finding was that scores of the students in the special classes decreased significantly between the beginning and end of 1st and 2nd grades, while the gap increased between their achievement and that of their peers without disabilities.

Educating Students with Learning Disabilities

Remember that a requirement of the IEP is to provide research-based supplementary aids and services that will enable students, including Louise, to make progress in the general education curriculum. Let's now turn our attention to how students with learning disabilities can benefit from intensive research-based instruction in math, reading, and writing. By implementing these strategies, you can enhance the likelihood that students with learning disabilities will make the progress that, in *Endrew F.*, the Supreme Court said is the essence of an appropriate education. You can ensure that your students will have "appropriately ambitious" IEPs that include "challenging objectives" in core academic subjects within the inclusive general education classrooms.

Tier 3 Math Curriculum-based Measurement and Interventions

Louise has significant math disabilities. She and many other students with math disabilities often require Tier 2 or 3 math instruction. In Tier 3 math instruction, a student's teacher calibrates the student's skill level with an appropriate intervention (Codding & Martin, 2016).

As you learned in Chapter 4, the vast majority of states have adopted Common Core Standards. At the elementary level, the Common Core Standards are consistent with research on learning math that stresses the critical importance of computational fluency. Computational fluency refers to accuracy and speed in completing math facts involving addition, substraction, multiplication, and division ranging from 1 to multiple digits with and without regrouping.

To pinpoint a student's skill level, you can use curriculum-based measurement (CBM) to identify the skills a student has mastered and those on which the student needs more instruction, as you also learned in Chapter 4. To use CBM, you will need an assessment tool comprising the math skills that align with the math standards adopted in your state. When Myra was initially planning Tier 3 math instruction for Louise, she created a CBM tool following the steps in the *Guidelines for Teaching*: *Developing and Using a Curriculum-Based Measurement for Computational Fluency* feature. We recommend this same process for creating CBM computational fluency measures for your students. CBM is one of those research-based practices that cross subject-matter boundaries.

Once you have developed your CBM tool, you should administer it starting at the current grade level of the student and moving downward until you identify the student's instructional level, as indicated in the *Guidelines for Teaching*: *Developing and Using a Curriculum-Based Measurement for Computational Fluency* feature. Once you have accurately identified the instructional level, you then should select an appropriate intervention strategy.

MyLab Education
Video Example 7.3
"The Cole Twins Overcome Learning Disabilities and Go to College" provides insight into what is possible for students with learning disabilities. What role do you think that high expectations might be playing in the twins' success? https://www.youtube.com/watch?v=lHWM9sZVSjc

Guidelines for Teaching

Developing and Using a Curriculum-Based Measurement for Computational Fluency

Determine objectives for math probe.

- Consider two types of objectives including:
  - Focus on similar problems using the same math operation that enable you to elucidate particular student skills
  - Focus on diverse problems using multiple math operations that enable you to elucidate a variety of student skills
- Select the appropriate objective for individual and/or groups of students

Prepare worksheets aligned with objective.

- Review Common Core Standards for types of problems to include
- Prepare single-skill worksheet by:
  - Selecting one computational objective—addition, subtraction, multiplication, and division including basic facts involving an increasing number of digits and regrouping or not
  - Identifying the math operation and problems that align with the objective
  - Constructing worksheets with 80–200 problems
- Prepare multiple-skill worksheet by:
  - Identifying the scope of math operations and problems conforming to objective
  - Constructing worksheets
- Consider using a free online tool, Math Worksheet Generator, to construct worksheets—Go to www.interventioncentral.org/ and enter Math Work-Worksheet Generator in the search function (http://www.interventioncentral.org/teacher-resources/math-work-sheet-generator/)

Administer CBM.

- Distribute face-down worksheet to target students
- Give directions based on single- or multiple-skill focus and tell students to turn the sheet over when instructed to do so
- Tell students to start and simultaneously start the stopwatch
- Observe students to make sure they are working through the problems
- After 2 minutes, tell the students to stop; collect papers
- Administer three probes and take the middle score for students being initially assessed
- Administer one probe for progress monitoring of students
- Administer one or more practice sessions for students new to computational fluency CBM

Score worksheets.

- Give credit for any accurate digit in the answer, even if the whole answer is incorrect
- Analyze errors to identify number skills developed and those requiring instruction

Apply norms.

- Identify student's instructional level based on the following norms for correct digits per end-of-year grade level:
  - Grade 1—20 (for 2 minutes)
  - Grades 2 & 3—14–31 (for 1 minute)
  - Grades 4 & 5—24–49 (for 1 minute)
  - Grade 6—40–79 (for 2 minutes)

Based on Louise's CBM results, the starting point for her computational fluency instruction was multiplication facts involving 2 and 3 digits without regrouping. Because two other students were at this same level, Myra set up a Tier 3 math intervention 3 times per week for this group of students. After considering a range of math interventions, Myra combined explicit instruction, self-instruction, and self-reinforcement.

To implement explicit instruction, Myra first modeled for students how to complete a problem; then provided guided feedback, such as hints, until the students were successful; and finally enabled them to practice once they had demonstrated success. She also broke down each new skill into small steps and supplied numerous examples of each step. The self-instruction portion involved having Louise and her classmates verbalize the steps they would follow to solve each problem. Finally, the self-reinforcement portion of the intervention focused on the students graphing their scores on progress monitoring checks and sending e-mails to their parents explaining their score increases. A "success synergy" developed in the group, characterized by students' excitement with their own and each others' progress and by friendly competition on the progress monitoring checks.

Orton-Gillingham Approach for Teaching Reading

Educators often believe that the most effective approach is the one that has most recently been developed to apply new solutions based on current technology. Sometimes, that belief is correct; other times, it may not be correct enough. What is research-based is not always the most recent strategy.

An approach based on explicit instruction that has clearly withstood the test of time is that developed by educator Dr. Samuel Orton and psychologist Anna Gillingham in the 1930s. It was not until almost 70 years later that Anna Gillingham and an associate, Bessie Stillman, codified the Orton-Gillingham instructional principles as a guide for teachers of students with learning disabilities (Gillingham & Stillman, 1997). These developers emphasized that Orton-Gillingham teaches to intellect and to automaticity. Teaching to intellect means teaching students how to think about language; teaching to automaticity means teaching to the point that sounding out words is immediate and leads to fluency. The key feature of the Orton-Gillingham approach is that it uniquely combines explicit instruction and multisensory methods. To ensure explicit instruction, the Orton-Gillingham approach incorporates a highly structured method of teaching sounds, syllables, words, sentences, and written composition. The Orton-Gillingham principles of explicit instruction include (Reed, 2016):

- Sequential skill building so that students learn simpler skills before progressing to moderate and complex skills
- Mastery of skills so that student responses become automatic
- Overlearning through many opportunities for repetition, practice, and success
- Regular progress monitoring to document students' progress in learning and generalizing rules.

Coupled with explicit instruction, Orton-Gillingham also emphasizes multisensory strategies that draw on visual, auditory, and kinesthetic/tactile learning channels to learning sequential skills. Given the multisensory approach, instruction enables students to combine all three of their senses in learning new material. For example, in teaching phonemes (single units of sound), students learn to associate:

- The symbol of a letter (visual) with the letter's name
- Symbol (visual) with the letter's sound (auditory)
- Symbol (visual) and the feel of tracing the letter on sandpaper (kinesthetic).

A fundamental emphasis in Orton-Gillingham is teaching phonemic awareness, which involves students being able to hear, recognize, and interchange phonemes—for example, breaking the word *ball* into each of its sound elements, *b*, *a*, and *l*. As students master the phonemes, they then proceed to master morphemes (the smallest meaningful language units, such as prefixes, suffixes, and roots). Students progress to learn about basic types of syllables to enable them to read and spell new words and to write sentences, paragraphs, and short stories.

In 12 studies, completed in a variety of settings including elementary general education classrooms, a juvenile detention facility, and college classrooms, researchers reported positive findings for word attack/decoding, reading comprehension, and spelling across settings and age groups (Ritchey & Goeke, 2006); such findings support the use of the Orton-Gillingham approach. Dr. Linda Mason, a national special education leader in learning disabilities, summarizes her expert opinion about the credibility of Orton-Gillingham as follows:

> When asked by a teacher, "What intensive reading program do you recommend for a student recently identified with dyslexia?" I recommend Orton-Gillingham or one of its derivative programs that uses its core principles. Why? Orton-Gillingham is sequenced and structured to meet the reading needs of

MyLab Education

Video Example 7.4

In the Orton-Gillingham Lesson (Figure 7.2) the student is reviewing the phonetic sounds of digraphs (th, sh), consonants and vowels. The teacher uses a deck of Phonogram Card Drill cards for this letter. Notice how the student traces the letters in the sand as he recognizes and says the letter sounds.

MyLab Education

Video Example 7.5

In this portion of the lesson the teacher leads the student in a review of closed and silent e-syllables. Reviewing concepts that have been previously taught is built into lesson plans.

MyLab Education

Video Example 7.6

A part of this Orton Gillingham lesson asks the student to engage in oral reading to apply what is being reviewed. If the student misreads a word, the student is guided to self-correct, never being prompted to guess a word.

If you want to learn more about the Orton-Gillingham approach, you will find information on the website of the Academy of Orton-Gillingham Practitioners and Educators, at http://www. ortonacademy.org/. There you will also find information about how you can participate in professional development programs that lead to accreditation and certification as an Orton-Gillingham teacher.

the individual student. It is language-based, giving students the foundational skills needed for word decoding and spelling. In addition, Orton-Gillingham teachers and tutors receive intensive training in the approach and are required to deliver instruction with fidelity.

The Orton-Gillingham approach can be used at Tiers 1, 2, and 3 for reading instruction at the elementary, middle, secondary, and postsecondary level. Students without disabilities, as well as those with a wide range of disabilities, can make progress with this approach. Although most of the history of the Orton-Gillingham approach has been with students having learning disabilities, its use expands far beyond this group of students alone.

Melanie Levitt, a non-categorical special education teacher in an elementary rural school, describes a lesson she designed for her students that incorporates the 10 components of an Orton-Gillingham lesson plan, presented in Figure 7.2.

Figure 7.2 Orton-Gillingham Lesson Plan*

Student: "N." 5th grader   Date: April 10, 2018   Lesson #:67

Teaching Objective: Review silent-e VCe syllable type

Key: T = Teacher   S = Student

N. has previously been taught:
- Closed syllables (VC)
- Digraphs: sh, ch, th, wh
- Beginning and ending consonant blends

◀ **Symbol to Sound**

---

1. Phonemic Awareness:

- N. will practice discriminating /sh/ and /ch/ at the beginning and end of words. These two sounds are often confused by N. and persistent error patterns are continually addressed across his individualized OG lessons.
- The teacher says a word or nonsense syllable that contains /sh/ or /ch/ at the beginning or end of the word.
- The student repeats the word, isolates /sh/ or /ch/, and points to either the "sh" or the "ch" card.

/sh/	/ch/
1. slosh	3. golch
2. shim	5. chut
4. swash	7. stench
6. rash	10. flunch
8. swish	12. clinch
9. stash	13. bench
11. flush	14. chock
15. blash	16. blatch

---

1. Handwriting:

- Introduce lowercase cursive s using the strategy of Trace Copy Cover Close.

---

2. Card Deck (Phonogram Drill):

- In addition to short vowel sounds, N. learned new key words for silent-e cards to remind him of the VCe pattern, such as a-[consonant]-e, ape, /A/.
- N. will write letters in cursive that he has been taught; otherwise he will write other letters in print.

Procedure:

T: shows card

S: trace letters as he says letter-name, keyword, sound

3. New Concept / Review:

- Review closed and silent-e syllable types, short and long vowel sounds.
- The teacher writes "cut" and then "cute" on the board and asks the student to read the words and identify the syllable type (cut—VC closed syllable with a short vowel sound, cute—VCe silent-e syllable with a long vowel sound). The teacher also spiraled back to review digraphs (e.g., sh, ch) and consonant blends.

4. Words to Read:

- N. is given a VC syllable. After reading it, he indicates if it is a real or nonsense word. A final -e is added to the VC word (e.g., scrap to scrape). N. reads the new VCe (silent-e) word and indicates if it is a real or nonsense word.
- Students with learning disabilities frequently memorize a small number of high-frequency words, so requiring N. to practice reading real and nonsense syllables forces him to focus on the vowel sound as being short or long based on the syllable type. Multisyllabic words consist of nonsense syllables, so practice with nonsense syllables is also preparing N. to tackle multisyllabic words.
- Examples of words he read (video presents an example):

a	e	i	o	u
plan-plane	get-gete	tribe-trib	not-note	cut-cute
scrap-scrape	let-lete	bit-bite	hot-hote	chup-chupe
nam-name	pet-Pete	rid-ride	slop-slope	rub-rube
mad-made	cret-crete	slid-slide	rod-rode	cub-cube
shap-shape				up-upe
				sun-sune

5. Oral Reading: *Nat and his Pal Nate*—decodable text

(Possible vocabulary needed to understand text: cod, code, tote, Pope)

- This decodable text included many closed and silent-e words, including the two characters' names, Nat and Nate. When the student misreads a word, the teacher uses a variety of tools to help the student attend to the letters in the word, guiding the student to self-correct. N. is never prompted to guess a word.
- At the end of the passage, the teacher monitors the student's comprehension by asking open-ended questions, such as "What was this story about? What pattern did you notice in the sentences?"

More Explanation:

In this OG lesson, N. reads a decodable text, meaning that the student has been explicitly taught to read each word in this passage, so he does not need to guess any word. Not all students need a decodable text in an OG lesson, but this 5th grader does to accurately identify the words and comprehend the text.

◄ ***Sound to Symbol***

6. Sound Dictation (Auditory Drill):

/p/	/sh/
/f/	/th/
/ch/	/Ā/ a-e
/e/	/Ī/ i-e
/i/	/Ō/ o-e

Procedure:

T: says sound

S: repeats sound and names letters orally first

S: writes and says all previously taught spellings of that sound

Sounds are selected based on previous errors in past lessons and the lesson objective.

7. Words to Spell (S.O.S.):

- N. uses chips to help him segment sounds in each word, improving his phonemic awareness and ability to map letters onto sounds.
- Based on N.'s difficulties reading closed and silent-e words earlier in the lesson, the teacher simplified the spelling list to only silent-e. Typically ~10 words are dictated to spell. Fewer words were given in this lesson due to lack of time because of filming.

1 blame		5 brute	
2 plebe		6 drape	
3 snipe		7 eve	
4 quote		8 bride	

8. Review of Previously Taught Learned Words:
what, where, who, many, says

- These words are phonetically irregular, meaning that you cannot sound them out. These words were selected by the teacher based on data from spelling assessments and student writing samples that the student had difficulty reading and/or spelling these words.

Procedure:

T: says word

S: repeats word and arm taps letter-names to spell the word aloud (do not sound out the word because it is phonetically irregular)

S: writes word, saying letter-names while writing

S: reads word back

9. Introduce New Learned Word:

- A new word was not introduced in this lesson.

Figure 7.2 *Continued*

10. **Sentence Dictation:**	Procedure:
A. *Brent will not give his bad joke.*	T: says sentence
• This sentence (1) contains the lesson objective, silent-e, (2) reviews previously taught concepts (such as Brent, which contains a closed syllable with a beginning and ending consonant blend), and (3) has two previously taught learned words (*will* and *give*). The word *will* is phonetic, but N. has not yet learned the spelling pattern of when to double "l" at the end of a one-syllable word, right after a short vowel.	S: repeats sentence after the teacher S: edits each sentence and rereads the sentence. The teacher uses the Socratic method of questioning to guide the student to self-correct if an error was made.
• Typically, 2–3 sentences will be spelled, but due to time constraints, only 1 sentence was dictated.	

Student's Level of Focus: *poor good great*
Comments/areas to address in next lesson:

• N. was very focused, but made multiple errors in identifying short vowels in closed syllables and long vowels in silent-e syllables. He requires continued review to increase accuracy before moving onto multisyllabic VCCV (e.g., dentist, reptile) words next in the teacher's scope and sequence. New concepts will not be introduced until the student demonstrates mastery at or above 90% throughout the lesson.

Source: Lesson plan provided by the Academy of Orton-Gillingham Practitioners and Educators. Sincere gratitude to Beth McClure, Sheila Costello, and Peggy Price.

* *Please note OG lesson plans vary in both format and procedures given the flexibility of the OG approach. This lesson was taught by a special educator learning how to teach OG during her year-long practicum toward OG Associate Level certification.*

In *My Voice*: *Melanie Levitt—My Journey as a Special Education Teacher Using the Orton-Gillingham Approach*, Melanie, who has earned her Orton-Gillingham accreditation, shares why she enrolled in the professional development program, her perspectives on what she learned, and how this professional development has made her a more effective teacher.

My Voice

Melanie Levitt—My Journey as a Special Education Teacher Using the Orton-Gillingham Approach

As a teacher for students with disabilities, my most notable strength stems from my personal experience. I was a student with exceptionalities. I still am. As a young child, I struggled to read and stay on task. For too long I was discouraged and frustrated with my learning, wondering why I was not at the level of my peers. It was not until I was a teenager that I was evaluated and diagnosed with dyslexia and attention-deficit hyperactivity disorder (ADHD). Truth be told, it was not until my undergraduate studies that I began not only to accept my learning disabilities, but also to be proud of who I am as a learner. Yes, I am proud to say I know how it is to be challenged. I use that knowledge when I teach.

As a special educator, I am committed to improving the lives and educational opportunities for children with exceptionalities. I strive to ensure that every child has access to an education that allows that child to thrive, grow, explore, and succeed. I am sure all teachers do, but I have a special perspective.

I connect with my students on a level that can only be achieved through shared experience. Our common ground, as well as my positive outlook on my own learning processes, informs my greatest strength when working with children with exceptionalities—empathy. I understand children who struggle amongst their peers, and I understand their frustration. I have learned to support these children in their learning process, but more importantly, I have learned to help them accept and appreciate their own unique way of learning. My students and I work together to ensure they are proud of who they are and how they learn. Let me explain.

I teach in a rural Vermont school of 150 students. While assessing my students' literacy at the beginning of the school year, I discovered that many of my 6th graders were reading up to 3 years below grade level. After I reviewed data from their previous years' interventions, I concluded that these students required a different approach to literacy. My students needed an approach that is tailored to their individual needs and honors their intellect. That is why I decided to become certified in the Orton-Gillingham approach through the Academy of Orton-Gillingham Practitioners and Educators. After all, Orton-Gillingham worked for me—I learned to read and to appreciate my intellectual capabilities. So, I figured, it would do the same for my students.

Here's what I have learned so far about the Orton-Gillingham (OG) approach: OG is language-based, multisensory, structured, sequential, cumulative, cognitive, and flexible. These characteristics can be easily individualized based on a student's individual needs. The basic purpose of everything that is done in the OG approach, from recognizing individual words to composing a poem, is assisting the student to become a competent reader and writer.

My most salient insight from my OG training is how critical it is for those who teach struggling readers to have a profound knowledge of the reading brain as well as the structure of the English language. A few topics I learned about are the neuroscience of reading and dyslexia, stages of normal reading development, phonology, morphology, history and structure of the English language, how to teach everything from phonemic awareness, handwriting, and spelling patterns, how to select appropriate reading material, and use and interpretation of formal and informal diagnostic assessment measures. Most of all, I learned how to think critically about what I teach and how I teach it. In a nutshell, OG training taught me how to teach literacy with flexibility and finesse to meet the numerous needs of my struggling students.

Before I studied the OG Approach, I only saw the complexities and irregularities of words in our language. Why is the word *bridge* spelled with -dge but the word *page* ends with -ge? How can I know if the letter "c" will say /k/ or /s/? I could not teach what I did not know. Now, I understand that every struggling reader needs to recognize that our language is actually predictable. The English language is complex, which is why our struggling readers deserve teachers who understand the complexity of the structure of the English language. Our students also deserve a teacher who understands how to teach literacy in a simple, concrete manner so that students are set up for success. There is an OG mantra which my OG Fellow repeatedly referenced and I find it very useful. With everything you teach, you should be able to answer three questions:

1. What am I teaching?
2. Why am I doing it?
3. How is it helping my student(s)?

As the school year came to a close, I anxiously awaited the results of the end-of-year benchmark literacy assessments. I was eager to know how the OG approach affected my students. I was delighted, but not surprised. Many of my students made up to 2 years of reading progress in just 1 year. Hanging up in my office I have a note from one of them which reads, "Ms. Mel, thank you for teaching me how to read better!" I am humbled to know that my students recognize me as an influence on their reading. I am inspired to know that my students recognize their own tremendous growth as readers. They have learned the same lesson I learned about myself: I learned to read, and I learned that I am intellectually capable.

Self-Regulated Strategy Development for Teaching Writing

Self-regulated strategy development (SRSD) is a research-based strategy used in a variety of academic areas; its major application has been to teach students how to write. SRSD was originally developed for students with learning disabilities (Graham & Harris, 2005), but has now been extended as a sound instructional strategy to enable all students to make progress—including ambitious progress—in writing (Harris, Graham, Mason, & Friedlander, 2008). It is frequently used across elementary, middle, and secondary levels at RTI Tiers 1, 2, and 3. In a word, it has wide flexibility and extensive application possibilities.

Research on SRSD has been extensively conducted in the United States and internationally, starting with students with learning disabilities and broadening to students with emotional and behavioral disorders, as well as students without disabilities who are not yet proficient writers. These students vary by age, type of classroom, and writing genre. Across the board, you can be absolutely confident that SRSD is a research-based instructional approach that has documented large gains for students that are maintained across time (Graham, Harris, & McKeown, 2013). In fact, it has more research documentation than any other instructional approach to writing. SRSD is an excellent example of the contributions that research-based special education instructional strategies have made for the benefit of all students.

Self-regulated strategy development synthesizes three major components: (1) mnemonic writing strategies, (2) self-regulation strategies, and (3) instructional stages.

MNEMONIC WRITING STRATEGIES As you learned in Chapter 3, mnemonic strategies include a pattern of letters or ideas that help you and your students remember important information. An example of a mnemonic strategy for teaching students to write a persuasive essay is presented in Figure 7.3 (De La Paz & Graham, 1979a; 1979b).

There are five mnemonic strategies for addressing different genres of writing, engaging in writing assessment, or writing to learn in the content areas. They are

- Story writing
- Narrative, expository, and persuasive writing
- Revising
- Taking a writing competency test
- Reading books (for example, science and social studies), making notes, and writing about what is learned.

SELF-REGULATION STRATEGIES In addition to mnemonic writing strategies, the SRSD also includes self-regulation strategies that students use to master the writing process. In short, students need to have not only fundamental writing skills but also fundamental self-regulation capacities; with these two combined, students, including those with learning disabilities, can learn how to write. The four self-regulation strategies include goal setting, self-instruction, self-monitoring, and self-reinforcement. *Guidelines for Teaching: Key Components of a Self-Regulation Strategy for Teaching Writing* offers useful suggestions.

Figure 7.3 STOP and DARE Mnemonic Strategy

STOP

Suspend judgment. Brainstorm ideas **for** and **against** the topic.

(For) _____ (Against) _____

Did I list ideas for both sides?
If not, do this now.

Can I think of anything else?
Try to write more.

Another point I haven't yet considered is....
Think of possible arguments.

Place a "**+**" to show the side you will take in your essay.

Put a ✓ next to ideas you want to use.

Put an "**✗**" next to an argument you want to dispute.

Number your ideas in the order you will use them.

Remember:

Develop your topic sentence,
Add supporting ideas,
Reject arguments, and
End with a conclusion.

Take a side. Place a "+" at the top of the box that shows the side you will take.

Organize ideas. Decide which ideas are strong and which ideas you can dispute.

Plan more as you write. Remember to use all four essay parts, and continue planning.

Now write your essay on another piece of paper.

SOURCE: Used with permission from Susan Delapaz.

Guidelines for Teaching

Key Components of a Self-Regulation Strategy for Teaching Writing

Goal setting: Have students set their goals and the steps to reach the goals to encourage strategic behavior.

- Students create a plan and timeline for meeting goals.
- Students track their progress.

Self-instruction: Teach students to overtly or covertly tell themselves what to do at each step of the writing process.

- *Problem definition*—students must understand the writing tasks that they are undertaking ("I need to write a report on Martin Luther King Jr.").
- *Focusing of attention and planning*—students use statements to focus their attention ("I need to write at least six paragraphs. I need to use at least three sources.").
- *Strategy implementation*—students use statements to review the strategy (for example, STOP and DARE; see Figure 7.3) they will be using.
- *Self-evaluation*—students use statements to align the criteria of the assignment with their performance: "Do I have six paragraphs?" "Have I used three sources?"
- *Coping and self-control*—students use statements to reduce their worry and to enhance their confidence: "I am halfway done, and I can keep making progress."

Self-monitoring: Teach students self-assessment and self-recording.

- *Self-assessment*—students use each step of the mnemonic strategy (for example, STOP and DARE; see Figure 7.3) to check their work and to make sure that all elements are addressed.
- *Self-recording*—students document their performance, typically on a chart or graph.

Self-reinforcement: Teach students to highlight their success when they meet their goals.

- Students make comments such as "I think the beginning of the report will grab attention."
- Seek to avoid tangible rewards by teaching students the value of self-reward.

Independent performance: Teach students to reach their writing goals automatically without needing to rely on the strategy.

- Transition from using strategy and self-regulation guidelines overtly to doing this covertly.
- Self-regulation procedures can be faded over time.
- Teachers provide booster sessions as needed by students.

Source: Based on Harris, K. R., Graham, S., Mason, L. H., & Friedlander, B. (2008). *Powerful writing strategies for students*. Baltimore, MD: Brookes.

STAGES OF INSTRUCTION   Instruction for writing and self-regulation consists of six stages. These apply regardless of the grade, tier, or needs of your students.

- Develop background knowledge
- Discuss it
- Model it
- Memorize it
- Support it
- Demonstrate independent performance

Lesson plans organize these stages flexibly, sometimes varying the order, modifying them, or combining two stages into one. Rather than moving through the stages in a linear fashion, students can circle back as needed to different stages. In *Into Practice Across Grade Levels: Self-Regulated Strategy Development Instruction for Teaching Writing*, you have an in-depth example of how Cindy Sherman, a speech and language pathologist, has taught two high school seniors (Tatianna and Carlos) to write argumentative essays.

Carlos Holley

Educator Cindy Sherman teaches Tatianna the STOP and DARE self-regulated strategy to improve her writing.

Into Practice Across Grade Levels

Self-Regulated Strategy Development Instruction for Teaching Writing

Meet the Students.

Carlos and Tatianna are 12th graders who have a learning disability. They each receive specialized instruction both in and out of the general education classroom, as well as speech-language services once a week for 30 minutes. Their speech-language goals focus on improving vocabulary, language formulation, and written language skills.

Tatianna requires significant support with organization, coherent ideas, sentence structure, and citing textual evidence. She especially benefits from graphic organizers during pre-writing activities, teacher-based rubrics, and checklists to support her grammar and spelling errors. Once Tatianna realized that strategy instruction was helping her improve her writing skills, she began for the first time sharing her papers on Google Docs and welcomed suggestions. She plans on going to college where she hopes to major in fashion design and business.

Carlos receives specialized instruction in reading, written expression, and math. Based on teachers' observations, Carlos needs assistance with stamina. He has a lot of responsibilities at home. He takes care of his five siblings when his mother is at work, feeds them, wakes them up, and gets them dressed for school. As a result, he often comes to school very tired. Carlos requires longer amounts of time to analyze text and articulate his ideas after reading text that is part of the curriculum. He does much better when he verbally expresses his personal opinion as contrasted to written expression. He plans on going to college and wants to be a computer engineer because he likes to work on computers and fix them.

Pre-Assessment.

Before instruction, I gave each student a public-released 12th-grade persuasive writing prompt from the National Assessment of Educational Progress. The prompt was to argue whether or not community service should be required. They were given a blank planning sheet, and told they had 5 minutes to plan what they wanted to write. Although Tatianna wrote fluidly, many of her sentences were grammatically and semantically incorrect (her essay also did not answer the prompt). Carlos produced sentences that were grammatically and semantically correct, but he often used slang rather than appropriate language in his writing (e.g., wanna/want to, post to/supposed to) and misspelled one homophone (there/their).

STAGES OF INSTRUCTION

Discuss the Strategy.

I introduced the STOP & DARE strategy along with each step in the first lesson (see Figure 7.3). I described "STOP" as a planning strategy and "DARE" as the writing strategy. In one of the activities, I presented a new writing prompt and instructed Tatianna and Carlos to brainstorm possible reasons for the argument under a "For" column and possible reasons against the argument under an "Against" column. Both students needed explicit instruction to understand the meaning of a couple of STOP & DARE steps, including "suspend judgment" and "reject the argument for the other side."

Develop Background Knowledge.

I presented an exemplar persuasive essay and asked the students to compare the exemplar essay to their pre-instruction essay. Because Tatianna and Carlos are 12th graders and are expected to write at least a five-paragraph persuasive essay, I provided a graphic organizer to serve as an outline suggesting how students could expand their ideas. Students received a list of transition words as an additional tool (e.g., another, furthermore). I explained to them that once they brainstormed their ideas and took a side, the graphic organizer would help them as they worked through each step in DARE, by prompting them to elaborate on their topic sentence, ideas, argument, and conclusion.

Model It.

I modeled the STOP & DARE strategy across two 45-minute sessions. Throughout this stage of instruction, I demonstrated how to use STOP & DARE along with the graphic organizer to plan a persuasive essay. Much of this instruction was modeled by thinking out loud, providing a sentence starter, using self-instructions and self-monitoring statements (e.g., "Ok, what do I need to do first."), and reciting the steps for STOP & DARE. I also modeled the use of transition words from one reason/idea to the next.

Memorize It.

From the time I introduced the STOP & DARE strategy, I asked Tatianna and Carlos to learn and memorize the meaning of the STOP & DARE mnemonic and its parts. Across three sessions, they were asked to complete a worksheet, take a quiz, and verbally name each part of the mnemonic. By the 4th session, both students had memorized the mnemonic and understood the steps for planning and composing; additionally, they were comfortable using the graphic organizer.

Support It.

I used the same writing prompt from before instruction a second time, but this time I added the STOP & DARE worksheet. I allowed Tatianna and Carlos to transfer ideas or topic sentences from their pre-instruction essays during this guided instruction. I provided explicit instruction—with both the mnemonic and the graphic organizer—as needed throughout the planning and writing process.

Independent Performance.

I presented a second writing prompt and removed all instructional supports to ensure Tatianna and Carlos were ready to write an essay independently.

Post-Assessment.
Once Tatianna and Carlos demonstrated a clear under-standing of STOP & DARE and were able to generate ideas and sentences without guidance, I again presented a post-instruction essay prompt from the National Assessment of Educational Progress. I gave Tatianna and Carlos a blank page to plan and the choice of writing or typing their post-instruction essay.

When comparing their work from pre-instruction to post-instruction, both Tatianna and Carlos demonstrated consider-able growth. Tatianna's pre-instruction essay was 180 words, did not specifically address the prompt, and lacked important essay elements. Although Tatianna continued to struggle with syntax and semantics, she did a much better job presenting her ideas after instruction. Her post-instruction essay included 252 words, contained all essay elements, was better organized, and clearly addressed the writing prompt. Carlos's pre-instruction essay was 98 words compared to 576 words in his post-instruction essay. He required two post-assessment sessions to complete his essay; however, no additional instruction was provided to him. He continued to have difficulty with sentence structure and semantics, but he demonstrated considerable improvement presenting his argument. It was especially gratifying to see that Carlos included self-generated quotes as evidence, then followed up with his analysis, something that the school consistently asked for in students' essays.

SOURCE: Written by Cindy K. Sherman, Ph.D., Founder and Director, The Write Turn. Strategy based on Susan De La Paz (2001). STOP and DARE: A persuasive writing strategy. *Intervention in School and Clinic, 36*, 234–243. Used with permission.

Developers of SRSD recommend that 20- to 60-minute lessons occur at least 3 times per week. SRSD's developers have written an extensive book that has detailed descriptions for implementing all three components (Harris et al., 2008). In addition to providing foundational content, the authors explain nine mnemonic strategies with three to nine detailed lesson plans for each strategy. The lesson plans are accompanied by numerous charts and worksheets needed to implement the lesson plans.

Because SRSD for writing has such a strong research base in terms of positive student outcomes, there are multiple resources you can draw on.

This IRIS instructional module will teach you more about SRSD and specifically how to use it in a middle school general education classroom. Bear in mind that SRSD is effective across grade levels and subjects. https://iris.peabody.vanderbilt.edu/modules/srs/#content

We encourage you to visit http://www.SRSDonline.org to review a comprehensive website that you can join to be part of the "SRSD Community." You will find teacher and student interviews, teacher resources, and a summary of research evidence shared by the developers, Dr. Harris and Dr. Graham.

Instructional Commonalities

Tier 3 math instruction, Orton-Gillingham, and SRSD all have their special features; however, they have much in common. Some commonalities include opportunities for being embedded in multi-tiered systems of supports (MTSS), explicit instruction, and self-instruction. Regarding embeddedness in MTSS, Orton-Gillingham and SRSD can be used at all tiers. Although the Tier 3 math instruction with its emphasis on curriculum-based measurement (CBM) is described as being specific to Tier 3, the use of CBM with computational fluency could be incorporated at Tiers 1 and 2 as well, especially in early elementary years, when all students are learning math facts. In terms of explicit instruction, each strategy emphasizes breaking larger skills down into smaller tasks and working sequentially with guided feedback and practice. Finally, a key link across strategies is the use of self-instruction; as students learn skills in a step-by-step fashion, they are encouraged to overtly and covertly guide themselves in staying focused on what they should do to demonstrate each specific skill. We hope you are "connecting the dots" that effective instruction for students with learning disabilities has many cross-cutting themes.

Now, pause for a moment before reading the summary of this chapter. Recall the student we described, Louise Hastings, and what we wrote about her. We wrote that her dignity within her school occurs because of her character and behavior. We wrote nothing about how she learns or how she is taught. However, it's time to say this: What Louise learns, and how her teachers instruct her, are components of her dignity. That is so because, for Louise and all students, their dignity—their capacity to earn their peers' and teachers' respect—will depend in part on how they approach their curriculum and how they master it. Character, behavior, and learning and teaching—these three components of a student—are elements of your students' dignity. You're in the dignity business.

MyLab Education **Self-Check 7.3**

MyLab Education **Application Exercise 7.3:** Self-Regulated Strategy Development for Teaching Writing

Summary

Defining Learning Disabilities

IDEA has two criteria for determining whether a student has a specific learning disability. One criterion is *inclusionary*—a disorder in one or more of the basic psychological processes involved in understanding or using written or spoken language. The other is *exclusionary*—the disorder is not due to an intellectual disability or environmental/economic disadvantages. Learning disabilities constitute the most prevalent disability category, comprising 36 percent of all students with disabilities.

Describing the Characteristics and Causes

Although students with learning disabilities typically have average or above-average intelligence, they represent a heterogeneous population with varied academic challenges related to reading and math. They often have difficulty with memory. Although they often experience higher levels of anxiety and depression, overall the majority of them do not experience mental health problems. Both neurological and environmental causes have been documented. Neurologically, research suggests that learning disabilities are linked to structural differences in the brain. Environmentally, key negative effects are low socioeconomic status and ineffective teaching practices.

Evaluating Students with Learning Disabilities

The traditional nondiscriminatory evaluation practice in the field of learning disabilities has been to use standardized intelligence and achievement tests to pinpoint a severe discrepancy between aptitude and achievement. IDEA also allows states to use response to intervention (RTI), rather than the severe discrepancy approach, to identify the presence of a learning disability.

Including Students with Learning Disabilities

Seventy percent of students with learning disabilities spend 80 percent or more of the day in general education classrooms.

Educating Students with Learning Disabilities

Students with learning disabilities benefit from receiving instruction in Tiers 2 and 3 in any academic subject. An approach to providing Tier 3 math instruction for students who have not attained computational fluency is to align their skill level with an appropriate intervention. You can use curriculum-based measurement (CBM) to assess skill levels. Once you have established the student's instructional level, you can use different interventions, such as explicit instruction, self-instruction, and self-reinforcement.

In teaching reading, Orton-Gillingham combines explicit instruction and multisensory methods (visual, auditory, and kinesthetic). It emphasizes phonemic awareness, breaking words down into their sound elements. It then proceeds to teaching morphemes, including prefixes, suffixes, and roots; thereafter, it focuses on basic types of syllables. The Orton-Gillingham approach can be used across all tiers, starting at the elementary and extending to postsecondary programs.

The self-regulated strategy development (SRSD) for teaching writing has three major components: (1) mnemonic writing strategies (such as DARE STOP in Figure 7.3), (2) self-regulation strategies (such as goal setting), and (3) instructional stages (such as "Model It"). You can organize these three components into flexible lesson plans calibrated with tiers across grade levels. Although SRSD was developed specifically for students with learning disabilities, it is highly effective for all students.

These three specific instructional approaches relating to instruction in math, reading, and writing have both unique and common features. Commonalities include implementation of MTSS, explicit instruction, and self-instruction.

Addressing the Professional Standards

In Chapter 7, Students with Learning Disabilities, we have covered the following Council for Exceptional Children (CEC) Initial Level Special Educator Preparation Standards: Chapter 7—1.0, 1.2, 2.0, 3.3, 4.2, 5.6, 5.7, 6.0, 6.2. Refer to the Appendix for a full listing of the CEC Standards with descriptions and supporting explanations.

Chapter 8
Students with Speech and Language Disorders

by Jane Wegner, Ph.D., University of Kansas, and Russell Johnston, M.A., University of Kansas

 ## Learning Outcomes

8.1 Define speech and language disorders, describe the common characteristics and causes of typical and delayed language development, and discriminate among specific speech and language disorders.

8.2 Identify the assessment practices for determining the presence of speech and language disorders (including for expressive and receptive skills), especially for non-native English language learners.

8.3 Describe tools and techniques to teach in inclusive classrooms, identify supplementary aids and service delivery models, and obtain measurements of students' educational progress.

Meet Kylie and Joey—Two Students and Five Steps Toward Progress

Kylie, age 11 and in 4th grade, and Joey, age 8 and in 2nd grade, attend their neighborhood school. Like their age peers, they have favorite parts of the school day—being with friends at school and playing outside during recess. They are, however, quite unlike their peers in other ways.

Their parents, Carrie and Paul, were working overseas at an international school when Kylie and Joey were born and while they attended preschool programs. Kylie and Joey had elephants, not dogs and cats, in their backyard. Instead of riding the bus or carpooling to school, they logged many frequent-flyer miles traveling back to the United States from Singapore, Saudi Arabia, and Indonesia. Compared with their same-age peers, they are apt to have a richer understanding of the world and its cultures. But unlike many of their peers, both use a variety of augmentative and alternative communication (AAC) tools to assist their communication. Yes, most of their peers use a computer and make facial expressions to communicate. But few use the AAC device that Kylie can activate with her eyes or Joey's iPad with voice output software. For Carrie and Paul, the question always has been, "What should we do to satisfy Kylie's and Joey's need to communicate?"

Step 1: Get Help. Carrie and Paul first observed changes in Kylie's development when she was 13 months old. After stressful months of observing her, visiting local physicians in Saudi Arabia, searching the Internet, and flying back to the United States, they obtained a diagnosis: Rett syndrome, "a disorder of the nervous system that leads to developmental reversals, especially in the areas of expressive language and hand use" (National Institutes of Health, 2011). Joey was diagnosed by a physician in Singapore with autism spectrum disorder (ASD) at approximately 2 years of age. Both diagnoses strongly suggested that further communication challenges were on the horizon.

Step 2: Provide Intensive Intervention. According to Carrie, these diagnoses did not change who her children were. They were still the same children she had always known. But what she and Paul needed now were people to help them secure early intervention services, so the family moved back to their home state so that Joey could attend kindergarten. Kylie and Joey now receive therapy services in their local school, at a nearby university, and within their community. They are involved in recreational activities in the community, music camp at the university, and art camp.

Kylie has explored and used a variety of low- and high-tech communication aids. For her simple, low-tech communication, she uses a pragmatic organization dynamic display (PODD) communication book (Porter & Burkhart, 2010). Each page of this book has nine choices. She accesses her choices with the assistance of a communication partner. Her partner points to each message, and Kylie indicates, "That's the one I want," either by activating a voice output switch at her left cheek or looking to the left while the partner touches the item she wants. She also uses eye gaze (looking at what she wants from choices held up) to select from a smaller set of choices.

Yet she has difficulty gaining attention to initiate communication without assistance, and her parents are concerned that she is not able to initiate communication unless someone approaches her. So Kylie has a high-tech device that reads her eye movements. Her eyes move the cursor similar to the way in which other people use a hand-controlled computer mouse to move a cursor. When she holds her gaze on a particular item for a set amount of time, she can activate the voice output or programmed command for that item.

Joey also uses low- and high-tech communication tools. He uses his speech, his gestures, and a communication book with picture symbols and written text to assist his communication. Joey comprehends many words and phrases and reads well. He accesses his technology by touching the picture or words he wants to use. He has explored a variety of mid- to high-tech voice output communication systems to assist his speech and gestures, and he currently uses an iPad with voice output communication software. None of these AAC tools and strategies would have been effective without parent-professional teamwork and careful observations by team members in all the settings in which Kylie and Joey participate.

Step 3: Assemble a Team. Carrie and Paul have chosen and lead a special group of individuals. This team includes extended family, friends, physicians, speech-language pathologists, physical therapists, college students to assist with child care for an occasional night out or work obligations, teachers, paraprofessionals, school principals, AAC consultants, and technical support personnel from AAC companies. Of course, they know that it's important to make sure that Kylie and Joey are members of their own teams as well. Consistent with the principle of self-determination, they have the ultimate say in choosing their own communication tools.

Step 4: Expect Great Results and Celebrate Them. Applaud Kylie and Joey; their parents, Carrie and Paul; and the professionals who work with them when Kylie and Joey make progress. Make it clear to everyone, including Kylie and Joey, that they should expect and work for great results, and then celebrate the results together.

Step 5: Face the Challenges. Carrie and Paul acknowledge that they still have much to learn. Both Kylie and Joey continue to learn how to use their communication systems.

Adults and peers also are learning strategies to communicate more and more effectively. Kylie is working to improve her motor skills for walking, transferring from her chair to a classroom chair, and activating switches. Both are continuing to learn literacy and math skills. At their school, professionals are determining how to increase the amount of time Kylie and Joey spend with their age peers in the general education classroom. The school and community team members meet with Carrie and Paul every other week to discuss current progress for each child and to plan for the future.

Research-based intervention coupled with state-of-the-art technology, inclusion in general education, partnerships, high expectations, and progress in communicating and learning—these are the foundations for Kylie and Joey, their parents, and their educators, the foundations for their education and for their futures of equal opportunity, independent living, full participation, and economic self-sufficiency.

Defining Speech and Language Disorders

The Individuals with Disabilities Education Act (IDEA) defines a speech and language disorder as "a communication disorder such as stuttering, impaired articulation, a language impairment, or a voice impairment that adversely affects a child's educational performance." Communication entails receiving, understanding, and expressing information, feelings, and ideas. It is such a natural part of our daily lives that most of us take our ability to communicate for granted. We participate in many communicative interactions each day. For example, we talk with others face-to-face or on the phone; we e-mail a colleague or a friend; we post messages on Facebook; we demonstrate social awareness by lowering our voices when we see a raised eyebrow or a frown; and we wink at friends over private jokes.

Although we usually communicate through speech, we also do so in other ways. Some people communicate manually, using sign language and/or gestures (Chapter 15). Others add nonlinguistic cues while speaking, such as body posture, facial and vocal expressions, gestures, eye contact, and head and body movements. Many speakers vary their voices by changing their pitch or rate of speaking. All of these skills make our communication more effective.

Communication by spoken or written language, or both, is the cornerstone of teaching and learning. Although most children come to school able to understand others and express themselves and thus are able to participate in school effectively, many children do not. Students with speech and language disorders can encounter challenges with classroom activities, social interactions, instructional discourse exchanges, acquisition of knowledge and language, and the development of literacy skills. So, what are the different types of speech and language disorders experienced by students? That's the preliminary to the next big question: What do educators do to ensure these students make progress in school?

Speech and language disorders relate to the components of the process affected: speech, language, or both (American Speech-Language-Hearing Association [ASHA], n.d.; Hulit, Howard, & Fahey, 2011; Justice & Redle, 2014). A **speech disorder** refers to difficulty producing sounds as well as disorders of voice quality (for example, a hoarse voice) or fluency of speech, often referred to as stuttering. A **language disorder** entails difficulty receiving, understanding, or formulating ideas and information. A **receptive language disorder** is characterized by difficulty receiving or understanding information. An **expressive language disorder** is characterized by difficulty formulating ideas and information. Both speech disorders and language disorders can adversely affect a student's educational performance.

Speech and language disorders are often associated with other disorders. Language disorders are sometimes the primary feature through which other disorders are identified. For example, a child with a hearing disorder may initially be referred for evaluation because the child is not talking as well as other children of the same age.

Cultural Diversity in Communication

Students from different cultural backgrounds may have speech or language differences that affect their participation in the classroom. Although many individuals have a speech or language difference, they do not necessarily have a language or speech disorder. Difference does not always mean disorder (Battle, 2012).

Some students are bilingual, while others have differences because of dialects or accents. Every language contains a variety of forms, called *dialects*. A **dialect** is a language variation that a group of individuals use and that reflects shared regional, social, or cultural/ethnic factors. An **accent** is a phonetic trait carried from a first language to the second (ASHA, 2007a). Examples of culturally and linguistically diverse populations that may use a social dialect or accent include African Americans, Latinos, Asian/Pacific Islanders, and Native Americans. Dialects and accents are not communication disorders; rather, they are differences (ASHA, 2007a).

Incidence

Of all students with disabilities served under IDEA, 20 percent have speech and language disorders (McFarland et al., 2017). Students with other disabilities may also have speech and language disorders that require intervention services from a speech-language pathologist. The prevalence of speech and language disorders is highest among students ages 3 to 6 compared to older students (National Institute on Deafness and Other Communication Disorders, 2016).

Describing the Characteristics and Causes

Characteristics

For most children, the development of communication is uneventful and follows a typical, predictable pattern and timetable. For others, such as Kylie and Joey, it does not; children such as they may need the assistance of a speech-language pathologist (SLP). Understanding the typical pattern of acquiring speech and language skills can help you recognize instances when disorders are present and then request assistance from an SLP.

SPEECH AND LANGUAGE DEVELOPMENT **Speech** is the oral expression of language. This expression occurs when a person produces sounds and syllables. Figure 8.1 illustrates the speech mechanism that, through a coordinated effort, allows for sound production. As a person pushes air from the lungs, the muscles in the larynx move the vocal folds, producing sounds. The larynx sits on top of the trachea and contains the vocal folds (ligaments of the larynx); voice is produced here. A person forms sounds by varying the position of the lips, tongue, and lower jaw as air passes through the larynx (voice box), pharynx (a space extending from the nasal cavities to the esophagus), mouth, and nose.

Language is a structured, shared, rule-governed, symbolic system for communicating. The five components of our language system are phonology (sound system), morphology (word forms), syntax (word order and sentence structure), semantics (word and sentence meanings), and pragmatics (social use of language). Each dimension works together with the others to create a robust language system.

MyLab Education

Video Example 8.1

In this video you will find a brief overview of the anatomy and physiology contributing to the production of speech.
https://www.youtube.com/watch?v=-m-gudHhLxc

Figure 8.1 Speech Mechanism

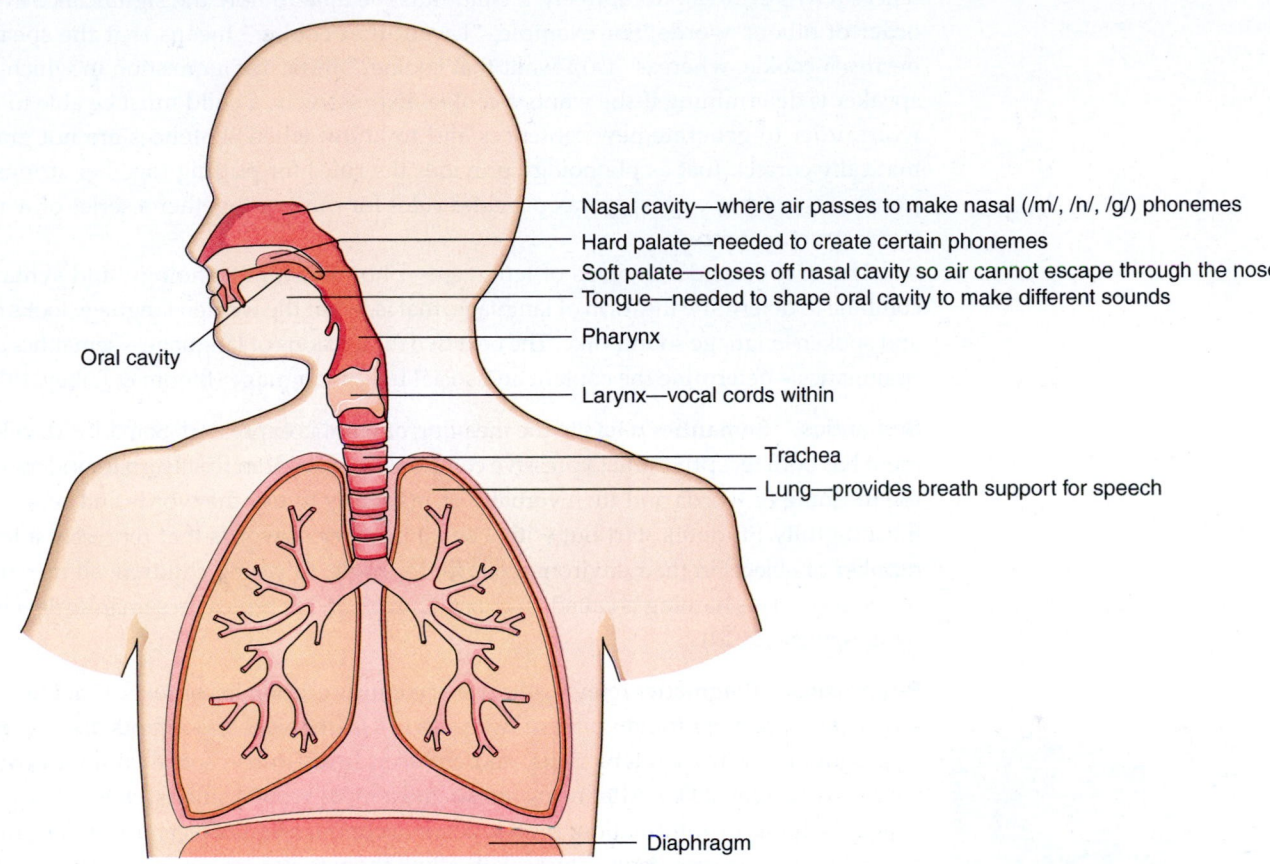

Nasal cavity—where air passes to make nasal (/m/, /n/, /g/) phonemes
Hard palate—needed to create certain phonemes
Soft palate—closes off nasal cavity so air cannot escape through the nose
Tongue—needed to shape oral cavity to make different sounds
Pharynx
Larynx—vocal cords within
Trachea
Lung—provides breath support for speech
Oral cavity
Diaphragm

Phonology.   **Phonology** is the use of sounds to make meaningful syllables and words. Phonology encompasses the rules and sequencing of individual speech sounds (called phonemes) and how they are produced, depending on their placement in a syllable or word. For example, consonants at the beginning of syllables or words (e.g., "tap") are produced slightly differently from those in the middle (e.g., "cattle") or at the end of syllables or words (e.g., "pat").

Phonological use requires correct pronunciation as well as awareness of sound differences as they signal change in meaning. In English, for instance, the word *bill* is different from *pill* by only one phoneme: /b/. By changing one phoneme, a speaker can produce a totally different word. Although English spelling has 26 letters, English speakers use them to produce 45 different sounds. For example, /th/, /sh/, /oy/, and /ou/ are four completely different sounds that are represented in spelling as different combinations of 2 of the 26 letters (Owens, 2012).

Morphology.   **Morphology** is the system that governs the structure of words (Owens, 2012). Phonemes or single sounds have little meaning on their own, but some can be grouped into syllables or words that have meaning. The smallest meaningful unit of speech is called a morpheme. For instance, when *s* is added to *bill*, the word becomes plural. Formerly having had one morpheme, the word now has two: *bill* (a mouth structure on a bird, a written document) and *s* (denoting plurality). Morphological rules allow speakers to add plurals, inflection, affixes, and past-tense markers to verbs. For example, correct use of morphological rules allows a child to change *swim* to *swimmed* and then, as the child matures, to *swam*, an irregular past-tense verb. An understanding of morphological rules allows us to recognize meaning just by hearing it.

Syntax. **Syntax** provides rules for putting together a series of words to form sentences (Owens, 2012). Receptively, a child must be able to note the significance in the order of others' words. For example, "I want that cookie" means that the speaker desires a cookie, whereas "Do I want that cookie?" indicates a question in which the speaker is determining if she wants a cookie. Expressively, a child must be able to use word order to generate new sentences and to know when sentences are not grammatically correct. Just as phonology provides the rules for putting together strings of phonemes to form words, syntax provides rules for putting together a series of words to construct sentences.

The first three dimensions of language—phonology, morphology, and syntax—combine to determine the form of language, that is, what the written language looks like and spoken language sounds like. The next two dimensions of language—semantics and pragmatics—determine the content and social use of language (Bloom & Lahey, 1978).

Semantics. **Semantics** refers to the meaning of what is expressed. Semantic development has both receptive and expressive components. Children first learn to understand the meaning of words and then verbally or manually to use the words and sentences meaningfully. Students start out with a small number of words that represent a large number of objects in their environments; for example, to young children, all men may be "daddy." This naming is called an overextension and is typical in semantic development (Owens, 2012).

Pragmatics. **Pragmatics** refers to the use of communication in contexts. Pragmatics is the overall organizer for language (Owens, 2012). Caregivers and infants use the rules of pragmatics in their interactions, and children learn to use social communication very early (Kuder, 2008). After using smiles and simple verbalizations, children request objects, actions, or information; protest actions; comment on objects or actions; greet; and acknowledge comments. These skills allow them to use language socially to interact within their environments and with people in those environments more efficiently.

No one knows for sure just how the five dimensions of language combine so that children acquire useful language. Theories explaining how children acquire language abound (Hoff, 2009). In the 1950s, linguist Norm Chomsky (1957) proposed that children are born ready to develop language skills because of an inborn language acquisition device. Later, behaviorists proposed that the ability to learn and use language is not inborn but happens as children imitate and practice. Today, researchers investigate the effects of a child's imitation, practice, and other social interactions on language development. Their research has been compiled into social interaction theories.

Most language development takes place in the preschool years and continues throughout the school years. This later development occurs in the areas of language structure, vocabulary, and language use. During the school years, students learn the language skills of reading and writing (Hulit et al., 2014). Similar to other areas of development, children are expected to achieve milestones in their speech and language skills. Although some variability is expected, when children do not achieve milestones it may be indicative of a delay. Typical milestones for speech and language development include the number of words spoken, the speech sounds produced, and the average length of sentences. When children have a speech or language delay, the recommended course of action is exactly the one that Carrie and Paul took for Kylie and Joey: the earliest possible intervention to diminish any negative impact that the speech and language disorder may have on children's progress in education and long-term quality of life, including how children regard themselves and how others respect them—that is, whether children regard themselves as having inherent worthiness and whether others have the same regard for them.

SPEECH DISORDERS Speech disorders include disorders of articulation, voice, and fluency (rate and rhythm of speech). These disorders can occur alone, in combination, or

MyLab Education
Video Example 8.2
A mother discusses her concerns about her son's speech and language development. What were LaKori's mother's concerns about his early language?

MyLab Education
Video Example 8.3
In this video, 3-year old LaKori participates in a shared reading activity. What concerns might you have about his language skills?

in conjunction with other disorders. For example, students who have hearing losses (Chapter 15) or cerebral palsy (Chapter 14) often have articulation or voice disorders as well as language disorders. Similarly, a few students with intellectual disability (Chapter 11) may demonstrate slight communication delays, whereas others demonstrate speech delays, language delays, or both speech and language delays.

It is important that young children learn and practice pragmatics in and outside of school.

Articulation Disorders.   Articulation disorders are among the most frequent communication disorders in preschool and school-aged children. Articulation is a speaker's production of individual or sequenced sounds. An articulation disorder occurs when the child cannot correctly produce the various sounds and sound combinations of speech. Articulation errors may be in the form of substitutions, omissions, additions, and distortions. For example, when a student says "wittle" for "little" the student is substituting /dw/ for voiced /l/. When a student leaves a sound out of a word, that is an omission. A simple example suffices to explain omission: if a student said "ike" instead of the word "bike." Distortions are modifications of the production of a sound in a word; a listener gets the sense that the sound is being produced, but it seems distorted. Common distortions, called lisps, occur when /s/, /z/, /sh/, and /ch/ are mispronounced.

Apraxia is a motor speech disorder that affects the way in which a student plans to produce speech. The preferred term for children is *childhood apraxia of speech* (CAS) (ASHA, 2007b). Apraxia can be acquired as the result of a trauma such as a stroke, a tumor, or a head injury, or may occur with other disorders. Apraxia can also occur early in life in isolation without trauma or other disorders.

Students with apraxia have difficulty with the voluntary, purposeful movements of speech even though they have no paralysis or weakness of the muscles involved in speech. They have difficulty positioning the articulators and sequencing the sounds. Students with apraxia may be able to say the individual sounds required for speech in isolation or syllables, but they cannot produce them in longer words and sentences. They may be able to say sounds and words correctly when there is no pressure or request to do so but not when there is.

Some characteristics of apraxia are errors in production of vowels, inconsistent speech errors, more errors as words or sentences get longer, voicing errors (for example, /b/ for /p/ or /g/ for /k/), and stress on the wrong syllables, also referred to as prosody. These errors are not usually present in students who have traditional articulation disorders. Students with apraxia need frequent therapy that focuses on repetition, sound sequencing, and movement patterns (ASHA, 2007b; Caruso & Strand, 1999). When individuals have significant difficulty with coordinating motor movements for sound production, as Kylie does, they usually benefit from evaluation for an AAC device while they continue to work on their speech.

Articulation problems, like all speech and language disorders, vary. Children often are identified in early childhood settings through school-based speech-language screenings. Many of them have mild or moderate articulation disorders; their speech is understood by others yet contains sound-production errors. Other children have articulation disorders that have a more significant impact on their interactions, making it nearly impossible for others to understand them. When children have serious articulation disorders, they, like Kylie and Joey, usually benefit from evaluation for an AAC device.

Teachers refer a student with articulation problems to a speech-language pathologist for many reasons. If a student's articulation problem negatively affects the student's interactions in class or the student's educational performance, referral is in order. Likewise, if a student's sound-production errors make speech difficult or impossible to understand, the teacher is justified in referring the student to an SLP. Furthermore, articulation problems resulting from neurological injuries (e.g., cerebral palsy or stroke) typically require therapy. Therapy is also needed to assist the student with clefts of the palate or lip if the student cannot produce speech sounds or sound combinations correctly. Therapy may also be required to help a student with a hearing loss who is experiencing difficulty in correctly producing speech sounds because of the inability to hear the sounds clearly.

Voice Disorders.   Each person has a unique voice. This voice reflects the interactive relationship of pitch, duration, intensity, resonance, and vocal quality.

- **Pitch** is determined by the rate of vibration in the vocal folds; men tend to have lower-pitched voices than women do. Pitch is affected by the tension and size of the vocal folds, the health of the larynx, and the location of the larynx.

- **Duration** is the length of time any speech sound requires.

- **Intensity** (loudness or softness) is based on the perception of the listener and is determined by the air pressure coming from the lungs through the vocal folds. Rarely do individuals believe that their voices are too loud. Rather, they may seek professional voice therapy because their voices are too soft.

- **Resonance**, the perceived quality of someone's voice, is determined by the way in which the tone coming from the vocal folds is modified by the spaces of the throat, mouth, and nose. Students with an unrepaired cleft palate may experience resonance problems because the opening from the mouth to the nasal cavity may be too large or differently shaped. This type of resonance trait is an example of **hypernasality**, in which air is allowed to pass through the nasal cavity on sounds other than /m/, /n/, and /ng/. Sometimes students have another type of resonance problem; they may sound as if they have a cold or are holding their noses when speaking. This is referred to as **hyponasality** because air cannot pass through the nose and comes through the mouth instead. These students may need speech therapy to learn how to produce non-nasal sounds.

The quality of the voice is affected by problems of breath support or vocal-fold functioning as well as resonance. You might have experienced short-term vocal-quality problems after cheering at a football game when your voice became hoarse. Repeated abuse of the vocal folds may cause vocal nodules, growths that result from the rubbing together of the vocal-fold edges. When the folds cannot vibrate properly or come together completely, the sound of a student's voice will change temporarily until the vocal nodules heal. This short-term problem usually heals because the vocal-fold abuse is not constant.

If, however, nodules develop and persist, therapy may help a student learn to talk in a way that is less abusive to the vocal mechanisms. In most cases, nodules disappear after rest and/or voice therapy. If vocal nodules are the result of an organic problem, therapy alone may not resolve them, and surgery may be required (Justice & Redle, 2014).

Kali9/E+/Getty Images

Students can learn pragmatics by working together; each can become a coach for the others to communicate in a particular environment.

Fluency Disorders.   Normal speech requires correct articulation, vocal quality, and **fluency** (rate and rhythm of speaking). Fluent speech is smooth, flows well, and appears to be effortless. Fluency problems are characterized by interruptions in the flow of speaking, such as atypical rate or rhythm, as well as repetitions of sounds, syllables, words, and phrases.

All children and adults have difficulties with fluency on occasion. They hesitate, repeat themselves, or use fillers such as "umm" at one time or another.

In other instances, dysfluency is considered stuttering, which is frequent repetition and/or prolongation of words or sounds. A student who stutters may repeat words such as "I I I I forgot my my my pencil," repeat sounds such as "W W W When is the papapapaper due," or interject sounds or words such as "I um um forgot um um my um homework." The cause of stuttering is not known, although research points to genetics and neurophysiological factors (ASHA, n.d.). Stuttering can interfere with classroom participation as well as social relationships at school.

LANGUAGE DISORDERS   Students may have language disorders that are receptive, expressive, or both. Their language impairment may be associated with another disability, or it may be a specific language impairment—not related to any physical or intellectual disability. Among students 3 to 17 years old, 3.3 percent have language disorders. Despite their causes, language impairments have a substantial effect on classroom participation and learning. Aspects of language that can be affected by a language disorder include phonology, morphology, syntax, semantics, and pragmatics.

Phonology.   Students with phonological disorders may be unable to discriminate between differences in speech sounds or sound segments that signify differences in words. For example, the word *pen* may sound no different from *pin*. Their inability to differentiate sounds, as well as similar, rhyming syllables, may cause reading and/or spelling difficulties (Apel & Swank, 1999; Lombardino, Riccio, Hynd, & Pinheiro, 1997). Phonological difficulties are common in students with language impairments and may affect their ability to read (ASHA, n.d.). You should be sensitive to these phonological disorders as young children develop their early literacy skills (Gillon, 2007).

Morphology.   Children with morphological difficulties have problems using the structure of words to get or give information. They may make a variety of errors. For example, they may not use *ed* to signal past tense, as in *walked*, or *s* to signal plurality. When children are unable to use morphological rules appropriately, the average length of their utterances is sometimes shorter than expected for the particular age because plurals, verb markers, and affixes may be missing from their statements (McCormick & Loeb, 2003). Students with morphological difficulties are unable to be as specific in their communication as others are. For example, if they do not use verb markers such as *ed*, it is difficult to know if they are referring to past or present tense.

Morphology errors can be associated with differences in dialects as well as with a variety of other conditions, including intellectual disability (Chapter 11), autism (Chapter 12), hearing loss or deafness and hard of hearing (Chapter 15), and expressive language delay. Incorrect use of morphology is also associated with specific language impairment.

Syntax.   Syntactical errors are those involving word order, such as ordering words in a manner that does not convey meaning to the listeners (e.g., "Where one them park at?"), using immature structures for a given age or developmental level (e.g., a 4-year-old child using two-word utterances, such as "Him sick"), misusing negatives (e.g., a 4-year-old child saying, "Him no go"), or omitting structures (e.g., "He go now"). As with phonology and morphology, differences in syntax sometimes can be associated with dialects and other conditions.

Semantics.   Children who experience difficulty using words singly or together in sentences may have semantic disorders. They may have difficulty with multiple-meaning

MyLab Education
Video Example 8.4
This video presents an example of a child with mixed receptive expressive language disorder. How might this disorder affect literacy development? http://www.youtube.com/watch?v=mFguWOufFrs

words and have restricted meanings for words (McCormick & Loeb, 2003). Some students with semantic disorders may have problems with words that express time and space (e.g., *night, tiny*), cause and effect (e.g., "Push button, ball goes"), and inclusion versus exclusion (e.g., *all, none*). Sometimes students with semantic language disorders rely on words with fairly nonspecific meanings (e.g., *thing, one, that*) because of their limited knowledge of vocabulary. Difficulty with semantics can affect both their understanding and expressing of concepts.

Pragmatics. Pragmatics focuses on the social use of language—the communication between a speaker and a listener within a shared social environment. Pragmatic skills include adapting communication to varied situations, obtaining and maintaining eye contact, using appropriate body language, maintaining a topic, and taking turns in conversations.

Pragmatic disorders occur in many different ways. Students who talk for long periods and do not allow anyone else an opportunity to converse may be displaying signs of a pragmatic disorder. Similarly, students whose comments during class are unrelated to the subject at hand or who ask questions at an inappropriate time may be exhibiting a pragmatic disorder (ASHA, n.d.). Students who have difficulty with pragmatics include those with autism (Chapter 12) and traumatic brain injury (Chapter 13).

Causes

Speech and language disorders can be classified according to their cause: (1) **biological**, those caused by an identifiable problem in the neuromuscular mechanism of the person; and (2) **environmental**, those with no identifiable biological or neurological cause.

Biological causes of disorders are numerous; they may originate in the nervous system, the muscular system, the chromosomes, or the formation of the speech mechanism. They may include hereditary malformations, prenatal injuries, toxic disturbances, tumors, traumas, seizures, infectious diseases, muscular diseases, and vascular impairments (Gillam & Gillam, 2015). As mentioned, the causes of environmental disorders are currently unknown. Examples of disorders with no current known biological or neurological cause include dysfluent speech (stuttering and cluttering) and phonological disorders.

Speech and language disorders can be classified further according to when the problem began. A disorder that occurs at or before birth is referred to as a **congenital disorder**. A disorder that occurs well after birth is an **acquired disorder**. For example, an acquired speech and language disorder may be present after a severe head injury (Chapter 13). A functional disorder may be congenital or acquired. Some causes have both organic and functional origins. In addition, portions of the speech and language disorder may have been present at birth, and other parts may have been acquired later in life. Kylie and Joey's disabilities, Rett syndrome and autism spectrum disorders, respectively, are both examples of congenital disorders. In Kylie's case the cause of her disability is known and is attributed to genetics. However, in Joey's case the cause is not currently known. Fortunately for speech-language pathologists, knowing the cause of the disorder is not necessary to provide intervention. In Kylie's case, the cause of her disability (genetics) does not inform treatment as much as research related to how individuals with Rett syndrome respond to certain teaching strategies and supports. In Joey's case, knowing the cause is not as important as knowing what the strengths (visual processing) and weaknesses (social language) generally are for individuals with autism.

MyLab Education Self-Check 8.1

MyLab Education Application Exercise 8.1: Types of Speech and Language Disorders

Evaluating Students with Speech and Language Disorders

Determining the Presence of Speech and Language Disorders

As defined by IDEA, a speech or language impairment is a communication disorder, such as stuttering, impaired articulation, a language impairment, or a voice impairment, that negatively impacts a student's educational performance. Educators, early intervention specialists, and speech-language pathologists (SLPs) try to meet the physical, cognitive, communication, social, emotional, and adaptive needs of infants and toddlers ages birth through 2 and young children ages 3 through 5 who have speech and language disorders.

Speech-language pathologists start by conducting a screening, creating a referral for an evaluation, or both. Many school districts also use short-term interventions to help determine if a referral for a full evaluation is needed (ASHA). The emphasis of the intervention or prereferral is to begin to explore the relationship between a student's communication abilities, the student's participation in school, and the student's response to direct intervention.

When determining whether a student has a speech and language disorder, the speech-language pathologist uses various sources of information, such as school records, parent and teacher interviews, hearing and vision screenings, observations, speech samples, language samples, classwork samples/portfolios, checklists, standardized tests, nonstandardized tests, and curriculum-based assessments. The SLP then determines if a speech and language disorder is present and if it affects the student's learning. Depending on the area of speech and/or language being assessed, the SLP may obtain certain types of information using the assessment tools shown in *Nondiscriminatory Evaluation Process: Determining the Presence of Speech and Language Disorders* and described in more detail here.

MyLab Education

Video Example 8.5

This video describes the evaluation process. Why should the SLP use a variety of sources of information during an evaluation? https://www.youtube.com/watch?v=Ssz_cutETTE

Nondiscriminatory Evaluation Process
Determining the Presence of Speech and Language Disorders

Observation	**Medical personnel observe:** The child is not achieving developmental milestones related to communication skills, or there is a change in a child's communication skills. **Teacher and parents observe:** The child has difficulty understanding or using language. The child may also have difficulty speaking clearly.
Screening	Assessment measures: **Classroom work products:** The student may be hesitant to participate in verbal classroom work. Written classroom projects may reflect errors of verbal communication or, in some instances, be a preferred avenue of expression for the student. **Vision and hearing screening:** The student may have a history of otitis media (middle-ear infection). Hearing may be normal, or the student may have hearing loss. Limited vision may impact language skills.
Prereferral	**Implementation of suggestions from a school-based team:** The teacher models speech sounds, expands language, asks open-ended questions, etc. If the child has been identified before entering school, the parents may implement suggestions from the school-based team.
Referral	If, in spite of interventions, the student still performs poorly in academics or continues to manifest communication impairments, the student is referred to a multidisciplinary team. The team may continue with more in-depth interventions.
Nondiscriminatory evaluation procedures and standards	**Assessment measures:** **Speech and language tests (articulation, phonology, language sample, speech sample, oral motor functioning, receptive language, and expressive language):** The student performs significantly below average in one or more areas. **Anecdotal records:** The student may have genetic or medical factors that contribute to speech or language difficulties. Some students with other disabilities are at risk for having speech and language disorders. **Curriculum-based assessment:** A speech and/or language difficulty may affect progress in the curriculum. **Direct observation:** The student experiences difficulty in communicating.
Determination	The nondiscriminatory evaluation team determines that the student has a speech and language disorder and needs special education and related services. The student's IEP team proceeds to develop appropriate education options for the student.

In a speech/language assessment where language is perceived to be the most significant deficit area, the SLP seeks to obtain information specific to how students understand information communicated to them (including when information is given to them verbally and in written form) and how they communicate what they know (verbally and through written language). The Test of Integrated Language and Literacy Skills (TILLS) is an example of a standardized test designed to procure information regarding a student's expressive and receptive language skills. The TILLS has 15 subtests, including vocabulary awareness, phonemic awareness, story retelling, nonword repetition, nonword spelling, listening comprehension, reading comprehension, following directions, delayed story retelling, nonword reading, reading fluency, written expression, social communication, digit span forward, and digit span backward. The SLP may administer all of the subtests or choose specific ones to obtain the information needed for a particular student.

Speech Assessments

When a student requires a speech assessment, the goal of the process is to determine the presence of articulation, voice, or fluency problems.

ARTICULATION Articulation assessments evaluate a student's abilities to produce speech sounds in single words, sentences, and conversation. Speech-language pathologists listen, noting the phonemes in error, the patterns of any errors, and the frequency with which the errors occur. Test instruments assessing articulation skills require that the student use consonants in the initial, middle, and final positions of words (e.g., for /p/, students might name a "pig," a "zipper," and a "cup"). An **oral motor exam**, which is the examination of the appearance, strength, and range of motion of the lips, tongue, palate, teeth, and jaw, is also a usual procedure.

VOICE Voice evaluations include information about the onset and course of the voice problem, environmental factors that might affect vocal quality, and typical use of voice (Verdolini, 2000), including pitch, intensity, and nasality.

FLUENCY When completing a fluency assessment, the speech-language pathologist measures the amount of dysfluency as well as the type and duration of dysfluencies while the student is speaking. The SLP also notes associated speech and nonspeech behaviors such as eye blinking or head movements (Haynes & Pindzola, 2012).

Language Assessments

The instrument mentioned earlier in the chapter, the TILLS, can be thought of in a broad sense to gain information about expressive and receptive language. However, when conducting language assessments, SLPs also focus on the specific components that constitute expressive and receptive language skills. These include phonological, semantic, morphological, syntactic, and pragmatic skills.

Although standardized tests are often used in the schools, they are not always appropriate for every student. The student who is nonverbal or who uses nonconventional means of communication requires more descriptive than standardized assessment measures (Downing, 2005). When assessing a student who is a nonverbal communicator, the SLP documents the communicative forms (conventional and nonconventional) and the functions these forms serve by observing the student in different environments and with various communication partners (Downing, 2005).

For example, the SLP might observe this interaction: Joey looks at a friend's snack and then at his friend. He repeats this behavior several times. When the friend gives Joey some of his snack, Joey smiles. The SLP then notes the communication functions observed and the form the student used, including that Joey initiated a communication interaction, requested an item, and expressed a social interaction (e.g., *thank you* or *please*). Joey's forms of communication included eye contact (to gain attention to initiate communication), eye gaze (to request), and facial expression (a smile as thanks). The SLP then determines how to shape and expand on Joey's communication forms (e.g., speech, pointing to pictures, voice output). When using a voice output communication device to expand Joey's communication forms, the SLP models how to use the device to fulfill the functions that nonverbal communication was used for. For example, when the SLP observes Joey's eye gaze between the friend and his friend's snack, the SLP may say, "It looks like you want to try his snack, Joey. You can tell him with your device. You can say I want [presses phrase: I WANT], chips [presses word: CHIPS], please [presses word: PLEASE]".

Sometimes it helps for a professional, such as this speech-language pathologist, to be of the same ethnic population as the student being evaluated.

Multicultural Considerations for Assessment

Sometimes a student will need specialized speech or language assessment, as when the student is bilingual or multilingual. The SLP must be particularly skilled when assessing the communicative capabilities of students for whom English is not the primary language. Fair, unbiased evaluation is difficult for a student who is **bilingual (uses two languages equally well) or bidialectal** (uses two variations of a language) or for whom language dominance (the primary language of the student) is difficult to determine.

To assess such a student, the SLP should not merely translate test items into the student's primary language. Rather, the SLP should test the bilingual student using both the student's dominant language and English (Paradis, Genesee, & Crago, 2011). The SLP can accomplish this by using appropriate diagnostic tools to determine whether a language difference or a disability exists. Similar to the process used when assessing students whose primary language is English, the SLP uses a combination of standardized and nonstandardized tools.

For example, a student learning English as a second language may have strengths and preferences that may be documented using both standardized (that are appropriate based on the sample of students the test was normed on) and unstandardized assessment tools. These may include observation and interviews with communication partners (Roseberry-McKibbin & O'Hanlon, 2005). Having observed a speech and language disorder, the SLP then can plan appropriate therapies using culturally sensitive standardized measures whenever possible. With that said, it is essential for school professionals to understand that disordered communication is different from communication difficulties resulting from dual/multilanguage use (i.e., those seen in students who are English language learners).

MyLab Education **Self-Check 8.2**

MyLab Education **Application Exercise 8.2:** Determining Speech and Language Disorders

Including Students with Speech and Language Disorders

According to the U.S. Department of Education (2016), 87 percent of students who receive speech and language services spend 80 to 100 percent of their time in the general education classroom (see Figure 8.2). Working in the classroom is one of the service delivery options available for an SLP's caseload (ASHA, n.d.). Benefits for the students and the professionals have been observed by teachers and the SLP practicing inclusive service delivery models (Clapsaddle & Palafox, 2013).

For students, inclusion practices have assisted with carryover and generalization of skills, provided an opportunity to work on skills in a natural and meaningful context of the curriculum, given an opportunity to observe what areas are difficult and what interventions support the student, and augmented the ability to assess skills in the context of the curriculum (ASHA, n.d.; Clapsaddle & Palafox, 2013). For professionals, inclusion practices create an opportunity for the SLP to become more familiar with the class content and instructional expectations of the student, which results in goals that align better with the curriculum, allows instructors to learn more about and to see strategies modeled that might be helpful, and provides instructors with the support needed to target the goals throughout the day even when the SLP is not present, which is important, as the teacher has much more contact time with the students (ASHA, n.d.; Clapsaddle & Palafox, 2013). In addition, other students who do not directly receive services can benefit from supports in place as well (Clapsaddle & Palafox, 2013). (See *Inclusion Tips for Students with Speech and Language Disorders.*)

Figure 8.2 Educational Placement of Students with Speech and Language Disorders

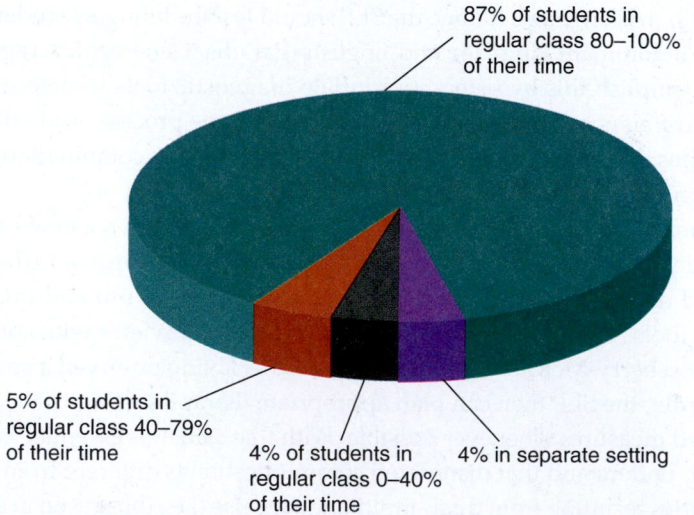

87% of students in regular class 80–100% of their time

5% of students in regular class 40–79% of their time

4% of students in regular class 0–40% of their time

4% in separate setting

SOURCE: U.S. Department of Education. (2017). *39th Annual Report to Congress on the Implementation of the Individuals with Disabilities Education Act.* Retreived from https://www2.ed.gov/about/reports/annual/osep/2017/parts-b-c/39th-arc-for-idea.pdf/

Inclusion Tips for Students with Speech and Language Disorders

	Behavior	Social Interactions	Educational Performance	Classroom Attitudes
What You Might See	The student appears shy and reserved. He may not participate in large-group setting. It may take him time to compose a response when speaking in front of the class.	The student is alone during unstructured times. The student does not ask friends to play. The student does not join peer interactions.	The student produces syntactically incomplete sentences verbally and in writing. The student avoids writing tasks.	The student expects the teacher to intercede when having difficulty with other students. The student might rely on the teacher to initiate interactions with other students.
What You Might Be Tempted to Do	Encourage the student to hurry or avoid calling on the student in large groups.	Assume the student is happy alone, and let the student be.	Constantly correct the student. Decrease the occurrence of writing assignments.	Tell the student to go play with others. Assume the students will work it out on their own.
Alternate Teacher Response	Provide a multiple-choice response option. Write the questions on the board, giving all students time to compose their answers before calling on specific students. Allow for small-group discussion and reporting.	Demonstrate that you value the student's contributions. Provide a model to help the student learn to interact with peers.	Provide visual and verbal models of complete sentences. Continue to provide lots of opportunities for writing. Provide positive feedback.	Teach all students ways to interact with one another and solve problems.
Ways to Include Peers in the Process	Provide multiple-choice response options or alternate response options for all students, along with other types of question formats.	Encourage peer buddies to help model and encourage interactions with other students in their classroom.	Allow small-group interactions with assigned roles that rotate to every student. The students can then provide models for each other.	Provide opportunities for the students to practice independent interactions with one another, offering assistance when needed.

It is important also to consider the social elements of the school setting. The concept of inclusion centers not only on academic topics but also the social aspects of school. Language skills are needed for navigating social interactions and establishing working relationships with others, both of which are important skills for future employment opportunities (Lowden, Hall, Elliot, & Lewin, 2011; Palilis, 2010). Students use these skills throughout the day, as in large-group discussions and small-group work (e.g., science experiments, group presentations). Conversations also occur with instructors for the purpose of understanding directions and assignments or explaining answers. In the hall and at lunch conversations take place with peers. And social conversations have a place in extracurricular activities.

Students need to be actively engaged in all aspects of the curriculum—the direct instruction and the indirect social instruction. During collaborative work, consulting, and co-teaching activities, the SLP and teacher can problem solve how to assist the student. For instance, the teacher may note that a student appears shy and reserved and does not participate in large-group settings. It may take the student time to compose a response when speaking in front of the class. The teacher may be tempted to encourage the student to hurry or avoid calling on the student in large groups. Any one of these reactions may well blunt the student's progress and limit inclusion.

Yet the SLP and teacher may jointly decide to co-teach during a large-group discussion to try a variety of strategies. They may try providing a multiple-choice response option after questions, write the questions on the board to give students time to compose their answers before calling on specific students, or allow for small-group discussion and reporting. They might also try providing multiple-choice response options or alternate response options for all students, along with other types of question formats. In these ways, they may be able to support even more than one student. Partnerships (co-teaching) and modifications (universal design for learning, which you learned about in Chapter 6) lead to progress.

Educating Students with Speech and Language Disorders

Importance of Language in the Classroom

Language occurs throughout the school day and is the vehicle for teaching the curriculum (Howell & Nolet, 2009; Losardo & Notari-Syverson, 2011). Additionally, communication takes part across all content areas. Whether a student is asked to discuss a topic verbally, answer questions, read language, write language, or work with others cooperatively, the student is practicing language throughout the entire curriculum while communicating.

As a teacher, you and your colleagues should pay careful attention to the environments where your students with speech and language disorders are placed and especially whether they are in inclusive settings with genuine access to the general curriculum and whether they have the types and amounts of support available or necessary for progress in those environments. To support students with speech and language disorders, it is advisable to think about teaching and learning using a framework, such as the universal design for learning (UDL).

When using a UDL framework in the general education classroom, you will decrease the barriers that students with speech and language disorders have in accessing the instructional content, and you will increase their participation in the general curriculum. A UDL approach takes into account different learning styles, differing proficiencies in English, and methods of communication. As such, it is useful for all students, not just those with speech and language disorders (Capp, 2017).

Planning for Universal Design for Learning

When planning universal design for learning for students with disordered communication, you must answer two questions: "How can I ensure that my students understand what I am teaching?" and "How can I ensure that my students can express what they know?" Universal design for learning includes modifications to how content is presented as well as options for expression. When you use only one or two methods to teach, especially if you use only verbal methods, some students with speech and language disorders, as well as some students without disabilities, are not able to access the material.

To assist your students, you can vary the format for relaying the information, such as by using both audio and text formats, visual representations with verbal information, graphics, graphic organizers, and controlled vocabulary. Similarly, you can vary the ways in which students demonstrate their knowledge. For instance, instead of assigning only a written report, also allow PowerPoint presentations, demonstrations with visual supports, taped oral reports, or dramatic performances. These and the facilitative language strategies described in *Guidelines for Teaching: Facilitative Language Strategies* provide access to the general curriculum.

Guidelines for Teaching

Facilitative Language Strategies

Key Components of Facilitative Language Strategies.

- Know the child's goals and objectives.
- View every interaction as an opportunity to use the strategies.
- Identify the goals and objectives that relate to specific activities of the day.

- Identify teaching strategies to be used during specific activities.
- Decide when to use strategies to emphasize targets within the activity.
- Use the strategies identified during the activity.
- Document the child's response.

Specific language strategies.

Focused contrast.

Highlight differences between the child's speech or language and the adult's. This can occur as feedback or a model.

- When the child says, "Otey," for "Okay," the adult could say, "Oh, you said 'Otey,' and I said, 'Okay.'"
- If the focus is on the past-tense marker *ed*, the adult, while playing house, may say, "She is walking," while moving the doll and then stop the movement and say, "She walked to the door." The adult then repeats this strategy with numerous actions during play.

Modeling.

Produce models of a particular language or speech structure that the child does not currently use.

- If the structure is the plural marker *s*, the adult may use it to describe the plurals in the ongoing activity, highlighting them with extra emphasis or stress.

Event casts.

Event casts provide an ongoing description of an activity, just as a sports broadcaster might. The events can be what the child or adult is doing.

- During dress-up play, the adult may say, "You are putting on the hat. Now you are putting on blue shoes."

Open questions.

Questions that have a variety of possible answers are open questions.

- Examples: "What should we do next?" and "What do you think happens next?"

Expansions.

The adult repeats the child's utterance, filling in the missing components.

- Child says, "Two horse," and the adult expands with "Two brown horses."

Recasts.

When recasting, the adult keeps the child's basic meaning but changes the structure or grammar of the child's utterance.

- Child says, "He has juice," and the adult can say, "Yes, he is drinking juice now."

Redirects and prompted initiations.

These strategies encourage children to interact with each other.

- Child approaches an adult and makes a request that could be made to another child; the adult redirects the child to ask a classmate: "You could tell Tom, 'I need a blue crayon.'" When a child does not make a request to an adult but has the opportunity to interact with another child, the child might be prompted to ask another child to play or request some item.

Individualizing Instructional Experiences and Identifying Necessary Supports

Although the UDL framework is useful for supporting students with varied needs, some educational environments employ traditional practices when developing lessons and activities. Regardless of the framework used, your duty under IDEA is to individualize the instructional experience for students. Students with speech and language disorders are heterogeneous; no single approach works for all, and so you must identify what supports are required for an individual student and implement them in the environments where they are needed. One of those supports might be uncovered by using an ecological inventory.

ECOLOGICAL INVENTORIES FOR COM-MUNICATION Ecological inventories are observation tools that help determine with specificity what supports a student with a speech and language disorder needs, and has a right to have, under IDEA. By observing typically developing peers engaged in an activity or task, you can see when students in general education are expected to communicate, what they typically say, and how they respond. (See Chapter 11 for more information on ecological inventories and how they apply

Assistive technology can be as simple and universal as a handheld device, and even that device can be specifically tailored for a designated user.

to students with intellectual disabilities.) In a word or two, ecological inventories can help you determine what communication demands exist in natural environments (Downing, 2005), and an ecological assessment can help you identify when a student is not meeting those communication demands.

Ecological assessment tools are not standardized. You may modify an inventory to meet your particular needs. You should, however, obtain certain information for all students. That information includes: (1) a description of the activity you are observing; (2) what language peers are using to participate or contribute; (3) why the students need to communicate; (4) how the students are communicating their response, such as verbally or in written form; and (5) how your student may communicate in order to participate. Steps identified that are not yet completed independently by a student may serve as a starting point for intervention.

When you conduct an ecological inventory, your first step is to collaborate with the SLP and others to determine what interactions occur within the natural environment. For example, assume a student needs to summarize current-events articles for a social studies class. You, the SLP, and others analyze the steps or components of the task, such as announcing the title, describing the main idea, including some of the facts disclosed, stating the conclusion, and offering an opinion.

This team then observes one of the student's peers completing the task and monitors the degree to which the peer is independent. Was the peer completely independent? Did equipment need to be set up first? Were verbal cues needed?

Now the student completes the task, and the team records the steps that the student needed assistance with or was not yet able to complete. The team then compares those data with the peer's data to determine the student's degree of discrepancy and target the areas of discrepancy for instruction, strategies, and possibly supplementary aids. See Figure 8.3 for an example of a completed ecological inventory.

Subsequent assessments based on the ecological inventory enable the team to determine whether the instruction, strategies, and/or supplementary aids are helping the student decrease the discrepancy in the performance observed. For instance, the student may need new vocabulary to be added to an AAC device, picture cues for the steps, pages of pictures of line drawings (called topic boards), or role playing and practice with others.

Go to http://communication .bridgeschool.org/docs/planning-success/ecological-inventory.pdf for an example of an ecological inventory.

DETERMINING SUPPLEMENTARY AIDS AND SERVICES In addition to identifying necessary supports, you and other team members must document those supports students need to access the curriculum and perform to the best of their abilities on tests. This documentation is done in the "supplementary aids and services" section within an individualized education program (IEP). (See Chapter 4 for a discussion of supplementary aids and services.) For Kylie and Joey, one of the most important supplementary aids was access to assistive technology. Kylie uses a program titled pragmatic organization dynamic display (PODD), and Joey uses an iPad that has voice output software. These technologies not only ensure that Kylie and Joey make progress in school but also make it possible for them to express themselves to others, to be the self-determined young people they already are, and to bring other people into their circles of self-determination.

Assistive technology (AT) includes any piece of equipment, commercial or handmade, that assists an individual to perform various functions, such as communication. One form of AT is an augmentative and alternative communication (AAC) system. AAC systems consist of integrated components that supplement the communication abilities of individuals who cannot meet their communication needs through speaking (Beukelman & Mirenda, 2013). An AAC system may include an AAC device, a physical object to transmit or receive messages, and other types of communication such as gesturing, speaking, and/or writing. AAC devices include communication books, communication/language boards, communication charts, mechanical or electronic voice output equipment, and computers.

Figure 8.3 An Ecological Inventory

Ecological Assessment for Communication

Student:

Observer:

Date:

Time:

Activity (Sharing a current event)	Peer use of language	Why is language used?	Possible Adaptations/ needed supports
1. Announce title 2. Describe main idea 3. Provide facts that support the main idea 4. State conclusion 5. State opinion	1. Short phrase 2. Sentence 3. Sentences 4. Sentence 5. Short phrase/Sentence	1. Convey information 2. Convey information/describe 3. Convey information 4. Convey information 5. Convey feeling/emotions	1. Use of speech generating device (need to program) 2. Picture supports to pick what the main idea is (2–4 options) 3. Facts represented symbolically, use core words on speech generating device to describe 4. Use programmed phrase on speech generating device 5. Use core vocabulary on device and/or pre-programmed phrases on device

An AAC device contains a set of symbols. A *symbol* is a visual, auditory, gestural, and/or tactile representation of a concept (ASHA, n.d.). Symbol sets include photographs, pictographs (symbols that look like what they represent), ideographs (more abstract symbols), printed words, objects, partial objects, miniature objects, braille, textures, or any combination of these symbols. Symbols that may be part of the AAC system, but not part of the symbol set for a physical device, include gestures, manual sign sets/systems, and/or spoken words.

A team approach—simply good partnership—is essential when determining what assistive technology may be needed. That is so because the team has to consider so many different aspects of the student and the technology. Input from the parents as well as information regarding the student's vision skills, fine-motor skills, gross-motor skills, hearing, and curriculum requirements all help SLPs and other team members, including the student's parents, to recommend the features the AAC system should have and whether the student needs additional forms of AT. Once the student is trying out or using an AAC device, the student's educational team will develop a plan to monitor its benefits and to provide the appropriate vocabulary.

If the student is using an AAC device, individualized vocabulary will have to be added to it. A variety of comprehensive vocabulary sets are available commercially that offer a range of frequently used vocabulary in both high- and low-tech versions and that may be customized for the student. Many of the high-tech devices also come with software so that the programming and editing can be completed on a separate computer and transferred to the student's device.

Students, especially those who are beginning to use symbols, depend on others to make vocabulary available for them to communicate. That is why you should carefully consider how to make vocabulary available throughout the school day. You should focus on vocabulary that occurs frequently instead of vocabulary used only once or twice a day. For example, choose high-frequency core words such as *like, go, more, want,* and so on. In addition, the ability to express a variety of communication functions (i.e., questions, comments, directives, and requesting) is also important. In the *My Voice* feature, Carrie points to ways Joey's educators encourage Joey to communicate orally, and in turn, facilitate a chance for Carrie and Paul to engage Joey in daily conversations at home about what Joey did at school.

Without vocabulary, students cannot express their thoughts or discuss topics with others; they cannot be as self-determined as they might otherwise be. The selection of a device, its features, and the degree of a student's needs and capacities all figure into establishing an AAC system.

My Voice

Carrie Lauds Joey's Educators

Literacy skills are important for all children, but especially so for Joey because he uses written text instead of oral discussion to learn new information and to learn speech. As his mother, Carrie, explained, "Joey has been reading words since he was 2."

Joey participates in guided reading groups with his 2nd-grade classmates. Determining his comprehension of grade-level text, however, is another issue. At first, "it was hard for the teachers to figure out what he knew as he is not good at answering oral questions." So, Carrie said, "to have a better understanding of what Joey was getting out of the stories, Joey's teachers typed out the questions" and provided multiple-choice answers. Usually he gets 70 to 75 percent correct. "If he doesn't get the answer correct, they go back to the page that relates to that question, talk about the picture, and give him the question again." Carrie noted, "They really do a great job of making him part of the class. The other kids talk to him and help him and he even helps them with reading."

But spelling challenges Joey. Once he has experience with a word, he generally is able to spell it; so spending time rewriting words he already knows does not engage him. He also has trouble writing with a pencil. So Joey's educators administer a pretest when presenting a new list of words to the class. Joey studies the words he missed and types them. His teachers and SLP then assess the definitions and comprehension purposes of those words so that they can teach them to Joey.

Carrie said, "I like that the teachers work on social skills with Joey. They understand that play is important, so they encourage play with him. When he goes to the resource room, one or two of his peers go with him." The teachers provide words, phrases, and questions in text form for Joey to use while playing. "Now he is starting to say these things on his own and getting more creative with his toys, and this draws other kids to him."

Carrie's favorite idea was to send a digital camera to school with her children. Joey's teachers take pictures through the day so when Joey and his sister, Kylie, arrive home and get off the bus they can discuss what happened at school, thus giving Carrie and her husband, Paul, a point of reference to build on and a way to practice communication. "This is great because Joey can't really answer the question 'What did you do today?'"

Service Delivery Models

Speech-language pathologists collaborate with special and general educators to determine how best to serve students with speech and language disorders during the school day. Different service delivery models could be appropriate for students, and no single model is appropriate for all students. IDEA mandates that the individual needs of the student be considered and that research-based practices be implemented in the least restrictive environment. Service delivery includes the setting in which the services take place, the intensity and frequency of services, and the role of the speech-language pathologist.

SETTING   The **setting** in which the speech-language services occur can be in a separate room where the student or small group meets with the speech-language pathologist. This is often called "pullout" intervention. This model may provide more focused intervention but takes students away from their peers and they miss classroom instruction.

An alternative is in-class intervention, sometimes called "push-in" intervention. In this model, the speech-language pathologist is in the classroom addressing student communication goals. This could mean team teaching with the educator, supporting a student with classwork, or supporting a small group in a specific activity. With this model, teachers can become more aware of effective supports or strategies for the student with the speech and language disorder and the speech-language pathologist can learn more about the curriculum. In a systematic review, McGinty and Justice (2006) found an advantage for classroom-based models. Classroom-based models have also shown better generalization of skills (Cirrin et al., 2010; McGinty & Justice, 2006).

The speech-language pathologist providing services to Kylie may use push-in intervention to support her communication within the classroom environment during academic activities. Supporting Kylie within the classroom also provides an opportunity for the SLP to demonstrate specific teaching strategies that other professionals can use to support Kylie when the SLP is not present. Likewise, the SLP supporting Joey may use a mix of push-in and pullout intervention. During pullout sessions, the SLP uses that time to teach Joey about how or why to initiate social interactions and ask partner-focused questions. During push-in services, the SLP supports Joey by having him practice using his device to initate and interact with peers during authentic academic or non-academic-related activities.

INTENSITY AND FREQUENCY OF SERVICES   In addition to where the services take place, how the services are **scheduled** is a factor in service delivery. The most frequent model is a traditional one in which the student is scheduled for services on the same day and time each week. Brandel and Loeb (2011) found this to be the most frequent scheduling model, as did Mullen and Schooling (2010).

Other models include receding schedules in which direct services are frequent initially and then reduced as indirect services increase (ASHA, n.d.). The cyclical schedule occurs when the speech-language pathologist provides direct services for a time and then no or indirect services (ASHA, n.d.).

The 3:1 model is an example of cyclical scheduling. In this scheduling model, there are 3 weeks of direct services to students and 1 week of indirect services. During the week of indirect services, the speech-language pathologist could engage in classroom observation, meeting with families, consulting with teachers, adapting materials, programming AAC devices, or training others.

Block scheduling is another option. In this model, the intervention sessions are longer but not as frequent. This scheduling option is often used in middle or secondary education settings (ASHA, n.d.). Blast or burst scheduling occurs when the speech-language pathologist provides services in short, intense bursts, such as 15 minutes 3 times per week. The student would miss less classroom content with this model.

Kylie's speech-language pathologist utilizes a traditional model due to her preference for a consistent schedule as she supports students across multiple schools. She sees Kylie for a total of 90 minutes per week, which is split into three 30-minute increments. Conversely, the speech-language pathologist supporting Joey also supports students in a variety of schools, but has adopted a 3:1 service delivery model. This allows her to see Joey 120 minutes per week in weeks in which direct services are provided in four 30-minute increments. In indirect weeks, she uses the time she would normally spend with Joey to complete paperwork reporting requirements, collaborate with Joey's general educator and special educator, and consult with Joey's family to identify words and phrases they would like programmed into his device. Although the service delivery models chosen by Kylie and Joey's speech-language pathologists differ in minutes per week, both models result in 360 minutes per month of direct service provision for each student.

THE ROLE OF THE SPEECH-LANGUAGE PATHOLOGIST The **speech-language pathologist's role** may vary in the provision of services. The speech-language pathologist can provide services directly to the student in the settings and with the schedules described above. An alternative or additional service delivery option is providing consultative services and indirect services. In this model, the speech-language pathologist supports teachers, paraprofessionals, and families instead of providing services directly to the student. Some of the ways in which the speech-language pathologist would indirectly support the student include adapting or creating instructional materials, programming AAC devices, teaching others how to use an AAC device or some other support strategy, monitoring student progress through observation, or collaborating with teachers (ASHA, 2010). Service delivery should be flexible and change with the changing needs of the student.

Teachers and speech-language pathologists must collaborate to support students with communication challenges if they are to succeed in school. It is important that the teacher and SLP discuss service delivery options that best meet students' needs and support students' participation in school in both academics and extracurricular activities. See *Into Practice Across Grade Levels: Three Partnership Options* to review examples of SLPs collaborating with classroom teachers to assist in meeting students' needs.

Into Practice Across Grade Levels

Three Partnership Options

Teachers and speech-language pathologists (SLPs) can work with each other in three usual ways (American Speech-Language-Hearing Association, 2003). Speech-language pathologists can help students succeed in the general education curriculum. They need to be aware of curriculum plans and upcoming instructional opportunities in which the student may be involved. Meeting with the general educator on a regular basis can be beneficial. Team members should define their roles and responsibilities to avoid confusion and misunderstanding, which will also leave them more time to focus on the student's outcomes.

Consultation.

Classroom teachers and SLPs meet to discuss lessons and to develop adaptations and accommodations for students in the classroom.

Example: Cristena, a **9th grader** with autism, loves science, music, and drama. The science curriculum presents many challenges for her, so her SLP works with her classroom teacher to adapt text materials, handouts, and tests so that they match Cristena's language abilities. The adapted science handouts also benefit students who need visual presentations of the content.

Supportive teaching.

Supportive teaching occurs when the teacher and the SLP plan lessons together. The SLP completes some pre- and

post-activities related to the lesson with the student, and the teacher and SLP co-teach the lesson.

Example: Andrew is a **2nd grader** with Down syndrome. His class is studying the life cycle of the frog. His SLP and teacher meet to plan for the unit and determine what extra supports Andrew will need to participate. They also discuss what responsibilities each will take during class. The SLP works with Andrew individually to preteach vocabulary and then teaches part of the unit to the whole class. She may meet individually with Andrew again to clarify any information he did not understand.

Complementary teaching.

Complementary teaching occurs when the SLP and the teacher co-teach material for the lesson in ways that reflect their levels of expertise.

Example: Beth is in the **5th grade**. She has language-learning difficulties that include auditory processing weaknesses, and she has a hard time taking notes during social studies. Her SLP takes notes while the teacher teaches. He also prepares study guides, teaches small groups that need more adaptation, and on occasion teaches organizational skills to the whole class.

Effective Instructional Strategies and Supports

FACILITATIVE LANGUAGE STRATEGIES   Most early education programs facilitate language development. Because communication is social in nature and is learned across all parts of a child's day, the child's communication partners should use strategies to promote speech and language development. The strategies you learned about in *Into Practice Across Grade Levels: Three Partnership Options* were researched and refined in the Language Acquisition Preschool at the University of Kansas (Bunce & Watkins, 1995; Rice & Wilcox, 1995). In the preschool classroom, the adults provide the intervention with no additional pullout therapy, so children do not receive individual therapy. These strategies rest on several foundations:

- Language intervention is best when provided in a meaningful social context.
- Language facilitation occurs across the preschool curriculum.
- Language begins with the child.
- Language is learned through interaction; valuable teaching occasions can arise in child-to-child interactions.
- Parents are valuable partners in language intervention programming.

Review the *Guidelines for Teaching: Facilitative Language Strategies* for specific activities to use while engaging students in language. Although these facilitative language strategies are used in preschool classrooms, they apply to students with speech and language disorders across grade levels.

VISUAL SUPPORTS   Teaching and learning across the grades depends in large part on how well you and your colleagues communicate to and with your students. Curriculum in the early elementary grades focuses on teaching them to read and write. Then in the later elementary and middle school years, they work on reading and writing to learn. Making these transitions can be difficult for students with speech and language disorders, but provision of visual supports can decrease these difficulties.

Visual supports can take a variety of forms. What they all have in common is that they assist in communicating what is expected to students and decrease demands on students when they are required to communicate what they know.

Graphic Organizers.   Graphic organizers are a form of a visual support that acts as an advance organizer. They assist students to comprehend and write more effectively (Cunningham & Allington, 2010; Sturm & Rankin-Erickson, 2002). Graphic organizers provide a visual representation in an organized framework, and they are especially useful for students with Down syndrome, autism spectrum disorders, and language-learning disabilities (Kumin, 2001; Myles & Simpson, 2003; Nelson & Van Meter, 2004), as well as for students who are learning English as a second language. Graphic organizers can be hand-drawn or computer-generated.

When using graphic organizers, you should first determine which organizer will best meet the desired curriculum outcome (Cunningham & Allington, 2010). You might choose a web design, a story map, a feature matrix, or data charts. You also should consider how students will participate when completing and using a graphic organizer and what adaptations they may need.

Oxfam International

Graphic organizers are simple yet effective methods for helping students with receptive language disorders remember information.

For example, if a student with a receptive language delay or disorder needs to learn and remember information for a science unit on insects, you may provide a web design using pictures to organize the insects' anatomical makeup, what the insects eat, what animals eat the insects, what habitats the insects live in, and so on. The information in a graphic organizer visually links together groups of important information for the student.

You can create a graphic organizer template on most classroom computers, using standard drawing tools found in word processing software or in the computer's accessory tools. You can also draw them by hand. Further, you can locate premade organizers by searching the Web for graphic organizers or obtaining books with premade organizers. Some textbooks come with online companions that have graphic organizer ideas. Also, commercial programs that create graphic organizers on the computer can be purchased. See Figure 8.4 for a sample graphic organizer.

You should consider the student's past experience with graphic organizers. Students may not necessarily know how to fill out a graphic organizer or how to use the information within one to answer questions. You may need to provide examples, model how to complete them, and model how to find information using them (Cunningham & Allington, 2010).

You should consider how the student feels about writing. If the student is concerned about making mistakes, reluctant to rewrite information, or hesitant to correct information, the student might choose to write ideas on sticky notes instead of directly onto a standard, prepared organizer, thereby gaining the option of easily changing the information or its placement (Foley & Staples, 2000). To assist some students, you can provide concepts, facts, ideas, and/or events. Then the students choose the information they want to display and place it into the organizer (Foley & Staples, 2000) or create their own organizer. You may also use photos, drawings, symbol sets, or a combination.

Figure 8.4 A Graphic Organizer Sample Based on the Californian Gold Rush for Middle Elementary Grade Level

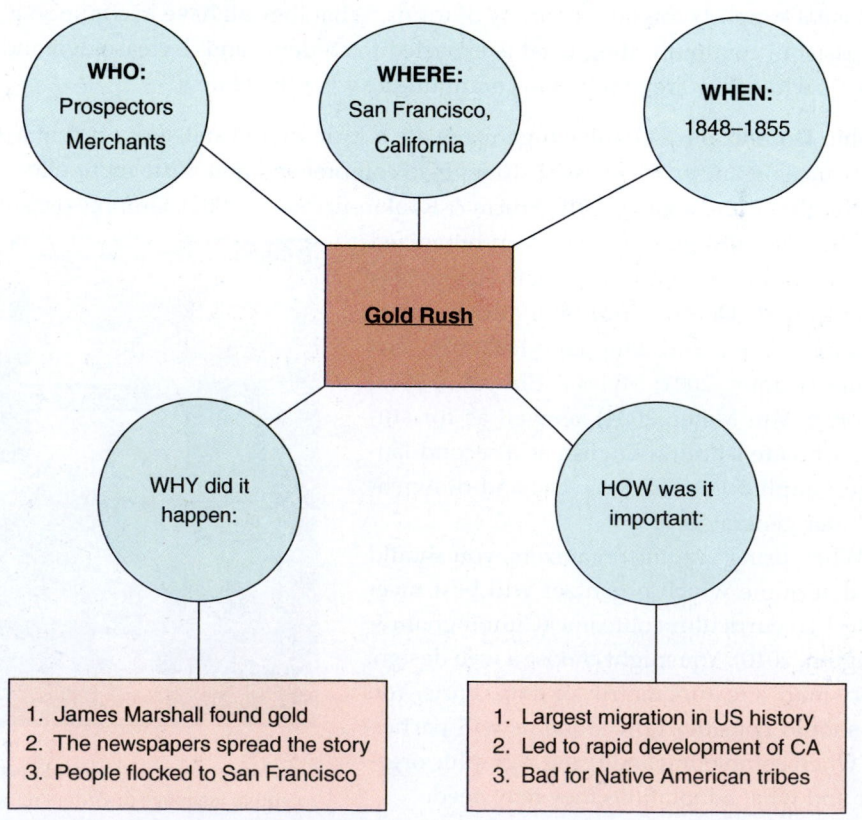

SOURCE: Reprinted with permission from Russell Johnston.

When comparing barter and trade with currency during a social studies lesson, Kylie's teacher relied on a computer-generated pro and con list found on a educationally related website. Kylie contributed to the organizer by taping pictures (representing main pros/cons of both barter and trade) to one side of the chart with tape. During a different lesson on the life cycle in Joey's science class, the symbols used on his communication device were printed and a timeline of the life cycle was drawn freehand by his teacher. Joey used vocabulary present within his device to represent important concepts on the life cycle, using words such as first, next, and last. Because Joey did not like using glue sticks (he had a "dispreferrance" for them), he contributed to his organizer by providing his answer with his device, and Joey's peer acted as a scribe and pasted the answer for him. Regardless of whether or not the graphic organizers were made ahead of time, their goal is to help organize information and help students comprehend academic content.

Visual Schedules.   Visual schedules are another type of visual support. The primary purpose of a visual schedule is to communicate to students the activities and events that are to be encountered during the day, or during a specific lesson. Activities and events may be provided in sequential order, using written text of the activity/event (i.e., order of content areas to be covered on the white board, and/or with symbols/picture support).

Different symbol sets exist, and the same ones used by special education professionals, such as Boardmaker, Lessonpix, and SymbolStix, may be used to generate visual schedules. These schedules also help decrease students' anxiety, as the schedule can help them anticipate what they are to do during a lesson or throughout their day. When you use visual schedules, explicitly tell students what the schedule is and how it is used, and identify what the symbols represent. Also, have the symbols represent less structured activities (i.e., free choice, stations, etc). Similar to the importance of remaining consistent regarding what symbols represent an activity or event, you need to be consistent in the use of a visual schedule, referring to it periodically as tasks are completed and transition to another activity occurs. For some students, crossing these items off their "to do list" can promote their engagement in various tasks.

Visual Timers.   In comparison to the visual schedules, visual timers relay information on how long a particular task is going to last. These come in a variety of types; some of your students may benefit from timers with numerical representations of the time (e.g., countdown timer), whereas others may need a timer that shows time elapsing in a visual format (e.g., amount of time on task indicated in red on a clock face, with time elapsing demonstrated by the red area disappearing). For students with more significant support needs, you may want to incorporate a sound signal when the time has elapsed. Whatever sound you choose, be sure to use it consistently.

AAC LANGUAGE INPUT STRATEGIES   AAC systems enable students to participate in the curriculum. But learning to use communication symbols requires a team effort from the student's familiar and frequent communication partners. AAC instructional strategies should focus on teaching communication rather than solely teaching the student to operate AAC systems. AAC is a means to an end, the end being communication and participation—in the language of the IDEA, progress and inclusion. To learn and express a wide range of daily communication functions, your students will need a comprehensive vocabulary. They will also need the ability to explain the strategies and equipment that benefit them. And they will require further instruction and support to meaningfully integrate their AAC systems into new communication environments.

One instructional strategy for modeling how to use AAC is the **system for augmenting language (SAL)** (Romski & Sevcik, 1988). SAL focuses on augmented input of language. Using SAL, communication partners augment their speech by activating the student's communication device in naturally occurring communication interactions at

MyLab Education
Video Example 8.6
Experience this video for an example of aided input. Why might using this technique be necessary for teaching students who use AAC new vocabulary words? http://www.youtube.com/watch?v=vUY6oQoSTXw

home and school and in the community, encouraging but not requiring the student to use the device (Romski & Sevcik, 2003). For example, during a literacy discussion, you could introduce the task by saying, "We will read this story. Then you will tell what happened first, second, third, and last in the story." While activating buttons on the device for "read," "story," "then," "tell," "first," "second," "third," and "last," the student has not only a model of what symbol vocabulary to use in that situation but also a model of how to use the vocabulary in conversation.

Although the SAL strategy was developed for use with electronic communication devices, augmented input can occur if your students have communication books or boards or sign language. It is sometimes called *aided language stimulation* when focusing on communication books or boards (Elder & Goossens, 1994; Goossens, Crain, & Elder, 1992). When your student uses sign language, the term *total communication* applies. Aided input can be effective with students of any age, regardless of whether a student is using SAL or the aided language stimulation strategy with a device (Romski & Sevcik, 1992, 1996; Romski, Sevcik, & Forrest, 2001).

The success of the augmented input instructional strategy depends on training the student's frequent and significant communication partners. Here, not only is the student learning, but so too are the student's partners; they are your partners, too.

A tool called Social Networks identifies these important partners (Blackstone, Hunt-Berg, Nygard, & Schultz, 2004). A student's communication partners should learn about the importance of input with respect to the physical operation of the device, and they should practice in providing input, feedback, and coaching in natural settings (Romski & Sevcik, 2003). Other communication partners who are less familiar may need training only in the operation of the device and how to model input (Blackstone, 2006). Two words express these ideas about training on how to use augmented input instruction: partnerships and inclusion. Indeed, these two words express so much about students' progress.

Progress in the General Curriculum

Educators use many different tools for measuring a student's progress, but they commonly use curriculum-based assessment because it focuses on a student's progress in the general curriculum (Howell & Nolet, 2009; Losardo & Notari-Syverson, 2011). You should consider using a data-based performance modification procedure to monitor a student's progress and make decisions about instructional strategies.

Here's how that measurement system works: With input from the student's IEP team, the SLP teams with the student's teachers to reduce the discrepancy between the student's current communication skill level and the curriculum standard against which the student's progress is assessed. For example, if a student exhibits atypical dysfluencies (or stuttering) and if the dysfluencies negatively affect participation in class, interaction with other students, or both, the SLP might set a goal of monitoring the amount of class participation that occurs as a result of the student's improved fluency, give the teacher and the parents suggestions that may be helpful when speaking with someone who stutters, work with the student to teach different fluency strategies, observe in class to monitor the use of the strategies in the classroom and the student's class participation, and ask the teacher to rate the student's fluency during the day and tally class participation at agreed-upon times. The measurement system does not depend on only one person; a partnership among various professionals and parents is necessary.

IMPLICATIONS FOR ASSESSMENT   Many students with speech and language disorders do not need accommodations for assessment. Others may need additional time for tests or access to a word processor and computer software when writing. When assessing a student with more significant speech and language impairments, you should ask,

"What is being assessed, how does the student best receive information, and how does the student best express ideas, thoughts, feelings, and so on?" You should consider the focus of the assessment to reduce the chances that the student will be assessed in more than one area at one time.

For instance, if the student's augmentative voice output communication system is new or unfamiliar and it is used during a science test, you may not be accurately assessing the student's understanding of science but, instead, the student's knowledge of the communication system. In other words, you may be finding it difficult to differentiate between whether the student did not answer a question correctly because the student did not know how to find the answer with the new system or because that particular science concept was unknown.

Similarly, if a student who exhibits difficulty understanding written complex language structures takes a science test but the test format is not adapted for that student, then you may be assessing the student's ability to read complex sentence structures as well as the student's knowledge about science. If you want to assess the student's understanding of complex language structures, then you should make sure that the test consists of complex structures. If, however, you are assessing science, you may need to take into account the student's preferred manner of receiving information. When the assessment is isolated, the student may concentrate solely on science knowledge.

You should present information in a manner that assists the student's comprehension of the assessment directions and questions. For instance, if your student finds it difficult to receive written information, you should explain it verbally or use visual supports. If a student has a problem understanding complex sentence structures, you should adjust the language and sentence structure, use visual supports, or both.

If a student has difficulty with self-expression in verbal or in written form, you should use an assessment format that does not require long verbal or written output. For example, a multiple-choice or true-false format may be helpful. The student may then only need to respond with a one-word answer, a switch activation, or a gesture indicating the correct answer. This change in format may decrease the probability that the student will not provide the answer because of the length of the response needed, an inability to clearly express an answer verbally, or both.

The format should complement the student's most common means of expression. For instance, if the student has begun to explore a new communication system, such as a device using a computer screen, you should use the more familiar previous system for assessment until the student has had time to learn the new system.

You have almost come to the end of this chapter; the official summary awaits you. You have learned about each theme of this book—research-based instruction, progress, inclusion, partnerships among professionals and between professionals on the one hand and parents on the other, high expectations, self-determination, and even cultural diversity. But you may have not yet taken into account that, because of how their parents and educators support Kylie and Joey, these two youngsters enjoy the dignity of being able to communicate. They can express what is in their hearts and minds; their inner voices now are heard. They speak; others hear; and the reciprocity dignifies these two students.

MyLab Education Self-Check 8.3

MyLab Education Application Exercise 8.3: Educating Students with Speech and Language Disorders

Summary

Defining Speech and Language Disorders

Speech and language disorders include speech impairments, language impairments, or both. A speech disorder is an impairment of one's articulation of speech sounds, fluency, or voice. Likewise, a language disorder reflects problems in receiving information; understanding it; and formulating a spoken, written, or symbolic response. Communication differences that are related to the culture of the individual, such as what is observed during second language acquisition, are not considered disordered communication. Language is a shared system of rules and symbols for the exchange of information. It includes rules of phonology, morphology, syntax, semantics, and pragmatics. Speech and language disorders can affect a student's academic, social, and emotional development.

Describing the Characteristics and Causes

Language is a structured, shared, rule-governed, symbolic system for communicating. The five components of our language system are phonology (sound system), morphology (word forms), syntax (word order and sentence structure), semantics (word and sentence meanings), and pragmatics (social use of language). Each dimension works together with the others to create a robust language system. Speech and language disorders are classified according to the cause: (1) biological causes refer to an identifiable problem in the neuromuscular mechanism of the person; and (2) environmental causes refer to those with no identifiable biological or neurological cause.

Evaluating Students with Speech and Language Disorders

The speech-language pathologist is the professional who determines the presence and extent of a speech and/or language impairment. When determining whether or not a student has a speech and language disorder, the speech-language pathologist uses a variety of information obtained from a variety of sources. The sources include school records, parent and teacher interviews, hearing and vision screenings, observations, speech samples, language samples, classwork samples/portfolios, checklists, standardized tests, nonstandardized tests, and curriculum-based assessments. When assessing a student who is bilingual, it is essential that the SLP test the bilingual student using both the student's dominant language and English (Paradis, Genesee, & Crago, 2011).

Including Students with Speech and Language Disorders

According to the U.S. Department of Education, 87 percent of the students who receive speech and language services spend 80 to 100 percent of their time inside general education classrooms. Inclusive educational practices assist with carryover and generalization of academic and nonacademic skills in natural and meaningful contexts of the curriculum. To include students, it is necessary for professionals to individualize the strategies and supports provided to students. This can be done through identifying supplementary aids and services within students' IEPs and through using a variety of service delivery methods to achieve inclusive education. Students transitioning to community-based instruction will need instruction and support to meaningfully integrate their AAC systems into this new environment.

Educating Students with Speech and Language Disorders

Language occurs throughout the school day and is the vehicle for teaching the curriculum. Students build their language skills when communicating throughout their school day in different content areas. Language skills are utilized in a variety of ways, like discussing a topic verbally, answering questions in written form, reading, and working with others cooperatively. Practitioners can create access to the curriculum by using a UDL framework in the general education classroom. By doing so, barriers to instructional content for students with speech and language disorders may be decreased and student participation may be increased. A UDL approach takes into account different learning styles, differing proficiencies in English, and methods of communication.

Addressing the Professional Standards

In Chapter 8, Students with Speech and Language Disorders, we have covered the following Council for Exceptional Children (CEC) Initial Level Special Educator Preparation Standards: Chapter 8—1.0, 1.1, 4.1, 5.3, 5.4, 6.1, 6.6, 7.1, 7.2. Refer to the Appendix for a full listing of the CEC Standards with descriptions and supporting explanations.

Chapter 9
Students with Emotional or Behavioral Disorders

 ## Learning Outcomes

9.1 Describe all characteristics in the IDEA definition, define externalizing and internalizing behavior categories, and describe two of the DSM-5 disorders that align with each category.

9.2 Compare and contrast the (a) purpose of the Scale for Assessing Emotional Disturbance and the Behavioral and Emotional Rating Scale and (b) inclusion rates for these students.

9.3 Describe how mindfulness, The Incredible Years, and DBT STEPS-A each reduce the likelihood that students will be suspended/expelled and increase the likelihood of their success.

Meet Anthony, Experiencing Challenges but Progressing Mindfully

"Put one hand on my heart, the other on my stomach, and breathe some." That's Anthony's advice to himself when he feels he is losing control of his emotions and especially when he wants to strike out at another person or damage someone's property. It's also what he tells his mother when she becomes frustrated with his behavior at home. And it's what he has learned at his school from PI School Administrator and Mindful Educator, Amelia Gallagher.

These three simple actions—two hands in place, breathing deliberately and slowly—may not seem to be a form of teaching, but they are one of many mindfulness practices that enable other teaching to occur. None of Anthony's teachers can instruct in the core subjects that a 14-year-old needs to know when his emotions create behaviors that block instruction. To be sure, Anthony wants to learn; he intends to graduate from high school, get a job and a driver's license, and become the person he wants to be. That may be hard to do, judging by Anthony's history. In elementary school, he was in fights daily, usually with the same student; Anthony thought the student was bullying him. He also sometimes destroyed property at school or in his community. Anthony presents two sets of challenges: aggression and property damage. He has been hospitalized in a psychiatric hospital. A court ordered him to be placed there for evaluation to determine whether he was competent to face criminal charges for destroying property in his community. He has had evaluations by educators, psychologists, and psychiatrists.

Anthony has an individualized education program (IEP); his teachers, counselors, and psychologist have conducted a **functional behavioral assessment** (FBA) of him and developed a **behavioral intervention plan** (BIP) for him. His school uses **positive behavior support** (PBS) on a school-wide, small-group, and individual basis; it practices the multi-tiered systems of support you learned about in Chapter 6, especially school-wide positive behavior interventions and supports (SW-PBIS). And, Anthony takes the state-approved alternate assessment of his academic progress—the assessment you learned about in Chapter 4. So, as we said, it may be difficult for Anthony to achieve his goals—difficult, but probable.

Why is it probable? One reason is that Anthony has three exceptional resources—his mother, a school staff that practices partnership across specializations, and a teacher, Amelia Gallagher. Amelia uses a research-based practice, mindfulness, to teach Anthony and other students how to control themselves when they are on the edge of losing control and also how to engage in self-regulation so that they remain grounded rather than venturing to the edge of losing control.

Amelia is clear about Anthony's needs:

> His thoughts are basically his triggers. If he believes that something is occurring, he will act as if it is. Many times his perceptions are inaccurate. We are working on supporting him in this area by using mindfulness strategies. He has aggressed toward staff and students. He has had several explosive episodes toward his mother and with property destruction in the community. I can't say what caused them in the community other than his inability to self-regulate and to reflect on what he perceives rather than what is actually happening.

Amelia meets weekly with Anthony's mother to discuss how Anthony can practice at home what he is learning at school and to address challenges that arise. The consequences? Anthony has changed his behavior at school and at home; indeed, his mother says:

> Anthony's using psychology on me. I'm an old-fashioned mom. There are rules in my home. I insist on him doing things he doesn't want to do, like picking up after himself. When I get on him for something, he tells me to do what he's learned to do, and I do what he has learned to do. Life at home is better for us. We've done a 360-degree change. He's just not hostile any more. He used to get all wound up. So did I. Not now.

It is also probable for another reason: Amelia and her colleagues address Anthony's academic and behavioral challenges as linked with each other. When he feels he is apt to be aggressive in class or elsewhere in school, he has permission to leave class and go to a room where, in privacy or with Amelia to guide him, he can use mindfulness techniques to calm down.

Finally, Anthony's achievement of goals is probable because he recognizes that his beliefs that others are "out to get me" are not based on fact and he can choose how to behave, that his aggression against others and his destruction of property can be under his control.

No single method ensures Anthony's progress in school, but he is making progress. His mother says he has "big ideas" and "high expectations" about his future, is no longer "explosive" at home and in the community, elects to solve problems and not react aggressively, and "knows himself."

Amelia has the same judgment:

> He's a 14-year-old teen-ager in a man's body. He's not as aggressive as he has been. He now has about one aggressive episode a month, compared to three or so per month. That's because we are meeting his emotional needs at the same time we are teaching him academically. It's a matter of having a partnership among Anthony, his mother, and our staff. He is learning not to go headlong into a problem, how to de-escalate and walk away. He is mindful of what he feels, so now he can control what he feels and act accordingly. That's a big step for this young man.

Defining Emotional or Behavioral Disorders

The Individuals with Disabilities Education Act (IDEA) uses the term *emotional disturbance* to refer to a condition that is (a) accompanied by one or more of the following characteristics over a long time and to a marked degree and that (b) adversely affects a child's educational performance:

- An inability to learn that cannot be explained by intellectual, sensory, or health factors
- An inability to build or maintain satisfactory interpersonal relationships with peers and teachers
- Inappropriate types of behavior or feelings under normal circumstances
- A general, pervasive mood of unhappiness or depression
- A tendency to develop physical symptoms or fears associated with personal or school problems.

Within the field of special education, the term *emotional and behavioral disorders* is generally used and is preferred to *emotional disturbance*.

In the 2015–2016 school year, 5.7 percent (338,381) of all students ages 3 through 21 in special education were classified as having emotional or behavioral disorders (EBD) (U.S. Department of Education, 2017). That prevalence rate conflicts with the judgment that experts in educating students with EBD reached after reviewing other prevalence data; they concluded that 12 percent of school-age students have at least a moderate impairment associated with EBD (Forness, Freeman, Paparella, Kauffman, & Walker, 2012). Three fourths of high school students identified as having EBD are male; however, the prevalence of EBD is higher for girls during adolescence (Rice, Merves, & Srsic, 2008). As you learned in Chapter 2, African American students are disproportionately classified as having EBD, as are students who are Hispanic (U.S. Department of Education, 2018). Although Black students represent 16 percent of the school population, they constitute 25 percent of students with EBD.

Describing the Characteristics and Causes

You may remember from Chapter 1 that IDEA applies to students who cannot, because of a disability, be successfully educated in general education. So, you should not be surprised to learn that not all students who have EBD receive services under IDEA. That is so because students with EBD may be underidentified or their emotional or behavioral needs may not interfere with their educational progress. For example, a student with a phobia of heights may not need special education services or specially designed instruction simply because of that phobia. However, a student who has a phobia of school may well qualify for IDEA services.

As a teacher, you will want to know about EBD and be alert to its characteristics in your students. If you question whether one of your students has EBD and qualifies for IDEA services or for reasonable accommodations in school under Section 504, you should review the student's education record, especially any evaluations of the student.

Characteristics

EMOTIONAL CHARACTERISTICS The *Diagnostic and Statistical Manual of Mental Disorders*—5th edition (DSM-5; American Psychiatric Association, 2013) describes the

Each student with emotional or behavioral disorders has a unique combination of strengths and needs, and each teacher should seek out and build on those strengths.

standard classification system for mental illness and EBD. We will describe five disorders that have particular relevance to you as an educator: (1) anxiety disorder, (2) depression, (3) oppositional defiant disorder, (4) conduct disorder, and (5) schizophrenia. We rely on DSM-5 throughout our discussion of characteristics.

Anxiety Disorder. **Anxiety disorder** is one of the most common childhood emotional disorders (Higa-McMillan, Francis, & Chorpita, 2014). It is characterized by excessive fear, worry, or uneasiness about the future. Some specific anxiety disorders include (American Psychiatric Association): **separation anxiety disorder**, **generalized anxiety disorder**, **specific phobia**, **panic disorder,** and **social anxiety disorder**.

Approximately 5 to 10 percent of children experience an anxiety disorder, namely, feelings of fear, worry, and irritability, and physical complaints (nausea, headaches) (Robb, 2013).

Compared with typical children, those with an anxiety disorder also encounter the social challenge of having fewer friends (Scharfstein, Alfano, Beidel, & Wong, 2011). Problematically, students with anxiety disorders are much less likely to receive services than children who experience other types of EBD (Merikangas et al., 2011).

Depression. The DSM-5 states that a student may be classified as having a diagnosis of depressive disorder if the student has one of the following symptoms and if the symptom occurs throughout 2 consecutive weeks:

- Depressed or irritable mood most of the time
- Loss of interest or pleasure in activities
- Significant weight loss when not dieting
- Sleeping too little or too much
- Slowness or agitation in movement
- Fatigue
- Feelings of worthlessness or guilt
- Dimensioned ability to think and make decisions
- Recurrent thoughts of death.

The overall prevalence of children who experience depressive disorder is almost 3 percent (Nabors, 2016). The prevalence of depression increases from early childhood to adolescence and is the highest for female adolescents (Thapar, Collishaw, Pine, & Thapar, 2012). If a person receives clinical treatment, the person's depression may last for 7 to 9 months, but it also may recur. Just because one of your students seems not to have depression does not mean a "cure" has occurred. That is so because depression frequently recurs. Watch for reccurrence, and also for whether a student seems to be using alcohol, because drinking may mean your student is depressed (Ranney et al., 2013).

Approximately 9 percent of all students attempted suicide during a 12-month period (Kann et al., 2016). The prevalence is 2 times greater for female students (12 percent) than male students (6 percent), with Hispanic females (15 percent) being most at risk for attempted suicide (Kann et al., 2016). In large urban school districts, the prevalence ranged from 6 to 21 percent. The suicide rate for students in 9th grade is highest as compared to other grades.

Bullying is often a catalyst for depression. There are four types of bullying:

- Verbal abuse, including calling a student by a stigmatizing name
- Social abuse, involving hurting someone's feelings or spreading rumors that cause embarrassment
- Cyber-abuse, using online forums or networks to attack a student's behavior or characteristics
- Physical abuse of any amount or degree, including sexual abuse.

Of all categories of disability, students with EBD are significantly more likely to be the target of verbal, social, and physical abuse, as well as to have their property stolen from their desk or locker (Lipscomb, 2017).

Victims of bullying sometimes—indeed, too often—can begin to have thoughts of suicide (suicidal ideation) or commit suicide. Compared with all students not involved in bullying, students who experienced both cyberbullying and bullying on school property are more than 5 times as likely to attempt suicide and 4 times as likely to report depression (Kann et al., 2016). Victims of bullying are more likely to be White and in 9th or 10th grade. Almost one fourth of female students and one tenth of male students in 9th grade reported being electronically bullied. Bullying on school property is high: Approximately one fourth of males and females reported being bullied. Gay students are bullied more than classmates who are not gay; they also are more likely to experience feelings of victimization, depression, and suicide attempts.

If a student admits to having suicidal thoughts or is being bullied, your best course of action is to take the student seriously and make a referral to a school psychologist, social worker, or counselor who, in turn, can provide support to the student and the parents. Also seek the advice of these professionals about other procedures to follow. School districts often have written guidelines; you need to learn and follow them. Not all students who are significantly depressed will talk about suicide, but you should not assume that not talking about it means that they are not thinking about it.

Oppositional Defiant Disorder. **Oppositional defiant disorder** causes a pattern of angry/irritable, mood, argumentative/defiant behavior, and/or vindictiveness (American Psychiatric Association, 2013). Students must have four of the following behaviors; they must exhibit these behaviors with at least one individual who is not a sibling; and they must exhibit them for at least 6 months:

- Loss of temper
- Easily annoyed
- Angry and resentful
- Frequent arguing
- Noncompliant with requests from authority figures
- Purposefully annoying others
- Blaming others for mistakes/misbehavior
- Being vindictive.

These behaviors must interfere with the student's functioning and cause distress to the student and others. As you have read, Anthony loses his temper easily, is easily annoyed, resents being teased by boys of his own age, and sometimes refuses to comply with his teachers' or his mother's requests.

Oppositional defiant disorder is usually diagnosed during the elementary school years and is sometimes a precursor to conduct disorders (Nabors, 2016). The majority of students who receive an early diagnosis of oppositional defiant disorder do not develop a conduct disorder, which you will learn about below (Munkvold, Lundervold, & Manger, 2011). Ensuring that students with oppositional defiant disorder can

MyLab Education
Video Example 9.1
As the video presents Amanda Todd's story, reflect on how bullying was a catalyst for her depression and suicide. As a future teacher, how do you see your role in addressing bullying? https://www.youtube.com/watch?v=ej7afkypUsc

appropriate services when they are younger could prevent them from having a more serious disorder at older ages.

Conduct Disorder. **Conduct disorder** consists of a persistent pattern of antisocial behavior that significantly interferes with others' rights or with schools' and communities' behavioral expectations. There are four categories of conduct disorders:

- Aggressive conduct, resulting in physical harm to people or animals
- Property destruction
- Deceitfulness or theft
- Serious rule violations, such as truancy and running away.

A diagnosis of conduct disorder is justified when a child or youth displays 3 of 15 criteria associated with these four categories. Anthony does not meet the criteria for conduct disorder, and his current improvement is promising that he will avoid this more serious diagnosis.

Unlike students with oppositional defiant disorder, students with conduct disorders have severe aggressive and antisocial behavior; they often infringe on other students' rights and demonstrate a lack of empathy. Although anger and aggression can emerge in infancy and throughout the early childhood years, it is typically during adolescence that students, especially boys, are identified as having conduct problems. Both oppositional defiant disorder and conduct disorder are diagnosed in boys about twice as often as in girls; the rates of diagnosis increase during adolescence (Kimonis, Frick, & McMahon, 2014). Students who have conduct disorders are often placed into juvenile correction programs (Thompson & Morris, 2016). Anthony has escaped the "school to prison" pipeline, largely because he is learning to control himself and because his teachers are his constant advocates when occasions call for advocacy for him.

Trauma- and Stressor-Related Disorder. **Trauma- and stressor-related disorder** is a new category included in DSM-5 that deals with incapacitating symptoms following exposure to a dangerous or traumatic event. In the past, you have heard of this condition as post-traumatic stress disorder (PTSD) and frequently in regard to veterans. Typically, the symptoms are re-experienced through flashbacks, nightmares, or other kinds of emotional distress, resulting in prolonged negative feelings. To obtain this diagnosis, symptoms must last for more than 1 month and result in everyday impairments in fulfilling expected tasks and responsibilities.

The largest study of the impact of childhood trauma and stress, conducted in the late 1990s, used a measure titled adverse childhood experiences (ACE) (Centers for Disease Control and Prevention [CDC], 2016). The ACE study is often highlighted in popular media in referring to children and families who experience a pile-up of environmental challenges associated with poverty, violence, and drug use.

Approximately 5 percent of adolescents meet the criteria for trauma- and stressor-related disorder, with the prevalence being approximately 4 times greater for female adolescents (U.S. Department of Veteran Affairs, n.d.). Furthermore, prevalence increases with age. You can gain insight into this emotional disorder by listening and reflecting upon a firsthand account.

> Link to https://acestoohigh.com/got-your-ace-score/ and find a short description of ACE; complete the questions yourself, compare your score to the study's norms, and gain information on the long-term impact of childhood trauma and stress.

Billy E. Barnes/PhotoEdit, Inc.

When a young person in special education becomes involved in the juvenile justice system, special and general educators should ask themselves what they might have done to prevent the child from being in court (to "divert" the child from the system) and what they should do when the child returns to school, such as using positive behavioral supports.

Schizophrenia. A diagnosis of **schizophrenia** is justified if a person experiences two or more of the following for a significant amount of time during a 1-month period: (a) **delusions** (strong and unusual beliefs that are thoughts, e.g., someone is trying to hurt me); (b) **hallucinations** (sensory perceptions without an environmental stimulus, e.g., hearing voices when no one is present); (c) **disorganized speech** (incoherent speech); (d) grossly disorganized or **catatonic behavior** (e.g., behavior that lacks typical movement, activity, or expression); and (e) other negative symptoms (e.g., reduced emotional expression). At least one of the criteria must be a, b, or c, that is, delusions, hallucinations, or disorganized speech (American Psychiatric Association, 2013).

The symptoms associated with schizophrenia must result in challenges associated with interpersonal and academic success and must be present for at least 6 months. Schizophrenia occurs in phases. Precursors are associated with atypical behavior, followed by an acute phase in which symptoms are most pronounced. The person then enters a recovery phase and, finally, a residual phase during which no symptoms are present. Most individuals with schizophrenia have multiple cycles, but some may have only one cycle. Children and youth with schizophrenia often have odd beliefs about make-believe people. Ten percent of suicides are by people with schizophrenia (Kuniyoshi & McClellan, 2014). As you have read, Anthony often is aggressive because he believes other children are teasing or trying to hurt him, even though he is far larger and stronger than they. Indeed, some children may bully him, but being the victim of bullying differs from having misconceptions about what a person—here, Anthony—thinks others are trying to do to him. Anthony is learning to know his context accurately and to be mindful that he can control himself in his environment.

BEHAVIORAL CHARACTERISTICS Students with EBD tend to have one or both of two easily identifiable behavioral patterns: externalizing or internalizing (Landrum, 2017).

Externalizing Behavior. **Externalizing behaviors**—persistently disruptive or annoying behaviors that are directed outwardly, or aggressive or acting-out and noncompliant behaviors, and bullying—often are associated with conduct and oppositional defiant disorders (Volpe & Chafouleas, 2011). Anthony has externalizing behaviors, fighting students who are bullying him and destroying property when he loses control of his emotions. The parents and other caregivers of children with externalizing behavior reported the following (Miner & Clarke-Stewart, 2008):

- Children's externalizing behavior declined in frequency from the ages of two to nine years.

- When mothers and caregivers/teachers rated the same children, the mothers rated them as having higher levels of externalizing behaviors.

- Caregivers/teachers identified African American children as having higher levels of externalizing behavior, but mothers reported the reverse.

Earlier we focused on the impact of being the victim of bullying; here we turn our attention to perpetrators of bullying. Engaging in **bullying** is a form of externalizing behavior. It can consist of verbal abuse, calling a student by a stigmatizing name; social abuse, involving hurting someone's feelings or spreading rumors that cause embarrassment; cyber-abuse, using online forums or networks to attack a student's behavior or characteristics; or physical abuse of any amount or degree, including sexual abuse. Perpetrators of bullying are more likely to have defiant and disruptive behavior, harsh discipline from parents or caregivers, and attitudes condoning violence.

Internalizing Behavior. **Internalizing behavior** includes withdrawal, depression, anxiety, and fearfulness (Kamphaus & Mays, 2011). You and other teachers may overlook internalizing behavior because it is not as disruptive as externalizing behavior. That is

MyLab Education
Video Example 9.2
In the rest of this chapter, keep Daniel in mind as you seek to learn as much as possible about what you, as his teacher, could do to give him an "honest chance." What does an "honest chance" mean to you?

one reason why students with anxiety disorders are less likely to receive special education services than their peers with externalizing behaviors (Schoenfeld & Janney, 2008).

Some researchers believe that girls are less likely than boys to be identified as having EBD because educators often overlook girls' internalizing behaviors (Rice et al., 2008). Girls, it is sometimes thought, tend to hold things in more than boys, whereas boys tend to be more externalizing in their behavior. Here's the caution for you: "Holding things in" is not always a gender-related trait; it can be a sign of an emotional disorder.

INTELLECTUAL AND ACADEMIC CHARACTERISTICS   Students with EBD may be gifted or have an intellectual disability, but most have IQs in the low-average range (Wagner, Kutash, Duchnowski, Epstein, & Sumi, 2005).

- Slightly less than two thirds of the students had reading scores in the lowest 25 percent of all students in the school population, and 43 percent were reported to be in the bottom 25 percent of scores in mathematics (Lane, Barton-Arwood, Nelson, & Wehby, 2008).

- The grade point average of students with EBD is lower than for students with disabilities as a whole, as well as for students in the general population (Wagner, 2014).

- Youth with EBD are more than twice as likely as students in all other categories of disabilities to have missed instructional time due to being suspended or expelled (Lipscomb et al., 2017).

- The graduation rate for students with EBD is 53 percent (U.S. Department of Education, 2016).

Causes

Typically, there is no single cause of an emotional and behavioral disorder (Thapar et al., 2012). Biological and environmental risk factors typically contribute to emotional and behavioral disorders, sometimes just by themselves but more often together and interactively.

BIOLOGICAL CAUSES   Genetics and temperament are two biological causes of EBD (Landrum, 2017). People who have genetic markers associated with EBD are predisposed to having EBD. Environmental factors, however, can exacerbate the genetic predisposition and influence the nature and extent of the specific disorder. For example, parents who have a disorder such as depression but who receive the appropriate pharmacological and therapeutic treatment are apt to carry out their parenting responsibilities quite differently than parents with depression who do not have appropriate treatment.

Genetics influence a child's temperament (Landrum, 2017). **Temperament** refers to behavioral tendencies that are biologically based. For example, a child's temperament might naturally be impulsive and resist guidance or supervision from others. Because temperament is biologically based, it interacts with numerous environmental factors within the family, neighborhood, school, and community to produce more positive or more negative outcomes. When genetic problems with

Echo/Juice Images/Getty Images

When a student is disengaged from studies, the student may be depressed and need mental health evaluation. Teachers should be quick to intervene positively, rather than to discipline the student.

temperament interact with environmental challenges, it is more likely that behaviors will become extreme and lead to an emotional or behavioral disorder. A child who is impulsive and resists others' guidance and supervision may establish behaviors that in time lead to oppositional defiant or even conduct disorder (Stringaris, Maughan, & Goodman, 2010). The child's temperament, even if biologically based, can be negatively and positively affected by environment, family, neighborhood, school, and community (McClowry et al., 2013).

ENVIRONMENTAL CAUSES School and family factors can contribute to EBD.

School Factors. Approximately 1500 general educators and special educators responded to a survey that asked about their preparation for teaching students with EBD by saying that they were not adequately prepared to teach social skills, develop and implement behavioral interventions based on data, and implement peer-mediated intervention and conflict resolution (Gable, Tonelson, Sheth, Wilson, & Park, 2012). These educators also reported they did not use many of the research-based practices that have been identified for students with EBD.

Moreover, teachers' personality factors seem to play a greater role than workplace conditions in determining whether teachers of students with EBD are satisfied with their jobs and likely to perform well in them (Prather-Jones, 2011). Among the most important personality characteristics are intrinsic motivation rather than relying on external rewards, learning to not take difficult encounters with students personally, accepting the limitations of what teachers can do, demonstrating flexibility, and having a genuine interest in students who have EBD. What is your temperament? Do you have any of those personality characteristics, and how might they affect your responses to students with EBD?

Family Factors. Families of students with EBD, as well as the students themselves, experience special challenges (Wagner et al., 2005). Slightly more than one third of elementary students with EBD live in a single-parent household, compared with about one fourth of students overall.

- Approximately one fourth live in households in which the head of the family is unemployed. The head of household in these families is 2 times less likely to be a high school graduate than are the heads of household in the general population.
- Approximately twice as many elementary or middle school students with EBD live in poverty compared with students in the general population.

On the last point related to poverty and as you learned in Chapter 3, we encourage you to embrace the pervasive impact that low socioeconomic status and poverty have on the emotional and behavioral health of children, as well as other family members (Yoshikawa, Aber, & Beardslee, 2012). A synthesis research report on this topic documented that 52 out of 55 published studies indicated a positive relationship between socioeconomic status and EBD problems in children and adolescents (Reiss, 2013). This review recounted that children and adolescents who experience socioeconomic challenges are 2 to 3 times more likely to develop problems associated with EBD. Furthermore, the longer the socioeconomic challenge within the family, the more likely it is that high rates of EBD will accrue.

Trusting partnerships between educators and families of students with EBD have been particularly problematic. That may be so because many parents of children with EBD believe that other people blame them for their child's problems. That's the perspective of the mother of an elementary school student, Marcel, who lives in Missouri.

Blaming parents impairs partnerships with families and does nothing to solve problems, as you learned in Chapter 3. Likewise, parents of students with EBD are significantly more likely to be dissatisfied with schools, teachers, and special

MyLab Education
Video Example 9.3
Take the "shoes" test with Marcel's mother in terms of how it feels to be blamed for her son's behavior. If you were her son's teacher, how might you establish a trusting partnership with her?

education services than are parents of students with other disabilities (Wagner et al., 2005). They are 3 times more dissatisfied than parents of students in the general population. They also are significantly less likely to spend time helping their child with homework at least weekly and to attend school or class events (Lipscomb et al., 2017).

Although you should avoid blaming parents for their children's emotional or behavioral disorder, you also should recognize that family factors can play a role:

- Maternal depression is related to a higher incidence of externalizing and internalizing behavior problems in children (Goodman et al., 2011).
- Parents' partner violence increases the likelihood of children experiencing externalizing behavior problems and antisocial behavior (Ehrensaft & Cohen, 2012).
- Parents who engage in more hostile behavior (e.g., getting into arguments, hitting or injuring others) increase the likelihood of their children having externalizing and internalizing behavior problems (Velders et al., 2011).

Interestingly, when parents were asked to rate the causes of their child's emotional or behavioral disorder, African American families were less likely to see causes related to the family and more likely to see causes related to prejudice (Yeh, Forness, Ho, McCabe, & Hough, 2004). Latino parents also tended to have this view, although the perception was not reported as strongly.

> **MyLab Education Self-Check 9.1**
>
> **MyLab Education Application Exercise 9.1:** Characteristics of Emotional Behavioral Disorders

Evaluating Students with Emotional or Behavioral Disorders

Determining the Presence of Emotional or Behavioral Disorders

Now, having given you some reason to wonder exactly how educators do determine whether a student may be classified into EBD, we describe exactly the process they follow to make that determination. *Nondiscriminatory Evaluation Process: Students with Emotional or Behavioral Disorders* highlights the nondiscriminatory evaluation process for students with EBD. The DSM-5 outlines diagnostic procedures for the assessment of emotional and behavioral disorders (American Psychiatric Association, 2013).

Although various evaluation measures help teachers and other professionals identify students with EBD (Flick, 2011), few of those measures align with or take into account IDEA's description of the five characteristics of EBD—namely, inability to learn, inability to build or maintain satisfactory relationships, inappropriate behavior, unhappiness or depression, and physical symptoms or fears.

One measure, however, is especially useful for educators. It's the one you and your colleagues should use. That's because it meets the research standards of being reliable and valid. It consists of a scale that specifically measures these five elements: the Scale for Assessing Emotional Disturbance—2nd edition (Epstein, Cullinan, Ryser, & Pearson, 2002; Lamb, 2011).

This scale has seven subscales. Each subscale corresponds directly to one of the five elements in the IDEA definition, to social maladjustment, and to adverse effect on educational performance. The second edition includes two supplemental

Nondiscriminatory Evaluation Process
Students with Emotional or Behavioral Disorders

Observation	**Teacher and parents observe:** The student may be unable to build and maintain satisfactory interpersonal relationships, may engage in aggressive behaviors, or may have a pervasive mood of unhappiness or depression. The student acts out or withdraws during classroom instruction and independent activities. Problematic behavior occurs in more than one setting.
Screening	**Assessment measures:** **Classroom work products:** The student may require one-to-one assistance to stay on task. The student has difficulty following basic classroom behavioral expectations during instruction or assignments, resulting in incomplete or unsatisfactory work products. **Group intelligence tests:** Most students perform in the low-average to slow-learner range. Performance may not accurately reflect ability because the emotional/behavioral disorder can prevent the student from staying on task. **Group achievement tests:** The student performs below peers or scores lower than would be expected according to group intelligence tests. Performance may not be a true reflection of achievement because the student has difficulty staying on task as a result of the emotional/behavioral disorder. **Vision and hearing screening:** Results do not explain behavior.
Prereferral	**Teacher implements suggestions from school-based team:** The student is not responsive to reasonable adaptations of the curriculum and positive behavior-support techniques.
Referral	The student should be referred to a multidisciplinary team for a complete evaluation if prereferral intervention is not successful.
Nondiscriminatory evaluation procedures and standards	**Assessment measures:** **Individualized intelligence test:** Intelligence is usually, but not always, in the low-average to slow-learner range. The multidisciplinary team makes sure that the results do not reflect cultural difference rather than ability. **Scale for Assessing Emotional Disturbance:** As described in the chapter, this scale is specifically tailored to IDEA's definition of emotional or behavioral disorders and is especially helpful in diagnosis in this area. **Individualized achievement test:** Usually, but not always, the student scores below average across academic areas in comparison to peers. The evaluator may notice acting-out or withdrawal behaviors that affect results. **Behavior rating scale:** The student scores in the significant range on specific behavioral excesses or deficiencies when compared with others of the same culture and developmental stage. **Assessment of strengths:** Use of the Behavioral and Emotional Rating Scale (as described in the text) enables evaluators to identify student strengths. **Assessment measures of social skills, self-esteem, personality, and/or adjustment:** The student's performance indicates significant difficulties in one or more areas according to the criteria established by testing and in comparison with others of the same culture and developmental stage. **Anecdotal records:** The student's problem behavior is not of short duration but has been apparent throughout time in school. Also, records indicate that behaviors have been observed in more than one setting and are adversely affecting the student's educational progress. **Curriculum-based assessment:** The student often is experiencing difficulty in one or more areas of the general curriculum. **Direct observation:** The student is experiencing difficulty relating to peers or adults and in adjusting to school or classroom structure or routine.
Determination	The nondiscriminatory evaluation team determines that the student has an emotional or behavioral disorder and needs special education and related services.

forms—Developmental/Educational Questionnaire and Observation Form—both of which are helpful in making a diagnosis of EBD. This scale includes 45 items, each of which is rated between 3 and 0 (3 equals a severe problem; 0 equals no problem). For example, 3 of the items on the relationship subscale ask the evaluator (who should know the student well and can be a teacher, parent, or other adult) whether any of the following applies to the student:

- Does not work well in group activities
- Feels picked on or persecuted
- Avoids interacting with people.

After completing the scale, the evaluator sums the subscale scores and converts them to percentiles, obtaining an overall indication of the student's emotional or behavioral functioning. The scale takes from 30 to 50 minutes to complete and includes items to help identify a student's diagnosis, IEP goals, and relevant behavioral information.

Determining the Nature of Specially Designed Instruction and Services

Consistent with the process you learned about in Chapters 1 and 4—namely, evaluation precedes planning for services—educators usually determine whether a student qualifies for IDEA services before they identify the student's areas of strengths and needs and build an appropriate IEP.

There are "tools," scales, that help you identify a student's strengths. The Behavioral and Emotional Rating Scale—2nd edition (BERS-2) is a companion to the Scale for Assessing Emotional Disturbance. It assesses strengths in five areas (Buckley, Ryser, Reid, & Epstein, 2006; Epstein, 2004):

- Interpersonal capacity
- Family involvement
- Intrapersonal competence
- School functioning
- Affective ability.

BERS-2 has 52 items across these five scales. Each item is scored on a 4-point scale ranging from "not at all like the child" to "very much like the child." Teachers, parents, or other adults who know the student well can complete the Behavioral and Emotional Rating Scale in approximately 10 minutes. It is suitable for assessing children ages 5 to 18. Assessment information is collected from three perspectives: child (Youth Rating Scale), teacher (Teacher Rating Scale), and parent (Parent Rating Scale). A Spanish version is also available (Sharkey, You, Morrison, & Griffiths, 2009). The scale is reliable and valid; it has strong psychometric properties and measures students' emotional and behavioral strengths (Epstein, 2004).

Including Students with Emotional or Behavioral Disorders

Figure 9.1 displays the percentage of students with EBD in four types of educational placements. Students with EBD are at great risk of not being included in the general education classroom and of being educated in a segregated setting: 47 percent of students spend 80 percent or more of their time in general education classrooms, as compared to 63 percent of all other students with disabilities combined. Furthermore, 17 percent are educated in separate schools, residential facilities, private schools, correctional facilities, or hospitals/home environments, as compared to 5 percent of all other students with disabilities combined (U.S. Department of Education, 2018).

What explains the fact that students with EBD are in the bottom three disability categories in terms of their extent of time in general education classrooms? Factors in play include conflicts between teachers and the student; externalizing behavior including oppositional defiant disorder and conduct disorder; students' poor academic performance; and the students' low opportunity for early, specially designed instruction particularly focusing on healthy social and emotional development (Stoutjesdijk, Scholte,

Figure 9.1 Educational Placement of Students with Emotional Behavioral Disorders

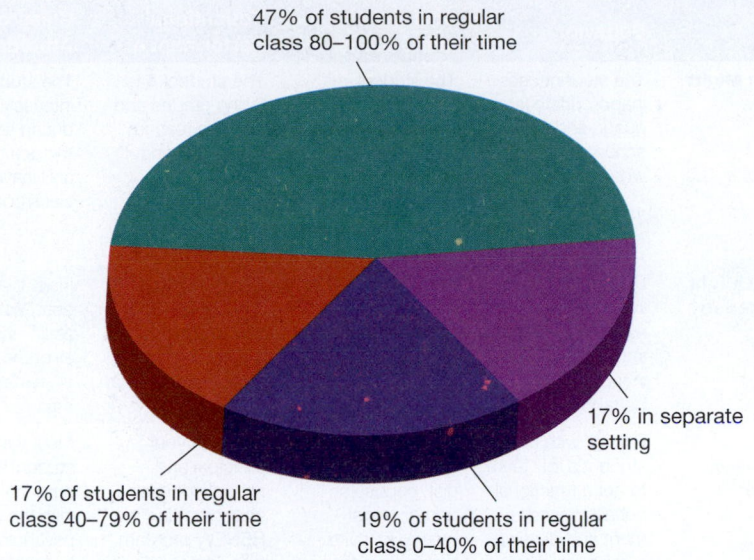

47% of students in regular class 80–100% of their time

17% in separate setting

17% of students in regular class 40–79% of their time

19% of students in regular class 0–40% of their time

SOURCE: U.S. Department of Education. (2018). *39th annual report to Congress on the implementation of the Individuals with Disabilities Education Act, 2017*. Washington, DC: Author.

& Swaab, 2012). We hope these reasons will caution you not to blame the students themselves but to consider whether you may be contributing to a conflict or whether your school is using research-based strategies, such as SW-PBIS (Chapter 5), to provide appropriately ambitious educational programs.

As Figure 9.1 displays, students with emotional or behavioral disorders are at risk for being served in separate schools, private schools, correctional facilities, residential settings, hospitals, or homes. Approximately 54,000 youth are in residential custody in a juvenile correction facility, and 30 to 60 percent have disabilities (U.S. Department of Education, n.d.). The students with disabilities who are incarcerated are most likely to be identified as having EBD or learning disabilities. Students with EBD are 3 times more likely to be arrested during their school years, as compared to all other students with disabilities.

As you might have expected, "intersectionality" often occurs. Black females and males with EBD have the highest enrollment in juvenile facility educational programs (U.S. Department of Education, 2016). For these students, the trajectory from childhood to adulthood is sometimes referred to as the school-to-prison pipeline. More than half of these incarcerated students do not receive special education services while incarcerated. This lack of service violates IDEA's zero-reject principle, which you learned about in Chapter 1. It is worrisome that students who do not receive instructional services while incarcerated have a higher likelihood of being rearrested and re-incarcerated within 12 months of their initial release.

In *Inclusion Tips for Students with Emotional or Behavioral Disorders*, you can review strategies you have considered using in your future teaching of students with EBD.

MyLab Education

Video Example 9.4

Consider how SW-PBIS Tiers 2 and 3 are important components of the educational programs of students with EBD who are at risk of segregation. What is your expectation of your capacity to reach this group of students in your future teaching roles?

Inclusion Tips for Students with Emotional or Behavioral Disorders

	Behavior	Social Interactions	Educational Performance	Classroom Attitudes
What You Might See	The student uses inappropriate language and throws school supplies when angry.	The student is withdrawn and sullen with peers and rarely has positive affect.	The student has failing grades and sees no reason to stay in school because the student has no hope of being successful.	The student gets intensely anxious during tests to the point of crying and leaving the classroom.
What You Might Be Tempted to Do	Place the student in time-out for extended periods immediately after inappropriate behavior occurs.	Remind the student repeatedly to be happy and upbeat in class.	Reprimand the student for a bad attitude and tell the student to set goals for after high school.	Insist that the student "act appropriately" and do what all of the student's classmates are doing.
Alternate Teacher Response	Partner with the student's IEP team to get a functional behavior assessment and develop a behavior intervention plan.	Confer with the school psychologist, counselor, and/or social worker to invite their expertise on the possibility that the student is experiencing depression.	Talk with your principal and school counselor about starting the RENEW program (see Chapter 5).	Meet with the student and his parents—along with the school psychologist, counselor, or social worker—to learn about previous test-taking experiences and to brainstorm testing accommodations.
Ways to Include Peers in the Process	Encourage the student's peers to ignore inappropriate behavior and to engage with the student when behavior is appropriate.	Identify the student's strengths and interests, and plan cooperative activities with peers who share the same strengths and interests.	Involve her and a peer whom she trusts as part of a planning team to start the RENEW program.	Provide some cooperative group assessment with peers who are supportive and reinforcing.

MyLab Education Self-Check 9.2
MyLab Education Application Exercise 9.2:
Jefferson is in Jeopardy

Educating Students with Emotional or Behavioral Disorders

You also learned that students with emotional and behavioral disorders have the highest rate of suspension—33 percent—which is over twice as high as that for students with learning disabilities and attention-deficit hyperactivity disorder (ADHD), as well as 3 to 10 times higher than for other categories of disability (Losen, Ee, Hodson, & Martinez, 2015). Once again, intersectionality is an issue: Male students from African American backgrounds who are identified as having EBD are especially at risk for poor school outcomes. In Chapter 2, you learned about several strategies to reduce suspensions and expulsions, including restorative justice practices that are highly appropriate to use with students with EBD.

All of the research-based instructional strategies that you will learn in this section can substantially contribute to creating appropriately ambitious programs for students with EBD that will transform the school-to-prison pipeline to the school-to-adulthood with dignity pipeline. We begin by asking you to reread the very first paragraph of the vignette about Anthony. Remember, he's the student who is "progressing mindfully."

Are you curious about why we described his education that way? It's because being mindful of yourself is a way to be open to progressing in academics and in extracurricular and other school activities—to making the progress that *Endrew F.* says is the core of an appropriate education.

Mindfulness for Educators and Students

"A potent description of mindfulness is from the movie *Kung Fu Panda*, in which the wise old turtle Oogway says, 'Yesterday is history, tomorrow is a mystery, but today is a gift.' That is why it is called the present" (Rechtschaffen, 2016, p. 3). What is it about the present that is so special? When teachers and students are fully attuned to each moment, they feel grounded and centered with open minds and open hearts. They experience a state of calmness that enables them to pay careful attention as they regulate their thoughts, emotions, and behaviors.

Mindfulness has been practiced for centuries and has roots in Buddhist traditions, although mindfulness is not considered a religious practice. One of the first mindfulness programs was Mindfulness Based Stress Reduction (MBSR), developed by Dr. Jon Kabat-Zinn in 1979 at the University of Massachusetts Medical Center. MBSR combines science, medicine, and psychology with Buddhist meditation practices. From the outset, mindfulness training has been focused on "paying attention in a particular way: on purpose, in the present moment, nonjudgmentally" (Kabat-Zinn, 1994, p. 4). MBSR benefits two types of people: those who experience a range of pain or challenges, and those who want to enhance their overall wellness. As MBSR expanded and diversified, research has consistently documented the improvement of brain wiring, physical health, emotional well-being, self-regulation, interpersonal effectiveness, and empathy (Rechtschaffen, 2014).

Although MBSR was initially provided primarily through health-related programs, the successful outcomes in these settings were a catalyst for incorporating mindfulness instruction in schools. A research review of 15 school-based mindfulness programs was undertaken; the programs involved approximately 1800 students ranging across grade levels and cultural contexts (Waters, Barsky, Ridd, & Allen, 2015).

Across the 1800 students, researchers had measured 76 student outcomes. The gains in approximately two thirds of the outcomes were statistically significant. Of these significant outcomes, 9 percent were considered to have a large effect, 24 percent a medium effect, and 61 percent a small effect. The positive outcomes occurred in overall well-being and social competence.

The researchers suggested that the programs with the strongest positive gains had longer duration, supported students to meditate 2 or more times a day, and had the teacher as the person who delivered the program. "Small effects should not be dismissed, and some would argue that 'every little bit helps' when it comes to fostering student success" (Waters et al., 2015, p. 129).

Mindfulness has grown rapidly over the past decade, and mindfulness leaders have developed dozens of school-based programs, videos, checklists, as well as other types of resources. A leading school-based program is Mindful Education, developed by Daniel Rechtschaffen. It is precisely the program that Amelia teaches Anthony and other students to use. Indeed, when Rechtschaffen offers his days-long training on mindfulness, Amelia, having received intensive training from him, sometimes is his co-presenter. She also has been trained and has her professional qualifications as a school psychologist, school counselor, and education administrator. She taught in New York public schools for 16 years before learning about Rechtschaffen's mindfulness intervention and adopting it as her main way of supporting students such as Anthony and his teachers.

The Mindful Education program incorporates five types of mindful literacy. These include:

- Physical literacy—slowing down, shedding your tension, relaxing, being present in the moment and safe in your body

MyLab Education
Video Example 9.5
Why is mindfulness useful to students? As you review this video, consider Daniel Rechtschaffen's ideas for using mindfulness as a tool to assist students and teachers.
https://www.youtube.com/watch?v=AzAA_EccTAM

- Mental literacy—avoiding distractions, directing your attention to a point of focus such as breathing, noticing your thought patterns
- Emotional literacy—bringing your emotions to the fore, acknowledging your negative emotions and fostering your positive emotions such as empathy, happiness, and gratitude, trying to find the place within your body where the emotion lies
- Social literacy—turning your attention toward others, avoiding making judgments about them, developing empathy and compassion for others, including those who trigger your negative emotions
- Global literacy—moving beyond your immediate network of family and friends to recognize the universal needs of all people, being aware of how your actions affect others, trying to leave a positive footprint in your community and this world.

In working with Anthony and other students, Amelia rigorously adheres to the mindfulness regimen. "I want a student to be able to use the five literacies, but I will take any one of them as the entry point to the others. In teaching mindfulness, we have to be pragmatic; we have to meet our students where they are and then sequentially build their capacities."

In the Mindful Education program, Daniel incorporates these five literacy types into an overall program that combines four sections.

1. *Beginning with Ourselves* starts the program with an emphasis on teachers and other educators learning mindfulness for their own practice. A teacher cannot teach mindfulness unless the teacher has learned it and practices it, as Amelia does.

2. *Introducing Mindfulness to Students: Resources and Recommendations* concentrates on moving from oneself to having tools to develop mindfulness teachings to students. Being a practitioner and having resources from Daniel's workshops and books, Amelia is superbly qualified to work directly with students such as Anthony and with his teachers.

3. *Mindfulness Lessons for Students: Classroom Activities, Practices, and Techniques* moves from tools to curriculum that embeds the five types of mindfulness into 25 lessons with suggestions for adaptations for different grade levels. Amelia's lessons for Anthony occur in his classroom, with the agreement of his teacher of the academic curriculum; or in a separate room where he, alone or with Amelia, can practice the physical, emotional, mental, and social literacies, thereby blunting the emotions that might become aggressive or destructive behaviors.

4. *Integrating Mindfulness: Recommendations, Insights, and Tools* provides guidance for bringing mindfulness teaching to whole schools and to the larger community. Amelia believes that mindfulness instruction belongs in every school and community.

Daniel begins his training by teaching educators themselves how to be mindful. If they do not know how to do it, they will not be able to teach it. His *Guidelines for Teaching: Beginning with Ourselves* provides an illustration of incorporating the five types of mindful literacy into the first section of the Mindfulness Education program. We encourage you not only to read this *Guidelines for Teaching: Beginning with Ourselves* feature but also to practice each of the five literacies. Daniel suggests practicing each literacy every day for 1 week before moving on to the next literacy. Amelia agrees: "I practice mindfulness daily; that way, I can be effective for my students. I am a mindfulness practitioner who becomes a mindfulness teacher."

Guidelines for Teaching

Beginning with Ourselves

Week 1: Physical Literacy

- Lie down in a comfortable position
- Notice what is happening in your body
- Starting with your feet, move your attention slowly up your body to focus on relaxing each muscle group
- Identify any tension and let it go
- Scan your body for tension and focus on letting it go
- Breathe deeply throughout
- Pay attention to how your body feels in a relaxed state and seek to return to a feeling of relaxation throughout the day

Week 2: Mental Literacy

- Sit in a comfortable position
- Take deep breaths to raise your height and then lower it
- Pay attention to four parts of your breathing process
  - Be aware of inhaling your whole breath
  - Be aware of your full lungs just before starting to exhale
  - Be aware of exhaling your whole breath
  - Be aware of your empty lungs before your next breath
- Let go of distracting thoughts when they arise and return to focusing on your breath
- Use this exercise throughout the day when you are distracted to bring your attention back to your task at hand

Week 3: Emotional Literacy

- Be aware of your natural breath
- Be aware of sensations in your chest and emotions in your heart
- Picture a child to whom you are devoted being engaged in a favorite activity
  - Be aware of the feelings in your heart of your genuine caring
- Transfer the feeling of genuine caring to yourself
  - Be aware with each breath of how your heart is feeling
  - If happy, relish the happiness
  - If sad, feel compassion for yourself
- Extend kindness and compassion to yourself on every breath

- Use this exercise throughout the day in celebrating happy moments and comforting yourself with compassion during frustrating moments

Week 4: Social Literacy

- Begin with the four parts of your breathing process (see Mental Literacy)
- Picture in your mind a frustrating incident with a student from beginning to end
  - Be aware of your thoughts
  - Be aware of your emotions
  - Be aware of your bodily tension
- Breathe in with thoughts about your tension and breathe out with a sense of relaxation
- Picture the student again with an open heart and say
  - Just like me, _____ (add name) has many worries.
  - Just like me, _____ (add name) wants to have happy days.
  - Just like me, _____ (add name) experiences challenges.
  - Just like me, _____ (add name) wants to feel calm and be at peace.
- Be attuned to how you feel when you practice empathy rather than judgment
- Use this exercise throughout the day when you experience frustration with students, families, and/or colleagues

Week 5: Global Literacy

- Sit in a relaxed position and focus on the breath
- Focus on relaxing by letting troubling thoughts and emotions pass by like clouds
- Turn your attention to the sounds around you and note how they come and go
- Go back and forth in shifting your attention to your inside world of relaxation and the outside world of sounds
- Experience the sounds and smells of your environment with an open mind and heart
- Be curious about your environment in terms of who were the first people who inhabited your land and their cultural background

SOURCE: Adapted from Rechtschaffen, D. (2016). *The mindful education workbook: Lessons for teaching mindfulness to students*. New York, NY: W. W. Norton & Co.

As you learn to develop a mindfulness practice, you will gain insight into the benefits of mindfulness and how you can support students to refine these same mindfulness skills.

Into Practice Across Grade Levels: Teaching Mindfulness is drawn from Daniel's third unit, titled *Mindfulness Lessons from Students: Classroom Activities, Practices, and Techniques*.

Into Practice Across Grade Levels

Teaching Mindfulness

Physical Literacy Lesson

Students in the **4th grade** learn to breathe like animals. They breathe like dolphins by inhaling as they curve their arms and jump like a dolphin and then exhale when they bring their arms down. They try a crocodile breath by inhaling when they open their arms to mimic a crocodile's jaw and then exhale when they clap their arms together. Students can make up their own breathing patterns for their favorite animals, then write a story about their favorite animals and how they breathe.

Mental Literacy Lesson

In **kindergarten**, use different musical instruments to teach students to actively listen. Ask students to mindfully listen to the sound of the instrument for as long as any sound lasts and then to raise their hand at the instant when they no longer can hear the music. As students are able to focus their listening, use longer and longer musical selections to encourage students to extend their listening for a greater period of time.

Emotional Literacy Lesson

7th graders practice using their breathing to handle difficult emotions. Have students, one at a time, imagine the following scenarios: being teased by a classmate for a bad grade, having a pop-test in class without having done the assignment, and being reprimanded by the principal and told that they may not attend an overnight field trip because of disruptive behavior. The students are guided to pay attention to where they feel stress in their bodies and to use mindful breathing to release the tension and become relaxed. Then the students imagine the opposite situation. Again, they note carefully their body sensations and the emotions that they experience. The lesson ends when students write in their journal about how emotions feel inside their bodies.

Social Literacy Lesson

11th graders with externalizing behavioral disorders meet in a small group with a counselor on a weekly basis. In one session, the counselor invites the students to think of a situation when someone was really nice to them and that made them feel happy. Each student has an opportunity to share that experience with others in the group. They ask each other questions in terms of what emotions they felt; they come up with a number of 1 to 10 in terms of the strength of the emotion. Then the students are encouraged to think of someone whom they think would benefit from having nice things directed to them. They should identify things they could say and do that would bring similar emotions in terms of type and intensity that they had experienced in their own nice interaction. Afterward, all students in the group share what they could do. The counselor encourages the students to try out the nice interaction during the next week.

Global Literacy Lesson

Students in the **9th grade** focus their meditation on elements of the natural world. Ask students to sit in a relaxed position and do breathing for several minutes. Then ask them to imagine the image of a tall pine tree that is strong and towering. With each breath, they should feel the strength and sturdiness of the tree. Then ask them to imagine sitting outside around a fire while feeling the warmth of the fire and the chill of the wind. Finally, they should imagine floating in outer space, enveloped by galaxies. For each of these guided meditations, they should put themselves in nature and experience increasing levels of relaxation.

SOURCE: Adapted from Rechtschaffen, D. (2016). *The mindful education workbook: Lessons for teaching mindfulness to students.* New York, NY: W. W. Norton & Co.

The Mindful Education program was designed primarily as a universal mindfulness program for all students. That's the approach Daniel advocates. It also works for Amelia:

> It does not matter so much what kinds of disabilities and challenges the students in any particular class have. What matters is that I work with a team. The teachers, the school psychologist, the school social worker, and I are the mindfulness team for any given student. The teachers invite us to use mindfulness in their classes. We work there 3 days a week, to start; then we fade down to 2 days a week; and then to 1.
>
> We pay careful attention to the details of how a student learns the academic material and how mindfulness supports the student to learn that material. The progress is slow but steady for the particular student. And then it expands to other students. We modify the classroom environment for one and then for all. We go step by step; we use visual and auditory exercises. We give one student, and then all, a practice that they can use for mindfulness. For example, we ask them to study a photograph or painting; we ask, "What do you see that no one else might see?" This way, the students are "playing attention." They become absorbed. You can hear a pin drop. They focus. They tell us what they found

in the photo. The exercise seems be about the photo and what's in it. But it's really about students with huge challenges in learning how to sit still, engage, and participate in a brain-changing exercise. We are re-forming their brains so they learn not to use old behaviors but to use new ones. Take Anthony as an example: When confronted by another boy, he would have resorted to fighting. Now he knows to study the situation he's in and then to handle it in a different way. He doesn't actually put his hands on his body and take deep slow breaths. Instead, he remembers what he has learned about being mindful of himself and his environment, and he acts differently than before, and so he changes his environment. Mindfulness is labor-intensive, but it has a high payoff.*

A small number of mindfulness studies have particularly focused on students with EBD. One of these included students with conduct disorder, which, as you have learned, is one of the most severe types of EBD. This study used an intervention known as *Meditation on the Soles of the Feet* (Singh et al., 2017). This intervention focuses on self-regulation to control aggression. One of the studies involved three 7th-grade teenagers who had been identified as having conduct disorder (Singh et al., 2017). The teenagers met with a therapist 3 times a week over a 4-week period for a 15-minute session each time. In the sessions, the therapist guided the students to learn each of the 10 steps of the *Meditation on the Soles of the Feet* program that is outlined in Figure 9.2.

After the training ended, the teenagers continued to practice the 10 steps and had a monthly meeting to share self-reported data. The results indicated that, although aggressive behavior did not have a sufficient reduction during the training, it did have substantial reductions during the 25 weeks of practice once the training had concluded. The students were able to engage in socially appropriate behavior to the extent that they achieved the milestone of graduation.

Teaching Social and Emotional Competence: Early Childhood and Elementary Years

One of the most research-based programs for increasing emotional and social (as well as academic) competence for all children, with a particular focus on children with emotional and behavioral disorders (and ADHD), is The Incredible Years® Series. Figure 9.3 provides an overview of the goals, curriculum, and immediate outcomes for all three target groups—children, parents, and teachers. It also includes long-term outcomes for children.

Figure 9.2 Training Steps for Meditation on the Soles of the Feet Procedure

1. If you are standing, stand in a natural rather than an aggressive posture, with the soles of your feet flat on the floor.
2. If you are sitting, sit comfortably with the soles of your feet flat on the floor.
3. Breathe naturally and do nothing.
4. Cast your mind back to an incident that made you very angry. Stay with the anger.
5. You are feeling angry, and angry thoughts are flowing through your mind. Let them flow naturally, without restriction. Stay with the anger. Your body may show signs of anger (e.g., rapid breathing).
6. Now, shift all your attention fully to the soles of your feet.
7. Slowly, move your toes, feel your shoes covering your feet, feel the texture of your socks, the curve of your arch, and the heels of your feet against the back of your shoes. If you do not have shoes on, feel the floor or carpet with the soles of your feet.
8. Keep breathing naturally and focus on the soles of your feet until you feel calm.
9. Practice this mindfulness exercise until you can use it wherever you are and whenever an incident occurs that may otherwise lead to you being verbally or physically aggressive.
10. Remember that once you are calm, you can walk away from the incident or situation with a smile on your face because you controlled your anger. Alternatively, if you need to, you can respond to the incident or situation with a calm and clear mind without verbal threats or physical aggression.

SOURCE: Used by permission from Nirbhay Singh.

*Used by permission from Jessica, Spnittley

Figure 9.3 The Incredible Years® Parent, Child, and Teacher Programs

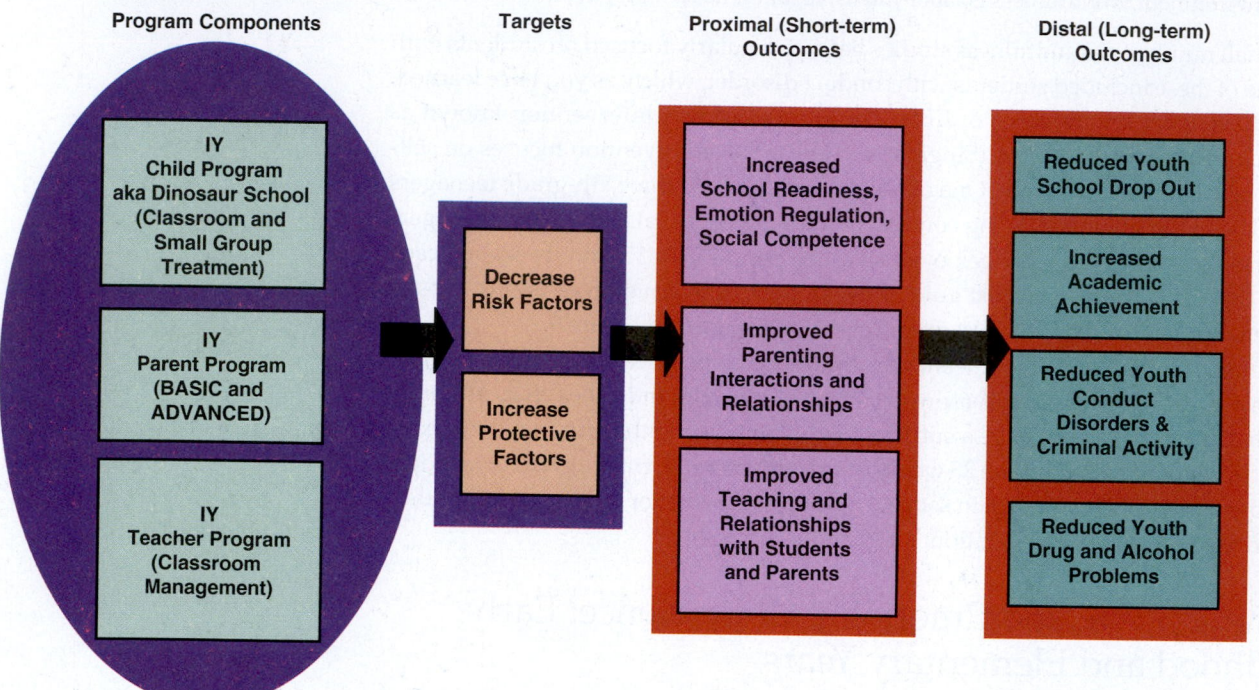

SOURCE: Program developed by Carolyn Webster-Stratton Ph.D, Professor and Director of the Parenting clinic at the University of Washington.

The child training program focuses on the key skills of self-control and problem solving, play skills, academic success, and self-esteem. A key strength of The Incredible Years® is that it was developed from the outset to be highly culturally sensitive. It has been implemented broadly with racial and ethnic groups throughout the United States, as well as in over 20 countries around the world.

The child training program is titled Child Dinosaur Social, Emotional and Problem-Solving Curriculum and covers the ages of 3 to 8 years. To individualize instruction in light of each child's developmental, social, and emotional skills, the program has lessons at three levels. It uses large puppets and dinosaur themes to enhance students' attention. The classroom dinosaur curriculum is a Tier 1 intervention used with all students 2 to 3 times a week for 20- to 30-minute lessons each time. In addition to the classroom program designed for all students, there is a Small Group Dinosaur Program used by counselors and therapists in a small-group setting (Tier 2), especially for students with conduct problems, externalizing and internalizing problems, and ADHD. The small-group curriculum is delivered in 2-hour sessions for 18 to 22 weeks.

The parent program focuses on positive discipline, nurturing relationships, anger management, and partnerships with educators. Developing a trusting partnership between parents and teachers is a key dimension of the program, and parents are supported to participate in the full range of partnership types, with a particular emphasis on extending learning in the home and community. The parent program is divided into four levels: babies (birth to 1 year), toddlers (1 to 3 years), preschoolers (3 to 6 years), and school age (up to 12 years). Both basic and advanced programs are available. Parent

MyLab Education

Video Example 9.6

In this video, the Child Dinosaur Curriculum is implemented in preschool classrooms. What do you perceive as two strengths in this curriculum? https://youtu.be/7ncHOZv2EJg

groups meet for 2 to 3 hours once a week for 12 to 20 group sessions, depending on the particular program selected.

A third component of The Incredible Years® is the teacher program. The curriculum for teachers focuses on classroom management skills, partnerships with families, instruction in problem solving, and enjoyment of teaching. The teacher program is focused on teachers of students 3 to 8 years of age. The heart of the program is classroom management that promotes positive social skills and academic readiness as well as prevention of problem behavior. The teacher training program entails 6 full-day workshops. A second teacher program focuses on teachers and childcare providers of children ages 1 to 5.

Of the 77 studies focusing on The Incredible Years® and examined by the What Works Clearinghouse, the most rigorous study involved a comparison of the program being delivered to children 4 to 8 years old with oppositional defiant disorder and, in some cases, the programs delivered to their families and teachers. The study examined the differential impact of providing child or parent training only versus combining child and parent training with each other and with teacher training. After implementing The Incredible Years® curriculum for 6 months, key results were impressive:

- Across all groups, children had fewer behavior problems with mothers, teachers, and peers, as compared to the control group.

- In addition to fewer behavior problems, children showed an increase in positive social skills with peers in all of the groups in which the children received training.

- All parent training groups resulted in less negative parenting for both mothers and fathers.

- When parent training and child training were combined with teacher training, parents and teachers reported being more satisfied with outcomes.

- Teacher training improved the classroom management that teachers were able to provide to students in their classrooms.

A meta-analysis of 50 studies reported a decrease in disruptive child behavior and an increase in positive social behavior. Children with the most severe problem behavior made the most improvement after their parents received parent training (Menting, de Castro, & Matthys, 2013). Most of the children 3 to 8 years old whose parents received training early on maintained positive outcomes 8 to 10 years later (Webster-Stratton, Rinaldi, & Reid, 2011). Their behavior problems during adolescence were less than the national norms.

To ensure program quality, The Incredible Years® headquarters provides professional development and certification for teachers, therapists, counselors, and other implementers. You can read *My Voice: "Switching How I Taught,"* written by Lisa Stinnett, a pre-kindergarten teacher in North Carolina. As you will discover, after Lisa attended the professional development program, she fully implemented the Child Dinosaur Social, Emotional and Problem-Solving Curriculum in her classroom, with outstanding results.

MyLab Education

Video Example 9.7
This video presents teacher training in action, as well as the teachers' perspectives on the value of this training for their overall classroom management effectiveness. What are your perspectives on the value of training along this line? https://youtu.be/qm-dFtIa4yk

---

My Voice

Lisa Stinnett—"Switching How I Taught"

I have been teaching preschool children for 19 years in different schools. Right now, I am teaching in a Title 1 preschool classroom and have 18 students, 5 of whom have Individualized Education Programs, or IEPs, through the public school system.

Four years ago, I was fortunate enough to have the opportunity to take The Incredible Years® (IY) Teacher Classroom Management Program, and my professional practices have not been the same for me since. I am like most people who go into teaching—I did it because I

(Continued)

Lisa Stinnet

Dinosaur School curriculum comes with excellent lesson plans that have guided me in knowing how to incorporate Billy into instruction with the children. They listen intently to him in our circle-time activities during which I teach core social and emotional skills.

In praising my students, I energize myself and change their behavior, too. The double effect surpasses any benefits from scolding my students; that brings me down and alienates them from me. I focus on catching children being good and letting them know how much I value their good behavior. I find that proximity praise works very effectively in terms of praising a child who is paying attention and complying with instructions as a way to remind students who are disengaged about what is the appropriate behavior that I expect. The children having a hard time pick up on this cue quickly and have a role model of the behavior that I want all students to have at that particular moment in time.

My whole goal is giving children every opportunity to shine. We have five basic rules that help the classroom work well—eyes on teacher, hands to self, listening ears, walking feet (rather than running), and inside voice. When rules are explicit and I praise the children for what they are doing right, the whole feel of the classroom is positive.

We spend lots of time in the circle and in our interactions throughout the day naming feelings. When I see kids with their faces scrunched up, I ask them to tell me their feelings. We also have a thermometer with a Velcro arrow. The colors on the thermometer are green in the calm stage, yellow in the moderate stage, and red in the intense phase. Children can use the arrow to express the strength of their feelings to themselves, to me, and to their classmates.

The circle instruction helps my students do more than express their feelings. It also helps them learn how to solve problems. Billy wears a detective hat during our problem-solving instruction. I use the lesson plans, with Billy's assistance, to guide the children through the steps of problem solving. Billy, the lesson, and I pose these questions, and the children then answer them:

- What is my problem and how do I know it's my problem (how am I feeling?)?
- What are the solutions?
- What are the consequences of solutions?
- What is the best solution?
- How do I use the skills to solve real problems?
- How do I evaluate the solution and the consequences?

Part of The Incredible Years® program is to practice calm-down techniques to use in everyday circumstances. I have an area of the classroom set aside as a place for children to calm down. As with many of the social-emotional skills we discuss in the curriculum, we practice using calm-down techniques when children are calm so that when they really need to use the skills, they know what to do. We relate the calm-down process to a turtle going into its shell, and children learn 5 steps to calming down: (1) recognize your feeling; (2) stop your body; (3) take a deep breath; (4) go into your turtle shell and tell yourself, "I can do it. I can calm

love kids, NOT because I want to manage the behavior of every kid in the class throughout every minute of the day. Classroom management was one of my biggest challenges, and it seems to be the biggest challenge of the vast majority of teachers. The year after I took the Teacher Classroom Management Program, I completed the training for Dinosaur School, the curriculum for children. Both of these programs enabled me to move away from scolding children after they have acted out to supporting them to be successful. In looking back, the way I reprimanded and punished children often contributed to their escalation and alienation. It did not do what I wanted from my work and my students: their trust in me and their social and emotional development. Thus, I learned to not add fuel to fire.

It is hard to put into words all of the many positive aspects of The Incredible Years® program. There is a very strong emphasis on children learning to understand and express feelings, as well as on self-regulation, such as learning to calm down. I adore the puppets that come with the Dinosaur School program. The puppets are almost child-sized and easy to manipulate to make them seem life-like. We named ours Billy, and he is like a member of our class and an active participant in circle time during Dinosaur School. He comes and shares things that have been happening to him, and our class helps him come up with solutions from things we have learned through the program. They react to the puppet in a completely different way than they do to me because he is like a peer to them, and they relate to him in a unique way. Interestingly, the puppets come in different skin colors. I particularly chose a darker African American puppet, since most of the students in my class are African American. Billy is one of us.

down"; and (5) when you are calm, come out and try again. The children meet Tiny Turtle, a puppet who practices the calm-down steps with them. He reminds them to take three deep breaths—smelling flowers/blowing candles—as a way to calm down emotionally and physically.

The Incredible Years® is helpful for every student in the class, including those who have some emotional challenges. One of my students frequently is defiant almost every time I provide instructions, screams throughout the day, hits frequently, and refuses to clean up the many messes that he makes. It is helpful for him to use the thermometer to illustrate his "red" feelings. Although I use lots of praise when things are going well for him, sometimes he needs stronger reinforcers, such as being the line leader, having free time, or picking a book for the class. I also use some of The Incredible Years® stickers with him, such as "Ask me how I shared" and "I can stop my anger." He thrives on being given chances to be successful and we really see improvement

with his behavior. Punishing him for his bad behavior wasn't a successful way for the behavior to change. We tried to highlight the things he was doing correctly and used it as an opportunity.

Overall, The Incredible Years® has been the best training and resource program that I have ever used. From my students, I know firsthand that they have learned to be in charge of their own feelings and behaviors rather than to have to rely on others. I deeply value how they learn to feel positive about themselves. That is such a critical foundation for them when they build positive self-concepts at the preschool level—it is catching them when they are young before shame builds up. Another positive outcome is related to trust. They trust themselves, each other, me, and adults in general. What more important outcomes could there possibly be?

—Used by permission Lisa Stnnett

We encourage you to reflect on how much Anthony would likely have benefited if he and his mother had experienced The Incredible Years® during his early childhood and elementary years.

The Incredible Years® professional development program also includes manuals and other written materials, videos, coaching, and consultation to ensure the program is delivered as intended by the developers. In the United States, approximately 4000 teachers have received professional development in the Classroom Dinosaur School Program over the past 20 years. In that same time frame, over 1000 people have been prepared to deliver classroom management training to teachers (numbers include the Teacher Classroom Management Program for children ages 3 to 8 and The Incredible Beginnings Program for children 1 to 5 years of age). If the school district where you eventually work is not part of The Incredible Years® network, we encourage you to share information with your principal and to explore whether or not there would be opportunities for you and other teachers to receive professional development.

A portion of the Incredible Years website, www.incredibleyears.com/for-administrators/, is designed specifically for administrators, providing them an overview of the program.

Teaching Emotional Problem Solving: Middle and Secondary Grades

DBT Skills Training for Emotional Problem Solving for Adolescents (DBT STEPS-A) is a curriculum designed to enhance the emotional problem solving of middle and high school students (Mazza, Dexter-Mazza, Miller, Rathus, & Murphy, 2016). DBT stands for dialectical-behavior therapy, which is a form of therapy begun in the early 1990s as a research-based therapeutic treatment for adults with complex mental health disorders (Linehan, 1993). Given its high success rate with adults, it then evolved to a research-based and clinic-based treatment for adolescents with complex emotional disorders (Miller, Rathus, & Linehan, 2007; Rathus & Miller, 2002). DBT STEPS-A is the next iteration in extending DBT for adolescents from the clinic to middle and secondary grades. Early research on school-based delivery and outcomes is "encouraging" (Mazza et al., 2016, p. 4).

The original dialectical behavior therapy and the current skill-building curriculum are rooted in dialectics, which is a way to understand how things are at a specific point in time and then the way things change. The opposing forces of a thesis and antithesis result in the emergence of a synthesis, which then evolves to a new thesis and antithesis.

Simply put, two opposing ideas can be true at the same time and exist as one idea. In DBT and DBT STEPS-A, dialectics is represented by skill development focusing on both acceptance and change—acceptance of current emotional and behavioral challenges and change in terms of learning new skills to prevent and/or resolve challenges.

The goal of dialectical thinking in DBT STEPS-A is to help students reduce "black-or-white," "all-or-nothing" thinking and increase their ability to recognize multiple perspectives to any situation. For example, when the going gets tough, students can think this way: "I'm doing the best I can in the moment, *and* I need to do better" (Mazza et al., 2016, p. 14). A goal for students is to embrace flexible thinking in accepting their challenges while coming up with sound solutions.

DBT STEPS-A addresses four key emotional challenges experienced by adolescents, especially those identified as having EBD. These include:

- Difficulty managing emotions—experiencing quickly changing emotions and behavioral dysregulation; limited insight into emotions

- Confusion about self/distraction—being out of touch with one's own values, emotions, and goals; being distracted from the task at hand; poor coping with emotional distress

- Impulsiveness—making spur-of-the-moment poor decisions about school attendance, hurting oneself, using drugs and alcohol, and so on; being unable to tolerate stress and painful emotions

- Interpersonal problems—difficulty with friendships and other relationships; not knowing how to ask for help; not knowing how to say "no" to others' requests; having low self-respect.

DBT STEPS-A systematically teaches youth to overcome these challenges by building skills to manage emotions, make wise decisions, and demonstrate constructive interpersonal relationships across all of the students' environments. The curriculum consists of 30 lessons divided into the following four modules: Mindfulness, Distress Tolerance, Emotional Regulation, and Interpersonal Effectiveness, as shown in Figure 9.4.

Figure 9.4 Key Skills Addressed in DBT STEPS-A

Mindfulness

Wise Mind

Making wise decisions using both logic and emotion

The "What" Skills—three skills practiced one at a time

- *Observing*—using the five senses to notice and observe things inwardly and outwardly
- *Describing*—using words to characterize observations without judgment or opinions
- *Participating*—putting 100 percent effort into mindfully engaging in activities

The "How" Skills—three skills practiced together

- *Nonjudgmentally*—to describe without evaluating
- *One-mindfully*—focusing on one task at a time without regard for what happened in the past or future
- *Effectively*—aligning actions with goals

Distress Tolerance

Crisis Survival Skills

- *Distracting with Wise Mind ACCEPTS*—distracting oneself from current challenges and emotions by mindful participation in <u>A</u>ctivities, <u>C</u>ontributing, <u>C</u>omparisons, <u>E</u>motions, <u>P</u>ushing away, <u>T</u>houghts, and <u>S</u>ensations
- *Improve the Moment*—tolerating the current moment through activities such as imagery, prayer, relaxation, and a brief vacation
- *Self-soothing with the Five Senses and Movement*—using the senses for comfort, such as listening to favorite music and lighting a scented candle

- *Tip Skills*—activating the parasympathetic nervous system to counter "fight-or-flight" through TIP: Temperature (putting face in a bowl of cold water), Intense exercise, and Pace breathing
- *Pros and Cons*—developing pros and cons for acting on impulsive urges and for tolerating the urges without acting on them

Reality Acceptance Skills

- *Radical Acceptance*—accepting something completely (radical) and terminating a focus on "shoulds", e.g., People should be nicer to me (acceptance)
- *Turning the Mind*—choosing to turn the mind to reality rather than feeling angry about what might have been
- *Willingness*—taking action on what is needed to deal effectively with the situation rather than refusing to deal with the situation's reality
- *Mindfulness of Current Thoughts*—recognizing and describing a distressful thought and letting it go rather than holding onto it

Emotional Regulation

Understanding and Naming Emotions

- *Goals of Emotional Regulation and Functions of Emotions*—understanding the biology and psychology of emotions
- *Describing Emotions*—observing and describing emotional cycles, e.g., from vulnerability factors/prompting event to final consequences of actions

Changing Emotional Responses

- *Checking the Facts*—teaching students to make sure that they have accurate information on the occurrence that prompted emotions
- *Opposite Action*—acting the opposite of an emotion one is experiencing, with the goal of changing the emotion
- *Problem solving*—solving the problem that is the trigger for the emotion

Reducing Vulnerability to Emotion Mind: ABC PLEASE

Accumulating Positives—doing at least one pleasant thing every day over the short term, while planning for the long term by aligning one's personal values with goals and action steps

- *Building Mastery*—participating in activities that are challenging but possible in order to increase self-efficacy
- *Coping Ahead of Time with Emotional Situations*—rehearsing coping skills in advance when one is anticipating difficult emotional situations
- *Please Skills*—taking care of the body by treating Physical illness, balance Eating, Avoid mood-altering drugs, balance Sleep, and get Exercise

Letting Go of Emotional Suffering

The Wave Skill, Mindfulness of Current Emotions—being mindful and experiencing the physical sensations of emotions rather than using distraction or avoidance

Interpersonal Effectiveness

Specific Interpersonal Effectiveness Skills

- *Overview and Goal Setting Prioritizing*—learning to ask what one wants or say no to things one does not want while maintaining or improving the relationship and enhancing one's own self-respect
- *Objectives Effectiveness Skills: DEAR MAN*—learning to be assertive in asking for what one wants or saying no to what one does not want through the following:

Describe the situation

Express your emotion or opinion

Assert your request

Reinforce the other person ahead of time

Stay Mindful of this moment

Appear confident

Negotiate as needed

- *Relationship Effectiveness Skills: GIVE*—delivering the DEAR MAN message to improve relationships; Gentle, act Interested, Validate, and use an Easy manner
- *Self-respect Effectiveness Skills: FAST*—asking or saying no in a way that enhances one's own self-respect; Fair, no Apologies, Stick to values, and be Truthful
- *Evaluating options*—asking for things or saying no to someone else with appropriate intensity

SOURCE: Based on Mazza, J. J., Dexter-Mazza, E. T., Miller, A. L., Rathus, J. H., & Murphy, H. E. (2016). *DBT® skills in schools: Skills training for emotional problem-solving for adolescents (DBT STEPS-A)*. New York, NY: Guilford Press.

MINDFULNESS   As you have already learned when reading about Anthony and Amelia, mindfulness involves "paying attention in a particular way, on purpose, in the present moment nonjudgmentally" (Kabat-Zinn, 1994, p. 4). Mindfulness skills enable students to increase their self-awareness of emotions, focus their attention, decrease their tendency to be judgmental, and focus on the present. The Mindfulness module is the foundational component of the DBT STEPS-A curriculum and includes six key skills (skills 1 to 6 in Figure 9.4). As you read about the next three modules, consider how Anthony might benefit from having DBT STEPS-A as an adjunct to his current mindfulness instruction.

DISTRESS TOLERANCE   The Distress Tolerance module teaches students to manage the distress of their current situation and to focus on learning and using new effective skills rather than making impulsive decisions leading to negative outcomes. Distress tolerance skills are divided into crises survival skills (five skills) and reality acceptance skills (four skills). Crises survival skills enable students to manage emotional stress in the short term, without making it worse. Reality acceptance skills focus on managing distress for problems that cannot be solved even in the long term. The reasons for being unable to change difficult circumstances may be due to present circumstances beyond the control of the student. Solutions to problems may take long-term planning and waiting, such as graduation from high school. Also, mistakes made in the past and their consequences cannot be changed. The key is to be able to accept present reality and make the best of an unfortunate situation.

EMOTIONAL REGULATION   The third module, Emotional Regulation, has the goal of teaching students to gain keen insight into their emotions and to develop the capacity to manage their emotions. The goal is to increase positive emotions while simultaneously reducing emotional helplessness. Students will learn to ride the wave of emotions and know that the intense emotion will not last forever.

INTERPERSONAL EFFECTIVENESS   The fourth and last module, Interpersonal Effectiveness, addresses interpersonal problems, with the goal of preparing students to have positive relationships through increasing self-respect, reducing conflict, and improving assertiveness. The focus on relationships helps to keep relationships steady at school with peers and adults, as well as at home with family members.

The DBT STEPS-A curriculum is best delivered during one class per week over two semesters or two classes a week for one semester. The 30 lesson plans are sufficiently detailed so that general and special education teachers can teach the curriculum for Tier 1 delivery. The curriculum can be delivered as a Tier 2 intervention for smaller groups of students who could benefit from more practice, as well as more extended feedback and coaching. The coaching is particularly important for students who have been identified as having EBD and/or who are confronting especially stressful situations at school, home, or in other environments. Tier 2 instruction might best be delivered by the counselor, school psychologist, social worker, or another school-based mental health professional. For students with more significant EBD challenges, Tier 3 intervention again should be delivered by a mental health professional with more intensive instruction, perhaps both individual and group sessions, which enable more in-depth coaching and progress monitoring. An additional component for Tier 3 can be having parents and

Victoria Lusk

Tier 1 instruction in DBT STEPS-A can be provided to all students during designated class sessions.

their teenagers working together in small groups or in individual sessions. You can gain keen insight about the impact of DBT STEPS-A on students with different intensities of need by reading the *Into Practice Across Grade Levels: Implementing DBT STEPS-A to Benefit High School Students.*

Before you read the summary of this chapter, take a moment to think about Anthony. He was frequently aggressive against others who teased him. When challenged by them, he challenged them in return, using his size as his weapon. Now, he

Into Practice Across Grade Levels
Implementing DBT STEPS-A to Benefit High School Students

Tier 1: Primary Prevention: 9th Grade

Context: A prevention program is delivered to all high school freshman through their general education classes. Students are introduced to the Dialectical Behavior Therapy: Skills Training for Emotional Problem Solving for Adolescents (DBT STEPS-A) curriculum once every 3 weeks throughout the school year. Students are taught two of the four modules (i.e., Mindfulness and Distress Tolerance). The goal is to teach skills and strategies that students can utilize when they are feeling emotionally dysregulated or stressed. During their sophomore year, students will learn the other two modules of Emotional Regulation and Interpersonal Effectiveness.

Intervention: The teaching of Mindfulness, the core of all DBT skills, occurs in the classroom setting. Students are taught how to work on being in the present, not focusing on the past or the future, through the use of visual aids and interactive activities. Too often, students stress about what they could have or should have done in the past or worry about future events and the "what if's." By remaining focused in the present, unnecessary stress regarding situations the students cannot control or change is reduced. Students are exposed to the mindfulness skill of Wise Mind, in which three states of mind (i.e., Emotion Mind, Reasonable Mind, and Wise Mind) are discussed, including the strengths and challenges of each. From these skills, students are able to identify Wise Mind as the ideal state of mind that is an integration of Emotion and Reasonable Mind. While fundamentals of Mindfulness are introduced, the students are also exposed to a variety of direct mindfulness activities that can help them achieve Wise Mind, remain focused, and be less judgmental of themselves and others. One mindfulness activity taught to the students in the classroom is A–Z. After the ringing of the mindfulness bell, the students are asked to write down a list of movie names that begin with each letter of the alphabet. This is a mindfulness exercise that can offer a distraction from their current emotion mind state, help them to stay focused on one thing at a time, and address self-judgments. The mindfulness bell is rung at the end of the activity, and observations are shared.

Tier 2: Response to Intervention (RTI) Tier 2 Intervention: STEPS-A for a 10th-grade General Education Student

Condition: A 10th-grade general education student was referred to the Child Study Team (CST) by her teacher, who was concerned that the student was not engaged in school, attendance was poor, she was often missing homework, and she had a difficult time managing her emotions with peers. This student would use harsh language with other students and then cry when students responded negatively. The CST recommended that the school psychologist meet with the student.

Intervention: The school psychologist met with the student and spoke with her family. The students' parents had recently separated, and the student was having a difficult time adjusting. She had a history of being highly emotionally sensitive and reactive, which caused her to have interpersonal difficulties. DBT STEPS-A was recommended, and both the student and her parent agreed.

The DBT STEPS-A group comprised 10 students in 9th through 12th grades. The group was offered during a lunch period; students ate lunch with the group, and group leaders provided snacks and drinks. Some students had an IEP or Section 504 Plan, while others were general education students. Emotional Regulation skills were taught, including how to identify and label emotions. Students learned to notice how thoughts about an event influence feelings, and to notice physical sensations in their body (e.g., a racing heart). It was demonstrated that thoughts and feelings about an event can impact actions and that these actions have consequences. This lesson (Describing Emotions) is pulled together with a diagram (model of emotions) that shows students how prompting events, vulnerability factors, thoughts about the event, and what happens inside and outside the body all lead to behaviors.

Tier 3: 11th Grade student with a 504 Accommodation Plan

Condition: An 11th-grade student, who previously (but not currently) had instruction in English as a second language, was referred for a 504 Plan after receiving a medical

(Continued)

diagnosis of attention-deficit hyperactivity disorder (ADHD). The student presented with the organizational and academic challenges typical of ADHD and had significant emotional distress. He reported engaging in risky behavior outside school as a means to cope with his emotions.

Intervention: The student was evaluated for 504 accommodations in response to the referral, and academic accommodations were provided, including extended time on tests and resource room every other day to assist with study skills and organization. It was determined that he would benefit from individual and group counseling to address significant difficulty tolerating emotional distress. In group counseling, he learned Distress Tolerance skills, including self-soothing and TIP skills (see Figure 9.4) for managing extreme emotions. Self-soothing skills included using the senses to calm emotions (e.g., lighting a scented candle, savoring a favorite snack, listening to music). TIP skills involve changing the physical experience of extreme emotions using ice or cold water, intense exercise, paced breathing, or progressive muscle relaxation. In individual counseling, the student was coached in using these skills to cope with intense emotions and as a replacement for the risky behaviors. He reported finding these skills helpful in dealing with distressing emotions.

Transitioning from Hospitalization to Tier 3: Comprehensive School-based DBT for 12th-grade Student Classified with Emotional Disability

Condition: A 12th-grade student who has always been conscientious with his work and grades was recently hospitalized

after he expressed suicidal ideation with a plan. Upon his return to school from hospitalization, he experienced difficulty getting out of bed for school, maintaining friendships, and completing school work. He received three failing grades on his report card due to poor attendance and incomplete school work.

Intervention: The Committee on Special Education referred the student for an evaluation, as his emotional distress issues were interfering with his education. He was classified as a student with an Emotional Disability. Group and individual counseling was added to his IEP. It was recommended that comprehensive DBT would be appropriate for this student to address life-threatening and quality-of-life interfering behaviors. The group comprised five students and took place during lunch. Individual sessions were held during his free period.

The school psychologist and the student identified his self-harming and suicidal behaviors using the diary card. These behaviors were processed and understood through the therapeutic strategy called behavioral chaining. Behavioral chaining is a technique in which the clinician and student discuss the events, thoughts, and feelings that lead up to and result in a behavioral incident. During group sessions, all DBT skill modules were taught. During one group session, Interpersonal Effectiveness Skills, the DEAR MAN skill, specifically, was presented. The student practiced the skill using an example of asking a teacher for an extension on a project. During the next group, the student reported that he was successful in utilizing the skill and getting what he wanted from his teacher by moving the deadline while keeping his relationship with the teacher stable.

SOURCE: This *Into Practice* feature was prepared by Dawn Catucci, Monique Johnson, Tara Wright, Michelle Myers, and Victoria Lusk based on the DBT STEPS-A work they do with their students. Used with permission.

challenges himself: "Find a place to go mentally or physically, put my hands where they belong, breathe some, think about what I should not do and what I can do instead."

Anthony is changing himself and his context. He is making academic progress in school. And he is presenting himself as worthy of others' respect. Amelia, his other teachers, and his school's administrators commit to educating him, not to suspending or expelling him. That's a way to dignify Anthony: respect him as capable of learning, teach him what research shows works, and then take deep satisfaction in watching him develop academically, behaviorally, and emotionally.

He's not the discipline problem that he once was. In Amelia's words, he is "a gentle person who needed to find a different way of being true to his real self."

MyLab Education Self-Check 9.3

MyLab Education Application Exercise 9.3: Strategies to Avoid Suspension or Expulsion

Summary

Defining Emotional or Behavioral Disorders

IDEA uses the term *emotional disturbance* to refer to a condition that is (a) accompanied by one or more of the following characteristics over a long time and to a marked degree and that (b) adversely affects a child's educational performance:

- An inability to learn that cannot be explained by intellectual, sensory, or health factors
- An inability to build or maintain satisfactory interpersonal relationships with peers and teachers
- Inappropriate types of behavior or feelings under normal circumstances
- A general, pervasive mood of unhappiness or depression
- A tendency to develop physical symptoms or fears associated with personal or school problems.

Approximately 5.7 percent of all students with disabilities are identified under IDEA as having emotional or behavioral disabilities.

Describing the Characteristics and Causes

Students may exhibit characteristics of anxiety disorder, mood disorder, oppositional defiant disorder, conduct disorder, and/or schizophrenia. Additionally, they may exhibit externalizing (aggressive, acting-out, noncompliant) behaviors and internalizing (withdrawn, depressed, anxious, obsessive, compulsive) behaviors. These students typically have normal intelligence, but they have significant challenges related to emotional, behavioral, and academic skills. Causes include interactions between biological (for example, genetics, and temperament) and environmental (for example, school and family) factors.

Evaluating Students with Emotional or Behavioral Disorders

For diagnosing students with EBD, the Scale for Assessing Emotional Disturbance, 2nd edition, is a norm-referenced scale tied directly to the five elements of the IDEA definition of EBD. The Behavioral and Emotional Rating Scale, 2nd edition, is also a norm-referenced tool with strong psychometric properties. It is designed to identify students' strengths and needs as a basis for educational planning.

Including Students with Emotional or Behavioral Disorders

Students with EBD constitute one of the most excluded groups from general education classrooms, with slightly less than half spending 80 percent or more time in inclusive classrooms. Seventeen percent of students are in separate settings, with many being in juvenile correction facilities. Black females and males with EBD have the highest enrollment in these restrictive settings.

Educating Students with Emotional or Behavioral Disorders

Mindfulness involves paying attention to the present moment in a nonjudgmental and calm way. Research has documented its beneficial impact for teachers and students alike. The Mindful Education program developed by Daniel Rechtschaffen involves five types of mindful literacies—physical, mental, emotional, social, and global. The Mindful Education program provides online professional development, curriculum activities, and a wide variety of resources for you to start with yourself in honing your mindfulness skills and then to teach mindfulness to students. Mindfulness can be an asset to students with EBD in learning to regulate their emotions and behavior.

The wIncredible Years® is a research-based program aimed at developing positive outcomes for children, parents, and teachers. Parents and teachers increase their competence in positive discipline and in forming trusting partnerships with each other. Together they support children to make positive gains in their emotional, social, and academic well-being. The child program, delivered at Tiers 1 and 2, uses puppets and dinosaur themes to engage children's attention. The parent program provides weekly workshops to teach parents key discipline skills, as well as how to nurture relationships with their child and with the teacher. The teacher program involves full-day workshops where teachers learn classroom management aimed at providing a context to maximize children's academic, social, and emotional growth.

DBT STEPS-A is a curriculum for supporting middle and high school students to strengthen their emotional problem solving. It is designed to teach students to accept their current emotional and behavioral challenges while also working on learning new skills to prevent and/or resolve challenges. Its four modules teach practical and specific skills related to mindfulness, distress tolerance, emotional regulation, and interpersonal effectiveness. It can be used in schools for whole classes and small groups at the Tier 1 and 2 levels, respectively. Furthermore, it can be used in individual therapy sessions at Tier 3.

Addressing the Professional Standards

In Chapter 9, Students with Emotional or Behavioral Disorders, we have covered the following Council for Exceptional Children (CEC) Initial Level Special Educator Preparation Standards: Chapter 9—1.1, 1.2, 2.3, 4.4, 5.5, 6.1, 6.5, 7.3. Refer to the Appendix for a full listing of the CEC Standards with descriptions and supporting explanations.

Chapter 10

Students with Attention-Deficit Hyperactivity Disorder

Learning Outcomes

10.1 Define ADHD, differentiate the three types, and describe the students' characteristics related to executive functioning; academic achievement; and behavioral, emotional, and social functioning.

10.2 Distinguish evaluation approaches, compare and contrast Conner's 3 and the ADDES-3 approaches; and summarize how to strengthen students' social connections.

10.3 Summarize two "take-away points" about implementing Section 504, providing accommodations and understanding the impact of medication.

Meet Will Sims—Taking Control of His Education

It has taken at least three people to take control of Will Sims' education—Will himself; his mother, Leigh Ann; and his teachers, especially his 4th-grade teacher. There's a partnership here, and a story worth your attention.

Will Sims is a 17-year-old 11th grader who has attention-deficit hyperactivity disorder (ADHD). He was in 4th grade when he and his mother, Leigh Ann, first learned that he has the disorder. He had been ill on the day when his school administered the state-required examination of students' proficiency, so he took his makeup examination in a room alone, not in a room with other students, as he would have done if he had not been ill. On that day, his teacher noticed how well Will was able to concentrate on the examination. "Isolation," she declared, "is a way to help him." She then wondered if this need for isolation was a clue that he might have ADHD. In a room with other students, Will became distracted, but in a room by himself, he focused intensely on his work.

Will's success has not come easily. After his 4th-grade teacher noticed how well he performed when he was alone, his mother asked his school administrators to test him for a disability. They said they could but that they had to arrange for the school psychologist to observe him over a period of

Leigh Ann Sims

6 to 8 weeks. "That was just too long," said Leigh Ann, "so we went and had him independently tested by an expert. He confirmed the diagnosis, and then when the school psychologist had finished his round of observations, he came to the same conclusion."

Leigh Ann adds that she had to pay not only for the independent evaluation but also for "learning remediation. That was another huge expense, almost $15,000 for getting him additional tutoring at a private center, 4 hours a week for 9 months."

In addition to his ADHD, Will has hearing loss in one ear, so he works with a speech therapist appointed by his school, reading and then speaking a sentence over and over again until he can say the words so well that he cannot be misunderstood.

Will is proud of his progress in school, but he is not satisfied with himself, even now. The accommodations and special services in school "helped me out a lot because they made me more responsible [for learning]. Now, it's like I have more responsibility to the point where I have to study a lot longer. I might have to study a lot longer than other peers in my classes do, but I can definitely understand the material more when I get all the help through my IEP and through my family, too."

What other support does Will get? His accommodations include taking practice tests at home, using a school online site called "Study Island," where he answers 20 questions at a time and instantly learns his score as well as which answers were correct or incorrect. "I take all the help I can get," he says. And despite the increasing difficulty of his curriculum, "every year my IEP has been reduced and reduced. It's getting a lot harder now, so I take control of my grades now. I want to go to college and I want to be successful. I just want to get all my time done and just put forth all the effort I can into my school work so I can improve everything."

Both Will and Leigh Ann have had to confront the fact that Will, like many students with ADHD, needs more than classroom accommodations. Throughout his school years, he has taken three different kinds of medication, but he now has finally found the one that suits him best—the one that allows him to concentrate but does not affect him so much that he is unable to learn.

Will characterizes himself as "athletically active." He quickly adds, "I want to get out of high school, graduate, and go to business school for four years and then after that I want to go to a maintenance school, like a car place, so I can get my car degree and then eventually open up my own car shop and redo cars."*

Are Will's goals realistic? He thinks so, and so does Leigh Ann. He knows what accommodations he needs. He has learned what medication works. He has become responsible for his own learning. He has ambition. Finally, he has a strategic plan for his future.

Asked if he is self-confident, he answers, "Yes, I am." And he has good reason to be self-confident: Special education services have boosted his abilities and his confidence. Will is more like than unlike so many students and young men and women: determined, responsible, self-confident, eager for support, and ambitious.

You get the sense, don't you, that Will is one fully self-determined young man. Some of that self-determination was inherent in him. And some was instilled in him, by his mother and by an observant teacher. It's a partnership that incubated Will's self-determination.

Defining Attention-Deficit Hyperactivity Disorder

If you read the Individuals with Disabilities Education Act (IDEA) and its definitions of a student with a disability, you will not find ADHD as a listed disability. Instead, IDEA includes it as a category within "other health impairments." The regulations implementing IDEA define students with other health impairments as those "having limited

*Used by permission of Leigh Ann Sims

strength, vitality or alertness, including a heightened alertness to environmental stimuli, that results in limited alertness with respect to the educational environment, that:

1. is due to chronic or acute health problems such as asthma, attention deficit disorder or attention deficit hyperactivity disorder, diabetes, epilepsy, a heart condition, hemophilia, lead poisoning, leukemia, nephritis, rheumatic fever, and sickle cell anemia; and

2. affects a child's educational performance."

The distinguishing feature for other health impairments is "limited strength, vitality, or alertness that adversely affects the student's progress in school." Students with ADHD, such as Will Sims, generally experience difficulty with alertness, as contrasted to strength or vitality. You will learn about another health impairment, asthma, in Chapter 14.

Because IDEA does not specifically define ADHD, most professionals adhere to the definition offered by the American Psychiatric Association (APA) (2013) in the *Diagnostic and Statistical Manual of Mental Disorders* (DSM-5). This definition focuses on two domains—inattention and hyperactivity/impulsivity that interfere with a student's development and functioning in multiple settings, including school. Some students with ADHD have a combination of both domains. To receive a diagnosis of ADHD, the symptoms must (1) occur before the student is 12 years old; (2) occur in two or more settings (home, school, or community); (3) not be explained by another disability; and (4) interfere with the child's functioning in typical activities and environments.

You should consider carefully the criterion that ADHD must interfere with development or functioning in typical activities and environments. Everyone forgets or is absentminded at times, especially during periods of stress. Also, some people are simply more or less active or energetic than others. But unless those characteristics meet the criteria in the previous paragraph, the person does not meet that specific ADHD criterion. And a student whose educational performance is not adversely affected will not qualify for IDEA services.

As you will recall, Will's teachers first suspected he might have attention deficit when he was required to take a 2-day standardized state assessment given to all 4th graders. He took the first day of the test in a classroom with his peers. He missed the second day of the test and so took the makeup in the quiet and uncrowded school library. The differences between the scores were remarkable: The classroom scores were much lower than the library scores, yet the classroom scores were typical of the scores Will had been receiving for several years. The discrepancy caused his teacher to think that Will might have ADHD. She was absolutely correct.

The DSM-5 (American Psychiatric Association, 2013) criteria also require that the symptoms occur before the age of 12, persist for at least 6 months, be present in at least two settings, and not be attributable to another disability. Approximately one fourth to one half of all children identified as having ADHD display the disorder into adolescence (Bussing, Mason, Bell, Porter, & Garvan, 2010).

Under the DSM-5 diagnostic criteria (American Psychiatric Association, 2013), there are three subtypes of ADHD: predominately inattentive, predominately hyperactive-impulsive, and combined.

MyLab Education
Video Example 10.1
In the "What ADHD Feels Like," video you are introduced to three students who experience ADHD. As you learn about the characteristics of ADHD, keep these students in mind. What is your hunch about whether each would be diagnosed as predominately inattentive, predominately hyperactive-impulsive, or combined? https://www.youtube.com/watch?v=NL483G4xKu0&t=1s

Predominately Inattentive Type

Students must exhibit difficulty with six or more of the following characteristics to be classified as having the predominately inattentive type:

- Paying attention to details/making careless mistakes
- Paying attention to academic and social activities
- Listening when someone speaks directly to them
- Following instructions/finishing tasks

Students with ADHD often have challenges in remembering routines and rules; it is advantageous to be explicit in teaching routines and rules and not to rely on waiting for students to make mistakes and then correcting them.

- Organizing tasks and activities
- Sustaining mental effort
- Keeping track of necessary supplies
- Avoiding distractions
- Remembering daily activities (American Psychiatric Association, 2013).

Will has many of these characteristics, such as not paying close attention to details, struggling to pay attention to academic activities, and being easily distracted. But like many students with ADHD, he does not have difficulty with all of them. Flexible time does not give him a special advantage over students who do not need it; instead, it enables him to show what he knows, and that is what examinations are all about—enabling students to prove they have learned the curriculum.

Because students with the inattentive type of ADHD usually are not as disruptive as those with hyperactivity-impulsivity, educators may overlook their needs. These students often display a slow tempo in their approach to academic tasks, boredom, lack of motivation, and self-consciousness. More boys than girls have the inattentive type of ADHD. They are more likely to experience anxiety and mood disorders and often face their biggest challenge with academic achievement (Glanzman & Sell, 2013).

Predominately Hyperactive-Impulsive Type

Students must exhibit difficulty with six or more of the following characteristics to be classified as having the predominately hyperactive-impulsive type of ADHD:

- Keeping hands and feet still/staying still in seat
- Staying seated
- Resisting running or climbing in appropriate situations
- Participating quietly in leisure activities
- Resisting being constantly "on the go"
- Talking excessively
- Blurting out answers prematurely
- Waiting for a turn
- Interrupting others (American Psychiatric Association, 2013).

Problems associated with hyperactivity and impulsivity typically start at the preschool level and may evolve to the combined type as children get older and confront higher expectations in school (Glanzman & Sell, 2013). These students are often described as displaying fidgetiness and being in constant motion. These characteristics align with hyperactivity. By contrast, characteristics with impulsivity align with difficulty in deferring gratification, withholding an inappropriate behavioral response, or blurting out answers or comments out-of-turn (Roberts, Milich, & Barkley, 2015). Although hyperactivity tends to decrease with age, impulsivity typically persists into adolescence and adulthood.

Combined Type

The third classification, which is also the most common, describes students who have features of both inattention and hyperactivity-impulsivity. The characteristics are academic challenges, social challenges, and increased prevalence of both internalizing and externalizing behaviors (Glanzman & Sell, 2013).

Because ADHD is not a separate category under IDEA, the U.S. Department of Education does not provide data on the extent to which students with ADHD participate in general education classrooms. Nonetheless, certain data are helpful to know.

In the United States, approximately 10 percent of children are identified as having ADHD (National Center for Health Statistics, 2017). The rates have increased by 42 percent between 2003 and 2011. Boys are approximately two times more likely to experience ADHD than girls. Also, elementary school–age students with ADHD are less likely to be from a diverse racial/ethnic background than from other disability categories (Morgan, Staff, Hillemeier, Farkas, & Maczuga, 2013).

Describing the Characteristics and Causes

Characteristics

EXECUTIVE FUNCTION "ADHD is far more than just a problem with attention, hyperactivity, or impulsiveness. It is a disorder of the brain's executive system—a system essential for effective functioning in school and in most other important domains of life . . ." (Barkley, 2016, p. xi). Barkley (2016) characterizes the four major executive function deficits as:

- Working memory challenges

  - Holding information in one's memory while also remembering what to do with that information to accomplish a goal
  - Attending to distractions rather than staying focused on a goal or task

- Goal-directed attention and persistence challenges

  - Determining what to do next
  - Experiencing more problems with planning for the future than with dealing with the present moment

- Inhibition challenges

  - Moving around, talking excessively, touching too much
  - Preferring immediate results rather than working hard for later results

- Problem-solving challenges

  - Generating multiple options for overcoming barriers
  - Developing an action plan to reach a solution

A common factor in these four major executive function deficits is the students' reduced capacity for self-regulation.

INTELLECTUAL FUNCTIONING The intellectual functioning of students with ADHD falls across the full spectrum of intelligence quotient (IQ) scores; the majority of students with ADHD have average intelligence (Brown, 2013). But children with ADHD have been found to have lower IQ scores than their brothers or sisters, averaging about a 7- to 10-point difference (Nigg & Barkley, 2014). In a comparison of students with ADHD and students who have normal and gifted IQs, both groups were identified at approximately the same age and had similar internalizing and externalizing behavioral challenges (Katusic et al., 2011). So, intellectual functioning is a factor, but it does not have to be as disabling as you might suspect. It certainly is not in Will Sims's case.

MyLab Education
Video Example 10.2
Learn the role of executive function in children's development from national experts. Although this video focuses on young children, the concepts you learn apply to students across the school years. What key points do you anticipate will apply to your future teaching position? https://www.youtube.com/watch?v=efCq_vHUMqs

ACADEMIC ACHIEVEMENT Although the majority of students with ADHD have typical intelligence, they, like Will, frequently have problems achieving academically.

- Students with ADHD, compared with other students, have lower academic achievement, lower grade point averages, and higher grade-retention rates (Bussing et al., 2012).
- Approximately one half of students with ADHD also have a learning disability (Nigg & Barkley, 2014).

Despite their academic challenges, each student with ADHD has a variety of strengths. Will, for example, has a strong interest in and a knack for car repair—a knack that prompts him toward automobile mechanics as a career.

BEHAVIORAL, EMOTIONAL, AND SOCIAL CHARACTERISTICS There is, however, a high degree of overlap in the categories of ADHD and emotional or behavioral disorders. For example:

- Children with ADHD are 11 times more likely than their peers without ADHD to experience oppositional defiant disorder and/or conduct disorder (Nigg & Barkley, 2014).
- Children with ADHD commonly have difficulty regulating their positive and negative emotions (Sjöwall, Roth, Lindqvist, & Thorell, 2013).
- Social challenges related to ADHD include the likelihood of having fewer close friends and more peer rejection (Rooney, 2017).

Causes

HEREDITY Multiple genes contribute to ADHD; each has a small effect, yet the additive impact of multiple genes is significant. Children are 6 to 8 times more likely to have ADHD if their parent also has ADHD (Barkley, 2016). Based on twin and sibling studies, the average estimate of genetic inheritability is 88 percent for males and 77 percent for females (Langner, Garbe, Banaschewski, & Mikolajczyk, 2013). When asked what has caused Will's ADHD, Will's mother, Leigh Ann, says that she believes heredity plays a role. She suspects that Will's father has ADHD, though he has not been formally diagnosed, and her sister (Will's aunt) was formally diagnosed with ADHD as an adult.

STRUCTURAL DIFFERENCES IN THE BRAIN Some of the brain differences between people with and without ADHD include variations in brain anatomy (significant reduction in total cerebral and cerebellar volume), variations in brain functioning (less activation in networks related to cognition, emotion, and sensorimotor functions), and neurochemical factors (dysfunction among several neurotransmitters, the chemicals that transmit signals between neurons and cells within the body) (Cortese, 2012). There is, then, a clear linkage between brain abnormalities and the reading comprehension of students with ADHD (Denckla et al., 2013).

ENVIRONMENTAL CAUSES Prenatal factors (e.g., prenatal exposure to cigarette smoke, lead, and alcohol), perinatal factors (e.g., low birth weight), and postnatal causes (e.g., environmental toxins, poor diet, low family income, and child abuse and neglect) also contribute to ADHD (Thapar, Cooper, Ayre, & Langley, et al., 2013). However, the evidence is much weaker with respect to environmental causes than heredity and structural brain differences. Environmental factors appear to interact with genetic factors rather than act as primary causes themselves. Symptoms of inattention are more strongly linked to environmental causes, whereas symptoms of hyperactivity-impulsivity are more strongly linked to biological factors (Freitag et al., 2012).

MyLab Education Self-Check 10.1

MyLab Education Application Exercise 10.1: Does Ryan Have ADHD?

Evaluating Students with Attention-Deficit Hyperactivity Disorder

Determining the Presence of ADHD

An accurate diagnosis of ADHD is difficult to establish before the child is 4 (American Psychiatric Association, 2013). Although diagnosis during preschool is possible, other students with ADHD may not be identified until they enroll in school or even until adolescence (Nigg & Barkley, 2014). Often students with ADHD encounter challenges in general education classrooms, and general education teachers may be the first people to develop concerns and initiate the referral process. As you may recall, it was Will's 4th-grade teacher who first suspected he had ADHD. School-based special education teams, pediatricians, family doctors, psychiatrists, clinical psychologists, and neurologists often provide the expert assistance—together, they exemplify partnership. See *Nondiscriminatory Evaluation Process: Students with ADHD*.

Nondiscriminatory Evaluation Process

Students with ADHD

Observation	**Teacher and parents observe:** **Predominately inattentive type:** The student makes careless mistakes, has difficulty sustaining attention, doesn't seem to be listening, fails to follow through on tasks, has difficulty organizing, often loses things, is easily distracted, or is forgetful. **Predominately hyperactive-impulsive type:** The student is often fidgety, does not remain seated when expected to be seated, runs or climbs excessively or inappropriately, has difficulty playing quietly, talks excessively, blurts out answers or comments, has difficulty taking turns, or acts as if always on the go. **Combined type:** Characteristics of both are observed.
Screening	**Assessment measures:** **Classroom work products:** Work is consistently or generally poor. The student has difficulty staying on task, so the student's work may be incomplete or completed haphazardly. **Group intelligence tests:** Tests may not reveal true ability because the student has difficulty staying on task. **Group achievement tests:** Performance may not be a true reflection of achievement because the student has difficulty staying on task. **Medical screening:** The physician does not find a physical condition that could cause inattention or hyperactivity-impulsivity. Medication may be prescribed. **Vision and hearing screening:** Results do not explain academic difficulties.
Prereferral	**Teacher implements suggestions from school-based team:** The student still experiences frustration, inattention, or hyperactivity despite reasonable curricular and behavioral accommodations.
Referral	The student should be referred to a multidisciplinary team for a complete evaluation if prereferral intervention is successful.
Nondiscriminatory evaluation procedures and standards	**Assessment measures:** **Psychological evaluation:** A psychiatrist or psychologist determines that the student meets DSM-V-TR criteria for ADHD. **Individualized intelligence test:** The student's intelligence may range from below average to gifted. **Individualized achievement test:** The student's performance on achievement tests may suggest that the student's educational performance has been adversely affected by the condition. **Behavior rating scale:** The student scores in the significant range on measures of inattention or hyperactivity-impulsivity. **Teacher observation:** The student's educational performance has been adversely affected by the condition. The behaviors have been present in more than one setting, were first observed before age 7, and have lasted for more than 6 months. **Curriculum-based assessment:** The student may be experiencing difficulty in one or more areas of the curriculum used by the local school district because the behaviors have caused the student to miss important skills. **Direct observation:** The student exhibits inattention or hyperactivity-impulsivity during the observation.
Determination	The nondiscriminatory evaluation team determines that the student has ADHD and needs special education and related services. The student's IEP team develops appropriate education options for the student.

The nondiscriminatory evaluation seeks to identify the following (Glanzman & Sell, 2013):

- ADHD symptoms as outlined in DSM-5 (American Psychiatric Association, 2013)
- Alternative conditions and factors that could cause the same symptoms

- Coexisting conditions (e.g., internalizing and externalizing behavior)
- Considerations related to medical, social, emotional, behavioral, and/or learning.

Link to http://www. pearsonclinical.com/psychology/ products/100000523/conners-3rd-edition-conners-3.html for more information about Conners 3.

Some students may need a medical evaluation to determine if they have ADHD. Under IDEA, the school district is responsible for paying for that evaluation, but parents may secure one at their own expense and require their child's educators to consider it. Frequently used evaluation tools include behavior rating scales, interviews, psychological testing, and behavioral observations (Barkley, 2015). Of these four techniques, rating scales are the most frequently used.

When conducting an initial evaluation to determine whether a student has ADHD, many psychologists use Conners 3rd edition (Conners 3). Conners 3 includes a focus on all three types of ADHD: hyperactive-impulsive, inattentive, and combined. It is available for teachers and parents to complete in long forms (20 minutes) and short forms (10 minutes) and is for students age 8 to 18. Conners 3 includes three rating scales (in long and short forms): Teacher Rating Scale, Parent Rating Scale, and Self-Report Rating Scale. The Teacher and Parent Scales are appropriate to use for students ranging in age from 6 through 18. The Self-Report Scale focuses on students age 8 through 18. The scales are available in English and Spanish. Additionally, there is an ADHD Index; the Index includes 10 items and is useful for screening children for ADHD. Other scales are useful for screening for externalizing behavior (oppositional defiant disorder, conduct disorder), learning problems, peer relations, and family relations.

Determining the Nature of Specially Designed Instruction and Services

After determining that a student has ADHD, the evaluation team must decide whether the student needs special education and related services. To make that decision, many teams use the Attention Deficit Disorders Evaluation Scale—3rd edition (ADDES-3) because it identifies interventions for students with ADHD (Demaray, Elting, & Schaefer, 2003). The ADDES-3 has three main scales:

Go to http://www.hawthorne-ed. com/ and then to ADHD in the left navigation bar. Find more information about the ADDES-3.

- Attention Deficit Disorders Evaluation Scale—3rd edition (ADDES-3)
- Early Childhood Attention Deficit Disorders Evaluation Scale
- Attention Deficit Disorders Evaluation Scale—Secondary-Age Student.

The ADDES-3 is suitable for evaluating students who are between 4 and 18 years old. It offers a home and a school version for parents and teachers, as well as a Spanish version and an intervention manual with suggested individualized education program (IEP) goals, objectives, and interventions.

Including Students with Attention-Deficit Hyperactivity Disorder

Consistent with IDEA's principle of education in the least restrictive environment and its national policy goal of full participation, Will receives most of his education in the general education classroom. There is one exception: He has one class period per day in a resource room, where he receives help on his schoolwork from a special educator. Within the general education classroom, he receives accommodations, including testing in a room by himself. Will is happy to declare that he has brought up his grades, first to a 2.9, then to a 3.0 (on a 4.0 scale), while annually reducing the types and extent of the accommodations he needs. Research-based practices make a difference for him, and for other students as well.

Figure 10.1 Percentage of Students with Other Health Impairment and ADHD in Educational Placement, 2015

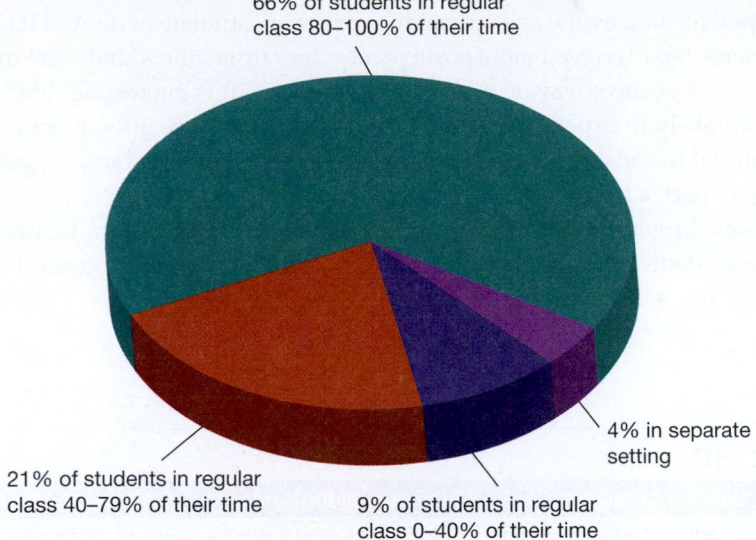

66% of students in regular class 80–100% of their time

4% in separate setting

21% of students in regular class 40–79% of their time

9% of students in regular class 0–40% of their time

SOURCE: U.S. Department of Education. (2017). *39th Annual Report to Congress on the Implementation of the Individuals with Disabilities Education Act.* Retrieved from https://www2.ed.gov/about/reports/annual/osep/2017/parts-b-c/39th-arc-for-idea.pdf/

Figure 10.1 displays the percentage of students with other health impairments according to their educational placement. Students with ADHD make up about two thirds of the students in the other health impairments category. Of all the students identified as having other health impairments, 65 percent spend 80 percent or more time in general education classrooms. IDEA's least restrictive environment (LRE) principle and educators' practice align well with students who have ADHD,

As you have learned, students with ADHD often have fewer friends and experience more peer rejection. Should you therefore assume that intervention to improve the appropriate behavior of students with ADHD will result in their social acceptance being increased? Don't answer until you read about the research.

A research study explored the differential effect of a behavioral intervention alone, as contrasted with the effect of a combined approach of behavioral intervention supplemented with a program to strengthen peer connections (Mikami et al., 2013). The behavioral intervention program consisted of all students receiving points for appropriate behavior with public acknowledgment (verbal and charts) of how many points each student received. The supplemental peer program switched the acknowledgment of points from being public to private based on the premise that students with ADHD frequently receive fewer points and therefore may be stigmatized when points are publicly acknowledged and praised. Furthermore, in the supplemental peer program, teachers:

- Developed warm relationships with all students, including those with ADHD
- Highlighted students' strengths and preferences
- Identified and communicated explicit classroom rules for social inclusion
- Deducted points for students who ostracized other classmates
- Used collaborative instructional strategies
- Encouraged students with similar interests to share those with each other

The purpose of all these activities was to strengthen social bonds between and among all students, with a special emphasis on those with ADHD. You might fairly conclude that LRE and full inclusion are compatible with research-based practice.

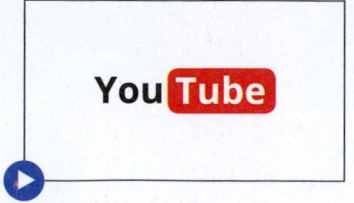

MyLab Education
Video Example 10.3
A 5th-grade teacher provides numerous suggestions for including students with ADHD in his classroom. Which two suggestions stand out for you? https://www.youtube.com/watch?v=Dd62-eL0JYI

So, what do you predict about the results of this study in comparing a behavioral intervention alone with behavioral intervention supplemented by a peer acceptance program? The behavioral program was effective in decreasing problem behavior. When it was supplemented by the peer acceptance program, students with ADHD had more mutual friendships, received more positive messages from others, and were more likely to be rated in a positive way on a social questionnaire. It is interesting that boys were much more likely to experience positive outcomes than were girls. Even more interesting, mutual friendships arose from the peer acceptance program, suggesting that dignity is, in part, a consequence of full participation.

Inclusion Tips for Students with ADHD provides an introduction to strategies for educating students with ADHD to achieve educational success in general education classrooms. You will learn these strategies in the following section.

Inclusion Tips for Students with ADHD

	Behavior	Social Interactions	Educational Performance	Classroom Attitudes
You Might See	The student is inattentive, withdrawn, forgetful, a daydreamer, and/or lethargic.	The student is constantly late in arriving at school and rarely turns in an assignment when it is due; the student has little conception for time.	The student's work is incomplete and full of errors.	The student's motivation is lacking. The student often lays head on the desk and falls asleep after lunch.
What You Might Be Tempted to Do	Overlook the student.	Have the student miss recess in order to catch up on classwork and previous homework.	Assign failing grades to the student.	Send frequent notes to parents about your disappointment in their child's lack of motivation.
Alternate Teacher Response	Provide Tier 2 and 3 interventions with the student to strengthen academic performance and motivation.	Set up a meeting with the student and parents to develop a time management plan; implement the same accommodations at school and home.	Break the student's larger assignment into smaller parts. Ensure the student understands instructions and adjust the length of the assignment to what is reasonable to complete in a specified time period.	Check out whether sleepiness could be tied to medication side effects by completing a rating scale and talking to the student's parents about the results.
Ways to Include Peers in the Process	Model acceptance and appreciation for the student. Then peers are more likely to do the same.	For projects, pair the student with another student who is conscientious about completing assignments on time.	Seat the student next to other students who are conscientious workers and who provide no distractions.	Be sensitive to any teasing or bullying that might occur from other students about afternoon naps and intervene immediately to curb it.

MyLab Education Self-Check 10.2
MyLab Education Application Exercise 10.2: Evaluating Ryan

Educating Students with Attention-Deficit Hyperactivity Disorder
Section 504 and Students with ADHD

It's now appropriate for us to bring you back to Chapter 1. There, you learned that one of the federal laws that benefits students with disabilities is Section 504 of the Rehabilitation Act. Under Section 504, a school may not discriminate against a student who does not meet IDEA criteria but still has, is regarded as having, or has a record of having a disability. (Take another look at Figure 1.10.) Many students with ADHD have Section 504 protection. Why? This is because their disability is not so great that they need special education, namely, specialized instruction. What they do need, however, are accommodations in general education. With that reminder, it is now time for us to discuss ADHD and the education of students with ADHD, under Section 504.

As you learned at the beginning of this chapter, the term ADHD has specific required diagnostic criteria; each criterion must be met. You are likely to have in your classes students who partially, but not fully, meet the ADHD criteria. For example, a student may meet four of the characteristics related to inattention, but not the required six. Still, these four characteristics may substantially limit one or more of the student's life activities in learning, concentrating, reading, thinking, and completing assignments (including multistep projects and homework).

We just taught you that IDEA may not apply to these students. Instead, Section 504 does. The consequence is that you may teach or otherwise support a student who does not meet the strict ADHD criteria but still needs help in school. These students are of two types: (1) students who are evaluated for ADHD and meet some, but not all, of the requirements, and (2) students who may have a physical or mental impairment that substantially limits one or more major life activities, who have a record of such impairment, and/or who are regarded as having such an impairment.

The federal Office for Civil Rights (OCR; Office for Civil Rights, 2016) issued a report interpreting Section 504 with respect to students who do not qualify under IDEA as having ADHD because they do not meet all of its criteria but still have an impairment that limits their ability to learn. OCR explained that, of more than 16,000 complaints of discrimination on the basis of disability in elementary and secondary schools during the years 2011 to 2015, approximately 11 percent alleged discrimination against students who have traits like those of ADHD but who do not meet all of the IDEA criteria for ADHD. OCR also reported that the most frequent complaints concerned faulty implementation of Section 504 for students with traits like ADHD. OCR highlighted what school districts must do for these students. You will learn about the complaints and obligations in *Into Practice Across Grade Levels: 504 Complaints and Obligations.*

Into Practice Across Grade Levels

504 Complaints and Obligations

Address life activities in addition to learning.

Complaint: A **5th-grade student** received a nondiscriminatory evaluation to determine if he had ADHD. He met four of the criteria for the hyperactive type of ADHD, but not six. The multidisciplinary evaluation team determined that he did not qualify to receive special education.

Obligation: Under Section 504, the school district must determine if the student has an impairment that substantially limits him in life activities of learning, concentrating, reading, thinking, and completing assignments (including multistep projects and homework).

Consider eligibility for 504.

Complaint: A **9th grader** consistently achieves above grade level, especially in math and science. She has received services for gifted students since early elementary school. She rarely finishes assignments during class, and she turns in homework on a haphazard basis. Her school team states that there is no duty on the part of the school to address these challenges of a student who is receiving gifted services.

Obligation: Under Section 504, her high school should evaluate her for Section 504 eligibility given her difficulty with organization and time management. She should receive accommodations and instruction in these areas.

Provide timely evaluation.

Complaint: The parents of a **1st grader** have complained that their son should be provided with a Section 504 Plan for ADHD. The school personnel insists that he will need to work through all three tiers of the multi-tiered systems of supports (MTSS) before they consider a Section 504 evaluation.

Obligation: Section 504 guidelines require that the implementation of more intensive intervention strategies and evaluation for a disability can occur simultaneously rather than sequentially. The implementation of an intervention is not a reason to postpone a Section 504 evaluation.

Recognize that evaluation can be less intensive than what IDEA requires.

Complaint: The parents of Jack, a **6th grader**, are concerned that their home life has been taken over by the need to help Jack with homework every night. They work for several hours, and he still has not completed his assignments. His parents request an evaluation in order to explore possible modifications in the amount of work assigned. The school psychologist reports that it will be at least 4 months before it will be possible to schedule a full multidisciplinary evaluation for him.

Obligation: Section 504 does not have detailed guidelines for evaluation and emphasizes that the evaluation does not

(Continued)

need to be extensive. Thus, it should be possible to conduct a less extensive evaluation at an earlier date.

Onus of responsibility for implementing 504 requirements.
Complaint: A father is very frustrated that his **11th-grade son** consistently is late in completing school work of any kind and is consequently making failing grades. He found out from a friend that the school has a responsibility to provide

instruction in time management and organization for students who have major challenges in these areas. When the father visits the principal and asks why his son has not been receiving these services, the principal responds, "Because you never asked for them."

Obligation: It is the school district's obligation to ensure that school personnel knowledgeable about the student's needs make appropriate referrals under Section 504.

Because of the frequent complaints and federal obligations identified in *Into Practice across Grade Levels: 504 Complaints and Obligations*, the U.S. Department of Education has summarized schools' obligation and students' opportunities (U.S. Department of Education, 2016, p. 29):

- With appropriate evaluation and support, many students with ADHD will qualify for advanced course placement and honors classes.

- School districts must not limit placement options under Section 504 for students with disabilities to a predetermined universe of options solely for the reason that the school district only offers certain options.

- Under Section 504, students with characteristics of ADHD are entitled to services the placement team decides are appropriate, regardless of the cost or administrative burden of those services.

- A student's Section 504 Plan should provide clear and detailed descriptions of the special education, related services, and accommodations aligned with the student's needs so that school personnel and parents clearly understand the federal requirements.

Accommodations Across Tiers

You have learned that one of the distinguishing characteristics of students with ADHD is that they have impairments in executive functioning, including working memory, goal-directed attention and persistence, inhibition, and problem solving. You also learned that a common factor in these four executive functioning challenges is self-regulation.

The good news is that executive functioning is malleable and can be improved (Zelazo, Blair, & Willoughby, 2016). Interestingly, improvement is especially likely during preschool years and during transition to adolescence. Without respect to a student's age, but certainly during preschool and transition to adolescence, you will want to incorporate instructional accommodations across all three tiers, thereby providing additional support related to executive functioning, especially during times when the students are particularly malleable. *Guidelines for Teaching: Accommodations to Enhance Executive Functioning* highlights accommodations that many teachers of students with ADHD have used with success.

A more comprehensive approach to the challenges identified in *Guidelines for Teaching: Accommodations to Enhance Executive Functioning* is a Tier 2 (group) or Tier 3 (individual) research-based instructional program for teaching organizational skills to students with ADHD. An excellent example is Homework, Organization, and Planning Skills (HOPS), which involves three skill areas:

- School material organization—skills focused on organizing one's backpack, school binder, and locker and transporting homework materials between school and home.

- Homework recording and management—skills focused on developing a habit of accurately recording homework assignments, projects, and tests in a planner.

Guidelines for Teaching

Accommodations to Enhance Executive Functioning

Enhance Attention.

- Enable students to take breaks at set intervals
- Break a long assessment into several parts and give one part only each day
- Provide seating in areas of the classroom as free of distractions as possible
- Encourage students to use mindfulness meditation (see Chapter 9)
- Have students run errands and do jobs around the classroom and school
- Arrange for students to have a standing desk and to stand while doing classwork
- Encourage students to engage in extracurricular activities characterized by physical exercise.
- Use instructional activities involving movement such as role plays and rotating from one learning center to another
- Provide seating with peers who are strong role models for paying attention

Enhance Organization.

- Use color coding for binders/notebooks according to subjects
- Provide clearly marked locations for students to store personal items such as coats, backpacks, and lunchboxes
- Encourage students to set up a study area at home where all school materials are kept
- Have parents sign homework when it is completed
- Have students complete a homework to-do list before leaving school
- Use smartphones, computers, or other tools to remember what needs to be done

- Guide students in generating options about how to get big assignments done
- Once options are generated, have students develop an action plan with tasks, resources, and timelines specified

Enhance Time Management.

- Communicate with parents about how much time homework takes and make appropriate modifications in length
- Encourage students to work for a time allotment and then to take a short break
- Delete peripheral work and ensure students focus on what is most relevant
- Have students use timers, stopwatches, smartphones, or other resources to provide clear delineation of the passage of time

Enhance Motivation.

- Provide instruction at the level of intensity necessary on school rules
- Enliven the learning of school rules through raps, music, and drama
- Pair the student with a classmate who is goal-directed during transitions
- Divide assignments into smaller portions and provide incentives for the completion of each portion
- Recognize that reinforcement will likely need to be more frequent and more immediate as compared to other students
- When teaching concepts, work to ensure that students receive information in visual, auditory, and kinesthetic ways
- Teach the student to make transitions between classrooms and other areas in the school

---

- Time management, accurate skills focused on subdividing large assignments and projects into smaller units, studying for tests, planning accurately for meeting assignment timelines, and planning evening schedules to balance school requirements and extracurricular activities. (Langberg, Epstein, Becker, Girio-Herrera, & Vaughn, 2012)

The instructional program includes sixteen 20-minute sessions that are delivered as a Tier 3 intervention to students on an individual basis. Of the 16 sessions, the first 11 focus on teaching skills; the next 5 focus on attending to problem-solving difficulties in implementing the skills, self-monitoring, and skill maintenance. Teachers provide points for skill completion at each session and then award additional points for having an organized binder, backpack, and planner at each session. Given parents' important role in supporting the skills their children are learning, the HOPS intervention involves two parent meetings. The meeting at the beginning of the program orients parents and encourages their support. The meeting at the end teaches parents about the point system and how to foster the continuous implementation of learned skills.

Is HOPS an effective intervention? In an earlier research study, parents of students (with ADHD) who received HOPS instruction reported that their children significantly improved;

MyLab Education
Video Example 10.4
In this video, focus on the perspectives of secondary students about the need and benefit of the HOPS intervention. Do you recognize any of your own characteristics or those of your classmates? Consider how learning the HOPS skills would be helpful to your future students and to yourself as a teacher intent on doing an excellent job in teaching students with ADHD. https://www.youtube.com/watch?v=nGUXbQqK2zE

Link to https://www.nasponline.org/ for a manual providing step-by-step directions for implementing the HOPS intervention and also for a parent manual. The link takes you to the National Association of School Psychologists website, where you will need to search for HOPS Interventions for Schools.

by contrast, students whose parents did not receive the intervention did not improve as much. Not only did the students improve at the end of the training, but 3 months later they were able to maintain these improvements. Additionally, students who received the intervention made small to moderate improvement in grades (Evans, Langberg, Egan, & Molitor, 2014). In the most recent study, parents reported large improvements and teachers reported moderate improvements in students' organizational and planning aspects of homework (Langberg et al., 2018). Students maintained these gains on a 6-month follow-up.

For a comprehensive review of other research-based programs specifically developed to enhance educational success for students with ADHD, we refer you to a chapter by Pfiffner and DuPaul (2015) in a book titled *Treatment of ADHD in School Settings*.

Medication as a Form of Treatment

In 2013, children and youth had over 6 million visits to a doctor, pediatrician, or psychiatrist to address ADHD issues, and 80 percent of those visits resulted in a prescription for medication (Thompson, 2017). Over two thirds of all students with ADHD took medication in 2011, and the percentage is likely higher since that time. The use of medication for students with ADHD increased by 28 percent between 2007-2011 (Visser et al., 2014).

When you teach students who are taking medicine to treat ADHD, you should be familiar with the types, effects, and side effects. There are two categories of ADHD-related medication: stimulant and non-stimulant.

Stimulant medication is the most effective and also the most frequently prescribed (American Academy of Child and Adolescent Psychiatry [AACAP] & American Psychiatric Association [APA], 2013). These drugs, including the often-used Adderall, Ritalin, and Focalin, have a long history and are safe and effective when used under medical guidance. These medications often come in the form of tablets that offer immediate-release, extended-release, and sustained-release options. The immediate-release tablet sometimes needs to be taken 2 to 3 times daily, while the extended- and sustained-release tablets can be taken once a day. In addition to tablets, stimulant medications are available in other forms, including liquid, chewable pills, capsules that can be opened and sprinkled into liquid or food, and patches.

Many students using stimulant medication experience significant decreases in hyperactivity, impulsivity, and inattention. But not all characteristics associated with ADHD are adequately addressed by these medications. The most common side effects include reduced appetite, weight loss, headaches, stomach pain, fatigue during the school day due to problems falling asleep at night, and increase in mood and anxiety challenges. In rare instances, children may slow down in their growth in height. When doses of stimulant medication are calibrated for their optimum impact, typically students with ADHD experience benefit within 30 to 90 minutes. A benefit of stimulant medication is that students can take a break from medication when they are on breaks from schools—such as at holiday times or in the summer—and thereby mitigate those undesirable side effects.

Non-stimulant medications, such as Strattera and Intuniv, have only recently been approved by the federal Food and Drug Administration. Often non-stimulants are a drug of choice for students with ADHD if stimulant medication is not effective for them or if they have complicating circumstances in addition to ADHD. In situations in which stimulant medications are partially but not fully effective, physicians may combine stimulant and non-stimulant drugs for a more successful outcome. Whereas stimulant medications typically have a rather quick impact, non-stimulant ones can take up to a couple of weeks to reach their maximum benefit. When students miss doses of non-stimulant medication, they also may experience withdrawal effects.

Regardless of which type of medication, when the match is right between a particular student and the type and dosage of medication, you can expect that the student's ADHD challenges, such as those associated with executive functioning, will decrease. Although symptoms decrease, medication does not cure ADHD, and often some characteristics persist.

You have opportunities and responsibilities when your students have ADHD and use medication. Of course, you should know which of your students has ADHD or is covered by a Section 504 plan; and you should know which of those students takes medication and, if so, the type and dosage during school hours.

You also should be a partner with the student, parents, and health-care providers by noting and even closely monitoring the effects of medication. Those physicians who prescribe ADHD medication may have rating scales that they want you, the student, and the student's parents to use to provide feedback about the student's functioning before medication starts and at regular intervals after the student has been on medication.

You should communicate with the parents of students about how you can participate in the preferred monitoring method of each student's physician. We encourage you to be an active partner with physicians, parents, and students in close monitoring of medication and its effects. If your students cannot complete the rating scale themselves, you should consider helping them to complete it, even by providing you with the information that you then can combine with your own feedback. This participation in medical management is a way for students to self-monitor and self-evaluate the impact that medication has on their performance inside and outside school. As part of the IEP process, your students can also learn to self-manage their medication, thereby increasing the likelihood that they will take their medicine as prescribed.

You can gain insight about medication by reading *My Voice: Dr. Kathleen Kyzar—Being Empathetic and Avoiding Judgment About Medication*, which is about Dr. Kyzar's own experience and the experience of her two children with medication for ADHD.

Will had an unwanted effect from the first drug he used—it tended to make him aggressive. Having now used three different medications, he has found an effective one

If the physician does not have a recommended rating scale for you to use, you can consider using the ADHD Monitoring System at www. helpforadd.com/monitor.pdf

My Voice

Dr. Kathleen Kyzar—Being Empathetic and Avoiding Judgment About Medication

In my experience as a former teacher, current teacher educator, researcher focusing on family-professional partnerships within early childhood/elementary education, and parent, one thing that concerns me about service provision related to ADHD is that people are *not qualified* to prescribe medication and are *not personally affected* by ADHD (i.e., neither they nor their immediate family members have ADHD), yet they hold judgments—favorable or unfavorable—about medication that they share with families of students who have ADHD. The people who pass judgment may be extended family members, friends, or educators, and they are often well meaning; they may have even done some research on ADHD. But, because they have not personally experienced how complicated and far-reaching the effects of inattention, hyperactivity, and impulsivity can be, their "book" learning only takes them so far. They have not felt what it is like to work harder than others to accomplish what to most seems like a simple task: reading and taking notes on a chapter excerpt, completing a few math or reading questions on a worksheet, cleaning out a desk. They have not watched their own children struggle in dealing with ADHD. They have not listened to the sobbing of their 1st-grade son, as I have, as he explained that he is "slow" at school (despite his recent identification for gifted programming) while recounting all the ways that he has been trying, but failing, to keep up with the other students.

For each precious student with ADHD, the effects are not just academic; these children are also affected emotionally by the disorder, which is, arguably, a more important consideration. I once read a quote that resonated with our family's experience: "Living with ADHD is like walking up a down escalator. You can get there eventually but the journey is exhausting" (https://www.adhdawarenessmonth.org/living-with-adhd-is-like-walking-up-a-down-escalator/). If my children with ADHD continue to feel as if they are "slower" than the other children, all the while working harder than the other children to complete tasks, the combination of these factors will wear on them over the long term. They might just want to give up. This is our family's experience with ADHD. Other families have different experiences, but one thing is constant: Parents of children with ADHD reflect on the unique effects ADHD has on their children when considering intervention options—medical and educational. These decisions are hard, and feeling judgment while making them adds an unnecessary emotional burden.

As a parent, I have felt the sting of judgment. Upon explaining to my daughter's 5th-grade teacher at our

Kathleen Kyzar

(Continued)

beginning-of-the-year conference that she has ADHD, the teacher looked down and shook her head. She said, "So many children in this school are medicated." I was taken aback because I had not even said anything about medication; I had only shared that my daughter has the diagnosis. I said, "I don't know about other kids, but I can tell you that my daughter's ADHD diagnosis is real and the effects of it on her education are very real."

How has medication for ADHD become an issue on which people who lack a personal connection to the disorder or medical qualifications believe they have a right to weigh in? It seems that children with ADHD are at risk of being stigmatized if they take medication because of issues with overmedication and that they are at risk of being stigmatized if they do not take medication because of the inattentive, hyperactive, and impulsive behaviors that manifest as a result of the disability. How can they win? And why does this phenomenon appear to be specific to ADHD? If a person has diabetes, no one judges that person for taking insulin.

I'm not advocating for or against medication. Choosing medication is personal and based on individual children's needs. Treatment decisions should be left to a family and their doctor. I'm advocating for schools to be a stigma- and judgment-free zone when it comes to the topic of medication. What you are learning in this book about treating students and families with dignity will help you accomplish this goal. Seek out training that enables you to become a good communicator, as this will help you in your interactions with families of students with ADHD. Remember that you are an educator, not a medical professional. When talking with the families of students with ADHD, offer to engage with them in shared decision making about *educational* strategies and interventions that might benefit their child. Finally, the best way to avoid judgment is to be curious: If you are genuinely curious about the experiences families of students with ADHD have, you will be less inclined to pass judgment because you will be gaining empathy and respect for their perspectives.

—Used with permission of Dr. Kathleen Kyzar

that has no undesirable side effects. Although medication can contribute to a substantial improvement in many students with ADHD, the treatment recommended as the most effective is to combine medication with research-based intervention; to teach parents how to support their child to make improvements; to support educators in their use of effective school-based interventions; and to help students improve their executive functioning, academic, and social skills.

Will Sims benefited from a partnership in which he himself was a key member; together with his mother, teachers, and others, he stood up for himself and proclaimed, in so many words: "I am worthy of the respect and dignity that I have gotten." That's self-determination coupled with dignity. Will you seek that for your students?

> **MyLab Education Self-Check 10.3**
>
> **MyLab Education Application Exercise 10.3:** What Education Plan Might Be in Place for Ryan?

Summary

Defining Attention-Deficit Hyperactivity Disorder

Under IDEA, ADHD falls under the larger category of other health impairments because of limitations in alertness that adversely affect students' educational performance. The DSM-5 identifies three subtypes of ADHD: (1) predominately inattentive, (2) predominately hyperactive-impulsive, and (3) combined. Approximately 10 percent of the student population experiences ADHD.

Describing the Characteristics and Causes

Students with ADHD have challenges related to executive functioning (working memory, goal-directed attention and persistence, inhibition, and problem solving); academic achievement; and behavioral, emotional, and social functioning. The causes of ADHD relate to a combination of genetics, structural brain differences, and environmental factors.

Evaluating Students with Attention-Deficit Hyperactivity Disorder

The nondiscriminatory process for students suspected of having ADHD addresses symptoms of the three types of ADHD as specified by DSM-5, alternative conditions that might be present, co-existing disabilities, and considerations related to the characteristics as set forth. Connors 3 is a sound measure for determining the presence of ADHD; the Attention Deficit Disorder Evaluation Scale-3 is especially helpful in planning a student's educational program.

Including Students with Attention-Deficit Hyperactivity Disorder

The majority of students with ADHD spend 80 percent or more of the time in general education classrooms.

Educating Students with Attention-Deficit Hyperactivity Disorder

Not every student who has ADHD qualifies for IDEA services, but they may qualify for Section 504 services in terms of accommodations being made for their educational needs related to learning, concentrating, reading, thinking, and completing assignments (including multi-step projects and homework). If a nondiscriminatory evaluation determines that such accommodations are necessary, these students are entitled to an appropriate special education, related services, and accommodations.

Although students with ADHD frequently have challenges associated with executive functioning, sound instruction can enable them to overcome many of these challenges. You can provide accommodations to enhance attention, organization, time management, and motivation. A research-based instructional program for teaching organizational skills is Homework, Organization, and Planning Skills (HOPS).

The majority of students with ADHD take stimulant medication. This medication produces decreases in hyperactivity, impulsivity, and inattention. You need to watch for side effects that can impact students' educational performance; these include headaches, stomachaches, fatigue (from difficulty sleeping at night), and increases in mood and anxiety problems. You can partner with the student, parents, and health-care providers in monitoring the positive and negative effects of the medication through the use of rating scales.

All three of these educational strategies—ensuring Section 504 compliance; accommodations for attention, organization, time management, and motivation; and medication—can address the challenges that students with ADHD experience. When students with ADHD have the support they need across all three tiers, they have a strong potential for educational success.

Addressing the Professional Standards

In Chapter 10, Students with Attention-Deficit Hyperactivity Disorder, we have covered the following Council for Exceptional Children (CEC) Initial Level Special Educator Preparation Standards: Chapter 10—1.0, 1.1, 1.2, 2.0, 2.2, 2.3, 3.0, 3.3, 4.0, 4.1, 4.3, 4.4, 5.0, 5.1, 5.6, 5.7, 6.0, 6.2, 7.0, 7.1, 7.2, 7.3. Refer to the Appendix for a full listing of the CEC Standards with descriptions and supporting explanations.

Chapter 11
Students with Intellectual Disability

⌄ Learning Outcomes

11.1 Explain why the assumptions from the definition of intellectual disability are important and discuss the characteristics, causes of and risk factors for intellectual disability.

11.2 Describe the processes to identify intellectual disability and compare benefits and disadvantages of intelligence testing and IQ scores to the education of students with intellectual disability.

11.3 Describe the benefits of inclusion for students with intellectual disability and discuss why embedded instruction and self-determination are important to educate students with intellectual disability.

Jawanda B. Mast

Jawanda B. Mast

Meet Rachel Mast—a Young Woman with High Expectations

Rachel sits across the table from you and begins her rapid-fire conversation, her eyes alight and her smile as broad as the nearby Missouri River. She shifts quickly from one topic to another; it is futile to take notes about the topics, much less to turn on the tape recorder. You just sit, listen, and, after a few minutes, you say, "Slow down, please. Rachel, I want to know all about you, but you've got to let me have time to take a few notes." Ignoring you, she resumes talking. Now, her mother, Jawanda, interrupts. "Rachel, let the man ask you a question, please."

What, you wonder, should you ask? About school? About life in the community? About her closest friend, whom you have just met? Start big, go to smaller, you think. "Rachel, what do you think about yourself?"

"I love my life," she declares. And then she fills in the details, rapid-fire, of course. "I love singing in the church choir, reading, acting, dancing, having sleepover parties, raising money for individuals and families impacted by Down syndrome, cheerleading, being in classes with my friends, getting an academic honors award, going to church camp, giving speeches, hanging out with my friends, talking with my senator on a trip to Washington, being on the 'welcome to school' team for the 6th graders, using my iPhone and iPad to keep myself on time and organized and to buy books, buying apps, putting off doing my homework, telling everyone that I have Down syndrome but I am just like you."

Just like you! Imagine that. Just like an 8th grader who does not have Down syndrome or any other disability. Rachel's got it right, or right enough. Consider what she likes, and you will span a wide range of the "likes" of other 8th-grade girls.

Some of the "dislikes" are also similar. "I don't like it when boys tease me. But I talk about it with my teachers and that helps. I don't understand enough about saying a boy is my friend and saying he's my boyfriend. Boys want to be my friend, not my boyfriend. Oh, I don't like studying math."

There you go again: typicality amidst difference.

Rachel shows you photographs of her with her friends at school and in theater and dance productions. You ask, "Rachel, why do you have so many friends?" She's quick to respond: "Because I am polite, friendly, kind, and loyal." You probe, "How are you loyal, Rachel?" She's quick to answer, "I help my friend remember that she cannot eat certain foods because she has a dangerous allergy."

Rachel's mother, Jawanda, and her general education teacher, Audra McClelland ("Miss Mac"), ask Rachel if she can tell more about her school, and Rachel, now busy having her afternoon snack of cheese and crackers, becomes silent.

Miss Mac confirms what Rachel has said about herself. And then she elaborates. "Rachel's never had a bad day, only some difficulty knowing that her friends don't always want to eat lunch with her but instead want to eat with other students. She sometimes gets upset about those social issues, so we say, 'Rachel, collect yourself, get over it.' She talks to herself to do just that."

What about academics, you ask Miss Mac. She answers, "Rachel does every bit of school work that every other student does, but I allow Rachel to dictate her answers rather than write them. Then she copies what I wrote, letter for letter, word for word, so she will learn how to spell. It takes time to include her in the general education curriculum; time is the big challenge. So the principal tries to put Rachel into the classes with the fewest students, and we make sure she understands what we expect of her and uses the strategies we have taught her for learning. She's intelligent—she gives comprehensive answers and details about her reading assignments. She knows what she wants, and she makes herself clear about that. She was in *Guys and Dolls* this year, but did not make the cheerleading team despite the fact that the coach made some accommodations for her. Not everyone succeeds, not even Rachel."

Jawanda adds, "I have to say I am worried about her going to high school next year. The expectations are so high, the grading so hard, the school so large, and I am tired of training another set of teachers. I've been doing that every year. It's exhausting. We have had many outstanding teachers, but every year you start over. As a mother, and every year, I have to remind many of her teachers what her IEP says about modifications, and then I usually have to help to do those. I think communication, especially at the beginning of the year, can also be a huge challenge. Some of the teachers understand about positive behavior support, or response to intervention, or universal design for learning. Some will have high expectations for Rachel; others won't. Some will take data to guide them and help Rachel make progress; others won't. Some paraprofessionals will do too much for Rachel. They don't believe her when she tells them she wants to learn independently. They don't get this idea about self-determination and accommodations. Others do. Some teachers focus on her IQ, but that's not a useful fact. Everything depends on the relationship Rachel and I have with educators, on their skills, and on Rachel's attitude, behavior, and self-determination."

Defining Intellectual Disability

The Individuals with Disabilities Education Act (IDEA) defines intellectual disability as "significantly subaverage general intellectual functioning, existing concurrently with deficits in adaptive behavior and manifested during the developmental period, that adversely affects a child's educational performance" (§300.8(c)(6)). Note these three features of the definition:

- Significant limitations in intellectual functioning
- Significant limitations in adaptive behavior as expressed in conceptual, social, and practical adaptive skills
- Origination of intellectual disability before age 18 (i.e., the developmental period).

Limitations in intelligence and adaptive behavior are not unchangeable; they are not features set in stone. That is so because the American Association on Intellectual and Developmental Disabilities (AAIDD) *Manual for Definition, Classification, and Systems of Supports* (Schalock et al., 2010) defined intellectual disability using the three-part definition, but also included five important assumptions. The premise of the assumptions is that intellectual disability is now regarded not as a never-changing limitation within a person, but rather as an outcome of the interaction between a person's capacities and the context in which the person wants to function successfully (Schalock et al., 2010).

Figure 11.1 Assumptions Regarding the Definition of Intellectual Disability and Their Application to Rachel Mast

Five Assumptions	Application to Rachel
1. Limitations in present functioning must be considered within the context of community environments typical of the individual's age, peers, and culture.	As we know, Rachel has intellectual disability. To support her cognitive needs in school, her teachers do not require her to answer every question on every test; it is enough for her to demonstrate what she has learned by answering the questions that reflect the core of a lesson. Further, her teachers do not require her to answer true-false questions but, instead, to answer multiple-choice questions. For some reason, those seem to be easier for Rachel to understand and answer. To support her in school and the community, her teachers and the staff at her theater program and church choir tell her well in advance of any action she must undertake, what they expect of her, and when they will expect her to comply. They also repeat and repeat, several times, their expectations, so that, with the advance notice and repetition, Rachel will be ready to do what she has to do when she has to do it.
2. Valid assessment considers cultural and linguistic diversity as well as differences in communication, sensory, motor, and behavioral factors.	Communication is a challenge for Rachel—not getting her thoughts together and expressing them, but doing so slowly enough that others can understand her. Jawanda has asked everyone working with Rachel to ask her to slow down and to use a special sign that tells Rachel to "speak more slowly" (put index fingers together, and then slowly separate them, indicating more time between words).
3. Within an individual, limitations often co-exist with strengths.	Rachel loves to put on make-up for her theater productions, and to be on stage. She doesn't mind mascara, but she is averse to eyeliner. So, mascara it is; forget the eyeliner. She wants to be stage center all the time, but sometimes she has to be on risers (elevated stairs/steps). She quivers about heights, so she takes the lowest step on the riser; the "blocking" of a scene is individualized for her.
4. An important purpose of describing limitations is to develop a profile of needed supports.	Rachel benefits from supports that were developed based on a knowledge of her profile of support needs. For example, her teachers and Jawanda give her advance notice (as we described above); remind her of her routine and any variations from it; help her maintain her own calendar on her iPad, so she will have a visual schedule; and rely on a paraprofessional to take notes for her in class so she can listen and pay close attention to her teacher without having to cope simultaneously with note taking.
5. With appropriate personalized supports over a sustained period, the life functioning of the person generally will improve.	With two technologies that people without disabilities use regularly, Rachel has been increasingly able to participate in general education. Those are her iPad and cell phone. Both contain calendars and note reminders that allow Rachel to stay organized. Moreover, she has learned how to cope with the lunch lines at school. She used to line up at the à-la-carte line, but it was always longer than the regular-meal line, and Rachel did not want to hurry through lunch. With just a bit of coaching, but mainly on her own, Rachel learned to use the regular line and, to keep her weight stable, avoid the treats of a sweet dessert.

SOURCE: Based on assumptions regarding the definition of intellectual disability, from Schalock, R. L., Borthwick-Duffy, S., Bradley, V., Buntinx, W. H. E., Coulter, D. L., Craig, E. M., Gomez, S. C., Lachapelle, Y., Luckasson, R., Reeve, A., Shogren, K. A., Snell, M. E., Spreat, S., Tassé, M. J., Thompson, J. R., Verdugo, M. A., Wehmeyer, M. L., & Yeager, M. H. (2010). *Intellectual disability: Diagnosis, classification and systems of support* (11th ed.). Washington, DC: American Association on Intellectual and Developmental Disabilities, Copyright 2010 by American Association on Intellectual and Developmental Disabilities.

You will understand that point by studying Figure 11.1. It lists the five assumptions of the AAIDD definition and shows how they apply to Rachel. Note that assumptions 4 and 5 call for professionals, teachers, family, and community members to understand and develop plans to support people with intellectual disability to flourish in everyday environments. **Supports** are resources and strategies that enhance how a person functions in typical environments and that promote the person's well-being, development, education, and interests (Thompson, Wehmeyer, Shogren, & Seo, 2017).

Prevalence and Incidence

It is difficult to obtain accurate **prevalence** (the total number or percentage of people with a given condition in the population at a given time) or **incidence** (the rate of newly diagnosed cases of a condition in a given time) estimates for intellectual disability. A review of all studies of the prevalence of intellectual disability between 2010 and 2015 found that these estimates ranged widely (0.05 percent to 1.55 percent of the total population) (McKenzie, Milton, Smith, & Ouellette-Kuntz, 2016).

Why do we find a range? The answer is that a lot of factors influence prevalence, including age (intellectual disability is diagnosed most frequently during school years), gender (more male than female students are diagnosed), and socioeconomic status (poverty is strongly related to intellectual disability) (Percy, Brown, & Fung, 2017). As a general rule, however, the prevalence of intellectual disability is about 1 percent of the general population; that is the conclusion of scholars who reviewed all of the studies about prevalence (McKenzie et al., 2016).

The incidence of intellectual disability is even more difficult to determine. Some conditions, like Down syndrome, can be determined at birth because the baby has medical and physical features associated with the condition. According to the World Health Organization, the incidence of Down syndrome worldwide is between 1 in 1000 and 1 in 1100 live births. In Australia, for example, the incidence is 1 in 1100 live births. In the United States, however, the Centers for Disease Control and Prevention estimates that about 1 in every 700 babies born has Down syndrome. Similar differences exist for other genetic conditions associated with intellectual disability.

The differences in such incidence figures relate to a number of factors. These include social conditions (older mothers are more likely to give birth to a child with Down syndrome, so in countries where women marry younger, the birth rates may be lower) and access to medical services (Down syndrome is identifiable through prenatal screening, so access to such medical services influences birth rates).

And, if conditions that are clearly linked to specific genetic or other medical causes show such variance in incidence, you can be certain that factors related to socioeconomic status, environment, and diet will vary even more. Poverty is associated with intellectual disability because, on average, poorer families have less access than other families to quality health care, fewer resources to plan and eat healthy meals, and greater exposure to more environmental toxins as a function of their living conditions. Indeed, two recent studies of the incidence of intellectual disability, both from Scandinavian countries, illustrate the variability (McKenzie et al., 2016). The incidences were found to be quite different: 0.62 percent versus 1.58 percent. Again, one can say that the incidence of intellectual disability is about 1 percent, approximately the average of those two figures. In a nutshell, the prevalence as well as incidence of intellectual disability is about 1 percent of the general population.

Poverty is too often correlated with disability, especially intellectual disability.

JW LTD/Photographer's Choice/Getty images

Intellectual Disability and Diversity

As you learned in Chapter 2 and Chapter 4, race plays an important role in special education. Does it also affect the incidence and prevalence of intellectual disability? Yes, it does. Black students are represented at higher percentages in the intellectual disability category than are students from any other racial or ethnic group (U.S. Department of Education, 2018).

At least three reasons explain why this is so. You should be familiar with them, given what you learned in Chapter 4. They are racial bias in the referral and placement process, low expectations, and cultural bias in the assessment process. In addition, there is reason to believe that Black students labeled as having intellectual disability benefit less from the special education services they receive than do their White peers. The evidence reveals that the growth trajectories of Black students with a learning disability or intellectual disability label were less positive than for White students with the same labels (Graves & Ye, 2017). That finding calls into question whether Black students are receiving equal treatment and high-quality instruction once they begin receiving special education services, as you read about in Chapter 2.

These data raise two questions. Does IDEA's goal of equal opportunity mean the same for Black students as for other students? In theory, yes, it does mean the same; in fact, it is doubtful. Will the *Endrew F.* decision make a difference for Black students as much as it might for other students? The answers to these questions depend in large part on new educators, such as yourself.

Describing the Characteristics and Causes

Characteristics

We have already taught you that two major characteristics of intellectual disability are limitations in intellectual functioning and limitations in adaptive behavior (Schalock et al., 2010). The third part of the three-part definition states simply that the disability emerges before the age of 18. This is because intellectual disability is associated with child development and from causes associated with development. It's time to consider the first two characteristics.

LIMITATIONS IN INTELLECTUAL FUNCTIONING Intelligence refers to a person's general mental capability for solving problems, paying attention to relevant information, thinking abstractly, remembering important information and skills, learning from everyday experiences, and generalizing knowledge from one setting to another. Psychologists measure a student's intelligence by administering intelligence tests, as you learned in Chapter 4.

Most major intelligence tests are normed with a mean score of 100 and **standard deviations** of 15 points. A standard deviation is a way to determine how much a particular score differs from the average. Among the general population, 95 percent of people have intelligence quotient (IQ) scores that fall between two standard deviations below and two standard deviations above the mean (i.e., IQ scores from 70 to 130). One standard deviation is 15 points. Students with intellectual disability have an IQ score approximately two standard deviations below the mean—namely, an IQ of around 70 or below. Approximately 85 percent of students with intellectual disability have an IQ ranging from 50–55 to 70. Students who have a lower IQ typically have greater needs for support to function successfully at school and in other settings (Schalock et al., 2010; Thompson et al., 2017).

Rachel has had an IQ test. When asked what Rachel's IQ score is, Jawanda, her mother, says, rather more forcefully than not, "I don't know. I don't pay any attention to it!" She pauses and then admits she does indeed know, but she repeats that she does not pay any attention to it. The score matters a lot. So does a teacher's support.

Rachel's score means she has intellectual disability. But her intelligence is obvious and blossoms with support. Rachel's teacher, Miss Mac, requires Rachel to do every assignment that every other student must do, believing that Rachel can learn what other students can learn but needs support to express what she knows. One support? Rachel dictates her answers to Miss Mac.

Rachel and Miss Mac are good examples of a key point: Regardless of their IQ score, students with intellectual disability often have support needs in three areas related to intellectual functioning: memory, generalization, and motivation.

Memory. People with intellectual disability often have impairments in memory; specifically, they have impairments in three types of memory: short-term, long-term, and working memory (Vicari, Costanzo, & Menghini, 2016). **Short-term memory** refers to the ability to recall information that has been stored for a few seconds to a few hours, such as the step-by-step instructions teachers give their students. **Long-term memory** refers to the ability to recall larger quantities of information for an extended period of time, including unlimited duration. **Working memory** refers to the ability to use information that has been retained to carry out a task.

Not surprisingly, these impairments create difficulties in reading, math, and other academic areas (Copeland & Keefe, 2017; Dekker, Ziermans, & Swaab, 2016). You should be encouraged to know, however, that memory training enhances memory skills (Bennett, Holmes, & Buckley, 2013). It's a research-based practice that helps ensure your students' progress inside and outside school; it aids their inclusion in several environments.

Generalization. Generalization refers to the ability to transfer knowledge or behavior learned for one task to another task (for example, identifying the main idea of a paragraph in a novel and in a history textbook) and to make that transfer across different settings or environments (for example, knowing how to add dollars and cents in the classroom and at the movie theater). People with intellectual disability often have difficulty generalizing skills they learn in school to home and community settings.

That is so because the cues, expectations, people, and environmental arrangements of one setting are usually very different from those factors in other settings. As the AAIDD definition makes clear, environments influence capacities. And, your high expectations for your students can change their environments and their progress inside and outside school.

Motivation. No single profile of motivation applies to all people with intellectual disability, any more than any single profile applies to all people without intellectual disability. But students with intellectual disability are often more externally oriented than their peers (Shogren, Toste, Mahal, & Wehmeyer, 2017). Many tend to wait for other people to prompt them before acting, and they believe that they have little control over outcomes in their day-to-day lives. That helps explain why they can be less hopeful about the future than, for example, their peers with learning disabilities or peers without disabilities (Wehmeyer & Shogren, 2018).

As a teacher, you can promote student motivation, especially in partnership with a student's parents. For example, Rachel wanted to be on the cheerleading squad of her middle school. Jawanda met with the squad's coach and an assistant principal of Rachel's school to explore how Rachel might participate. The competition for membership was fierce; even with some accommodations for movements the cheerleaders must make, Rachel was not invited to join the squad. That disappointed her and Jawanda, but they moved on to secure Rachel membership in the school's drama club and performances in its two most recent shows. Rachel understands she will not get everything she wants, and she wants a lot, but she also understands that there is much she will achieve, and she has the determination to achieve as much as she can. It is not correct to say that Rachel is externally motivated and nothing more. Of course, external motivation is part of her life, but so, too, is her inherent desire, her self-determination.

LIMITATIONS IN ADAPTIVE BEHAVIOR   **Adaptive behavior** refers to the conceptual, social, and practical skills that people learn and perform to function in everyday life (Schalock et al., 2010). Adaptive behavior has three domains:

- Conceptual skills include language (receptive and expressive), reading and writing, money concepts, and self-direction.
- Social skills include responsibility, self-esteem, gullibility, and compliance with rules.
- Practical skills include activities of daily living, occupational skills, and maintenance of safe environments.

Adaptive behavior, a characteristic of intellectual disability, includes the practical skill of knowing how to use money. Here, a student and her teacher practice buying, paying, and receiving change. The student is learning a skill that will help her live independently in her community.

Robin Nelson/PhotoEdit, Inc.

You learned some information about adaptive behavior in Chapter 4. By definition, people with intellectual disability have significant limitations in adaptive behavior. A significant limitation occurs when a student scores at least two standard deviations below the mean on (1) one of the three types of adaptive behavior: conceptual, social, and practical skills; or (2) an overall score on a standardized measure that includes conceptual, social, and practical skills (Schalock et al., 2010).

Students' adaptive behavior relates to contextual considerations, such as their culture, environment, and age (Tassé, 2017). The causes of their significant limitations may include not knowing how to perform a skill, not knowing when to perform a skill, and motivational factors that influence whether skills are performed. Rachel's adaptive skills are impressive at the middle school level. The chances are they will remain impressive as she moves into high school and then adulthood. That certainly is a reasonable, not too-high, expectation.

Causes

There is no single cause of intellectual disability. In fact, researchers have identified a number of different risk factors that contribute to the occurrence of intellectual disability. The timing of these risk factors also makes a difference, in both the occurrence and extent of intellectual impairment. However, even though risk factors have been identified, the exact cause of intellectual disability can be difficult to determine. A cause can be pinpointed for less than half of the students identified with less intensive support needs and for about three fourths of the students with extensive support needs (Shapiro & Batshaw, 2013).

TIMING   Timing refers to when the causal factors occurred and whether these factors affected the parents of the child with intellectual disability, only the child with intellectual disability, or both:

- Prenatal (before birth, such as chromosomal disorders and disorders of brain formation—in Rachel's case, a prenatal chromosomal disorder: the extra chromosome that causes Down syndrome)
- Perinatal (during the birth process, such as prematurity and birth injury)
- Postnatal (after birth, such as brain injury and infections).

The vast majority of people with mild disability have a postnatal cause, and the vast majority of people with severe disability have a prenatal cause (Shapiro & Batshaw, 2013).

RISK FACTORS   Four main risk factors can cause intellectual disability (Schalock et al., 2010):

- Biomedical factors relate to biological processes, such as genetic disorders and nutrition.

- Social factors relate to social and family interaction, such as stimulation and adult responsiveness.
- Behavioral factors relate to potentially causal behaviors, such as dangerous activities and maternal substance abuse.
- Educational factors relate to the availability of educational supports that promote development of adaptive skills.

BIOMEDICAL CAUSES   Biomedical causes typically originate prenatally (Shapiro & Batshaw, 2013). An example of a biomedical cause is a chromosomal disorder that occurs at or soon after conception. When the egg and sperm unite during conception, they bring together genes from the mother and the father. These genes determine the personal characteristics of the developing embryo and are found on threadlike structures called chromosomes. Chromosomes direct each cell's activity.

Humans have 23 pairs of chromosomes in each cell, with one chromosome in each pair coming from the mother and one from the father. A chromosomal disorder occurs when a parent contributes either too much genetic material (an extra chromosome is added) or too little (all or part of a chromosome is missing). The most common autosomal chromosomal disorder is Down syndrome, which typically occurs when there is an extra 21st chromosome (Esbensen & MacLean, 2017). A person with Down syndrome has 47 individual chromosomes rather than 46. Rachel has Down syndrome; the cause of her disability is biological, and it occurred during the prenatal period. You can check out a video on students with Down syndrome to get a better understanding of the condition.

MyLab Education
Video Example 11.1
In this video you will learn about children with Down syndrome. What do you know about the biology of Down syndrome?

My Voice

Sarah Carlson

I come from a house of all girls. There are three of us in total. Despite having the same parents and growing up in the same household, my sisters and I are quite different. I am every bit the oldest child. I organize and take charge of situations to make sure things get done. Emily, the baby of the family, has bright red hair. Quick-witted and sarcastic, Emily keeps our whole family laughing. Alison, the middle child, is just under 5 feet tall and is always wearing a pair of bright-framed eyeglasses. Alison is thoughtful and caring, much more so than Emily and I. We readily admit this fact. Alison also has Down syndrome.

While you might think that Down syndrome is what sets Alison apart, I can tell you this isn't true. As mentioned before, that would be her thoughtfulness. Really, though, Alison is more like us than not. Alison has strengths and interests. Her biggest strength is her emotional awareness. She always seems to know when someone in our family is upset or sad. Alison also loves celebrations! She dutifully tracks important dates, commemorating birthdays and anniversaries with elaborate countdowns. Despite being a shy person, Alison loves to perform. Whether dancing or acting in a play, Alison turns into a whole different person when she is on stage. Alison also loves to bake. Chocolate chip cookies are her specialty. Alison sets her own goals. For the past 5 years, Alison has been in a swimming club. She has been working toward promotion to the Level 2 Swim Team. This past month, Alison video messaged my husband and me to let us know she had met her goal. "Guys—you

know how the pool has the deep end? I SWAM IN THE DEEP END OF THE POOL TODAY!"

Although Down syndrome doesn't change the fact that Alison has strengths, interests, and goals, it does influence the supports she needs. For example, Alison isn't a strong reader. The traditional recipe card isn't accessible to her. As a result, she uses a picture recipe card to bake her signature chocolate chip cookies. Also, Alison needs to practice her dance routines and play lines more than others to make sure she is prepared for her performances. So, she practices at home using a video recording made by her instructors. To be successful and independent, Alison tends to require more supports than other people. I must note that Alison needs no supports to remember important dates. She does so without the aid of a calendar or reminders.

The most significant impact that Down syndrome has on Alison's life is the impact that it has on others. People see Alison's short stature and almond eyes, they hear her speech, and they make assumptions. They make assumptions about who Alison is. And, they make assumptions about what she can and can't do. These assumptions are problematic, as they influence people's expectations of Alison and the opportunities they provide her. If you have a student like Alison in your class, I hope you'll remember my sister. I hope you'll remember that disability is just one part of your student. More importantly, I hope you'll remember to consider how your student's disability is influencing you.

—Reproduced with permission of Sarah Carlson

We caution you: Do not dwell too much on the condition that caused the intellectual impairment at the expense of getting to know the person.

In *My Voice: Sarah Carlson*, Sarah shares her perspectives about the important impact of her sister with Down syndrome on her life and that of her family.

Other biomedical risk factors are more health related, specifically to the health of the mother and, thus, the developing fetus. Some maternal infections can be associated with intellectual disability, including cytomegalovirus and rubella. A recent example of such a biomedical factor is the Zika virus, which is transmitted through mosquito bites and, if a mother is bitten during certain periods of fetal development, may result in microcephaly (small head size) and intellectual disability (Percy, Machalek, Brown, Pasquali, & Fung, 2017). Maternal exposure to alcohol and drugs during pregnancy may also negatively affect the child's development and result in intellectual disability. Fetal alcohol syndrome (FAS), caused by exposure of the developing fetus to alcohol in utero, is the most common cause of intellectual disability in the United States (McClain, Kodituwakku, & Kodituwakku, 2017).

SOCIAL, BEHAVIORAL, AND EDUCATIONAL CAUSES Social, behavioral, and educational risk factors interact with each other and with biomedical risk factors to influence whether intellectual disability exists and, if so, the extent of intellectual impairment. For example, a study of the prevalence and causes of intellectual disability in a cohort of more than 4250 children born in 2004 found that, of children with intellectual disability diagnosed by age four, 44 percent of the cases were caused by environmental factors and another 13 percent of the cases could not have a cause identified (Karam et al., 2016). As we taught you earlier in this chapter, social, behavioral, and educational risk factors influence whether a child has intellectual disability; specifically, poverty during childhood is associated with additional risk factors, such as limited access to health care, inadequate diet and nutrition, and unequal access to high-quality child care and education opportunities (Percy, Brown et al., 2017). Other social, behavioral, and educational risk factors include parental education level (Shapiro & Batshaw, 2013), exposure to environmental toxins such as lead, and social isolation and high levels of familial stress (Percy, Machalek et al., 2017). Diversity plays its pernicious role. That is a point of Chapter 2; it is a point of this chapter as well.

MyLab Education **Self-Check 11.1**

MyLab Education **Application Exercise 11.1:** Assumptions About Intellectual Disability

---

Evaluating Students with Intellectual Disability

Determining the Presence of Intellectual Disability

To determine whether a student has intellectual disability, professionals evaluate the student's intellectual functioning and adaptive behavior; you will recall that these are the two, of three, major characteristics of intellectual disability (Schalock et al., 2010). The evaluation process includes observation, screening, and the IDEA nondiscriminatory evaluation process, depicted in *Nondiscriminatory Evaluation Process: Students with Intellectual Disability*.

NONDISCRIMINATORY EVALUATION PROCESS Evaluators use intelligence tests to assess intellectual functioning, whose results, Jawanda declares about Rachel, do not by any means determine what Rachel's life is or will be. Progress in school and high expectations play important roles.

Evaluators must also assess a student's adaptive behavior. They need to know whether students have conceptual, social, and practical adaptive skills that are appropriate to their age and environments and typical of their community. A new adaptive behavior measure, *The Diagnostic Adaptive Behavior Scale* (DABS) (Tassé, 2017; Tassé et al., 2016), provides a comprehensive, standardized process to assess adaptive behavior.

Nondiscriminatory Evaluation Process
Students with Intellectual Disability

Observation	**Medical personnel observe:** The child does not attain appropriate developmental milestones or has characteristics of a particular syndrome associated with intellectual disability. **Teacher and parents observe:** The student (1) does not learn as quickly as peers, (2) has difficulty retaining and generalizing learned skills, (3) has low motivation, and (4) has more limitations in adaptive behaviors than do peers in the general education classroom.
Screening	**Assessment measures:** **Medical screening:** The student may be identified through a physician's use of various tests before the child enters school. **Classroom work products:** The student has difficulty in academic areas in the general education classroom; reading comprehension and mathematical reasoning are limited.
Prereferral	**Teacher implements suggestions from school-based team:** The student still performs poorly in academics or continues to manifest limitations in adaptive behavior despite interventions. (If the student has been identified before entering school, this step is omitted).
Referral	If, in spite of interventions, the student still performs poorly in academics or continues to manifest limitations in adaptive behavior despite interventions, the student is referred to a multidisciplinary team.
Nondiscriminatory evaluation procedures and standards	**Assessment measures:** **Individualized intelligence test:** The student has significantly subaverage intellectual functioning (bottom 2 to 3 percent of population) with IQ standard score of 70 or below. The nondiscriminatory evaluation team makes sure the test is not culturally biased. **Adaptive behavior scales:** The student scores significantly below average in two or more adaptive skills domains, indicating deficits in skill areas such as communication, home living, self-direction, and leisure. **Anecdotal records:** The student's learning problems cannot be explained by cultural or linguistic differences. **Curriculum-based assessment:** The student experiences difficulty in making progress in the general education curriculum used by the local school district. **Direct observation:** The student experiences difficulty or frustration in the general education classroom.
Determination	The nondiscriminatory evaluation team determines that the student has intellectual disability and needs special education and related services. The student's IEP team develops appropriate education options for the student.

The DABS is based on the three components of conceptual, social, and practical skills you learned about previously in this chapter. It determines a cutoff point for significant limitations in adaptive behavior that is approximately two standard deviations below the mean of individuals without intellectual disability.

The DABS was normed on the general population; this means that the scholars who developed the DABS identified the range of scores in the general population and used those scores to determine significant limitations in adaptive behavior. That is important because, in the past, scholars normed adaptive behavior measures only with people with impairments in adaptive skills. The significant contribution of the DABS is that it evaluates adaptive behavior based on what is typical or expected in the general population. That basis promotes inclusion and becomes a focus of education and its *Endrew F.*–based standard of progress.

Dr. Marc Tassé, who is the lead author for the DABS, talked about why this new approach to measuring adaptive behavior is important from yet another perspective:

> *The DABS was standardized using a national sample that was representative of the general population (i.e., people with and without disabilities) because this assessment must provide information regarding how the person's performance compares to same-age peers from the general population. The very nature of adaptive behavior requires that we assess the person's functioning in comparison to her/his same-age peers and if limitations are present, establish the extent and nature of these limitations as compared to the general population. Providing a reference back to the general population is a must when assessing adaptive behavior for the purpose of making a determination of intellectual disability.*

Determining the Nature of Specifically Designed Instruction and Services

In Chapter 4 you learned that IDEA requires that a student's individualized education program (IEP) must ensure that students are involved with and make progress in the general education curriculum; the IEP must also address the student's other educational needs. Accordingly, when a student is in secondary school, the student's IEP will emphasize, in part, the skills needed to be successful at work and in the community as an adult. You will learn more about community-based services later in this chapter. Remember, special education is about inclusion and full participation, not segregation.

A useful procedure for advancing a student's inclusion by determining the strengths and needs of older students and planning services and supports for them is the Transition Planning Inventory-2 (TPI-2) (Patton & Clark, 2013). It focuses on the following areas of adulthood: career choice and planning, employment knowledge and skills, further education/training, functional communication, self-determination, independent living, personal money management, community involvement and usage, leisure activities, and interpersonal relationships. Within each area, the inventory identifies the knowledge, skills, or behaviors associated with successful postsecondary outcomes.

The TPI-2 has student, home, and school versions as well as forms for documenting a student's preferences and interests—the student's self-determination—and for developing profiles and further assessment recommendations. Students, parents (or other family members or guardians), and a school representative independently complete a five-point rating scale (strong disagreement to strong agreement) for each transition-related item.

A practical guide, *Informal Assessment for Transition Planning,* instructs educators on how to use the inventory (Erickson, Clark, & Patton, 2013). Using the inventory during transition planning results in IEPs that have more transition-related goals as well as greater parental satisfaction with the IEP process (Rehfeldt, Clark, & Lee, 2012). When using the TPI-2 with students who have extensive support needs, teachers and parents varied in terms of their perspectives about students' strengths and needs related to transition (Carter, Brock, & Trainor, 2014). Encouragingly, however, they found that students with the most significant intellectual impairments have transition strengths, as well as needs.

> **MyLab Education** Self-Check 11.2
>
> **MyLab Education** Application Exercise 11.2: Intelligence Testing and Special Education Services

Including Students with Intellectual Disability

Rachel's general education teacher, Miss Mac, along with special educators and other school personnel, Rachel's mother, and, indeed, Rachel herself, have worked hard to ensure her success in the general education classroom. As you learned before, Miss Mac insists that Rachel complete the work that other students do, but she provides accommodations, such as allowing Rachel to dictate her answers (rather than write them), giving her extra time to complete assignments, and arranging for her to be in smaller classes. There are lots of strategies, many of which you've learned about in this text, that can be used to promote the inclusion of students with intellectual disability, and there are lots of examples of students with intellectual disability being successfully included in general education, like Rachel. Unfortunately, too many students with intellectual disability don't have the same opportunities as Rachel to participate in general education. Figure 11.2 illustrates where students with intellectual disability were educated (U.S. Department of Education, 2018).

Students with intellectual disability now spend more time in general education classes than in years past. That is probably because more educators are using strategies like those used by Miss Mac, Rachel's teacher. However, work still needs to be done to improve the number of students with intellectual disability who are included in general education classes. It may be that *Endrew F.* and its emphasis on progress and its complaint about students "sitting idly" while waiting to "drop out" will make a difference. It can. It's up to you.

Fifty percent of students with intellectual disability spend less than 40 percent of their day in general education classes, and only about 17 percent spend most of their

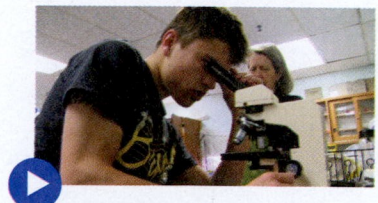

MyLab Education
Video Example 11.2
In this video you will learn about Garrett and some of the accommodations that assist him to be successful in school. What are some of the benefits to Garrett of having been included in general education classrooms?

Figure 11.2 Extent of Inclusion for Students with Intellectual Disability

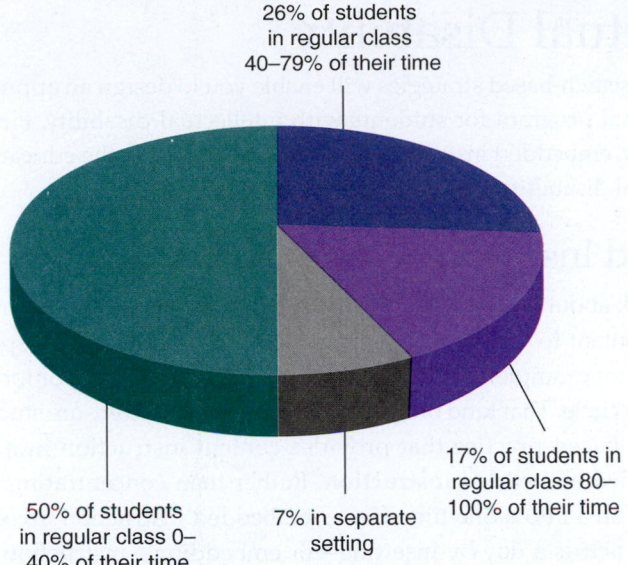

26% of students
in regular class
40–79% of their time

17% of students in
regular class 80–
100% of their time

7% in separate
setting

50% of students
in regular class 0–
40% of their time

SOURCE: U.S. Department of Education. (2017). *39th Annual Report to Congress on the Implementation of the Individuals with Disabilities Education Act.* Retrieved from: https://www2.ed.gov/about/reports/annual/osep/2017/parts-b-c/39th-arc-for-idea.pdf/

day (80 percent or more) in the general education setting (U.S. Department of Education, 2018). In fact, in only one other categorical area did students spend less time in the general education classroom (multiple disabilities), and, from among all categorical areas, students with intellectual disability had the highest percentage of time spent in the general education setting 40 percent of the day or less.

As you've learned, it is hard to gain access to the general education curriculum if you're not in the general education classroom. For several reasons this remains the case, from the ongoing focus on impairment and deficits rather than strengths for students with intellectual disability to the impact of racial/ethnicity discrimination in labeling and placement (Zhang, Katsiyannis, Ju, & Roberts, 2014). The feature *Inclusion Tips for Students with Intellectual Disability* will help you to increase the number of students who are included in general education (the least restrictive environment principle and the national policy goal of full participation). The *Inclusion Tips* will also help you with *Endrew F.* and its standard of an appropriately ambitious education program.

Inclusion Tips for Students with Intellectual Disability

	Behavior	Social Interactions	Educational Performance	Classroom Attitudes
What You Might See	The student demonstrates potentially distracting behavior, such as loud laughing.	On the student's job training sites, the student feels very shy around co-workers.	The student lacks interest in and expresses boredom with class activities.	The student demonstrates learned helplessness with new activities.
What You Might Be Tempted to Do	Tell the student to stop the behavior (laughter) and be quiet or leave the room.	Tell the student that to get and keep a job the student will need to learn to interact with others on the job.	Discipline the student for lack of cooperation.	Let the student be excused from the activity.
Alternate Teacher Response	Teach skills to enable the student to self-regulate behavior. For example, teach the student to self-monitor loud laughter.	Include social skills as an important component of transition instruction.	Create opportunities for community-based instruction.	Encourage the student to identify motivational strategies that have worked in the past and incorporate them into the activity.
Ways to Include Peers in the Process	Encourage peers to ignore inappropriate behavior and praise classmates when they regulate their own behavior.	Gather information from co-workers about preferences for social interactions at work.	Include other class members as part of community-based instruction.	Pair the student with a partner who needs help in an area of the student's strength, e.g., music.

Educating Students with Intellectual Disability

A number of research-based strategies will enable you to design an appropriately ambitious educational program for students with intellectual disability. First, you'll learn about a strategy, embedded instruction, that is widely used in the education of students with intellectual disability, particularly in elementary years.

Embedded Instruction

When you think about how to structure instruction, you may have in mind instruction that delivers content to a student in a specific time period. During a specific lesson in geometry class, for example, students might be instructed on angles or formulas to calculate the area of a circle. That kind of thinking is not sufficient to ensure students' progress.

A research-based practice that provides content instruction in a different time sequence is called **embedded instruction**. Rather than concentrating instruction on a content topic area into a one-time frame, embedded instruction involves spreading instruction out across a day by inserting—or embedding—instruction into naturally occurring activities during that day. The instruction is still intensive and systematic, but instead of delivering it all at once, teachers embed such instruction at different points during the day (Kurth, Marks, & Bartz, 2017).

Embedded instruction has strong, powerful effects for students with intellectual disability, including in science (Jimenez, Browder, Spooner, & Dibiase, 2012), reading and literacy (Hudson, Browder, & Wood, 2013), mathematics (Jimenez & Staples, 2015), and social studies (Wood, Browder, & Flynn, 2015), as well as across ages, from preschool and elementary years (Williams-Diehm & Palmer, 2017) to middle and high school (Heinrich, Knight, Collins, & Spriggs, 2016).

Embedded instruction has emerged from behavioral learning theories and, specifically, from applied behavior analysis (ABA). Its critical features are the following:

- *Expected learning outcomes are clearly delineated.* Teachers develop explicit goals and objectives for the student and specific criteria for determining student progress. Embedded instruction involves instruction in naturally occurring contexts, but it is not haphazard; instead, it is planned and purposeful.

- *Instruction occurs within typical routines or activities.* Having identified goals and objectives, teachers (special and general educators partnering) do an environmental scan to see when instruction can be embedded into naturally occurring times during the day.

- *Instructional opportunities are distributed across the day in a planned, scheduled manner.* Instead of massing or grouping instruction at one time, instruction occurs throughout the day, delivered according to a pre-arranged time and schedule.

- *Instruction implements research-based instructional procedures.* A number of strategies are typically implemented during embedded instruction trials, including discrete trial training and prompting (Chapter 14).

- *Instructional decisions are data-based.* Data on the student's performance in attaining instructional goals and objectives guide the decision-making process for embedded instruction (McDonnell, Johnson, & McQuivey, 2008).

Into Practice Across Grade Levels: Effectively Implementing Embedded Instruction provides step-by-step instructions on implementing embedded instruction across classrooms and age levels.

Under embedded instruction, a student with intellectual disability may receive prompts from a peer who does not have a disability or from a teacher. Sometimes it is easier and more natural for peers to interact with a student, rather than a teacher or a paraprofessional. Peer prompting may give new meaning to inclusion and full participation.

Into Practice Across Grade Levels

Effectively Implementing Embedded Instruction

Identify the student's learning goals and objectives.
Learning goals and objectives are drawn from familiar sources: the general education curriculum and the student's unique learning needs. Know something about student performance on these goals from the present levels of performance activities and from working with the student. Collect data about specific student performance on the selected instructional goal up to this point. For example, a **3rd-grade** student might benefit from repeated trials using math skills that are being taught in the general education curriculum, while an **11th-grade** student might benefit from embedded instruction in naturally occurring social skill communication settings.

Develop an instructional distribution schedule.
Consider the naturally occurring activities that take place during the school day and across the school week and work with your colleagues in general education to do likewise. Where and when might instruction on the targeted goals and objectives take place? Embedded instruction that promotes communication initiations for a **5th grader** can occur across multiple environments, but if, for example, the focus is on reading instruction for a **1st-grade** student, specific instructional time should be allotted in the general education classroom. Figure out when and where to embed instruction by spending a week quietly observing and recording when, during the day, opportunities for instruction might be best included. After collecting a week of data, decide when and where to deliver instruction.

Collect baseline data on student performance in naturally occurring activities and contexts.
Baseline data provide information confirming the student's present level of performance in naturally occurring contexts. Use these data to examine progress over time and implement the embedded instruction program. For example, a goal to increase the money skills of a **7th-grade** student might involve observations in the cafeteria when the student pays for lunch or in the middle school student-run coffee shop where students work and make change for purchase.

Design and implement the embedded instruction program.
Determine what strategies will be used (prompting, discrete trial training, other strategies) in the instructional events, and begin to implement the program. If, for example, verbally prompting a **5th-grade** student to initiate a communication event is the first instructional strategy, begin by asking a question (e.g., Do you have something to say/ask?) or by providing the student a discrete prompt (What do you say about that?). Over time, fade the verbal prompt and provide only gestural prompts. Decide, too, when to have peers deliver prompts in social circumstances.

Collect data on student progress.
Data-based decisions require ongoing data collection. Utilize various ways to collect data on student progress, tracking either changes in the level of prompts needed or changes in the number of communication situations. If deciding that the best option for ongoing data collection is to randomly take 1 day a week, then instead of delivering the instruction to your **1st-grade** student during reading instruction, provide the student a chance to show comprehension by reading a paragraph and summarizing the key elements. Record the scores each week to track progress.

Troubleshoot problems if necessary.
If a student is not making progress, a number of reasons could explain it. Try providing different types of instruction or provide more frequent instructional events. Be certain that other factors are not limiting the student's opportunity to respond. If someone else is implementing the instruction, be sure the person is doing so according to the schedule. A **6th-grade** student who is part of a social studies cooperative learning group in which peers deliver embedded instruction and who is not progressing may need different prompts, may need the teacher to deliver the prompts, or may just need peers to do so more consistently.

SOURCES: Based on Kurth, J., Marks, S., & Bartz, J. (2017). Educating students in inclusive classrooms. In M. L. Wehmeyer & K. A. Shogren (Eds.), *Handbook of research-based practices for educating students with intellectual disability* (pp. 274–295). New York, NY: Routledge; McDonnell, J., Johnson, J. W., & McQuivey, C. (2008). *Embedded instruction for students with developmental disabilities in general education classes.* Reston, VA: Council for Exceptional Children.

The Self-Determined Learning Model of Instruction

Promoting self-determination has become an important educational focus for all students receiving special education services, especially for students with intellectual disability given their tendency to experience challenges related to motivation. As you learned in Chapter 1, **self-determination** refers to acting volitionally—that is, making or causing things to happen in your life based on your preferences, interests, values, and beliefs. Self-determined people are goal-oriented. And they achieve remarkable success because they are goal-oriented. Indeed, young people with disabilities, including students with intellectual disability, who leave high school as more self-determined young people achieve more positive employment and community-inclusion outcomes than their peers who are not self-determined (Shogren, Wehmeyer, Palmer, Rifenbark, & Little, 2015).

MyLab Education
Video Example 11.3
In this video, Garrett's father talks about the importance of having high expectations for Garrett and Garrett talks about his high expectations for himself. In what ways does Garrett benefit from these beliefs about him?

You can find the full Teacher's Guide to the Self-Determined Learning Model of Instruction at http://www.self-determination. org. Go down the page to find the link to the PDF. You can download the PDF to your computer.

One empirically validated instructional model to promote self-determination is the *Self-Determined Learning Model of Instruction* (SDLMI) (Shogren, Wehmeyer, Burke, & Palmer, 2017). The SDLMI builds on the principles of self-determination and student-directed learning and supports teachers in teaching students to teach themselves! Students who have been taught using the SDLMI have improved in self-determination, attained academic and functional goals at higher rates than their peers who have not received instruction using the model, and improved their access to the general education curriculum (Shogren, Palmer, Wehmeyer, Williams-Diehm, & Little, 2012; Wehmeyer, Shogren, Palmer, Williams-Diehm, Little, & Boulton, 2012).

The SDLMI involves three phases. In each, the teacher presents the student with a problem to solve. In Phase 1, the problem is "What is my goal?" In Phase 2, it is "What is my plan?" In Phase 3, it is "What have I learned?" The student learns to solve the problem in each phase by answering a series of four questions. Although the questions vary in each phase, each question represents one of four steps in a typical problem-solving process: (1) identify the problem, (2) identify potential solutions to the problem, (3) identify barriers to solving the problem, and (4) identify consequences of each solution. Figures 11.3, 11.4, and 11.5 show the student questions in each of the three phases.

Figure 11.3 Self-Determined Learning Model of Instruction Phase 1: Set a Goal

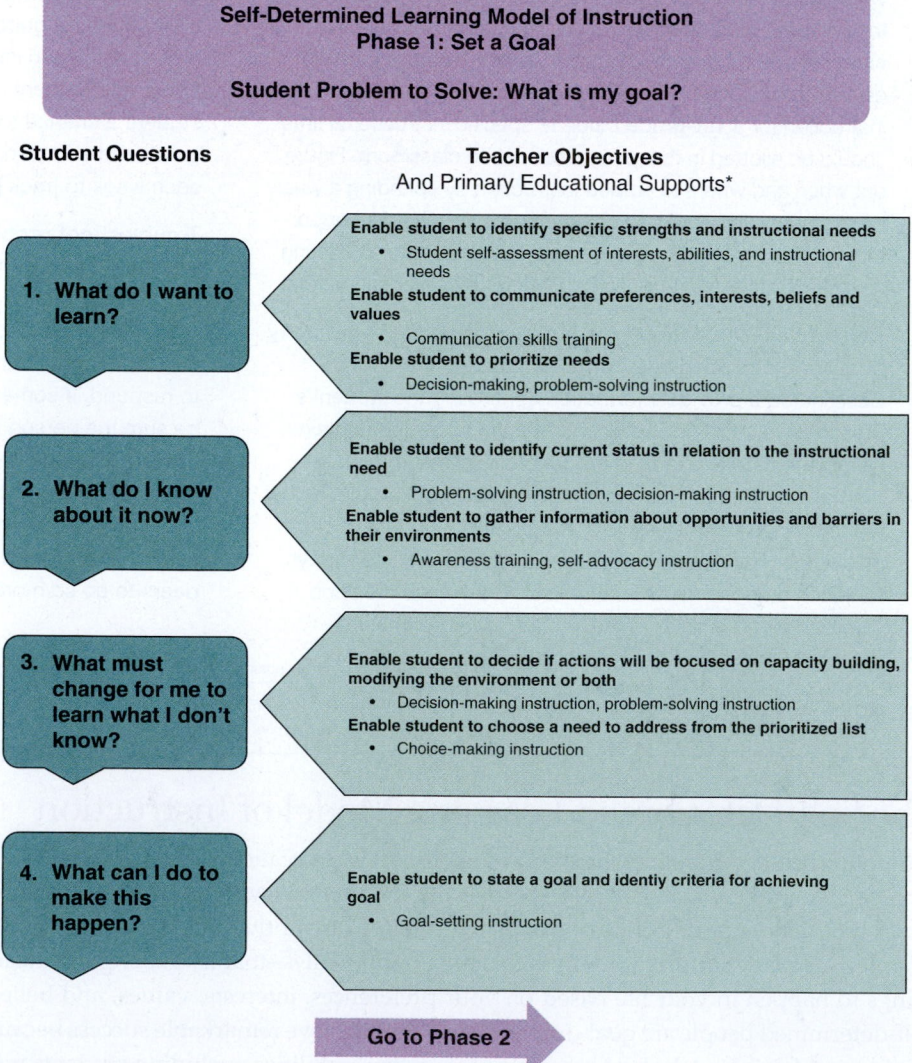

*In addition to the primary educational supports, other supports may be used as needed. See the Teacher's Guide for more information. ©2017 – Kansas University Center on Developmental Disabilities, Lawrence, KS US.

Figure 11.4 Self-Determined Learning Model of Instruction Phase 2: Take Action

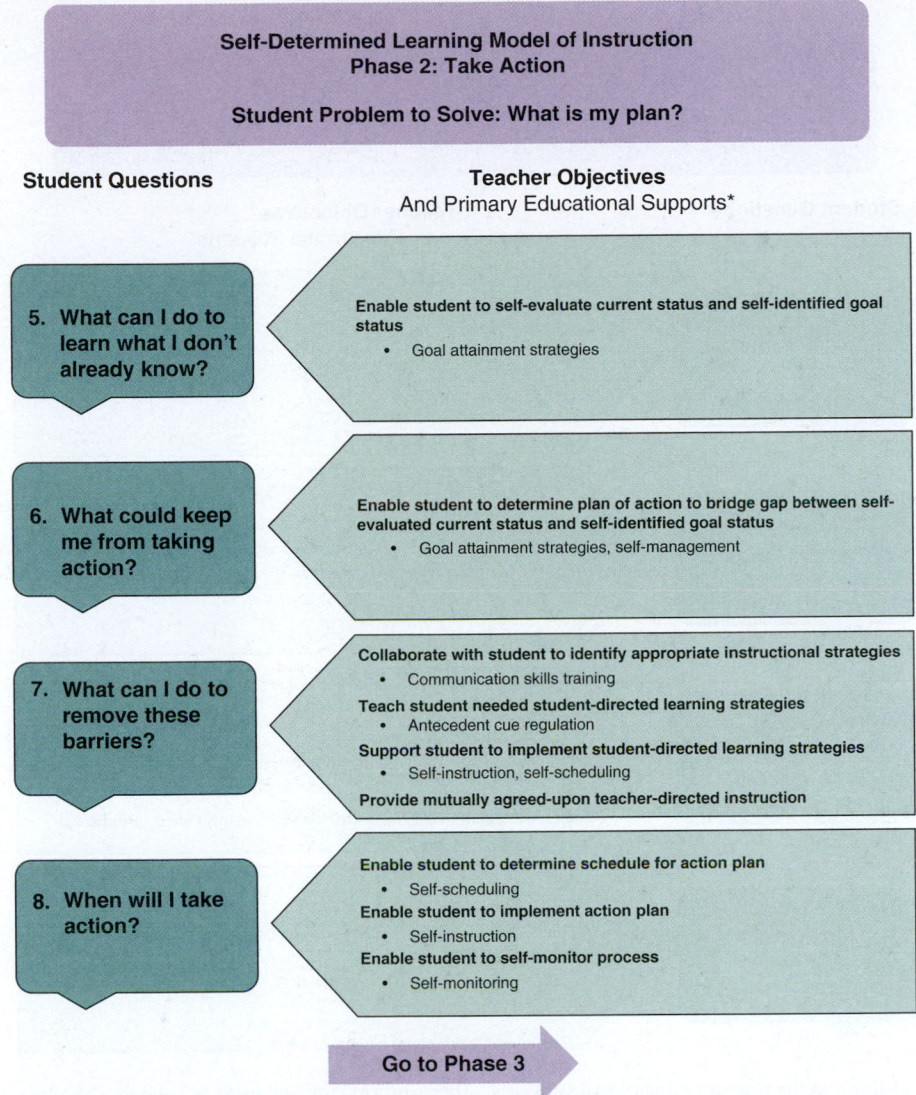

*In addition to the primary educational supports, other supports may be used as needed. © Kansas University Center on Developmental Disabilities, Lawrence, KS US.

These questions connect to a set of teacher objectives, also shown in Figures 11.3, 11.4, and 11.5. In each phase, the student is the person who makes the choices and takes actions, even as the teacher remains in charge of the teaching. Each phase includes a list of educational supports that teachers can use to enable students to direct their own learning. Some students will learn and use all 12 questions exactly as they are written. Other students will need to have the teacher reword the questions. Still others will need to have the teacher explain what the questions mean and give examples of each question.

The outcome of Phase 1 is that students set an instructional goal based on their preferences, interests, abilities, and learning needs. The outcome of Phase 2 is that they design a plan for achieving their goal and self-monitor their progress toward the goal. The outcome of Phase 3 is that they evaluate data from their self-monitoring and, if necessary, alter their action plans or change their goal. *Guidelines for Teaching: Teaching Students to Self-Direct Learning Using the Self-Determined Learning Model of Instruction (SDLMI)* provides information on how to teach your students to self-direct learning using the questions in the SDLMI.

Among the skills that students acquire using the SDLMI is self-advocacy. **Self-advocacy** involves speaking up for yourself and for others and advocating for your best interest.

MyLab Education
Video Example 11.4
In this video, Garrett runs his own IEP meeting and talks about what he likes, what he's good at, and where he has support needs. How does your perception of Garrett change when you see him in charge of his planning meeting?

Figure 11.5 Self-Determined Learning Model of Instruction Phase 3: Adjust Goal or Plan

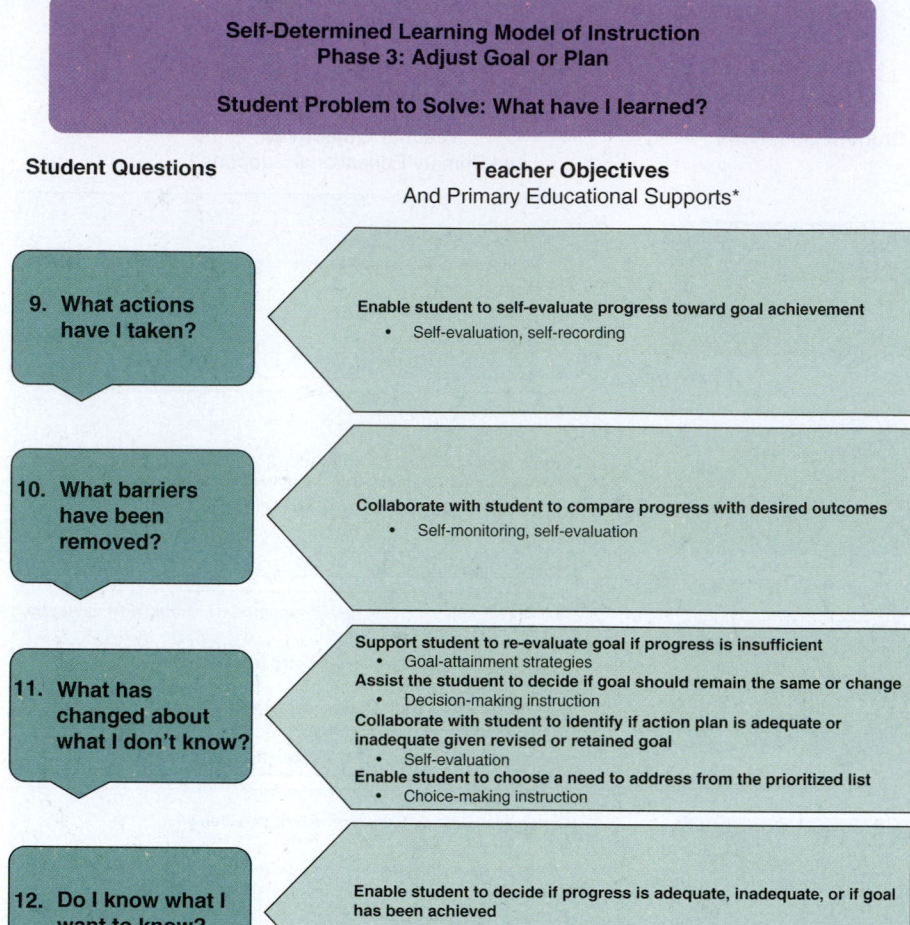

Self-Determined Learning Model of Instruction
Phase 3: Adjust Goal or Plan

Student Problem to Solve: What have I learned?

Student Questions

Teacher Objectives
And Primary Educational Supports*

9. What actions have I taken?

Enable student to self-evaluate progress toward goal achievement
• Self-evaluation, self-recording

10. What barriers have been removed?

Collaborate with student to compare progress with desired outcomes
• Self-monitoring, self-evaluation

11. What has changed about what I don't know?

Support student to re-evaluate goal if progress is insufficient
• Goal-attainment strategies
Assist the studuent to decide if goal should remain the same or change
• Decision-making instruction
Collaborate with student to identify if action plan is adequate or inadequate given revised or retained goal
• Self-evaluation
Enable student to choose a need to address from the prioritized list
• Choice-making instruction

12. Do I know what I want to know?

Enable student to decide if progress is adequate, inadequate, or if goal has been achieved
• Self-evaluation, self-reinforcement

*In addition to the primary educational supports, other supports may be used as needed. © Kansas University Center on Developmental Disabilities, Lawrence, KS US.

Guidelines for Teaching

Teaching Students to Self-Direct Learning Using the Self-Determined Learning Model of Instruction (SDLMI)

As you have learned, the SDLMI has three phases. In each phase, students answer a series of questions that enable them to solve the problem posed in that phase (What is my goal? What is my plan? What have I learned?). There is, however, an initial "phase" that involves teaching students how to work through the process. The following guidelines provide information on how you can set up instruction to ensure students' self-directed learning.

Keep the student at the center of the process.
• Support the student to answer the student's questions; don't answer them for the student.

• Engage the student in a conversation, keeping the student at the center of the process.
• Find ways to keep the student engaged.

Discuss teacher and student roles with the student.
• Be an advocate and facilitator as well as an instructor.
• Believe in the student's abilities and tell the student so.
• Support the student in the student's quest for success.
• Emphasize that self-directed learning does not mean that the student has to do everything independently, but that the student is the driver for the process.

- Emphasize that the student is an active learner and a self-advocate and is the change agent for the process.

Discuss key terms used in the SDLMI.
- Tell students that a goal is something they set to help them achieve outcomes they desire.
- Explain that problems are barriers to getting what one wants and achieving one's goals and that the SDLMI provides a problem-solving procees.
- Emphasize that goals require action plans if they are to be successful.
- Discuss the three phases and how solving the problem posed in each phase by answering the questions leads to the next phase and, eventually, meeting their goal.

Provide the supports a student will need to self-direct learning.
- Use principles of universal design for learning to support the student who has difficulty reading or communicating to answer questions.
- Use assistive technology to support the student with communication difficulties.

- When supporting the student to answer questions pertaining to Phase 2 action planning, use student-directed learning strategies whenever possible.

Have the student practice going through the questions with a topic the student chooses.
- Work with the student to modify the questions to be more understandable and to create a personal set of questions.
- Have the student practice setting a recreation and leisure goal as a way to learn the process and to restate the questions.

Emphasize the problem-solving and goal-setting process.
- Emphasize the process of setting goals and solving problems and not just the outcomes.

The key to the SLDMI is the adjustment process.
- Emphasize to students that it is in their control to change their plan or goal if they are not at first succeeding.
- Emphasize to students that, in the end, if they follow the process, they will achieve a goal that they have set and that is important to them.

SOURCE: Based on Shogren, K. A., Wehmeyer, M. L., Burke, K. M., & Palmer, S. B. (2017). *The Self-Determination Learning Model of Instruction: Teacher's Guide.* Lawrence, KS: Kansas University Center on Developmental Disabilities.

Community-based Instruction

"Learn it where you'll need to do it." That's good advice for any student with intellectual disability who experiences challenges in generalizing and adapting to community expectations. "Teach it where you want your students to practice it." That's good advice for teachers, especially those whose students struggle with memory and with generalizing skills to the community. "Where you do/teach it" is all about full participation and inclusion. How you do it is all about partnerships, as you are about to learn.

To address these issues, teachers can use community-based instruction (CBI), a technique that special education teachers have reported to be highly beneficial in increasing the likelihood that students will achieve positive postschool outcomes (Kim & Dymond, 2010). Because students with intellectual disability typically learn fewer skills than do their peers without disabilities, it is critical for them to learn functional skills that are relevant to the community and that are identified on the IEP, as discussed in Chapter 4.

Students with intellectual disability in high school and, particularly, students who are ages 18 through 21 and who are eligible to receive special education services, should receive instruction in their communities. Under IDEA, some students who need more work on transition goals or who have not graduated with a diploma are eligible for special education services through their 21st birthday. Best practice in community-based instruction includes the following:

Go to https://thinkcollege.net and learn more about postsecondary education opportunities and resources for students with intellectual disability.

> High-quality education services are provided in an age-appropriate environment that allows for social interaction and promotes community inclusion. During high school, this can be the high school campus. But because the high school is no longer an age-appropriate environment for students ages 18 through 21, educational supports should be provided in environments that are age-appropriate and promote interaction with same-age peers, such as a community

or a junior college. In fact, there is a growing network of 2- and 4-year colleges and universities that provide postsecondary education for students with intellectual disability (Grigal & Hart, 2010).

High-quality educational services are ecologically valid and community-based. As students grow into adulthood, they should receive more of their instruction in community-based settings that approximate the environments in which they might live, work, learn, or play as adults.

High-quality transition services are results-oriented. IDEA requires transition services, which as you learned in Chapter 4 must be considered by at least the student's 16th birthday, to be results-oriented, especially with respect to employment, independent living, postsecondary education, and community participation. Transition programs are effective when students obtain competitive work, are integrated into and participate in their community, live where they prefer with needed supports, and engage in a full array of leisure and recreation activities.

Academic instruction in quality programs is functional and focused on outcomes. Students continue to need academic instruction, so educators must teach academic and functional skills in inclusive settings, such as community and junior colleges.

Quality services emphasize person-centered planning and active family involvement. Education leads to employment when families and community leaders, not just the school team, are involved.

Adult service providers actively participate in planning and implementing quality services. IDEA requires interagency collaboration in transition planning, especially with agencies that serve adults with and without disabilities and community businesses where students may someday work or become customers.

Quality transition services implement best practices. Among the best practices are job shadowing, job sampling, and leisure training.

Community-based instruction is most effective when founded on an ecological inventory, which was introduced in Chapter 4. To conduct such an inventory, you and your teacher colleagues should:

1. Select the instructional area (e.g., vocational, recreation-leisure, independent living)
2. Identify current and future environments where the student needs to learn skills to succeed
3. Prioritize the need for instruction in specific subenvironments in each environment
4. Identify activities within each subenvironment
5. Task-analyze the highest-priority activities.

For example, if a student wants to work with animals, the ecological inventory should identify a specific environment (e.g., pet store) and subenvironments within that environment (e.g., stock room, checkout counter, and animal cages). Then teachers should give priority to the subenvironments in which the student will most likely work; identify tasks within those subenvironments (e.g., cleaning cages, feeding animals, cleaning windows); and conduct a task analysis to use in teaching each task.

Like any other type of instruction, community-based instruction can be heavily teacher-directed, or it can become heavily student-directed. Given the importance of self-determination for successful outcomes for students with intellectual disability, consider these guidelines:

Goal setting and instructional planning should be student-directed. Implementing student-directed learning strategies, which you will learn more about in Chapter 12, and the SDLMI (Self-Determined Learning Model of Instruction) can ensure that students have a meaningful voice in planning for their future.

Instructional goals should be based on student preferences, interests, and strengths. The rule of thumb is that students should not see any difference between their final day of school and the first day of the rest of their lives. That outcome can be achieved when students learn skills in environments in which they will work or live. Obviously, if the student's preferences, interests, and strengths do not significantly influence teachers' decisions, students are unlikely to use the skills they have learned.

Job development should begin with the student. Although high-quality transition programs focus on more than employment, employment affects the student's life in a great many ways. Using a student-directed approach, job development begins with student preferences and interests.

The challenge comes in aligning these community-based instructional approaches with the IDEA principle of least restrictive environment and the policy goal of full participation. For some helpful suggestions, see *Into Practice Across Grade Levels: Strategies for Ensuring Success in Community-based Instruction.* If students with disabilities are in the community but not at school, how can they also be included in the general education curriculum with students who do not have disabilities? The answer is that it depends on educators. At some schools, teachers are demonstrating how to make community-based learning an important part of the curriculum for all students. They are showing that community-based instruction is good for all students, not just students with intellectual disability.

Into Practice Across Grade Levels

Strategies for Ensuring Success in Community-based Instruction

Ensure that planning for community-based instruction adheres to the Principle of Ultimate Functioning.

- Focus on instruction in ecologically valid, naturally occurring environments; the ultimate environment in which the student is to function.
- Generalize learning to real settings to help alleviate student difficulty.

Examples: For a **3rd-grade** student, the school itself is an ultimate environment, because 3rd grade leads to 4th and then higher grades, allowing less need for community-based instruction (CBI). For an **11th-grade** student learning job skills related to food preparation, however, it may be critical that the student learn those skills in a restaurant and not in the school.

Maximize a student's participation by partial participation.

- Set up activities for students that contribute to the quality of their life to the maximum degree possible.
- Ensure access to an environment that allows students to function independently and learn skills they are able to acquire even if they are unable to acquire all of them.

Example: A **4th-grade** student may not be able to perform every step in solving a problem in science class, but it's likely that task can be broken into steps and the student can perform some of the steps and get support to do others.

Determine how much time will be spent in the community and how much time will be spent in typical school settings.

- Set up time for students to spend in community-based learning, recognizing that student needs vary by the student's age, their instructional needs, and their competing learning needs.
- Engage students who get closer to graduation to participate in activities with more functional content (and CBI).

Examples: By the time a student with intellectual disability is in **12th grade**, that student may benefit from spending more time in the community, while a **7th-grade** student may need less instructional time outside school.

Identify environments that students currently access and that they will need to access in the future.

- Choose natural environments, settings in which students generally use the skills being taught and places that are frequented by peers without disabilities.

Examples: For a **1st-grade** student, that is primary school and home. For a **10th-grade** student, however, myriad environments may become a target for instruction, from grocery stores to movie theaters to job sites to restaurants as part of the student's day (while, of course, the student is being educated in general education settings for academic content as needed).

(Continued)

Determine when students with disabilities are learning in the community and align community-based instruction with those times.

- Plan for ongoing, systematic instruction in ecologically valid settings (CBI).
- Offer opportunities, as possible, for middle school or secondary students with disabilities to learn a trade in the community by going to vocational or technical school for part of their day.
- Focus on student participation on project-based learning and community-based instruction, if/when available, to assist in removing the stigma that might be associated with CBI.

Examples: For a student who is 20 years of age and receiving **18–21 services**, because the focus of instruction is primarily on the transition to adulthood, community-based instruction can occur for the majority of the student's day in the settings that the student is most likely to frequent as a young adult. For an **8th-grade** student, however, CBI needs to be scheduled around the student's general education classrooms, and ideally when the student's classmates are engaged in project-based learning. Scheduling community-based learning for the end of a day, for example, might minimize disruption in the student's day.

Use data to determine where and what to teach in community-based instruction.

- Ensure community-based instruction is based on data-driven decisions.
- Collect information on student needs in the community by interviewing the student, parents and family members, and others; by conducting observations; and by conducting an ecological inventory.

Examples: For a **2nd-grade** student, interviewing family members about what types of things the student does outside school might be important. For a **10th-grade** student, interviewing employers in job areas in which the student expresses interest may yield more useful information than just interviewing the student or the student's family. And, of course, collect data as you implement CBI, to track student progress.

Figure out what instructional personnel will participate in community-based instruction.

- Determine who will accompany students in community-based instructional activities and who will stay at school to provide instruction there.
- Use the nature of the learning activity as a determinant for who will do what.

Examples: A vocational teacher might accompany several **11th-grade** students to a work site, while a special education teacher might be the right person to teach **3rd-grade** students how to use a library. In addition to teachers, related services personnel (speech therapist, occupational therapist, etc.) may be available to teach students in the community, or a paraprofessional can do so.

Solve the problems of transportation and funding.

- Check the district's policy with regard to public transportation, use of personal cars, or walking.
- Be creative to find transportation and funding to get to community-based learning sites (riding in teacher's car, exploring the use of district's vans, and so on).

Examples: **2nd-grade** students learning about the library might walk to a nearby library branch. A **12th-grade** student learning specific job skills might take the bus to a restaurant.

MyLab Education **Self-Check 11.3**

MyLab Education **Application Exercise 11.3:** Educating Anna

Summary

Identifying Students with Intellectual Disability

Intellectual disability involves significant limitations in intellectual functioning (determined by intelligence tests), significant limitations in adaptive behavior (determined by adaptive behavior assessments), and origination before the age of 18 years. Five assumptions of this definition are that limitations must be considered in typical, age-appropriate environments; that limitations must take into account cultural and linguistic diversity issues as well as differences in communication, sensory, motor, or behavioral factors; and that limitations co-exist with strengths, can improve over time, and should be considered as important only if they result in needed supports (like special education services). In general, the incidence as well as prevalence of intellectual disability is about 1 percent of the general population. There are, however, clear disproportionalities in who receives the intellectual disability label as a function of socioeconomic, racial/ethnicity, and/or linguistic considerations.

Describing the Characteristics and Causes

The two major characteristics of intellectual disability are limitations in intelligence and limitations in adaptive behavior. But, intelligence tests don't always capture what a person knows or is good at and often are not useful in planning for instruction. Limitations in intelligence are often reflected in difficulties with short-term, long-term, and working memory; limits in generalizing information from one task to another; and difficulty with motivation. All of these limitations, however, can improve if students receive high-quality instruction; these limitations are not static characteristics of the person. Adaptive behavior assessments provide information about conceptual skills (language, reading, writing, etc.), social skills, and practical skills.

Intellectual disability has many causes, from biological to environmental. Many biological causes occur prenatally, including common chromosomal disorders like Down syndrome. Other causes involve injury in the perinatal period (during birth, such as a lack of oxygen or prematurity). Still other causes are postnatal, occurring after birth from injury, diseases, or environmental toxins like lead in paint. Social, behavioral, and education risk factors are associated with intellectual disability, including the important impact of poverty, which often is linked with limited access to health care, poor nutrition, and substandard housing that increases the exposure to environmental toxins.

Evaluating Students with Intellectual Disability

Determining the presence of intellectual disability involves the use of intelligence tests and measures of adaptive behavior. Although intelligence tests provide some information useful for diagnosis, they do not measure how successful students can be. Adaptive behavior measures provide more useful information for instructional purposes, and can be used as part of the process of determining present levels of functional performance. The Diagnostic Adaptive Behavior Scale (DABS) is a new and highly effective measure of adaptive behavior because it has been normed with students and youth with and without disabilities.

Including Students with Intellectual Disability

Progress has been made in including students with intellectual disability in general education classrooms, but that progress has been slow. Almost half of all students with intellectual disability spend less than 40 percent of their day in general education settings. This is among the lowest levels of inclusion for all students receiving special education services. Among the reasons for such low levels of inclusion are low expectations of students with intellectual disability and the impact of racial and ethnic discrimination in labeling and placement.

Educating Students with Intellectual Disability

Embedded instruction is an instructional strategy that involves embedding instruction in naturally occurring activities throughout the day, rather than grouping or massing instruction into a single time period. There is strong evidence of the impact of embedded instruction across multiple content areas and across grades and ages. Embedded instruction typically involves the implementation of other instructional strategies, especially prompting and discrete trial training, in a distributed manner across a student's instructional day. Embedded instruction trials can be implemented by teachers, but also by other educational personnel (paraprofessionals) or by the student's peers.

Promoting self-determination has been shown to be an important instructional focus for students with intellectual disability and other disabilities. The Self-Determined Learning Model of Instruction (SDLMI) enables teachers to instruct students on how to self-direct problem solving to set goals; create action plans to achieve the goal; and monitor and evaluate progress toward the goal, modifying the action plan or goal as necessary. Students receiving instruction using the SDLMI have improved school and postschool outcomes.

Community-based instruction (CBI) involves teaching students with disabilities in typical environments in their communities. Students who are older or who have more difficulty generalizing a learned task to another context may benefit from CBI, but all students with intellectual disability should be involved in CBI, with varying times and activities differing as a function of age, proximity to graduation, and other instructional needs. Assessment to plan for CBI involves multiple sources, but particularly the ecological inventory process, which provides a systematic way to determine current environments, future environments, and critical activities and learning needs.

Addressing the Professional Standards

In Chapter 11, Students with Intellectual Disability, we have covered the following Council for Exceptional Children (CEC) Initial Level Special Educator Preparation Standards:

Chapter 11—1.0, 1.2, 2.0, 2.2, 3.2, 3.3, 4.2, 5.3, 5.4, 5.6, 6.5, 6.6, 7.2. Refer to the Appendix for a full listing of the CEC Standards with descriptions and supporting explanations.

Chapter 12
Students with Autism

⌄ Learning Outcomes

12.1 Identify changes in the definition of autism, describe the characteristics in the DSM-5 pertaining to communication and behavior, and discuss how these characteristics result in student isolation and low rates of inclusion.

12.2 Consider how positive behavior supports and student-directed learning strategies might support the inclusion of students with autism and consider how social stories might support inclusive practices.

Meet Thasya Lumingkewas—Included by Communicating and Entertaining

Now hear this!

"If you are not willing to differentiate instruction for your students, you are in the wrong profession. They're all your kids. You need to have that philosophy. You need to be willing to work hard at it. You need to know you're not always going to be perfect, but you need to have a team of people you can rely on to help you, and you should create a community where your students get to be a support for you, too, because you're all in it together."

Sounds like a commencement address at a school of education, doesn't it?

It should but it isn't.

Those are the words of Holly Prud'homme, a general education teacher at Maple Wood Elementary School, Somersworth, New Hampshire.

She's speaking specifically about Thasya, her 8-year-old student with autism whose mother is Indonesian and does not speak English.

Holly is clear that she is concerned about all students, whether or not they have a disability such as autism.

She has found inclusion to be "so incredibly powerful, not just for students with disabilities but also for just a general education classroom to have that experience together."

"I work hard to create a community where everyone feels like they want to help each other and love each other and support each other." Her students with and without disabilities, including autism, "learn how to challenge each other, how to support each other, to encourage each other to do their best. They remind each other of behavioral expectations. They include each other."

Here is where you might say, "So much for generalities. Tell me what to do." Fair enough.

MyLab Education
Vignette Video 12.1

In this video, you will meet Thasya and learn about her experiences at Maple Wood Elementary School. How did Holly and the other teachers take advantage of Thasya's strengths to individualize instruction for her?

Here's what Holly, a teacher with 10 years' experience in including students with autism and other disabilities into her general education elementary school classroom, says:

- Be passionate about teaching.
- Expect to be "frustrated and anxious." There will be days when you feel you "just don't measure up" to your expectations for yourself.
- Keep learning. Do that by "observing, interacting, going into this profession and each classroom with an open heart and open mind, knowing that the students are going to teach you as much as you will teach them."
- Go back to college to earn an advanced degree.
- Take advantage of in-service education.
- Differentiate. "Find a different way to teach to the best of a student's ability." If it means letting Thasya work under her desk, let her work there.
- Think outside the box. Use your imagination. Work hard.
- Be patient. It takes time to get results.
- Have high expectations for your students, for all of them. "Never underestimate the ability of the students you are teaching, especially those with autism. They know so much more than they let on or that we understand that they know."
- Rely on a team of professionals. Treat every member of the team as an equal to every other member.
- Use universal design for learning, so all of your students will benefit.
- Use assistive technology for those who need it, such as Thasya, who uses a word-board to communicate.
- Put the research to use in your classroom.
- Bear in mind that, if you teach your students to be together despite their differences, you are teaching them how to live in a "safe world," one where accepting and believing in other people, where an atmosphere in a community is filled with respect and empathy, is much more important than teaching them about long and short vowels.
- Most of all, remember that "we're all in it together," this business of education and this longer-term business of changing America.

How did Holly arrive at talking about changing America when her job is teaching in an elementary school in New Hampshire? This shift came about simply by asking a question regarding Thasya's future: "What do you foresee for Thasya when she graduates from secondary school?"

And how did Holly answer the question? "She's going to blow people away. I would put money on the fact that she's going to have some famous CD or be on stage somewhere famous. She'll speak through her music."

Defining Autism

The regulations that the U.S. Department of Education promulgated to implement the Individuals with Disabilities Education Act (IDEA) defines autism as a developmental disability that significantly affects verbal and nonverbal communication and social interaction, is generally evident before the age of 3, and adversely affects a student's educational performance. The regulations further provide that the following characteristics are often associated with autism: repetitive activities and stereotyped movements, resistance to change environmentally and in daily routines, and unusual responses to sensory stimulation. Thasya shows many of these behaviors.

The definition of autism has evolved since it was first described in 1943. The most recent definition was published in the *Diagnostic and Statistical Manual of Mental Disorders*—5th edition (DSM-5; American Psychiatric Association, 2013) and represents a significant change from previous editions. The earlier editions defined autism as being part of a broader group of disorders referred to as pervasive developmental disorders, which included five discrete conditions: autistic disorder, Rett syndrome, childhood disintegrative disorder, Asperger syndrome, and pervasive developmental disorder not otherwise specified. DSM-5, however, renamed this broader group of disorders as **autism spectrum disorder**. That term refers to a developmental disability resulting in and characterized by persistent impairments in social interactions and communications, and stereotyped or repetitive movements, including inflexibility in routines or patterns. **Developmental disability** refers to a condition that emerges during the developmental period, typically described as from birth to 18 years of age. Even though DSM-5 has switched the name of the condition to autism spectrum disorder, many people still refer to this condition just by the term autism. Because IDEA's regulations define "autism," we will use that term when referring to all students diagnosed with autism spectrum disorder.

Typically, students with autism are initially identified by a physician during early childhood years rather than by a school-based eligibility process. Instead of using the IDEA definition, most physicians and diagnostic clinics rely on the DSM-5 criteria. In brief, DSM-5 defines autism as comprising two domains—social-communication impairments and restrictive, repetitive behaviors and interests. These must occur during the early childhood years and must create challenges in everyday functioning.

Significantly, DSM-5 removed the **Asperger syndrome** category (Lauritsen, 2013). In the previous classification, this term referred to people who have significant challenges in social functioning but do not have significant delays in language development or intellectual functioning. Rather than continuing to use the term Asperger syndrome, these individuals will likely increasingly be referred to as having high-functioning autism.

In 2015, approximately 9.1 percent of all students ages 6 through 21 received special education services under the category of autism (U.S. Department of Education, 2018). That is compared with only 5 percent of students served under the autism category in 2008. You may have read about the increasing prevalence of autism; the increase is obvious in education.

Let's consider the prevalence of autism, since it is often a topic of discussion. You learned in Chapter 11 that prevalence refers to the total number or percentage of people with a given condition in the population at a given time. A recent study of data from the National Health Interview Study, which involves data collection on health-related issues conducted annually by the U.S. Centers for Disease Control and Prevention (CDC), found that from this large, representative national database, the prevalence of autism spectrum disorder from the period 2014–2016 was 2.47 percent of children and adolescents ages 3 to 17 years, or about 1 in every 45 children (Xu, Strathearn, Liu, & Bao, 2018). The prevalence in this study was 3.63 percent for boys and 1.25 percent for girls, which is a gender-related trend that has been consistent for years. Also, there were differences by race or ethnicity:

- Prevalence for Hispanic children and adolescents was 1.82 percent.
- Prevalence for White children and adolescents was 2.76 percent.
- Prevalence for Black children and adolescents was 2.49 percent.

The prevalence rate increased each year, from 2.24 percent in 2014 to 2.41 percent in 2015, to 2.76 percent in 2016. To illustrate the complexity in determining prevalence, you should consider that the Centers for Disease Control and Prevention estimates that

Go to https://www.psychiatry.org/patients-families/autism to learn more aobut the American Psychiatric Association resources on autism spectrum disorder.

the prevalence of autism is 1 in 68 children and adolescents in America (Christensen et al., 2016). Why are there differences? One reason may be that the National Health Interview Study surveyed parents, so that prevalence rate is based on parental report. By contrast, the CDC estimate is based on an active surveillance system of 8-year-olds in multiple states. That is to say, the CDC estimates are based on reviews of medical and school records, so it is likely that some children may be missed if they are not receiving such services.

What might you conclude about the "true" prevalence of autism? Instead of worrying about "true" prevalence, consider instead the trends and commonalities across these studies. First, it is clear that the number of boys diagnosed with autism is higher than the number of girls diagnosed with autism by between a 3:1 and a 4:1 ratio. That is, for every 1 girl diagnosed with autism, 3 or 4 males are diagnosed (Loomes, Hull, & Mandy, 2017).

Why? As is the case with many complex issues, the answers are not clear. There are, certainly, issues pertaining to biology and brain development. Studies have shown that males are more likely than females to inherit genetic mechanisms associated with autism (Tick, Bolton, Happe, Rutter, & Rijsdijk, 2015). But, a systematic analysis of multiple studies found a role for gender bias in, essentially, the underrepresentation of females in the autism category (Loomes et al., 2017). One aspect of this gender bias is that the display of characteristics used by scientists or educators to diagnose autism may differ between males and females; the different "displays" may mean that females are not adequately identified through assessment. Another reason seems to be that professionals such as teachers and physicians may believe that autism is mainly a male condition; they may be less aware of the characteristics being exhibited by females. As a teacher, you should be aware that gender bias may influence which students get support and which students do not.

In addition to gender bias, there is a history of bias in relation to autism diagnosis as a function of race and ethnicity. You saw in the National Health Interview Study data that Hispanic children and youth had much lower rates of diagnosis and that White children and youth had the highest percentage of diagnosis. In the CDC disability monitoring data, the same trends held, with White children diagnosed at higher rates than Black and Hispanic children (Christensen et al., 2016). These trends play out in schools as well, creating a potential area of underrepresentation as a function of race and ethnicity, rather than the overrepresentation as a function of race and ethnicity in the category of intellectual disability.

A study examining the representation of racially diverse students receiving special education services under the category of autism found that White students were twice as likely as Hispanic students to be identified with autism, and Black students were underrepresented (compared to White students) as well (Travers, Tincani, & Krezmien, 2013). So, school trends mirror trends in prevalence with regard to the diagnosis of autism. Once more, we need to ask why this is so.

This study's authors provide two suggestions. First, given that students of color are overidentified in categories such as intellectual disability, the underidentification in autism may reflect the fact that biases in the diagnostic process lead to students of color being labeled with intellectual disability when, perhaps, they might have otherwise been identified as having autism. Second, and importantly, it is clear that families of students of color have less access to high-quality health care and may not have access to the clinical and other medical services that often result in the early identification of autism (Travers et al., 2013). It bears repeating: As an educator, you need to be aware of the kinds of biases that lead to underrepresentation by gender or by race or ethnicity, even as you should bear in mind that a student's disability may depend also on the student's family's socioeconomic status and accompanying access to professional services.

Describing the Characteristics and Causes

Characteristics

We begin this section by addressing the two general diagnostic criteria in DSM-5—first, social-communication impairments and, second, restrictive, repetitive behaviors and interests. We will then focus on additional characteristics, including atypical language development, problem behavior, sensory and movement disorders, and differences in intellectual functioning.

SOCIAL-COMMUNICATION IMPAIRMENTS DSM-5 identifies three particular criteria that must be present as social-communication impairments before a student may be classified as having autism; Thasya shows impairments in these areas:

- Social-emotional reciprocity—taking turns in communication and throughout activities, interacting with others around shared interests, taking initiative in social situations, and sharing of affect with others

- Nonverbal communication—body language, facial expression, gestures, eye contact, and the alignment of language and nonverbal behaviors

- Maintaining relationships—adapting behavior to the expectations of particular contexts, making friends, and lacking interest and initiative in approaching peers.

These three particular criteria for social-communication impairments have been documented in research to occur consistently for people with autism and to be consistent across the lifespan (Lord & Jones, 2012) and, together, too often result in social isolation for students with autism. A recent study of friendships and social participation of adolescents with autism found that only 4 percent of participants with autism had a mutual friend, that is someone they called a friend who would also call them a friend. Not surprisingly, given this, the same study found that adolescents with autism spent very little time with friends and neighbors and did not participate in hobbies (DaWalt, Usher, Greenberg, & Mailick, 2017).

Another study using data from a large national study of transition from school to adult life, the National Longitudinal Transition Study-2 (NLTS-2), found that youth with autism in the sample were significantly less likely than their peers with other disabilities (intellectual disability, emotional behavioral disorder, or learning disability) to see friends, get calls from friends, and be invited to activities and, accordingly, were significantly more socially isolated (Orsmond, Shattuck, Cooper, Sterzing, & Anderson, 2013). In yet another study, adolescents with autism were significantly less likely to participate in their community autonomously when compared to youth with intellectual disability or youth with learning disabilities (Chou, Wehmeyer, Palmer, & Lee, 2017).

The clear message from these studies is that young people with autism are at high risk for social isolation. An equally clear message for you and other educators is that the education of students with autism involves supporting them to get and keep friends, to participate in activities in which others participate, and to become part of

DK images

Some children with autism may withdraw—or be excluded from—their peers' activities. But IDEA requires them to have opportunities to participate in extra-curricular activities, not just academic ones.

and not apart from their community. As you may recall, one of IDEA's six principles—the principle of the least restrictive environment—presumes students with autism and other disabilities will participate in the general education curriculum, that is, in the academic, extra-curricular, and other school activities that are open to students who do not have disabilities.

REPETITIVE, RESTRICTED BEHAVIORS AND INTERESTS   DSM-5 also identifies four particular criteria that must be present as repetitive, restrictive behaviors and interests before a student may be classified as having autism. Thasya shows impairments in these areas:

- Repetitive speech (**echolalia**, repeating of other people's words or phrases), motor movements (finger flicking, hand flapping), and/or interaction with objects (lining objects up)

- Excessive reliance on routines, use of verbal and nonverbal rituals, or insistence on sameness

- Highly circumscribed and fixated interests that are atypical in terms of intensity or focus (preoccupation with objects such as door locks, lights, bus schedules, or particular movies)

- Unusually excessive or limited reaction to sensory input, excessive touching or smelling of objects, fascination with spinning objects or lights, aversive response to environmental sounds.

Like all human behavior, the reasons for and causes of these behaviors are varied and often complex. Clear brain structures are associated with repetitive motor movements among people with autism (Ha, Sohn, Kim, Sim, & Cheon, 2014). Also, research has linked insistence on sameness and reliance on routines to anxiety; that is, these behaviors help the person to control feelings of anxiousness (Lidstone et al., 2014). Further research has shown that sensory-related behaviors are highly related to environments and contexts (Kirby, Boyd, Williams, Faldowski, & Baranek, 2017). Brain? Anxiety? Environment? Yes, yes, and yes. The take-home-message is that although these behaviors are grouped under an overall heading, they are, in fact, diverse behaviors that occur for and are caused by many reasons.

If the causes of these behaviors are wide-ranging, quite a bit is known about restrictive, repetitive behaviors and interests, including:

- A 30-year review of literature on children's repetitive behavior identified 25 behavioral categories, with the most frequent being rocking or swaying of the body or head; vocalizations not recognizable as words; hand flapping or waving; noncontextual words or phrases; tapping objects with body, finger, or hands; and spinning, flipping, or waving objects (Reed, Hirst, & Hyman, 2012).

- Restrictive, repetitive behaviors and interests tend to remain stable over time between the ages of 2 and 7, rather than improving (Joseph, Thurm, Farmer, & Shumway, 2013).

- Compared with the social-communication domain, restricted, repetitive behaviors and interests are more heterogeneous and contribute more to the need for families, teachers, and others to make accommodations (Lord & Jones, 2012).

Robin Nelson/PhotoEdit, Inc.

Students with autism often display stereotypical behavior, such as flapping their hands, sometimes near their bodies.

Finally, whatever the cause of these behaviors, instruction and education can improve outcomes for students with autism. For example, increases in the language (receptive and expressive) of young children are related to decreases in restrictive, repetitive behaviors (Ray-Subramanian & Weismer, 2012). Similarly, teaching students with autism the skills to engage their environment has been shown to reduce repetitive motor and sensory behaviors (Boyd, McDonough, & Bodfish, 2012).

Thasya certainly "qualifies" with respect to the behavioral characteristics of swaying, unrecognizable vocalizations, and hand flapping. What differences do those behaviors make? Certainly, they make it more difficult to understand her and to respond to her. "More difficult" is the main phrase in that sentence. None of Thasya's behaviors make it "impossible" or "extremely difficult" to understand, respond to, and teach her. The proof lies in Thasya's performance in the school musical, where she displays her significant strengths in music. Her teachers have taught her, indeed; "impossible" and "extremely difficult" differ from each other—the former signified "cannot" and the latter signified "can but with unusual effort." You are likely to find that the kind of talent Thasya showed at the concert is worth your effort to develop.

ATYPICAL LANGUAGE DEVELOPMENT   Unlike earlier editions, DSM-5 now provides that atypical language is not one of the key domains. Rather, aspects of what previously had been diagnostic criteria for autism related to language have been merged in the social-communication domain (nonverbal communication) and in the domain of restrictive, repetitive behaviors and interests (echolalia, repeating words and phrases). In the past, language delay has been considered a major diagnostic criteria of autism; however, the majority of children who have significant language delays do not have autism, and not all individuals with autism have language delay (Lord & Jones, 2012). Thus, language delays are considered one of the associated characteristics that can occur in conjunction with the two major diagnostic domains.

You learned that impairments in social-communication behaviors are diagnositic criteria of autism. These impairments often involve the following communication patterns or irregularities (Anagnostou, et al., 2015):

- Interrupting when others are communicating and experiencing difficulty in knowing when it is appropriate to speak

- Focusing attention on one topic only

- Limiting a communication topic to fewer than a couple of interactions

- Reversing pronouns (e.g., the student may look at the teacher and say, "You want to have a snack now," meaning that the student, not the teacher, wants a snack)

- Repeating or echoing other people's language (echolalia).

Like restrictive and repetitive behavior patterns, irregular or impaired social-communication behaviors can be improved by social-communication interventions. These interventions focus on age-appropriate communication outcomes, improve social-communication skills, and address both communication and context (Watkins, Kuhn, Ledbetter-Cho, Gevarter, & O'Reilly, 2017).

Thasya has significant communication support needs. She speaks through gestures, her facial expressions, her behaviors, and her music. She is easily distracted. If, however, you understand that her behavior is her way of communicating, then you address her behavior, not her speaking ability.

Students with autism have a broad range of language abilities, ranging from no verbal communication to quite sophisticated communication abilities (Boucher, 2012). Approximately one third of children with autism are minimally verbal, meaning they do not speak or only minimally use verbal language even after intervention (Tager-Flusberg & Kasari, 2013). These students can greatly benefit from alternative and augmentative communication (AAC) to facilitate their communication opportunities (Chapter 8).

PROBLEM BEHAVIOR   IDEA requires educators to consider using positive behavior support (Chapter 5; we discuss behavior support in more detail later in this chapter) when students engage in behavior that impedes their or other students' learning. Students with autism commonly may exhibit any of four categories of problem behavior: self-injurious behavior, aggression, tantrums, and property destruction. We will focus on the first two.

Self-injurious Behavior.   **Self-injurious behavior** is a self-explanatory term. It occurs when people engage in behavior that might cause them to injure themselves. These behaviors include hitting, biting, or cutting oneself and head banging. Obviously, these behaviors can result in significant physical harm. Over their lifetime, almost half of people with autism will, at some point, engage in some form of self-injurious behavior; indeed, the prevalence of self-injurious behavior among people with autism (that is, the percentage of people with autism engaging in self-injurious behavior at any point in time) is 25 percent (Minshawi, Hurwitz, Fodstad, Biebl, Morriss, & McDougle, 2014).

The most common forms of self-injurious behavior among people with autism are self-biting, self-scratching, skin picking or pinching, self-hitting, and head banging. Health consequences associated with such behavior can include skin lacerations and wounds, infections, detached retinas (from banging one's head), bruising, and, in extreme cases, fractured bones. Obviously, these self-injurous behaviors significantly impair a student's daily life activities, including educational activities (Minshawi et al., 2014).

As is the case with repetitive, stereotyped behaviors, self-injurious behavior has no single cause; indeed, the multiple causes are complex and overlapping. Some factors that seem to be related to or predict the occurrence of self-injurious behaviors include:

- Severity of the core autism spectrum disorder symptoms
- Appearance of stereotyped or repetitive behaviors before age 3
- Presence of intellectual disability co-occuring with autism
- Limited receptive or expressive communication skills
- Limited social or self-care skills
- Restricted mobility and limited motor skills
- Co-occurrence of problem behavior
- Co-occurrence of mental or psychiatric disorders (Minshawi et al., 2014).

Fortunately, as is true with respect to other behaviors, there are interventions that reduce or eliminate self-injurious behaviors. These include multiple behaviorally based interventions (reinforcement-based strategies) using functional behavioral assessment (about which you will learn more later in this chapter) and positive behavior supports that can reduce the frequency of or completely eliminate these dangerous behaviors from a person's repertoire (Moskowitz, Walsh, & Durand, 2016).

Aggression.   Aggressive behaviors are similar to self-injurious behaviors, but the behavior is directed toward others. Approximately half of all students (ages 2 through 17) with autism have been found to engage in mild-to-severe aggressive behavior; this incidence rate compares to a rate of approximately 5 percent of adolescents in the general population (Mazurek, Kanne, & Wodka, 2013). Aggression by children with autism is highest during the preschool years (ages 2 through 4) and decreases across the elementary and secondary years. Students who engage in aggression also frequently engage in self-injury. Students with autism are much more likely to engage in aggressive behaviors than are students with intellectual disability or other disabilities (Hill et al., 2014).

MyLab Education
Video Example 12.1
In this video, you will learn about Thasya's use of an augmentative communication device to communicate with her teachers, her peers, and her family. How does the AAC device enable Thasya to be involved with the curriculum in the classroom and to network with her classroom peers?

Problem behavior typically serves a communicative function, enabling students to obtain something positive, avoid or escape something unpleasant, and/or increase or decrease sensory stimulation (Dunlap, Strain, & Fox, 2012). Given the functions that problem behavior serves, you will want to teach your students other ways to communicate to get what they want. Thasya does not have any of these challenging behaviors. Instead, she has hyperactivity, sometimes needing her own space in which to run alone, sometimes needing to join a dance circle with her peers, and sometimes needing to pound a keyboard. None of those behaviors constitute "problem behaviors," but each reflects her reaction to her environment.

SENSORY AND MOVEMENT DISORDERS   Increasingly, researchers are focusing on sensory and movement impairments that are experienced by children and youth with autism. Some of the recent research findings are as follows:

- Approximately three fourths of preschool children with autism have sensory impairments, and the extent of their sensory impairments is not influenced by their intelligence quotient (IQ; O'Donnell, Deitz, Kartin, Nalty, & Dawson, 2012).

- Environmental stimuli trigger alternative sensory and movement responses due to differences in how individuals with autism experience intensity, rhythm, frequency, duration, and timing of movement (Robledo, Donnellan, & Strandt-Conroy, 2012).

- Students with autism have significant difficulty in using visual information to guide the nature and timing of their movements (catching a ball, crossing the street) (Whyatt & Craig, 2013).

- Nonverbal communication involves motor movements such as gestures, facial expressions, and eye contact. There is increasing evidence that, from the earliest years of their lives, children with autism experience delays in motor development that contribute to social-communication challenges (McCleery, Elliott, Sampanis, & Stefanidou, 2013).

DIFFERENCES IN INTELLECTUAL FUNCTIONING   Autism occurs in children with all levels of intelligence, ranging from students who are gifted to students classified as having intellectual disability. A recent national study concluded that 38 percent of children with autism were identified as having intellectual disability (IQ less than 70), 24 percent were in the borderline range of IQ (e.g., 70 to 85), and 38 percent had IQs of 85 or above (Centers for Disease Control and Prevention, 2016). Keep in mind that the mean, or average, IQ score is 100, so about two thirds of students with autism will have some cognitive challenges that may affect their learning, even if they are not identified as having intellectual disability.

One of the strongest predictors of the severity of autism symptoms is IQ (Mehling & Tassé, 2016). Autism symptoms are more severe when individuals have lower IQs. It is hard to know what Thasya's IQ is because the assessments used are not as effective for students with more extensive support needs and who use augmentative and alternative communication devices.

It is, however, clear that she has sufficient intelligence to be a soloist in the elementary school orchestra—proof that she has the ability to learn what she should do and how to display her understanding of her role among her peers.

Some people with autism also display the unusual savant syndrome, which consists of extraordinary talents, most typically being music, art, calendar calculating, mathematics, and mechanical/visual-spatial skills (Treffert, 2014). For example, a student with savant syndrome may be able to recite the baseball game scores and the batting averages of all players who ever participated on a particular team in the major leagues or have a calendar range of 6000 years in being able to describe weather and to answer questions such as "What date was the second Sunday in October in 1947?" The same students who can answer these questions may not be able to add or subtract. The majority of individuals who experience the savant syndrome have IQs between 50 and 70, although some individuals have IQs in the gifted range (Treffert, 2014).

Causes

HISTORICAL PERSPECTIVE ON CAUSES When autism was first diagnosed and described in the early 1940s, parents of children with autism were often regarded as intelligent people of high socioeconomic status who were also "cold." At that time, incredibly, some professionals referred to mothers of children with autism as "refrigerator mothers" (Bettelheim, 1967).

By the 1970s, however, researchers had established that autism is caused by brain or biochemical dysfunction that occurs before, during, or after birth and that blaming parents is totally unwarranted. In 1977 the National Society for Autistic Children (now known as the Autism Society of America) stated, "No known factors in the psychological environment of a child have been shown to cause autism." Today parents are not seen as the cause of problems; they are seen as partners with educators, contributing to solving their children's problems.

BIOMEDICAL CAUSES Significant progress has been made in understanding the cause of autism. However, scientists have not yet been able to pinpoint the definitive cause (Buxbaum & Hof, 2013). It is clear, however, that autism is primarily biological in origin and that multiple biological factors are implicated, including genes, brain structure, and neural pathways. With respect to genetic causation, hundreds of genes have been explored but only a relatively small number have been identified as having a major effect in autism causation (Ramaswami & Geschwind, 2018). Other research supports a genetic explanation for autism, showing that a family with one child with autism has a higher chance of having a second child with autism than families without a child with autism. Similarly, studies of twins show that in cases of identical twins, who share the same genetic makeup, when one twin has autism, the second twin is more likely to have autism than are fraternal twins, that is, when twins do not share the same genetic makeup (Perry, Koudys, Dunlap, & Black, 2017).

One consistent finding regarding brain structure has been that the brains of children with autism grow at an accelerated rate during the first few years of life. Specifically, expansion of the cortical surface (the outer layer of the cerebral cortex, which controls brain functions related to memory, attention, cognition, awareness, and language) between ages 6 and 12 months is highly related to a diagnosis of autism at 24 months (Hazlett et al., 2017).

In addition to size differences, the connectivity between different parts of the brain appears to be a cause of autism and is linked to differences in how people with autism process language (Herringshaw, Ammons, DeRamus, & Kana, 2016). Additionally, connectivity issues between frontal and posterior areas of the brain have been implicated in terms of the **etiology** of autism (Just, Keller, Malave, Kana, & Varma, 2012).

ENVIRONMENTAL CAUSES Aside from biological factors, environmental contributions to autism include toxic exposure to chemicals and radiation, exposure in early pregnancy to maternal medications (thalidomide, valproic acid), and maternal infection (rubella) (Hyman & Levy, 2013). Although there has been much publicity on the possible link between childhood immunization and autism, multiple studies and reviews have consistently found no credible evidence of this link (DeStefano, Price, & Weintraub, 2013; Jain, Marshall, Buikema, Bancroft, Kelly, & Newschaffer, 2015). It is important for you to know about and to refer to this scientific finding, especially given that some parents refuse to immunize their children against deadly diseases because they fear that immunizations will cause autism (Bazzano, Zeldin, Schuster, Barrett, & Lehrer, 2012).

MyLab Education
Video Example 12.2
A man with savant syndrome draws the Singapore skyline from memory. What might account for his memory and drawing skills? https://www.youtube.com/watch?v=iXrvL7IlEtw

MyLab Education
Video Example 12.3
A mother talks about her son's development with autism and the lack of help she received from the medical community during that time. Blaming mothers for autism seems a cruel thing today; why do you think that occurred in the 1950s? https://www.youtube.com/watch?v=TQY2oB3Rqdg

Overall, research on the causes of autism is one of the most heavily funded areas across the entire disability field. Although the prevalence of autism is increasing, researchers are optimistic that the scientific commitment to discovering the cause of autism is also on an upward trajectory. Someday, probably sooner than later, we will be able to identify, with certainty, why Thasya has autism. In the meantime, we must rely on teachers such as Holly Prud'homme to bring her education, experience, knowledge, and passion to bear so Thasya can be educated with her peers. That education begins with evaluating her and other students to determine whether they have autism and, if so, what difference that fact makes for their education.

Evaluating Students with Autism
Determining the Presence of Autism

Many children receive the initial diagnosis of autism from a psychologist, psychiatrist, and/or interdisciplinary evaluation team, typically during their early childhood years (Woolfenden, Sarkozy, Ridley, & Williams, 2012). *Nondiscriminatory Evaluation Process: Determining the Presence of Autism* highlights the standard techniques used for observations, screening, and nondiscriminatory evaluation.

NONDISCRIMINATORY EVALUATION PROCESS Various diagnostic tools can detect the presence of autism (Timimi & McCabe, 2016). One of the standard tests is

Nondiscriminatory Evaluation Process
Determining the Presence of Autism

Observation	**Medical or psychological professionals and parents observe:** The child is challenged by social conversations, does not play with others, is frequently unresponsive to voices, may exhibit echolalia or other unusual speech patterns, has language development delays, has problem behavior, is disrupted by changes in daily routine, engages in stereotypical behaviors, and has sensory and movement disorders.
Screening	**Assessment measures:** **Physical examinations:** A physician notes that the child is not reaching developmental milestones, especially in areas of social and language development. The child's physical health is usually normal. The physician may refer the child to a psychiatrist or psychologist for further evaluation. **Psychological evaluations:** The child meets the *Diagnostic and Statistical Manual of Mental Disorders* (DSM-5) criteria for autism spectrum disorder, including (1) persistent deficits in social communication and social interaction across multiple contexts; and (2) restricted, repetitive patterns of behavior, interests, or activities. These must be present in early development, must significantly impact current functioning, and must not be explained by intellectual disability or global developmental delay.
Prereferral	The student is usually identified before starting school. In rare circumstances in which the student is not identified before starting school, the severity of the disability may make prereferral unnecessary.
Referral	Children with autism should be referred by medical personnel or parents for early intervention during infancy or the preschool years. The child is referred for special education on reaching school age.
Nondiscriminatory evaluation procedures and standards	**Findings that suggest autism:** **Individualized intelligence test:** About half of students with autism perform two or more standard deviations below the mean, indicating intellectual disability. Others have average or even gifted intelligence. Evaluating intelligence is generally difficult because of challenging social and language behaviors. **Individualized achievement tests:** Students with autism who have average or above-average intelligence may perform at an average or above-average level in one or more areas of achievement. Some individuals with autism have unusual giftedness in one or more areas. Students with autism typically have below-average achievement. **Adaptive behavior scales:** The student usually scores significantly below average in areas of adaptive behavior, indicating severe deficits in skills such as communication, daily living, socialization, gross- and fine-motor coordination, and socially appropriate behavior. **Autism-specific scales:** The student's scores meet the criteria for being identified as having autism. **Direct observation:** The student's self-initiated interactions with teachers and peers are limited. The student exhibits language delays and may use unusual speech patterns such as echolalia. The observer may notice that the student has difficulty with changes in routines and manifests stereotypical behaviors. **Anecdotal records:** Records suggest that performance varies according to moods, energy level, extent and pile-up of environmental changes, and whether or not individual preferences are incorporated.

the Autism Diagnostic Interview—Revised (LeCouteur, Lord, & Rutter, 2003). It consists of three domains: Language/Communication; Reciprocal Social Interactions; and Restricted, Repetitive, and Stereotyped Behaviors and Interests. The Autism Diagnostic Interview—Revised was developed to be used with children through adulthood. An algorithm for this tool extends its valid use to toddlers starting at 12 months of age (Kim & Lord, 2012). Only specially trained professionals administer and score the interview because scoring is based on clinical judgment regarding the caregiver's description of the child's development and behavior. The interview consists of 93 questions and takes about 1½ to 2½ hours to complete. The professional conducting the interview calculates summary scores for each domain and compares scores to a cutoff metric that then allows the professional to conclude that a child has or does not have autism. The reliability and validity of this tool have been carefully established (Zander et al., 2017).

Determining the Nature of Specially Designed Instruction and Services

As you have already read, many students with autism exhibit problem behaviors, especially when a mismatch exists between their need for accommodations on the one hand and environmental expectations on the other. To reduce or eliminate those behaviors, teachers and other professionals often use positive behavior support. You learned about positive behavior supports in Chapter 5, and you'll learn how it is applied with young children later in this chapter.

Before offering that support to a student with problem behavior, someone must conduct a functional behavioral assessment. You read a little about this process in Chapters 4 and 5, and now it's time for you to learn the "how to" of conducting a functional behavioral assessment.

A **functional behavioral assessment (FBA)** identifies specific relationships between a student's behaviors and the circumstances that trigger those behaviors, especially those that impede the student's or others' ability to learn. Although a functional behavioral assessment is helpful for many students who do not have autism, it is particularly apt for the student with autism. The *Guidelines for Teaching: Functional Behavioral Assessment* feature includes a sample functional behavioral assessment and associated behavior intervention plan for a student struggling with completing academic work and engaging in off-task behavior.

You will use these basic steps when conducting a functional behavioral assessment (Chandler & Dahlquist, 2014):

Guidelines for Teaching

Functional Behavioral Assessment

A functional behavioral assessment (FBA) is a systematic process for gathering information that helps teachers and related service providers determine why a student engages in problem behaviors and how teachers can influence events and circumstances to change these behaviors. As the text describes, there are a few basic steps in conducting an FBA. The first is to complete the analysis (FBA); then develop a behavior intervention plan (BIP); and finally incorporate that plan into the student's IEP, thereby addressing the student's behavior and enabling the student to interact with peers and teachers in the general education classroom. Below is a sample of a completed FBA for a 4th-grade boy.

(Continued)

Student: Grade: *4*	School:	Date:
FBA/BIP developed for: Programming purposes	IEP requirement	Participants:

	ANTECEDENTS	**CONSEQUENCES**

In your own words, describe the behavior that prompted this FBA
 	
Issues with off-task behavior
	Ask yourself: What is likely to set off (precede) the problem behavior?
	
	Directions to do academic work
	
	WHEN is the problem behavior most likely to occur?
	
	Morning **x** Approximate times(s)
	Afternoon **x** Approximate times(s)
	Before/after Lunch/recess school
	
	WHERE
	
	x Reg. Ed Classroom Hallway
	    Spec. Ed Classroom Cafeteria
		Ask yourself: What payoff does the student obtain when she/he demonstrates the problem behavior?
		
		The student GAINS:
		
		x Teacher/adult attention
		
		   Peer attention
		
		   Desired item or activity
		
		x Control over others or the situation
		
		The student AVOIDS or ESCAPES:
		
		   Teacher/adult interaction
		
		   Peer interaction

PROBLEM BEHAVIOR
 	
If the above explanation addresses multiple behaviors, identify the ONE BEHAVIOR to be targeted for intervention.
 	
Avoiding a nonpreferred activity by resting head on desk and covering ears
	During what SUBJECT/ACTIVITY is the problem behavior most likely to occur?
	
	Subject(s) *reading, social studies, science*
	
	x Seatwork Classmates Group Activities
	
	   Other Lesson Presentation peers
	
	Are there OTHER EVENTS or CONDITIONS that immediately precede the problem behavior?
	
	x A demand or request
	
	  Unexpected changes in schedule or routine
	  Consequences imposed for behavior
	  Comments/teasing from other students
		x Nonpreferred activity, task, or setting
		
		   A difficult task or frustrating situation
		
		What has been tried thus far to change the problem behavior?
		
		Implemented rules and consequences for behavior as posted
		
		Implemented behavior or academic contract
		
		Implemented home-school communication system. Adapted curriculum. How?
		
		Picture symbols, one on one

	When is the student most successful? When DOESN'T the problem behavior occur? *When preforming an academic task he enjoys*	Modified instruction. How? *Shorter lessons*
The behavior I have targeted for intervention is: x x OBSERVABLE MEASURABLE		Adjusted schedule. How? Conferenced with parents: Dates: Sent to office: Dates:

Function of Problem Behavior

Ask yourself: Why is the student behaving this way? What function/need is being met by the student's behavior?

Complete the following preliminary analysis by summarizing information from the three columns in part one of the **functional behavioral assessment**.

When: *Teacher has asked student to perform academic work he cannot do* (summarize antecedents)

This student *will at times lower head onto desk and cover ears* (identify the problem behavior)

In order to *avoid doing work he cannot perform (temporarily)*. (summarize payoff)

EXAMPLES:

1. When in the halls before school, after school, and during transitions, this student pushes other students and verbally threatens to beat them up in order to gain status and attention from peers.

2. When working on independent seatwork during his regular education math class, this student puts his head on his desk in order to escape work that is too difficult/frustrating.

Replacement Behavior

Ask yourself: What alternative behavior would meet the same function/need for the student?

Complete the following:

Rather than: *Tuning out, lowering head, covering ears* (identify the problem behavior)

I want this student to:

Attempt to perform his academics or explain to teacher that work is too difficult for him.

(Note: This replacement behavior should represent an IEP goal.)

This definition is:

     (OBSERVABLE)   (MEASURABLE)

EXAMPLES:

1. Rather than pushing students and threatening to beat them up, I want this student to walk in the halls with his hands to his side and say "hello" to those with whom he wishes to interact.

2. Rather than putting his head on his desk because he doesn't know how to do the problem, I want this student to raise his hand for help and move onto the next problem while waiting for my assistance.

Behavior Intervention Plan

Name: _____

Date of Implementation: _____

Behavior:
Avoidance of work
Challenging academics

Preventative Measures:
Determine correct academic levels at all times!
Quietly redirect to complete work.

Hypothesis:
From observation of antecedence, appears to display this behavior to avoid academic work that he cannot (or will not) do.

Reinforcement Schedule:
Computer time, 10 minutes per "successful" day. For a successful week, 20 minutes at the end of the week, Friday afternoon.

1. Through careful observation, describe as precisely as you can the nature of the behaviors that are impeding the student's or others' ability to learn. Remember Holly Pru-d'homme's advice: observe, interact, go into your work with an open heart, and expect your students to teach you, even as you teach them.

2. Gather information from teachers, related service providers, family members, the student, and any other people who have firsthand knowledge about the circumstances regularly associated with the student's problem behavior. Determine as specifically as you can the events that occur before, during, and after the student's appropriate and inappropriate behavior.

3. Determine why the student engages in the problem behavior. What is the student trying to accomplish or communicate? Does the student want to obtain something positive, avoid or escape something unpleasant, or increase or decrease certain sensory stimulation?

4. Hypothesize the relationship between the problem behavior and the events occurring before, during, and after the behavior.

5. Incorporate the functional assessment information into the student's individualized education program (IEP). Focus on changing the environmental events and circumstances so that the student does not need to use problem behavior to accomplish an outcome.

6. Help the student develop alternative behaviors and new skills to accomplish the same outcome in more socially acceptable ways.

> **MyLab Education** Self-Check 12.1
>
> **MyLab Education** Application Exercise 12.1: The Prevalence of Autism

Including Students with Autism

Although research demonstrates that students with autism can be effectively included in general education classes, these students have low rates of inclusion. As illustrated in Figure 12.1, only 40 percent of students with autism spend more than 80 percent of their time inside general education classes, and 42 percent of students are educated in self-contained or separate settings (U.S. Department of Education, 2018). Figure 12.1 illustrates where students with autism were educated during the 2015–2016 school year.

MyLab Education
Video Example 12.4
In this video, Thasya shows her musical abilities in a concert for the entire school. What are some things that Thasya's teachers and peers learned because she was included in the general education classroom?

Figure 12.1 Extent of Inclusion for Students with Autism

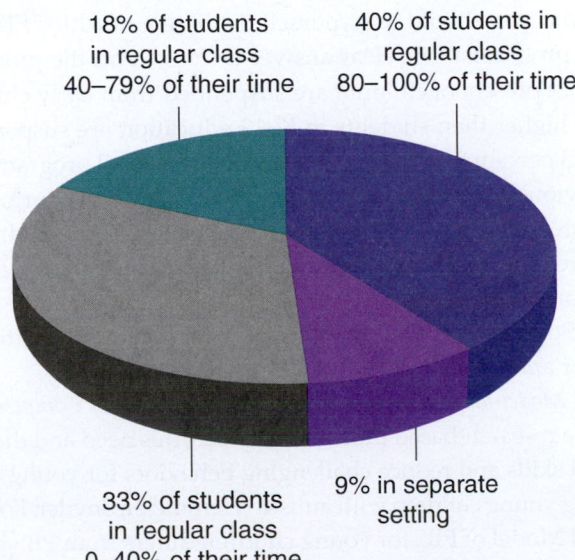

18% of students in regular class 40–79% of their time

40% of students in regular class 80–100% of their time

33% of students in regular class 0–40% of their time

9% in separate setting

SOURCE: U.S. Department of Education. (2018). *39th Annual Report to Congress on the Implementation of the Individuals with Disabilities Education Act.* Retrieved from: https://www2.ed.gov/about/reports/annual/osep/2017/parts-b-c/39th-arc-for-idea.pdf/.

The *Inclusion Tips for Students with Autism* feature provides ideas for how you might include students with autism.

Inclusion Tips for Students with Autism

	Behavior	Social Interactions	Educational Performance	Classroom Attitudes
What You Might See	The student often rocks back and forth over and over during class activities in which she's not interested.	On the playground the student is almost always left out of group interactions.	The student learns slowly and needs a great deal of extra help to learn simple concepts.	The student becomes antagonistic during activities in which there is noise or confusion.
What You Might Be Tempted to Do	Ignore the student's behavior or tell the student to stop.	Assume that being alone is how the student prefers to spend time.	Expect less and make the requirements less structured.	Remove the student from class activities to work alone in the library.
Alternate Teacher Response	Conduct a functional behavioral assessment to understand why rocking is occurring.	Teach the student to ask if the student can be included and to develop the skills to participate in play with one or two peers.	Use visual images and music to teach abstract concepts.	Use social stories to help the student learn ways to concentrate in noisy environments.
Ways to Include Peers in the Process	Help peers to understand the student's behavior. Encourage and support their acceptance.	Pair the student with peers who understand the student's preferred communication method.	Provide opportunities for peer tutoring with visual images and music.	Teach peers to write social stories that include all students. Have small groups, including the student, review and work out different scenarios.

Educating Students with Autism

A number of research-based strategies will enable you to design an appropriately ambitious educational program for students with autism. We begin with an innovative model to implement positive behavior supports with children in early childhood and preschool programs.

Positive Behavior Supports in Early Childhood and Preschool Programs

The most common application of school-wide positive behavior supports (SW-PBS) is in K–12 schools: elementary, middle, and high schools. You learned a lot about SW-PBS in Chapter 5. Positive behavior supports are important for children in their early childhood and preschool years, but there are quite a few differences between these programs and those in K–12 schools that must be addressed when implementing PBS in early childhood settings (Dunlap, Smith, Fox, & Blase, 2014).

First, however, you should ask yourself, is there a need for PBS interventions in early childhood programs? The clear answer is "yes," and the proof for that answer lies in the fact that preschool children are suspended from early childhood programs at a rate 3 times higher than students in K–12 education are suspended. Young boys are involved in 78 percent of all suspensions from preschool programs. From what you have read in previous chapters about racial biases, it shouldn't surprise you that Black children constitute about 50 percent of all preschool and early childhood suspensions, and young children of American Indian and Native Alaska origins are suspended from early childhood programs at a rate 3 times their representation in the population (Allen & Smith, 2016). So, unfortunately, there is a strong need for positive approaches to problem behavior among young children.

The *Pyramid Model for Promoting Young Social Emotional Competence in Infants and Young Children* is a research-based process that meets this need and that has been shown to improve social skills and reduce challenging behaviors for young children with disabilities, including young children with autism (Hemmeter, Snyder, Fox, & Algina, 2016).

The Pyramid Model of PBS for young children differs from PBS in K–12 settings in that it was derived from research on effective instructional practices for young children, focuses on social and emotional skill development, and has a strong family engagement

You can find more information about the Pyramid Model from the Pyramid Model consortium website at http://www.pyramidmodel.org/

component. Like PBS in K–12, however, the Pyramid Model relies on functional behavior assessment to inform the design and implementation of strategies to promote social and emotional skills and is a multi-tiered framework that models the PBS process in K–12 schools (Dunlap & Fox, 2015).

Like school-wide PBS in K–12 schools, implementation of the Pyramid Model is program-wide (not just in one classroom). Some components to the program-wide implementation of the Pyramid Model include:

- *Establishing a Leadership Team.* This program-level team meets regularly, often monthly, to plan for the implementation of the model, to implement the model, to evaluate the model's implementation and effectiveness, and to problem solve if issues arise. Stakeholders who are represented on the Leadership Team include, at a minimum, program administrators, teachers, coaches who support the teachers, and someone with expertise in behavioral interventions. In addition to planning for, implementing, and evaluating the model, the team works to provide training and professional development, technical assistance, data-collection and analysis procedures, and a plan to meaningfully involve family members in the process. The Leadership Team also ensures that all program staff are willing to participate and supports the model's implementation.

- *Actively involving families.* Family involvement is a critical component of the Pyramid Model. The model emphasizes active communication with families, the provision of information on and help in supporting the social and emotional needs of the child, and collaborative teaming to support each child.

- *Adopt program-wide expections.* Establishing high expectations for children's behavior and clearly communicating these expectations are critical features of all PBS systems, and this is true for the Pyramid Model. Expectations for behavior are posted in common spaces for the early childhood program in classrooms, and are shared with families.

- *Develop policies and practices for behavior support plans and procedures.* In a number of ways the Pyramid Model addresses the details of providing behavior supports, from the Leadership Team establishing policies for crisis situations, to implementing fidelity tools in classrooms, to developing behavior support plans for children who need them (Dunlap et al., 2014).

Importantly, the Pyramid Model has been found to incorporate culturally responsive elements. First, the focus on partnerships with families and building positive relationships can ensure that a family's cultural values are included. Second, the focus on social-emotional instruction has the potential to bring culturally responsive practices to the forefront, though educators need to make sure that instruction is not bound to one cultural practice or another. Third, by building diverse Leadership Teams, schools can better ensure that the teams respect the cultural diversity of a school population (Allen & Steed, 2016). Figure 12.2 provides the story of an unusual school that is implementing the Pyramid model . . . at a zoo!

MyLab Education
Video Example 12.5
The Pyramid Model has been adopted in many states, including Kansas. As you experience this video, what elements of the Pyramid Model did you find most important? https://www.youtube.com/watch?v=_8Rl00F49Hg

Social Stories

One widely used strategy for students with autism, particularly in their elementary years, involves the use of social stories. You have already learned that students with autism have difficulty in social situations: knowing what is cool and uncool behavior, understanding others' perspectives, and knowing the unwritten codes of conduct— what educators call the "hidden curriculum" (Myles, Trautma, & Schelvan, 2013). Social stories are written by educators, parents, or students and describe social situations, social cues, and appropriate responses to those cues. These stories usually consist of four types of sentences (Gray, 2013):

Figure 12.2 Tampa Zoo School Hatches New Methods for Positive Behavior Support

---

A Zoo of Possibilities

Tampa's Park Zoo is one of the most popular zoos in the southeastern United States. Built in the 1930's, it has grown to include a 24-acre facility of about 1,200 animals.

But the zoo isn't just home to swinging monkeys and happy hippos. They host an Education Center or "Zoo School" for children. The school, which has enrolled over 1,000 students, was the first full-time early education center in an accredited zoological facility.

Finding a New Buddy System

Leslie Moat is an Early Childhood Education Instructor at the Lowry Park School. She's the two-year-old Lead Teacher and has worked with young children for over ten years.

Moat values continuing her education when it comes child development. She earned her Associate Degree in Child Development in 2009 and continues to participate in a variety of training courses each year.

Through her experience, she has seen challenging behaviors in her classroom increase. "In a two-year-old class, you often find children using other solutions, instead of words, to describe their feelings," Moat says, "For example, hitting usually comes first."

While Lowry Park School has explored methods for supporting social-emotional enhancement, they hadn't found the right solution. As a result, the program decided to partner with The Pyramid Model Consortium, previously called Program-Wide Positive Behavior Support.

"Challenging behavior in young children is almost always cited as the number one training need by the early childhood workforce," says Rob Corso, "Our goal is to help a district, region, or program develop systems that ensure infants and young children develop social-emotional skills."

Transitioning to Success

Lowry Park School participated in PMC's Program-Wide Capacity Building training. This process included:

- Selecting demonstration classrooms as a model for performance
- Onsite training events for leaders and the program's workforce
- Planning meetings to establish policies and procedures
- Ongoing support to address new challenges and collect classroom data

In the classroom, PMC provided targeted training to help teachers design high-quality environments and increase their confidence in identifying and enhancing positive behavior.

PMC also assisted the teachers in improving communication with parents, from creating take-home books for children who need additional support at home to handing out visual schedules and behavior support research.

"As we entered into a partnership, we could see the difference in how working with the Pyramid Model helped the children understand their feelings and emotions," says Moats.

Moat adds her children are developing nurturing and responsive relationships with classmates and the transition from preschool to elementary school is smoother.

Pyramid Model Consortium. Reprinted from http://www.pyramidmodel.org/case-studies/tampa-zoo-school-hatches-new-methods-for-positive-behavior-support/ with permission.

- Descriptive sentences provide details about the situation, including where the story occurs, who is involved, what they are doing, and why.
- Perspective sentences describe the person's thoughts, feelings, beliefs, and motivations.
- Directive sentences define what is expected as a response to a cue or in a particular situation.
- Control sentences identify strategies students may use to recall the information in a social story, reassure themselves, or define their responses.

The goal of social stories is to expose the student to a better understanding of an event and to encourage alternative, and appropriate, responses. Here are tips for successfully implementing social stories:

- Social stories should be presented (typically) to the student before a situation occurs so as to allow the student to rehearse the situation.
- A story should include both positive and problem behaviors.

- Using illustrations may help students with autism who are younger or have cognitive limitations (Ryan, Hughes, Katsiyannis, McDaniel, & Sprinkle, 2011).

The accompanying video presents social stories inventor Carol Gray discussing how to develop social stories.

You may well ask whether social stories are effective in changing students' behavior. The short answer is "Yes." Researchers found moderate-to-strong evidence of their effect on reducing inappropriate skills or behaviors and increasing social-communication skills and appropriate skills and behaviors (Qi, Barton, Collier, Lin, & Montoya, 2018).

MyLab Education
Video Example 12.6
Carol Gray discusses social stories in this video. What do you think about using social stories with Drew? https://www.youtube.com/watch?v=vjllYYbVIrI

Student-directed Learning Strategies

Consider this question: "If students were floated in life jackets for 12 years, would they be expected to swim if the jackets were suddenly jerked away?" (Martin, Marshall, Maxson, & Jerman, 2016, p. 4). The obvious answer is "Of course not." Students would sink without specific instruction on how to swim. Depending on a life jacket does not ensure success once the life jacket is removed. Unfortunately, "the situation is similar for students receiving special education services. All too often these students are not taught how to self-manage their own lives before they are thrust into the cold water of post-school reality" (Martin et al., 2016, p. 4).

To avoid the life-jacket situation, you can use **student-directed learning strategies**. These strategies teach students with and without disabilities to modify and regulate their own learning (Wehmeyer, Shogren, Little, & Lopez, 2017). The educational supports that you should use to implement the Self-Determined Learning Model of Instruction (Chapter 11) include many student-directed learning strategies, but several are particularly important for students with autism: **self-instruction strategies**, **self-scheduling strategies**, **self-modeling strategies**, and **self-monitoring strategies**. As you read this section, you will find similarities to what you learned in Chapter 7 regarding the Self-Regulated Strategy Development for Teaching Writing.

SELF-INSTRUCTION Self-instruction strategies involve teaching students to use their verbal or other communication skills to direct their learning. Students use self-instructions as cues for what they need to do next to perform the task. Self-instruction strategies are flexible because students use something they have with them at all times: their means of communication (Wehmeyer & Shogren, 2016). Several research-based templates for self-instruction exist, including:

- In traditional problem-solving self-instruction, students learn to verbally instruct themselves to identify the problem ("What do I do next in this task?"), identify a solution to the problem ("I place the silverware in the napkin."), evaluate the effectiveness of the solution ("Does this look right?"), and reinforce themselves ("Yes, that looks good!").

- In the task-sequencing, or "did-next-now," strategy, students learn self-instruction statements related to the step they just completed ("I placed the silverware in the napkin."), the next step ("I need to roll the silverware in the napkin."), and when they will perform the next step ("I'll do the next step now.").

- In the "what-where" strategy, students learn statements about what they need to do ("I need to roll the silverware in the napkin.") and where they will do it ("I roll the silverware in the napkin at my workstation in the restaurant."), which helps them remember the context in which they engage in certain activities.

- In the interactive, or "did-next-ask," strategy, students learn self-instruction statements similar to the task-sequencing strategy but complete the statement by instructing themselves to ask someone about the next step or about some aspect of the task. It is helpful to teach this in conjunction with the task-sequencing strategy in case students forget the next step.

In the *My Voice: Using Visual Supports in Biology and Zoology* feature below, Rebecca Trillo, a general education biology and zoology teacher for middle and high school students in Phoenix, Arizona, discusses how she uses visual supports that illustrate a form of self-instruction for students with autism in her classrooms.

My Voice

Using Visual Supports in Biology and Zoology

I'm Rebecca Trillo and I've taught biology and zoology to middle and high school students for 2 years. My school primarily serves academically advanced students who thrive on an accelerated curriculum. Due to the environment at the school, I teach a number of students with autism who are higher-functioning. My position presents the challenge of engaging students with ASD in scientific discourse, when many, due to their social-communication challenges, and/or anxiety, would prefer not to interact with the class during whole group discussions.

Early in my career as an educator, I noticed that many of my students with ASD often interacted in class less often than their peers without disabilities. And when some of my students with ASD do interact, it sometimes is not in an appropriate way for the situation. For example, a statement may be far off topic and not relevant to the lesson being discussed. When students refrain from socially interacting or attempt to engage in class but do so in a way that prevents their meaningful participation, these students also often miss out on one of the most important parts of a science education: discourse and debate. A primary component of my instruction involves encouraging students to discuss topics such as bioethics and current research in the field of biology, enhancing their understanding of the fundamental nature of science. Students with ASD frequently miss this very important (and often exciting) aspect of class due to their reluctance or inability to engage effectively with their peers.

Through research of recent literature and conversations with my colleagues and university faculty, I learned that visual supports are often a useful tool to assist students with ASD as they navigate social situations, such as those that are expected during science discussions. I then began to develop examples of visual supports that my students could use to guide themselves through scientific discourse. For example, when participating in a discussion on a bioethics situation, a student will plan out in advance a personal opinion on the topic, provide evidence to support the opinion, and identify how

someone who disagrees might respond, using a discussion guide.

A script may also be used with sentence prompts such as "I think the strongest piece of evidence I found is _____" or "My favorite fact I discovered is _____." Students are then able to prepare for discussions using these visual scripts to cue themselves and then read their responses to a classmate, as well as prepare for what to do while their peer responds (e.g., "Next, a member of my group will reply. I will be polite and respectful of this student's opinion."). This script enables the student to engage in the back-and-forth nature of the discussion successfully.

I have seen firsthand that, when students with ASD are able to plan out a conversation in advance and prepare for possible rebuttals, they are much more engaged with the conversation and willing to talk to their classmates. This opportunity to participate meaningfully not only improves students' understanding of science but also enhances their social skills and relationships with peers. The use of visual supports and scripts in a classroom is a vital tool for any teacher of students with ASD.

Discussion Guide

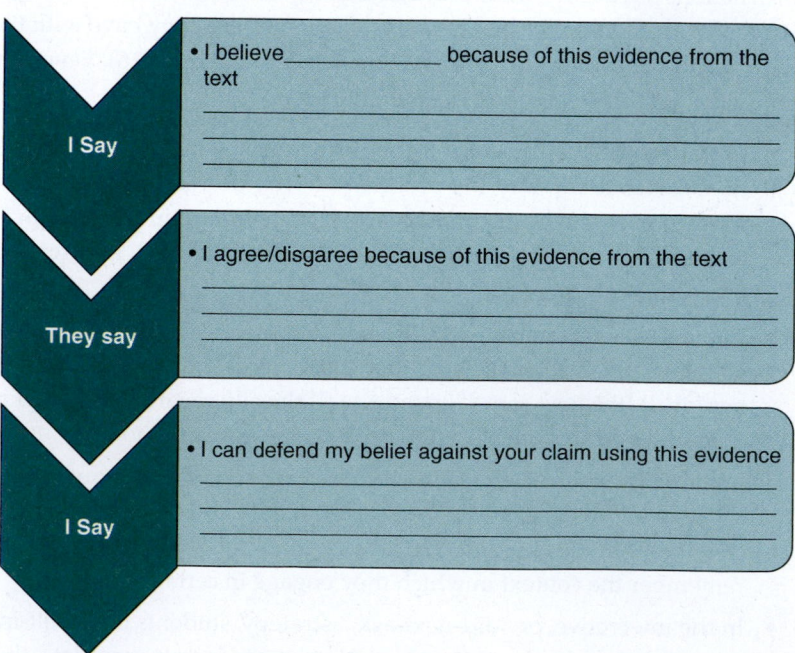

I Say
- I believe _____ because of this evidence from the text

They say
- I agree/disagree because of this evidence from the text

I Say
- I can defend my belief against your claim using this evidence

Reprinted with permission of Rebecca Trillo, Secondary Biology/Zoology Teacher, BASIS of Phoenix, Phoenix, AZ

SELF-SCHEDULING   Self-scheduling involves the self-regulation of one's schedule, rather than relying on someone else to regulate the activities of the day. Think about the number of times you need to "self-schedule" during the day, from incremental times like knowing when to change to a different activity to larger scheduling activities that involve setting up appointments. Students with autism often have difficulty transitioning from one event to the next, so providing instruction and supports that enable students with autism to do this more independently can have multiple purposes, promoting self-determination and minimizing disruptions due to transitions.

Providing a support for self-scheduling can be as simple as posting a print-out of a student's schedule for the school day on a desk or in a place where the student can consult it. Providing such supports has become increasingly simple with technology advances. Most mobile devices, from smartphones to tablets, include calendar apps that can be set up to provide sensory (vibration), sound, or visual reminders of a scheduled activity or time. For example, students with developmental disabilities, including autism, were taught to use an iPad to self-schedule their involvement in exercise activities during their day as part of an effort to teach these students about healthy living (Uphold, Douglas, & Loseke, 2016).

The *Into Practice Across Grade Levels: Implementing Visual Schedules* feature provides step-by-step examples on implementing visual schedules for students with autism.

Into Practice Across Grade Levels

Implementing Visual Schedules

Use visual schedules to illustrate activities and show what will happen next for children who do not read well.
Example: Many **kindergarten** students with autism may have difficulty reading. Use visual schedules to show, incorporating video or photos into a calendar printed out and taped to the student's desk, what activity will occur next. Take videos or photos using a smartphone or tablet to make graphic information very personal to the student, incorporating images into the calendar app on these mobile devices. Similarly, use video or photos in visual schedules to indicate when a task or activity has been completed.

Use visual schedules to reduce anxiety for stressful events.
Example: Students with autism in **3rd grade** can use visual schedules to reduce anxiety and limit possible problem behavior. The transition from one class to another is often a stressful time, associated with lots of noise and stimulation in the hallway. It is also a time, however, for social interactions that may be important. Students can use a tablet that has a notification set 10 minutes prior to change of classes to be notified of and begin preparing for that transition. They can be provided with scripts that enable them to interact more successfully in the hallway with peers.

Implement visual schedules to support students to succeed in academic instruction in inclusive classrooms.
Example: Create a printed calendar to illustrate the activities for **6th-grade** students in the classroom for the day. Use the calendar app on a smartphone to indicate the time at which it is appropriate to ask a question or to get up from a work station. Have all students in a cooperative learning group use the same calendar app on a tablet PC to identify the beginning of group work and the end. Implement a visual schedule to indicate when it is time to put work away for the class session.

Support families to use visual schedules in the home and community.
Example: Students with autism are less autonomous than students with other disabilities. Use calendar supports on smartphones to alert **8th-grade** students that it is time to catch a bus home from school or time for a preferred leisure activity. Teach students to use the visual schedule to participate in preparing meals at home by setting calendar appointments for meal preparation times or grocery shopping times, or as a prompt to do the dishes after a meal. Prepare a sheet with images of tasks needing completion in getting ready to go to school each morning or images of what to do after school to complete chores around the house or homework.

Support students to follow a daily schedule during community-based learning activities.
Example: A **10th-grade** student with autism may spend a portion of the day learning functional skills in community-based settings. Use pictures on the smartphone to provide a sequence of activities that must be performed during the time in the community. Use the calendar app on the smartphone to provide vibrating and visual input (e.g., notification from calendar) for times to switch from one learning task to another in a community setting.

(Continued)

Use visual schedules to teach postsecondary or transition skills.

Example: As **12th-grade** students prepare for their graduation, use visual schedules to structure vocational-learning tasks that may require multiple, complex steps. Teach students with autism to use notifications and photos on smartphones to get from one class to another in learning how to navigate the community college campus. Work with graduating seniors to use visual supports and calendars so that they can fully participate in the senior-class activities and graduation activities.

SELF-MODELING Another important student-directed learning strategy involves the use of self-modeling. Self-modeling is simply observing videos or pictures of oneself doing an activity that is targeted for improvement or that the person is trying to learn. Far and away the most popular form of self-modeling, particularly with students with autism, is video self-modeling (VSM). In the *Guidelines for Teaching: Using Video Self-Modeling with Students with Autism* feature, you will find specific instructions for implementing video-self-modeling.

Guidelines for Teaching

Using Video Self-Modeling with Students with Autism

Identify the behavior to target for instruction using video-self-modeling.

- Determine the domain in which instruction is needed.
- Conduct observations of the student in the domain area.
- Collect and interpret data from multiple sources.
- Identify areas of needed instruction in a given area.
- Prioritize target skills.
- Break down the target behavior into discrete steps.
- Observe the behavior being performed.
- Record steps from the behavior as performed.

Create videos of the student performing the targeted behavior.

- Obtain any needed permission (parent, school) to video the student.
- Support the student in performing each step of the behavior.
- Video the student successfully performing each step of the behavior.
- Edit the video to create a positive example of the student successfully completing the behavior.
- Create a second video in a different context if appropriate.
- Edit all videos to be no more than 5 minutes each.

Implement the video self-modeling instruction.

- Have the student view the video right before the student is to demonstrate the skill being taught.
- Begin in only one setting.
- Set up any needed materials in the same way that such materials are set up in the video.

- After the student views the video, have the student practice the skill.
- Provide supports for the student to successfully complete the skill.
- Continue to have the student view the video and practice the skill over time.

Evaluate the student's progress and ensure generalization.

- Collect data on the student's performance of the target behavior in a natural setting.
- Continue to provide instruction until the student performs the behavior at the expected level.
- Implement video self-modeling instruction in the new setting.
- Collect data on the student's performance of the target behavior in the new setting.
- Observe the student in other settings to determine generalization of learning.

Solve problems that arise through the video self-modeling process.

- Give the instruction time to work.
- If the student is not making progress, consider re-filming the video to provide more detailed information.
- Ensure that the student is receiving adequate reinforcement for successful performance.
- Determine that the student has prerequisite skills to perform the task if progress does not occur over time.
- Consider the instructional environment and minimize distractions and stimuli that might impede learning.

SOURCE: Based on Ganz, J. B., Earles-Vollrath, T. L., & Cook, K. E. (2011). Video modeling: A visually based intervention for children with autism spectrum disorder. *Teaching Exceptional Children, 43*(6), 8–19.

As you consider *Guidelines for Teaching: Using Video Self-Modeling with Students with Autism*, it is important for you to know that VSM is a very well-researched strategy for students with autism across ages and across learning areas. One area in which VSM has shown effectiveness is in reducing problem behavior and increasing adaptive behavior. For example, a recent study used VSM to improve the on-task behavior of elementary school age children with autism in a math class. Teachers video recorded each student appropriately involved in on-task behavior, and students viewed the videos before class each day. The VSM improved on-task behavior for all children (Schatz, Peterson, & Bellini, 2016). VSM has also shown effectiveness in increasing social initiations, reducing stereotyped behavior, and improving communication (Gann & Umbreit, 2017; Nikopoulos & Panagiotopoulou, 2015).

Of course, behavioral issues are not the only learning activities for which VSM can be used. A recent review of VSM found positive benefits (in addition to communication and behavioral issues) related to academic performance, independent living, and self-care activities (Mason, Davis, Ayres, Davis, & Mason, 2016).

SELF-MONITORING   One of the most effective student-directed learning strategies involves teaching students to monitor their own behavior or actions. Essentially, when using self-monitoring strategies, students learn to collect data on their progress toward educational goals. They can do this through traditional formats, such as charting their progress on a sheet of graph paper or completing a checklist, or you can get creative—any way that students can count their behavior is a form of self-monitoring. Even when students are not entirely accurate, there are benefits to the use of self-monitoring. Suggestions for implementing self-monitoring strategies include:

- Implement self-monitoring strategies after the student has already learned to do the task that is being monitored
- Teach the self-monitoring strategy to the student before implementing the strategy
- Build in checks to determine the accuracy of the student's self-monitoring.

Which of the major themes of this book did you find in this chapter? The answer is that you learned about cultural-racial-ethnic issues, research-based practices, inclusion, and partnerships. In learning about research-based practices, you learned how to ensure that students such as Thasya and Endrew (Chapter 1) can make progress in their education—that's a theme. You had hints about the great expectations that educators are justified in having. And you learned that, all together, these themes reflect how educators can dignify their students. There is dignity in Thasya's playing the piano and in Ms. Prud'homme's admonitions about what to do and what to expect as a teacher.

MyLab Education Self-Check 12.2
MyLab Education Application Exercise 12.2: Educating Students with Autism

---

Summary

Identifying Students with Autism

Autism is a disability that significantly affects verbal and nonverbal communication and social interaction, is usually present before the age of 3, and has a negative impact on students' educational performance. Most diagnosis involves the *Diagnostic and Statistical Manual of*

Mental Disorders, 5th edition (DSM-5), which refers to a developmental disability resulting in and characterized by persistent impairments in social interactions and communications, and stereotyped or repetitive movements, including inflexibility in routines or patterns. It is difficult to determine the "true" prevalence of autism, but it is clearly on the rise, with about 9 percent of all students who receive special education services being classified as having autism. Males have always outnumbered females in the autism diagnosis, although part of that discrepancy may be due to gender bias. Similarly, issues in racial bias may result in the underrepresentation of Hispanic, Black, and Native American/Alaska Native students in the autism category.

Describing the Characteristics and Causes

The DSM-5 defines autism spectrum disorder as having two major criteria—social-communication impairments and restrictive, repetitive behaviors and interests. DSM-5 identifies three particular criteria that must be present as social-communication impairments before a student may be classified as having autism: impairments in social-emotional reciprocity, in nonverbal communication, and in maintaining relationships. These characteristics often result in social isolation for students with autism. Repetitive, restricted behaviors and interests refer to repetitive speech, motor movements, or interactions with objects; reliance on routines and rituals; fixation on objects; and excessive or limited reaction to sensory input. Impairments in two of these four particular areas must be present for a student to be diagnosed with autism. The causes of these behaviors are complex and include brain mechanisms or the person's response to anxiety or sensory stimuli in the environment.

Another common issue with students with autism involves problem behavior, directed either at themselves (self-injurious behavior) or at others (aggressive behavior). Self-injurious behaviors are serious and can result in injury and affect life functioning. At some point in their lives, almost half of people with autism will engage in some form of self-injurious behavior. Similarly, almost half of students with autism will engage in mild-to-severe aggressive behavior sometime in their lives. Such behavior is highest during preschool years. Problem behavior serves a communicative function. Interventions can reduce or eliminate self-injurious or aggressive behavior. Many students with autism also experience cognitive impairments, with about one third of students with autism also being identified as having intellectual disability, although people with autism range widely in their intellectual ability. Indeed, some students with autism have exceptional talents in math, memory, art, and other areas; this exceptional talent is referred to as savant syndrome.

The causes of autism are not well known but clearly involve biomedical (brain, genetic) factors and environmental (exposure to toxic chemicals) factors. What is absolutely evident, however, is that a commonly cited cause of autism, immunizations, has no effect on autism. Despite these definitive findings, some people continue to blame immunizations for causing autism.

Evaluating Students with Autism

Medical or psychological professionals use valid assessments to detect the presence of autism; in addition, parent and teacher observations of child behavior, interviews with people who know the child well, and other strategies assist in identifying whether a student has autism. When a student with autism has problem behavior, IDEA requires educators to perform a functional behavioral assessment. The FBA identifies relationships between a student's behaviors and the circumstances that trigger those behaviors, especially those that impede the student's or others' ability to learn.

Including Students with Autism

Students with autism have low rates of inclusion in general education settings. Only 40 percent of students with autism spend more than 80 percent of their time inside general education classes, and 42 percent of students are educated in self-contained or separate settings. This is so despite evidence showing that students with autism can be educated in the general education classroom.

Educating Students with Autism

Research-based strategies are effective in educating students with autism. Just as positive behavior supports are important in elementary, middle, and high school, so, too, are such supports important in preschool and early childhood programs. That is so in part because preschool children are suspended from early childhood programs at a rate 3 times higher than students in K–12 education. The Pyramid Model is an evidence-based PBS model for implementation in preschool and early childhood that improves students' social skills and reduces challenging behaviors for young children with disabilities, including young children with autism. The Pyramid Model focuses on improving social and emotional learning for young children and is particularly centered on meaningful involvement with families.

Social stories are written by educators, parents, or students to provide a scenario that will assist students with autism to navigate what might be difficult transitions. The goal of social stories is to expose the student to a better understanding of an event and to encourage alternative, and appropriate, responses. Social stories typically should be presented to the student before a situation occurs so as to allow the student to rehearse the situation. Social stories have a positive effect on reducing a student's inappropriate skills or behaviors and increasing the student's social-communication skills and appropriate skills and behaviors.

Student-directed learning strategies teach students with and without disabilities to modify and regulate their own learning. Several are particularly important for students with autism, including self-instruction, self-scheduling, self-modeling, and self-monitoring strategies. Self-instruction strategies involve teaching students to use their verbal or other communication skills to direct their learning. Self-scheduling involves the self-regulation of one's schedule, rather than relying on someone else to regulate the activities of the day. Self-modeling entails observing videos or pictures of oneself doing an activity that is targeted for improvement or that the person is trying to learn. The most popular form of self-modeling, particularly with students with autism, is video-based self-modeling. Self-monitoring strategies involve students learning to collect data on their progress toward educational goals. They can do this through traditional formats, such as charting their progress on a sheet of graph paper, completing a checklist, or otherwise monitoring their behavior.

Addressing the Professional Standards

In Chapter 12, Students with Autism, we have covered the following Council for Exceptional Children (CEC) Initial Level Special Educator Preparation Standards: Chapter 12—1.0, 2.1, 2.3, 3.1, 3.3, 4.0, 5.2, 5.3, 5.4, 6.3, 7.1. Refer to the Appendix for a full listing of the CEC Standards with descriptions and supporting explanations.

Chapter 13
Students with Multiple Disabilities and Traumatic Brain Injury

⌄ Learning Outcomes

13.1 Discuss the evaluation processes for students in each of these groups and identify the role of special educators in contributing to knowledge about specially designed instruction for these students.

13.2 Describe how paraprofessionals and assistive technology support students in both groups to be included in general education and identify barriers that limit the success of these strategies.

13.3 Identify how person-centered planning and assistive technology benefit transition services and are beneficial to students in both groups in achieving positive independent living and employment outcomes.

In this chapter, we discuss two categories of exceptionality: multiple disabilities and traumatic brain injury. We begin by providing an overview of these categories, including their characteristics and causes. Because students in these categories share issues involving evaluation and education, we address these commonalities in the sections on evaluating and educating students. As we describe multiple disabilities and traumatic brain injury, we introduce you to two students—Alana Malfy, who has multiple disabilities, and Dylan Outlaw, who has a traumatic brain injury.

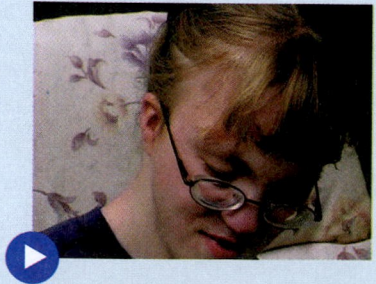

MyLab Education
Vignette Video 13.1
How do you think you would have responded if you had been Kristina and were told what she was told about her newborn daughter?

Meet Alana Malfy—The Importance of High Expectations

Who is Alana Malfy?

The year is 1987. Kristina Malfy, age 19, has just given birth to her first child, Alana. The doctors look at Alana and declare, "She's a freak of nature. Kristina, our best advice is to institutionalize her."

Kristina, immediately postpartum, looks at them and says, "No! Never!!"

Time passes. Alana grows up, goes to school, takes most of her courses in the general education curriculum, graduates, is discovered to have a rare genetic condition attributable to her father, and now lives with Kristina and is active in her community.

It is uncomfortable to encounter the word "freak." It is wrong to use it. But it is the word Kristina heard from Alana's early doctors. It is a word that, from time to time, she and Alana hear; only now it is the R-word. Freak and the R-word dehumanize and stigmatize.

Yes, Alana does have disabilities. They are caused by a gene that her father carries. He didn't know it at the time Alana was conceived. Indeed, the best geneticists at New England's best university hospital could not explain Alana's disability except to say that it was a mysterious result of nature.

But genes are not destiny, not entirely. Who your parents and teachers are also affect your destiny. In the Malfy family, context controls at least as much as genes. Here's the proof of that assertion.

Kristina's family "broke down" when they learned about Alana's disability. Kristina could not afford to. "I was shell-shocked. I had a trillion questions. My family 'lost it.' I couldn't afford to. I had to be strong, to stay positive. I learned to move forward, day by day, to find humor in our life together, to realize that not everyone 'gets it' about Alana."

Moving forward meant enrolling Alana soon after she was born into a program for infants and toddlers, where she received physical therapy, occupational therapy, and speech-language therapy, and where Kristina herself found support from the early intervention providers and other parents.

When it came time for Alana to enter preschool at age 4, Kristina insisted that Alana be included in the school's general education curriculum. There, Alana took the same courses as children without disabilities. In time, she learned to read, use an iPad, do chores at home and at school, and care for animals.

Alana sometimes was in a resource room where she could have more one-on-one instruction. She and Kristina did not like that separation from her general education classmates, so they successfully pressed for inclusion. It helped that she always had her own supports, such as a paraprofessional in the general education classroom to facilitate learning. It also helped that most of her teachers believed in inclusion and had the skills to accomplish it for Alana, and that they recognized her strengths and had high expectations for her.

Alana, Kristina, and most of her teachers defied a taunt and proved that inclusion works for Alana. Alana graduated with her peers, and with a general education diploma. That was unpredictable, and not easy.

Alana has friends—not a large number, but a circle of close friends. In school, she tried hard to be thoughtful of other students and to be humorous and eager to learn. But she was acutely aware she had differences; her needs for structure and routine were greater than those of her friends. Also, she did not tolerate disappointments easily; when one of her teachers or paraprofessionals would change jobs or when Alana could not get what she wanted exactly when she wanted it, she would often cry or shout out loudly, protesting. Or she would become depressed and withdrawn. In time, she found that shouting was not a good strategy for getting what she wanted.

If you ask Kristina to explain the big message for new teachers, she pauses for a moment and then answers: "You won't learn it all from a book. There is more to every person than you will see at the beginning. Get to know the person. Celebrate them for who they are, not what they can do. Pay attention not just to your students, but also to yourselves. Don't be distant from the person; give them the benefit of the doubt; listen to their parents; and expect more than you ever think you have a right to expect."

Defining Multiple Disabilities

As you might guess by the term "multiple disabilities," students who receive special education services under that classification have more than one disability. Specifically, the Individuals with Disabilities Education Act (IDEA) defines multiple disabilities by the presence of "**concomitant** impairments," the combination of which causes such intense educational needs that they cannot be accommodated by solely addressing one of the impairments. Alana meets the definition—she has more than one disability and has intensive educational needs because of the combination of her disabilities. Students with multiple disabilities are a diverse group and will have diverse profiles of strengths and support needs. Some students will have intellectual disability and blindness; others will have emotional or behavioral disorders and orthopedic impairments. But all usually require more intensive supports to address their unique learning needs.

Most students with multiple disabilities will need intensive supports to address their intellectual, adaptive, motor, sensory, or communication needs. For example, Alana has physical, intellectual, and behavioral support needs, and each requires intensive support for her to access and progress in the general education curriculum. In the 2015–2016 school year, approximately 2.0 percent (131,140) of all students ages 3 through 21 receiving special education services were classified as having multiple disabilities (U.S. Department of Education, 2018).

Describing the Characteristics and Causes of Multiple Disabilities

Characteristics

Given the different combinations of disabilities that can lead to students receiving special education services under the multiple disability category, it is difficult to describe accurately all possible characteristics of students within this category. Students with multiple disabilities are a widely heterogeneous group in terms of their characteristics, capabilities, and educational needs. Their strengths, needs, interests, preferences, personalities, socioeconomic levels, and cultural heritages are as varied as those of any of their peers who do not have disabilities. Each has a right to individualized instruction based on specific needs. As you consider how to individualize, think about these five domains of development:

- Intellectual and academic functioning
- Adaptive skills
- Motor development
- Sensory functioning
- Communication skills.

Robin Nelson/PhotoEdit, Inc.

Students with multiple disabilities have two or more significant disabilities. This student, benefiting from peer teaching, has at least two: physical disabilities and intellectual disability.

INTELLECTUAL AND ACADEMIC FUNCTIONING Many students with multiple disabilities have significant impairments in intellectual functioning, meaning they will need intensive supports for completing cognitive tasks (Brown, McDonnell, & Snell, 2015). Cognitive tasks include making decisions and solving problems and are often critical to academic learning and engagement. For example, solving math problems or identifying the meaning of the sentences and paragraphs in a novel requires the use of cognitive skills such as decision making and problem solving.

Not all students with multiple disabilities have impairments in intellectual functioning. Some students with multiple disabilities may function intellectually in the typical or even in the gifted range, but they still may be classified as having multiple disabilities because of their adaptive, motor, sensory, or communication impairments and needs. So, an initial step in supporting students with multiple disabilities is to identify what their needs are related to cognitive tasks and to individualize instruction based on those needs.

Alana has intellectual disability in addition to her other disabilities and needs support for completing cognitive tasks. But, Alana's other support needs make it difficult to determine the extent of her impairments in intellectual functioning. It often is difficult to document the intellectual capabilities of students who have multiple disabilities. As you read in Chapter 4, schools typically measure a student's intellectual functioning by administering an intelligence test. Yet these traditional methods can be inappropriate for many students with multiple disabilities who have significant impairments in intellectual functioning (Orelove, Sobsey, & Gilles, 2016). That is so in part because students with multiple disabilities usually are not included in the normative samples of standardized intelligence tests. Why? The reason is they have difficulty engaging with the items presented on the tests, as most intelligence tests rely heavily on verbal abilities, and many students with multiple disabilities also have communication needs that limit their ability to respond verbally. So, if students cannot engage with the tests, then information generated from attempting the tests will have limited utility when designing appropriate educational programs. Professionals will have to consider other means for determining students' intellectual support needs and how students can access and progress in the general education curriculum.

MyLab Education
Video Example 13.1
In this video, some of Alana's teachers and classmates talk about inclusion. What are the most important points they make?

ADAPTIVE SKILLS   As you learned in Chapters 4 and 11, **adaptive skills** include conceptual, social, and practical competencies for functioning in typical community settings (Tassé, Luckasson, & Schalock, 2016). Self-care skills also may be especially important for students with multiple disabilities. **Self-care skills** include eating, dressing, and going to the bathroom. In partnership with other educators, related services providers, and students' families, you will want to make sure the right supports are in place across home and school to enable students to fully participate in these tasks.

Students need yet another adaptive skill—how to communicate about their own needs and goals for the future (Diegelmann & Test, 2018). That is why, for example, adaptations can be made to processes to teach students to lead their own individualized education program (IEP) meetings, such as creating a picture-based self-monitoring checklist to prompt students to complete the steps involved in an IEP meeting.

MOTOR DEVELOPMENT   Students with multiple disabilities can also have significant motor and physical support needs (Orelove et al., 2016). For example, some students have motor impairments that produce abnormal muscle tone. They may have underdeveloped muscle tone or, contrarily, increased muscle tension and extremely tight muscles, causing spasticity. Any abnormal muscle tone can interfere with the ability of students to perform self-care tasks such as eating, dressing, using the bathroom, playing with toys, or sitting or standing in the general education classroom. Nevertheless, many students learn to perform these skills and/or use supports that enable them to fully participate in these activities. For example, something as simple as a stander, which is an assistive device that supports students to stand upright, can be used to enable complete participation in general education classroom activities. You may recall that Jack Steinberg (Chapter 6) has a specially designed standing device.

Another example of a motor support for students with multiple disabilities is a switch. Switches are designed to assist students who have motor needs to activate a device; switches can be attached to a wheelchair or a desk or anywhere that is convenient for the student. Switches for students with multiple disabilities are no different than switches that you use all the time, like light switches. The only difference is that switches for students with disabilities are highly individualized for students' needs. For example, a switch might activate a computer or it might activate a specialized device that turns pages in a book so students who cannot turn pages on their own can

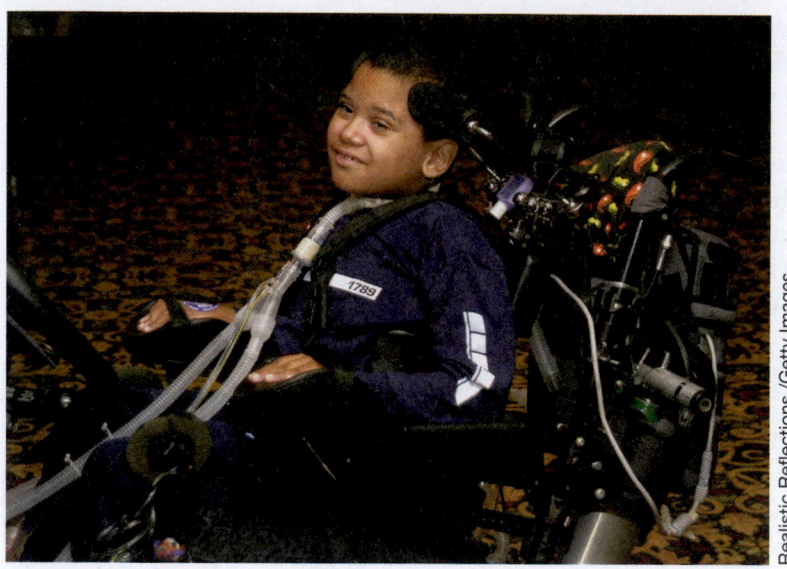

Realistic Reflections /Getty Images

Wheelchairs, oxygen tanks, and other technologies make inclusion possible for students with multiple disabilities.

Visit and bookmark the National Center on Deaf-Blindness— https://nationaldb.org/—to review a wide array of resources focused on supporting students who experience deaf-blindness.

MyLab Education

Video Example 13.2

In the video "My Child Is Deaf and Blind: National Deaf Children's Society Family Story," you meet Gethin, an elementary-age boy who experiences deaf-blindness. Do Gethin's abilities surprise you based on what you thought when you found out he was deaf-blind? http:// www.youtube.com/watch?v=7d2d5 nB3QOshttp://www.youtube .com/watch?v=7d2d5nB3QOs

participate in literacy and reading activities in the general education classroom. Switches can also be used to activate a communication system that "speaks" for students, speaking aloud something they have written to enable communication with peers. Switches can be set up to be activated by students using their heads, fingers, arms, or feet, depending on the motor needs. The switches enable students to express themselves, to indicate they want to answer a question, or to activate a device that communicates for them as they participate in learning tasks (Schaefer & Andzik, 2016).

SENSORY FUNCTIONING Hearing and vision impairments are also common among students with multiple disabilities (Orelove et al., 2016). In fact, because of the unique educational needs of students who experience deafness and blindness, IDEA includes a separate category of disability, called **deaf-blindness**, and defines it this way: "concomitant hearing and visual impairments, the combination of which causes such severe communication and other developmental and educational needs that they cannot be accommodated in special education programs solely for children with deafness or children with blindness." According to the National Center on Deaf-Blindness (2017), in 2016, approximately 10,000 children experienced deaf-blindness. However, like all students with multiple disabilities, students with deaf-blindness are a heterogeneous group, varying in the type and degree of visual impairment and hearing loss.

Many research-based strategies are available for teaching behavior, communication, daily living, and vocational skills to students with deaf-blindness (Parker, Davidson, & Banda, 2007). As a teacher, you will need to be a partner with specialists trained in deaf-blindness to access visual and hearing aids that make it easier for students to use whatever vision or hearing capacities they have. Specialists can also help devise tactile teaching techniques, enabling students to engage with materials using their sense of touch to learn.

Students with deaf-blindness require consistent support. So you will also need to have a trusting partnership with their parents and other family members (Chapter 3). Indeed, families themselves benefit from strong connections with professionals who focus on building both family and student capacity; not surprisingly, families' interactions and overall well-being depend on partnerships with professionals (Kyzar, Brady, Summers, & Turnbull, in press). Likewise, expert educational services and instructional partnerships enhance family quality of life (Kyzar, Brady, Summers, Haines, & Turnbull, 2016).

COMMUNICATION SKILLS Many students with multiple disabilities, including those who are deaf-blind, have communication support needs (Downing, 2011). They have what are often called **complex communication needs**. That is, they have difficulties producing speech, which can affect their communication and social development (Douglas, Kammes, Nordquist, & D'Agostino, 2018). Your job, then, is to make sure the right supports are in place so your students can build their communication skills and to use technology-based supports, including augmentative and alternative communication (AAC) systems (Chapter 8). Similarly, you will want to make sure that their communication partners, especially other students, teachers, or family members, have the skills to support your students' communication and social development.

You should not be surprised to know that, when a student's teachers, paraprofessionals, family members, including brothers and sisters (Douglas et al., 2018), and peers in school have been trained how to communicate with children who have complex communication needs, the students themselves acquire greater communication capacities and can progress in school. Like other partners, you yourself can benefit from those research-based strategies, learning how to ask questions or how to prompt speech using technology like AAC. The bottom line is that trained partners can ensure students' progress (Kent-Walsh, Murza, Malani, & Binger, 2015).

If you have the impression that students need several types of interventions, you are correct. Multicomponent interventions occur when the student's peers receive training and when the training takes into account the context in which the student and peers interact—a general education classroom, playground, or lunchroom, for example. Teaching peers to prompt or model communication using AAC during motivating activities seems to be particularly powerful, probably because these activities make students with and without complex communication needs want to communicate using whatever supports are in place (Therrien, Light, & Pope, 2016).

Nor should you be surprised to know that, without the right communication supports, students with disabilities may use their behavior to communicate. This is why it is so important for you to create motivating contexts and consider both students with complex communication needs and their peers when teaching communication skills and building peer supports (Biggs, Carter, & Gustafson, 2017). For example, Alana will sometimes use disruptive or inappropriate behaviors to communicate when she is stressed and does not feel comfortable using her communication tools. To prevent these problems as a teacher, a key part of communication supports will be supporting not only students with communication needs but also their peers as communication partners.

Causes

Sometimes the cause of a student's disability is simply unknown. Indeed, when students have multiple disabilities, the specific causes of each disability may be unknown. At other times, however, the cause is easy to pinpoint. In the majority of children with severe or profound intellectual impairments, a biomedical factor often causes the impairments. For example, specific genetic or chromosomal differences can lead to intellectual disability. The most commonly understood causes of intellectual disability include Down syndrome, 22q11.2 deletion syndrome, and fragile X syndrome. Down syndrome (Chapter 11) typically involves having an additional copy of chromosome 21. 22q11.2 deletion syndrome (also known as DiGeorge syndrome and velocardiofacial syndrome) involves a missing piece of chromosome 22. Fragile X syndrome is caused by a single gene mutation on the X chromosome; for this reason male individuals with fragile X have a more significant intellectual disability than do female individuals with fragile X, as male individuals only have one X chromosome (Percy, Brown, & Fung, 2017).

Other biomedical factors can contribute to the presence of multiple disabilities. Those factors include malnutrition and vitamin deficiencies during development, as well as toxic threats (e.g., exposure to lead or other environmental toxins during development).

The prevalence of vision and hearing impairments is estimated to be 40 times more common in people with intellectual disability, perhaps because of genetic disorders or specific conditions that impact intellectual and sensory functioning. Young people with one biomedical risk factor (e.g., genetic, environmental factors) may also be at risk for other mental health–related disabilities, such as depression or bipolar disorder (Percy, Brown, et al., 2017). Because of the frequency of these co-occurrences, you should expect that any evaluation of your students with multiple disabilities will take into account those five domains we listed earlier in this chapter—intellectual, adaptive, motor, sensory, and communication.

MyLab Education

Video Example 13.3
In the video "Are You Happy?" you will meet Morgan and learn about her strengths and intellectual, adaptive, motor, sensory, and communication needs. How are her skills enhanced by being included? https://www.youtube.com/watch?v=Y_r3KkRK2h4

By now, you know that understanding the labels and the causes is only one step in providing appropriate supports based on students' individualized learning needs. When Alana was born, she seemed to the doctors to be "a freak of nature." No one now knows why they thought that. But clearly they were incorrect. Yes, Alana has multiple disabilities and a number of support needs that arise from these disabilities. But, even though no one knew the causes when she was born, the most important consideration for her family and educational team was determining the intellectual, adaptive, motor, sensory, and communication supports she needed. With the right combination of supports, Alana grew and developed academically and socially. Yes, she made progress in school. Equally importantly, Alana has grown to be her own person; she is self-determined. As Kristina admonished: Don't write anyone off, but don't disregard their needs. That's just another way of saying: Dignify my daughter by ensuring her progress in school and her independence and self-determination.

Defining Traumatic Brain Injury

The category of multiple disabilities is covered under IDEA. However, traumatic brain injury, because it is an acquired disability, is covered under either IDEA or Section 504. Dylan Outlaw, whom you will meet next, has been covered under both.

Meet Dylan Outlaw—Many Times a Graduate

For 12-year-old Dylan Outlaw, graduation has occurred six times. Yes, six. Each time, it has consisted of far more than the awarding of degrees or diplomas. Think of graduation as moving from one stage of life to another. Then apply that meaning to Dylan.

Dylan graduated from the category of students who do not have disabilities into the category of those who do when a two-ton refrigerated truck plowed into his family's car and caused a traumatic brain injury. Dylan was only 4 years old.

He graduated again by defying the dire prognoses of physicians after the accident. They had warned Dylan's mother, Renee, and her family that he might not survive the injury. He was evaluated as having the most severe form of brain injury. Shards of bone from his eye sockets and temples were floating in his cerebral fluids, near his optic nerves. To prevent the shards from moving, doctors placed Dylan into an induced coma for 5 days. Seemingly miraculously—Renee attributes his recovery to prayer—Dylan's body digested the shards. Yet even though his many magnetic resonance imaging (MRI) scans revealed no bone residue, the brain injury nonetheless affected him.

Dylan graduated from the hospital's critical care unit to its rehabilitation unit in a near-record time of 6 weeks, and then graduated from that unit to rehabilitation at home. From there he went to kindergarten.

Through 5th grade, Dylan was classified as a student with a disability under IDEA and had the requisite IEP. When it came time for him to enter 6th grade, however, Renee had learned that, under Section 504 of the Rehabilitation Act (Chapter 1), Dylan had a right to "reasonable accommodations." She told Dylan that, for him, having those accommodations was like, for another boy, having a cast for a broken arm; it was no big deal to accept those benefits. Together, Renee and Dylan insisted that he receive Section 504 accommodations and that he graduate from his status as a student covered by IDEA. So instead of benefiting from the federal special education law (IDEA), Dylan now benefited from the federal antidiscrimination law, Section 504.

No student graduates without first having been educated. Typically, the student learns from professionals, family, and peers.

His physicians saved his life. Occupational therapists, speech-language therapists, and physical therapists restored most of his functional abilities. His mother, Renee, resigned from her job and stopped taking college courses to coordinate his care at home. His father, Bob; his aunt, Laura; and his grandmother, Ruby, delivered the therapies they had learned from professionals. Dylan's older brother, also named Bob, was Dylan's model: No matter his circumstances, Dylan was determined to follow Bob into kindergarten and then through the grades ahead.

Dylan's classmates in special education also played a role, however accidentally. By having an IEP and being educated with them, Dylan learned that he could do a lot more for himself than his teachers were allowing him to do. He learned the importance of high expectations. Armed with Renee's knowledge about Section 504, Dylan decided that he would abandon his IDEA rights, the special education pullout programs, and (truth be told) the labeling that came with being in special education.

Dylan is bright enough to have understood something profound about himself: He wants to be more typical than not. He's determined enough to have persevered through physically challenging therapies and to have "relabeled" himself. And he's so values-driven that he, with his family wholly behind him and with support from his teachers (Patti Whipple and Kate Simsek), seeks inclusion and independence.

Yet he still needs therapy and accommodations. Because he injured the right side of his brain, he has functional limitations on the left side of his body. Occupational therapists target his fine-motor skills. He receives accommodations in taking tests and doing homework because traumatic brain injury scrambles a person's executive functions: the ability to plan and to execute a plan.

Because he still has not fully recovered his strength, simply getting from one place to another in school exhausts him, often to the point that he physically cannot carry out his homework assignments as well as his classmates without disabilities are able to do. Because academic demands increase from grade to grade, school work is becoming more difficult, despite the fact that Dylan is an excellent reader.

His teacher Patti Whipple cautions us all: "Don't judge before you deal with the student. Traumatic brain injury is not a death sentence. Indeed, I'd love to teach a classroom of a thousand Dylans."

IDEA's Definition of Traumatic Brain Injury

IDEA defines traumatic brain injury (TBI) as:

> an acquired injury to the brain caused by an external physical force, resulting in total or partial functional disability or psychosocial impairment, or both, that adversely affects a child's educational performance. Traumatic brain injury applies to open or closed head injuries resulting in impairments in one or more areas, such as cognition; language; memory; attention; reasoning; abstract thinking; judgment; problem-solving; sensory, perceptual, and motor abilities; psychosocial behavior; physical functions; information processing; and speech. Traumatic brain injury does not apply to brain injuries that are congenital or degenerative, or to brain injuries induced by birth trauma.

We call your attention to three aspects of this definition: First, TBI must be an **acquired injury** (occurring after a child is born, as in Dylan's case). It is inappropriate to classify a student as having TBI if their brain injury was **congenital** (present at birth) or if it occurred at the time of delivery. Second, TBI must be caused by an external physical force (as in Dylan's case). Thus, if a student had **encephalitis** (inflammation of the brain) and the brain was injured as a result of this, the student would not be classified as having TBI. Finally, the term TBI applies to both open and closed head injuries. An **open head injury** penetrates the bones of the skull, allowing bacteria to have contact with the brain and potentially impairing specific functions, usually those controlled by the injured part of the brain. A **closed head injury** (Dylan's type) does not involve penetration or fracture of the bones of the skull. It results from an external blow or from the brain being whipped back and forth rapidly, causing it to rub against and bounce off the rough interior of the skull.

In the 2015–2016 school year, approximately 0.4 percent (32,785) of all students ages 3 through 21 receiving special education services were classified as having a traumatic brain injury (U.S. Department of Education, 2013). The U.S. Department of Health and Human Services (2013) reports the following statistics:

- Approximately 1.7 million people annually sustain a TBI.
- Approximately one third of all injury-related deaths in the United States are related to a TBI.
- Children from birth to age 4, adolescents ages 15 to 19, and older adults over age 65 are most likely to sustain a TBI.
- Male individuals are much more likely to sustain a TBI than female individuals are.
- Male children from birth to age 4 have the highest rates of emergency room visits.
- The annual cost of TBI in the United States (direct medical costs and indirect costs related to lost productivity) is approximately $76.5 billion.

Describing the Characteristics and Causes of Traumatic Brain Injury

Characteristics

Ian Cook/Image Source/Superstock

Students with traumatic brain injury often receive assistance from a school-based physical therapist. Here, the therapist is helping the student recover her sense of balance and her torso strength.

Students with TBI differ from each other in terms of onset, complexity, and recovery (Trovato & Schultz, 2013). Their injuries may affect them in many areas of their functioning; however, they often share similar characteristics with students who have learning disabilities (Chapter 7), communication disorders (Chapter 8), emotional or behavioral disorders (Chapter 9), intellectual disability (Chapter 11), and other health impairments (Chapter 14). Dylan's injury caused learning, communication, emotional, and physical challenges. Of these, the emotional challenges were the greatest, says his mother, Renee. Interestingly, his teacher, Patti, downplays those challenges: "When any student has any emotional problem, we deal with it right then. It doesn't take long. All kids have problems, especially during puberty. Then we move along in class." She knows that Dylan is not so unlike other students and that a short deviation from lesson plans to address behaviors makes teaching easier and learning more effective.

The characteristics of students who experience TBI align with the particular site and extent of their injury. Injuries are classified as mild, moderate, or severe. The extent of functional changes and the course of recovery depend largely on whether the injury was mild, moderate, or severe. Approximately 80 to 90 percent of TBIs are classified as mild (Lajiness-O'Neill, Erdodi, & Lichtenstein, 2017).

PHYSICAL CHANGES   Coordination problems, physical weakness, and fatigue are common effects of TBI (Trovato & Schultz, 2013), as they are for Dylan. Students who were previously athletic often find these changes to be especially frustrating. Fortunately, coordination and physical strength usually improve after the injury as students' brains heal and they undergo rehabilitation, especially occupational therapy, to reacquire their fine-motor skills. Dylan's injury was on the right side of his brain, so his left side is impaired; his occupational therapy targeted his left-side fine-motor skills (holding eating utensils, for example). Students' fatigue often lingers, though; and if occupational therapy and other rehabilitation interventions are not brought to bear, the students' muscles may atrophy, resulting in lost or reduced muscle strength.

COGNITIVE AND ACADEMIC CHANGES   A ten-year follow-up study of students who sustain a TBI between age 2 and age 20 reported that their intelligence quotients (IQs) were within the low average to average range (Anderson, Catroppa, Godfrey, & Rosenfeld, 2012). Students who had sustained a severe brain injury had increased rates of intellectual impairment, particularly related to nonverbal skills. The cognitive impact of brain injury often results in problems associated with memory, planning, problem solving, and abstract reasoning (Ganesalingam et al., 2011).

The extent of injury, ranging from mild to severe, is an important determining factor of the extent of cognitive changes (Recla et al., 2013). When a TBI injury is mild, students usually do not face significant changes in their academic or language abilities; by contrast, students with moderate TBI often have variable outcomes that are influenced by the amount of time since injury and the specific skills being targeted. Students with

MyLab Education

Video Example 13.4

Check out the video "Overview of Traumatic Brain Injury" to learn about different areas of the brain, their related functions, and the impact of brain injuries on particular areas. How does the brain compensate for an injury? http://www.youtube.com/watch?v=T0WBMM7WKL4

moderate TBI tend to have an early small drop in academic skills that persists on a long-term basis, compared with those who have a less severe injury and are able to catch up academically after their injury (Vu, Babikian, & Asarnow, 2011). Finally, students with a severe TBI initially have the most significant impairments in academic and language performance. It is encouraging to note, however, that these students tend to show the most improvement over time in math, spelling, reading, and language. The cognitive impairments associated with severe TBI include difficulties with processing speed and recall of detailed new information.

The student's age at the time of injury is a second factor affecting cognitive functioning (Karver et al., 2012). Those injured under the age of 4 demonstrate greater rates of cognitive impairment than those over the age of 4 (Recla et al., 2013). Very young children have greater brain vulnerability, and the impairment often becomes more evident over time, especially as cognitive demands increase.

Undoubtedly, Dylan has improved cognitively. For a full month after his accident, he was unable to speak. His therapists elicited responses by asking him to play video games. By mastering one game and then another, he began to talk about himself and the games. They soon learned that Dylan was a competitive young boy. He was determined to succeed, as indeed he has.

EMOTIONAL, BEHAVIORAL, AND SOCIAL CHANGES Emotional, behavioral, and social changes can be especially problematic for children and youth with TBI. From time to time Dylan has meltdowns: His frustration gets the better of him when tasks he thinks he should be able to do elude him. One of Patti's accommodations is subtle; she allows him to leave the classroom, compose himself, give himself a pep talk, and return. Often he is out of the room for only a few minutes, so he does not lose much real instructional time and he regains his ability to learn.

Depending on the extent and location of their injuries, students with TBI have an increased likelihood of experiencing a multitude of challenges:

- Mild TBI has few long-term social consequences; however, students with moderate and severe TBI have an increased risk for problems in building close friendships, solving social problems, and recognizing emotions (Rosema, Crowe, & Anderson, 2012).

- Students who experience severe TBI at an earlier age have significantly higher levels of internalizing and externalizing behavior problems (Karver et al., 2012).

- Depending on the severity and age of injury, students with TBI have an increased risk for challenges related to inhibiting, stopping, or redirecting their ongoing actions (Sinopoli & Dennis, 2012).

Causes

There are four major causes of acquired TBI (Faul, Xu, Wald, & Coronado, 2010):

- Falls (accounting for 35 percent) are the number-one cause of TBI. They are most frequent among young children from birth to age 4 and adults age 75 or older. Falls also account for the greatest number of emergency room visits and hospitalizations due to TBI.

- Automobile accidents (accounting for 17 percent) are the leading cause of death from TBI and occur most frequently among adults ages 20 to 24 years. A leading contributor to automobile accidents is driving under the influence of alcohol.

- Being struck by or against something (accounting for 17 percent) typically occurs in sports or recreation when a person collides with a moving or stationary object (for instance, sledding, skiing, snowboarding, diving, skateboarding, playing contact sports, or being hit by a baseball). You have probably seen the increased awareness of the long-term negative effects of concussions from collisions in sports like football or even soccer. These are, essentially, forms of traumatic brain injury.

- Assaults (accounting for 10 percent) frequently involve firearms. Non-firearm assaults include child abuse that results in head injuries in infants.

- Unknown/other causes account for 21 percent.

In infants, **shaken baby syndrome** refers to TBI resulting from a caregiver shaking a child violently, often in situations in which the caregiver is frustrated because of the child's crying (Lopes, Eisenstein, & Williams, 2013). The size of the baby's head, relative to the rest of its body, and the immaturity of the muscles in an infant's neck make even what seems to be a nonviolent shake have the potential to result in TBI.

In *My Voice: Megan's Story*, Megan talks about her experience with a TBI and how she built up her strength and stamina after her accident.

My Voice

Megan's Story

Four days after graduation, my friends Dan, Elizabeth, Sundance, and I went on a fishing trip for steelhead at C. J. Strike Reservoir outside Boise, Idaho. We were driving down a dirt road when our vehicle was in a head-on collision with another vehicle. Dan and Sundance suffered many external injuries and were flown by helicopter to a local air force base. Elizabeth was a life-saver; she managed to get herself free and with a broken arm ran to the nearest house, which was a few miles away. Guided only by a porch light, she made a sling for her arm out of her shirt as she ran along the road. Covered in blood, Elizabeth arrived at the house and called for help. Within 25 minutes a Life Flight crew had arrived and transported me to Saint Alphonsus Hospital for immediate surgery.

I received multiple injuries, but the one that was the most severe was to my head. At Saint Alphonsus, I immediately underwent a craniotomy. Dr. Michael Henbest repaired my skull, correcting a posterior displacement of the cranial vault. My skull was basically destroyed, and it took titanium mesh and plates to piece my skull back together. During surgery, a priest administered last rites, figuring that it was unlikely

I would live through the night. A day after the surgery, I was transported to the Elk's Rehabilitation Center, where I remained in a coma for a week. My prognosis was not good, and the chance of a full recovery was very slim.

After nearly 2 weeks in a coma, I awoke at the Elk's Rehabilitation Center, where my family and the Brain Injury Program's staff had already begun my rehabilitation. My parents, brothers, and friends were by my side 24 hours a day, assisting in shifts, talking to me, holding my hands, and letting me know what was happening. Although I didn't respond (nor do I remember this), the Elk's staff explained to me that this interaction served as the beginning of the slow road of recovery for me. After I came out of the coma, I began a more strenuous rehabilitation. Although I cried a lot and was often frustrated, I approached it as I had other athletic endeavors and simply figured I was preparing for next season. Each day I worked with a series of staff members, working my way through a series of physical and mental exercises designed to build my physical strength and mental acuity.

—Megan Kohnke

Evaluating Students with Multiple Disabilities and Traumatic Brain Injury

The following sections on the nondiscriminatory evaluation (NDE) process highlight the NDE approaches to determining the presence of multiple disabilities and traumatic brain injury, respectively.

Determining the Presence of Multiple Disabilities

As you know, IDEA's nondiscriminatory evaluation process determines whether the student has a disability and requires specially designed instruction and, if necessary, the student's special education and related service needs. The *Nondiscriminatory Evaluation Process: Determining the Presence of Multiple Disabilities* feature describes this process.

Nondiscriminatory Evaluation Process
Determining the Presence of Multiple Disabilities

Observation	**Physicians/medical professionals observe:** The newborn may have noticeable disabilities associated with a syndrome or may have medical complications that are often associated with severe disabilities. **Parents observe:** The child has difficulties nursing, sleeping, or attaining developmental milestones.
Screening	**Screening measures:** Apgar scores are below 4, indicating the possibility of severe disabilities.
Prereferral	Prereferral is typically not used for these children because the severity of the disability indicates a need for special education and related services.
Referral	Students with health impairments that adversely affect their learning or behavior need to be referred for education assessment.
Nondiscriminatory evaluation procedures and standards	**Assessment measures:** **Genetic evaluations:** Evaluation leads to identification of a genetic cause. **Physical examinations:** Medical procedures, including vision and hearing tests, blood work, metabolic tests, spinal tests, etc., reveal the presence of a disabling condition. **Individualized intelligence test:** The student scores at least two standard deviations below the mean (i.e., 70 to 75 or lower), indicating that intellectual disability exists. Most students with multiple disabilities have IQ scores that are significantly below 70, indicating severe cognitive impairment. **Adaptive behavior scales:** The student scores significantly below average on two or more areas of adaptive behavior, indicating severe deficits in skills such as communication, daily living, socialization, gross- and fine-motor coordination, and behavior. **Assistive technology assessment:** The student receives a comprehensive assessment for assistive technology needs in all of the environments in which the student participates. This evaluation should be consistent with IDEA's definition of assistive technology device and assistive technology service. The student's IEP team develops an IEP for the student.
Determination	The nondiscriminatory evaluation team determines that the student has "multiple disabilities" and needs special education and related services.

NONDISCRIMINATORY EVALUATION PROCESS Students with multiple disabilities are often identified at birth or in their early years (as Alana was), so physicians, not educators or psychologists, usually make the initial diagnosis. This diagnosis can be based on problems identified during pregnancy, immediately after birth, or as early developmental milestones are not attained (Percy, Lewkis, et al., 2017). For chromosomal disorders, such as those you read about in the previous sections, specific genetic tests may be undertaken (Percy, Brown, et al., 2017). To identify the causes and severity of sensory disabilities, specific screenings to understand the functioning of the nervous system will be performed (MacKay & Percy, 2017). Each of these sources will be useful in identifying the causes of the disability. However, remember that a critical component of determining the need for special education services and supports is evaluating—as IDEA states in its definition of multiple disabilities—the intense education needs that arise from concomitant impairments.

Determining the Nature of Specifically Designed Instruction and Services

To determine the nature of specially designed instruction and supports for students with multiple disabilities, assessing the need for support in the multiple domains that may affect students with multiple disabilities—intellectual, adaptive, motor, sensory, and communication—will be important. Throughout this chapter, you've learned about the various support needs that students with multiple disabilities have. It might not surprise you, then, to learn that assessments of support needs are available that provide information that can be used in planning for and implementing supports tailored to the needs of students with disabilities.

The *Supports Intensity Scale—Children's version* (SIS-C; Thompson et al., 2016) was developed for children and youth ages 5 to 16 with intellectual and developmental disabilities (including multiple disabilities) to provide information on the support needs of children with disabilities in home, community, and school activities. A trained interviewer talks with two people who know the student well (e.g., teacher, family member) to gather information to complete the SIS-C. SIS-C interviewers ask about the type, frequency, and daily support time needed by students to participate in typical environments. Ratings are made on seven subscales: Home Life, Community and Neighborhood, School Participation, School Learning, Health and Safety, Social, and Advocacy. This information is the basis for an individualized support plan that includes the educational supports a student needs to make progress in school (Thompson, Hughes, Walker, & DeSpain, 2017).

In developing educational supports, two types of support call for your special attention:

- Supports to Enhance Personal Competencies
- Supports to Make the Environment More Accessible and Welcoming (Thompson, Hughes, et al., 2017).

Both types of supports are critical for students with multiple disabilities. Supports for personal competencies work to build skills and abilities and can include the instructional strategies you have read about in this chapter and others (e.g., systematic instruction, prompting). Supports that make the environment more accessible and welcoming include training communication partners in preparation for communicating and engaging with students who have multiple disabilities. You will want to understand what specific support needs a particular student has (based on the student's evaluation) and then—with other professionals, the student's parents, and the student (where appropriate)—in the IEP process, arrive at the accommodations, modifications, and supplementary aids and services that will enable the student to access and progress in the general education curriculum (Thompson, Hughes, et al., 2017).

Determining the Presence of Traumatic Brain Injury

The evaluation of students with TBI needs to be comprehensive (across the student's physical, intellectual/cognitive, emotional-behavioral, and developmental support needs) and ongoing because children change (Bodin & Shay, 2012), just as Dylan changed after his injuries.

Nondiscriminatory Evaluation Process

Determining the Presence of Traumatic Brain Injury

Observation	**Parents observe:** The student receives a head injury from an accident, fall, sports injury, act of violence, or other cause. **Physicians observe:** The student has an open or closed head injury caused by an external physical force. **Teacher observes:** In the case of a mild head injury that might not have been treated by a physician, the teacher observes changes—physical, cognitive, communication, social, behavioral, and/or personality.

Screening	**Assessment measures:**
	    Scanning instruments: Electroencephalograms (EEGs), computerized tomography (CT) scans, magnetic resonance imaging (MRI) scans, positron emission tomography (PET) scans, and other technology determine the extent of injury.
	    Neurological exam: A neurologist examines the student for indications of brain injury.
	    Coma scale: In instances of moderate-to-severe head injuries that induce comas, these scales provide some information about probable outcome.

Prereferral	Prereferral typically is not used with these students because the sudden onset and severity of the disability indicate a need for special education or related services.
Referral	Students with moderate-to-severe TBI should be referred for special education evaluation while still in rehabilitation. Teachers should refer students with mild head injuries if they notice any changes—physical, cognitive, communication, social, behavioral, and/or personality.

	Assessment measures:
	    Individualized intelligence test: The student tends to score higher on the verbal section than on the performance section.
	    Individualized achievement tests: The student usually has peaks and valleys in scores. The student often retains skills in some areas, whereas other skills are affected adversely by the injury.

Nondiscriminatory evaluation procedures and standards	**Adaptive behavior scales:** The student may have difficulty in social, self-care, household, and community skills as a result of the injury. **Cognitive processing tests:** The student may have difficulty in areas of attention, memory, concentration, motivation, and perceptual integration. **Social, emotional, and behavioral changes:** The student may demonstrate difficulty relating to others and behaving in socially appropriate ways. The student may have problem behavior and/or emotional disorders. **Anecdotal records:** The student's cognitive, communication, motor, and behavior skills appear to have changed from what was indicated in records before the accident. **Curriculum-based assessment:** The student may have difficulty in areas of curriculum that were not problematic before the injury. **Direct observation:** The student appears frustrated, has a limited attention span, tires easily, or lacks motivation to perform academic tasks. The student may have difficulty relating appropriately to others. Skills can improve rapidly, especially during the early post-injury stage.
Determination	The nondiscriminatory evaluation team determines that special education and related services are needed.

NONDISCRIMINATORY EVALUATION PROCESS (see the *Nondiscriminatory Evaluation Process: Determining the Presence of Traumatic Brain Injury* feature) details the nondiscriminatory evaluation process for students with traumatic brain injury. In Chapter 4, you learned about the role of progress monitoring in the NDE process. Progress monitoring involves frequent and repeated (usually at least monthly) assessments of student learning and performance that, when charted or graphed, provide information about progress. For students with TBI, those data may be particularly important for determining a student's needs with regard to special education services. A recent White Paper on statewide systems to support students with TBI stated that "[t]o improve academic supports for students with TBI, school-based management plans must include explicit protocols for identifying, assessing, and tracking those students" (Gioia, Glang, Hooper, & Brown, 2016, p. 399). Progress monitoring is identified by these authors as a means to such assessment and identification. The *Guidelines for Teaching: Progress Monitoring* feature shows how progress monitoring can be performed across multiple content areas and across grades and ages as part of the response to intervention (RTI) process you learned about in Chapter 5.

Guidelines for Teaching

Progress Monitoring

Pre-Reading.
- *Phoneme Segmentation Fluency*
  - Pronounce a word or a series of words to a student.
  - Be certain that the student says the sounds that make up each word.
  - Record correct responses to graph across time.
- *Letter Sound Fluency*
  - Show the student a sheet of paper with the 26 lowercase letters displayed in random order.
  - Be certain that the student says the sound of each letter within 1 minute.

Reading.
- *Word Identification Fluency*
  - Show the student a random list of high-frequency words.
  - Be certain that the student reads words aloud for 1 minute.

- Record the number of words read correctly.
- *Passage Reading Fluency*
  - Find a reading passage that is at the level you expect for students at the year's end.
  - Present the passage to the student.
  - Be certain that the student reads the passage aloud for 1 minute.
  - Record the number of words read correctly.
- *Maze Fluency*
  - Find a reading passage that is at the level you expect for students at the year's end.
  - Replace every seventh word with three possible word choices.
  - Show the student the passage for 2½ minutes.
  - Be certain that the student reads the passage, selecting word choices.
  - Record the number of correct word choices.

(Continued)

Mathematics.
- *Computation*
  - Show the student a sample of computation (e.g., addition, subtraction, multiplication, fractions) problems to be covered during the year.
  - Provide the student with a fixed time, depending on the student's age, to write answers.
  - Record the number of correct digits written in answers.
- *Concepts and Applications*
  - Show the student a sample of concept and application problems (e.g., measurement, money, word problems) to be covered during the year.
  - Provide the student with a fixed time, depending on the student's age, to write answers.
  - Record the number of correct answers.

Spelling.
- Create multiple 20-word spelling tests from words the student is expected to master during the year.
- Dictate a word to the student.
- Be certain that the student spells out the word on the paper.
- Dictate another word after the student completes spelling or after 10 seconds, whichever occurs sooner.
- Provide 2 minutes for the test.
- Record the number of letter sequences (pairs of letters) spelled correctly.

Writing.
- Provide the student a short topic sentence to begin a written piece.
- Provide a fixed time (3–10 minutes, depending on the age of the student) for the student to write in response to the topic sentence.
- Record the number of correct word sequences.

SOURCE: Adapted from: Fuchs, L. S., & Fuchs, D. (n.d.). *What is scientifically-based research on progress monitoring?* Washington, DC: American Institute for Research National Center on Progress Monitoring. Accessed at https://files.eric.ed.gov/fulltext/ED502460.pdf on June 19, 2018.

Determining the Nature of Specifically Designed Instruction and Services

As you have learned earlier, students with TBI often have impaired executive functions (McCauley et al., 2012). A helpful tool to assess behaviors related to executive functions relevant in educational settings is the Behavior Rating Inventory of Executive Function (BRIEF). BRIEF has scales to cover behavioral regulations (inhibit, shift, emotional control) and meta-cognition scales (initiate, working memory, plan/organize, organization of materials, and monitor). It includes 86 items and requires approximately 10 to 15 minutes for administration. BRIEF is appropriate for use with students ages 5 through 18. Additionally, a preschool version for children ages 2 through 5 is available. Researchers have documented that BRIEF has sound reliability and validity (McCauley et al., 2012).

> MyLab Education **Self-Check 13.1**
> MyLab Education **Application Exercise 13.1:** Identifying Needs for Supports

Including Students with Multiple Disabilities and Traumatic Brain Injury
Multiple Disabilities

Leaders in the field of multiple disabilities have long advocated for inclusive education to enhance students' academic and social development and supports (Quirk, Ryndak, & Taub, 2017). The major professional organization in the field of multiple disabilities, TASH, has had a long-term commitment to inclusive education. Nevertheless, Figure 13.1 shows that most students with multiple disabilities still spend most of their time outside the regular classroom (U.S. Department of Education, 2018). Only 13 percent of students with multiple disabilities spend 80 percent or more of their

Figure 13.1 Extent of Inclusion for Students with Multiple Disabilities

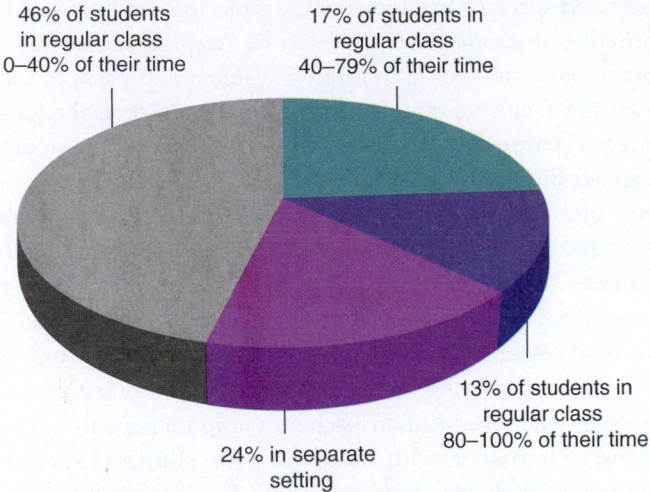

46% of students in regular class 0–40% of their time

17% of students in regular class 40–79% of their time

13% of students in regular class 80–100% of their time

24% in separate setting

SOURCE: U.S. Department of Education (2018). 39th Annual Report to Congress on the Implementation of the Individuals with Disabilities Education Act, 2017. Washington DC: U.S. Department of Education, Office of Special Education and Rehabilitation Services, Office of Special Education Programs.

day in general education classrooms, while almost 25 percent are in completely separate settings. Takeaway message? Students with multiple disabilities, even compared to students with one disability label, are at high risk for being educated in separate special education classrooms or in separate schools (Morningstar, Kurth, & Johnson, 2017).

In Chapter 4 and in other places in this book, you've read about supplementary aids and services. Paraprofessionals play essential roles in ensuring students' inclusion and progress in the general education curriculum. **Paraprofessionals** are school staff who, under IDEA, are regarded as supplementary aids and services. They often are IEP team members.

A paraprofessional is defined as a person hired to:

> provide instructional support including those who (1) provide one-on-one tutoring if such tutoring is scheduled at a time when a student would not otherwise receive instruction from a teacher; (2) assist with classroom management, such as organizing instructional and other materials; (3) provide instructional assistance in a computer laboratory; (4) conduct parental involvement activities; (5) provide support in a library or media center; (6) act as a translator; or (7) provide instructional support services under the direct supervision of a teacher. (U.S. Department of Education, 2018)

Paraprofessionals are an important part of Alana's team to support inclusion. For her and other students with multiple disabilities, paraprofessionals are nearly indispensable for ensuring access to and progress in the general education curriculum. In 2014 (the most recent data available) 415,781 full-time paraprofessionals were employed across the United States to support students with disabilities ages 6 through 21. By contrast, there were 339,833 special education teachers (U.S. Department of Education, 2018).

No doubt, paraprofessionals are essential for students with disabilities, including students with multiple disabilities. A survey of 313 paraprofessionals across 77 elementary, middle, and high schools found that 44 percent reported supporting students with multiple disabilities; 80 percent reported supporting students with autism spectrum disorders; and 75 percent reported supporting students with intellectual disability (Carter, O'Rourke, Sisco, & Pelsue, 2009).

The use of paraprofessionals is not without controversy, as some have argued that paraprofessionals are not adequately trained to implement supports for students with disabilities and that special and general education teachers are more qualified to design and implement supports. In fact, researchers have suggested that there is an "overreliance" on paraprofessionals in today's schools that negatively impacts student outcomes (Giangreco & Suter, 2015). Researchers have developed guidelines for school teams to

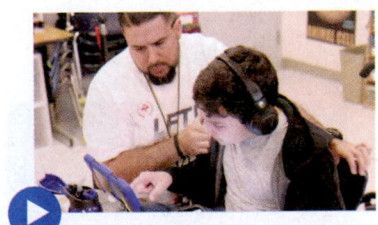

MyLab Education

Video Example 13.5

The role of paraprofessionals is important to inclusion. What strategies is this paraprofessional using to support Jack?

think critically about how they can effectively and creatively use resources in schools to provide all students, including students with disabilities, greater access to highly qualified teachers and special educators. For example, in a study of 26 schools using the *Guidelines for Selecting Alternatives to Overreliance on Paraprofessionals* framework over six states, researchers found that going through a systematic process of identifying alternatives led to greater inclusive opportunities, changes in special education teachers' caseloads, changes in paraprofessional utilization, and greater classroom collaboration practices (Giangreco, Suter, & Hurley, 2013).

When paraprofessionals assist you to provide instruction and other support in inclusive classrooms, be sure they are trained and supported; learn what they know and what they need—that's part of your duty to ensure your students' progress and a sure way to be an effective partner with paraprofessionals (Carter et al., 2009). There is an emerging body of research on effective strategies for training paraprofessionals. In a recent review of research studies on the effectiveness of training procedures directed toward practitioners—special education teachers, paraprofessionals, and related services personnel working with students with disabilities—106 studies (22 percent of all studies included in the review) involved paraprofessionals. The only practitioners targeted more frequently in studies were special education teachers themselves. Across the studies and the practitioners, providing specific training improved the practitioner's ability to implement instruction and supports needed by students with disabilities. This finding did not differ for paraprofessionals. Modeling, written instruction, and oral descriptions were all training practices that positively impacted the implementation of research-based practices with students with disabilities by practitioners (Brock & Carter, 2017).

In terms of training specifically for paraprofessionals, teachers can learn how to train paraprofessionals to use research-based practices. For example, teachers delivered a 2-hour training to paraprofessionals about peer support arrangements and how these arrangements differed from current instructional practices. The training focused on enabling paraprofessionals to shift toward a facilitator role, enabling the students' peers to take on a more targeted social and academic support role. As a result of the training, three of four students with disabilities experienced greater academic engagement (Brock & Carter, 2016).

Special educators are likely to be called on to train and supervise paraprofessionals. It is important to keep in mind that paraprofessionals may spend quite a bit of time in general education settings, so it is vital to provide training across settings. In addition, special educators will need to work with general educators to understand the roles of paraprofessionals and how to support them to be successful. In training and supervising paraprofessionals, the first step is to clarify that paraprofessionals are to deliver instruction and supports under the guidance of a licensed teacher. Developing concrete roles and responsibilities will help ensure this guidance occurs. Then, in providing support and guidance to paraprofessionals, the following training components have been found to be effective:

- Provide a clear description of the educational practice, its purpose, and its implementation

- Model the practice (e.g., role play or have the paraprofessional learn from videos of the practice being implemented)

- Provide performance feedback (e.g., monitor the paraprofessional implementing the practice and provide coaching or ongoing feedback) (Brock, Biggs, Carter, Cattey, & Raley, 2016).

MyLab Education
Video Example 13.6
As you've learned, inclusion has been important for Alana. How have Alana's teachers supported her inclusion?

Traumatic Brain Injury

Figure 13.2 indicates the educational placement of students with TBI. Among students with TBI, 50 percent spend more than 80 percent of their day in general education classes. However, 8 percent are educated in a separate setting, including at a hospital or at home. So, this is better than for some categories, but over a quarter of all students

Figure 13.2 Extent of Inclusion for Students with Traumatic Brain Injury

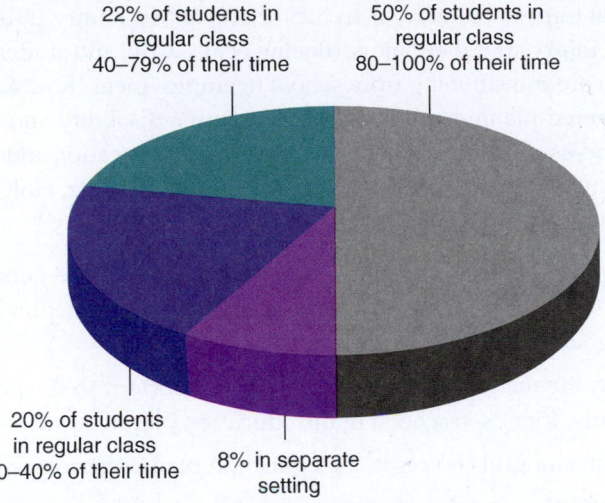

22% of students in
regular class
40–79% of their time

50% of students in
regular class
80–100% of their time

20% of students
in regular class
0–40% of their time

8% in separate
setting

SOURCE: U.S. Department of Education (2018). 39th Annual Report to Congress on the Implementation of the Individuals with Disabilities Education Act, 2017. Washington DC: U.S. Department of Education, Office of Special Education and Rehabilitation Services, Office of Special Education Programs.

Inclusion Tips for Students with Multiple Disabilities or Traumatic Brain Injury

	Behavior	Social Interactions	Educational Performance	Classroom Attitudes
What You Might See	The student has temper tantrums and hits self or others.	The student is unable to communicate needs or wants using words.	The student is not able to read or write, and functional skills are extremely limited.	The student is confused about exactly what is expected on assignments.
What You Might Be Tempted to Do	Discipline and isolate the student from the rest of the class.	Allow the student to remain a class observer rather than a participant.	Give up and let the student color or do something quiet.	Excuse the student from assignments.
Alternate Teacher Response	Learn to identify cues that trigger positive behavior. Reward appropriate behavior.	Use assistive technology to enable the student to communicate self needs and wants.	Create opportunities for the student to benefit from peer tutoring.	Use rubrics as a way to delineate expectations for assignments.
Ways to Include Peers in the Process	Support the peers closest to the student and teach them to recognize and give cues that encourage positive behavior in a way that is respectful.	Teach peers to communicate with the student using assistive technology.	Arrange for peers to assist the student with task completion. Support the student's opportunities to be friends and have relationships with peer tutors.	Pair the student with a partner and friend who can help the student focus and participate meaningfully during instruction.

with TBI spend little or no time in general education settings. Dylan and his mother were right to fight for his inclusion.

Inclusion Tips for Students with Multiple Disabilities or Traumatic Brain Injury describes how you can include students with multiple disabilities and traumatic brain injury.

MyLab Education Self-Check 13.2
MyLab Education Application Exercise 13.2: Support and Guidance for Paraprofessionals

---

Educating Students with Multiple Disabilities or Traumatic Brain Injury

Person-centered Planning

Person-centered planning is a practice that you and other teachers will often use as you partner with students and their families (as well as paraprofessionals and related services providers) to identify goals, values, and visions for the future and to use this information to design IEPs and plan for transitions (Mazzotti, Kelley, & Coco, 2015). Person-centered planning can benefit students who are deaf-blind and are in transition from school to postsecondary activities (Zatta & McGinnity, 2016), students with traumatic brain injury after their injury (Boeing et al., 2010), and students with multiple disabilities who are transitioning from school to employment (Katz & Barol, 2017).

Person-centered planning puts the student with a disability and the family at the center of the process of building systems of supports in education and community contexts. Its key features in the education context include (Schwartz, Holburn, & Jacobson, 2000; Wells & Sheehey, 2012):

- Aligning special education services and supports with the person's values and dreams. A long-term planning approach is utilized and action steps to achieve long-term goals are identified.
- Focusing on the inclusion of people who are important to the person with a disability (family, friends, teachers) in the education planning process.
- Providing meaningful choices in the education planning process.
- Building natural supports (e.g., peer supports).
- Building relationships and networks that foster participation in inclusive environments.
- Creating opportunities and experiences in inclusive contexts by providing effective instruction and supports.
- Planning collaboratively and frequently to address changing needs.
- Fostering leadership by the student with a disability.

A number of different approaches have been developed to implement person-centered planning. The names of some of the available approaches include Group Action Planning (GAP; see Turnbull et al., 1996), Essential Lifestyles Planning (ELP; see Smull & Burke Harrison, 1992), Personal Futures Planning (PFP; see Mount & Zwernik, 1988), and Planning Alternative Tomorrows with Hope (PATH; see Pierpoint, O'Brien, & Forest, 1995). In the education context, one of the most popular person-centered planning approaches is the MAPs (formerly McGill Action Planning) process. Through that process, you will partner with students and their families to customize their educational programs to their specific visions, strengths, and needs (Wells & Sheehey, 2012).

Person-centered approaches are especially effective in planning transitions from school to postschool activities (Kelley & Buchanan, 2017; Mazzotti et al., 2015), building stronger family and professional partnerships and enhancing student and family expectations for postschool outcomes (Hagner et al., 2012). Indeed, by integrating person-centered planning with other instructional approaches, young people with multiple disabilities can take steps toward attaining their transition goals (Nittrouer, Shogren, & Pickens, 2016).

The MAPs process can be divided into three phases—preparation, meetings, and follow-up. The preparation phase involves identifying and getting participants ready for the activities that will occur in the series of meetings. The meetings phase typically involves two to three meetings (each lasting a couple of hours) and culminates with the creation of a plan. The follow-up phase includes additional meetings or activities needed to promote the sustainability and implementation of the plan. MAPs participants should include the person with a disability, family and friends, and relevant professionals (both special and general education teachers, paraprofessionals, and related services providers). It is also highly recommended that same-age peers be included in the meetings (Wells & Sheehey, 2012).

The following goals drive the meeting phase:

1. Hear the Person's Story—What is the person's history?
2. Honor the Dream—What is the dream for the person?

3. Recognize the Nightmare—What is your nightmare?

4. Name Strengths—Who is the person?

5. Name Needs—What are the person's needs?

6. Agree on Actions—What would the person's ideal day at school and in the community look like?

7. Develop a Plan—What must be done to make it happen?

Questions 1 through 5 are the focus of the first meeting, and Questions 6 and 7 drive subsequent meetings. MAPs calls for a facilitator to lead the discussion and ensure that everyone has the opportunity to contribute. Also, there is a recorder who documents the discussions using markers and flip charts; both text and pictures are used to document information and build the action plan (O'Brien, Pearpoint, & Kahn, 2010; Wells & Sheehey, 2012). See *Into Practice Across Grade Levels: Implementing MAPs* for examples of how this process works.

Into Practice Across Grade Levels

Implementing MAPs

Implement the MAPs process to ensure that planning for students with multiple disabilities or traumatic brain injury is person-centered.

Hear students' and their family's story.

Example: Bachir is a **3rd-grade** student at Barnard Elementary School. His family emigrated from Sudan to flee the civil war in the south of the country. Bachir had been injured when a land mine exploded near his home in south Sudan, resulting in ongoing traumatic brain injury. He and his parents speak only halting English, but are working to improve their language skills and to make a life in Omaha. During the MAPs meeting, Bachir's mother wanted to share information about their life in Sudan before the civil war and talk about Bachir's skills and abilities that she still sees in him, even though he has greater difficulty performing some of these tasks and activities after the TBI.

What is the dream for the student?

Example: Jennifer is a **5th-grade** student with multiple disabilities, including physical disabilities (cerebral palsy), cognitive disabilities (intellectual disability), and communication disabilities. She uses The Proloquo2go app on her iPad as an alternative communication device. For most of her life, Jennifer's parents have been told she'll never work, but during the MAPs meeting, Jennifer's mother shares that she has a dream that Jennifer will be able to work somewhere where she can be happy and make friends when she leaves school. All the MAPs members talked about Jennifer's strengths and asked Jennifer to talk, using her iPad, about what she thought she might like to do. The meeting resulted in some career exploration activities for Jennifer to learn more about different jobs.

What is the nightmare for the student?

Example: Jose's **6th-grade** year at Highlands Middle School—his first year in middle school—triggered a number of concerns on the part of Jose's parents and Jose himself. Jose experienced TBI as a result of a fall down stairs at his home when he was a 1st grader, and although he has steadily improved, he still requires more time to process information and has difficulty expressing what he knows using written language. At his MAPs meeting, Jose and his parents brought up the difficult time he was having with going from content class to content class throughout the day, and expressed the "nightmare" that Jose would fall behind in math, reading, and science each year and not be ready for high school and beyond. The MAPs team discussed short-term and long-term accommodations that could enable Jose to keep up with the work without having to spend every evening doing homework. This included using a self-organizer to keep him on track and meeting with his teachers at the start of each week to decide how best to prepare for the week's work expectations.

What are the student's needs and strengths?

Example: Linda is a **9th-grade** student with TBI from an automobile accident when she was in elementary school. Linda had a difficult time in middle school as a function of her difficulties with attention and organization. Some of her general education teachers were good at providing accommodations, but some were not. Linda's special education teacher suggested that a MAPs meeting might be good to make plans as Linda transitions from middle school to high school in the coming year to avoid these issues in high school. In the MAPs meeting, Linda, her family, and the school faculty began by considering Linda's strengths—she has strong musical abilities, she is good at math, and she likes to read—and areas of instructional need—she does not learn well sitting for long periods of time and has a difficult time organizing her work to get it done and turned in. Linda, her family, and the school faculty talked about what had worked

(Continued)

in middle school (scheduled breaks to walk around, linking coursework to music), what had not worked (going from course to course without support to help her get everything she needed), how supports might capitalize on her strengths, and what accommodations she might benefit from.

What would the person's ideal day at school and in the community look like?

Example: Michael is a **12th-grade** student at Nathan Hale High School. He is an avid fan of the school's basketball and football teams. Michael has multiple disabilities from a genetic disorder that resulted in intellectual disability and an orthopedic disability. Michael and his family know he is eligible for the 18 to 21 services in his school district, but he's more interested in going to a local 4-year university that has a program for students with developmental disabilities. His teacher suggests that a MAPs meeting might enable them to plan for his senior year in high school in preparation for the postsecondary education program. They know Michael's dream is to go to the local university, so the next step is to envision what the time he had left at Hale and the first year at the university would look like so they could create a plan to meet the instructional needs arising from that vision.

How does person-centered planning affect students and adults with disabilities? A review of the research on person-centered planning published in 2010 found 15 articles that examined the effect of person-centered planning. The review found that person-centered planning was commonly combined with other approaches, including positive behavior support or transition planning. It concluded that, overall, person-centered planning led to improvements in social networks and greater involvement of students with disabilities in activities in their daily lives. Some studies found that active involvement of the person with a disability and their team led to increased communication and development of a vision for the future. For example, one study with transition-age students found that when person-centered planning was used, parents spoke more during IEP meetings, suggesting more involvement in the education planning process (Claes, Van Hove, Vandevelde, van Loon, & Schalock, 2010). Another study found that when integrating person-centered planning into leadership education for people with disabilities and their family members, engagement and advocacy increased (Schuh, Hagner, Dillon, & Dixon, 2016). This body of research suggests that person-centered planning can be a meaningful way to engage young people with disabilities and their families in educational and transition planning, leading to enhanced outcomes.

Assistive Technology

In Chapter 6, you learned about assistive technology (AT) and how it can be used to promote access, inclusion, and progress for students with disabilities. You may remember that assistive technology can be used to address needs in many areas, including:

- Environmental access
- Mobility
- Positioning
- Communication
- Learning.

In this chapter, you are learning that different types of assistive technologies benefit students with multiple disabilities to access their environment (e.g., switches to turn book pages), to address positioning needs (e.g., standers to enable students to be in the same position as their peers without disabilities), or to communicate (e.g., augmentative and alternative communication systems). In addition, students with TBI can benefit from technology supports related to memory, language, and cognitive supports (audio recorder to capture a lecture, a calendar app on a smartphone to help remember appointments and medication, or screen reading software to support literacy and text comprehension).

A multidisciplinary evaluation is almost always necessary for students with traumatic brain injury and multiple disabilities to determine what they need by way of assistive technology. Assistive technology specialists, speech-language pathologists, orientation and mobility specialists, and occupational and physical therapists usually should be involved as partners with you, the teacher, and the students and families. Together, these people should pay particular attention to students' needs for assistive technology so students can have access to and make progress in those five critical domains we identified earlier—intelligence, adaptation, motor, sensory, and communication.

A helpful guide for an assistive technology evaluation is the SETT (Student, Environment, Tasks, Tools) framework (Zabala, 2005). SETT provides a framework for identifying, trying, and evaluating assistive technology (Thompson, Shogren, & Wehmeyer, 2017) related to the:

- Student's needs, interests, and abilities
- Environment in which the technology could potentially be used
- Tasks for which the technology could be used
- Technology that might be able to meet the student's needs.

Any assistive technology evaluation also should take into account the student's needs across the five domains.

Assistive technology can be high-tech (e.g., electric wheelchair, computer-based communication systems) or low-tech (e.g., picture-based communication systems, adding a grip to a spoon for a student with motoric needs). For students with traumatic brain injury and multiple disabilities, assistive technology can increasingly be provided through the technology that is part of our day-to-day lives. For example, smartphones can be used as a cognitive support for a student with TBI who is having difficulty with memory and completing tasks with apps that provide memory and organizational supports on a smartphone (Wong, Sinclair, Seabrook, McKay, & Ponsford, 2017). Those apps can assist a student who has had a brain injury to remember the steps needed to complete a task, promoting greater independence (Rumrill et al., 2016). For example, a number of apps provide picture prompts, using photos taken by the student or a teacher, and present these photos (with audio prompts if necessary) in the order of the vocational task. Another example of technology benefiting adolescents with TBI involves an app-based coaching model (with videos made by peers of adolescents with TBI related to a variety of social situations and appropriate responses) that resulted in enhanced social participation (Bedell, Wade, Turkstra, Haarbauer-Krupa, & King, 2017). When using these assistive technology tools, however, it is critical to provide training and support for students with TBI to learn how to effectively use these tools and integrate them throughout instructional activities.

Further, assistive technologies can increase independence and self-direction in people with multiple disabilities (Stock, Davies, & Gillespie, 2013). Simplified interfaces that integrate cognitive supports have even been developed to enable people with multiple disabilities to access Facebook, increasing their social communication (Davies et al., 2015). Programs exist that can assist with decision making by integrating decision points into visual or audio prompts. Other technological tools that can benefit people with traumatic brain injuries and multiple disabilities are transportation apps that provide highly individualized personal navigation supports so that people with cognitive support needs can more independently navigate public transportation (Livingstone-Lee, Skelton, & Livingston, 2014). These apps, run on smartphones, not only use Global Positioning System (GPS) data to provide information about where a user is on a map (such as standard map applications) but also can identify for the user, through audio information, whether the user is at the desired location. You will want to make certain a student's IEP team considers these types of technologies when planning transition from secondary school to postsecondary activities.

Overall, there is little doubt that people with TBI and multiple disabilities can benefit from technologies to support cognition and memory. For example, a review of

43 studies found that providing people who have TBI with access to technology that addressed needs for supports related to memory had a large impact (Jamieson, Cullen, McGee-Lennon, Brewster, & Evans, 2014).

However, it is always vital to keep the needs of people with disabilities at the center of decisions regarding the development and selection of assistive technologies. For example, a review of the literature related to communication technologies for people with TBI stated that it was highly important to consider the "user" (person with TBI) in terms of experience with the technology and to address motivation and goals (Brunner, Hemsley, Togher, & Palmer, 2017). Promoting access to assistive technology, particularly cognitive support technology, can also impact how educators view students with disabilities. For example, when students have access to technology, teachers perceive students with disabilities as having greater self-determination (Shogren, Wehmeyer, Davies, Stock, & Palmer, 2013). Clearly, the research leaves little question that assistive technology should be considered for students with multiple disabilities and traumatic brain injuries.

As you learned in Chapters 1 and 4, IDEA requires that IEP teams consider and make informed decisions about the need for assistive technology devices and services and the nature and extent of such devices and services required for students to benefit from the educational program. The *Guidelines for Teaching: Planning for Assistive Technology Use* feature provides guidance with regard to planning for appropriate AT use by students with multiple disabilities and TBI and meeting the requirements of IDEA. Of course, much of this planning will be done in conjunction with related services professionals, including speech and language therapists, physical therapists, occupational therapists, AT experts, as well as students and their families.

Guidelines for Teaching

Planning for Assistive Technology Use

Identify the Skills to Be Addressed Through Assistive Technology Use.
- Assess student skills pertaining to a desired activity or outcome.
  - Identify student strengths pertaining to a desired activity or outcome.
  - Identify student instructional needs pertaining to a desired activity.
  - Identify skills to be taught and skills to be supported with assistive technology (AT).
- Assess student current technology use skills.
- Identify environments in which skills related to desired activity or outcome will be performed.

  - Assess student performance of desired activity or outcome in specific environments.

Identify the Assistive Technology Devices to Be Used.
- Consider student characteristics and preferences pertaining to AT use.
  - Identify potential devices that meet student preferences and abilities.
- Consider environmental factors that influence which device to use.

- Consider universal design features needed by the student.
- Consider funding, cost, and availability factors that impact the decision regarding what device to use.
- Consider maintenance and reliability factors that influence the decision regarding what device to use.
- Generate a list of device options, with pros and cons, for presentation to students and families.

Identify School and Related Services Personnel Who Can Provide Instruction and Support on the Assistive Technology Devices to Be Used.
- Examine the primary function of AT and identify school and related services personnel who are involved in instruction and support in that area of function.
- Examine skills pertaining to a desired activity or outcome to determine what school and related services personnel might be needed.
- Examine device maintenance and reliability factors to determine what school and related services personnel might be needed.
- Consider instructional needs associated with AT device use to determine what school and related services personnel might be needed.

Create Plan for Assistive Technology Services and Device Use.

- Identify appropriate AT services associated with student adoption and use of AT device.
  - Write goals pertaining to AT device adoption and use.
- Identify time required with device and time associated with device training.
  - Specify time (daily, weekly) associated with AT training and device use.
- Provide for trial uses of device and modifications to device or device to be used to ensure usability.
- Identify barriers to implementing AT device use.
  - Write goals and specify modifications to remove barriers.
- Create data collection plan to ensure that AT device is utilized, is maintained, and supports successful performance of skills leading to desired activities and outcomes.
  - Ensure that data are reviewed and, if needed, the team is called together to make revisions.

Transition Strategies

For more than a quarter of a century, IDEA has required that students receiving special education services be given needed transition services when they become adolescents. In Chapter 4 you learned that, beginning no later than the first IEP after the student turns 16, or earlier if deemed necessary by the IEP team or mandated by the state, the IEP team must consider what transition services are needed for a student to successfully transition from school to adulthood. Transition services are defined in IDEA as *a coordinated set of activities that promote movement from school to such post-school activities as post-secondary education, vocational training, employment, adult services, independent living and community participation. They must be based on the individual student's needs, taking into account his or her preferences and interests. Transition services must include instruction, community experiences, and development of employment and other post school adult living objectives. If appropriate, daily living skills and functional vocational evaluation may also be included.* In addition to being required by law, however, transition efforts are critical for students with multiple disabilities and students with TBI, as both groups fared poorly in achieving transition outcomes like employment or independent living in a longitudinal study of the impact of transition outcomes for youth with disabilities (Mazzotti et al., 2016).

In Chapter 11, you learned about transition planning using the Transition Planning Inventory. There are a host of strategies that can be implemented to support the transition of students with multiple disabilities or traumatic brain injury (and, for that matter, all students with disabilities) from high school to adulthood, including some you have already learned about. For example, the *Self-Determined Learning Model of Instruction* (Chapter 11) is an important transition strategy to promote self-determination and positive transition outcomes. Person-centered planning (this chapter) and student-directed learning (Chapter 12) are also important transition strategies. The federally funded National Technical Assistance Center on Transition (NTACT) has identified effective practices in transition, including practices that are evidence-based and research-based, across multiple outcome areas. These are grouped according to various practices, from transition planning to graduation to independent living strategies. We highlight a few of these in the areas of independent living and employment.

You can find more information about research-based transition practices on the NTACT website at https://www.transitionta.org/effectivepractices.

RESEARCH-BASED TRANSITION PRACTICES TO PROMOTE INDEPENDENT LIVING   Among the research-based practices identified by NTACT to foster independent living are those promoting student involvement in educational planning, the Self-Determined Learning Model of Instruction, and a number of prompting strategies. For all students, particularly perhaps those with multiple disabilities, prompting strategies are important (and not only for transition), so it is important that you know something about them. Prompts are "any teacher behaviors presented to increase the probability of correct responding" (Westling & Fox, 2009, p. 128). There are levels of prompts, referred to as a prompt hierarchy. In a prompt hierarchy, physical prompts are considered to be the most intrusive, followed by modeling, verbal, and gestural prompts.

Prompting strategies are part of the systematic instruction process, which involves instruction that is delivered through discrete instructional sessions composed of instructional trials. These trials are composed of three behavioral components, referred to as the A-B-C of instructional trials (antecedent, behavior, consequence). The antecedent is any stimulus that precedes a behavior or response and, logically, the consequence is anything that follows the behavior (Collins, 2012). The systematic delivery of stimuli and consequences form the fundamental process in systematic instruction, and the delivery of prompts to students ensures that they will learn. Prompts can be given with the antecedent (stimulus prompts) or the response (response prompts). Generally, stimulus prompts are in place prior to instruction, while response prompts are inserted into instruction. Printing the word "red" in the color red is a stimulus prompt (Collins, 2012). Pointing to a correct response immediately after giving a verbal instruction (stimulus) to find a picture with the color red is a response prompt.

One research-based prompting strategy for teaching independent living skills is constant time delay, which involves providing a stimulus prompt (such as "For the next task . . . "), presenting the antecedent (such as a verbal direction), and then waiting for a predetermined time (e.g., 3 seconds, 5 seconds) before providing the response prompt (e.g., pointing to the correct answer). For students who need more support, in the first few trials of a new task, instead of a 5-second delay, the teacher might use a zero-second delay, meaning the response prompt is delivered immediately after the task direction (stimulus), with no delay. After those trials, the delay moves to the 5-second delay. The level of prompting (e.g., physical, gestural, verbal) can change as students respond accurately.

Another evidence-based prompting strategy to promote independent living is the systems-of-least-prompts (SLP) strategy, also called least-to-most prompting, which uses the time delay, but also uses "a hierarchy of prompts that moves progressively from having a minimal influence to having a maximal influence" (Westling & Fox, 2009, p. 132). The teacher uses the least invasive or minimum intensity prompt necessary to elicit the behavior.

An alternative to SLP is the most-to-least prompts strategy, which follows the same logic as SLP, but in the opposite direction—that is, from maximum- to minimum-intensity prompt. This is used particularly with the student who has multiple disabilities to ensure that the student is always reinforced for the correct behavior. The *Guidelines for Teaching: Systems-of-Least-Prompts* feature provides steps for implementing the systems-of-least-prompts strategy.

Guidelines for Teaching

Systems-of-Least-Prompts

Identify Skill to Be Taught Using Systems-of-Least-Prompts (SLP).
- Assess the student's independent living needs.
  - Conduct observations in independent living environments.
  - Compare the student's task performance with typical task performance.
- Identify independent living skills that need to be taught.
- Prioritize independent living skills that need to be taught.
- Select skills to be taught using SLP.
- Determine the instructional strategy to be used to teach skills.

Identify the Prompts to Be Used.
- Determine if a stimulus prompt is needed.
- Determine if a response prompt is needed.

- Determine what type of prompt will be used (physical, modeling, gestural, verbal) for the stimulus prompt.
- Determine what type of prompt will be used (physical, modeling, gestural, verbal) for the response prompt.

Implement Instruction Using SLP Strategy.
- Deliver task direction.
- Give the student time to respond independently.
- If there is no response or the student performs the task incorrectly, deliver a stimulus prompt.
  - Prompt the student using a stimulus prompt when delivering task direction.
- Give the student time to respond independently.
- If there is no response or the student performs the task incorrectly, deliver a stimulus prompt and a response prompt

- Prompt the student using a stimulus prompt when delivering task direction.
- Prompt the student using a response prompt after delivering task direction.
- Use the "least intrusive" prompt that elicits the behavior.
- Provide reinforcement for completion of the task.

Collect Data on the Student's Performance.

- Set goals that establish criteria for the student's mastery of the skill.
  - Write objectives that break the steps to achieving the goal into smaller steps incorporating the level of prompting.
- Record data on the student's performance (percent correct, frequency correct, time to completion, etc.).

- When the student meets the criteria in an objective, implement instruction using the next level of prompting (e.g., the next least restrictive level, such as going from physical prompting to modeling).

Fade Prompting When the Student Masters Skill or Task.

- Provide systematic instruction until the student can perform task when provided task direction (no stimulus prompt) and without a response prompt.
- Link task performance to naturally occurring stimuli instead of task direction.
- Fade reinforcement and prompting from the teacher.

NTACT has identified research-based practices other than prompts that promote independent living. They include inclusion in the general education classroom; teaching self-care and independent living skills; teaching self-advocacy skills; community-based instruction (Chapter 11) to teach purchasing, safety, food preparation, and grocery shopping skills; and video modeling and video self-modeling (Chapter 12).

RESEARCH-BASED TRANSITION PRACTICES TO PROMOTE EMPLOYMENT

Research-based practices identified by NTACT to promote employment include student involvement in transition planning and the Self-Determined Learning Model of Instruction as well as inclusion in the general education setting, participation in occupational courses, paid employment or work experiences during high school, vocational education courses, and work-study opportunities. In addition, using student-directed learning strategies (Chapter 12) to promote employment skills and specific job skills has been shown to be effective. Providing career awareness activities, work-based social skills training, travel skills training, and youth autonomy skills (Chapter 17) has demonstrated evidence of positive impact on employment outcomes.

You can easily conclude that numerous educational strategies are associated with promoting the transition from school to adulthood for students with disabilities. Your duty under IDEA is to ensure that students with multiple disabilities and TBI receive instruction that uses one or more of these strategies. Why? It is your duty, first, because IDEA requires research-based instruction; and, second, because some people (including educators) may incorrectly assume that some students with multiple disabilities or TBI cannot learn transition skills. There is strong evidence for the positive impact of transition instructional strategies for both students with multiple disabilities (Dymond, Butler, Hopkins, & Patton, 2018) and students with TBI (Inge et al., 2016).

The fact of the matter is that the high expectations that IDEA asks you to have rest on research-based practices and partnerships; together, the expectations, practices, and partnerships ensure students' inclusion, progress and self-determination; and all of these approaches—these themes—dignify the students whom you will teach.

MyLab Education Self-Check 13.3

MyLab Education Application Exercise 13.3: Educational Planning

Summary

Defining Multiple Disabilities

IDEA defines multiple disabilities by the presence of "concomitant impairments" (such as intellectual disability and blindness; emotional or behavioral disorder and orthopedic impairment), the combination of which causes such intense educational needs that they cannot be accommodated by solely addressing one of the impairments. About 2 percent of students receiving special education services are classified as having multiple disabilities. Most students with multiple disabilities will require intensive supports to address intellectual, adaptive, motor, sensory, or communication needs.

Describing the Characteristics and Causes of Multiple Disabilities

Students with multiple disabilities are a widely heterogeneous group in terms of their characteristics, capabilities, and educational needs. Many students with multiple disabilities have significant impairments in intellectual functioning, though some students may function typically. It is clear, though, that with appropriate cognitive supports, even students with intellectual impairments can progress in the general education curriculum. Students with multiple disabilities can also have significant motor and physical support needs, as well as hearing and vision impairments. Students who have both blindness and deafness are served in another IDEA category, deaf-blindness. Many students with multiple disabilities have communication difficulties of some sort. Research is clear that for students with multiple disabilities to be able to effectively communicate, they may need communication supports, like augmentative and alternative communication devices, and their communication partners will need training to interact effectively. Multiple disabilities have a wide array of causes, including biomedical, genetic, chromosomal, environmental, and nutritional causes.

Defining Traumatic Brain Injury

IDEA defines traumatic brain injury (TBI) as "an acquired injury to the brain caused by an external physical force, resulting in total or partial functional disability or psychosocial impairment, or both, that adversely affects a child's educational performance." Children from birth to age 4, adolescents ages 15 to 19, and older adults over age 65 are most likely to sustain a TBI. Male individuals are much more likely to sustain a TBI than are female individuals. Approximately 0.4 percent of all students ages 3 through 21 receiving special education services are classified as having a traumatic brain injury.

Describing the Characteristics and Causes of Traumatic Brain Injury

Students with TBI differ in terms of onset, complexity, and recovery. Their injuries may affect them in many areas of functioning. The characteristics manifested by students who experience TBI are aligned with the particular site and extent of their injury. Injuries are classified as mild, moderate, or severe. The extent of functional changes and the course of recovery depend largely on whether the injury was mild, moderate, or severe. Coordination problems, physical weakness, and fatigue are common effects of TBI. The cognitive impact of brain injury often results in problems associated with memory, planning, problem solving, and abstract reasoning. The severity of the injury and the age of the child can influence the degree of cognitive impairment. Emotional, behavioral, and social changes can be especially problematic for children and youth with TBI. The four major causes of TBI are falls, automobile accidents, being struck by or against something, or assaults. In infants, shaken baby syndrome refers to TBI resulting from a caregiver shaking a child violently, often in situations in which the caregiver is frustrated because of the child's crying.

Evaluating Students with Multiple Disabilities and Traumatic Brain Injury

Students with multiple disabilities are often identified at birth or in their early years, so physicians, not educators or psychologists, usually make the initial diagnosis. This diagnosis can be based on problems identified during pregnancy, immediately after birth, or as early developmental milestones are not attained. To determine the nature of specially designed instruction and supports for students with multiple disabilities, assessing the need for support in the multiple domains that may impact students with multiple disabilities—cognitive, adaptive, motoric, sensory, and communication—will be important. The Supports Intensity Scale—Children's version is a measure that can be used to determine support needs for students with multiple disabilities.

The evaluation of students with TBI needs to be comprehensive (across the student's physical, cognitive, emotional-behavioral, and developmental support needs) and ongoing because children change. One means of doing this involves progress monitoring, which entails frequent and repeated assessments of student learning and performance that, when charted or graphed, provide information about progress. For students with TBI, such data may be particularly important for determining a student's needs with regard to special education services. In addition, tools like the Behavior Rating Inventory of Executive Function (BRIEF) scale provide information about behavioral regulation and executive functioning.

Including Students with Multiple Disabilities and Traumatic Brain Injury

Most students with multiple disabilities still spend most of their time outside the regular classroom. Only 13 percent of students with multiple disabilities spend 80 percent or more of their day in general education classrooms, while almost 25 percent are in completely separate settings. It is clear from these data and from research that students with multiple disabilities, even compared to students with one disability label, are at high risk for being educated in separate special education classrooms or in separate schools. One support to promote the inclusion of students with multiple disabilities involves the use of paraprofessionals in the general education classroom. Paraprofessionals are school staff included under the IDEA term supplementary aids and services. In 2014 (most recent available data), 415,781 full-time paraprofessionals were employed across the United States to support students with disabilities, ages 6 through 21. While paraprofessionals are important in promoting inclusion, there may be an overreliance on them that negatively impacts student outcomes. When paraprofessionals are used to provide instruction and other support in inclusive classrooms, it is highly important to ensure that paraprofessionals receive training and support to effectively deliver instruction.

Among students with TBI, 50 percent spend more than 80 percent of their day in general education classes. However, 8 percent are educated in a separate setting, including at a hospital or at home. So, this is better than for some categories, but over a quarter of all students with TBI spend little or no time in general education settings.

Educating Students with Multiple Disabilities and Traumatic Brain Injury

Person-centered planning is an approach increasingly used by teachers to collaborate with students who have disabilities and their families, to identify goals, values, and visions for the future and to use this information to design IEPs and plan for transitions. The emphasis in person-centered planning is putting the students with disabilities and their families at the center of the process of building systems of supports in education and community contexts. A number of different approaches have been developed to implement person-centered planning. In the education context, one of the most popular person-centered planning approaches is the MAPs (formerly McGill Action Planning) process. It enables teachers to work with students and families to customize educational programs to their specific visions, strengths, and needs.

Assistive technology can be used to promote access, inclusion, and progress for students with disabilities. Given the range of assistive technologies that are available and the various needs that can be addressed by assistive technology, it is useful to begin planning for technology supports using a multidisciplinary approach to assistive technology evaluation. Assistive technology specialists, speech-language pathologists, orientation and mobility specialists, and occupational and physical therapists usually should be involved, alongside teachers, students, and families. A helpful guide for an assistive technology evaluation is the SETT (Student, Environment, Tasks, Tools) framework. When supporting adolescents with multiple disabilities, cognitive support technologies can also be very useful. These technologies, a form of assistive technology, address cognitive needs.

For more than a quarter of a century, IDEA has required that students receiving special education services be given needed transition services when they become adolescents. Research suggests that transition efforts, in addition to being required by law, are critical for students with multiple disabilities and students with TBI, as both groups fared poorly in achieving transition outcomes like employment or independent living in a longitudinal study of the impact of transition outcomes for youth with disabilities. The federally funded National Technical Assistance Center on Transition (NTACT) has identified effective practices in transition, including practices that are evidence-based and research-based, across multiple outcome areas. Myriad practices show evidence of their impact in promoting independent living and employment outcomes, including prompting strategies such as systems-of-least-prompts. Prompting strategies are part of the systematic instruction process, which involves instruction that is delivered through discrete instructional sessions composed of instructional trials.

Addressing the Professional Standards

In Chapter 13, Students with Multiple Disabilities and Traumatic Brain Injury, we have covered the following Council for Exceptional Children (CEC) Initial Level Special Educator Preparation Standards: Chapter 13—1.0, 1.2, 2.0, 2.1, 2.2, 2.3, 3.1, 3.3, 4.3, 4.4, 5.0, 5.1, 5.2, 5.3, 5.4, 5.5, 6.0, 6.1, 6.3, 6.6, 7.1, 7.3. Refer to the Appendix for a full listing of the CEC Standards with descriptions and supporting explanations.

Chapter 14
Students with Physical Disabilities and Other Health Impairments

 Learning Outcomes

14.1 Discuss how physical and health conditions may affect students' learning and achievement and explain why students from non-White families have higher rates of some physical and health conditions.

14.2 Identify how genetic and environmental factors that contribute to physical disabilities and other health impairments impact public health initiatives and how students benefit from such initiatives.

14.3 Discuss the importance of learning with and from peers and how programs can be structured to promote self-directed learning for students with physical disabilities and other health impairments.

Like the previous chapter covering multiple disabilities and traumatic brain injury, this chapter discusses two categories of exceptionality: physical disabilities and other health impairments. We begin by providing an overview of these categories. Note that because students with physical disabilities and students with other health impairments share issues involving education, we address these commonalities in the section on educating students. In explaining the characteristics of these categories, we focus on two of the most common physical conditions, cerebral palsy and spina bifida, and two of the most common other health impairments, epilepsy and asthma. As we describe physical disabilities and other health impairments, we introduce you to two students: Samuel Habib, who has cerebral palsy, and Shiloh Thomas, who has epilepsy.

Meet Samuel Habib—Doing It His Own Way

Samuel Habib has cerebral palsy and an underlying mitochondrial disorder. It impairs his ability to communicate. At age 14, Samuel had a medical device implanted in his body that automatically infuses a medicine called baclofen to relax his muscles so that he will be able to function more independently. The surgery itself is not life threatening, but malfunctioning of the implant is: Either an overdose or an underdose of the medication can jeopardize Samuel. The device has all sorts of monitors to prevent the wrong dosage, but, still, there is risk, as well as great benefit.

Dan Habib and Betsy McNamara, Samuel's parents, calculated the risk and decided to go forward with the surgery. And so did Samuel: He made the final decision. That's right: Samuel, at the young age of 14, made the decision.

Are you surprised? You shouldn't be. After all, Samuel has a mind of his own. His big challenge is not intellectual; it is physical, and it is not inconsequential.

Indeed, throughout his lifetime, and especially in his early years, Dan and Betsy's biggest fear and focus of their energies was always Samuel's health. It was the predominant factor in their lives. Making sure he was getting the right therapies, and being available to him physically and emotionally when he was not feeling well—that was Dan and Betsy's past.

It is also part of their future. "The fear I have for the future," Betsy says, "is that we're never going to not be doing this, and we're always going to be spending a lot of our time managing all this, and I think that's a reality. It's tiring to think about. What I want for him is to have a full and independent life. I worry that he won't and the consequence of that will be that we'll be his very involved hands-on managers when we'd like to retire."

Dan agrees: "The day-to-day kind of obsession with Samuel's health and well-being is just nonstop for me." Don't get the wrong idea about "nonstop." Dan and Betsy have another son, Isaiah, for whom they also go nonstop. Samuel is in general education, but that fact does not mean that Dan and Betsy have any let-up in his case. Their advocacy, like that of nearly all parents who have more than one child, including a child with a disability, is an integral part of their life. That is particularly so, since Samuel and Isaiah are the best of friends.

The future holds promise for Samuel, even as it does for Isaiah. Dan and Betsy want and expect Samuel to live a full life, to be happy, discover love, live independently, find fulfillment in work or volunteer work, not be poor and live on only Medicaid, have health that is as good as it can be, and not live with them. Not remarkably, that is what they want for Isaiah, too.

Part of that future is for them, and Samuel's teachers have high expectations for him. Another part is to know his passions and to respond to them, setting a trajectory for him based on what he wants in his life.

Right now, that means responding to Samuel's passion for sports, especially NASCAR. It also means that Dan and Betsy are working with Samuel's teachers to develop an internship for Samuel at the nearby NASCAR race track, learning about marketing, communication, engineering, and business management, and, equally important, getting to know people in the NASCAR networks. That internship might lead to a paid one when Samuel is in high school, and, in turn, that might lead to a job. Those results will be elusive unless Dan and Betsy, and Samuel, give a lot of intentional effort and organize around preparing for higher education and a job. Does that future seem improbable? Betsy and Dan think not. Indeed, their advice to educators increases the chances that Samuel will have the future they all want:

- See students and families as full and complete individuals
- Presume all students are competent
- Set aside low expectations for high ones
- Respond to the students' passions
- Regard students as experts about themselves
- Recognize that when there is a hiccup in a student's education, it is not because of the student but because educators and the family have not found a way to reach the student
- Create teams whose members support each other—educators, families, and students alike
- Learn and apply the practices that work

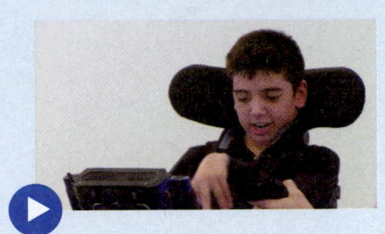

MyLab Education
Vignette Video 14.1
You met Samuel and his family earlier in this text and at 14, Samuel is a leader who can voice his own desires, laugh at his teenage foibles, and share his hopes for the future.

- To the maximum extent possible, let students make decisions for themselves
- Make sure that students have access to everything written or said about them.

Take Samuel's 14 years of life, double it by a factor of two (Betsy and Dan), sum them, and you have 42 years of advice. Is it worth following? Absolutely. Just consider where Samuel is now: learning in the general education curriculum. And, he's on the honor roll.

Defining Physical Disabilities

The regulations implementing the Individuals with Disabilities Education Act (IDEA) define the term physical disability as a severe orthopedic impairment that adversely affects a student's educational performance. The term includes impairments resulting from a **congenital** impairment caused by disease (e.g., poliomyelitis, bone tuberculosis) or other causes (e.g., cerebral palsy, spina bifida, amputations, and fractures or burns that cause contractures).

Although the regulations use the term orthopedic impairments, educators typically use the term physical disabilities. So there are two terms in use, the IDEA term and educators' term. But special educators also sometimes refer to students with severe and multiple disabilities or traumatic brain injury (see Chapter 13) as having physical disabilities. The term physical disabilities can refer to students who experience conditions that are quite different from each other, either by their causes or their implications for functioning, although most students experience mobility limitations. In this section we focus on two common physical disabilities: cerebral palsy and spina bifida.

Because physical disabilities often occur in combination with other disabilities, it is hard to determine their prevalence. Nevertheless, some data are available. In the 2015–2016 school year, approximately 1.0 percent (61,716) of all students ages 6 through 21 in special education were classified as having an orthopedic impairment (U.S. Department of Education, 2018).

Cerebral Palsy

Cerebral refers to the brain. Palsy describes the lack of muscle control that affects a student's ability to move and to maintain balance and posture. The term cerebral palsy refers to a group of neurological impairments that affect movement and posture and occur before birth or during infancy. Cerebral palsy is a lifelong condition, but it is not a disease. A word of advice to you: You will be wrong to consider children and youth with cerebral palsy as being sick.

Cerebral palsy is the most common motor disability in childhood. According to the U.S. Centers for Disease Control (CDC), Autism and Developmental Disabilities Monitoring (ADDM) Network, the prevalence of cerebral palsy is about 3.1 to 3.6 children for every 1000 children (in a nationally representative population of 8-year-old children). Almost 60 percent of the children in this study were able to walk independently. About 40 percent of children with cerebral palsy had epilepsy, which you will also learn about in this chapter. The level of epilepsy is highest in children with limited or no walking ability. The prevalence of cerebral palsy is higher for boys (3.6 per 1000) than girls (2.5 per 1000), or at a rate of about 1.5 boys for every 1 girl diagnosed with cerebral palsy (Christensen et al., 2014). A number of reasons could account for the gender differences in prevalence. The most prominent is that male individuals are biologically vulnerable because of genetic or other conditions that exist prior to birth (Romeo et al., 2016).

The CDC ADDM study also found that prevalence was higher for Black children than for White or Hispanic children (at about a 1.5 to 1 ratio). That may seem surprising to you, since it may be more difficult to imagine how bias might contribute to a differential diagnosis of cerebral palsy, as it does with other categories like autism or intellectual disability. But, keep in mind that in the other categories of disabilities (such as emotional-behavioral disorders and intellectual disability—Chapters 9 and 11, respectively), factors such as poverty and socioeconomic status play a role, as seems to be the case with cerebral palsy. Another analysis of the ADDM data indicated that low socioeconomic status was associated with a 67 percent higher risk of cerebral palsy (Durkin et al., 2015).

Spina Bifida

Spina bifida, which means "open spine," refers to a malformation of the spinal cord occurring before birth. The spine is made up of separate bones called vertebrae, which normally cover and protect the spinal cord. In a person with spina bifida, the spinal column does not close completely and cover the spinal cord, usually resulting in a protrusion of the spinal cord, its coverings, or both. A saclike bulge may occur in any part of the person's spine, from neck to buttocks. The higher on the spinal column the impairment appears, the more severe the person's loss of function. Typically, the impairment occurs in the lower region of the spine and causes loss of skin sensation and complete or partial paralysis of the person's lower extremities. However, as with cerebral palsy, it is incorrect to consider children with spina bifida as sick.

Spina bifida belongs to a larger group of birth impairments associated with the spinal cord, brain, and vertebra that are referred to as **neural tube defects**. The prevalence of spina bifida in the United States is 38.7 out of 100,000 individuals, but prevalence rates of spina bifida vary widely across the world as a function of the availability of folic acid in the diet of pregnant women. You'll learn more about that later in the chapter, but for now, in countries across the world with mandatory folic acid laws, the birth rate is 33.86 per 100,000 live births, while in countries where the folic acid laws are simply voluntary, the rate jumps to 48.35 per 100,000 (Atta et al., 2016).

Unlike most of the disability categories you've learned about, neural tube defects like spina bifida occur more frequently in girls than boys. The effects of race and ethnicity are related to both the effectiveness of treatment (folic acid) and access to treatment. Accordingly, it appears that folic acid supplements to prevent neural tube defects are less protective among Hispanic women, though findings are inconsistent and not well studied (U.S. Preventative Services Task Force, 2017). Further, children with birth defects, including neural tube defects, born to Black and Hispanic mothers have a greater risk of mortality than do White children (Wang et al., 2015), probably due to unequal access to health care.

Describing the Characteristics and Causes of Physical Disabilities— Cerebral Palsy and Spina Bifida

Characteristics of Cerebral Palsy

As you've learned, the primary characteristic of cerebral palsy involves motor difficulties that impact balance, posture, gait, and other motor activities. Diagnosis of the condition is a function of the severity and observability of the motor impairments. The diagnosis of cerebral palsy consists of four main features:

- Onset before, during, or after birth, usually by 2 years of age
- Motor difficulties as a function of brain injury or development
- Limited control of motor movements, poor motor coordination and balance, muscle stiffness
- Symptoms that are permanent but nonprogressive (Fehlings & Hunt, 2017, p. 263).

In addition, there are four main types of cerebral palsy, but a fifth consists of any combination of the other four (Hoon & Tolley, 2013):

1. **Spastic**, which is characterized by tightness in one or more muscle groups and affects approximately 78 percent of people with cerebral palsy (Christensen et al., 2014)

2. **Dyskinetic**, which involves impairments in muscle tone affecting the whole body

3. **Athetoid**, which involves abrupt, involuntary movements of the head, neck, face, and extremities, particularly the upper ones

4. **Ataxic**, which involves unsteadiness, lack of coordination and balance, and varying degrees of difficulty with standing and walking

5. **Mixed**, which combines two or more movement patterns when one type does not predominate over another.

In addition to characterizing cerebral palsy by the nature of a person's movement, professionals also refer to parts of the person's body that are affected. In this topographical classification system, the specific body location of the movement impairments correlates with the location of the brain damage (Hoon & Tolley, 2013). Figure 14.1 describes the topographical classification system.

Many health and developmental problems may accompany cerebral palsy. These include a higher than typical rate of seizures (20 to 30 percent), visual impairments, difficulty swallowing, higher risk for aspiration pneumonia, high levels of reflux diseases, and complications from orthopedic limitations, including hip and knee problems and the risk for sores from sitting for long periods. In addition, some portion of people with cerebral palsy also have intellectual disability. Too many times, people assume a person with cerebral palsy has a cognitive impairment, but that is true only for between 30 and 60 percent, and varies from intellectual disability to learning disabilities (Fehlings & Hunt, 2017). Neither Samuel Habib nor Jack Steinberg (Chapter 6) has cognitive limitations.

They do, however, have communication challenges. That is not unexpected. One common complication for people with cerebral palsy involves speech and language difficulties. Estimates are that 3 out of 5 children with cerebral palsy have speech impairments, which range from articulation (speech production) difficulties, to language development delays, to language comprehension difficulties (Hustad et al., 2017). Many of these children can benefit from the use of augmentative and alternative communication systems (Chapters 4 and 8).

MyLab Education

Video Example 14.1
Communication is important not only for social interactions but also for learning. How does the use of a communication device to support Isaiah allow him to participate in the same learning task as his classmates?

Figure 14.1 Topographical Classification System

Monoplegia: one limb

Paraplegia: legs only

Hemiplegia: one half of body

Triplegia: three limbs (usually two legs and one arm)

Quadriplegia: all four limbs

Diplegia: more affected in the legs than the arms

Double hemiplegia: arms more involved than the legs

Causes of Cerebral Palsy

Cerebral palsy is caused by **prenatal** (e.g., gestational infection, brain malformation before birth, prematurity), **perinatal** (e.g., stroke, lack of oxygen or infection during birth), or **postnatal** (e.g., brain injury or meningitis after birth) factors (McIntyre et al., 2012). It used to be thought that the primary cause of cerebral palsy was a lack of oxygen during the birth process, often as a result of the umbilical cord being around the fetus's neck. We now know, however, that multiple and complex causes may result in or contribute to cerebral palsy. In fact, risk factors for cerebral palsy can go back to issues prior to the conception of the pregnancy. Maternal age, low socioeconomic status, and maternal health are all related to having a child with cerebral palsy.

During the prenatal period, infections of the placenta or other maternal infections, such as **cytomegalovirus (CMV)**, are possible causes. During the birth itself, the baby's position, the position of the cord, and the length of the labor are risk factors. And, after the birth, diseases such as neonatal (newborn) encephalopathy, respiratory distress syndrome, neonatal stroke, or other neonatal infections can result in cerebral palsy (Fehlings & Hunt, 2017).

Children with cerebral palsy may have difficulties in the development of gross- and fine-motor skills, speech and language skills, learning and academic skills, and interpersonal skills and relationships. That said, physical and occupational therapy, speech therapy, high-quality instruction, and technology and other supports can (and do!) enable young people with cerebral palsy to lead full, rich lives. You'll learn more about strategies that might benefit young people with cerebral palsy later in this chapter.

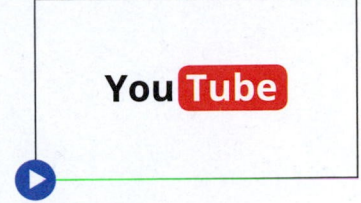

MyLab Education

Video Example 14.2

Dr. Darcy Fehlings discusses the different types of cerebral palsy and their causes. Why is it important to look at each person's strengths and areas of support in order to understand how to be an effective teacher? https://www.youtube.com/watch?v=vFrdANVTYGk

Characteristics of Spina Bifida

Like cerebral palsy, spina bifida is not a progressive condition and has three common forms (Liptak, 2013):

- **Spina bifida occulta**. An opening occurs in one or more bones of the spinal column, with no damage to the spinal cord. This is the mildest and most common form.

- **Meningocele**. The covering of the spinal cord, but not the cord itself, protrudes through the opening created by the defect in the spine. This more serious form can be repaired through surgery and usually does not lead to mobility impairments.

- **Myelomeningocele**. The spinal cord's covering and a portion of the spinal cord or nerve roots protrudes or forms a sac that protrudes through the opening created by the defect in the spine. This is the most serious form and results in alterations in brain development during the early stages of gestation that lead to physical and cognitive impairments.

The extent of mobility and sensory loss in children and youth with myelomeningocele depends on the location of the spinal impairment. Thus, 42 percent of children with spina bifida could walk with walking aids, and approximately one quarter of them always needed to use a wheelchair (Pauly & Cremer, 2013).

Mobility limitations can impair students' active participation in unstructured peer activities, such as those that occur at recess (Peny-Dahlstrand, Krumlinde-Sundholm, & Gosman-Hedstrom, 2013). It is encouraging that students with spina bifida are frequently present in most school activities and settings; however, without supports and accommodations, their active participation is lower than that of their peers. Approximately 75 percent of individuals with spina bifida have average intelligence, although many of these students struggle with attention, abstract reasoning, memory, and executive functioning (Liptak, 2013).

Myelomeningocele almost always occurs above the part of the spinal cord that controls the bladder and bowels (Wiener et al., 2017). Constipation, bladder paralysis, urinary tract infections, and resulting incontinence are common. Kidney failure can also result. Many students can be taught the technique of clean intermittent catheterization (CIC) (inserting a tube into the urethra for urination) (Liptak, 2013). Approximately three fourths of students who receive CIC and medication are able to be continent during their elementary years (Liptak, 2013). School nurses are typically trained in CIC techniques and are valuable resources to teachers in addressing issues associated with CIC.

Causes of Spina Bifida

Spina bifida occurs within the first month of gestation (Liptak, 2013). Genetic and environmental factors interact to cause the spinal malformations associated with spina bifida. Although more than 100 genes have been examined, fewer than 20 percent have been found to have even a minor impact on the risk of spina bifida. Environmental contributors include maternal exposure to valproic acid (Depakote), acne medication (Accutane), hyperthermia (excessive use of saunas), maternal diabetes, and obesity (Liptak, 2013).

Fortunately, a very effective means to reduce the risk that a child will be born with spina bifida and other neural tube defects involves maternal ingestion of folic acid. Folic acid is a B vitamin that enables bodies to build healthy cells. In 1992, the U.S. Public Health Service recommended that women who were planning to become pregnant should take folic acid supplements daily, and, beginning in 1998, the federal Food and Drug Administration required breads and enriched cereal-grain products to be fortified with synthetic folic acid. The highest rates of prevention occur when women take 0.4 mg of folic acid per day during childbearing age as well as multivitamins containing folic acid just before the time that they anticipate conception. Since 1998, this regimen seems to have prevented approximately 1300 neural tube defect–impacted pregnancies per year (Williams et al., 2015). It also seems that the individual risk for a woman who is pregnant can be reduced by up to 70 percent (Atta et al., 2016).

Defining Other Health Impairments

As you learned when studying about attention-deficit hyperactivity disorder (ADHD) (Chapter 10), IDEA's regulations define students with other health impairments as those "having limited strength, vitality or alertness, including a heightened alertness to environmental stimuli, that results in limited alertness with respect to the educational environment, that:

1. is due to chronic or acute health problems such as asthma, attention deficit disorder or attention deficit hyperactivity disorder, diabetes, epilepsy, a heart condition, hemophilia, lead poisoning, leukemia, nephritis, rheumatic fever, and sickle cell anemia; and

2. affects a child's educational performance."

Note the terms "chronic" and "acute" in the definition of other health impairments (OHI). A chronic condition develops slowly and has long-lasting symptoms. For example, the student with diabetes, another chronic condition, has lifelong medical needs. The word *other* in the categorical name distinguishes these from conditions such as multiple disabilities (Chapter 13), traumatic brain injury (Chapter 13), and physical disabilities (this chapter) that involve health-related issues. To be served under the "other health impairments" category, the student's health condition must limit strength, vitality, or alertness to such a degree that the student's educational progress is adversely affected. That said, let us introduce you to Shiloh Thomas, a student who has an "other health impairment," namely, epilepsy.

Meet Shiloh Thomas—Misunderstood, Yet a Source of Hope

"I just want to give hope to other families. That's our purpose. I want it so that, 10 years down the road, other families won't have to have the heartbreak and frustration we have had with our son's education."

Those are the words of Tanya Thomas. She and her husband, Ward, have four biological children and four adopted children. One of their adopted children is Shiloh, aged 10, who is a 4th grader in a rural school. He has not one, not two, but three different disabilities. He has had seizures since he was born and was diagnosed as having epilepsy when he was 3 years old. Add to that disability two others—autism and legal blindness—and you begin to get to know Shiloh.

The picture is incomplete, however, until you learn that Shiloh has significant communication problems. Yes, epilepsy, autism, and a vision impairment challenge him, his family, and his teachers. Individually, each condition would be challenging. Together, they cause him to have huge difficulties in communicating with his teachers. His type of epilepsy alone (Lennox-Gastaut syndrome) is rare (1 in 50,000 to 100,000 children) and is associated with intellectual, communicative, and behavioral challenges.

Because of his epilepsy, Shiloh has "absence" seizures—short and sudden episodes of a few seconds. When having one, Shiloh stops what he is doing—he seems "absent"—and then resumes his activities. Tanya and the school nurse have trained everyone in Shiloh's school who has direct contact with him about epilepsy. Fortunately, Shiloh has never had a major seizure at school, just the absence seizures.

Shiloh also has behavioral challenges that are associated with his kind of epilepsy. He often acts out at school and home, throwing himself to the floor, slapping his face but not so hard as to bruise himself, screaming, and sometimes banging his head against the floor.

Tanya, Ward, and their other children know why Shiloh behaves this way (he wants attention) and what to do to protect him (put a pillow under his head or carefully restrain him, following the procedures of a research-based intervention program). They also know how to prevent these behaviors (try to understand what he wants, because his behavior is his only means of communication), and then de-escalate his behavior (tell yourself he just wants attention, so ignore him and then he will stop, within a minute or so). That's the situation at home. At school, the situation is different.

Despite the fact that Shiloh's individualized education program (IEP) provides that he will have communication supports and his behavior intervention plan provides that he will benefit from prevention and intervention strategies, these supports are not available for Shiloh at school. What is the consequence? At home, Shiloh's behaviors are few and not as alarming as those he has at school. Why?

Tanya thinks it is because the school does not implement Shiloh's IEP and has not obtained a functional behavioral assessment (FBA) that accurately describes why Shiloh behaves as he does—to get what he wants. His behavior is not a result of his epilepsy but of the lack of teachers' understanding about him and his condition.

Is there something wrong here? Yes, of course: It is wrong that the school cannot or will not implement Shiloh's IEP, conduct an accurate FBA, or apply research-based interventions or the prevent-intervene-recover strategies that Tanya and her family use.

What's right here? What's right is that Tanya wants other families and educators to learn from their experiences. Tanya says she and Ward—and Shiloh, too—want to "give hope." She and Ward are university educated; they confront facts, identify problems, seek solutions, and apply them. That's exactly what they want Shiloh's teachers to do: evaluate accurately and then apply research-based interventions to ensure progress and inclusion.

As you read the *My Voice: Much More Than "No Sugar"* feature about Austin Lorenzo, you may find differences between the perspectives of Tanya and Ward Thomas, Shiloh's parents (epilepsy), and those of Diane, Austin's mother (diabetes, an OHI category). Tanya and Ward focus on education; Diane focuses on Austin's daily quality of life. The types of other health impairments vary and elicit different but not inconsistent responses. Why are they different but not inconsistent? The reason is that educational consequences remain basically the same—to promote progress by using evidence-based interventions and never to lose hope in one's child or the partnerships that educators and other professionals create. That's also the message about students with physical disabilities, such as Samuel Habib (this chapter) and Jack Steinberg (Chapter 6).

My Voice

Much More Than "No Sugar"

Diane Lorenzo

When our then fifteen-month-old child Austin was diagnosed with juvenile diabetes (type I), we thought, "Oh—we can handle this—he just can't have any sugar." After he was hospitalized for one week, we realized we were drastically wrong. We were told what this disease was and how hard it would be to maintain. We were trained on how to give insulin injections (three times a day), how to test his blood sugar

(Continued)

by drawing blood from his finger with a needle (six times a day), how to count every gram of carbohydrate that entered his body, and how to monitor his exercise to keep him from dangerously low blood sugars that could lead to seizures and/or a coma. We also had to learn how to avoid high blood sugars that could lead to a coma and very serious long-term effects such as blindness, kidney failure, heart disease, and amputations. When we left the hospital, we felt completely alone and afraid to be unsupervised in taking care of our own son.

Austin is now five years old, and he has bravely faced more than 2,555 insulin injections and 7,665 blood tests since he was diagnosed. I have had people comment that they would never know from looking at Austin that there was anything wrong. In reality, diabetes is wearing down every organ in his body, and every day is a battle to keep his blood sugar at the right level to avoid immediate danger.

As he gets older, he is becoming more aware of his special needs and that he is different from most kids. There are days where he embraces the fact that he is "special," as he calls it, and performs his own blood tests, and there are days that he screams, "I hate diabetes!" when we try to give him his shots. We try to keep him focused on the things he likes—like Batman, and dinosaurs, and sugar-free chewing gum—and try to give him the most normal childhood he can possibly have facing these hourly medical responsibilities.

Being a parent of a child with type I diabetes has its challenges. Every day I hope for a cure that will allow Austin the freedom to live without insulin injections, blood and urine testing, and having to eat regulated, scheduled meals. The freedom to play without interrupting him to test his blood because he might be low from too much activity. The freedom to eat when he is hungry and stop eating when he is full. The freedom to wake up each morning without being poked by needles. The freedom to sleep in when he is tired instead of being woken up because he must follow the same daily schedule. Austin often wonders why he does not get to enjoy these normal freedoms of childhood. And we wonder if maintaining this rigid schedule will be enough to prevent him suffering from the devastating complications of diabetes such as blindness, amputations, and kidney and heart failure.

As a result of Austin's disease, we have become very involved with the Juvenile Diabetes Foundation (JDF). JDF was started in 1972 by parents of children with diabetes; their main goal is to find a cure through funding research. We were recently asked by JDF to travel to Capitol Hill and tell Congress what our son endures. As a result of many such efforts, Congress has for the first time formed a Diabetes Caucus, which currently has 250 representatives from across the country whose goal is to pass legislation for funding to help find a cure.

—Reprinted with permission from Diane Lorenzo

Having read the perspective of parents of students who have an other health impairment, you should be ready to learn more about the impairments. Let's start by recalling that a chronic condition, such as Shiloh's epilepsy, is one characteristic of an other health impairment. It is a permanent condition.

Another characteristic of a student with OHI is that the student's condition can be acute, not chronic. What's the difference? An acute condition develops at an identifiable point in time and its symptoms last for a relatively short period. For example, students with mononucleosis may need special education services for the duration of their mononucleosis. Once they recover from this acute condition, however, they no longer are eligible for special education services under the category of other health impairment. That's not the case for Shiloh Thomas; his epilepsy is chronic.

We will focus on two common OHI conditions, epilepsy and asthma, but Figure 14.2 provides a list of conditions that may be covered in the OHI category. Some of these are listed in the definition of OHI in IDEA's regulations, but others are not. The regulations

Figure 14.2 Common Conditions Served Under Other Health Impairments

Asthma	Heart conditions
Attention-deficit hyperactivity disorder	Lead poisoning
Diabetes	Leukemia and related diseases
Epilepsy	Sickle cell anemia
Fetal alcohol syndrome	Tourette syndrome
Hemophilia	

accordingly provide that "[t]he list of acute or chronic health conditions in the definition of other health impairment is not exhaustive, but rather provides examples of problems that children have that could make them eligible for special education and related services under the category of other health impairment."

Epilepsy

Epilepsy is a condition characterized by recurrent and unprovoked seizures, which are temporary neurological abnormalities that result from unregulated electrical discharges in the brain, much like an electrical storm (Li, Ding, & Wu, 2013). If a person has seizures only once or temporarily, perhaps from a high fever or brain injury, that person does not have epilepsy. To be classified as having epilepsy, a person must have at least two seizures that are unprovoked on separate days at least 24 hours apart (Zelleke, Depositaro-Cabacar, & Gaillard, 2013). This is certainly the case for Shiloh Thomas.

Seizures are "periods of neural hyperactivity, caused by an imbalance between excitation and inhibition in the central nervous system" (Burnham, 2017, p. 313). What that means is that during a seizure, neurons in the brain fire at levels much higher than is typical. How that affects the person (e.g., what the seizure looks like) varies, as you will learn shortly.

About 4 percent of the population will have epilepsy at some time in their lives, and about 1 percent of the population has epilepsy at any given time (Burnham, 2017). Epilepsy often co-occurs with other conditions. For example, children with intellectual disability (Chapter 11) experience epilepsy at much higher rates than the general population (van Ool et al., 2016).

There are differences in diagnosis with epilepsy as a function of race, although the mechanisms are not well known. Black children have significantly higher rates of temporal lobe epilepsy (Allen et al., 2018)—a condition in which the elevated neuron firing levels originate from the temporal lobe. This is the most common type of epilepsy. Susceptibility to certain autoimmune impairments may explain some of the differences in this type of epilepsy, though the research is not clear (Allen et al., 2018).

Asthma

Asthma is a chronic lung condition characterized by airway obstruction, inflammation, and hyperirritability of the bronchial tubes (Sheen, 2011). You probably have heard about asthma attacks, but you may never have been in the presence of someone who is experiencing an attack. Usually, asthma attacks are characterized by a shortness of breath with signs of struggles, such as heaving of the chest and using neck muscles to breathe. Wheezing and coughing are often present, and individuals struggle so hard to breathe that they may not be able to talk or respond to questions.

Asthma is the most common chronic disease among children in the United States. Approximately 10 percent of children have a diagnosis of asthma (Centers for Disease Control and Prevention, 2017). Triggers of asthma attacks include dust, tobacco smoke, polluted air, pets, mold, and strenuous exercise. Ask yourself whether any of these "triggers" occur in your classroom or school; if they do, alert your students and their families and consult your school's administrators to determine how to mitigate them and how your students themselves might avoid them.

Students who have asthma often experience fatigue during the school day; that's because their breathing difficulties can keep them awake at night. And they often are absent from school because of their symptoms. The impact of asthma on a student's educational performance is complicated. A recent study of all Dutch school children found that there was no relationship between asthma symptoms themselves and school performance, but when the number of days that students missed school due to illness and family socioeconomic status were included, those with asthma performed more poorly (Ruijsbroek, Wijga, Gehring, Kerkhof, & Droomers, 2015).

MyLab Education

Video Example 14.3

In this video you will learn about the symptoms of asthma. How many of these myths about asthma have you heard? https://www.youtube.com/watch?v=IkvYjbbo3pc

Link to www.cdc.gov/asthma/children.htm to find many resources you can use in helping your students with asthma understand their condition and in guiding other students to understand how asthma affects their peers.

In general, children from Black and Hispanic families have higher rates of asthma, presumably because of the environments in which many non-White families live—environments having high rates of poverty and limited access to quality health care. A recent large study of urban and non-urban children found that the presence of asthma was higher for Black and Hispanic children from lower household incomes (Keet et al., 2015). Another study showed that Black children had significantly fewer visits with an asthma care provider in a 12-month period than did White children and were less likely to have a written asthma treatment plan (Trivedi et al., 2018).

Describing the Characteristics and Causes of Other Health Impairments— Epilepsy and Asthma

In this portion of the chapter, we describe the characteristics and causes of two common other health impairments, epilepsy and asthma, but we remind you that you have met only Shiloh Thomas, who has epilepsy, and that you have not met a student with asthma.

Characteristics of Epilepsy

Now is a good time for you to review Figure 14.3 and to note that there are two types of seizures: partial seizures and primary generalized seizures (Zelleke et al., 2013). **Partial seizures** begin in one side of the cerebral hemisphere and typically involve only one motor or sensory system. Simple partial seizures usually involve motor symptoms, such as uncontrollable bending and flailing. Complex partial seizures involve an alteration of consciousness encompassing mood, memory, typical behavior patterns, and/or personality traits. Children and youth with complex partial seizures are more likely to have stereotypic, repetitive movements, such as pursing or smacking their lips, or moving in a repetitive way, such as marching (Zelleke et al., 2013).

The second type of seizure is primary **generalized seizures**. In contrast to partial seizures, primary generalized seizures involve both cerebral hemispheres. An alteration of consciousness is a primary characteristic, and the seizure affects both sides of the body (partial seizures typically affect only one side of the body). Primary generalized seizures can be further classified into tonic-clonic seizures and absence seizures.

Tonic-clonic seizures (once known as grand mal) cause the student to lose consciousness and go back and forth through rigid extensions of extremities (tonic phase) and rhythmic contractions of extremities (clonic phase). The students may make unusual

Figure 14.3 Overview of Seizure Types and Subtypes

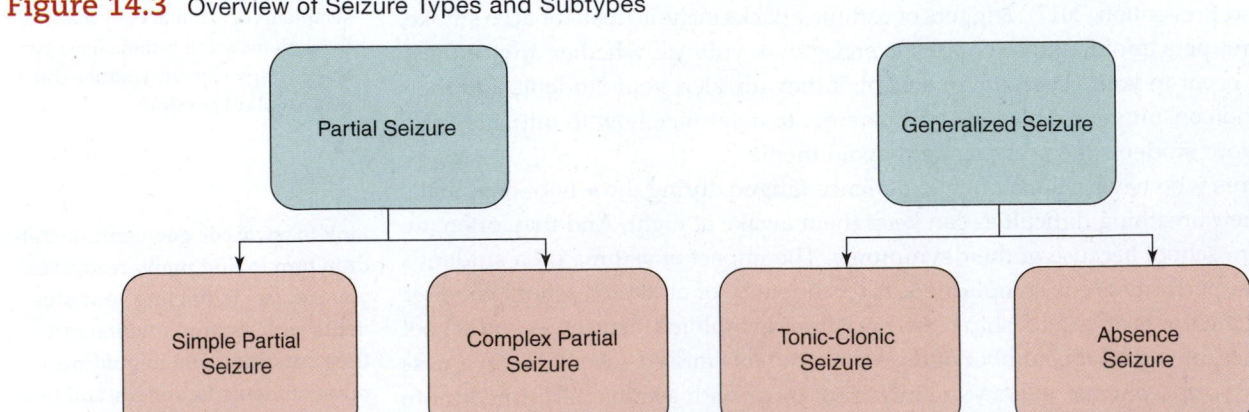

noises during tonic-clonic seizures, have a bluish hue, lose bladder control, and require sleep or rest after the seizure. The student typically has no memory of the seizure.

During **absence seizures** (formerly known as petit mal), the student—Shiloh Thomas is a good example of such a student—also loses consciousness but only for a brief period lasting about 10 seconds. Frequently, the student also has motor movements such as blinking the eyes or changing the position of the head. The student, teachers, and peers might not realize a seizure has taken place. Absence seizures can occur hundreds of times a day and can severely affect learning. It is encouraging that approximately 70 to 90 percent of individuals with epilepsy can, with appropriate medical treatment, become seizure free (Alarcón & Valentin, 2012).

We know that students with intellectual disability are at higher risk for epilepsy (van Ool et al., 2016), but although the majority of children with epilepsy have intelligence quotient (IQ) scores in the typical range, chronic epilepsy is associated with high rates of cognitive impairments, as might be expected from a condition impacting neural activity. Students with epilepsy often have difficulty in school, as epilepsy can affect memory and attention and the medications used to treat epilepsy can create further difficulties, including side effects related to sleepiness (Burnham, 2017).

Among students with epilepsy who did not have intellectual disability (thus, IQ scores in typical ranges), 70 percent had significantly lower academic achievement scores (Wo, Ong, Low, & Lai, 2017). Further, anxiety, depression, irritability, and emotional problems have a higher prevalence among students with epilepsy. Indeed, up to 60 percent of students with epilepsy have some sort of psychosocial problem, and 20 to 30 percent of students with epilepsy also have ADHD (Burnham, 2017). The take-home message is that even if students with epilepsy do not have an identified intellectual disability, many of them will need additional supports to be successful in school.

Causes of Epilepsy

Epilepsy can be caused by a combination of genetic and environmental factors (Engel, 2013). For some people, certain disorders are clearly associated with the onset of epilepsy. Epilepsy can be caused by genetic disorders, as in conditions such as tuberous sclerosis or Huntington's disease, or by non-genetic disorders, such as multiple sclerosis. Environmental factors may cause epilepsy, including certain nutritional or dietetic factors that result in vitamin deficiencies. Epilepsy also may result from neural insult, such as tumors, head injuries, or scars to the brain. Some forms of epilepsy, such as Lennox-Gastaut syndrome, which Shiloh has, is caused by other diseases or illnesses, including encephalitis and meningitis. In other people, no obvious neural impairment, disorder, or environmental factor causes seizures, and the epilepsy results from inherited genetic factors. In most cases, this involves multiple genes and not a simple mutation (Burnham, 2017).

Drug therapies are the most common treatment for epilepsy, with a number of anticonvulsant drugs prescribed to control the seizure activity, though not to cure the condition. For a small number of people, the seizure activity is so disruptive and drug treatment so ineffective that surgery to remove the part of the brain where the seizures are centered can either stop the seizures or make drug treatment more effective (Shorvon, Perucca, & Engel, 2015). Epilepsy can be very difficult to treat and control, and what works for a while may not work for a long time, so you need to work closely with parents, families, medical professionals, and related services professionals to support students with epilepsy.

Characteristics of Asthma

The symptoms and severity of asthma vary widely from person to person. The U.S. Department of Health and Human Services National Heart, Lung, and Blood Institute

MyLab Education
Video Example 14.4
In this series of eight videos on different types of seizures, you will "meet" a wide range of individuals who experience epilepsy and learn about how you can be helpful when you are with someone who has a seizure. How might a teacher confuse an absence seizure, like those that Shiloh Thomas has, with inattention?
https://www.youtube.com/watch?v=men1or169Xo&list=PLBDAD161FD15E3BC3

Link to https://www.nhlbi.nih.gov/files/docs/guidelines/asthma_qrg.pdf. **The National Heart, Lung, and Blood Institute offers Guidelines from the National Asthma Education and Prevention Program on all aspects of the care and control of asthma.**

(NHLBI) classifies asthma severity as intermittent or persistent, with three levels of persistent:

- Intermittent (asthma attacks 2 or fewer days per week or 2 or fewer nights a month)
- Mild persistent (asthma attacks more than 2 days per week, 3 to 4 nights a month)
- Moderate persistent (asthma attacks daily, more than 1 night per week)
- Severe persistent (asthma attacks are continual and interfere with physical activity).

Causes of Asthma

Individuals with asthma have airways that are especially sensitive. Asthma attacks have been linked to genetic and environmental factors (Blumenthal, 2012). Genes can increase susceptibility to inflammation from environmental pollutants, which raises the chances that an asthma attack will occur (von Mutius & Hartert, 2013). Environmental factors include air pollution that is associated with traffic, industry, and smoke, as well as pollen, pet dander, dust, and molds.

Although asthma has a genetic basis, it is closely linked to pollution in a student's environment and to respiratory infections during infancy. The prevalence rate of 10 percent for all children with asthma increases to 13.4 percent for African American children. Indeed, asthma among African American children has increased by almost 50 percent from 2001 to 2009 (Centers for Disease Control and Prevention, 2017). As you learned earlier in the chapter, poverty is the environmental factor most strongly associated with their childhood asthma. These children have the lowest levels of checkups and medication for asthma. Typically, they are exposed to pollutants in their home, neighborhood, and school environments. The cumulative toll of this exposure negatively affects their readiness for school, achievement in school, participation in extracurricular activities, and emotional and behavioral well-being.

www.cdc.gov/asthma/video/childhood/
This excellent video provides a broad overview of asthma and also demonstrates the use of inhalers. How might students with asthma need support to be successful in general education classrooms?

MEDICATION   Students with asthma often take two types of medicines—one for long-term control of asthma and the other for quick relief during an asthma attack. The medication decreases swelling, airway hyperresponsiveness, and mucus production (Crawford, 2011). It also can have side effects such as hoarseness, yeast infections, easy bruising, and decreased bone density. Your students may use an inhaler to prevent the debilitating effects of an acute attack of asthma. You need to make sure that you understand the proper use of an inhaler so that you can supervise students in your class when they are using it.

Physicians prescribe inhalers and school nurses often help to supervise students' use of medication. Students should have ready access to their inhalers even before but especially at the very beginning of an asthma attack. They and you also should know and practice the usual sequential steps for responding to an attack, namely, removing the cap, priming the inhaler, blowing out the air in your lungs, putting your mouth around the inhaler and administering the puff or puffs the doctor recommended, and holding the puff in your lungs for a few seconds before exhaling (Nabors, 2016, p. 17). Remember, these are the usual steps for responding to a non-emergency asthma attack. Figure 14.4 highlights the actions to take when seeking emergency care for an asthma attack. Your students' IEPs or Section 504 plans should describe the non-emergency and emergency steps.

Levent Kornuk/Shutterstock

Students need guidance from parents, school nurses, and teachers on the appropriate use of their inhaler.

Figure 14.4 When to Seek Emergency Care for Asthma

- The student's symptoms worsen, even after the medication has had time to work (generally five to ten minutes).

- The student cannot speak a sentence without pausing for breath, has difficulty walking, and/or stops playing and cannot start again.

- The student's chest and neck are pulled or sucked in with each breath.

- The student's peak flow rate lessens or does not improve after bronchodilator treatment or drops below 50 percent of the student's personal best.

- The student's lips and fingernails turn blue: emergency care is needed immediately.

- A second wave occurs after an episode subsides; the student is uncomfortable and having trouble breathing but does not wheeze.

MyLab Education Self-Check 14.1

MyLab Education Application Exercise 14.1: Physical Disabilities and Other Health Impairments May Affect Language and Achievement

Evaluating Students with Physical Disabilities and Other Health Impairments

The following sections on the nondiscriminatory evaluation (NDE) process highlight the NDE approaches to determining the presence of physical disabilities and other health impairments, respectively. In both cases, a physical examination from a physician is often the first step in determining whether the student has a disability.

Determining the Presence of Physical Disabilities

Although medical exams are individualized according to the particular symptoms of each student, a neurological exam is frequently administered when there is any concern about the brain's involvement in a particular condition. **Neuroimaging** provides detailed pictures of various parts of the brain. Neuroimaging is exceedingly helpful in determining the presence of cerebral palsy, spina bifida, and epilepsy. Neuroimaging can involve multiple procedures including magnetic resonance imaging (MRI), functional magnetic resonance imaging (fMRI), and positron emission tomography (PET).

NONDISCRIMINATORY EVALUATION PROCESS For students with physical disabilities, measures of motor functioning and the attainment of developmental milestones with regard to motor development are essential. Physical and occupational therapists have important roles in this process, and you will work closely with related services personnel in the evaluation process.

Although you may think that motor impairments and physical disabilities might be detected by medical professionals early in a child's life, that may or may not be true. Children with spina bifida will be detected at birth because of the presence of medical issues related to the spine and neural cord. But many times children with cerebral palsy are not identified until they begin to show delayed motor development or atypical muscle or motor coordination patterns. That is why, as you can see in the *Nondiscriminatory Evaluation Process: Determining the Presence of Physical Disabilities* feature, parents' and teachers' observations of motor development affect identification and evaluation.

Nondiscriminatory Evaluation Process

Determining the Presence of Physical Disabilities

Observation	**Parents or teacher observe:** The student has difficulty with moving in an organized and efficient way; with fine-motor activities; with gross-motor activities; with activities of daily living, such as dressing; with postural control; and with speaking. **Physician observes:** The student is not passing developmental milestones. Movement is better on one side of the body than the other. Muscle tone is too floppy or stiff. The student has problems with balance or coordination or has neurological signs that suggest a physical disability.
Screening	**Assessment measures:** **Developmental assessment:** The student is not meeting developmental milestones or shows poor quality of movement on measures administered by a physician, physical therapist, occupational therapist, and psychologist. **Functional assessment:** Activities of daily living are affected.
Prereferral	Prereferral is typically not used with these students because of the need to quickly identify physical disabilities. Also, most children with physical disabilities will be identified by a physician before starting school.
Referral	Students with physical disabilities who are identified before starting school should receive early intervention services and a nondiscriminatory evaluation upon entering school. Because some physical disabilities may develop after a student enters school, teachers should refer any student who seems to have significant difficulty with motor-related activities.
Nondiscriminatory evaluation procedures and standards	**Assessment measures:** **Individualized intelligence test:** Standard administration guidelines may need to be adapted because the student's physical disability interferes with the ability to perform some tasks. Results may not be an accurate reflection of ability. The student may be average, above average, or below average in intelligence. **Individualized achievement test:** The student may be average, above average, or below average in specific areas of achievement. Standard administration guidelines may need to be adapted to accommodate the student's response style. Results may not accurately reflect achievement. **Motor functioning tests:** The student's differences in range of motion, motor patterns, gaits, and postures may present learning problems. Also, length and circumference of limbs and degrees of muscle tone or muscle strength may affect the ability to learn specific skills. **Tests of perceptual functioning:** The student is unable to integrate or has difficulty in integrating visual/auditory input and motor output in skills such as cutting and carrying out verbal instructions in an organized manner. **Adaptive behavior scales:** The student may have difficulty in self-care, household, community, and communication skills because of the physical disability. **Anecdotal records:** Reports suggest that the student has functional deficits and requires extra time or assistance in mobility, self-care, household, community, and communication skills because of the physical disability. **Curriculum-based assessment:** The student's physical disability may limit accuracy of curriculum-based assessments. **Direct observation:** The student is unable to organize and complete work or has difficulty doing so.
Determination	The nondiscriminatory evaluation team determines that the student has a physical disability and needs special education and related services.

Determining the Nature of Specially Designed Instruction and Services: Physical Disabilities

Physical therapists and occupational therapists test a student's activity and participation (Hilton, Goloff, Altaras, & Josman, 2013). A tool that can assist in this process is the School Function Assessment (SFA); it measures a student's performance of functional tasks related to participation in school activities. SFA has three parts:

- "Participation" evaluates students' level of participation in school activities and environments.

- "Task Supports" evaluates the extent to which students need supplementary aids and services to participate in school activities and environments.

- "Activity Performance" evaluates students' ability to complete functional activities requiring cognitive and physical skills.

The SFA is composed of 28 scales (with three additional optional scales) that include 266 items. Questions focus on issues such as using school materials, hygiene, following social conventions, and compliance with adult directives. Each item is scored on a 4-point scale in terms of the frequency of the student's performance. Educators who are very familiar with the student in school settings are the respondents.

The SFA differentiates among students with and without disabilities and also distinguishes between groups of students with different disabilities, including students with cerebral palsy (Rabinovich, Patel, Gates, & Otsuka, 2015). The reliability, validity, and psychometric characteristics of the SFA have been established (Hwang & Davies, 2009).

Determining the Presence of Other Health Impairments

Because by definition other health impairments involve health-related issues, conditions such as epilepsy, asthma, and diabetes, you will have to collaborate with professionals from the medical and public health systems. As you can see from the *Nondiscriminatory Evaluation Process: Determining the Presence of Other Health Impairments* feature, medical testing is necessary to identify conditions that might affect your students' learning. So be alert to whether the students you teach have access to quality health care. If they do not, you may refer students for medical evaluation (or re-evaluation) that pays particular attention to conditions that affect students' progress in school.

Nondiscriminatory Evaluation Process
Determining the Presence of Other Health Impairments

Observation	**Parents or teacher observe:** The student may seem sluggish or have other symptoms that suggest illness. The parent takes the student for a medical examination. **Physician observes:** During a routine physical or a physical resulting from symptoms, the physician determines why the student needs further medical assessment. Some health impairments are determined before or shortly after birth.
Screening	**Assessment measures:** **Battery of medical tests prescribed by physician and/or specialists:** Results reveal that the student has a health impairment. A physician makes the diagnosis.
Prereferral	Prereferral may or may not be indicated, depending on the severity of the health impairment. Some students function well in the general classroom. A decision may be made to serve the student with a 504 Plan if accommodations are needed solely to monitor medications and/or to make sure the faculty knows what to do if the student has a medical emergency.
Referral	Students with health impairments that adversely affect their learning or behavior need to be referred for educational assessment.

Nondiscriminatory evaluation procedures and standards	**Assessment measures:**
	    Medical history: Completed jointly by parents and medical and school personnel, the history yields information needed to develop a health-care plan.
	    Individualized intelligence test: The student's condition or treatment may contribute to a decrease in IQ.
	    Individualized achievement test: The student's medical condition and/or treatment regimen may affect achievement.
	    Behavior rating scales: The student is not mastering the curriculum in one or more areas as a result of the condition, treatment, and/or resulting absences.
	    Curriculum-based assessment: The student is not mastering the curriculum in one or more areas as a result of the condition, treatment, and/or resulting absences.
	    Direct observation: The student may experience fatigue or other symptoms resulting from the condition or treatment, detrimentally affecting classroom progress.

Determination	The nondiscriminatory evaluation team determines that the student has an "other health impairment" and needs special education and related services.

NONDISCRIMINATORY EVALUATION PROCESS In many cases, children with other health impairments will have been identified before they come to school, particularly if they are delayed in the attainment of motor or other developmental milestones that might result in the need for early childhood education. In other cases, public health screening might be in place to identify children. You've learned a lot about several conditions under other health impairments—epilepsy and asthma in this chapter and ADHD (Chapter 10)—so let's consider another condition that has become a part of the public discussion again, lead poisoning. Exposure to even trace amounts of lead through the environment, from lead-based paint to chemical residues in soil to lead from old water pipes, can result in multiple developmental and intellectual impairments. Serious problems with exposure to lead by the latter means (old water pipes) occurred in the past few years in the United States, creating significant risk for many children. Most states suggest that children living in high-risk areas, children from families of low socioeconomic status who might live in more contaminated areas, or children in programs such as Head Start be screened for lead levels during routine health appointments using various blood tests. These and other public health initiatives can greatly improve detection and head off detrimental outcomes, as you learned when reading about the public health campaign to introduce folic acid into the food supply. You may also recall that asthma and other conditions (emotional-behavioral disorders, Chapter 9, and intellectual disability, Chapter 11) arise in part from environmental conditions; disability is an issue not only in education but also in public and environmental health and welfare.

Determining the Nature of Specially Designed Instruction and Services: Other Health Impairments

You can use the Child Asthma Risk Assessment Tool (CARAT) to help determine whether one of your students has asthma. CARAT is an online survey of 36 items about a child's asthma status, environmental triggers, medication routines, overall child well-being, and attitudes toward asthma (Wilson et al., 2015). Bear in mind, however, that a health-care provider makes the final decision on whether one of your students has asthma. You will use CARAT only as an early-detection technique.

Let's assume that a health-care provider has diagnosed one of your students as having asthma. What's next? The National Lung, Heart, and Blood Institute recommends that health-care providers, parents, educators, and the student work together to develop an Asthma Action Plan. This plan documents emergency names and contact information. It also describes the action that you should take when the student is not experiencing symptoms of asthma, is experiencing them, or is on medical alert for an asthma attack. You especially need to clearly understand the precise symptoms that should trigger your call for emergency assistance.

The Asthma Action Plan can become part of the student's IEP or Section 504 Plan. (You may want to review Chapters 1 and 4 about Section 504 plans.) All teachers and related services providers for the student should have a copy of the student's Asthma Action Plan, given that an asthma attack can happen at any point throughout the school day. You may want to suggest to the student's parents that the student should have a "wallet card" or other document to carry all the time; after all, an asthma attack is not always predictable and some people may not know that the student has asthma or what to do for the student.

Many other types of health impairments also have action-plan templates online. For example, the American Diabetes Association has a sample Section 504 Plan for students with diabetes.

Link to www.nhibi.nih.gov/health/resources/lung/asthma-action-plan for an action plan available in both English and Spanish and an asthma wallet card.

Including Students with Physical Disabilities and Other Health Impairments

More so than for students receiving special education services in other IDEA categories, students with physical disabilities and other health impairments spend the majority of their time in the general education setting. That's good, in that they will get access to the general education curriculum, but you and your colleagues in general and special education need to be certain that students are receiving the specially designed instruction and supplementary aids and services they need to be successful (Chapters 1 and 4).

Figure 14.5 Extent of Inclusion for Students with Physical Disabilities

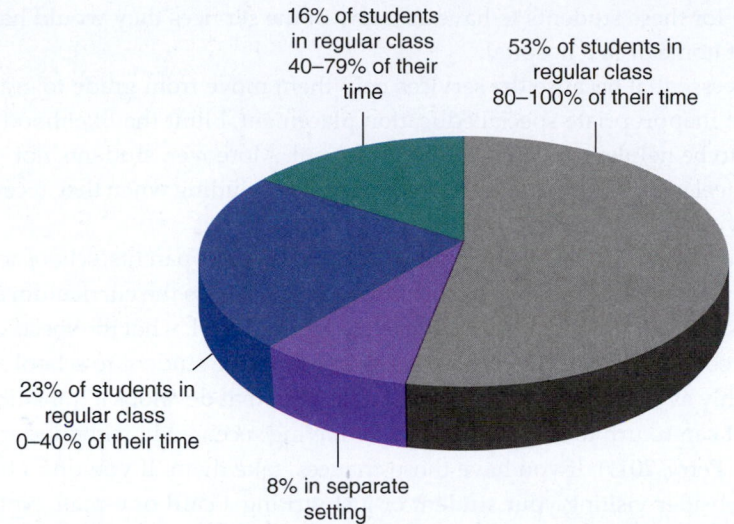

16% of students in regular class 40–79% of their time

53% of students in regular class 80–100% of their time

23% of students in regular class 0–40% of their time

8% in separate setting

SOURCE: U.S. Department of Education. (2017). *39th Annual Report to Congress on the Implementation of the Individuals with Disabilities Education Act.* Retrieved from: https://www2.ed.gov/about/reports/annual/osep/2017/parts-b-c/39th-arc-for-idea.pdf/.

Physical Disabilities

More than half of students with physical disabilities are educated in the general education classroom for 80 percent or more of the day, and 16 percent for between 40 and 79 percent. That still leaves 31 percent of students served in segregated settings for most of their day (U.S. Department of Education, 2018). Eight percent of students with physical disabilities are educated in other settings. What we don't know is whether students educated outside the general education classroom have other co-occurring disabilities, such as intellectual disability. Still, work remains to be done to ensure that students with physical disabilities are included in the general education curriculum. That is one point you should draw from the vignettes about Samuel and Shiloh. Figure 14.5 illustrates where students with physical disabilities were educated during the 2015–2016 school year.

Including students with physical disabilities in general education settings often involves the use of assistive devices, such as communication devices or mobility support devices. But, like all students, using innovative teaching strategies with students with physical disabilities is equally important. A recent study of how to promote inclusion in a math course for a student with cerebral palsy who did not have intellectual disability utilized a cued self-monitoring process to improve student math problem completion. You learned about self-monitoring in Chapter 12. Self-monitoring strategies enable students to learn to collect data on their progress toward educational goals. They can do this through various formats, such as by charting their progress on a sheet of graph paper or completing a checklist. In this study, the student learned to self-graph his progress on completing math problems. The student used a small silent device that vibrated to let him know when he would record his progress. Not only did he make progress, but also the teachers indicated that he greatly enjoyed being in charge of graphing his progress (Sheehey, Wells, & Rowe, 2017).

Other Health Impairments

Figure 10.1, in the chapter on ADHD, displayed the percentage of students with other health impairments according to their educational placement; you might want to review it now to refresh your memory. Of students identified as having other health impairments, 65 percent spend 80 percent or more time in general education classrooms. But 4 percent of students are in separate settings, which may include medical facilities due to the child's health impairment. In some cases, students with health impairments are educated in home or hospital settings when they are having intense health episodes. It is essential for these students to have as many of the services they would have if they were not at home or in a hospital.

This is essential because the services help them move from grade to grade, avoid subsequent inappropriate special education placement, blunt the likelihood that they will learn to be helpless, or prevent early dropout. Moreover, students not with their peers may feel isolated by out-of-school placements, including when they receive homebound services (Boonen & Petry, 2011).

You may have the chance to partner with your student's parents, school administrators, and primary care physician to consider how to address the curriculum standards and IEP goals that the student would achieve if still in school, what the specific duration of the homebound services will be, and how to return the student to school as quickly and smoothly as possible. You also may be on an IEP that develops a transition plan so the student can return to the classroom after having received homebound instruction (Boonen & Petry, 2011). If you have those chances, take them. If you don't have those chances, consider visiting your student or just writing a card or e-mail. Not only can you continue the student's education; you can also boost your student's morale and say, "We will welcome you back in school!" What a simple way to dignify your student. Having done that much, now ensure your student's progress by adhering to *Inclusion Tips for Students with Physical Disabilities or Other Health Impairments*.

Inclusion Tips for Students with Physical Disabilities or Other Health Impairments

	Behavior	Social Interactions	Educational Performance	Classroom Attitudes
What You Might See	The student becomes very anxious when not able to complete assignments at the same speed as classmates.	The student may be self-conscious or embarrassed and withdraws from others.	Lack of strength and use of a wheelchair hinder the student's capacity for full participation in physical education.	The student appears to be overwhelmed by class activities when feeling fatigued.
What You Might Be Tempted to Do	Tell the student to be realistic and face self limitations.	Allow the student to work alone, assuming the student is merely low on energy or needs to be alone.	Excuse the student from physical education and have the student attend a study hall instead.	Tell the student that the only choice is to deal with it.
Alternate Teacher Response	Develop a 504 Plan that incorporates the use of technology to enable the student to complete assignments more quickly.	Work with the school counselor to provide the student with self-awareness instruction.	Use curriculum-based assessment to evaluate the student's strengths and needs related to adapted physical education.	In a 504 Plan, specify the appropriate length of work and rest periods for the student.
Ways to Include Peers in the Process	Explore ways in which all class members can benefit from assistive technology.	Recognize that all students deal with self-esteem issues and involve the class in self-awareness instruction.	Explore opportunities for the student to participate in a wheelchair basketball league.	Have classmates serve as scribes for the student and offer other support as needed.

> **MyLab Education** Self-Check 14.2
>
> **MyLab Education** Application Exercise 14.2: Environmental Factors and Their Impact on Children's Health

Educating Students with Physical Disabilities and Other Health Impairments

A number of research-based strategies will enable you to design an appropriately ambitious educational program for students with physical disabilities and other health impairments. You've learned that although many students with physical disabilities or other health impairments do not necessarily have cognitive impairments, your students may struggle academically because of factors such as frequent school absences and health crises. In this section you will learn about three strategies that enable your students to make progress.

Cooperative Learning

Students with physical disabilities or other health impairments can, like other students with disabilities, feel alone and isolated. They may not be able to go everywhere that other students go and, particularly for students with physical limitations, physical environments may impede their full participation. You'll learn more about providing accommodations and modifications to address some of these issues in a moment, but let's look first at how you can ensure that students with physical disabilities or other health impairments have access to high-quality instruction and that they interact with their peers. This can be accomplished through cooperative learning strategies.

Cooperative learning is a strategy for ensuring progress in the general education curriculum for students with disabilities, including students with physical disabilities or other health impairments. Cooperative learning strategies involve small groups of students who focus on a common learning task or activity. This strategy differs from classroom-wide learning because the learning task is one that all of the group members, not just the student with the disability, are responsible for learning. To implement cooperative learning, you need to do more than simply put students together in small groups and give them an assignment. A haphazard approach to group learning can result in a few students doing most of the work and, indeed, most of the learning.

Early seminal research in cooperative learning (Johnson & Johnson, 1991) identified the primary characteristics of cooperative learning groups. Two of them warrant your careful attention: positive interdependence and individual accountability.

Positive Interdependence.   **Positive interdependence** refers to creating situations where students have to work together to succeed (Johnson, Johnson, & Holubec, 2008). In essence, students support and enable their fellow group members to succeed individually and as a group. Each group member has tasks that are critical to the overall goal and are individualized to the student's ability level. Students engage in different levels of learning and their tasks vary, but each task is essential to the overall success of the group.

Individual Accountability.   In haphazardly created learning groups, all students equally benefit or not by the group outcome, not necessarily according to their individual contribution. One student may do all the work and the group may earn an A, but other students may not have deserved that grade. Similarly, one student may perform a portion of the task at a high-quality level, but the overall quality of the product may be dragged down by other students' performances; that one student is unfairly punished with a grade lower than what is deserved.

By assigning each student in cooperative learning groups discrete, identifiable tasks that contribute to the whole, you can individually assess students on the quality of their component task. However, most important to the implementation of cooperative learning is that students understand that each group member has a role and that the group as a whole will be accountable for the quality of the product.

The teacher can structure cooperative learning groups in several ways to ensure both individual and group success (Johnson & Johnson, 1991). One factor is group size: The smaller the group, the easier it is to fairly distribute tasks and to individualize those tasks according to the unique needs of students. A second factor is detailing each student's individual task, providing examples of quality outcomes pertaining to that task, and making sure that the student understands the contribution of the personal task to the group's task or goal. Instead of waiting until the group is finished, you should use frequent assessments of what each group member is doing and learning. A third factor is accountability, peers holding each other accountable. For instance, you might assign one group member to be a "checker" and to question other group members to ensure that everyone understands the task (Johnson et al., 2008).

Learning with peers has multiple benefits to students with physical disabilities or other health impairments. There is strong evidence across all grade levels that cooperative learning supports students with and without disabilities to acquire knowledge and skills across multiple content areas (Jolliffe, 2016). And, the interaction with peers can facilitate friendships and social interactions and provide role models for students with disabilities. See *Guidelines for Teaching: Cooperative Learning* for how to incorporate cooperative learning into your teaching.

Guidelines for Teaching

Cooperative Learning

Plan.

- Set academic content goals you hope to achieve using cooperative learning.
- Identify social skills objectives that may also be a focus of the learning project.
- Determine the group size depending on the size of the project and learner strengths and support needs.
- Identify students for each group to ensure students with different strengths, knowledge sets, and abilities are included.
- Work with group members to identify specific roles within the group that contribute uniquely to the group achieving the goal.

Train.

- Teach group members about group decision-making processes.
- Support group members to understand the importance of consensus and compromise.
- Support group members to set criteria for addressing the problem and evaluating options.
- Teach group members what will be expected with regard to project outcomes.
- Ensure that group members understand how they will report out and that all group members will have a role in that.
- Explain the criteria you will use to determine if each person is successful.

Introduce.

- Describe the academic task or project to the group, including objectives and major tasks.

- Make sure students understand they are, together, responsible for the outcome and, individually, responsible for their role in the outcome.
- Explain each group member's role to the student and the group.
- Set time limits for the activity on the project and communicate expected work pace.
- Work with students to create a process for monitoring progress toward the goal.
- Answer students' questions.

Observe and Support.

- Create a process to record group and individual student performance during work on the project.
- Determine what actions, interactions, and activities you will observe.
- Determine how often you will observe.
- Conduct regular observations.
- Provide information to correct or improve group performance through positive, clarifying statements.
- Have students generate suggestions for correcting or improving group performance.
- Ensure that peers/peer teams have an opportunity to interact socially, outside an instructional context, so that relationships may grow.

Provide Feedback.

- Provide group feedback on project outcomes.
- Provide individual feedback on each group member's role.
- Support the group to reflect on what went well and what could be improved.
- Celebrate progress on the goal and emphasize improved outcomes from cooperation.

Adapted from Johnson, D., Johnson, R., & Holubec, E. (2008). *Cooperation in the classroom* (8th ed.). Boston, MA: Allyn & Bacon.

Accommodations and Modifications

In Chapter 4 you learned that accommodations are changes to the presentation of instructional content or test or assessment administration that support a student to participate in the learning activity or assessment; you learned about a number of testing accommodations. You also learned about supplementary aids and services that involve modifications and supports to promote student participation and progress in the general education classroom. Figure 4.6 (in Chapter 4) showed domains for and examples of supplementary aids and services.

In this section, you will learn about instructional accommodations and modifications that particularly benefit students with physical disabilities or other health impairments. Because you learned about universal design for learning in Chapter 6 and assistive technology and paraprofessional support in Chapter 13, you will learn here about ensuring access, modifications to the classroom, and other task modifications for students with physical and health-related disabilities.

ACCESS You can't learn if you can't get into the classroom or the school building. Accommodations and modifications to ensure physical access are familiar to many, particularly since the passage of the Americans with Disabilities Act (Chapter 1), but a surprisingly high number of environments, including school environments, remain inaccessible for physical access. Perhaps doorways are too narrow for a student using a wheelchair, or a student with cerebral palsy has a difficult time opening a door due to the type of door handle or the weight of the door. Perhaps a student with asthma can't tolerate climbing multiple flights of stairs to get to a class. Or, maybe fluorescent lighting in a room is a trigger for a student with epilepsy. There are a lot of access issues that people just don't think about that you may need to point out and advocate to change.

CLASSROOM ECOLOGY You will have some say in how to organize the classrooms in which you teach. Again, physical access is often the first issue to consider. If your student with a physical disability uses a wheelchair, are desks spaced far enough apart to create aisles that allow easy navigation? Do desks facilitate an easy transfer from the chair to the desk? Are tables high enough that a student can wheel close to the table? If a student with spina bifida walks using hand crutches, are there uneven floor surfaces due to carpets or raised floors that create a barrier to navigation? You are not powerless to modify and accommodate:

- Ensure furniture is wheelchair accessible, with adjustable legs. The regulations for implementing the Americans with Disabilities Act require that at least 5 percent of the tables in a classroom are wheelchair accessible.

- Store supplies and instructional materials in low, open shelves rather than higher cabinets with doors.

- Consider where students are seated and provide options that accommodate for the student's needs. Perhaps it is easiest for a student with cerebral palsy who does walk to be seated nearer to the entrance of the room to minimize the time spent trying to go around other desks or other furniture. Or, perhaps a student with absence seizures should be seated near the teacher so that the teacher is aware when the student is having difficulties.

- Keep access in mind when designing learning centers. Free-time reading centers where students sit on a carpet or in a bean bag to read may need to include seating that is accessible for a student with a physical disability. Learning centers should be relatively clutter free with easy access to instructional materials.

- Make sure there is a private space in the class or elsewhere near your classroom that your students may use if they need to administer their medications or do some other medical procedure.

- Secure sloped or standing desks for your students who have difficulty writing because they have a physical impairment or weakness or if they cannot sit still for long periods. Enlist note takers or allow tape recording of lectures by students who have trouble writing.

TASK MODIFICATIONS Your students with physical disabilities or other health impairments also will benefit when you modify their tasks and assignments. Some of those modifications are similar to those for assessments: extended time or deadline extensions. You may also assign work to be done in a cooperative learning situation or

MyLab Education

Video Example 14.5
Being aware of students' accommodations as well as their physical needs is important for students with physical disabilities. How did the teacher in the video use both support strategies?

assign your student with a disability to perform a reasonably accomplished task, such as by reducing the number of items on a class-based assignment or homework. Some students may benefit from more frequent breaks and less time seated in one location.

Students with physical or health-related disabilities will need modified physical education. The very nature of the "curriculum" in physical education—physical activity, sports, exercise, games—uniquely challenges those students. The barriers are both attitudinal and environmental (Shields, Synnot, & Barr, 2012). They are not insurmountable.

Adapted physical education uses modifications and accommodations described in the *Into Practice Across Grade Levels: Accommodations and Modifications in Physical Education* feature. The modifications address both the environment in which the sport or physical activity will occur and the equipment used in the sport. Adapted physical education also focuses on students' specific educational needs related to sensory awareness systems, reflexes, fine- and gross-motor skills, body image, locomotor skills, manipulation skills, muscular endurance, and agility or speed (Hodge, Lieberman, & Murata, 2012). Enabling students with physical disabilities or other health impairments to participate in sports and recreation activities may link that student to a source of lifelong enjoyment.

Into Practice Across Grade Levels

Accommodations and Modifications in Physical Education

Recess and playground.
Students in Ms. Oliver's **2nd-grade classroom** often play soccer during recess. To ensure that Myra, a student with spina bifida who uses hand crutches to walk, can participate, Ms. Oliver implemented a set of modified rules for the game. Instead of running, students walk. Students have assigned positions in specific locations of the reduced-size field and do not range outside that location. The ball is slightly deflated so that it stops more easily and doesn't roll as far. These changes enable Myra to participate with her peers during recess.

Softball.
The **4th-grade** students at Arrowhead Elementary do a unit on softball every year. To accommodate for the needs of two students in the class this year, Ms. Russo made several modifications. First, because one student had asthma and had difficulty running long distances, she used the smaller of two softball diamonds and shortened the bases by 10 feet. This modification also helped reduce the risk of an asthma attack because there was less dust on this field than the other. For a student with cerebral palsy who could run with assistance, she also allowed the student to hit from a tee, rather than from a pitched ball, and allowed the student to select one other student to be her designated runner. All students wear protective helmets, protecting the one student with epilepsy for whom a head injury would be an emergency without making her seem to be so different than the other students.

Track and Field.
The entire **6th-grade** class at Oxnard Middle School has an annual track meet toward the end of the school year. Several students have physical or health-related disabilities that limit the types of activities in which they can participate. To make sure that all students participated and benefited from the track meet, Coach Johnson did not require all students to

participate in any one event, but allowed students to choose two that they wanted to compete in. Instead of the running long jump, there was a standing long jump event that didn't require as much energy or lung capacity. The softball-throw replaced the shotput activity. Instead of a discus, the coach had students fling Frisbees for distance and accuracy.

Basketball.
The **9th-grade** curriculum requires that students at Tyler High School participate in basketball during the fall semester. To ensure that all students benefit, the coaching staff designed a series of units that emphasize skill development and individual improvement, rather than team competitions. Students evaluate their ability to dribble and shoot at the start of the semester. Students who use a wheelchair have modified equipment (lower basket, closer to the basket) and comply with International Paralympics rules (catch ball, dribble once, put in lap, push wheelchair to next spot). Students can choose from basketballs of several sizes.

Swimming.
Jonathan loves to swim, but has epilepsy, and he and his parents are concerned about his safety. Ms. Butler is the **11th-grade** counselor and has worked with Jonathan's physical education teacher to put in place the safety measures necessary for him to swim with his peers. They make sure that there is always one adult in the pool area who knows that Jonathan has seizures and is alert to where he is and what he is doing. In addition, for much of the swim period, a buddy system pairs students with and without disabilities who perform the same activities at the same time. If Jonathan has had a seizure within the past 24 hours, he and his parents decided he should stay out of the water for that period, and instead Ms. Butler assigns him some coaching duties.

Health Education

Since one of the themes of our book and of special education itself is self-determination, you need to know that students with physical disabilities or other health impairments should and can learn about and plan for their own health maintenance and care. They will not learn and plan alone; you and health-care–related professionals will be involved, as teachers, school nurses, or staff in school-based health centers.

Some schools have set up school-based health centers to provide comprehensive support for students with health impairments (Keeton, Soleimanpour, & Brindis, 2012). Be sure your students know about those centers and how to access their many services (School-based Health Alliance, 2013):

- Eighty-two percent of the centers are located in traditional public schools.

- Twenty-nine percent are staffed by a primary care provider such as a nurse practitioner, physician assistant, or physician; 33 percent provide primary care and mental health in terms of having the services of a social worker, psychologist, or substance abuse counselor; and 37 percent provide primary care and mental health "plus" (in terms of also having a health educator, oral health provider, social service case manager, or nutritionist).

- In addition to serving students from the school, 51 percent are open to serve students from other schools, 37 percent serve families of student users, and 37 percent serve faculty/school personnel. All of the school-based health clinics are open during school hours and 71 percent have after-hours care available.

In a comparison of students who had access to a school-based health center and students who did not have access, the students with access reported not only a greater likelihood of having a regular health-care provider, but also a greater likelihood of having a provider who respected their concerns, spent adequate time during the visits, and provided clear explanations of important topics (Gibson, Santelli, Minguez, Lord, & Schuyler, 2013).

Health services within schools vary from state to state because no federal legislation covers the provision of school health services (Council on School Health, 2013). IDEA, however, requires that school health services be available to students with disabilities and that these services address educationally related health needs through the services of a school nurse or another qualified professional, so there will be something that the student can learn about accessing. In addition, students can be involved in creating their health-care intervention plans, such as those you learned about earlier in the chapter for students with asthma.

Beyond all this knowledge, your students need instruction to understand how their disability affects their overall functioning and how to maintain optimal health. The *Into Practice Across Grade Levels: Health Education* feature provides examples of such educational focus across school ages and grades.

Before reading the summary of this chapter, take a moment to reflect on the themes we have covered. They include research-based intervention, progress, inclusion, partnerships, and, yes, the "welcoming" words that signify dignity.

Into Practice Across Grade Levels

Health Education

How healthy behaviors impact health.
Students in Ms. Round's **1st-grade** class are involved in a study unit that helps them understand the basics of health, ways to prevent communicable disease, how to prevent injury, and when to seek health care. Lauren is a student with spina bifida in Ms. Round's class, and because children with spina bifida are at increased risk for infections, Lauren works with several children on a unit that focuses on general ways to reduce risks for common infections.

Choosing healthy alternatives when making decisions.
Rolanda is a **3rd-grade** student with diabetes. Her classmates are studying how to identify healthy versus unhealthy habits and situations and what the benefits are from healthy choices. Her teacher, Ms. Lofton, knows that Rolanda struggles with making choices of foods that are good for her diabetes, so she includes in the lesson on healthy eating choices information about vegetables, low-carbohydrate foods, and low-fat foods and their positive benefits for health to all students, knowing that this information will be of particular benefit to Rolanda. Each student prepares a week-long menu using healthy foods and works with the family to cook and prepare some healthy meals to enjoy.

Understanding how the environment affects personal health.
The principal of the Dewey-Mann Middle School had tracked a gradual increase in the rate of asthma in students in her school and the steady increase of emergency health situations associated with asthma attacks, and decided she needed to increase student awareness of environment risks and triggers for poor health. To that end, she worked with **7th-grade** teachers to prepare a science lesson that all students would be involved with on the effects of environmental allergens (dust, mold, pollens) on breathing and lung performance and what precautions to take to minimize problems.

Identify personal susceptibility to injury or illness and links to unhealthy behavior.
Mr. Jones requires all of his biology students to create a personal health plan during their **11th-grade** year. Ryan is a student with cerebral palsy who uses a wheelchair; in selecting a topic, Mr. Jones encouraged him to think about what health factors were particularly important to him. Ryan knew wheelchair users often develop painful and sometimes life-threatening pressure sores. To learn how to prevent those sores, Ryan researched their causes and then developed a health plan that involved shifting positions within the chair frequently, getting out of the chair on a regular basis, making sure that his skin was dry, and making sure that the supports in his chair kept him upright and in a stable position.

MyLab Education **Self-Check 14.3**

MyLab Education **Application Exercise 14.3:** Accommodating Students

---

Summary

Defining Physical Disabilities

IDEA uses the term orthopedic impairments, but most people refer to physical disabilities, those that adversely affect a student's educational performance. Two common physical disabilities are cerebral palsy and spina bifida. Cerebral palsy comprises a group of neurological impairments that affect movement and posture and occur before birth or during infancy. Spina bifida refers to a malformation of the spinal cord prior to birth that results in motor impairments.

Describing the Characteristics and Causes of Physical Disabilities—Cerebral Palsy and Spina Bifida

Cerebral palsy involves motor difficulties that are a function of brain injury or development; these affect a student's balance, posture, gait, and other motor activities. There are four main types of cerebral palsy: spastic, dyskinetic, athetoid, and ataxic (plus any combination). Other health and developmental problems may accompany cerebral palsy, including intellectual limitations. Cerebral palsy can be caused by prenatal, perinatal, and postnatal factors.

There are three forms of spina bifida: spina bifida occulta, meningocele, and myelomeningocele. Mobility and sensory impairment can vary according to form. Students with spina bifida usually have typical intelligence but may struggle to be included with other students and may have associated conditions related to bladder and bowel function. Spina bifida is caused during the first month of gestation by genetic and environmental factors. Maternal ingestion of folic acid significantly reduces the risk of having a child with spina bifida.

Defining Other Health Impairments

IDEA defines other health impairments as those that limit a student's strength, vitality, or alertness (including a heightened alertness to environmental stimuli); that are chronic or acute; and that negatively affect a student's educational performance. Two common OHI conditions are epilepsy and asthma. Epilepsy is characterized by recurrent and unprovoked seizures (unregulated electrical discharges in the brain). Asthma is a chronic lung condition characterized by airway obstruction, inflammation, and hyperirritability of the bronchial tubes that results in wheezing, shortness of breath, and coughing. Asthma is the most common chronic disease among children in the United States. Black and Hispanic families have higher rates of asthma because they may live in impoverished environments and have limited access to quality health care.

Describing the Characteristics and Causes of Other Health Impairments—Epilepsy and Asthma

There are two types of seizures in epilepsy. Partial seizures typically involve only one motor or sensory system and can be simple (motor) or complex (involving consciousness and behavior). By contrast, primary generalized seizures involve both brain hemispheres and multiple motor and sensory systems. There are two types of these seizures—tonic-clonic seizures and absence seizures. Tonic-clonic seizures cause the student to lose consciousness and go back and forth through rigid extensions of extremities (tonic phase) and rhythmic contractions of extremities (clonic phase). Absence seizures involve brief loss of consciousness and motor movements, such as blinking or head movements. Most children with epilepsy have typical IQ scores, but may have memory or attention problems resulting from the seizures. Epilepsy is caused by a combination of genetic and environmental factors.

The symptoms and severity of asthma vary widely from person to person, from intermittent to severe assaults on a person's airways. Asthma attacks are linked to genetic and environmental factors. Genes can increase susceptibility to inflammation from environmental pollutants, which increases the chances that an asthma attack will occur. Environmental factors include air pollution that is associated with traffic, industry, and smoke, as well as pollen, pet dander, dust, and molds. Asthma can be controlled by medications, though awareness of the oncoming attack and when to intervene early is important.

Evaluating Students with Physical Disabilities and Other Health Impairments

A physical examination by a physician, preferably a neurologist, is often the first step in determining whether the student has a physical disability. Physical and occupational therapists also participate in evaluating students; parents' observations are valuable, too. The School Function Assessment determines a student's motor functioning and participation in school activities. Medical evaluation determines other health impairments. Blood tests determine whether a student has lead poisoning, which often results from exposure to environmental lead and can affect a student's intellectual functioning. The Child Asthma Risk Assessment Tool determines the severity of a child's asthma and is an early detection technique. Students who have asthma should have an Asthma Action Plan.

Including Students with Physical Disabilities and Other Health Impairments

More so than for students receiving special education services in other IDEA categories, students with physical disabilities and other health impairments spend the majority of their time in the general education setting. However, a high percentage of students with these disabilities are still not included in schools but are educated in hospitals or at home.

Educating Students with Physical Disabilities and Other Health Impairments

Cooperative learning strategies involve small groups of students focused on a common learning task or activity. Cooperative learning differs from group-based peer tutoring because the learning task is one that all of the group members, not just the student with the disability, are responsible for learning. Effective coordinated learning emphasizes positive interdependence (all students have a role and must perform their role for the team to succeed) and individual accountability.

Accommodations change the presentation of instructional content; they also change how tests or assessments are administered. Modifications refer to changes in the instructional content or product that enable students to be successful. Accommodations and modifications to classroom environments include seating arrangements, wheelchair-accessible furniture, accessible materials storage, and areas for privacy. Task modifications involve extended time, deadline extensions, using cooperative learning teams, frequent breaks, and other strategies. Physical education modifications are essential for students with physical disabilities and OHI.

Finally, students with physical disabilities and OHI often experience health-related issues. Teaching them to take a meaningful role in their health maintenance and care is a means for ensuring that they are self-determined, such as by including students in developing and implementing their individual health-care plan and making them aware of what health-related supports are on their campus. Also, students need to be taught, across ages and grades, how their own efforts to manage health can improve the quality of their lives.

Addressing the Professional Standards

In Chapter 14, Students with Physical Disabilities and Other Health Impairments, we have covered the following Council for Exceptional Children (CEC) Initial Level Special Educator Preparation Standards: Chapter 14—1.0, 1.2, 2.1, 4.3, 4.4, 5.1, 6.1, 6.5, 6.6, 7.1. Refer to the Appendix for a full listing of the CEC Standards with descriptions and supporting explanations.

Chapter 15
Students with Hearing Impairments

by Heather Grantham, Washington University in St. Louis

 Learning Outcomes

15.1 Define and describe the characteristics and causes of hearing loss; explain why hearing loss affects language and literacy development; and identify assessments and their service-related roles.

15.2 Evaluate classroom accommodations; describe those that account for students' communication and age; and describe three instructional strategies for improving students' vocabulary.

Meet Martae Allen—Wired to Progress

Nine-year old Martae Allen is wired to make progress in 3rd grade—indeed, to keep making progress. He has had profound hearing loss since he was born, but he has a device that enables him to hear remarkably well in his general education classes and to make good grades in the general education curriculum. The device is really two separate but identical devices. Each is a cochlear implant, an amplification system surgically implanted into his ears.

By itself, the device does not ensure that Martae hears everything his teacher says. His teacher wears a microphone that transmits her voice directly to Martae's implants. Think about an FM sound system that you might use, and you'll understand what Martae and his teacher use.

His teacher also modifies how she teaches him. She gives directions orally and in writing; she repeats her directions, clarifies them, paraphrases them, seats him near her, allows him to use a screen-reader and closed captioning of the material he needs to read, checks frequently to be sure he understands what she is teaching, and arranges for him to have extra time to complete the state-mandated testing of students' progress on the state-designed core curriculum.

She's not alone in her efforts to ensure that Martae makes progress in the general curriculum and among students who do not have disabilities in Port St. Lucie, Florida. Martae's mother, Erika, his only parent, is acquiring an advanced degree in speech-language pathology and expects to work with bilingual students with and without hearing challenges. She herself is Hispanic and, with her parents Edgar and Elba Baculima, is teaching Martae how to understand and speak Spanish.

She and Martae's teacher are not the only partners in Martae's education. A general education teacher at Martae's school, Christina, is Martae's tutor at

Christina Perez

Christina Perez

home. Erika's friends (happily, a former teacher of the deaf and an educational audiologist) are the other partners. There's a group of "junior partners," too—students in Martae's school who are deaf or hard of hearing, or have no disabilities, who have joined a club to learn American Sign Language, a language that some deaf and hard of hearing students use.

With so much support, you might expect Martae to progress easily through the general curriculum. You would be partially correct. Martae has been in the general curriculum since 1st grade, is on grade level in reading and writing but needs help in comprehending concepts, acquiring vocabulary, and using grammar and structuring sentences correctly. Yet he is earning As and Bs. Why? He achieves those high grades in part because he is a perfectionist; he strives for excellence and does not yet understand that he may not always attain it; his deafness may impede his pursuit but it will never totally block him.

Like him, Erika and his teachers have high expectations for him. His strength is in mathematics; he is a problem solver; he loves to read; he delights in building LEGO models and in STEM building projects; he draws and paints creatively. Long term, Erika and his teachers think that Martae will be an engineer or an architect, and that his occasional upset at not achieving perfection in some subjects will dissipate as he finds those subjects in which he can excel.

Pause for a moment to develop the big picture of Martae. Here's what you might well put into the picture: a naturally talented boy whose limitation in language is partially corrected by technology and teaching practices, whose high expectations and self-determination are strong, whose talents are bolstered at home and by a circle of peers and adult partners, and who is fully included in and most likely will always be included in the general curriculum and in the ordinary life of his community. Does your picture include an icon for dignity? It should, for that is what he has inside himself—a sense of self-worth; and that sense of worthiness is what technology, his teachers' practices, and, most of all, his family contribute to him. He's on his way to equal opportunity in his school and community, to being independent and making his own choices, to being fully a member of his school and community, and to earning his way.

Martae is wired for progress. There's no doubt about it.

Defining Hearing Loss

To better understand what students who are deaf or hard of hearing are able to hear, you should first know how professionals describe the degrees (or severity) of hearing loss. Hearing loss is determined by an **audiologist**, who is a special clinician trained to identify and treat problems in hearing or balance. Pediatric audiologists use a number of different tools to identify how loud sounds must be before a child can hear them, and then they map the results on a chart called an **audiogram**. Figure 15.1 is a familiar sounds audiogram; it shows how loud common sounds are (on the left vertical axis), how highly pitched the sounds are (on the horizontal axis), and the categories most audiologists use to describe hearing loss (on the right vertical axis).

For example, imagine that you have a student in your classroom who has a moderate hearing loss. You can get a sense of how much the student is able to hear by drawing an imaginary line horizontally across the chart at 50 **decibels** (dB). The student is able to hear sounds that are louder (or below) this line. Importantly, without hearing aids, a student with a moderate loss will not be able to hear sounds softer (or above) this line. This means that the student will not be able to understand speech sounds, which are crucial to language and reading development.

Figure 15.1 Familiar Sounds Audiogram

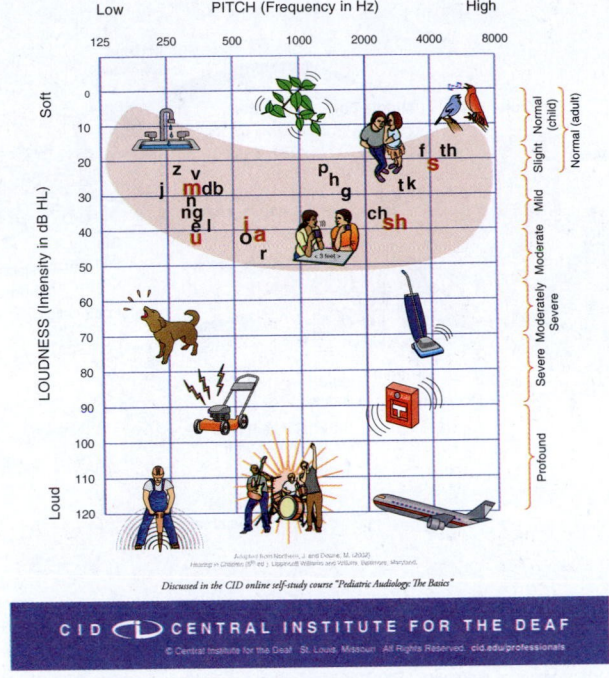

Discussed in the CID online self-study course "Pediatric Audiology: The Basics"

C I D — CENTRAL INSTITUTE FOR THE DEAF

SOURCE: Reprinted with permission from CID – Central Institute for the Deaf, St. Louis, MO. All rights reserved.

An audiologist's job, after identifying a loss, is to find the best devices that will give a child access to as many sounds as possible, especially speech. Students with mild, moderate, and even severe losses can often use **hearing aids** to "boost" the loudness levels of sounds around them so that they can detect most speech. However, even the best hearing aids are not powerful enough for students with profound hearing loss.

Cochlear implants (either one or two) are possible options for students with profound hearing loss to be able to hear speech. We will discuss those devices later, but just keep in mind that students can have varying degrees of loss, across varying **frequencies** (or pitches), and that the presence of devices like hearing aids can give many students access to the quietest sounds (like speech).

Types of Hearing Loss

To complicate matters further, there are a few different types of hearing loss. Take a look at Figure 15.2, which shows the anatomy of the ear.

First, hearing loss can be **conductive**, which means there is a problem with how the outer ear (what you see) or middle ear (ear canal, tiny bones, ear drum) works. Conductive hearing losses can be temporary (e.g., an ear infection that causes the ear drum to be less flexible, and thus not transmit sounds as loudly to the brain) or permanent (e.g., the ear canal is too narrow because the three tiny bones are fused together). Think about how your voice sounds when you have a cold—this is a good reminder of how conductive hearing loss might sound to a student. Thankfully, conductive hearing loss is often able to be corrected.

The second type of hearing loss is **sensorineural**, which means there is a problem with how the inner ear (snail-like cochlea, auditory nerve) works. Sensorineural hearing loss is the most common type of hearing loss and is not able to be corrected medically. Sounds are not only softer but also unclear and distorted. The third type of hearing loss is **mixed**, or when both conductive and sensorineural causes are present.

MyLab Education
Video Example 15.1
This video demonstrates how we hear. What are several ways in which the process can be disrupted, resulting in difficulty hearing? https://www.youtube.com/watch?v=fIIAxGsV1q

Figure 15.2 Anatomy of the Ear

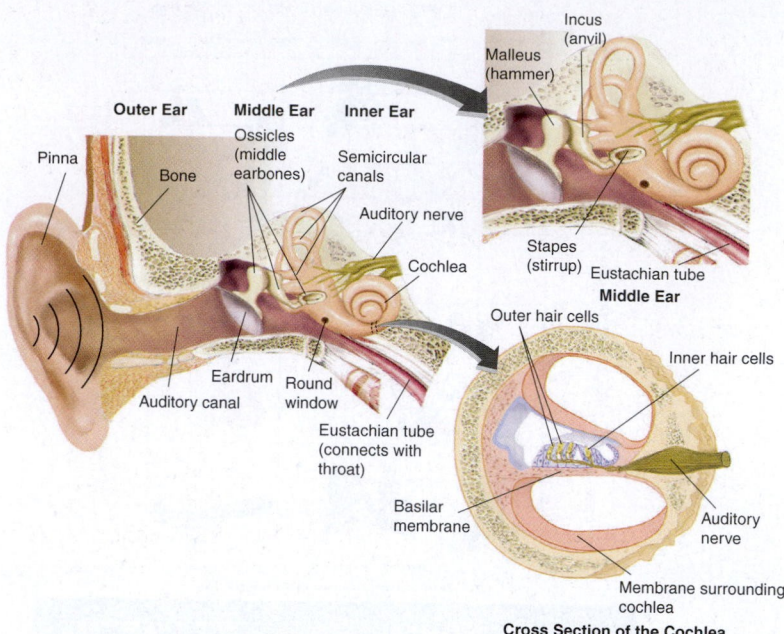

SOURCE: From *Physiology of Behavior with Neuroscience Animations and Student Study Guide CD-ROM* (8th ed.) by Neil R. Carlson, 2004. Upper Saddle River, NJ: Pearson Education, Inc. Reprinted and electronically reproduced by permission of Pearson Education, Inc.

Hearing loss can be one-sided (**unilateral**) or two-sided (**bilateral**). It can be mostly for low-pitched sounds, mostly for high-pitched sounds, or flat across all frequencies.

In summary, keep in mind that each student's hearing loss can vary in terms of severity, type, one- versus two-sided loss, age at loss (birth vs. an older child), cause of hearing loss (disease, genetics), and many other characteristics. All of these (and others) contribute to how a student performs in an academic setting. If you would like to learn more about audiology and hearing loss, the American Speech-Language-Hearing Association (www.asha.org) provides excellent resources in the *Public* section of their site.

It is important to note here that not all individuals who are deaf consider their hearing loss something to be treated with devices or medical intervention. Some individuals who are deaf identify as culturally Deaf by using a capital D—this represents a perspective that deafness is not considered a loss in any way. **Deaf culture** in the United States has a long and rich history (Moores, 2010), with a strong sense of community and shared language (American Sign Language). Throughout this chapter we will refer to students who are deaf or hard of hearing using a lowercase "d" to reflect our specific discussion of students in an educational context, rather than a cultural context.

Prevalence

Approximately 2 to 3 of every 1000 babies are born with some degree of hearing loss (Centers for Disease Control and Prevention, 2010). In fact, about 95 percent of students who are deaf or hard of hearing are born to *hearing* parents (Mitchell & Karchmer, 2004). Only 5 percent of students who are deaf are born to deaf parents. This is an important fact to keep in mind as we discuss communication modes later in this chapter.

The most recent data from the U.S. Department of Education reveal that approximately 65,000 students who are deaf or hard of hearing are served under the Individuals with Disabilities Education Act (IDEA) in public schools (2017). Indeed, 88 percent of

To learn more about Deaf culture and community, visit www. handsandvoices.org in the *Communication Considerations* section of the website.

students with hearing loss are educated in inclusive settings, with most of those students spending more than 80 percent of the school day in a typical classroom (IDEA, 2017). Figure 15.3 shows the educational placement of students with hearing loss. Take a moment to consider Martae's story—he was born with hearing loss, he is the only person with hearing loss in his family, and he attends his local public school while receiving services per an individualized education program (IEP). Martae is representative of the vast majority of students with hearing loss.

Identifying Students Who Are Deaf or Hard of Hearing

As of the writing of this chapter, every state in the country has a program to identify students born with hearing loss (National Center for Hearing Assessment and Management, 2018). The goals of these programs—often called newborn hearing screening programs or **early hearing, detection, and intervention (EHDI)** programs—is to screen for hearing loss by 1 month of age, diagnose the degree and type of hearing loss by 3 months of age, and have the child fitted with hearing devices and receive early intervention services before the child is six months old. This 1-3-6 principle is necessary for successful outcomes for speech, language, and literacy development (Yoshinaga-Itano, Sedey, Wiggin, & Chung, 2017).

If a child does not pass the initial screening test, the child is referred for additional diagnostic testing with a pediatric audiologist. To repeat: a pediatric audiologist is someone who specializes in working with very young students to determine what the child is able to hear, and then to determine which devices may provide the most benefit to the child. Young babies might have a test called an **auditory brainstem response (ABR)**, which measures how well the auditory nerve functions. By the time a child is a toddler, the child typically is able to be tested using behavioral or conditioned play measures, such as dropping a block in a bucket upon hearing a sound.

Ideally, students who are deaf or hard of hearing begin receiving **early intervention** services from a qualified teacher of the deaf immediately after diagnosis and fitting of hearing aids. Unfortunately, not all students receive timely or frequent early

Figure 15.3 Educational Placement of Students Who Are Deaf or Hard of Hearing

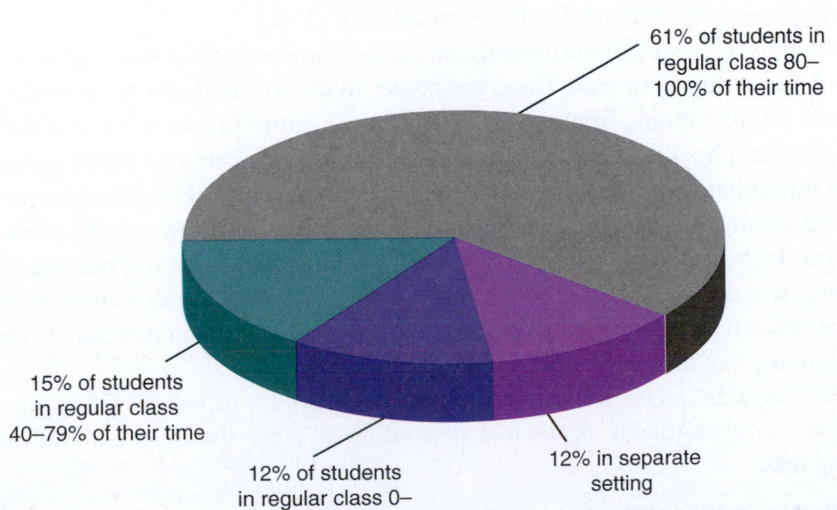

61% of students in regular class 80–100% of their time

15% of students in regular class 40–79% of their time

12% of students in regular class 0–40% of their time

12% in separate setting

SOURCE: U.S. Department of Education. (2017). *39th Annual Report to Congress on the Implementation of the Individuals with Disabilities Education Act*. Retrieved from: https://www2.ed.gov/about/reports/annual/osep/2017/parts-b-c/39th-arc-for-idea.pdf/.

intervention, although efforts such as **teletherapy** are making strides, especially in more rural communities (Behl et al., 2017).

Early intervention involves coaching parents on how best to encourage language and listening development in everyday scenarios. For example, an early intervention-ist might help guide a mother on how to make an everyday activity such as changing her baby's diaper as rich with language and "conversation" as possible. Research has shown that parental language has a significant effect on later outcomes (Hart & Risley, 1995), especially for students with hearing loss who are already at risk for language delay (Suskind et al., 2016). The goals of early intervention are to empower and edu-cate parents on the importance of exposing students to as much language as possible, whether spoken or signed.

As you know from reading Chapter 1 and other chapters, Part C of IDEA provides that parents and teachers must develop an **Individualized Family Service Plan (IFSP)** to guide instruction up until the child's 3rd birthday. An IFSP is a road map of a fam-ily's goals for their child. It is similar to an IEP in that it summarizes the child's present levels of development and needs and lays out a plan for special education services for the family and the child. The IFSP is a crucial part of securing services for children and families and can be of great benefit in developing an IEP after the child turns 3 years old.

Hearing Devices

Most students who are identified with hearing loss are fitted with hearing devices. Depending on the severity and type of the loss, students might wear one or two hear-ing aids, one or two cochlear implants, or a combination of the two. A student who has a unilateral loss might not wear hearing devices (although it is strongly recommended by audiologists and teachers of the deaf) or might choose to wear one. After all, there is the principle of self-determination.

HEARING AIDS   Hearing aids are devices that make sounds louder for students—most importantly, *speech* sounds. Students who have conductive hearing loss often wear a **bone-anchored hearing aid**. This small nugget-like device is placed on the mastoid bone (the part of the skull behind the outer ear) and is often held onto a student's head with a soft headband. Older students might have the bone-anchored aid surgically implanted, depending on the student's age. The microphone on the device picks up sound in the environment and transmits the sound to the inner ear via the bones of the skull, bypassing the damaged outer or middle ear.

Students who have sensorineural hearing loss, however, often have specially fitted **behind-the-ear hearing aids**. These are powerful devices that sit on top of the outer ear, with a tube running from the hearing aid to an earmold that sits inside the outer ear. The microphone on the aid picks up sound in the environment and transmits the sound through the earmold and into the middle and inner ear. Hearing aids can make speech accessible to students with mild-to-severe hearing loss; however, it cannot make that speech clearer. Remember that students who have sensorineural hearing loss are listening to a distorted signal. So, simply wearing hearing aids does not change the fact that speech and other sounds are unclear and challenging to understand. The aids simply make that distorted signal louder.

Hearing aids can be fitted to students in the first days or weeks of life, providing access to sound as quickly as possible, depending on when the child is identified with hearing loss.

COCHLEAR IMPLANTS   Students who have profound, sensorineural hearing loss typically do not benefit from wearing behind-the-ear hearing aids. The aids are not powerful enough to make speech sounds loud enough for students with this level of hearing loss. However, a different type of device—a cochlear implant—can provide many profoundly deaf students like Martae with access to spoken language that they would otherwise not be able to hear.

Cochlear implants have two parts: external and internal. The external components consist of a small hearing aid–like device that sits either on top of the ear or behind the ear on the skull. It contains a powerful speech processor and a microphone. This external device is connected via a magnet to an internal device, which is surgically placed inside the inner ear. An electrode array is coiled along the **cochlea**, which is the organ of hearing. When sound is picked up by the external microphone, the speech processor converts the sound to electrical signals, which are transmitted along the internal electrode array into the cochlea and ultimately perceived by the brain.

See the external pieces of the cochlear implant on this student; they consist of a behind-the-ear speech processor, an earmold, a magnet, and a cord connecting the processor to the magnet.

Listening to sound via a cochlear implant is very different from listening to sound via a hearing aid. Consider the difference between an acoustic signal (sound traveling through the air in waves) and an electrical signal. For many students (and even adults who have progressive or later-developing hearing loss), listening through a cochlear implant requires years of intensive rehabilitation therapy. However, the potential for a profoundly deaf child to be able to listen to speech, listen to music, talk on a cell phone, and learn through listening is often considered by many parents to be worth the effort and risks associated with childhood surgery.

Cochlear implants are typically restricted to children no younger than 9 to 12 months old. However, under certain circumstances (such as medical reasons that cause the inner ear to ossify, or grow bony, thus requiring the implant to be placed as soon as possible) children can receive cochlear implants at much younger ages. To be eligible for a cochlear implant, children must demonstrate that they cannot perceive any speech using hearing aids.

Describing the Characteristics and Causes
Communication Methods

Students who are deaf or hard of hearing are a diverse group of individuals in terms of how they communicate with their families, their friends, and their environments. One language used by some students who are deaf or hard of hearing in the United States is **American Sign Language (ASL)**. ASL is a visual-spatial language with a unique syntax, or word order, among other distinctive linguistic elements. ASL is "visual" because it uses hands, facial expressions, and body orientation to communicate with another person. It is also "spatial" because it uses the space around a person to "place" or "assign" individuals or ideas in a story as visual reference points. For example, if a signer wants to tell a story about a brother who is not in the room, the signer might sign "my brother" and point to an adjacent space, effectively "assigning" the space to the brother. Then, orienting the body accordingly, the signer can use that space as a reference point each time this brother is mentioned in the story. Students in general education classrooms who use ASL typically have an **educational interpreter** to relay information that is spoken by teachers or other students. The interpreter will also be the "voice" for the student if the student uses ASL to communicate with others.

MyLab Education
Video Example 15.2
This video is designed to orient general education teachers to interpreting services. What are three rules to follow when working with an educational interpreter in the classroom? https://www.youtube.com/watch?v=bXiwEKVbUs0

AMELIE-BENOIST/BSIP SA/Alamy Stock Photo

As you already know, the vast majority of people who are deaf or hard of hearing are born to hearing parents, and most hearing parents' native language is spoken language (Mitchell & Karchmer, 2004). You should not be surprised to know that many hearing parents with deaf or hard of hearing children want them to be able to talk, as this allows effective communication with family members and others in their schools and communities. Such desires are entirely reasonable.

It is possible for students who are deaf or hard of hearing to learn how to talk if they receive appropriately fitted hearing devices as soon as possible in life and if they have early and intensive speech/listening/language intervention (Niparko et al., 2010; Moog & Geers, 2010). Some early intervention professionals used to think it was too confusing to expose babies who are deaf to more than one language. In fact, it is certainly possible for students who are deaf or hard of hearing to be bilingual or multilingual. Consider Martae—his primary language is spoken English, but several of his family members are fluent in spoken Spanish, so he's learning that at home, too. The most important thing for children who are deaf is to be exposed to high-quality language input, regardless of whether it is spoken English, other spoken languages, or signed language. Both quality *and* quantity of input matter for babies with hearing loss.

Some students who are deaf or hard of hearing communicate using signs that are in English order while speaking. This is sometimes called **Simultaneous Communication, Total Communication,** or **Signed Exact English**. Note that this is not the same as using American Sign Language, which has a syntactic structure (or word order) that is distinctly different from that of English, making it impossible to speak English at the same time as using ASL.

Many students use some combination of spoken language and visual communication to converse with friends and family, and in school settings. The presence of a hearing loss does not immediately mean that a teacher should expect the student to know only sign language. In fact, general education teachers are quite likely to encounter students in their classrooms who wear hearing aids and/or cochlear implants, who do not know sign language, and instead who listen and talk. However, even students who primarily use spoken language may use ASL or other sign communication methods in certain situations.

The take-home message is that students who are deaf or hard of hearing are not a one-language-fits-all sort of population. The language used by students depends heavily on the language of the home, the best-fitting accommodations for school, and the peer group, who may be more linguistically diverse than the family (e.g., students may have deaf friends who use ASL, but no family members who are deaf).

> Go to https://hearingfirst.org to learn about the development of listening and spoken language (LSL) and their connection with literacy skills. Search for videos of children and their families who tell their stories.

Effects of Childhood Hearing Loss

When hearing loss occurs at birth or within the critical period of language development (approximately the first 3 years of life), significant delay can occur for several reasons. Typically developing babies' brains are particularly sensitive to auditory information, especially speech. Babies listen to the steady speech in their environments and "collect data" like little scientists about all of the interesting differences between sounds in words (Eimas, Siqueland, Jusczyk, & Vigorito, 1971). These databases of spoken language continue to get larger and more complex as the listening experience of babies increases. By the time babies reach their 1st birthday, they have heard millions of words and are ready to start producing some of these wonderful words themselves.

By contrast, the brain of the deaf or hard of hearing baby has fewer opportunities for listening (e.g., reduced quantity—the baby cannot hear as much or any speech information). Even when these listening opportunities do exist, they are typically of poor quality (e.g., sensorineural hearing loss means that the speech sounds are distorted because certain parts of the ear's anatomy are missing or malfunctioning). Accordingly, students who are deaf or hard of hearing typically have delayed language compared to hearing students, especially in the areas of vocabulary and syntax (Lederberg, Schick, & Spencer, 2013).

In general, the more hearing a child has for a longer period, the less the language delay. For example, students who are born with typical hearing and who contract meningitis as a toddler, resulting in profound deafness, should be expected to have less language delay than a child who has been profoundly deaf since birth. Listening to any amount of spoken language during the critical first years of life can make a tremendous difference in speech and language development. This is precisely why parents who would like their child to learn spoken language must make sure to get hearing aids or cochlear implants placed on their child as early as possible so that the child's brain can start listening to speech.

Also, some deaf students receive visual language input from birth. These are students who are born into families whose native language is ASL. When deaf or hard of hearing babies are exposed to high-quality, fluent ASL from birth, their signed language development is on track compared to hearing babies' spoken language development (Bonvillian, Orlansky & Novak, 1983). The bottom line is this: Babies must be exposed to language—either via listening to spoken language or watching native signers use ASL—in order to learn new words, learn word order, and be able to communicate with other people.

Not surprisingly, reading is a challenging task for students who have poor vocabularies, deficient syntax knowledge, and poor phonological awareness (the knowledge that words can be broken up into chunks, like syllables or individual sounds). On average, students who are deaf or hard of hearing tend to struggle with all aspects of language, and so tend to be poorer readers and spellers than hearing students of the same age (Geers & Hayes, 2011).

It has often been reported that students with hearing loss struggle to read beyond a 3rd- or 4th-grade level (Traxler, 2000). However, the most recent research shows that a particular subset of deaf students—those who receive hearing aids or cochlear implants at young ages, and who receive intensive early intervention—can achieve reading scores that are well within the normal range of hearing peers (Geers et al., 2017). This is a direct consequence of being able to hear more speech and subsequently acquire better vocabulary, syntax, and the very important skills of phonological awareness.

Students who are deaf and who have native ASL exposure have stronger language skills than those who did not have native ASL input, which is important for text comprehension, but decoding is challenging because written English is based on spoken English (Perfetti & Sandak, 2000). There is no written correlate of ASL. However, some reading programs have been developed for use with students who use ASL and/or who do not have functional hearing (Trezek, Wang, Woods, Gampp, & Paul, 2007). Students in these programs, who receive supplemental visual phonics instruction on the parts of words and corresponding letters, are able to improve their decoding skills.

Causes

Hearing loss can be present at birth (called **congenital hearing loss**) or after birth (called **acquired hearing loss**). Let's first describe hearing loss that occurs after a child is born.

The most common cause of hearing loss (either congenital or acquired) in students is **otitis media**, or fluid buildup in the middle ear behind the eardrum (American Speech-Hearing-Language Association, n.d.). It is estimated that 75 percent of students will have had one instance of otitis media by age 3 years (American Speech-Hearing-Language

Association, n.d.). This buildup of fluid causes the eardrum to be inflexible, and thus sound does not transmit very well. Students with otitis media can experience a mild-to-moderate hearing loss, meaning that they may be missing out on speech. Take a look at Figure 15.1, the familiar sounds audiogram, for a reminder of the loudness levels of many speech sounds.

The age range of birth through 3 years is a critical period of language development, a time during which the brain is primed and ready to listen to speech (or *see* language, in terms of signed language). Any degree of hearing loss can be problematic for speech and language development, even if just for a short period. Fortunately, otitis media usually does not cause permanent hearing loss; however, even a short-term fluctuating hearing loss can pose problems for speech and language development in the early years.

Other causes of acquired hearing loss during infancy or childhood include diseases such as meningitis, measles, mumps, or chickenpox, among others. Some students with life-threatening illnesses must take drugs that save their lives but that damage the auditory system. Head injury and noise exposure can also cause hearing loss in students.

Importantly for those of us in educational settings, most students who have an acquired hearing loss have been able to hear sounds at some point in their development. Even just hearing speech for a few months can make a tremendous difference in later speech and language development. Students who have congenital hearing loss, however, are at a distinct disadvantage because they have experienced a hearing loss since birth, without any periods of typical hearing.

Congenital hearing loss occurs at or prior to birth. It can be caused by prenatal illnesses such as rubella, diabetes, cytomegalovirus (CMV), or other complications during pregnancy. However, 50 percent of congenital hearing loss is caused by genetics, or hereditary factors. These factors can be related to dominant or recessive gene transmission by parents. Some students who are deaf have other characteristics that are part of a broader syndrome of genetic abnormalities, such as Down syndrome, Treacher Collins syndrome, and CHARGE syndrome, among others.

Auditory skills begin developing as early as 18 weeks during pregnancy, so listening to spoken language (albeit muffled because of amniotic fluid) begins in utero. In fact, as soon as a few days after birth, babies show a preference for a passage read by their mother during the last trimester of pregnancy compared to a new passage their mother had never read before (DeCasper & Spence, 1986). Listening—as well as learning—is happening well before the baby arrives in the delivery room. This fact is important for teachers of students who are congenitally deaf to keep in mind: These students have missed out on important listening opportunities from the very beginning stages of auditory brain development, and thus may be at significant risk of language (and subsequent academic) delays without intensive intervention.

Evaluating Students Who Are Deaf or Hard of Hearing

Assessments

Because students who are deaf or hard of hearing are at risk for language delay and may struggle to achieve age-appropriate academic outcomes, assessments of language and reading ability are often administered. These assessments may include standardized tests of language (such as receptive or expressive vocabulary, syntax, and pragmatics) and reading (decoding, fluency, and comprehension). These tests normally are administered by a school psychologist or possibly a speech-language pathologist. A complete assessment battery includes in-class data on how the student is responding to interventions, typically administered by the teacher of the deaf and/or the general education teacher. *Nondiscriminatory Evaluation Process: Determining the Presence of a Hearing Loss* provides an overview of the standard techniques used for observations, screening, and nondiscriminatory evaluation.

Some students who are deaf or hard of hearing use sign language, such as ASL, as their primary method of communication. Test accommodations must be made to ensure that these students understand all directions and requirements of the test. The accommodations include having an interpreter present during administration or having printed directions (instead of oral directions) available to the student. When supporting students who use listening and spoken language, the test administrator must make sure that the students' devices are functioning correctly and that any **assistive listening devices** (such as **FM/DM systems**, discussed later) are used as well. As in all testing situations with all students, it is crucial to ensure that they understand the directions, whether spoken, written, or signed. Martae does not require any test-taking accommodations. See Figure 15.4 to review what Martae's IEP states regarding his participation in assessment.

Nondiscriminatory Evaluation Process

Determining the Presence of a Hearing Loss

Observation	**Medical personnel observe:** The baby does not show a startle reflex to loud noises. As the child matures, speech and language are delayed. **Teachers and parents observe:** The child (1) does not respond to sound; (2) does not babble or engage in vocal play; and (3) experiences communication misunderstandings, speech difficulties, and inattention.
Screening	**Assessment measures:** 　**Newborn screening:** Most states require newborn screening for hearing loss. 　**Auditory brainstem response:** Results may show inadequate or slow response to sound. 　**Transient evoked otoacoustic immittance:** Results may show that measurement of sound in the ear is lower than normal. 　**Behavioral audiological evaluation:** Hearing thresholds are higher than 15 dB.
Prereferral	Prereferral is typically not used with these students because of the need to identify hearing loss quickly.
Referral	Students receive nondiscriminatory evaluation procedures as soon as they enter school. Intervention should occur as soon as the student is diagnosed. Students with mild hearing loss may be referred.
Nondiscriminatory evaluation procedures and standards	**Assessment measures:** 　**Audiological reassessment:** Recent audiograms may indicate that the student's hearing loss has stabilized or is worsening. Testing for hearing aid function is a regular need. 　**Speech and language evaluation:** The student may have significant problems with receptive and expressive language. The student's speech is usually affected. 　**Individualized intelligence test:** The student's scores show a discrepancy between verbal and nonverbal measures. Nonverbal tests are considered the only reliable and valid measures of intelligence for this population. 　**Individualized achievement test:** The student may score significantly lower than peers. 　**Adaptive behavior:** The student may score below average in communication and possibly in other areas of adaptive behavior. 　**Anecdotal records:** The student's performance may indicate difficulty with reading, writing, or language arts. 　**Curriculum-based assessment:** The student may be performing below peers in one or more areas of the curriculum because of reading and/or language difficulties. 　**Direct observation:** The student may be difficult to understand and may misunderstand others.
Determination	The nondiscriminatory evaluation team determines that the student has a hearing loss and needs special education and related services. The student's IEP team proceeds to develop appropriate education options for the student.

Figure 15.4 Partial IEP for Martae: Participation in Assessment

---

Student: RMartae

Meeting Date: 02/15/2018

<u>Participation in Assessment</u>

    Not applicable for this student.

X   The student will participate in the **general statewide assessment** (e.g., Florida Standards Assessment (FSA), Statewide Science Assessment, End-of-Course Examination (EOCs), ACCESS for English Language Learners).

    Specific statewide assessments the student will take include (if known):
FSA: Reading, Math

    The student will participate in the **Florida Standards Alternate Assessment (FSAA),** including Access End-of-Course exams and Alternate ACCESS for ELLs as applicable.

Districtwide Assessments

The following districtwide assessments will be administered:

    I Ready: Reading, Math

    District unit assessments: Reading, Math, Science

Assessment Accommodations

Assessment accommodations may be used only if they do not alter the underlying content that is being measured by the assessment or negatively affect the assessment's reliability or validity. Assessments include classroom as well as districtwide and statewide assessments. Note that only accommodations allowed by individual test administration manuals can be implemented on standardized tests.

Presentation

    Oral presentation of items and answer choices; Oral presentation of directions; Directions repeated, clarified; Student to demonstrate understanding of directions (e.g., repeating or paraphrasing); Verbal encouragement (e.g., "keep working," "make sure to answer every question")

Paper-Based Presentation Options

    Highlighter to mark key phrases or words in directions, items, and passages

Computer-Based Presentation Options

    Screen reader; closed captioning

Responding

    Periodic check by administrator to be sure student is entering answer choices correctly

Scheduling

    Extended time (100%); Time management tools like checklists, assignment planners, or visual schedules

Setting

    Assessments or tests administered by a familiar person who has been appropriately trained; Assessments or tests administered in a small-group setting (no more than 12 students); Special acoustics, such as FM system or special room (FM system); Preferential seating

Other Assistive Devices

    Auditory amplification device (FM system)

Unique Accommodations or Special Exemption Requests

In accordance with Rule 6A-1.0943, F.A.C., school districts may request unique accommodations or special assessment exemptions that are based upon medical complexity, extraordinary circumstances, or extraordinary conditions for individual students with disabilities. Such requests must be approved by the district superintendents or Florida Commissioner of Education.

    The team is not submitting a request for a unique accommodation or special assessment exemption.

At this point in the discussion of assessments, you should note that the presence of a hearing loss does not automatically guarantee that a student will have an individualized educational program (IEP). In fact, many students with hearing loss do not receive formal special education services via an IEP. Remember, from Chapter 1, that to be eligible for an IEP, a disability must prevent a student from benefiting from general education; the key is that the student cannot function in the general education curriculum. Alternatively stated, the student's disability must lead to unexpectedly poor performance, not otherwise explained by cognitive ability (Stanberry, n.d.). Many students who are deaf or hard of hearing are able to achieve academic outcomes on par with their classmates and thus do not qualify for an IEP, depending on the school district's interpretation of poor performance. However, even these students may have a Sec. 504 Plan, ensuring that the school setting and curriculum are accessible to them. A 504 Plan can be provided to all students with hearing loss, regardless of whether the loss causes problems with academic outcomes.

Finally, do not overlook the fact that approximately 40 percent of students with hearing loss have concomitant disabilities or overlapping diagnoses (Gallaudet Research Institute, 2005). Disabilities such as attention-deficit hyperactivity disorder (ADHD), learning disabilities, or dyslexia may be very difficult to detect because of the presence of hearing loss. ADHD or dyslexia may have some of the same effects as those that may arise from hearing loss. Thus, numerous sources of data must be collected to best assess a student who is deaf or hard of hearing.

MyLab Education Self-Check 15.1
MyLab Education Application Exercise 15.1: Language Considerations for Students with Hearing Impairments

---

Including Students Who Are Deaf or Hard of Hearing
Accommodations in the Classroom

In many simple ways teachers can ensure that students who are deaf or hard of hearing are included in all classroom activities. Some of these are just good practice and are not necessarily stated as formal accommodations on an IEP.

Many of the strategies are designed to improve the learning environment for students who are deaf or hard of hearing. When they are talking, teachers can simply make sure that students are able to see their face. This means that teachers should avoid talking while writing on a whiteboard, while standing behind students, or while the lights are low in the room (during a video, for example).

Another strategy is to improve the listening environment in the classroom. Many classrooms are noisy places for even hearing students, but they pose particular challenges for students with hearing loss. Any hard surfaces, like hard floors and walls, cause noise to reverberate. Teachers should consider adding throw rugs or soft wall coverings to lessen the reverberation. Even putting tennis balls on the bottoms of chairs can reduce the loud background noise of chairs constantly scraping on the hard floors as people maneuver throughout the room. More formal accommodations, like adding acoustic tiles to walls and ceilings, are ideal but often not available in most schools.

Another way to indirectly reduce noise for students who are deaf or hard of hearing is to make sure they are seated away from noisy objects, such as air conditioning or heating units, windows, and fans, and as close as possible to where the teacher typically provides instruction.

Finally, one of the most inclusive ways to make sure that students who are deaf or hard of hearing participate in the curriculum is to ensure that all videos shown in the classroom are captioned. Interestingly, many of the above informal accommodations not only are helpful to students with hearing loss but also may be beneficial for other learners. These strategies are additive, in that other students clearly benefit from less background noise, being able to see the speaker (visual input adds a great deal to interpretation of content, even for hearing students), and having captions available to improve and practice reading skills. Specific ideas for making the classroom more inclusive for students who are deaf or hard of hearing can be found in the *Inclusion Tips for Students Who Are Deaf or Hard of Hearing* feature.

Inclusion Tips for Students Who Are Deaf or Hard of Hearing

	Behavior	Social Interactions	Educational Performance	Classroom Attitudes
What You Might See	The student does not participate in cooperative learning activities.	The student's speech is difficult to understand, and other students do not know how to sign, limiting the student's ability to interact during small-group discussions.	The student misses some things other students say and appears not to understand.	The student appears bored or inattentive due to not hearing all that is said or not watching the interpreter.
What You Might Be Tempted to Do	Tell the student in front of the rest of the class to participate appropriately.	Randomly assign the student to a group; assume the group will work out roles for participation.	Tell the student to ask the interpreter.	Discipline the student for inattentiveness.
Alternate Teacher Response	Be sure the student understands the activity and what is expected before beginning to work on it.	Discuss the situation with the teacher of the deaf so that the student can practice certain social situations through role play and turn-taking activities.	Ask the interpreter to move to the student who is talking so the student can see both the interpreter and the student who is talking.	Be sure the student is wearing the assistive listening devices properly.
Ways to Include Peers in the Process	Use a buddy system to foster greater participation.	Use a student to facilitate a more structured approach that allows comments and input from everyone.	Tell students to wait until the interpreter is nearby before they speak up in class.	Group the student with peers who are helpful and caring but do not mother the student.

MyLab Education
Video Example 15.3
This video reveals how difficult it is for a student with a hearing aid to listen in a noisy environment, and how an FM system can significantly improve a student's listening experience. https://www.youtube.com/watch?v=1l37lzLIgQU

More formal accommodations may also be incorporated per the student's IEP. These might include, but are not limited to, a sign language interpreter, the use of a personal or sound field FM/DM system, and CART (Caption Assist in Real Time) transcription service.

Students who know American Sign Language often use interpreters in classrooms and in other school activities. The ways in which students use interpreters can vary greatly. Some students might only need the interpreter as a support and choose to voice for themselves when answering questions or engaging in group conversations. Other students might want the interpreter to interpret the spoken language instruction and also voice for them as the interpreter signs. Regardless of the student's personal preference, the sign language interpreter is not expected to serve as an additional teacher or aide, but is considered a valuable member of the student's educational support team.

For students who use hearing aids and cochlear implants, an FM or DM system is often considered an essential accommodation.

A personal FM/DM system has two components: a wireless microphone that is either worn or held by the teacher or by anyone providing instruction, and a receiver that is connected wirelessly to the student's hearing aids or cochlear implant(s). The student hears the speaker regardless of distance. It is as if the teacher is sitting right in front of the student; instead, the teacher might be across the room providing instruction. The FM/DM system is particularly important for small-group work and reducing background noise. Martae uses an FM system in school—his teacher wears a microphone so that he can hear her voice above any other noise that is happening in his classroom. An alternative to a personal FM/DM system is a sound field system, which pipes the speaker's voice through speakers in the classroom (either via a sound bar or speakers mounted in the ceiling or other locations). The benefit of a sound field system is that all of the students receive a more direct signal regardless of where the teacher is in the room.

CART (Communication Access Realtime Translation) writers are individuals who transcribe all spoken language in the classroom. CART is an accommodation that is typically requested only for older students with good English reading proficiency. The CART writer either is present in the classroom during instruction or can be listening remotely through a microphone that the teacher uses. The writer captions all spoken information, which is then transmitted in real time to a handheld screen at the student's desk or on a laptop. An added benefit of CART is that the student receives a transcript of the class session and can refer to it when studying.

Review the *Guidelines for Teaching: Accessibility* to determine accommodations that can make the classroom more accessible for students who are hard of hearing or who have a hearing loss.

MyLab Education
Video Example 15.4
CART is realtime translation of all spoken language in the classroom. What are the advantages for students who have access to CART? https://www.youtube.com/watch?time_continue=8&v=qn4B0gyDosA

Guidelines for Teaching

Accessibility

To provide students who are deaf or hard of hearing with complete access to information, teachers should:

- Ensure that the other classmates face the student when they are talking.
- Make sure the other classmates raise their hands before speaking so the student can visually orient to the speaker.
- Use a remote microphone as part of an FM/DM system, so that it can be passed among classmates during a discussion, or in small-group activities.
- Provide a study guide of upcoming topics to the teacher of the deaf so that the teacher can pre-teach unfamiliar vocabulary.
- Avoid talking while writing on the whiteboard or when behind the student who is deaf or hard of hearing.
- Ensure that the student's hearing aid(s) and/or cochlear implant(s) are working.

- Check the notes taken by the student note taker to be sure they are adequate.
- Arrange for peer tutoring of unfamiliar vocabulary.
- Arrange instruction for peers to learn more sign language, if that is the student's primary method of communication.
- Ensure a well-lit space at all times so that the student can see the speaker and/or the interpreter clearly.
- Caption all video segments that are shown in the classroom.
- If a student uses an interpreter, speak directly to the student, not the interpreter.
- Avoid seating the student near sources of noise, such as a fan or open window. If the classroom has hard floors, consider laying down throw rugs or put tennis balls on the ends of chairs.

Educating Students Who Are Deaf or Hard of Hearing

Effective Instructional Strategies

EARLY INTERVENTION As you have read repeatedly throughout this book, the most important intervention for students who have special needs is *early* intervention. The same is true for students who are deaf or hard of hearing. Students in early intervention programs are typically taught by teachers of the deaf or speech-language pathologists who specialize in hearing loss. Most early intervention contains a parent-coaching component. This means that the early interventionist goes into the family's home and teaches the caregiver how to provide an enriched language model for the child in everyday, routine activities. The concept behind this coaching model is that

---

Into Practice Across Grade Levels

Vocabulary Instruction

Vocabulary instruction must be frequent and intense for students of all ages who are deaf or hard of hearing.

For students who are in preschool.

- Teach related vocabulary through thematic units. For example, in a unit on *weather*, you can teach and practice words such as *cloudy, sunny, rainy,* and *windy* by charting the weather each morning on a calendar during circle time.
- Choose words that are vital to the student's everyday experiences. For example, send home a survey to parents about the student's favorite foods, favorite family traditions, and favorite holidays to ensure that the student knows all the related vocabulary words, enabling the student to express thoughts with ease.

For students who are in elementary school.

- Pre-teach vocabulary prior to introducing a concept. For example, several weeks before teaching a unit on rocks and minerals, provide the student and the student's teacher of the deaf with a list of important vocabulary words and phrases. The teacher of the deaf can then expose the student to the words and related concepts prior to the first day of the unit. This provides the student with an important opportunity for extra practice.
- Use graphic organizers or concept maps to help students retrieve newly learned concepts. For example, provide students with a Venn diagram and ask them to list the similarities and differences between reptiles and mammals. Tell them to recall as many ideas as possible, to provide them with retrieval practice of new vocabulary.

For students who are in middle school.

- Ask students to highlight all unknown words and phrases in a textbook chapter. This metacognitive strategy is important for students who are deaf or hard of hearing and who may not realize which words are actually unknown. Sometimes students have an illusion of fluency—they can decode the words easily but may not know what they mean.
- Teach broad categories of words, along with exemplars. For example, students may be able to identify specific items, such as *forks, steak knives, ladles*, or *spatulas*, but struggle to label the category of items as *utensils*. Requiring them to sort and categorize vocabulary will help with learning broader labels.

For students who are in high school.

- Space out the practice of vocabulary words so that the student has the opportunity to practice new words over time, rather than cramming in the practice prior to an exam. Although spaced practice is difficult and may seem to cause poorer performance in the short term, research shows that it is far better for long-term retention of new words than massed, or crammed, practice (the latter having only short-term benefits).
- Teach students to use contextual information to determine the definitions of new words. For example, students can divide unknown words into morphemes (the smallest meaningful units of words) to gain insight into a word's meaning. Words like *antiestablishment* can be broken down into a prefix (*anti-*), root word (*establish*), and suffix (*-ment*), all of which have meaning and can provide clues about the definition.

the parents or caregivers are around the child for the most hours of the child's day in these early years.

Some students are able to attend center-based programs in addition to home visits. Center-based programs, typically for students ages 18 months to 3 years, provide small-group instruction along with one-on-one therapy. Research shows that students who attend both a toddler classroom with a teacher of the deaf and who receive home visits from a teacher of the deaf show greater gains in language development at age 5 years (Moog & Geers, 2010). Again, the purpose is to reduce the amount of language delay with intensive, early instruction.

VOCABULARY   The next area of instruction that must be considered for students who are deaf or hard of hearing is vocabulary. Most students who are deaf or hard of hearing struggle to hear language around them, unlike hearing students who can overhear and learn new words indirectly from other people's conversations. Additionally, much of new vocabulary knowledge comes from print, and if students who are deaf struggle to read, then they will miss out on opportunities that a good reader gets to learn new and more uncommon vocabulary through books. Clearly, vocabulary intervention is critical for this population of students. Read more about specific vocabulary teaching strategies in *Into Practice Across Grade Levels: Vocabulary Instruction* at the end of this section.

First, students must be taught new words in a systematic and direct approach. Many teachers of the deaf pre-teach vocabulary, such as practicing new words that will be used during a field trip or prior to discussing a new topic in science. Those new words must be practiced repeatedly, and links must be made to prior knowledge. For example, a teacher might be working with kindergarten students on a thematic unit about fall, which will culminate in a field trip to the local apple orchard. The teacher might send home a survey to parents about the types of fall activities the students do at home, with the goal of learning which experiences and vocabulary words should be familiar to students during the unit, and which may be new. The teacher might learn that none of the students have visited an apple orchard, but they have visited a pumpkin patch. The teacher can begin a discussion by using a graphic organizer to elicit all of the information the students know about pumpkin patches, and then explicitly point out to students all the ways that apple orchards are similar to (or different from) pumpkin patches. In the process, the teacher is helping students not only to learn new vocabulary words but also how to organize those new vocabulary words into existing schemas, or categories of words. For students who are deaf or hard of hearing, this systematic instruction on how to connect known and unknown information is a crucial strategy for vocabulary instruction.

Once students have been taught new vocabulary, they must be able to retrieve and use the new words—otherwise there is no point to learning them in the first place. Scaffolded retrieval practice of new vocabulary is an effective memory strategy for all students, including those at risk for language delay. Studies have shown that simply rereading vocabulary words along with their definitions is a poor way to retain new vocabulary. However, it is typically what students do: reread a chapter several times to study for a test. Instead, students should practice *retrieving* vocabulary from their mental dictionaries to have better retention of those words (Karpicke, Blunt, Smith, & Karpicke, 2014). One way to practice retrieving vocabulary is to use a partially completed concept map. Students are taught new vocabulary and then are asked to complete a concept map. You will find an example about clouds in Figure 15.5.

Figure 15.5 Example of a Partially Completed Concept Map for Vocabulary Instruction

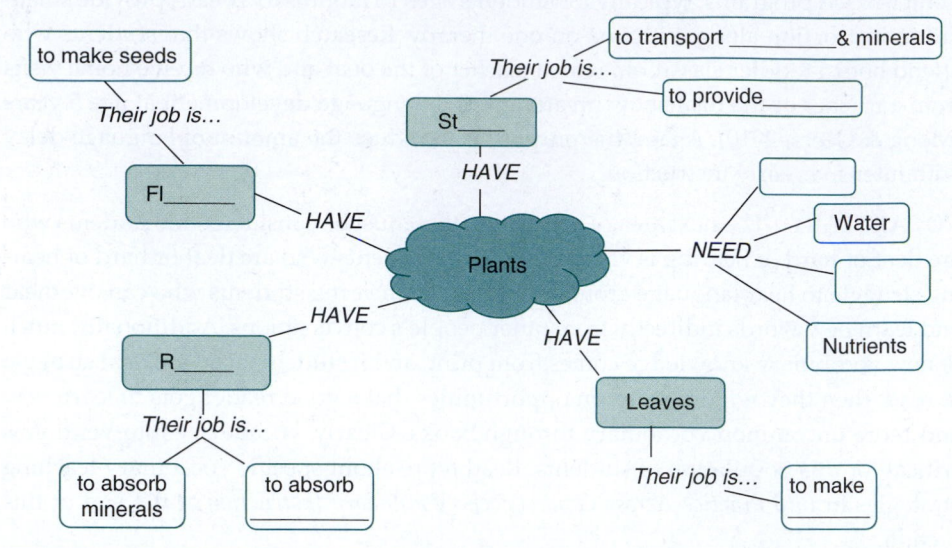

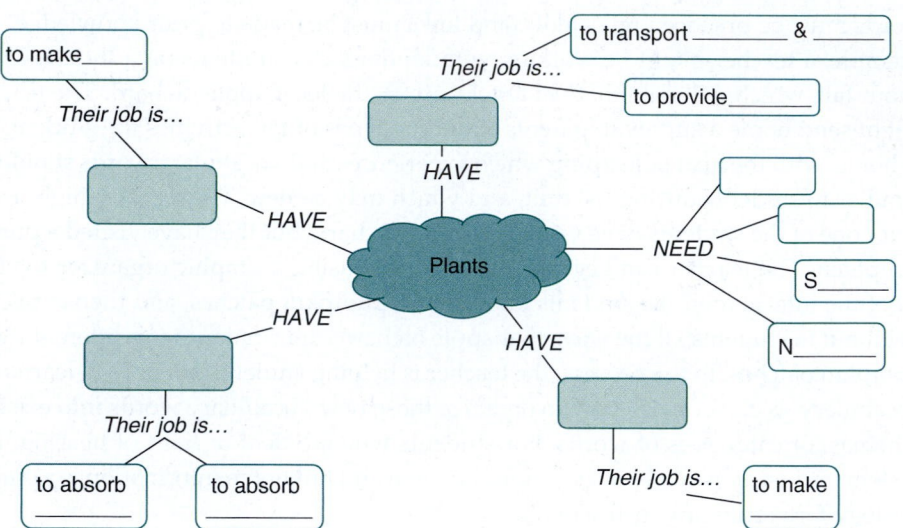

Students must dig deep into their memories and pull up the appropriate concept or vocabulary word to complete the partially filled-in map. This process of retrieving words helps cement the words in long-term memory far more effectively than simply rereading words and their definitions in a textbook. For students who are deaf or hard of hearing, this process is critical to ensuring better retention of learned words over time.

READING AND SPELLING Literacy skills are often delayed in students who are deaf or hard of hearing. Students who struggle to hear speech also struggle to hear the different parts of spoken words. Phonological awareness, and specifically phonemic awareness, is challenging for students with hearing loss, so explicit instruction must be made in these areas. Practice with manipulating syllables or individual sounds in words is a critical foundational skill to develop in students with functional hearing.

For example, teachers of the deaf may practice phonemic awareness tasks auditorily with students who have functional hearing. A task might be "Say the word 'top.' Add a /s/ to the beginning of the word. What new word do you have?" The task of blending phonemes, as in this example, along with adding, deleting, or substituting phonemes, is crucial for all students, but particularly for those who are deaf or hard of hearing. For students who are not able to rely on listening skills for these sorts of tasks, teachers have other ways to make individual sounds more "visible," and thus the same segmenting skills can be practiced. Teachers who employ a method called Visual Phonics use hand cues to represent individual sounds in words. This approach tries to make visible the sounds that cannot be heard, and to stress that words have individual components that are assigned to letters.

To learn more about Visual Phonics, visit http://seethesound.org/

Along with a strong foundation of phonemic awareness, subsequent phonics instruction—the linking of individual sounds to letters—must be included in all literacy programs for students who are deaf or hard of hearing (Miller, Lederberg, & Easterbrooks, 2013). Deaf students cannot rely on rote memorization of word spellings alone to be successful readers. Fortunately, many students who are deaf or hard of hearing and who are able to listen through their device(s) are able to learn phonics alongside their hearing peers, using traditional curricula, provided the students have strong phonemic awareness skills.

Fluency is an important component of literacy development, reflecting decoding abilities and comprehension of print mechanics, such as punctuation. Students cannot be fluent readers without having a level of automaticity in decoding words, nor can they read fluently without some degree of comprehension during reading. Fluency is like a bridge between decoding and comprehension and an important skill for students who are deaf or hard of hearing to practice. Strategies used with hearing students, such as reading aloud or signing while reading, both with feedback, can also be effective with students who are deaf or hard of hearing.

True reading, of course, means that students understand what they have just decoded. Comprehension relies on knowing the meanings of print vocabulary words, as well as knowing the syntax (or word order) in which those words occur. Compared to hearing peers, students who are deaf or hard of hearing often have a delay in vocabulary and syntax knowledge (Svirsky, Robbins, Kirk, Pisoni, & Miyamoto, 2000). Even if students can decode all of the words in the sentence, if they are unfamiliar with a complex syntax structure or the vocabulary presented, then they are not going to comprehend the sentence.

Teachers of the deaf and speech-language pathologists may provide systematic language instruction on various English syntax structures and vocabulary to improve not only general language skills but also literacy. Strategies for teaching syntax may include using a criterion-referenced form such as the Teaching Assessment of Spoken Language (TASL; Moog & Biedenstein, 1998). Forms like the TASL can be used by teachers or other professionals to assess what types of syntax structures students can understand and use, and guide lesson planning for structures that are not yet acquired. For example, a teacher might plan lessons to teach and practice the conjunction "while" in sentences of 6 to 10 words, because a 4th-grade student is not yet able to use (and so likely is not able to understand) that structure, even though it appears in the reading texts quite often. For students who primarily use ASL or for whom spoken English is a second language, spoken language rating forms can still be very useful because

MyLab Education

Video Example 15.5

Check out this video to learn more about the widening gap between good readers and poor readers. What are some ways that teachers can battle the Matthew Effect?

students are required to read texts in written English and so their English syntax skills must be strong.

Finally, it is important for all teachers to remember that students who are deaf or hard of hearing are at particular risk of the so-called Matthew Effect (Stanovich, 2009)—the rich get richer, and the poor get poorer. In education, the effect is that good readers improve more quickly than poor readers; the gap between them widens.

Students who are better at reading tend to read more, and thus get better at reading. Because of all the barriers present for many students who are deaf or hard of hearing (poor vocabulary due to lack of overhearing and learning opportunities, poor phonemic awareness due to degraded auditory signal, etc.), teachers must provide reading opportunities that allow students to feel successful. Literacy skills drive most academic outcomes, and thus it is crucial that students who are deaf or hard of hearing continue to be monitored for literacy development, particularly in the earliest years of school.

Imagine yourself as Martae, unable to stimulate his mind and imagination because he has an impaired sense, the sense of hearing. How much richer and fuller his life could be if he were as able to read, just as you or his mother or teachers are able. To enable Martae to read is to enliven his mind and soul through books. To do that is to proclaim that he is as worthy as a person who has the sense of hearing. It is to dignify him.

MyLab Education Self-Check 15.2

MyLab Education Application Exercise 15.2:
Low-Tech Accommodations

Summary

Defining Hearing Loss

Hearing loss in children can be described in terms of severity of loss (mild, moderate, severe, profound), types of loss (conductive, sensorineural), and sidedness (unilateral, bilateral). Students may wear hearing aids and/or cochlear implants. Professionals called audiologists manage the care of students with hearing loss by diagnosis, evaluation, and fitting devices.

Describing the Characteristics and Causes

Students with hearing loss may use spoken language, signed language, or some combination of both. When hearing loss occurs at birth, significant language delay can occur because the critical period of language development is within the first few years of life. Babies with hearing loss, particularly those born to hearing parents who are not fluent in a visual language, miss out on listening opportunities and experiences that build the brain's mental dictionary. Hearing loss can be described as congenital or acquired, with congenital deafness causing the most potential for delayed language. Getting

appropriate hearing devices and receiving intensive early intervention can mitigate some of the effects of auditory deprivation.

Evaluating Students Who Are Deaf or Hard of Hearing

Common assessments for students with hearing loss include standardized tests of language, reading, and cognition to determine eligibility for special education services. Other sources, such as response to intervention and audiological testing results, as well as administering the assessment in the student's primary method of communication, are necessary to best assess a student who is deaf or hard of hearing.

Including Students Who Are Deaf or Hard of Hearing

Accommodations can include having an educational interpreter, a CART writer, or a note taker in the classroom. Other accommodations include seating the student away from sources of noise, using an FM/DM system, captioning videos, and avoiding talking while writing on the whiteboard or behind the student with hearing loss.

Educating Students Who Are Deaf or Hard of Hearing

Students with hearing loss often require intensive early intervention, systematic vocabulary instruction, and phonics-based reading instruction. Strategies that involve repetition and explicit practice, as well as connecting known to unknown information, are considered best practices for students who are deaf or hard of hearing.

Addressing the Professional Standards

In Chapter 15, Students with Hearing Impairments, we have covered the following Council for Exceptional Children (CEC) Initial Level Special Educator Preparation Standards: Chapter 15—1.0, 1.1, 1.2, 2.1, 2.2, 3.2, 3.3, 4.0, 4.3, 5.1, 5.2, 5.4, 5.5, 6.1, 6.3, 7.1, 7.2. Refer to the Appendix for a full listing of the CEC Standards with descriptions and supporting explanations.

Chapter 16
Students with Visual Impairments

Sandra Lewis, Florida State University

∨ Learning Outcomes

16.1 Differentiate terms that describe students with visual impairment, explain how their commonalities impact student learning, and describe the evaluations necessary to determine students' academic and functional needs.

16.2 Summarize the inclusion challenges in the general and expanded core curriculum, progress in it and reading needs (including via braille) and nonacademic functioning.

Lottie Thornbury

Lottie Thornbury

Meet Corbin Thornbury—Headed Toward Independent Living

Imagine a bright, inquisitive, upbeat 7-year-old, actively involved in tae kwon do, swimming, music, cooking, nature exploration, school, and adventures with family and friends. Imagine a boy with a zest for living, and you have imagined Corbin Thornbury.

At 7, Corbin aspires to go to college and has mentioned an interest in several different occupations, including radio announcer, policeman, and firefighter. Recently, however, he told his mother, Lottie, "I am blind, so I won't have a job." Taken aback, she responded that lots of people who are blind have jobs. She asked, "Why do you think that they don't?"

Corbin's reply was quick: "We can't drive. What do they do, ride horses?" This was a logical conclusion, certainly, as he loves riding ponies, and Lottie smiled as she explained the transportation options for people who are blind. She didn't say that policemen and firemen need to be able to see and that those jobs are not in his future. They just aren't; others are, however.

Blind since birth, Corbin functions quite well with the use of his cane and braille books. He doesn't dwell on differences for long, though, as he benefits from living with a busy family. They take trips to Disney World, playgrounds and parks, beaches, restaurants, grocery stores, and other public places. On a family campout, he helped pitch the tent, unroll sleeping bags, and set up battery-operated lanterns. Naturally inquisitive about nature and science, Corbin discovers and explores items often overlooked by sighted individuals and adds to his collections of cocoons, honeycomb, acorns, shells, and other objects he finds with his cane.

Lottie Thornbury

At the grocery store, Corbin loves to grind coffee beans. He puts the beans into the grinder, places the bag under the chute, and operates the machine. At home, he uses the talking microwave independently, sets the timer, and uses the timed cooking settings to prepare his own breakfast of waffles and bacon.

Each morning, Corbin and Lottie discuss what he needs for school. His tasks are listed in braille on a magnetic strip and are aligned on the left side of a divided magnet board. As he completes each task, he moves the strip to the right side of the board. When finished, he receives a marble with Velcro on the back to attach to his chore chart on the refrigerator door. He also earns marbles for completing other chores, such as sweeping the floor, feeding his pet, wiping the table, or helping with the dishwasher. Corbin helped his mother organize his room so that he can find his toys, games, instruments, and books. He also has a system for organizing personal belongings, such as his cane, lunchbox, and backpack, so they are easily located and returned. He has learned to put things away, not just put them down!

Lottie and Nathan have never had a negative, limiting perspective about blindness. Lottie is a teacher and recognized in Corbin's infancy that it was important to challenge him every day, to have high expectations for him, and to take the role of being his first teacher very seriously. She has created unique materials to enhance new concepts, as when she molded clay representations of the life stages of a butterfly after Corbin received a caterpillar that formed a chrysalis and completed the transformation into a butterfly. Knowing that Corbin's peers in kindergarten would be opening snack packs and other food items independently, Lottie decided to pack his lunchbox during the summer before he started school, with the goal of helping him hone his skills at unpacking it. So every day, Corbin practiced opening the lunchbox, packages, and drink cartons. He learned strategies for opening the containers so that he could eat independently and then learned how to check his eating area for what needed to be discarded. Not surprisingly, he started school with confidence, having mastered the same skills in this area as his classmates had.

Corbin also helps his dad pump gas, check the oil, and do other routine mechanical work on the family car. The key to their interaction is that Nathan patiently answers Corbin's questions and demonstrates his responses through hands-on activities.

Corbin is increasingly independent: He visits friends after school and spends the night with his grandmother. His competence is blossoming. As an adult, he may not get around by riding horses, but he will definitely have a job. He will be able to live independently, to advocate for himself, and to communicate the clear message to the world that, although society often says blind people can't, Corbin *can!* Think about what he is telling us:

> I, Corbin Thornberry, can. I'm going to be an independent person. Don't worry about my dignity. I've got it inside me. And my family and my teachers know that and act accordingly. I'm Corbin, the can-do kid.

Defining Visual Impairments

When you think about blindness, you might imagine someone such as Corbin, who sees almost nothing and must use adaptive techniques for tasks that typically require vision, such as braille for reading or a cane to detect objects when traveling. So it may surprise you to learn that most individuals with **legal blindness** have a great deal of useful vision and that most students who have visual impairments read print.

The legal definition of blindness is based on a clinical measurement of visual acuity. **Acuity** is determined by having an individual read the letters on a chart, each line of which is composed of letters written with a certain size of print. The ability to read the line that is composed of symbols with a measurement of 20 from a distance of 20 feet is typical; a person who can read at that line has 20/20 acuity. Individuals who from 20 feet can read only the top line, where the print size is 200 (the big *E*), even when using both eyes and wearing glasses, have 20/200 acuity; these people are legally blind. People are also legally blind if their **field of vision** (the area around them that they can visually detect when looking straight ahead) is less than 20 degrees (normal is 160 degrees), even if their visual acuity is normal. These individuals have **tunnel vision**. Figure 16.1 shows what people with various types of visual impairment might see.

The legal definition of blindness is an arbitrary clinical measure used to determine eligibility for federal Social Security benefits (Social Security Act, §1614 [42 U.S.C. 1382c] (a)(1)). It does not provide reliable information about the way in which a person experiences and learns about the world (Corn & Lusk, 2010). But how a person experiences and learns about the world is at the core of the definition of visual impairments as set forth by the Individuals with Disabilities Education Act (IDEA).

The U.S. Department of Education combines "visual impairment" and "blindness" to describe students who need support because of visual issues. The term *visual impairment*, then, is an umbrella term used to refer to anyone who qualifies for special education services under this IDEA category.

The current regulations implementing IDEA define **visual impairment (including blindness)** as "an impairment in vision that, even with correction, adversely affects a

Figure 16.1 Estimate of How a View Appears for (a) Individuals with 20/20 Vision, (b) Reduced Visual Acuity, and (c) and (d) Restricted Fields of Vision

(a)

Lori Whitley/Merrill Education/Pearson Education

(c)

Lori Whitley/Merrill Education/Pearson Education

(b)

Lori Whitley/Merrill Education/Pearson Education

(d)

Lori Whitley/Merrill Education/Pearson Education

child's educational performance. The term includes both partial sight and blindness." Key to this definition is that the student has some kind of disorder of the visual system, including the parts of the brain controlling vision, that interferes with learning. For the most part, we will refer to students with visual impairment in this chapter, as most of the principles discussed here refer to all students who experience difficulties because of a disorder of the visual system.

Because state and local educational agencies vary so widely in how they measure and report visual impairments, it is extremely difficult to count accurately the number of students with visual impairments who are served in schools. Best estimates indicate that approximately 1 to 2 students in 1000 have a visual disorder that interferes with learning; those students are eligible to receive special education services (Wall & Corn, 2004).

Students with visual impairments have a wide range of visual abilities. Educators often classify these students by their tendency or need to use visual or tactile means for learning (Corn & Lusk, 2010):

- **Low vision** describes individuals who read print, although they may depend on optical aids, such as magnifying lenses, to see better. A few read both braille and print; all rely primarily on vision for learning. Individuals with low vision may or may not be legally blind.

- **Functionally blind** describes individuals who typically use braille for efficient reading and writing. They may rely on their ability to use functional vision for other tasks, such as moving through the environment or sorting items by color. Thus, they use their limited vision to supplement a combination of tactile and auditory learning methods. Corbin is typical of a student who is functionally blind.

- **Totally blind** describes those individuals who do not receive meaningful input through the visual sense. These individuals use tactile and auditory means to learn about their environment, and they generally read braille.

Every individual with visual impairment uses vision differently and in a way that is difficult to predict. So when you teach these students, observe carefully how each student functions and then present instructional activities to maximize the student's learning.

Describing the Characteristics and Causes

Characteristics

Students with visual impairments are surprisingly heterogeneous. They differ from each other in how they learn and in their visual functioning, socioeconomic status, cultural background, age of onset of visual impairment, presence of other disabilities, and cognitive abilities. Some are gifted or have special talents. A large number also have multiple disabilities (Garber & Huebner, 2017). Yet each possesses a characteristic in common: limited ability to learn incidentally from the environment (Lewis & Allman, 2014b).

Almost from the moment they are born, children with good vision learn seemingly without effort through their visual sense. Their vision helps them organize, synthesize, and give meaning to their perceptions of the environment (Ferrell, 2011; Lewis & Allman, 2014b). For example, babies with unimpaired vision spend hours looking at

MyLab Education
Video Example 16.1
The video presents a simulation of what someone with tunnel vision might see when traveling through the environment. What kinds of challenges confront this traveler?
https://www.youtube.com/watch?v=v9CawJSUy2c

their hand before that hand becomes an efficient tool. Young children will drop a toy repeatedly, watching its path to the floor until they learn to understand *down*. Through these recurring observations, the children are learning how to move their hands and watching the effects of their hand movements on themselves, the toy, and caretakers. As similar and diverse experiences occur with various objects, they gradually learn about the properties of nature (sound, gravity, weight, etc.). This learning occurs almost exclusively through the power of observation without direct instruction from others.

Think about the way in which young children learn the concept of *table*. Even before they have a name for that object, they have observed a variety of tables in their environment: in the kitchen, in the living room, at the homes of relatives and friends, and at preschool. Tables are everywhere, and children with unimpaired vision begin to recognize that the objects people call *tables* have certain features in common. Soon they perceive a relationship between the object and the word. Later, after more visual experiences, they will distinguish among desks, counters, and other flat surfaces. Children learn this kind of conceptual information incidentally—that is, with little or no direct instruction.

Incidental learning is, however, problematic for all children with visual impairments (Ferrell, 2011; Hatlen & Curry, 1987; Lewis & Allman, 2014b), so they need other forms of instruction. Children with limited visual access to their environment may need opportunities to explore carefully and completely, either visually at a close distance or through tactile means, every part of a variety of tables before they can acquire, organize, and then synthesize information about "tableness." But they certainly can achieve these levels of understanding.

Incidental learning also affects how children learn new skills. For example, most children need little training when they make toast for the first time. They have few problems with any of the steps involved because they have watched adults make toast, perhaps hundreds of times, before trying on their own. Without hands-on instruction, however, children with visual impairments may not be aware that a special machine is used in this task. Even children with low vision, who may not see clearly beyond a distance of 2 or 3 feet, usually need special instruction and practice time to perform this and other tasks. Remember how Corbin's father involves him in helping pump the gas for the car? And how his mother teaches him skills for independent living?

Because it influences the important role of incidental learning, a visual impairment can influence the development of motor, language, cognitive, and social skills. Generally, however, these influences are not long-lasting if students receive appropriate interventions (Ferrell, 2011; Lewis & Allman, 2014b). Visual impairment primarily affects how students learn skills, but it does not prevent them from acquiring skills. Interventions must address the unique needs of students with visual impairments, including those that arise from limitations in range and variety of experiences, ability to get around, and ability to interact with the environment.

LIMITATIONS IN THE RANGE AND VARIETY OF EXPERIENCES Vision allows a person to experience the world meaningfully and safely from a distance. Touch is not always an effective substitute for vision: Some objects are too big (skyscrapers, mountains), too small (ants, molecules), too fragile (snowflakes, moths), too dangerous (fire, boiling water), or too distant (the sun, the horizon) for their characteristics to be learned by touch (Lowenfeld, 1973). The other senses do not fully compensate for what can be learned visually (Ferrell, 2011). The song of a bird or the smell of baking bread may provide evidence that those objects are nearby but do not provide useful information about many of their properties. Individuals with visual impairment often have not had the experiences of their peers with typical vision, so their knowledge of the world may be different.

Students with visual impairments also experience different social interactions because they cannot easily share common experiences with sighted friends. Students who have not seen the latest movie, played the newest video game, or taken a driver's training course have markedly different experiences from peers with unimpaired vision. The potential for inadequate development of social interaction skills and the related negative impact on self-esteem may have a lifelong effect (Sacks & Page, 2017). However, with appropriate instruction and supports, social interaction skills can develop, as Corbin's have.

Similarly, career development can be limited. Although individuals with visual impairments are employed in a variety of occupations, many young adults struggle with determining an appropriate vocation because they are unaware of the jobs that people with or without vision perform (Crudden, 2012). That is why you will need to use alternative strategies to introduce careers to students. Corbin's parents and teachers expect that, through the collaboration of his teachers of students with visual impairments (TVIs) and general educators, he will graduate from high school and pursue a career that he chooses for himself, based on his own understanding of his interests, strengths, and abilities.

LIMITATIONS IN THE ABILITY TO GET AROUND Individuals who have visual impairments are limited in their spontaneous ability to move safely in and through their environment. This restriction influences children's early motor development and exploration of the world and thus affects their knowledge base and social development. The ability to move through the environment spontaneously is one area over which probably only moderate control can be exercised and is a continuing source of frustration for many adults (Gallagher, Hart, O'Brien, Stevenson, & Jackson, 2011; Lee & Ponchillia, 2010) because it directly affects opportunities for experiences. Children with impaired vision may not know what is interesting in the environment. Even if they are aware of something to explore, they may not know how to get to the desired object. These children can become passive and in turn have fewer opportunities for intellectual and social stimulation (Sacks & Page, 2017; Pogrund, 2002). That is why you should encourage students to explore their environment and engage with objects they enjoy. In other words, do for your students what Corbin's parents do for him.

LIMITATIONS IN INTERACTIONS WITH THE ENVIRONMENT Knowledge about and control over the environment often are areas of concern for individuals with visual impairments. In some cases, their limited vision reduces their level of readily acquired information about their environment and their ability to act on that information. For instance, they cannot determine at a glance the source of a loud crash or a burning smell, so they cannot quickly determine an appropriate reaction. Similarly, they cannot adequately inform themselves about the effects of their actions on the people and things around them.

In young children, reduced vision correlates with poor motivation to move through the environment, manipulate toys, and initiate interactions (Ferrell, 2011; Sacks, 2006). Their tendency toward physical and social detachment (Sacks, Lueck, Corn, & Erin, 2011) and low motivation can have the long-lasting consequence of limiting their sense of competence and mastery. Individuals who have a poor sense of their ability to effect change in their lives are at risk for poor self-esteem, poor academic achievement, and reduced social skills (Wilton & MacCuspie, 2017). Identifying alternative ways to enable students to acquire information from their environment from an early age is critical to reducing these negative outcomes. Again, Corbin's life at home shows how well his family has helped him discover alternative ways to acquire necessary information for his independent living. When skills are taught early, many of the negative effects of blindness can be overcome.

MyLab Education
Video Example 16.2
In this video, the orientation and mobility specialist helps a preschooler avoid potential limitations related to her blindness as she learns to travel safely on the sidewalks at her school. How does the child use her cane to discover things in the environment that she wants to explore https://www.youtube.com/watch?v=rIGN44XJ7bY

Causes

Damage to the structures involved in the visual process can result from an event that happens during the development of the embryo, at or immediately after an infant's birth, or at any time during development. **Congenital** visual impairment occurs at birth or, in the case of blindness, before visual memories have been established. Corbin has a congenital visual impairment. That type of impairment can affect the child's earliest access to information and experiences.

Students who acquire a vision loss after having unimpaired vision have an **adventitious visual impairment**. That is, their impairment results from an advent (e.g., loss of sight caused by a hereditary condition that has just manifested itself) or an event (e.g., loss of sight caused by trauma). Although the educational needs of students with adventitious and congenital visual impairments may be similar, even a short period of unimpaired vision can enrich the student's understanding of self, others, and the relationships among people, objects, and events in the environment (Hupp, 2003).

Evaluating Students with Visual Impairments

Like students with other disabilities, a student with visual impairment receives a nondiscriminatory evaluation. However, evaluation of the student with visual impairment has several highly specialized aspects. Once a medical diagnosis of uncorrectable visual impairment has been made, educators must identify how a student uses any remaining vision, in what form educational materials are best accessed by the student, and whether specialized instruction and services are needed to help the student function across the several areas known to be impacted by visual impairment. *Nondiscriminatory Evaluation Process: Determining the Presence of Visual Impairments* highlights the standard techniques used for observations, screening, and nondiscriminatory evaluation.

Determining the Presence of Visual Impairments

Medical specialists usually determine whether a disorder of a child's visual system is present. Physicians often detect a serious visual disorder when a child is very young or has just experienced a trauma. Their diagnosis generally is followed by a search for medical solutions to correct vision to typical levels. When no such correction is possible, referrals to the schools occur.

When a school district receives a referral for services, the TVI will read the doctor's report to learn the cause, or **etiology**, of the visual disorder. Although a diagnosis of the etiology may not provide accurate information about how much a student sees, an accurate diagnosis suggests typical characteristics associated with a particular eye condition, including probable lighting needs, a potential prognosis, and possible related medical disorders or learning problems. The next steps in the evaluation are to determine how any available vision is used and whether the student learns best using visual or tactile sense.

Determining How a Student Uses Vision

Even given an accurate diagnosis and standard visual acuity measurements, teachers and family members will find it impossible to predict exactly how a student with a visual impairment will learn incidentally from the environment and will learn to perform age-appropriate tasks. That is why TVIs work with a student and the family to

Nondiscriminatory Evaluation Process
Determining the Presence of Visual Impairments

Observation	**Parents observe:** The child may not respond to visual stimuli as expected. **Physicians observe:** The newborn or infant may have an identifiable visual disorder. **Teacher observes:** The student squints or seems to be bothered by light, the student's eyes water or are red, the student holds books too close, or the student bumps into objects.
Screening	**Assessment measures:** **Ophthalmological:** Medical procedures indicate the presence of a visual disorder or reduced visual functioning that cannot be improved to typical levels through surgery or medical intervention. **Direct observation/functional vision evaluation:** The TVI and orientation and mobility (O&M) specialist determine how the student uses vision to accomplish daily tasks and identify strategies that will facilitate increased efficiency in the student's use of vision. **Low vision specialist:** A specialist evaluation indicates ways to improve visual efficiency through the use of low vision devices (magnifiers), electronic devices, and nonoptical approaches. **Vision screening in school:** For students with low vision who have not been identified before entering school, screening indicates the need for further evaluation.
Prereferral	Prereferral typically is not used with these students because the severity of the disability indicates a need for special education or related services.
Referral	Students with visual impairments should be referred by medical personnel or parents for early intervention during the infancy/preschool years. Many states have Child Find organizations to make sure these students receive services. Teachers should refer any students with possible visual impairments for immediate evaluation.
Nondiscriminatory evaluation procedures and standards	**Assessment measures:** **Curriculum-based assessment:** The TVI and O&M specialist will assess a student's competence in all areas of the expanded core curriculum, including use of technology, independent living, self-determination, career education, recreation and leisure, sensory efficiency, social functioning, use of compensatory skills, and orientation and mobility. **Direct observation—learning media assessment:** This involves determination of the most efficient method or methods that students with visual impairments will use to access general education materials. **Individualized intelligence test:** Standardization may need to be violated because the student's visual impairment interferes with the ability to perform some tasks. Therefore, results may not be an accurate reflection of ability. The student may be average, above average, or below average in intelligence. **Individualized achievement tests:** The student may not have had the experiences to achieve in concept development and academic areas at the levels of peers. Also, standardization of these tests, unless developed for the student with visual impairments, may have to be violated because of the visual impairment. Results may not accurately reflect achievement but instead be more indicative of opportunity and experience. **Adaptive behavior scales:** Because of limited experiences and low expectations, the student may have difficulty in self-care, household, and community skills because of vision and mobility problems. **Anecdotal records:** Unless the student has received specific instruction and is supported, age-appropriate self-help, social, and recreational activities in home, community, or school may be limited.
Determination	The nondiscriminatory evaluation team determines that the student has a vision impairment or blindness and needs special education and related services.

determine the effects of the disorder on the student's visual functioning. To do so, they conduct a **functional vision assessment (FVA)** (Holbrook, Wright, & Presley, 2017). Although the results of an examination by an eye specialist are reported in clinical terms (such as 20/120), the results of an FVA are reported in language that informs educators and others in more concrete ways. For example, an FVA report might read, "The student can see three-inch-high printed letters at a distance of no more than five feet," or "The student can pick up a raisin on a white table when seen from six inches."

Functional vision assessments describe how a student uses vision in a variety of natural environments, such as under the fluorescent lights in a grocery store, on the playground in the glare of the midday sun, or in a dimly lit corridor leading to the school library. These assessments also consider the different activities that occur in these environments. For example, a student at a grocery store may be able to see the products on the shelves but not be able to read the aisle labels that hang directly below the bright lights or the value of paper money at the checkout counter. Obviously, information about how the student functions in various environments helps educators design relevant instructional strategies (Erin & Levinson, 2007; Erin & Topor, 2010).

Most students with usable vision benefit from periodic evaluations by a **low vision specialist**, a person with special training who can prescribe optical and nonoptical devices appropriate to the individual's functioning (Lueck, 2004; Wilkinson, 2010). Ideally, an FVA should occur before an examination by a low vision specialist so the TVI can share information about the student's functioning. If optical aids are recommended, a follow-up FVA may be necessary to describe the student's improved functioning while using these devices.

Determining the Appropriate Learning Medium

For students such as Corbin, it is easy for teachers to determine how educational materials should be presented. Because he can see very little, braille clearly is the appropriate learning medium for him. Remember, however, that most students who are visually impaired have some usable vision; determining the appropriate learning medium for them is more complex.

Learning medium describes the options for accessing literacy materials; these may include braille, print, audio, and access technology. Many students who can read print do so at such slow speeds or with such inefficiency that they also benefit from using braille. Teachers determine the appropriate reading media for students by conducting a **learning media assessment (LMA)** (Holbrook et al., 2017; Koenig & Holbrook, 1993). The LMA begins with a functional vision assessment but also includes additional considerations, such as the use of touch and vision in new situations or environments, the stability of the eye condition, visual stamina, and motivation.

Like an FVA, the LMA needs to be repeated at regular intervals to determine whether circumstances or students' skills have changed and whether additional instruction in a different reading medium is necessary. Students who use both braille and print have the advantage of being able to choose the reading medium that works best for them under different conditions—for instance, when they are in a dimly lit restaurant or when reading assignments are long and eye fatigue occurs.

IDEA requires individualized education program (IEP) teams to assume that the reading medium for all students with visual impairments is braille and that evidence must be presented to challenge this assumption, when appropriate.

Determining the Nature of Specially Designed Instruction and Services

The provision of special education and related services must be based on a student's specific needs as identified through a comprehensive assessment of the student's current level of functioning and knowledge in both the general education curriculum and the **expanded core curriculum** (Allman & Lewis, 2014). The expanded core curriculum includes the following areas: compensatory and communication skills, social and interaction skills, **orientation and mobility (O&M)** skills, independent living skills, recreation and leisure skills, self-determination skills, use of assistive technology, sensory efficiency skills, and career/vocational skills. Figure 16.2 describes the skills educators will evaluate in a complete assessment.

Assessment is best accomplished by a team of individuals who have experience working with students with visual disabilities. In addition to those people who, under IDEA, must be included on the team, the team also should consist of an O&M specialist and a TVI. The outcome of a comprehensive assessment should be a description of the student's current level of functioning in all areas of the general and expanded core curriculum and the identification of skills to be addressed for that student to function optimally in current and future home, school, and community environments (Barclay, 2003; Lewis & Allman, 2014a).

Few teachers would consider it important to evaluate a straight-A high school student's ability to order a meal at a fast-food restaurant or to launder clothes, yet

Figure 16.2 Skill Areas with the Domains of the Expanded Core Curriculum

Compensatory Skills, Including Communication Modes
- Concept development
- Listening and speaking skills
- Study and organizational skills
- Use of reference skills
- Determination of reading modes
- Communication modes for students with additional disabilities (such as tactile symbols, a calendar system, sign language, and recorded materials)

Social Interaction Skills
- Socialization
- Affective education
- Knowledge of human sexuality
- Knowledge of visual impairment

O&M Skills
- Development of body image
- Understanding physical environment and space
- Orientation to different environments
- Ability to travel in school and community environments
- Opportunities for unrestricted, independent movement and play

Daily Living Skills
- Personal hygiene
- Dressing
- Housekeeping
- Clothing care
- Food preparation
- Eating
- Basic home repair
- Money management
- Telephone
- Time and calendar
- Shopping
- Use of community services

Recreation and Leisure Skills
- Competitive sports
- Noncompetitive sports
- Hobbies and games
- Choosing recreational activities

Career/Vocational Skills
- Relationships between work and play
- Understanding value of work
- Job and career awareness
- Job acquisition skills (want ads, résumés, applications, interviews)
- Typical job adaptations made by workers with visual impairments
- Prevocational skills (work habits, attitudes, motivation)
- Awareness of vocational interests
- Work experience

Assistive Technology
- Keyboarding skills
- Braille access devices
- Visual assistive software and devices
- Auditory assistive software and devices
- Choosing appropriate options
- Device maintenance and troubleshooting

Visual Efficiency Skills
- Use of nonoptical low vision devices
- Use of optical low vision devices
- Use of a combination of devices
- Use of environmental cues and modifications
- Recognizing when not to use vision

Self-Determination Skills
- Knowledge of laws protecting people with disabilities, particularly visual impairment
- Assertiveness skills
- Negotiation skills
- Public interaction skills
- Management of readers and drivers

SOURCE: Reprinted with permission from the California Department of Education.

a student with a visual impairment who achieves at grade level may not function appropriately outside the classroom. Many students with visual impairments lack these outside-school skills. Informal assessment techniques, including family and student interviews, the use of checklists, observation in natural environments, and authentic and performance assessments, are the most valuable methods for determining the level of functioning of students with visual impairments in the expanded core curriculum.

When assessing a student's needs, you should evaluate the age appropriateness of a task from two perspectives. First, what are the student's peers doing? If Corbin's friends are at the stage of social development when participating in groups, such as Cub Scouts, is common, an assessment of Corbin's visual and social skills should be relevant to his potential to be a scout with his peers.

Second, because students with unimpaired vision are incidentally learning to perform some skills long before it is age appropriate to expect mastery of them, you should evaluate students' involvement in these tasks earlier than you might for sighted students. For example, although Corbin's friends will not be expected to launder clothes independently until their late teens, his ability to participate in this task's component parts, such as scooping soap or folding freshly laundered towels and socks, should be assessed, because these skills are within the range of his capability now and are being learned visually by his peers.

You also should avoid making assumptions about a student's previously learned information. Because visual impairment often results in gaps in information, you should assess whether a student does, in fact, have knowledge common to that of sighted peers. For example, a TVI was surprised to learn that one 18-year-old female student with low vision was unaware that men's sexual organs differ from her own. The TVI used the result of the assessment to work with the family in designing an appropriate program to ensure that the student graduated with this knowledge so critical to her social functioning.

MyLab Education Self-Check 16.1

MyLab Education Application Exercise 16.1: Evaluations for Students with Visual Impairments

---

Including Students with Visual Impairments

Determining the Location of Special Education and Related Services

Having decided what is going to be taught, the IEP team then must determine where that instruction should take place. In 2017, 67.66 percent of students with visual impairments spent 80 to 100 percent of their time in the general education classroom, as Corbin does. Another 12 percent were in general education for 40 to 79 percent of the school day (U.S. Department of Education, 2017). Other students are served in a variety of placements, including special purpose or residential schools. Figure 16.3 illustrates patterns of educational placement.

As you have learned, blindness and low vision do not affect what a student can learn as much as they affect *how* a student learns. Inclusion is successful when educators address both academic needs and those related to the expanded core curriculum. Sometimes it is more appropriate to provide initial instruction privately and then to practice emerging skills within the general education classroom. To meet other needs, such as the acquisition of skills related to human sexuality, cooking, or shopping, instruction in specialized environments is usually essential.

Corbin is included in a general education 2nd-grade class and is expected to complete the same work as other students do. When appropriate, he occasionally leaves that class to work with his TVI or O&M specialist in another classroom or the community. Depending on the subject of instruction, however, there are times when his TVI will support Corbin in his general education class. This flexible approach to placement benefits many students with visual impairments. The needs of other students, however, are so intense that they are best met in less inclusive environments; the IDEA requirement that a range of placement options be made available to all students supports these specialized placements.

Figure 16.3 Educational Placement of Students with Visual Impairments

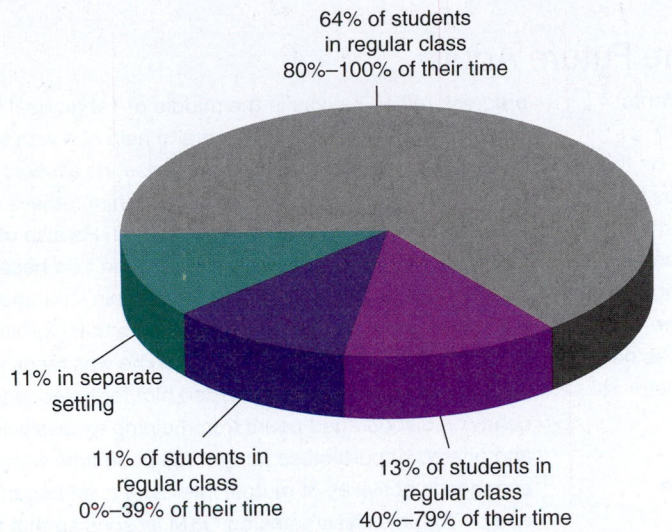

64% of students
in regular class
80%–100% of their time

11% in separate
setting

11% of students in
regular class
0%–39% of their time

13% of students in
regular class
40%–79% of their time

SOURCE: U.S. Department of Education. (2017). *Digest of Education Statistics—Children and Youth with Disabilities.* Retrieved 3/13/18 from http://nces.ed.gov/programs/digest/d13/tables/dt13_204.60.asp.

NOTE: Percentages have been rounded and collapsed across categories.

Communicating to Meet Students' Needs

For students who rely on adapted materials and who need increased opportunities for meaningful, hands-on activities, collaboration is essential for successful inclusion. Close communication to meet students' needs is also necessary when determining accommodations and modifications to assigned work. Corbin requires at least twice as much time as his peers to complete a typical math assignment, in part because the braille math code is still unfamiliar to him. His teachers have discussed the possibility of reducing the length of his assignments, but it was obvious that, because of his lack of experience with numbers and math concepts, he needed additional opportunities to achieve at the level of his classmates. His IEP team had to deal with his competing needs for more time to complete the assigned work and more experiences to understand it. They ultimately decided that his need to practice these basic mathematical skills was critical to his long-term academic success and, as a result, did not recommend this modification.

Students with visual impairments often need additional supports to learn in the general education classroom. To include these students successfully in the general curriculum, close partnerships must be formed among the general educator, the TVI, the O&M specialist, the parents or guardians, and other professionals involved in the students' education. In particular, these individuals must collaborate to make important decisions about providing instruction to support students' success in the general education curriculum and to determine on which nonacademic priorities they will focus.

MyLab Education

Video Example 16.3

Note that the teacher invites students to change their seats too and, thereby, advances students' self-determination. In what way does this approach preserve the dignity of the child with visual impairment?

Educating Students with Visual Impairments

To participate in general education, students who are blind or have low vision require adapted materials and curriculum accommodations to facilitate access to general education activities, the provision of which is usually facilitated by the TVI. Another responsibility of the TVI is providing instruction in the nonacademic areas of the expanded core curriculum that have been identified as priorities by the IEP team. As you review the *Inclusion Tips for Students with Blindness or Vision Impairments*, you'll see each of these activities reflected.

My Voice

Mickey Damelio—Focusing on the Future Adult

Corbin begins his school days with his teacher of students with visual impairments (TVI) in a quiet space in a small learning area, where they work together on braille and on the Nemeth code, which he uses for mathematics. He goes to his general education class, where his teacher has learned the adaptations she needs to ensure that Corbin has access to all class activities. She collaborates with his TVI to accommodate the instructional materials so that he can do the same work and meet the same educational standards as her other pupils do. Assistive technology will continue to help Corbin maximize his potential.

When he's with me, his orientation and mobility instructor, Corbin works on areas of the expanded core curriculum, emphasizing skills that will prepare him to become a fully participating member of society. He has studied traffic; grown and harvested vegetables; learned to do headstands; and explored faucets, fire extinguishers, thermostats, playground equipment, and other objects at the school. He visits the librarian, the custodial staff, and the cafeteria workers in their various workplaces. I allow him to "get lost" and find his way back to our starting point, a game that increases Corbin's level of confidence.

Although technically my job is to teach independent travel skills to Corbin, the 2nd grader, I really see my job as facilitating the gradual emergence of "Grown Up Corbin." I am constantly monitoring to ensure that he is showing progress. When he was in the middle of 1st grade, I noticed that Corbin began to rely on peers to help him with tasks that he could do independently. For instance, he allowed students to guide him to the lunchroom and help him retrieve and put away materials more often than expected. He also began telling me that there were things he couldn't do because he was blind. Concerned, I met with Corbin's parents and teachers to discuss the matter. Guessing that Corbin was being reinforced by the peer attention he was receiving, we agreed on a plan that rewarded him for independent behavior, discouraged peers from helping excessively, and offered opportunities for him to spend time with peers engaged in activities of mutual interest. I even began taking one of Corbin's classmates on O&M lessons so that they could share that experience together. These students think they are having fun as they roll down hills and climb into drainage pipes, but I know I'm doing serious work—teaching Corbin all sorts of skills that will make a difference both today and in the future.

I find that when I keep the image of my students as adults in mind when I'm teaching, when I think beyond what they need right now to the people they will become, my instruction is more real and meaningful, and, I'm sure, will have a longer-lasting impact.

—Albert M. Damelio IV (Mickey Damelio). Used with permission.

Inclusion Tips for Students with Blindness or Visual Impairments

	Behavior	Social Interactions	Educational Performance	Classroom Attitudes
What You Might See	The student is a loner on the playground, choosing to play or walk by herself.	The student doesn't say hello to peers in hallways or acknowledge peers' presence when entering the room.	The student is completing arithmetic assignments more slowly than peers are.	The student seems bored or uninterested during classroom demonstrations or teacher-directed activities.
What You Might Be Tempted to Do	Allow the student to stay in class and read or do homework.	Assume the student is stuck up or unfriendly.	Immediately shorten the assignment for the student.	Assume the lesson is too difficult or simply ignore the inattention.
Alternate Teacher Response	Teach the student board or card games.	Have the entire class prepare autobiographies, including life history, special interests, photos or objects for the student and others to study.	Assess to determine if the student understands the arithmetical concepts. Provide concrete objects and manipulatives if they are necessary for mastery. Shorten the assignment if concepts are mastered.	Make sure that the student can "see" the teacher's materials by having copies of materials that are printed/translated into braille and real objects at the student's desk during the lesson.
Ways to Include Peers in the Process	Once the student has mastered the games, set up a game table during recess where anyone who wants to play can do so.	Teach peers to say both the student's name and their own in greeting because the student may not be able to recognize them from their voices alone.	Have the student act as a cross-age tutor for younger students who benefit from use of concrete materials in learning.	Have the student and peers help the teacher prepare a lesson by getting out materials and preparing overheads and hands-on materials for class use.

Instructional Accommodations

Often students with visual impairments have difficulty understanding some of the ideas that their teachers are presenting because they have not directly experienced them. They may need many additional experiences to make up for their lack of incidental learning. Universally designed instruction provides these meaningful experiences and can benefit all students. For example, early reading books designed for children rely heavily on pictures to convey the meaning of the story. In addition, the pictures reveal to young readers information about the world that they may not have directly experienced. Not all new readers have been for a walk in a forest or have gone for a ride in a rowboat, but from pictures they can discern what the words in the story convey (Koenig & Farrenkopf, 1997). Even older students with visual impairments benefit from instruction that incorporates real experiences that employ a tactile/kinesthetic approach to learning. General educators of students with visual impairments must provide more experiential activities in their classrooms to ensure that all students understand the text.

Providing Adapted Materials

Corbin's teachers often collaborate to create meaningful lessons for his class based on the principles of universal design. Because Corbin cannot see print materials, most instructional materials and activities must be adapted for him. About a week in advance of her lesson, his teacher provides his TVI with copies of her lesson plans and any worksheets she plans to use in class. The TVI transcribes these worksheets in braille, staples the print version to the braille copy, and delivers it to the teacher to hand to Corbin in class. When pictures are involved, the TVI may need to create a tactile version of the worksheet. Usually, she doesn't try to replicate the picture because these often have little meaning to students who are blind. Instead, she determines (often in consultation with the classroom teacher) the primary educational purpose of the assignment and creates a slightly different worksheet that preserves the purpose. So instead of counting pictures of rabbits on a graph for a mathematics assignment, Corbin might count buttons on a tactile graph. The means of representation has changed, but the expectation of the student has not.

A variety of adapted materials are available for use by students with visual impairments, including braille and large-print maps, measuring devices, graph paper, writing paper, calendars, flash cards, and geometric forms. A good source of adapted materials is the American Printing House for the Blind.

TVIs often must adapt materials for assignments designed by general educators. Making such adaptations requires careful judgment by the TVI, who must determine what the primary and secondary purposes of the lesson are and what information can reasonably and meaningfully be represented in a tactile form. Adaptations can be simple, as when a student is given real coins instead of pictures to complete a math assignment. Occasionally, meaningful adaptations are impossible to create, and alternative assignments that focus on the same skill must be prepared.

Students with low vision access print primarily through the use of optical devices, such as glasses, telescopes, and magnifying lenses. In some instances, they may read large-print books, though some researchers suggest that this practice does not lead to faster reading rates or more comfortable reading distances (Lussenhop & Corn, 2002). One of the advantages of magnification devices is that they allow the student access to printed materials not only at school but also at home, at work, and in the community.

Specialized Academic Instruction

Because of the complex or highly visual nature of some academic areas, students with visual impairments may need specialized instruction to master the curriculum. For example, some students need to master a variety of compensatory skills, such as writing braille with a **braillewriter** or **slate and stylus**; using the **abacus** for calculating; or developing listening, study, and organizational skills. For these purposes, special and general educators collaborate to provide appropriate learning experiences. As you read about how students who are blind learn braille, think about the level of interaction that must occur between the general and special educators.

READING INSTRUCTION   Students who do not learn efficiently through their visual sense may access the academic curriculum through **braille**, a tactile method of reading. Like the print alphabet, braille is a code, a way of presenting spoken language in written form. As Figure 16.4 shows, there is one braille symbol for each of the 26 letters of the English alphabet. You can see numerous shortcuts, called **braille contractions**, are used for writing common words or letter combinations. Because of the contractions, there is not a one-to-one correspondence between print and braille. In Figure 16.5, you can compare a print passage with its braille translation.

TVIs collaborate closely with general educators to introduce the over 175 braille symbols and the specific rules for using them in a way that allows the student to become competent in literacy skills. The early introduction of contractions correlates with better literacy skills, including performance in spelling, vocabulary, and general reading level (Emerson, Holbrook, & D'Andrea, 2009).

This finding challenges educational teams who are serving students in the general education environment. The fast pace of whole- and small-group reading instruction often does not meet the needs of young

A trip to the sculpture garden at the zoo provides a natural opportunity to encourage peer interactions.

Scott Cunningham/Merrill Education/Pearson Education

Figure 16.4 Unified English Braille Symbols, Including Some Contractions

1 a	2 b	3 c	4 d	5 e	6 f	7 g	8 h	9 i	0 j
k	l	m	n	o	p	q	r	s	t
u	v	w	x	y	z				

about	ab	bb		can	
above	abv	be		cannot	
according	ac	because	bec	cc	
across	acr	before	bef		
after	af	behind	beh	ch	
afternoon	afn	below	bel	character	
afterward	afw	beneath	ben	child	
again	ag	beside	bes	children	chn
against	agst	between	bet		

SOURCE: Courtesy of Victor S. Hemphill. Used with permission.

Figure 16.5 Comparison of "Old Mother Hubbard" in Braille and Print

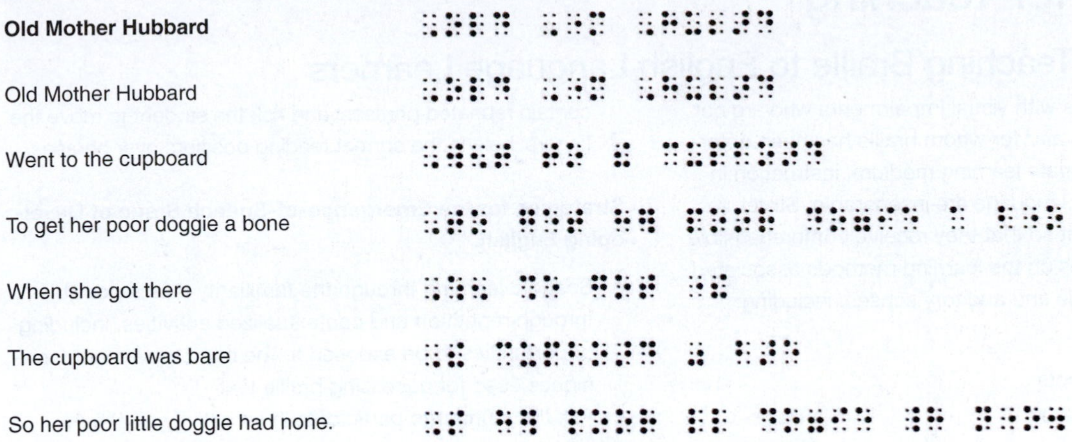
Old Mother Hubbard
Old Mother Hubbard
Went to the cupboard
To get her poor doggie a bone
When she got there
The cupboard was bare
So her poor little doggie had none.

braille learners, who typically benefit from an individualized approach to master initial literacy skills of identifying braille letters and contractions, using phonics, developing vocabulary, and reading connected text. Swenson (2016) suggests that a flexible approach combining the strengths of individualized and general education instruction is most likely to be successful. As students develop basic skills, they can increase the time they spend in class with peers. Before long, they can become full members of the classroom's reading and writing community, and the primary responsibility for teaching reading can shift to the classroom teacher. Corbin is in this period of transition now.

You can imagine that the situation becomes even more complex for students who are English-as-second-language learners. No curriculum exists for teaching literacy skills to students with visual impairments whose first language is not English (Topor & Rosenblum, 2013). In the *Guidelines for Teaching: Strategies for Teaching Braille to English Language Learners* feature, you'll see some strategies for teaching braille to these students.

Many students with visual impairments may not have had the same kind of exposure to literacy events as their sighted peers have had. Think of all the opportunities that Corbin's 3-year-old peers had to see letters, long before they were expected to read. Letters are everywhere: They appear on cereal boxes, on toys, on billboards, on street signs, on television, in books, and on educational games. Even if these children were not learning the letter names, they saw them and incidentally compared their outlines and shapes, setting the stage for future learning.

That is why you and your colleagues need to make certain that young students who have low vision are exposed to letters and words that can be seen clearly. For preschoolers who are blind, two essential components of an early literacy program include systematically introducing braille and flooding the environment with incidental opportunities to find braille, such as on labels, notes, books, schedules, and lunch menus.

ASSISTIVE TECHNOLOGY INSTRUCTION Today, several types of devices make access to the curriculum much easier for people with visual impairment. Figure 16.6 describes some of these technologies.

Corbin already independently uses many features of his iOS devices. Like many students, however, he likely will use a variety of technologies in combination. For example, when he is older and is required to write an essay, Corbin will probably access electronic search engines with JAWS (Job Access with Speech), which speaks the text on the monitor aloud to him. He may take notes with his electronic braille note taker about which books and articles to review further. Then, when he has copies of articles that aren't available electronically, he will scan them with his optical character reader, which will convert the print to an electronic form that he can either emboss in braille or read aloud using the computer's voice synthesizer. Corbin no doubt will choose to

Guidelines for Teaching

Strategies for Teaching Braille to English Language Learners

When teaching students with visual impairments who are not native English speakers and for whom braille has been determined to be the appropriate learning medium, instruction in braille and their second language are inseparable. Structure the learning environment so that they receive comprehensible language that capitalizes on the learning methods associated with the use of the tactile and auditory senses, including:

- Predictable routines
- Use of concrete objects
- Contextualized language.

General Strategies.

- Draw from both the foundations of teaching students who are blind and the principles of second language learning to identify potentially valuable teaching techniques and strategies.
- Collaborate with the English as a second language (ESL) teacher, the O&M specialist, and others involved with the students' education to coordinate teachers' activities and address students' language and visual needs.
- Sequence language activities and structure lessons based on the school district's ESL curriculum.
- Use real objects instead of visual examples.
- Use thematic instruction whenever possible.

Strategies for the Early Production Stage of Developing English.

- Provide students who are blind the opportunity to associate words presented both orally and in written form with real objects.
- Bring real objects that belong to a single category, such as fruits, to school. Make braille cards with words that match the objects. Assist the student in creating first oral and then written sentences using adjectives that describe the objects (e.g., "The orange is bumpy.").
- Create braille cards on which are written the names of classroom objects, such as *door, desk,* and *book*. Read each noun, give the card to the student, and ask the student to place the card on the correct classroom item.
- Provide the student with a braille copy of material presented orally, such as simple stories, poems, and rhymes that contain repeated phrases, and ask the student to move the fingers, held in the correct reading position, over phrases.

Strategies for the Emergence-of-Speech Stage of Developing English.

- Scaffold learning through the familiarity that is possible through repetition and contextualized activities, including opportunities to be exposed to the hand movement techniques used for accessing braille text.
- Ask the student to participate in an activity and then assist the student in writing about the activity on the braillewriter.
- Give the student an audiotape and a braille version of an age-appropriate story. Encourage the student to read the braille while listening to the story.
- Have the student participate in a daily living or an O&M activity, audiotape the sequence of activities, and then write related keywords on the braillewriter.

Strategies for the Intermediate Fluency Level.

- Integrate the oral and written forms of the new language in a variety of contexts, whether the learning medium is print or braille.
- Ground experiences in language activities even as the student grows less dependent on real situations and concrete objects.
- Have the student create a book about an experience and share it with classmates.
- Require the student to keep a braille list of vocabulary words and a journal related to each of the content areas.
- Create meaningful activities that require the student to speak, listen, read, write, and interact with others.

Resources:
Conroy, P. W. (2005). English language learners with visual impairments: Strategies to enhance learning. *RE:view, 37*(3), 101–108; Milian, M. (1997). Teaching braille reading and writing to students who speak English as a second language. In D. P. Wormsley & F. M. D'Andrea (Eds.), *Instructional strategies for braille literacy* (pp. 189–230). New York, NY: AFB Press.

---

emboss his last draft for proofreading and then will use braille translation software to submit a print copy to his teacher. In fact, students who use assistive technology have been found to have better postschool outcomes (Kelly, 2011).

You might be thinking that since people who are blind can access print through assistive technology, learning braille may not be as important today as it once was. These technologies create the opportunity for students with significant visual impairments

Figure 16.6 Using Technology to Ensure Progress

Students with visual impairments often need to use a variety of technologies to access print materials and to create the products expected of all students in the general curriculum.

- *When you have a student with low vision who needs to view a small object closely,* the student can use a handheld magnifier or a closed-circuit television (CCTV). CCTVs come in either handheld or desktop models that enlarge the image to the desired size and project it onto a television screen or computer monitor. The camera on some CCTVs can be adjusted to focus on a distant object, such as a demonstration or a whiteboard, thereby bringing the information to the computer screen directly in front of the student.

- *When you have a student who needs to scan a print document that is not available electronically,* the student can use an optical character reader (OCR) or scanner. Special software combined with an off-the-shelf scanner will increase the accuracy with which material is scanned. Some OCRs are specifically designed for people who are visually impaired and can even scan information in columns accurately.

- *When you have a student with low vision who needs to read information displayed electronically on a computer screen,* the student can use a screen enlargement and navigation system. These systems increase the size of the characters on the screen, the cursors, and the menu and dialogue boxes and provide features that allow easy access to displayed information.

- *When you have a student for whom electronic text on a computer screen is difficult to see,* the student can use a screen reader. Using synthesized speech, screen readers read the text aloud as the user moves the cursor (usually using keyboard strokes, not the mouse) or inputs from the keyboard.

- *When you have a student who needs to take notes in class,* the student can use a note-taking device. Several lightweight electronic note-taking devices (with either braille or qwerty keyboards) are available. The student can then download these notes to a computer for study or to be printed or embossed as braille. Most of these devices have audio output; some also create braille on an electronic display.

- *When you have a student who needs to create a personal braille copy of an assignment that has been created electronically,* the student can use a braille embosser, which, when connected to a computer and used in conjunction with braille translation software, will "print" a braille version of the text. Some braille embossers also print the ink-print translation on the same page.

to access and participate in the general education curriculum. However, as teachers supplement more and more of the general education curriculum with graphics-based sources, such as interactive software programs, they make it less likely that the curriculum will be accessible to students who cannot see the images on the screen. Even if these materials are presented with audio descriptions, they may be meaningless to students who are blind simply because they have limited or no experience with the concepts being described.

The challenge for classroom educators is to remain flexible, using interesting materials that are accessible to all students, including those with visual impairments. Through careful attention to students' needs and incorporating the principles of universally designed instruction, teachers can make a positive difference in the learning of all their students, not just those with visual impairments.

Nonacademic Priorities

As you reviewed Figure 16.6, you may have felt a bit overwhelmed by the list of areas in which a student with visual impairment may need specialized instruction. Once a student's performance in these areas has been assessed and any needs for instruction identified, the IEP team must prioritize those needs. Often, not all of the skills of the expanded core curriculum can be addressed every year. Nonetheless, the team should not ignore needed skills in these areas in favor of the academic skills that are the focus of statewide achievement and accountability testing. That is so because all are skills needed for success in adult life. Ideally, the team will identify some skills in each expanded core curriculum area for intensive instruction each year. The TVI must carefully monitor a student's acquisition and use of these skills so that by the time the student is ready to transition from school to adult life, the student has the skills necessary for success. The IEP team should maintain and annually review a checklist of expanded core curriculum skills. That way, the team will include one year's low-priority skills in the next year's list of skills to be developed.

You might ask yourself how instruction in these areas affects students' progress in the general education curriculum. When students with visual impairments have had the same experiences as their sighted peers, are encouraged to be autonomous, and are expected to make decisions for themselves, they are more interested and engaged in the content of the general curriculum and understand and appreciate it better. Mastery of these kinds of skills is critical to students' long-range educational and life outcomes. Students will need social, living, travel, and career skills to manage as competent adults and to apply the content and performance standards acquired in their general education programs. Typically, professionals need to focus on three areas in the expanded core curriculum of students with visual impairments: daily living skills, orientation and mobility, and self-determination.

DAILY LIVING SKILLS   Students with visual impairments require ongoing instruction in important skills of daily living, such as clothing management and kitchen skills. Generally, effective teaching strategies involve repeated visual or hand-under-hand kinesthetic

Katelyn Metzger/Merrill Education/Pearson Education

A student who is blind often needs hand-over-hand instruction to learn independent living skills.

Into Practice Across Grade Levels

Age-Appropriate Food Preparation That Can Easily Be Taught at School

Teach students in **preschool** to:

- Place sliced cheese on crackers
- Take slices of bread from a bag
- Put toothpicks in cheese cubes
- Pour juice from a small pitcher into a drinking glass
- Make cold chocolate milk
- Hull strawberries.

Teach students who are in **kindergarten, 1st grade, and 2nd grade** to:

- Make waffles in toaster
- Spread butter and other soft substances on toasted bread
- Tear lettuce and rinse vegetables for a salad
- Slice bananas with a knife
- Squeeze oranges, limes, or lemons
- Pour cereal and milk in a bowl.

Teach students who are in **3rd, 4th,** and **5th grade** to:

- Use a can opener

- Cut carrots, celery, onions, and other vegetables with a sharp knife
- Make juice from frozen concentrate
- Pare fruits and vegetables
- Make popcorn in a microwave
- Prepare simple sandwiches with meat and cheese.

Teach students in **middle school** to:

- Prepare no-bake cookies
- Prepare, then use a toaster oven to bake a potato
- Make hot tea or cocoa
- Use an electric frying pan, blender
- Prepare snack mixes
- Make sandwiches that involve mixing ingredients, like egg salad or tuna fish salad sandwiches.

Using the kitchen in the home economics or culinary arts classroom, teach students in **high school** to:

- Use an oven for baking and broiling
- Use food processors or juicers
- Prepare scrambled or fried eggs on a stovetop.

SOURCE: Based on Naughton, F., & Sacks, S. (1978). *Hey! What's cooking? A kitchen curriculum for the parents of visually impaired children.* Austin, TX: Texas School for the Blind and Visually Impaired. Retrieved from http://www.tsbvi.edu/instructional-resources/1070-hey-whats-cooking-a-kitchen-curriculum-for-the-parents-of-visually-impaired-children.

demonstrations (or both), systematic instruction, gradual fading of assistance and prompts, and significant periods of practice (Holbrook & Rosenblum, 2017).

Review the list of food preparation skills that are recommended for students with visual impairments in the feature titled *Into Practice Across Grade Levels: Age-appropriate Food Preparation That Can Easily Be Taught at School* and think about how you might design interesting content-based lessons for the entire class that incorporate these skills.

Often people do not think to include children with visual impairment in simple activities of daily living. Involving students in an activity and having high expectations that the skill can be acquired are critical factors in the acquisition of daily living skills. Because many adults think of people who are blind as helpless, they have low expectations for students with visual impairments. In addition, because adults may assume that students with low vision see more clearly than they do, the adults do not show them how to perform some of the activities that sighted children learn incidentally, such as buttoning a shirt, holding a spoon correctly, or making a bed. When students do not spontaneously develop these skills, teachers may mistakenly think that the students also have cognitive disabilities and may reduce their expectations even more.

Low and inaccurate expectations of their abilities are students' worst enemies. Skilled teachers know to be constantly alert to what students are not doing for themselves. These teachers are prepared to challenge students to promote independence and self-motivation, just as Corbin's parents do with him.

ORIENTATION AND MOBILITY   O&M, an IDEA-related service, encompasses skills that people with visual impairments use to know where they are in their environment and how to move around that environment safely. Unlike sighted students, those with visual impairments must learn to listen to the flow of traffic; react to changes in street and road surfaces; and use their vision, other senses, and perhaps a cane or other mobility device to detect objects in the environment and to help them know where they are.

The development of O&M skills begins in infancy and continues until students can reach desired destinations safely by using a variety of techniques. Young children concentrate on developing body image, mastering spatial and positional concepts, learning the layout of their homes and schools, and developing environmental awareness. Older students focus on crossing streets safely and negotiating travel in increasingly complex situations, such as a town's business district or a shopping mall.

Some blind adults learn how to travel with a dog guide. Primarily because of the responsibility associated with the care of these service animals, individuals under the age of 18 who still attend local schools rarely learn to use a dog guide, but students can be prepared to use dog guides by learning to care for animals as pets and by becoming proficient at orientation skills, which are necessary for efficient traveling.

SELF-DETERMINATION   As adults, most people with visual impairments are required to explain their abilities and special needs to people they meet: bus drivers, prospective employers, landlords, restaurant workers, and flight attendants. Sometimes these explanations are simple, such as asking a bus driver to announce the name of every bus stop, but sometimes they require more detailed descriptions. For example, as a college student, Corbin may need to ask each of his teachers for permission to record lectures, explain that it will be necessary for them to say aloud what they write on the board, and describe special accommodations that he needs (e.g., a reader or additional time

These students work with an O&M specialist to learn how to move safely within their school neighborhood before tackling the challenge of a busy city street.

during testing). He may also need to convince each of his professors that he can do the work for the class. In brief, he will have to be an effective self-advocate.

Corbin has already begun developing self-advocacy skills. For now, he simply listens as his TVI explains his needs to his teachers; but soon he will be expected to participate in this task, taking responsibility for explaining the special tools that he uses to his general education teachers. As an adult, Corbin may need to advocate for his rights with landlords and, if he has a dog guide, for access to public buildings. His teachers will need to help him learn the laws (especially the Americans with Disabilities Act) and the communication techniques he can use to avoid confrontations (if possible) and to assert himself (as necessary). As part of Corbin's lessons in self-determination, his TVI is introducing him to successful adults who are blind.

OTHER EXPANDED CORE CURRICULUM SKILLS In addition, and depending on the students' needs, the TVI emphasizes the development of sensory efficiency skills, recreation and leisure pursuits, career development, and critical social interaction competencies, including knowledge of human sexuality, understanding of their own visual impairment, and awareness of how to protect themselves in potentially dangerous situations. All of these, and the other ECC skills you've learned about, are essential as students prepare to be adults who will function in the familial, social, and work environments in which they spend time.

As students enter the transition years, TVIs generally spend more time with students to meet needs related to the expanded core curriculum while students are enrolled in general education classes to satisfy graduation requirements. Sometimes students choose to delay graduation in order to master all the skills needed for a successful transition to independent adult living. TVIs and O&M specialists who work with students at the high school level might work with students on transition skills that will assist them in living and in maneuvering through the community as adults, such as exploring an apartment complex or navigating bus routes to get to destinations of higher education, the grocery school, and other community areas they will be using. When students with visual impairments are provided with the necessary supports, including instruction to meet both the core and expanded core curriculum needs, they are more likely to develop the skills they require to achieve success in school and postschool environments.

Partnering Is Key to Effective Instructional Strategies

Meeting the academic, social, and functional life skills needs of students with visual impairments frequently becomes a balancing act that demands considerable finesse, goal prioritization, and creative problem solving. Creativity is the answer to many questions: in scheduling, in instruction, in use of free time, and in collaboration among the many adults involved in each student's program. That is why IEP team members must assume responsibility for the instruction and practice of newly learned skills whenever the natural opportunity to do so occurs. Each member also must believe that successful adult functioning depends on the student's attainment of skills in all of the curriculum areas—that no one area is more or less important than the others.

IDEA requires that parents are members of IEP teams. Be sure to use these team members to identify families' routines, preferences, and their dreams for their children and incorporate that information as goals and objectives are developed.

We have just counseled you to take into account the dreams and aspirations of the family of a student with vision impairment. We have also taught you, in this chapter and throughout the entire book, that the dreams and aspirations of the student are worthy of our respect. Let us end this chapter with these words: Though a student may not be fully able to see, yet the student is fully able to hope. To see is one thing, to fore-see one's future is another. It's a capability you should develop and share; it's your way of dignifying the student. Let Corbin see; more than that, let him fore-see.

Education includes training for job skills. Economic self-sufficiency is an obtainable goal for people with visual impairments.

Bob Rowan/Corbis Documentary/Getty Images

MyLab Education **Self-Check 16.2**

MyLab Education **Application Exercise 16.2:**
Curriculum for Students with Visual Impairments

Summary

Defining Visual Impairments

Students identified as being visually impaired are heterogeneous and include those who are blind, who are functionally blind, or who have low vision. They differ from each other not only in how they function visually but also with regard to age of onset of visual impairment as well as the presence of other cognitive and physical disabilities. Some are gifted or have special talents; a large number have multiple disabilities. A characteristic they have in common is the limited ability to learn incidentally from the environment.

Describing the Characteristics and Causes

Visual impairment can be caused by congenital or adventitious damage or malfunction of the structures of the eye or the parts of the brain that process visual input. The presence of a visual impairment primarily affects the easy ability to understand concepts and acquire incidental information, which further results in limitations in the range and variety of experiences available to them, their ability to get around, and their ability to interact with people and things in the environment.

Evaluating Students with Visual Impairments

A report from an eye specialist indicating the presence of an uncorrectable visual impairment usually triggers a nondiscriminatory evaluation, which includes a functional vision assessment, a learning media assessment, and a complete assessment of the student's functioning in all areas that typically are impacted by a visual impairment, which is known as the expanded core curriculum.

Including Students with Visual Impairments

Most students with visual impairments are educated for most of the school day in general education classrooms, with services provided by a TVI who is assigned to that school on a full- or part-time basis and who collaborates with the general educator to ensure that students have full access to the curriculum.

Educating Students with Visual Impairments

Blindness and low vision do not affect what a student can learn as much as they affect *how* a student learns. To facilitate learning, educators collaborate to ensure that the student is provided with needed accommodations, adapted materials, and the specialized instruction necessary to access the general curriculum and to develop the functional skills needed to be a successful adult. The skills that are the focus of instruction include those identified as the expanded core curriculum, which encompasses compensatory, assistive technology, sensory efficiency, independent living, social interaction, recreation and leisure, career education, self-determination, and orientation and mobility skills.

Addressing the Professional Standards

In Chapter 16, Students with Visual Impairments, we have covered the following Council for Exceptional Children (CEC) Initial Level Special Educator Preparation Standards: Chapter 16—1.0, 1.1, 1.2, 2.1, 2.2, 3,1, 3.3, 4.3, 5.1, 5.4, 5.5, 6.1, 6.3, 6.6, 7.1, 7.2. Refer to the Appendix for a full listing of the CEC Standards with descriptions and supporting explanations.

Chapter 17
Students Who Are Gifted and Talented

 Learning Outcomes

17.1 Discuss how biological and environmental factors influence the development of giftedness and whether these factors adequately explain the underrepresentation of students of color in gifted or talented programs.

17.2 Discuss ways in which students who are gifted and talented can be educated in general education settings and how those strategies and practices can benefit all students.

Meet John Tabb—Exceptionally Gifted, Indeed

Ownership. Ownership has been a key theme throughout John Tabb's life. His parents have worked to instill in him and his three older siblings a sense of ownership over their lives, their learning, and their decisions.

The Tabb family is unique. John's parents, Charles and Linda, were both identified as gifted. So were John's three older siblings: Rebecca, Natalie, and Charles, Jr. John followed in their footsteps, starting in the gifted program in elementary school. But even though all six members of his family are gifted, John has always made his own path. In fact, he's been encouraged to do so. As Linda says, "Our philosophy is to give the kids a lot of space, let them make a lot of choices, and give them a lot of credit to be able to do that. We've always encouraged them to be really independent and confident."

John has definitely carved out his own niche in his family and community. He chose to go to an elite boarding school for his freshman year where he could play soccer and access a challenging academic curriculum. He joined the wrestling team in his senior year (even though he had never wrestled before), just to try something different. As he says, "I try to live life without regrets. . . . I don't want to live with any 'what ifs.'"

John has many gifts and talents, as shown by the fact that he recently received a perfect score on the math portion of the American College Test (ACT). Yet he feels that many aspects of his gifted education helped him develop his academic skills and talents. In elementary school, he was in a self-contained gifted program, with 15 to 20 other students who were also identified as gifted. He remembers that his teachers oversaw many hands-on projects, such as taking apart electronic devices. He feels that he really benefited from such unconventional teaching and from teachers who challenged him and his peers to achieve their full potential.

Middle school was a bit more of a challenge (which was one of the reasons he chose to go to boarding school for his freshman year). John was no longer in a self-contained gifted program and sometimes did not feel challenged in his classes. He felt as if some teachers were trying to teach important life lessons while others just addressed problems and didn't teach very much. But he also felt that middle school taught him a lot about responsibility and taking ownership over this life. "Middle school is like a transition. You go from being in one class all day to switching classes. You have more responsibility, learn life lessons, and mature a lot."

John is also gifted in sports: He competed nationally in tennis when he was 10 years old and is now playing competitive soccer. He has also played baseball and golf and, more recently, has wrestled. He's had to make decisions about which sports to play because of the challenges of balancing multiple sports and academics. Eventually he chose soccer because he not only excels at it but also enjoys its social aspects. Once again, John is owning his decisions and carving out the best path for himself.

John also considers his social skills a gift. He says, "I didn't have much to say in conversations when I was younger, but I was really observant. I'd pick up subtle things, people's emotions. I was always studying my parents' and siblings' emotions. I found them interesting." Now he wants to follow a career that lets him integrate his social abilities with his academic skills.

As the youngest child, John says that he always wanted to keep up with his brothers and sisters. "When your oldest sister goes off to one of the top universities in the country, you want to do well yourself; you don't want to be the straggler left behind." But he admits that much of the pressure is internal. "I have expectations for myself to do well and succeed." John knows that pressure, both internal and external, is a downside of being identified as gifted. But he also says that "IQ can only take you so far. You get to a point where you have to learn to manage things for yourself, and learn what is good and bad for you and work to live up to your potential."

John is taking ownership of living up to his potential. He is working hard, even in his senior year, and plans to major in business at a top college next year. While math is his strong suit, he wants to pursue a major that also allows him to use his social strengths and gives him options for the future. As he says, education is what you make of it.

Defining Giftedness

Unlike the laws benefiting students with disabilities, such as Individuals with Disabilities Education Act (IDEA), Section 504, and Americans with Disabilities Act (ADA), there is no federal legislation that requires state or local educational agencies to offer special education services to students who are gifted or talented. State and local laws or regulations, however, may apply to these students.

The National Association for Gifted Children (2015) surveyed states to identify state policy related to gifted education in the 2014–2015 school year. Of 39 states, 27 indicated that local school districts received some funding to provide gifted education. Thirty-two states (out of 40) had some type of legal requirements pertaining to gifted education. Twenty-three states, out of 40, had state laws specific to gifted education, from which seven states had gifted education included in state laws governing the education of exceptional children. From the 32 states with some form of gifted education mandates, only 4 states provided full funding, with 20 providing partial funding, and 8 providing no funding.

Unlike most of the disabilities you have learned about in this book, giftedness is not well or easily defined. Historically, most states adopted (sometimes with modification) the definition the federal government introduced in 1978—a definition that applies to John Tabb:

> [T]he term "gifted and talented children" means children and, whenever applicable, youth, who are identified at the preschool, elementary, or secondary level as possessing demonstrated or potential abilities that give evidence of high performance capability in areas such as intellectual, creative, specific academic,

or leadership ability, or in the performing and visual arts, and who by reason thereof, require services or activities not ordinarily provided by the school. (Gifted and Talented Children's Education Act, 1978).

However, many states have been expanding their definitions. McClain and Pfeiffer (2012) found in a survey of the states that 48 states have established definitions of giftedness, and these states recognized diverse aspects of giftedness in their definitions:

- Forty-five states address intellectual giftedness.
- Thirty-nine states address high achievement.
- Twenty-eight states address a specific category of giftedness, such as giftedness in performing and visual arts.
- Twenty-seven states address creativity.
- Fifteen states address leadership or leadership ability.
- Three states address motivation.

To account for the fact that giftedness spans more than one area of human development and achievement, researchers have proposed models recognizing the multiple forms of intelligence demonstrated by students who are gifted and talented. Psychologist Howard Gardner (1983, 2011) introduced a multidimensional model of intelligence that is broader and includes eight specific intelligences found across cultures and societies: musical, bodily-kinesthetic, linguistic, logical-mathematical, spatial, interpersonal, intrapersonal, and naturalistic. Figure 17.1 lists the characteristics and distinctive features common in gifted individuals in each of these eight areas.

Data showing how many students in America receive gifted and talented services in schools are difficult to locate. A 2015 report from the U.S. Department of Education indicated that just over 3.2 million public school students were enrolled in gifted and talented programs (Snyder, de Brey, & Dillow, 2016). But, those data are from 2006. There are more recent data.

The National Association for Gifted Children (2015) estimates there were about 3 million students receiving gifted and talented services for the 2014–2015 academic year. The lack of routine data collection at the federal level in gifted education introduces issues when determining which students are served in gifted and talented programs, but they provide some information.

More female students are enrolled in such programs than male students, though that ranges across states from 57 percent female students, 43 percent male students in Hawaii, to several states in which the distribution was even, to 52 percent male students, 48 percent female students in Colorado (2015). The U.S. Department of Education reported that for the 2011–2012 school year, 6.2 percent of all male public school students were served in gifted and talented programs, while 6.4 percent of all female public school students were likewise educated (Snyder et al., 2016).

You may remember that, in Chapter 2, we introduced you to the concept of cultural justice and reviewed data about the intersection of disability and race. Let's return to that concept as it applies within the field of gifted-talented education.

Image Source/Getty Images

Students of color often—and incorrectly—are disproportionately underrepresented in classes for especially intellectually gifted peers.

Figure 17.1 Potential Areas of Giftedness: An Adaptation of Gardner's Eight Areas of Intelligence

Area	Gifted Person	Possible Characteristics of Giftedness	Early Indicators of Giftedness
Musical	Ella Fitzgerald Itzhak Perlman Ray Charles Carlos Santana Yo Yo Ma	Unusual awareness and sensitivity to pitch, rhythm, and timbre Ability may be apparent without musical training Uses music as a way of capturing feelings	Ability to sing or play instrument at an early age Ability to match and mimic segments of song Fascination with sounds
Bodily-kinesthetic	Michael Jordan Nadia Comĕneci Marla Runyan Jim Abbott	Ability can be seen before formal training Remarkable control of bodily movement Unusual poise	Skilled use of body Good sense of timing
Logical-mathematical	Albert Einstein Stephen Hawking John Nash	Loves dealing with abstraction Problem solving is remarkably rapid Solutions can be formulated before articulated: Aha! Ability to skillfully handle long chains of reasoning	Doesn't need hands-on methods to understand concepts Fascinated by and capable of making patterns Ability to figure things out without paper Loves to order and reorder objects
Linguistic	Virginia Woolf Maya Angelou Helen Keller Ralph Ellison Sandra Cisneros	Remarkable ability to use words Prolific in linguistic output, even at a young age	Unusual ability in mimicking adult speech style and register Rapidity and skill of language mastery Unusual kinds of words first uttered
Spatial	Pablo Picasso Frank Lloyd Wright I. M. Pei Maya Lin	Ability to conjure up mental imagery and then transform it Ability to recognize instances of the same element Ability to make transformations of one element into another	Intuitive knowledge of layout Able to see many perspectives Notices fine details, makes mental maps
Interpersonal	Martin Luther King, Jr. Madeleine Albright Rosa Parks Nelson Mandela	Great capacity to notice and make distinctions among people, contrasts in moods, temperaments, motivations, and intentions Ability to read intention and desire of others in social interactions; not dependent on language	Able to pretend or play-act different roles of adults Easily senses the moods of others; often able to motivate, encourage, and help others
Intrapersonal	Sigmund Freüd Elizabeth Kübler-Ross	Extensive knowledge of the internal aspects of a person Increased access to one's own feelings and emotions Mature sense of self	Sensitivity to feeling (sometimes overly sensitive) Unusual maturity in understanding of self
Naturalist	Rachel Carson John James Audubon Jane Goodall Jacques Cousteau	Relates to the world around him or her In tune with the environment	Recognizes and differentiates among many types of an environmental item, such as different makes of cars Recognizes many different rocks, minerals, trees

Clearly, Black and Latino students are underrepresented in gifted and talented education. A 2016 report from the U.S. Department of Education's Office for Civil Rights (OCR) examining data from the 2013–2014 school year provides current data on this area of concern. The OCR report showed that Black and Latino students represented 42 percent of all students enrolled in public schools that offered gifted and talented education programs, but represented only 28 percent of students enrolled in gifted education. White students represented 49 percent of all students enrolled in public schools that offered gifted and talented education programs, but represented 57 percent of students enrolled in gifted education programs. Similar disparities exist with English language learners, who constitute 11 percent of all students in schools offering gifted programs, but less than 3 percent of students in gifted programs (U.S. Department of Education, 2016).

Why the discrepancy as a function of race or language status? Ford (2014) argues that the underrepresentation of Black and Hispanic/Latino students in gifted education programs is a function of social inequality (income and wealth, discrimination, lack of opportunities), deficit thinking, and discrimination. What is **deficit thinking** and how does it impact access to gifted education? Pay attention to one student of color talk about these issues and give some thought to whether you've experienced anything like this before. You may conclude, as prominent researchers do, that it is defensible to take the position that the relationship between access to gifted education, race, and wealth is so intertwined as to suggest that gifted education is more a reflection of privilege than actual giftedness (Ford & King, 2014). You may also justifiably conclude that cultural justice intersects with another core element of our book, namely, high (or low) expectations.

Describing the Characteristics and Causes

Characteristics

It is difficult to identify the characteristics of all people who are gifted and talented. Nevertheless, people who are gifted and talented typically have one or more of these characteristics: high general intellect, specific academic aptitude, creativity and leadership ability, and visual or performing artistry. Paradoxically, high-ability students may also have language, hearing, visual, physical, or learning disabilities. So-called **twice-exceptional** students are students who have high cognitive abilities or distinctive talents, but also have a disability that affects their ability to express those high abilities (Coleman & Roberts, 2015).

Strategies for educating twice-exceptional students include focusing on their strengths and interests, providing accommodations for areas of needed support, and providing a supportive learning environment that enables students to understand their abilities and how they can succeed (Baldwin, Omdal, & Pereles, 2015).

HIGH GENERAL INTELLECT   From its earliest conceptions, giftedness has been associated with high general intellectual ability, as is the fact for John Tabb. The majority of states define giftedness, at least in part, by intellectual giftedness. And, not surprisingly, intelligence tests and IQ scores are the primary means by which high intellect is determined. You learned in Chapter 4 that most major intelligence tests are normed with a mean score of 100 and standard deviations of 15 points and that among the general population, 95 percent of people have IQ scores that fall between two standard deviations below to two standard deviations above the mean (e.g., IQ scores from 70 to 130). Most states use IQ scores approximately 2 standard deviations above the mean (so between 125 and 130) to indicate eligibility for gifted education.

Exceptionally gifted individuals are sometimes referred to as prodigies. The term **prodigy** refers to a child who, by 10 years of age, reaches professional status in a valued domain (such as the visual or performing arts or specific academic pursuits) (Ruthsatz, Ruthsatz, & Stephens, 2014). A child identified as a prodigy usually focuses on a specialized domain (e.g., music, chemistry) and exhibits highly developed giftedness within that domain.

Specific cognitive characteristics are associated with students who have high general intellectual ability. Those characteristics include superior functioning related to memory, concentration, abstraction, generalization, and reasoning (Ritchotte, Suhr,

MyLab Education

Video Example 17.1

In this video a student discusses deficit thinking. How often do you think these examples happen in school? https://www.youtube.com/watch?v=ZvF9_pzT8QY

MyLab Education

Video Example 17.2

In this video, Professor Kristie Speirs Neumeister highlights a study on the importance of family support for twice-exceptional children and adults who are successful. What concerns does Dr. Neumeister raise? https://www.youtube.com/watch?v=ym0ichhhu7k&t=4s

Alfurayh, & Graefe, 2016). Given these characteristics, students who are gifted typically develop vast knowledge in one or more areas.

CREATIVITY Although high general intellect has received significant attention in the identification of giftedness, increasingly, creativity has received attention. Creativity is often described as the ability to produce novel and useful ideas that solve problems and/or entertain. Creativity has been recognized in the "hard" sciences (e.g., engineering, science, and technology) as well as in "soft" sciences (e.g., humanities, music, literature, and the arts) (Kerr & McKay, 2013). There are multiple characteristics of children who are creative. As you read about these characteristics, note that at least the second and third of them relate to a student's self-determination, one of the core elements of our book. Kettler and Bower (2017) examined rating criteria on scales of creativity and found that students who are creative are:

- Fluent, flexible, imaginative, and original thinkers
- Intrinsically motivated and curious
- Adventurous, risk takers, and persistent problem solvers
- Able to generate multiple ideas and solutions to problems
- Intellectually playful and willing to manipulate ideas
- Able to improvise and comfortable with uncertainty.

LEADERSHIP ABILITY Key characteristics associated with leadership include the ability to engender others' trust, to assess situations quickly, and to take direction for the benefit of a group (Lee & Olszewski-Kubilius, 2012). But, leadership goes beyond typical understanding of what it means to be a leader and to exhibit leadership skills. Students who persist in college were not necessarily the ones who excelled on measures of aptitude, like achievement tests or intelligence tests, but the ones with exceptional character strengths such as optimism, persistence, and social intelligence that enable them to lead and be creative (Renzulli & D'Souza, 2014).

TALENTS IN VISUAL AND PERFORMING ARTS The visual and performing arts include the areas of fine arts, music, dance, and theater. Families and peers are catalysts for nurturing interest in and commitment to the long-term development of artistic talents. Important types of support include encouragement, commitment to practice, financial support for lessons, and instrumental support related to transportation and performances.

How can you, as a teacher, know if a student has gifts and talents in visual and performing arts? Well, for one, those students apply their creativeness to these realms, pursuing ideas and paths in the arts that other students do not. We often talk about this as being imaginative. Students with talents and gifts in visual and performing arts often pursue these avenues with determination, seeking opportunities to create and perform whenever they can. Determining "giftedness" in these areas can be subjective; those determinations involve the use of portfolios, performance evaluations, and product assessment activities. You will need to enlist the assistance of people who are knowledgeable about evaluating these portfolios, performances, and products, like the school psychologist or the gifted and talented specialist in your school, and to assist in developing rubrics that identify students who have gifts in these areas (Matthews, 2017).

EMOTIONAL AND SOCIAL CHARACTERISTICS Students who are gifted and talented experience the same range of emotions and feelings that all children experience, though research suggests that children who are gifted experience lower levels of anxiety and depression than their typical peers, although this can change as children enter adolescence, particularly for girls (Weeks et al., 2014). Many students who are gifted tend to develop a sense of perfectionism that can lead to negative self-judgments.

Perfectionism, often described as setting unreasonable standards and expectations, is a two-edged sword. On the one hand, self-oriented perfectionism (that is, setting unrealistic standards for oneself) has been shown to be linked to conscientiousness, a mastery goal focus, and high achievement. On the other hand, socially prescribed perfectionism, which refers to a student's perceptions that others are placing unrealistic standards or expectations on the student, are associated with stress and anxiety, and a performance goal orientation (Miller & Neumeister, 2017). Put more simply, self-oriented perfectionism may result in a focus on and achievement of goals that improve competence and internal motivation, while student-perceived perfectionism may lead to a focus on goals related to performance (e.g., grades, test scores).

Many factors influence these relationships, from the personality characteristics of students, to parenting dynamics and styles, to early school experiences. John mentioned such pressures as a downside of being labeled as gifted, but he also felt that he often put more pressure on himself than his parents did (self-oriented perfectionism) and that this pressure could, at times, be helpful when he was going after goals.

Students who are gifted, like all students, can face bullying and cyberbullying. Researchers suggest that some gifted students may be at increased risk for bullying because of stereotypes and alienation from same age peers; they also may be less likely to communicate with parents or teachers because of a perception that they should be able to manage it by themselves (Smith, Dempsey, Jackson, Olenchak, & Gaa, 2012). Encouragingly, in this study, students ranked feeling stereotyped by others and feeling punished by others for being smart as the lowest of all negative aspects of giftedness.

MyLab Education
Video Example 17.3
Learn more about emotional and social characteristics of students with gifts and talents. What can you, as a teacher, do to ensure that students who are gifted and talented don't experience social and emotional difficulties?

Causes

Whether giftedness originates from nature and/or nurture has long been debated. In terms of nature, neuroimaging techniques have enabled scientists to document differences in the structure of the brains and the neurological functioning of students who are gifted (Kalbfleisch & Gillmarten, 2013). For example, **neuroimaging** studies of students who are gifted in mathematics suggest that such talents require extensive coordination among several systems in the brain and that students who are mathematically gifted have more extensive such networks in both hemispheres of the brain (Singer, Sheffield, Freiman, & Brandl, 2016). Those studies, combined with studies that use techniques related to task speed, complexity, and response time, show that students who are mathematically gifted use the same neural networks that govern mathematical abilities, but that there is greater cooperation between left and right hemispheres, and higher levels of activity across that system (Singer et al., 2016).

But, as with all aspects of development, nurture plays a role, too. Families, mentors, teachers, and others can substantially influence accelerated development leading to giftedness (Callahan & Hertberg-Davis, 2017). John feels that his home environment influenced him a great deal. "Being at home, you hear more big words, you hear more intelligent discussions; it's the environment you grow up in. I think it really influences you a lot in terms of how you progress. You almost learn more at home. It can influence you more than your schoolwork."

A study of parent perspectives on how they promote the academic motivation of their gifted children indicated the following (Garn, Matthews, & Jolly, 2010):

- Parents view themselves as the experts on their gifted children and seek to counteract their child's lack of challenge at school by modifying homework and increasing opportunities for the child to be academically motivated.

- Parents use techniques at home to increase academic motivation by instructing their child interactively, aligning homework with interest, providing structure for learning, and developing their child's intrinsic motivation.

- Parents use behavioral techniques (for example, rewards such as computer games, computer time, and money) to encourage their children to complete homework and to accomplish academic goals.

Of course, both nature and nurture are important in the development of giftedness. The student's genetic patterns and environment interact because the environment enables the student to develop abilities to the point at which the student becomes gifted. Conversely, the environment can impede the student's development.

Evaluating Students Who Are Gifted and Talented

Determining the Presence of Giftedness and Talents

You've learned that Black and Latino students have less access to gifted education than their white peers and that several reasons account for this, from income inequality and discrimination to deficit thinking. One of the ways that these historic trends—this distressing issue about cultural justice/injustice—may be reversed is to move away from traditional models of evaluating for giftedness that overemphasize intelligence scores on tests, which may be culturally biased, and to focus on alternative assessments that provide a different approach to identifying students who are gifted and talented.

For example, researchers developed the Hispanic Bilingual Gifted Screening Instrument, a teacher rating scale, to provide a culturally appropriate tool to assess bilingual Hispanic students and determine their gifts and talents (Fultz, Lara-Alecio, Irby, & Tong, 2013). Some aspects of the assessment process that could lead to greater equity for Black and Latino students include implementing tools that can universally screen for potential giftedness instead of relying on teacher or family/caregiver referral; giving traditional and non-traditional (e.g., non-verbal) intelligence tests; setting scores for eligibility from achievement tests to be at the building level, not the district or the assessment's norms; beginning gifted programming early (by 1st grade); and setting equity goals for the school (Ford, 2015).

Programs have also been developed to assess and support gifted students from underrepresented minorities and their families. For example, DISCOVER (Discovering Intellectual Strengths and Capabilities through Observation while allowing for Varied Ethnic Responses) is a performance-based and research-validated assessment for identifying giftedness in students from diverse backgrounds (Sarouphim & Maker, 2010). It requires the student to undertake problem-solving tasks in six of Howard Gardner's domains of intelligence: spatial, logical-mathematical, linguistic, bodily-kinesthetic, interpersonal, and intrapersonal. The tasks increase in complexity and openness as the assessment progresses. Assessments are available at four grade levels: K–2, 3–5, 6–8, and 9–12. Using DISCOVER, educators identify a higher proportion of students from diverse ethnic, socioeconomic, and linguistic backgrounds as gifted and talented (Sarouphim, 2009).

The DISCOVER instrument draws on Maker's (1993) definition of giftedness that emphasizes problem solving in highly efficient and effective ways. During the evaluation process, students work in small groups while highly trained observers use standard observation sheets, pictures, and a video camera to note their problem-solving processes and products. Over a 2½-hour period, observers accept all products, give helpful clues when asked, adopt a nonjudgmental attitude, and rotate regularly to minimize bias. Afterward, observers work as partners to rate the students' strengths on a scale of 1 to 5, from "no strength observed" to "definite strength observed." Students with superior problem-solver ratings are those with definite strength ratings in two or more activities.

In addition to using DISCOVER to identify children and youth who qualify for gifted education, a DISCOVER curriculum model has been developed that fosters students' multiple intelligences and problem-solving abilities. The model emphasizes hands-on learning, group activities and student self-direction, learning centers based on the domains in multiple intelligences, a problem-solving approach, visual and performing arts, and integration of technology. The model is also intended to support the integration of a student's cultural and linguistic preferences, including supporting bilingual education (Maker, Zimmerman, Gomez-Arizaga, Pease, & Burke, 2015).

Nondiscriminatory Evaluation Process
Evaluating Whether or Not a Student Is Gifted, Using an IDEA-like Process

Observation	**Teacher and parents observe:** The student may be bored with school or intensely interested in academic pursuits, has high vocabulary or specialized talents and interests, shows curiosity and frequently asks questions (especially *how* and *why*), is insightful, and has novel ideas and approaches to tasks.
Screening	**Assessment measures:** **Classroom work products:** The student's work is consistently superior in one or more academic areas; or in the case of the gifted student who is underachieving, products are inconsistent, with only work of special interest being superior. **Group intelligence tests:** Tests often indicate exceptional intelligence. **Group achievement tests:** The student usually performs above average in one or more areas of achievement. (Cutoff for screening purposes is an IQ of 115.)
Prereferral	Generally, prereferral is not used for students who may be evaluated as gifted.
Referral	Schools vary in their procedures for referral; in some cases, referral will be handled very similarly to the process of referring students who have disabilities.
Nondiscriminatory evaluation procedures and standards	**Assessment measures:** **Individualized intelligence test:** The student scores in the upper 2 to 3 percent of the population. Because of the cultural biases of standardized IQ tests, students from minority backgrounds are considered if their IQs do not meet the cutoff but other indicators suggest giftedness. **Individualized achievement test:** The student scores in the upper 2 to 3 percent of the population in one or more areas of achievement. **Creativity assessment:** The student demonstrates unusual creativity in work products as judged by experts or performs exceptionally well on tests designed to assess creativity. The student does not have to be academically gifted to qualify. **Checklists of gifted characteristics:** These checklists are often completed by teachers, parents, peers, or others who know the student well. The student scores in the range that suggests giftedness as established by checklist developers. **Anecdotal records:** The student's records suggest high ability in one or more areas. **Curriculum-based assessment:** The student is performing at a level beyond peers in one or more areas of the curriculum used by the local school district. **Direct observation:** The student may be a model student or could have behavior problems as a result of being bored with classwork. If the student is a perfectionist, anxiety might be observed. Observations should occur in other settings besides the school. **Visual and performing arts assessment:** The student's performance in visual or performing arts is judged by individuals with expertise in the specific area. The student does not have to be academically gifted to qualify. **Leadership assessment:** Peer nomination, parent nomination, and teacher nomination are generally used. However, self-nomination can also be a good predictor of leadership. Leadership in extracurricular activities is often an effective indicator. The student does not have to be academically gifted to qualify. **Case-study approach:** Determination of a student's giftedness looks at all areas of assessment just described without adding special weight to any one factor.
Determination	The nondiscriminatory evaluation team determines that the student is gifted and needs special education.

NONDISCRIMINATORY EVALUATION PROCESS Because the category of gifted and talented is not included in IDEA, this specific process is not required, although *Nondiscriminatory Evaluation Process: Evaluating Whether or Not a Student Is Gifted, Using an IDEA-Like Process* incorporates the recommendations of leaders in the gifted education field (Callahan & Hertberg-Davis, 2017; Ford, 2015). A national survey of school psychologists (Robertson, Pfeiffer, & Taylor, 2011) found that general education teachers, school psychologists, and gifted consultants tended to be the most involved in the gifted identification process. Further, the most common factor used to determine eligibility for gifted education was scores on intelligence tests, although classroom performance and reviews of academic work were also frequently used. As we've discussed, however, the overreliance on intelligence tests may be one factor serving as a barrier to gifted education for students of color.

Determining the Nature of Specially Designed Instruction and Services

In addition to measuring intellectual functioning, educators evaluate students' creativity. Having measures that specifically tap creativity are especially important, given the research finding that traditional intelligence tests and academic achievement tests may miss students who are highly creative (Kaufman, Plucker, & Russell, 2012). The Torrance Tests of Creative Thinking are the most frequently used tools for assessing creativity. They have been translated into 35 languages, and research has shown that they are a

MyLab Education
Video Example 17.4
Learn how one district is trying to address the underrepresentation of students of color in gifted education programs. In what ways might these procedures benefit all students?
https://www.youtube.com/watch?v=07QCN1iKAbo

stronger predictor of creative achievement than IQ scores. They are frequently used in the identification of gifted and talented students and for admission into gifted programs. They are also highly relevant for students from diverse backgrounds and who express their gifts in diverse ways (Yarbrough, 2016; Yoon, 2017).

These tests were initially designed to foster the development of creativity and not simply assess students' creativity. However, they can be used to assess creativity with both words and pictures. Thinking Creatively with Words focuses on students' verbal or linguistic creativity from kindergarten through adulthood. Six exercises assess fluency, flexibility, and originality with words. You'll learn more about fluency, flexibility, and originality later in the chapter. Thinking Creatively with Pictures evaluates students' figural and spatial creativity from kindergarten through adulthood. Exercises assess the five mental characteristics of fluency, elaboration, originality, resistance to premature closure, and abstractness of titles. For both tests, a manual is provided for scoring that includes national norms with standard scores and national percentiles by grade and age.

MyLab Education Self-Check 17.1

MyLab Education Application Exercise 17.1: Nature vs. Nurture

---

Including Students Who Are Gifted and Talented

The U.S. Department of Education does not collect data with regard to where students who are gifted and talented are educated. The absence of data may explain why, within the field of gifted education, there is an ongoing debate regarding student placement. On the one hand, approaches such as the all-school **enrichment** programs provide proven ways to educate students who are gifted in the general education classroom, to the benefit of all students (Callahan & Hertberg-Davis, 2017; Firmender, Reis, & Sweeny, 2013). On the other hand, some leaders within the field of gifted education have expressed concern about the lack of curriculum breadth, depth, and specificity in many general education classrooms (Pfeiffer, 2012). They have underscored the need to consider a broad range of options, including **acceleration**:

- *Cluster grouping.* Assign three to six students who are gifted and talented to the same general education classroom so that they can work together.

- *All-school enrichment programs.* Address the top 20 percent of students in a school through special interest groups, specialized instruction in small groups, and mentoring on individual projects.

- *Acceleration.* Students start kindergarten or college early, skipping one or more grades in order to experience higher levels of instruction, and/or attend a higher-grade-level program for part of the school day.

SCHOOL-WIDE ENRICHMENT   One strategy to deliver gifted services involves school-wide enrichment efforts. To address gifted students' unique cognitive characteristics and to promote their motivation, attention, and social-emotional development, teachers match the content of their courses to students' aptitudes, sophistication, and interests. Often they use enrichment strategies to engage students. The term enrichment refers to curricular and program delivery services that expand the curriculum by adding instruction in domains beyond what is in the general curriculum; present more challenging content; and teach critical thinking, problem-solving, and goal-setting skills (Callahan & Hertberg-Davis, 2017). In *My Voice: Graham*, Graham talks about how enrichment services made a difference in his education.

My Voice

Graham

My name is Graham. I was in gifted education programs starting in the 2nd grade. In many ways, I think the different instructional opportunities I had made the difference in me being successful. During elementary school, there was a whole-school enrichment program and I received some specialized supports from my gifted teacher. She worked a lot on critical thinking skills, problem solving, and, for me, how to be more organized. Being in the enrichment program in elementary school really helped me challenge myself, and it opened me up to a lot of really good ideas and ways of thinking.

For me personally, being gifted means that I need something more from school than what is taught in the general classroom. I need to be challenged mentally so I can learn. During middle school, this was harder. I could go to my enrichment coordinator for some extra work, but there was no school-wide enrichment, so many of the classes seemed too simple and, honestly, it was boring. But, fortunately, in 6th grade, I got to test out of 6th-grade math and skip to 7th-grade math, along with about 12 other kids. This kept me a lot more interested in the work and prevented me from getting too bored in school. When I got to 8th grade, I went to the high school campus to take algebra.

One benefit of being in gifted education was that I had an IEP, which set year-long academic goals. These goals helped me manage my time and learn how to set reasonable goals. Another opportunity is that in 8th grade I got the whole semester to investigate five colleges that I might want to go to. It helped me learn a lot more about the colleges I investigated and about the entire higher education system.

In high school, some of the difficulties with classes happened again. They were all lecture-based and over material I either knew or could learn quickly. My enrichment coordinator at the high school worked with some of the teachers to compact the curriculum so I could move through material more rapidly. Then, when I was a junior in high school, I began a life sciences program at a career and professional school that my school district opened. There were small classes, individualized teaching, and when we learned something in the classroom, we spent part of the semester applying that in a project outside of the school. It really got me interested in science and biology in a way that the lecture classes had not.

Because of my work in the life sciences program, I was able to get an undergraduate research appointment in the microbiology laboratory at the university I was going to attend the summer before I started. I worked in the lab the entire time and graduated with a microbiology degree. This past year, I started medical school. I honestly think that had I not had the enrichment opportunities and the chance to do project-based learning, I would never have been interested enough to commit the time to do well in college so I could get into medical school.

—Reprinted with permission of Graham Wehmeyer

The school-wide enrichment model (SEM) (Renzulli & Reis, 2010) is a good example of an enrichment model. It promotes challenging, high-end learning by creating approaches that can be integrated across the general education curriculum to assist all students, not just those who are gifted. There are three types of enrichment experiences within the school-wide enrichment program. Type I enrichment exposes students to a wide variety of topics, disciplines, occupations, hobbies, people, places, and events that ordinarily would not be included in the general education curriculum. For example, Type I experiences may involve community speakers, demonstrations, performances, multimedia presentations, or other illustrative formats. Type II experiences involve group training activities in which students learn to brainstorm solutions to problems, apply critical thinking skills, and acquire learning-to-learn strategies. Type III experiences involve tackling real world problems with the skills that students have learned and practiced in the first two types of experiences. The SEM is an excellent fit within all levels of the multi-tiered systems of supports (MTSS) model you learned about in Chapter 5. The SEM recently added an online process to support all of these experiences (Housand, Housand, & Renzulli, 2016).

John's family has experienced multiple models of gifted education. Both his mother and father, Linda and Charles, were in accelerated programs when they were in school. John and his siblings have been in public- and private-school gifted programs and have received self-contained and integrated supports in the classroom. All have benefited from diverse options that can be individualized to each student's needs, strengths, and talents. *Inclusion Tips for Students Who Are Gifted and Talented* provides suggestions for students who are gifted.

Inclusion Tips for Students Who Are Gifted and Talented

	Behavior	Social Interactions	Educational Performance	Classroom Attitudes
What You Might See	The student asks so many questions that there is time for nothing else.	The student is unable to see another person's perspective.	The student is very bored in class and is refusing to do homework.	The student is achieving slightly below grade level, but has unusual talents related to leadership and emotional intelligence.
What You Might Be Tempted to Do	Tell the student to be quiet and pay attention.	Avoid calling on the student in class to avoid potential conflict.	Discipline the student for inattentiveness or give additional work to reinforce the lesson.	Assume that the student is becoming academically lazy and give the student extra work to try to boost the student up to grade level.
Alternate Teacher Response	Begin a dialogue journal. Ask the student to write down any questions the student has. Then research and discuss some of the answers.	Build on the student's leadership skills by giving the student responsibility for leading a class discussion of major concepts.	Modify the scope and sequence of the curriculum through acceleration or compacting to create more challenge.	Recognize the student's gifts and strengths and work with the school principal to find a school citizenship project for which the student can provide leadership.
Ways to Include Peers in the Process	Have an all-class "Challenge Box," where students can write questions they think are difficult. Enable the students who are gifted to work on these questions in small groups with their peers.	Have the student work with small groups, teaching other students to be discussion facilitators.	Explore the possibility of this student attending one or more classes in the next grade.	Identify other students with similar talents and get them involved in a cooperative citizenship project.

Educating Students Who Are Gifted and Talented

Autonomous Learner Model

Personalized learning involves student self-directed learning that capitalizes on the availability of technology to support learning. In the 21st century, autonomous learning is important for all students, but given the unique characteristics of students who are gifted or talented with regard to critical thinking, problem solving, and creativity—and given their inclination to be self-directed—autonomous learning becomes even more important. Autonomous learners are internally motivated; they have a passion for learning; they are problem solvers and rarely satisfied with what they have learned (Betts, Carey, & Kapushion, 2016). The Autonomous Learner Model enables students to:

- Explore what it means to be gifted
- Explore what intelligence and creativity mean
- Explore aspects of their personal/social development
- Consider their strengths and limitations
- Learn organizational skills
- Engage in self-directed study about topics in which they are interested
- Learn the importance of autonomous lifelong learning.

The Autonomous Learner Model was developed to promote independent, self-directed learners who are not just exceptionally intelligent but also well developed in social, emotional, and cognitive domains. The model includes five areas in which students receive support and enrichment experiences. Each of these dimensions, the focus of those dimension, and actions that facilitate learning within each are below:

1. Orientation. Dimension focus: Promoting self-awareness of giftedness, talent, intelligence, and creativity

2. Individual development. Dimension Focus: Inter/intrapersonal skills, learning skills, technology, college and career involvement, organizational skills, productivity

3. Enrichment. Dimension Focus: Explorations, investigations, cultural activities, service, adventure trips

4. Seminars. Dimension Focus: Futuristic thinking, problem-based learning, knowledge dissemination

5. In-depth study. Dimension Focus: Individual projects, group projects, mentorships, presentations, assessments.

The strength of the ALM lies in its flexibility. As students and teachers work together, roles change and adapt. The teacher may become the student and the learner may become a facilitator of others' learning. By changing roles, all students develop and appreciate their own strengths and become independent learners. The activities and strategies within the ALM have been validated by research within classrooms (Betts, Kapushion, & Carey, 2016), and the model incorporates practices that have been validated by research independently (VanTassel-Baska, 2000).

Through these dimensions, students can differentiate their own learning, become engaged in open-ended learning experiences, and develop skills that enable them to be lifelong learners (Betts, Kapushion, & Carey, 2016). The *Guidelines for Teaching: Autonomous Learner Model* feature provides details on implementing the model. Note that the ALM process can benefit all students, not only students with gifts and talents; it can be a means for inclusion. There is a fit between the ALM and response to intervention (RtI), in that the dimensions of the ALM can be infused into all tiers of an RtI or MTSS framework, with the intensity of supports varying among the tiers (Betts & Carey, 2010). Both RtI/MTSS and ALM focus on cognitive, academic, emotional, and physical needs of students and emphasize student autonomy and self-direction—what you know as self-determination.

Differentiated Instruction

Differentiated instruction is a prevalent strategy for promoting participation and progress in the general education curriculum for all students. But, the strategies that constitute differentiated instruction were first developed for students who were gifted and talented. To differentiate means to make something different by altering or modifying it. Differentiated instruction modifies traditional instruction. In differentiated instruction, a teacher uses more than one instructional methodology, such as increasing students' access to instructional materials in a variety of formats, expanding test-taking and data collection options, and varying the complexity and nature of content presented during the course of a unit of study (Tomlinson, 2017). Differentiated instruction is a good strategy for all students, not just students who are gifted, so you should almost always consider it when developing an individualized education program (IEP) for a student with a disability. But, in this section, you'll learn about some specific differentiation strategies that have been shown to benefit students who are gifted.

Your role as a teacher changes in a differentiated classroom from "keepers and dispensers of knowledge" to "collaborators with students and organizers of learning opportunities" (Tomlinson, 2017, p. 35). Another important role for the teacher in differentiated classrooms is to create an effective learning community. Learning communities are classrooms in which students feel free to explore and take risks, feel safe to give

Will Hart/PhotoEdit

Co-teaching, which involves a general and special education teacher working together, is often an essential element of including students who are gifted in the general education classroom.

Guidelines for Teaching

Autonomous Learner Model

Actions to Facilitate Dimension 1: Orientation.

- Support students to identify their interests and strengths.
- Stress that people have talents in many areas.
- Have students explore ways in which they prefer to learn.
- Teach students self-advocacy skills to enable them to facilitate their own learning.
- Include a focus on student emotions and personal feelings about giftedness.
- Include a focus on social and interpersonal relationships and how students interact with other students through group activities.
- Help students create "identities" around being problem solvers, being creative, and being able to facilitate change, rather than just around being "smart."

Actions to Facilitate Dimension 2: Individual Development.

- Support students to find ways to use their talents across emotional, social, cognitive, and physical dimensions and not just in one dimension.
- Enable students to take a lifelong approach to learning rather than focusing solely on short-term, performance-based objectives like tests or grades.
- Introduce age-relevant career and college readiness and involvement activities, from levels of exploration to future planning.
- Teach organizational and self-regulation skills like time management, self-scheduling, self-monitoring, self-instruction, or self-evaluation.
- Teach goal-setting and attainment skills.
- Integrate technology into instruction to augment student learning opportunities.
- Teach problem-solving skills.

Actions to Facilitate Dimension 3: Enrichment.

- Provide opportunities to go beyond the curriculum to explore additional or new topics.
- Encourage students to identify topics they are interested in investigating or that relate to current social or culturally relevant issues.

- Assist students to become problem finders; that is, teach them to look for problems worth exploring and investigating.
- Provide opportunities to investigate topics within the curriculum at a more detailed or expanded level.
- Help students identify opportunities for service-learning.
- Engage students in community-based learning that expands learning in the classroom and opens the door for exploration and investigation.

Actions to Facilitate Dimension 4: Seminars.

- Provide students opportunities to investigate relevant problems and make presentations on those problems to a larger group.
- Emphasize future-oriented thinking, such as how to solve current problems with future actions.
- Assist students to explore controversial topics in a balanced manner.
- Emphasize the value of the student's work in benefiting others and society.
- Emphasize the role of planning and goal setting in future-focused action.
- Encourage collaboration with others to achieve group goals in relation to presentation and problem-based learning.

Actions to Facilitate Dimension 5: In-Depth Study.

- Assist students to identify topics that require longer times to learn and examine problems, rather than only a focus on short-term problems.
- Turn control for making decisions about projects and activities over to students to facilitate self-direction.
- Teach problem-solving, self-regulation, and self-determination related skills that will facilitate self-directed learning.
- Connect students with mentors who have extensive knowledge about the topic.
- Help students identify products that can result from in-depth study.
- Teach students to self-evaluate progress toward goals and to determine what they want to learn next.

SOURCE: Based on Betts, G., Carey, R., & Kapushion, B. (2016). *Autonomous Learner Model resource book.* Waco, TX: Prufrock Press.

answers without fear of being wrong, and regard each other with respect. In learning communities, all members feel welcome and contribute, expect to succeed, and value growth and progress and not just outcomes (Tomlinson, 2017). Do you agree that these elements of learning communities reflect the fact that members of these communities attribute dignity to each other? Each member is respected by—dignified by—the others.

Differentiated instruction involves not only providing multiple ways in which learning occurs but also recognizing that not all students have the same skill sets and that objectives and lessons need to include differentiated indicators of progress and growth. There are many ways to differentiate learning opportunities, from providing students opportunities to choose from instructional materials or tasks to creating learning centers or **compacting the curriculum**. Tomlinson (2017) provides some ways in which instruction can be differentiated:

- From structured, well-laid out activities to open-ended, improvisational activities
- From teacher-directed instruction to independent work by the student
- From slowly unfolding lessons and information to quickly paced learning opportunities
- From introductory content to complex content
- From group-focused instruction to instruction focused on the individual learner's interests.

Differentiation can be done in a number of ways, including the following:

- **Create a learning community.** Create learning communities in which all students feel safe to take risks, are expected to learn and succeed, and are welcomed and appreciated by communicating clear expectations of and for success, providing directions that assume student ownership over learning and supply adequate detail and structure, and teach using multiple modalities and universally designed materials. Provide students access to technology, to examples of successful work, and to supports such as graphic or advance organizers. Learning communities incorporate center-based and small group learning in which every student has a meaningful role in achieving the learning goal. In addition, students are involved in setting rules in learning communities, rather than having rules imposed upon them.

- **Differentiate instruction by content.** Differentiating instruction by content involves differentiating what you teach and what students learn. An often used strategy is to set up learning centers that vary by content. Another is to use educational technology, particularly computers and tablets, to provide students different learning experiences on the same topic. Compacting and expanding content is a form of differentiation that involves providing the same content in a shorter time frame or expanding the content so that students who get through it quickly can learn more content or at a greater depth. Be careful, though, that students don't just see this as doing more work! Tiered activities provide opportunities for students at different levels of readiness to be successful. Universal design elements, such as presenting information in graphic formats, using advance organizers, and ensuring that all students have access to the content are forms of differentiation.

- **Differentiate instruction by process.** Differentiating instruction by process involves differentiating how students think about or make sense of information. This often involves matching students with appropriately challenging work and varying activities by degrees of difficulty. Students can be provided directions that are simpler to understand, information can be highlighted, students can be given additional practice opportunites before a learning activity, or students may be provided greater flexibility in deadlines. Students can work on a topic individually, in a small group, or through computer-based instruction as a function of how the student will be most successful. Learning can occur in the classroom, in other areas of the school, and in the community. Teachers also can differentiate by process, creating lesson objectives that vary across levels of complexity and expectations for how the student will engage with the information (from memorizing to applying to analyzing to creating).

- **Differentiate instruction by product.** Differentiating instruction by product involves differentiating what students produce to provide evidence of their learning. Teachers give multiple options for products, rather than one option (e.g., a written report), to ensure that a greater number of students will be able to show evidence of their learning. The types of products may vary from traditional written products, to digital products (both audio and video/image), to presentations, to websites. For students for whom English is not their first language, differentiation may mean providing options for products in their first language. You may also want to supply different timelines for products; some students may do better providing more frequent responses to illustrate learning, other students may want to present a long-term project as a product.

- **Differentiate instruction by interest.** Another means to differentiate instruction for gifted students is to do so by a student's interest areas. Work with students to identify how their interest areas overlap with the content being covered. These interest areas can be used to expand learning opportunities for students who are gifted and talented and to individualize content presentation for all students. A student who has a strong interest in photography can incorporate that into almost any lesson or unit topic. A frequently used differentiation that takes advantage of interests is the use of WebQuests—which teachers use to guide students through problem-solving activities using web-based resources. Another strategy is to create interest groups, whereby students have opportunities throughout the year to learn alongside classmates who share the same interest.

- **Differentiate instruction by learning profiles.** Students also vary by how they prefer to learn. One student may prefer to have opportunities to move around, and another student may learn best in a quiet context. Refer back to Gardner's multiple intelligences to think about how students who are gifted and talented might best learn. Differentiating based on learning profile preferences may involve arranging environments to support student strengths, or providing more opportunities for social interactions. A student's culture also may provide ways to differentiate instruction, and offering such differentiation may help the student feel more welcomed in the class.

Differentiated instruction has strong support in the research literature, having been shown to have positive impact on literacy and reading acquisition (Valiandes, 2015), science (Pablico, Diack, & Lawson, 2017), and math (Prast, Weijer-Bergsma, Kroesbergen, & Van Luit, 2018).

The *Into Practice Across Grade Levels: Differentiated Instruction* feature provides detailed information on ways in which to differentiate instruction across ages and grades.

Creativity and Critical Thinking

As you have learned, students who are gifted tend to be highly original, independent, curious, motivated, and attracted to complexity. They are creative and effective critical thinkers. It would be wrong, however, to assume that students who are gifted are already highly skilled in creativity and critical thinking and do not need instruction in these areas (Callahan & Hertberg-Davis, 2017). Instead, you should focus on enhancing your students' innate strengths by honing their creative talents and thinking abilities. According to Rimm, Siegle, & Davis (2017), you can promote their creativity by

- Fostering creative attitudes
- Improving student understanding of creativity
- Practicing and exercising creativity
- Teaching critical and creative thinking skills
- Engaging students in creative activities.

Promoting creativity goes hand-in-hand with efforts to enhance critical thinking and effective problem solving. Teachers who are focused on promoting creativity use active verbs such as *brainstorm, invent, imagine,* and, indeed, *create* when designing activities and providing direction and instruction, and they engage students in exploring and investigating problems and challenges (Sternberg, Jarvin, & Grigorenko, 2015). Smutny,

Into Practice Across Grade Levels

Differentiated Instruction

Create a Learning Community: In Ms. Armstrong's **3rd-grade** class, the first week of school was spent with students identifying their own character strengths through an online assessment. Once all students identified their five top character strengths, these were posted on the bulletin board. Each day, students were asked to identify one of their top strengths and use it 3 times during the day. The class also used this information when they talked about class rules and identified how each student's strengths might be used in the classroom to meet class goals.

Differentiate Instruction by Content: In Mr. Martinez's **6th-grade** science class, he sets up learning centers that concentrate on multiple aspects of the unit focus on the planetary system for the first 9 weeks of the semester. In one center, students build papier-mâché models of each planet in the solar system. In another center, students use the National Aeronautics and Space Administration (NASA) website to identify and label major geographical formations on the moon and Mars. In a third center, students explore how black holes form, and how they have impacted the evaluation of galaxies.

Differentiate Instruction by Process: In Ms. Washington's **11th-grade** biology class, students working on a unit pertaining to the life cycle of insects begin with activities studying honey bees through web-based sites, studying the anatomy of samples, and reading about bee habitat. The lesson objectives are differentiated so that all learners can meet challenging objectives based on their readiness level. For the second half of the semester, students spend part of their day in field-based activities observing bees and recording data about the number of bees, their activity, weather patterns, and time of day.

Differentiate Instruction by Product: In Ms. Patel's **8th-grade** social studies class, students choose from multiple product options in the unit on the industrial revolution, including presentations on major inventions that propelled the industrial age, a video report on the role of the railroads in the industrial revolution, a written report on child labor in the industrial age, and a debate of the pros and cons of unionization in that era.

Differentiate Instruction by Interest: In Ms. Wolowic's **4th-grade** class, students spend one session per week in groups aligned with their interests. This time is guided by the students in the group, who decide how they will apply their interest to the topic at hand.

Differentiate Instruction by Learning Profiles: In Mr. Pool's **10th-grade** algebra class, he uses multimodal instructional activities to teach concepts like slope and angles, providing opportunities for students not only to listen to presentations but also to manipulate materials to solve geometric problems. He assigns students to working groups organized according to the multiple intelligences focus that the school has adopted, matching students to groups as a function of their areas of strengths, interests, and abilities.

SOURCE: Based on Tomlinson, C. A. (2017). *How to differentiate instruction in academically diverse classrooms* (3rd ed.). Alexandria, VA: ASCD.

Walker, and Honeck (2015) provide five dimensions of creative thinking that can direct teachers in efforts to promote greater creativity:

- **Fluency:** generating multiple ideas and solutions easily. Students learn to generate multiple ideas and solutions by doing so time and again. As with most skills, practice is the best way to enhance fluency; providing frequent opportunities to generate ideas and solutions is critical for children at all ages.

- **Flexibility:** generating alternative ideas and solutions. The intent of instruction to promote fluency is to teach students to generate multiple ideas with ease. The purpose of flexibility instruction is to come up with ideas from different perspectives, angles, and alternatives.

- **Originality:** generating original ideas, thoughts, and solutions. As with fluency, generating original ideas, thoughts, and solutions is as much a matter of practice as anything else.

- **Elaboration** and **Evaluation:** generating details to further develop ideas, thoughts, and solutions. From simply generating ideas and alternatives, students must eventually be able to generate details that further develop their ideas and solutions and evaluate the success of these ideas and solutions. Elaboration and evaluation often go hand-in-hand, so they are presented together here.

MyLab Education
Video Example 17.5
In this video, a teacher assigns gifted students a problem-based learning task. How does this generate fluency and flexibility skills?

The *Into Practice Across Grade Levels: Promoting Creativity* feature provides examples of how to enhance each of these dimensions for younger children who are gifted and talented (and, for that matter, all children!).

Into Practice Across Grade Levels

Promoting Creativity

Promote Fluency.

- Present a situation that poses a problem or a dilemma and ask students to brainstorm as many ideas (as a group) as possible, without evaluating any idea.
- Provide the beginning of a story and an end and ask students to think of all the different ways to link the beginning of the story to the end.
- Provide a scenario that poses a problem or dilemma and ask students to think about the ways in which the dilemma or problem might be resolved. Ask each student to keep a list of all of the possible solutions the student can come up with over a week.
- Present a painting or photograph and ask students to imagine what the subjects are thinking, what happened before the scene depicted in the painting/photo, and what happened after the scene depicted in the painting/photo.

Example: Ms. Owens's **6th-grade** science class is studying Mars. Students have learned about some of the basic properties of Mars, from the geography, climate, soil composition, and so forth. At the start of class on a Monday, Ms. Owens explained that students should imagine they have landed on Mars several miles from where the original spaceflight was intended to land and that they need to make their way over to the original landing location to be transported home. She provided a list of what the students had at hand and asked them to generate as many ways of getting to their destination as possible. Each student was paired with another student, and at the end of the week, all students presented their ideas in multiple ways.

Promote Flexibility.

- Have students role play characters in a story with different perspectives on a problem or issue and ask each student to generate ideas about how the character might solve the problem or resolve the issue.
- Provide a description of a situation or problem from one person's perspective, then ask students how the situation might be different from another person's perspective.
- Provide a description of a character with three different histories (childhood experiences, countries, etc.) and have students identify how that character might act in the same situation, taking into account each different history.
- Tell a story with a beginning, middle, and end; then ask students to imagine "what if" one thing changed in the beginning of the story or the middle of the story, and to generate ideas about how the story might have differed based on the change.

Example: In Ms. Ramirez's **1st-grade** class, students were fond of the popular book *If you Give a Mouse a Cookie* by Laura Joffe Numeroff. The story has a logical if/then sequence, so Ms. Ramirez changed one element of the story and asked her students to draw pictures that illustrate how that would change the sequence from the original story.

Promote Originality.

- Have students identify 10 things that make them "original" and not like anyone else and then write a story or draw an illustration of these original characteristics.
- Explain to students that they are to create a new language (using symbols and codes) and that they should use that language to communicate a predetermined short story to a peer by teaching the peer the language. The peer, in turn, does the same.
- Ask students to compare and contrast two similar, though not identical, items, pictures, or photographs and have them list what makes each unique and original.
- Draw random shapes on a piece of paper and give to small groups of students, and ask each group to turn the shape into something new.

Example: **3rd-grade** students in Mr. Wagner's class did a unit on understanding animal species. Working in small groups, they identified the characteristics of ducks that could be used to identify specific species. Then they were asked to compare and contrast those features to identify what makes each species unique and original.

Promote Elaboration and Evaluation.

- From a list of ideas that a student has generated for responding to an issue or solving a problem, have the student identify one idea and describe how the idea would be implemented in detail and what changes might need to be made to be successful in the implementation.
- Provide an outline of a story and have students fill in the details to flesh out a complete story.
- Teach students self-directed learning strategies like self-monitoring or self-evaluation to enable them to better evaluate their ideas and solutions.

Example: Ms. Winter's **4th-grade** class members were studying the role of climate in water shortages in parts of the world. They generated a list of ideas for addressing the water shortage. On the basis of this list, students selected one idea and provided detailed information about how it might be implemented, identified possible barriers to implementing the idea, and described how they would evaluate the success of the idea.

SOURCE: Based on Smutny, J. F., Walker, S. Y., & Honeck, I. E. (2015). *Teaching gifted children in today's preschool and primary classrooms: Identifying, nurturing, and challenging children ages 4–9.* Minneapolis, MN: Free Spirit Publishing.

Gifted students are still just students. They are no more or less worthy of being respected and accorded dignity than any other students.

MyLab Education **Self-Check 17.2**

MyLab Education **Application Exercise 17.2: Differentiating Instruction**

Summary

Defining Giftedness

Giftedness can be difficult to define, in part because children can be gifted and talented in so many ways. Unlike disabilities, giftedness is not a categorical area under IDEA. However, many states have policy regarding the education of gifted children. It appears that about 6 percent of students in public schools are gifted or talented. Children of color, particularly those who are Black or Latino, are underrepresented in gifted programs for a variety of reasons, from social inequality—cultural injustice—to deficit thinking to discrimination.

Describing the Characteristics and Causes

Students who are gifted or talented can have gifts and talents in multiple areas, and gifts and talents can co-exist with a disability. Students who are twice-exceptional are those who have high cognitive abilities or distinctive talents, but also have a disability that impacts the expression of those high abilities. The most prevalent characteristic of giftedness is high general intellect, but educators are focusing more on other areas to describe gifted students, particularly high levels of creativity and critical thinking abilities, leadership skills and abilities, talents in visual and performing arts, and emotional and social abilities.

The causes of giftedness involve both biological and environmental factors. Neuroimaging studies of children who are gifted show that they process information more rapidly and with greater complexity and activity in the brain than do children who are not. But, it is also clear that a child's environment, family practices, and other environmental factors can promote or impede development and, thus, giftedness. High expectations play a role.

Evaluating Students Who Are Gifted and Talented

Using alternative or nontraditional ways to evaluate giftedness can be one way to more equitably identify Black and Latino students for their giftedness and talents. The Discovering Intellectual Strengths and Capabilities through Observation while allowing for Varied Ethnic Responses (DISCOVER) process is both an assessment and a curriculum model that focuses on problem solving within multiple domains of intelligences. Because IDEA does not include the category of gifted and talented, its NDE process is not specifically mandated, although recommendations from leaders in the field of giftedness mirror activities that are reflected in the NDE process. A widely used set of tools, the Torrance Tests of Creative Thinking, provide culturally sensitive ways to examine dimensions of creativity, including fluency, flexibility, and originality.

Including Students Who Are Gifted and Talented

Although there are no federal data with regard to where students who are gifted and talented are educated, there is general agreement that cluster grouping, all-school enrichment models, and acceleration can enable students to be supported and educated in typical settings. The term enrichment refers to curricular and program delivery services that expand the curriculum by adding instruction in domains beyond what is in the general curriculum, present more challenging content, and teach critical thinking, problem-solving, and goal-setting skills. Enrichment programs can be tiered, much as is done in RtI or Multitiered Systems of Supports. In school-wide enrichment programs, teachers match the content of their courses to students' aptitudes, sophistication, and interests. Often they use enrichment strategies to engage students.

Educating Students Who Are Gifted and Talented

Creating autonomous learners is a major focus in the education of gifted and talented students. The Autonomous Learner Model (ALM) focuses on students' self-awareness, development of individual talents, enrichment, learning new knowledge, and engaging in individualized projects, among other features. Another approach to educating learners who are gifted involves differentiated instruction. In differentiated instruction, a teacher uses more than one instructional methodology, such as

increasing students' access to instructional materials in a variety of formats, expanding test-taking and data collection options, and varying the complexity and nature of content presented during the course of a unit of study.

Creativity and critical thinking are important dimensions of gifted learners. Promoting creativity goes hand-in-hand with efforts to enhance critical thinking and effective problem solving. Teachers who are focused on promoting creativity use active verbs like *brainstorm, invent, imagine,* and, indeed, *create* when creating activities and providing direction and instruction, and they engage students in exploring and investigating problems and challenges. A focus on student fluency (generating multiple ideas), flexibility (generating alternative ideas), originality, elaboration (generating details for ideas), and evaluation can promote creativity and critical thinking.

Addressing the Professional Standards

In Chapter 17, Students Who Are Gifted and Talented, we have covered the following Council for Exceptional Students (CEC) Initial Level Special Educator Preparation

Standards: Chapter 17—1.0, 1.2, 2.2, 3.3, 4.1, 4.2, 5.5, 5.6, 6.3, 7.1. Refer to the Appendix for a full listing of the CEC Standards with descriptions and supporting explanations.

Epilogue

An epilogue is the last word, our time to say goodbye. It is also our final chance to teach you, to remind you that you are in the profession of education and the culture of dignifying.

When you met Endrew in Chapter 1, you learned about students' and families' *rights* and your *duties*. You also learned about special education and its themes—*progress* through *research-based practices*, *high expectations* and *partnerships*, the *diversity* of the students you will teach and their claim to *cultural justice* and *self-determination*, their right and ability to be *included* in the general curriculum, and their inherent *dignity*, which you can enhance.

When you met McKyla and the Stuckey family in Chapters 2 and 3, you learned about *diversity* and *cultural justice*, and about families as your *partners*.

When you met Pablo in Chapter 4, Kelsey in Chapter 5, and Jack in Chapter 6, you learned that school-wide education is *inclusive education* and that what is good education for students with disabilities is also good education for all students.

You then met other students—Louise (learning disability), Kylie and Joey (communication), Anthony (emotional and behavioral disorder), Will (ADHD), Rachel (intellectual disability), Thasya (autism), Alana and Dylan (multiple and traumatic brain injury), Samuel and Shiloh (physical disability and epilepsy), Corbin and Martae (vision and hearing impairments), and John (gifted and talented).

When you met them, you learned how to teach them and that some of the practices you will use for them are practices you will use for other students, too: *research-based practices that ensure progress.*

What will happen to students like them if you do your job effectively?

Remember Samuel, whom you learned about in Chapter 14? He hasn't graduated yet from school, but is shining. Yes, he has cerebral palsy, but that fact doesn't prevent him from telling his story to his peers, their families, and his teachers. Would you have predicted his achievement? Did you have *high expectations* for him? You probably did and certainly should have. Special education's outcome includes Samuel's choice—his *self-determination*—and his capacity to teach others.

Remember Kelsey, whom you met in Chapter 5? After graduating from high school, she joined the staff of Project RENEW and taught about her journey and its support in schools and universities throughout the United States. She is another example of how *independent living* and *economic self-sufficiency* are outcomes of effective special education.

Now, meet Micah, whom you have not met before now. He has intellectual disability, but—don't be surprised!—he is a co-teacher in special education classes at Syracuse University, although his parents live in Detroit. His life is all about IDEA's principle of *equal opportunity, full participation, independent living,* and *economic self-sufficiency.*

Why do these students—each one in the 17 chapters you have read, and Micah, too—matter to you? It's not just because they are *emblems of the outcomes* that IDEA proclaims and that you will educate your students to attain. It is because they are *emblems of dignity.*

These students, each and every one of them, are like the students you will teach. Each has inherent dignity, that quality of worthiness that resides in them, that is part of them, no matter who they are and what they do or do not have ability to do.

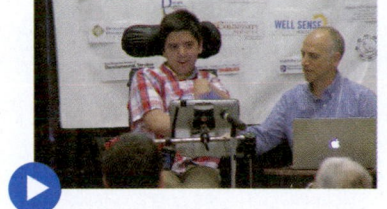

MyLab Education
Video Example EP.1
Samuel himself will tell you about his inclusive life in high school—his classes, his friends, and what else he has been doing.

MyLab Education
Video Example EP.2
Kelsey has a no-nonsense attitude when she shares her story with high school students.

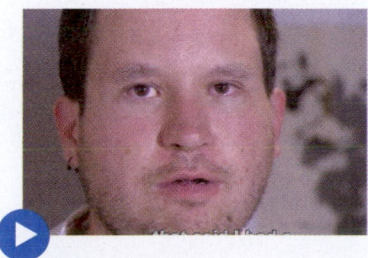

MyLab Education
Video Example EP.3
What surprises you about Micah Feldman or Samuel or Kelsey?

And each of them teaches you that you are not just in the education profession. Instead, they tell you that you are respecting their inherent worth, acknowledging their strengths, supporting them to prevail over the challenges that face them, making their rights come true, ensuring that their education is a truly progressive enterprise, and proclaiming dignity by carrying out what you have learned in our book. That's what your students will tell you. It's what we have tried to teach you.

Thank you for taking this journey with us. We wish you well.

Rud, Ann, Mike, and Karrie

CEC Initial Level Special Educator Preparation Standards[1]

Among the sine qua non characteristics of mature professions are the identification of the specialized knowledge and skill and the assurance to the public that practicing professionals possess the specialized knowledge and skill to practice safely and effectively (Neville, Herman, & Cohen, 2005). Through credentialing of professionals and professional recognition of preparation programs, special educators assure the public that practicing professionals have mastered the specialized skills for safe and effective practice.

Reflective of the personalized needs of individuals with exceptionalities, agencies prepare and credential special educators in a variety of specialty areas. To address these important specialty preparation areas, CEC has developed the seven CEC Preparation Standards on a three-step foundation. CEC uses a rigorous consensual validation process to identify sets of knowledge and skills for entry-level and advanced special educators in the variety of specialty areas. These specialty sets capture the professional knowledge base, including empirical research, disciplined inquiry, informed theory, and the wisdom of practice for their area of expertise for each proposed knowledge and skill. As a part of the validation process, CEC uses a rigorous consensual validation process (CEC Validation Study Resource Manual, 2010).

CEC synthesizes the specialty sets into seven major preparation standards organized under four areas of focus: learners and learning environments, curricular knowledge, assessment, specialized pedagogical skills, and professional and collaborative skills. CEC has further analyzed the seven preparation standards into key elements with which preparation programs align program assessments of special education candidates for CEC Professional Program Recognition.

While the CEC Preparation Standards cross special education specialty areas, CEC uses the specialty sets to inform and differentiate the content, contexts, and issues among and between the respective specialty areas (e.g., early childhood, mild/moderate, developmental disabilities, and learning disabilities). Preparation program faculties align their program assessments to the seven preparation standards with the key elements, and program reviewers review for alignment between the program assessments and the seven preparation standards with the key elements.

---

[1]NCATE approved November 2012.

Headings and Foci for the CEC Initial Preparation Standards
Learner and Learning
1. Learner Development and Individual Learning Differences
2. Learning Environments
Content Knowledge and Professional Foundations
3. Curricular Content Knowledge
Instructional Pedagogy
4. Assessment
5. Instructional Planning and Strategies
Professionalism and Collaboration
6. Professional Learning and Practice
7. Collaboration

Republished with permission of Council for Exceptional Children, from *What Every Special Educator Must Know: Ethics, Standards, and Guidelines for Special Educators* (2009); permission conveyed through Copyright Clearance Center, Inc.

CEC Initial Preparation Standard 1: Learner Development and Individual Learning Differences
1.0 Beginning special education professionals understand how exceptionalities may interact with development and learning and use this knowledge to provide meaningful and challenging learning experiences for individuals with exceptionalities.
Key Elements
1.1 Beginning special education professionals understand how language, culture, and family background influence the learning of individuals with exceptionalities.
1.2 Beginning special education professionals use understanding of development and individual differences to respond to the needs of individuals with exceptionalities.

Supporting Explanation

From its roots, special educators have placed the learning needs of the individual at the center of special education instruction. Historically, pedagogy or teaching skill has been at the heart of special education. Whether helping individuals with exceptionalities master addition, cooking, independent living, or philosophy, special educators have altered instructional variables to optimize learning for individuals with exceptionalities. The raison d'être for special education lies in the specialized professional knowledge and skills to individualize[2] access to learning in both specialized and general curricula for individuals with exceptionalities. Development of expertise begins with a thorough understanding of and respect for similarities and differences in human growth and development. Like all educators, beginning special educators first respect individuals with exceptionalities within the context of human development and individual learning differences.

Additionally, beginning special educators understand the characteristics between and among individuals with and without exceptionalities. They know exceptionalities can interact with multiple domains of human development to influence an individual's learning in school, in community, and throughout life.

Moreover, beginning special educators understand that the beliefs, traditions, and values across and within cultures can influence relationships among and between students, their families, and the school community. Furthermore, the experiences of individuals with exceptionalities can influence families, as well as the individual's ability to learn, interact socially, and live as a fulfilled contributing member of the community.

[2]As used herein the term "individualize" is used as synonymous with terms such as "personalize," "customize," "adaptive," and "differentiated."

However, beginning special educators' knowledge of human development goes beyond listing and ordering developmental milestones, and reciting legal definitions of exceptionalities. Beginning special educators understand how exceptionalities can interact with development and learning, and modify developmentally appropriate learning environments to provide relevant, meaningful, and challenging learning experiences for individuals with exceptionalities. Beginning special educators are active and resourceful in seeking to understand how primary language, culture, and family interact with the exceptionality to influence the individual's academic and social abilities, attitudes, values, interests, and career and post-secondary options.

These learning differences and their interactions provide the foundation upon which beginning special educators individualize instruction to provide developmentally meaningful and challenging learning for individuals with exceptionalities.

CEC Initial Preparation Standard 2: Learning Environments

2.0 Beginning special education professionals create safe, inclusive, culturally responsive learning environments so that individuals with exceptionalities become active and effective learners and develop emotional well-being, positive social interactions, and self-determination.

Key Elements

2.1 Beginning special education professionals, through collaboration with general educators and other colleagues, create safe, inclusive, culturally responsive learning environments to engage individuals with exceptionalities in meaningful learning activities and social interactions.

2.2 Beginning special education professionals use motivational and instructional interventions to teach individuals with exceptionalities how to adapt to different environments.

2.3 Beginning special education professionals know how to intervene safely and appropriately with individuals with exceptionalities in crisis.

Supporting Explanation

Like all educators, beginning special educators develop safe, inclusive, culturally responsive learning environments for all students. Beginning special educators also collaborate with education colleagues to include individuals with exceptionalities in general education environments and engage them in meaningful learning activities and social interactions.

Beginning special educators modify learning environments for individual needs. Knowledge regarding an individual's language, family, culture, and other significant contextual factors and how they interact with an individual's exceptionality guide the special educator in modifying learning environments and providing for the maintenance and generalization of acquired skills across environments and subjects.

Beginning special educators structure environments to encourage the independence, self-motivation, self-direction, personal empowerment, and self-advocacy of individuals with exceptionalities, and directly teach them to adapt to the expectations and demands of differing environments.

Frequently, special educators safely intervene with individuals with exceptionalities in crisis. Special educators are also perceived as a resource in behavior management that include the skills and knowledge to intervene safely and effectively before or when individuals with exceptionalities experience crisis, e.g., lose rational control over their behavior.

CEC Initial Preparation Standard 3: Curricular Content Knowledge

3.0 Beginning special education professionals use knowledge of general[3] and specialized curricula[4] to individualize learning for individuals with exceptionalities..

Key Elements

3.1 Beginning special education professionals understand the central concepts, structures of the discipline, and tools of inquiry of the content areas they teach, and can organize this knowledge, integrate cross-disciplinary skills, and develop meaningful learning progressions for individuals with exceptionalities.

3.2 Beginning special education professionals understand and use general and specialized content knowledge for teaching across curricular content areas to individualize learning for individuals with exceptionalities.

3.3 Beginning special education professionals modify general and specialized curricula to make them accessible to individuals with exceptionalities.

Supporting Explanation

The professional knowledge base in general education has made clear that the educators' understanding of the central concepts and structures of the discipline, and tools of inquiry related to the academic subject-matter content areas they teach make a significant difference in student learning. There is good reason to generalize this conclusion to special educators.

Within the general curricula, beginning special educators demonstrate in their planning and teaching a solid base of understanding of the central concepts, structures of the discipline, and tools of inquiry of the academic subject-matter content areas they teach so they are able to organize knowledge, integrate cross-disciplinary skills, develop meaningful learning progressions, and collaborate with general educators in:

- Teaching[5] or co-teaching the content of the general curriculum to individuals with exceptionalities across a wide range of performance levels.

- Designing appropriate learning and performance accommodations and modifications for individuals with exceptionalities in academic subject matter content of the general curriculum.

Additionally, beginning special educators use a variety of specialized curricula, e.g., academic, strategic, social, emotional, and independence curricula, to individualize meaningful and challenging learning for individuals with exceptionalities.

CEC Initial Preparation Standard 4: Assessment

4.0 Beginning special education professionals use multiple methods of assessment and data sources in making educational decisions.

Key Elements

4.1 Beginning special education professionals select and use technically sound formal and informal assessments that minimize bias.

4.2 Beginning special education professionals use knowledge of measurement principles and practices to interpret assessment results and guide educational decisions for individuals with exceptionalities.

4.3 Beginning special education professionals in collaboration with colleagues and families use multiple types of assessment information in making decisions about individuals with exceptionalities.

4.4 Beginning special education professionals engage individuals with exceptionalities to work toward quality learning and performance and provide feedback to guide them.

Supporting Explanation

Like all educators, beginning special educators understand measurement theory and practice for addressing issues of validity, reliability, norms, bias, and interpretation of assessment results. Like their general education colleagues, beginning special

---

[3]As used, "general curricula" means the academic content of the general curricula including math, reading, English/language arts, science, social studies, and the arts.

[4]As used, "specialized curricula" means the content of specialized interventions or sets of interventions including, but not limited to academic, strategic, communicative, social, emotional, and independence curricula.

[5]Because of the significant role that content specific subject matter knowledge plays at the secondary school level, special education teachers routinely teach secondary level academic subject matter content classes in consultation or collaboration with one or more general education teachers appropriately licensed in the respective content area. However, whenever special education teachers assume sole responsibility for teaching a general curriculum academic subject matter course at the secondary level, the special educators possess a solid subject matter content knowledge base sufficient to assure the students can meet state curriculum standards.

educators regularly monitor the learning progress of individuals with exceptionalities in both general and specialized content and make instructional adjustments based on these data.

Beginning special educators also use assessment information to support a wide variety of decisions within special education. Beginning special educators understand the legal policies and ethical principles of measurement and assessment related to special education referral, eligibility, program planning, individualized instruction, learning, and placement for individuals with exceptionalities, including individuals from culturally and linguistically diverse backgrounds.

Beginning special educators understand the appropriate use and limitations of various types of assessments, and collaborate with families and other colleagues to assure nonbiased, meaningful assessments and decision-making.

Beginning special educators conduct formal and informal assessments of behavior, learning, achievement, and environments to individualize the learning experiences that support the growth and development of individuals with exceptionalities.

Beginning special educators make multiple types of assessment decisions, including strategic adaptations and modifications in response to an individuals' constellation of social, linguistic, and learning factors, in ways to minimize bias.

Beginning special educators use assessment information to identify supports and adaptations required for individuals with exceptionalities to access the general curriculum and to participate in school, system, and statewide assessment programs.

Beginning special educators integrate the results of assessments to develop long-range individualized instructional plans anchored in both general and special education curricula, and translate these individualized plans into carefully selected shorter-range goals and objectives. They also have a central role integrating the results of assessments in developing a variety of individualized plans, including family service plans, transition plans, behavior change plans, etc.

Beginning special educators use available technologies routinely to support their assessments. With the rapid advance and use of technology, special educators use technologies to support and manage assessment of individuals with exceptionalities. The appropriate and efficient use of technology to support assessment tasks is rapidly becoming an essential tool for special education professionals.

CEC Initial Preparation Standard 5: Instructional Planning and Strategies

5.0 Beginning special education professionals select, adapt, and use a repertoire of evidence-based instructional strategies[6] to advance learning of individuals with exceptionalities.

Key Elements

5.1 Beginning special education professionals consider an individual's abilities, interests, learning environments, and cultural and linguistic factors in the selection, development, and adaptation of learning experiences for individuals with exceptionalities.

5.2 Beginning special education professionals use technologies to support instructional assessment, planning, and delivery for individuals with exceptionalities.

5.3 Beginning special education professionals are familiar with augmentative and alternative communication systems and a variety of assistive technologies to support the communication and learning of individuals with exceptionalities.

5.4 Beginning special education professionals use strategies to enhance language development and communication skills of individuals with exceptionalities.

5.5 Beginning special education professionals develop and implement a variety of education and transition plans for individuals with exceptionalities across a wide range of settings and different learning experiences in collaboration with individuals, families, and teams.

5.6 Beginning special education professionals teach to mastery and promote generalization of learning.

5.7 Beginning special education professionals teach cross-disciplinary knowledge and skills such as critical thinking and problem solving to individuals with exceptionalities.

[6]Instructional strategies, as used throughout this document, include intervention used in academic and specialized curricula.

Supporting Explanation

In individualizing access to general and specialized content, individualized decision-making and individualized instruction are at the center of special education practice. In the selection, development, and adaptation of learning experiences for individuals with exceptionalities, beginning special educators consider an individual's abilities, interests, learning environments, and cultural and linguistic factors. The interactions of these factors with the implications of an individual's exceptionality guide the special educator's selection, adaptation, and use of a repertoire of evidence-based instructional strategies in promoting positive learning results in general and special curricula and in modifying learning environments for individuals with exceptionalities appropriately.

Beginning special educators teach personalized literacy and numeracy to individuals with exceptionalities who are often non-responsive individuals in tiered intervention models. In their planning and teaching with these individuals, beginning special educators emphasize explicit instruction with modeling and guided practice to assure acquisition and fluency, as well as the development, maintenance, and generalization of knowledge and skills across environments, settings, and the life span through approaches such as cross-curricular lesson planning. Moreover, they enhance 21st century student outcomes such as critical thinking, creative problem solving, and collaboration skills for individuals with exceptionalities, and increase their self-awareness and reliance, self-management and control, and self-efficacy and advocacy.

Beginning special educators provide effective language models and use communication strategies and resources to facilitate understanding of subject matter for individuals with exceptionalities whose primary language is not English. Beginning special educators match their communication methods to an individual's language proficiency and cultural and linguistic differences. Beginning special educators are familiar with augmentative and alternative communication systems and assistive technologies to support and enhance the language and communication of individuals with exceptionalities, and use individualized strategies to enhance language development and teach communication skills to individuals with exceptionalities.

Beginning special educators implement a variety of individualized learning plans across a wide range of settings and a range of different learning experiences, including individualized family service plans, individualized transition plans, and individualized behavior change plans.

Transitions are specific points of potential difficulty for individuals with exceptionalities. Beginning special educators develop a variety of individualized transition plans, such as transitions from preschool to elementary school and from secondary settings to a variety of postsecondary work and learning contexts.

For individuals with exceptionalities in early childhood, special educators focus the individualized instruction plan within the context of family services, taking into account the needs, priorities, and concerns of families as the primary providers of instruction.

Beginning special educators facilitate all personalized instructional planning within a collaborative context including the individuals with exceptionalities, families, professional colleagues, and personnel from other agencies as appropriate.

Beginning special educators use technologies routinely to support all phases of instruction planning. With the rapid advance and use of technology, special educators use technologies to support and manage all phases of planning, implementing, and evaluating instruction.

CEC Initial Preparation Standard 6: Professional Learning and Ethical Practice

6.0 Beginning special education professionals use foundational knowledge of the field and their professional Ethical Principles and Practice Standards to inform special education practice, to engage in lifelong learning, and to advance the profession.

Key Elements

6.1 Beginning special education professionals use professional Ethical Principles and Professional Practice Standards to guide their practice.

6.2 Beginning special education professionals understand how foundational knowledge and current issues influence professional practice.

6.3 Beginning special education professionals understand that diversity is a part of families, cultures, and schools, and that complex human issues can interact with the delivery of special education services.

6.4 Beginning special education professionals understand the significance of lifelong learning and participate in professional activities and learning communities.

6.5 Beginning special education professionals advance the profession by engaging in activities such as advocacy and mentoring.

6.6 Beginning special education professionals provide guidance and direction to paraeducators, tutors, and volunteers.

Supporting Explanation

Beginning special educators practice in multiple roles and complex situations across wide age and developmental ranges that require ongoing attention to legal matters and serious consideration of serious professional and ethical issues. The Ethical Principles and Professional Practice Standards of the Council for Exceptional Children guide beginning special education professionals. These principles and standards provide benchmarks by which special educators practice and evaluate each other professionally.

Beginning special educators understand special education as an evolving and changing discipline based on philosophies, evidence-based principles and theories, policies, and historical points of view that continue to influence the field of special education and the education of and services for individuals with exceptionalities and their families in both school and society. Beginning special educators understand how these factors influence professional practice, including assessment, instructional planning, implementation, and program evaluation.

Beginning special educators are sensitive to the aspects of diversity with individuals with exceptionalities and their families; how human diversity can influence families, cultures, and schools; and how these complex issues can each interact with the delivery of special education services. Of special significance is the growth in the number and prevalence of English Language Learners (ELL) and the provision of effective special education services for ELL with exceptionalities and their families.

Beginning special educators understand the relationships of the organization of special education services to the organization of schools, school systems, and education-related agencies within the country and cultures in which they practice. Beginning special educators are aware of how their own and others' attitudes, behaviors, and ways of communicating can influence their practice, and use this knowledge as a foundation to inform their own personal understandings and philosophies of special education.

Beginning special educators engage in professional activities and participate actively in professional learning communities that benefit individuals with exceptionalities, their families, colleagues, and their own professional growth. Beginning special educators view themselves as lifelong learners and regularly reflect on and adjust their practice, and develop and use personalized professional development plans. Beginning special educators plan and engage in activities that foster their professional growth and keep them current with evidence-based practices. Beginning special educators also know how to recognize their own skill limits and practice within them.

There has been substantial growth in the use of special education paraeducators over the past few years, and beginning special educators frequently provide guidance and direction to paraeducators and others, such as classroom volunteers and tutors.

CEC Initial Preparation Standard 7: Collaboration

7.0 Beginning special education professionals collaborate with families, other educators, related service providers, individuals with exceptionalities, and personnel from community agencies in culturally responsive ways to address the needs of individuals with exceptionalities across a range of learning experiences.

Key Elements

7.1 Beginning special education professionals use the theory and elements of effective collaboration.

7.2 Beginning special education professionals serve as a collaborative resource to colleagues.

7.3 Beginning special education professionals use collaboration to promote the well-being of individuals with exceptionalities across a wide range of settings and collaborators.

Supporting Explanation

One of the significant changes in education over the past several decades is the rapid growth of collaborative educational teams to address the educational needs of students. The diversity of the students, complexity of curricular demands, growing influence of technology, and rising targets for learner outcomes in the 21st century have created the demand for teams of educators collaborating together to ensure all students are effectively learning challenging curricula.

Special educators view general educators as possessing knowledge and expertise in curriculum, and general educators reciprocally view special educators as having knowledge and expertise in the education of individuals with exceptionalities. Beginning special educators embrace their role as a resource to colleagues and use the theory and elements of collaboration across a wide range of contexts and collaborators.

Beginning special educators collaborate with their general education colleagues to create learning environments that meaningfully include individuals with exceptionalities, and that foster cultural understanding, safety and emotional well-being; positive social interactions; and active engagement. Additionally, special educators use collaboration to facilitate personalized instruction planning and transitions of individuals with exceptionalities in promoting the learning and well-being of individuals with exceptionalities across a wide range of settings and different learning experiences.

Beginning special educators routinely collaborate with related-service providers, other educators including special education paraeducators, personnel from community agencies, and others to address the needs of individuals with exceptionalities.

Special educators have long recognized the positive significance of the active involvement of individuals with exceptionalities and their families in the education process, and special educators involve individuals with exceptionalities and their families collaboratively in all aspects of the education of individuals with exceptionalities.

Glossary

Abacus is a tool composed of beads on vertical rods that is used by students with visual impairments to help them with mathematical calculations. The abacus is not a calculator but is similar to solving a math problem with paper and pencil.

Absence seizures are a type of generalized seizure that cause the person to lose consciousness only briefly.

Academic achievement standards define the knowledge, skills, and understanding that students should attain in academic subjects.

Acceleration involves students' skipping one or more grades in order to experience higher levels of instruction and/or attending a higher-grade-level program for part of the school day.

Accommodations are changes to the presentation of instructional content or test or assessment administration that support a student to participate in the learning activity or assessment, but that does not in any way modify the content or assessment.

Acquired disorder is a disorder that occurs well after birth.

Acquired hearing loss occurs after a child is born.

Acquired injury means that the injury occurred after a child was born.

Acuity is a measure of the sharpness and clarity of vision. It is determined by having an individual stand at a specified distance to read a standard eye chart, each line of which is composed of symbols printed at a certain size.

Adaptive behavior refers to the typical performance of individuals without disabilities in meeting the expectations of their various environments.

Adaptive skills include conceptual, social, and practical competencies for functioning in typical community settings.

Additions occur when students place a vowel between two consonants.

Adventitious visual impairment means that the impairment results from an advent (e.g., loss of sight caused by a hereditary condition that has just manifested itself) or an event (e.g., loss of sight caused by trauma).

Agoraphobia is a childhood anxiety disorder in which a person is extremely afraid related to at least two of the following three circumstances: (1) being in a situation in which getting help or escaping is difficult, (2) using public transportation, and (3) being in an open space.

Alternate academic achievement standards are academic achievement standards for students with the most significant cognitive disabilities. Such standards must align with the state's academic achievement standards, promote access to the general education curriculum, and ensure students are on track to pursue postsecondary education or competitive integrated employment.

Alternate assessment means evaluating performance for students for whom test accommodations are not sufficient to enable them to participate in the typical state- or district-wide assessment.

Alternate assessments based on alternate academic achievement standards (AA-AAAS) are assessments aligned with alternate academic achievement standards for students with the most significant cognitive disabilities.

Alternate assessments based on grade-level achievement standards (AA-GLAS) enable students to demonstrate skills and knowledge on grade-level assessments, but the assessments are modified versions of the general assessment.

Alternate assessments based on modified achievement standards (AA-MAS) are used for students across disability categories (other than primarily students with the most significant cognitive disabilities) who need both accommodations and some modifications to the grade-level standards.

American Sign Language (ASL) is the most widely used sign language among deaf adults in North America.

Anxiety disorder is characterized by overwhelming fear, worry, and/or uneasiness. The condition includes phobia, generalized anxiety disorder, panic disorder, obsessive-compulsive disorder, and post-traumatic stress disorder.

Apgar test is a method for determining the health of a newborn immediately in transition to life outside the womb. The screening occurs in the first minute after birth and again at the fifth minute after birth.

Applied behavior analysis (ABA) uses the principles of operant psychology to develop techniques that reduce problem behavior and/or increase positive behavior.

Appropriate education is an IDEA principle that requires schools to provide an individualized educational program for students with disabilities that is appropriate to their educational strengths and needs.

Apraxia is a motor speech disorder that affects the way in which a student plans to produce speech.

Articulation is a speaker's production of individual or sequenced sounds.

Asperger syndrome describes the traits of individuals on the autism spectrum who have significant challenges in social and emotional functioning but without significant delays in language development or intellectual functioning.

Assistive listening device (ALD) amplifies sound to help people hear speech better, such as an FM/DM system or a hearing aid.

Asthma is a chronic lung condition characterized by airway obstruction, inflammation, and increased sensitivity.

Ataxic cerebral palsy involves unsteadiness, lack of coordination and balance, and varying degrees of difficulty with standing and walking.

Athetoid cerebral palsy involves abrupt, involuntary movements of the head, neck, face, and extremities, particularly the upper ones.

Atrophy refers to lost or reduced muscle strength.

Audiogram is a graphic representation of an individual's response to sound in terms of frequency (hertz) and loudness (decibels).

Audiologist has special training in testing and measuring hearing.

Audiometer is a machine that measures hearing threshold, the softest level at which sound can first be detected at various sound frequencies.

Audiometry refers to a hearing test, using a device called an audiometer, which provides a graph showing hearing thresholds at various levels of pitch and loudness.

Audition is the hearing process.

Auditory brainstem response (ABR) assessment is a test that determines how well a child's auditory nerve responds to sound, usually conducted with very young babies who cannot be tested using traditional audiological methods.

Augmentative and alternative communication (AAC) refers to the devices, techniques, and strategies used by students who are unable to communicate fully through natural speech and/or writing.

Auricle or pinna is the top of the external ear; it channels sound into the ear canal.

Autism spectrum disorder refers to a developmental disability resulting in and characterized by persistent impairments in social interactions, social communication, and stereotyped or repetitive movements, including inflexibility in routines or patterns.

Autonomous learning model assists students in dealing with the social-emotional issues that might accompany their giftedness.

Bacterial meningitis is an infection of the meninges, the three membranes enveloping the brain and the spinal cord.

Behavior intervention plan is a document that educators, parents, and students prepare based on the functional behavior assessment to prevent and/or ameliorate a student's behavior that impedes learning or causes discipline under IDEA.

Behavioral audiological evaluations are hearing tests that require a child to respond to a series of beeps called pure tones to indicate that she hears a sound.

Behind-the-ear hearing aid is worn on the outside of the outer ear.

Bidialectal refers to someone who uses two variations of a language.

Bilateral is a hearing loss that occurs in both ears.

Bilingual refers to someone who uses two languages equally well.

Bipolar disorder refers to a condition in which a person experiences exaggerated mood swings—for example, sometimes feeling depressed and other times experiencing heightened activity, energy, and a sense of strength. (These latter experiences are sometimes referred to as mania.)

Bone-anchored hearing aid transmits sound via vibrations of the skull rather than sending sound down the ear canal and through the middle ear, like a traditional hearing aid.

Braille is a method of writing that uses raised dots in specific configurations that can be read and interpreted by people who are blind (and who have received appropriate instruction) by running their fingers across the dots.

Braille contractions are shortcuts for writing letter combinations in braille. Intended to save space and reading time, these contractions may represent a whole word or part of a word. As a result, the braille version of printed material is usually composed of fewer symbols than the print version, even though both include the same words.

Braillewriter is a mechanical tool that the blind use to create written materials in braille, manipulating the 6 keys (one for each dot) and a space bar.

Bullying is a form of externalizing behavior. It can consist of verbal abuse—calling a student by a stigmatizing name; cyberabuse—using online forums or networks to attack a student's behavior or characteristics; or physical abuse of any amount or degree, including sexual abuse.

Catatonic behavior is behavior that lacks typical movement, activity, and/or expression.

Cerebral palsy refers to a lack of muscle control that affects a student's ability to move and to maintain balance and posture; it has a neurological basis.

Chromosomes direct each cell's activity and contain DNA and genes that determine a person's physical and mental condition.

Circle of friends refers to the individuals who surround a person with a disability with support that is consistent with the person's choices and that advances the person's self-determination, full citizenship, relationships, positive contributions, strengths, and choices.

Classroom-centered intervention refers to classroom-based strategies to intervene against poor academic achievement and aggressive or shy behavior.

Clean intermittent catheterization (CIC) refers to the procedure whereby a person or an attendant (a trained health aide) inserts a tube into the person's urethra to induce urination. It is "clean" because the procedure is done under sterile conditions, and it is "intermittent" because it is done as needed or on a regular schedule; the tube is not permanently placed in the person's urethra.

Cleft palate or lip describes a condition in which a person has a split in the upper part of the oral cavity or the upper lip.

Closed head injury results when the brain whips back and forth during an accident, causing it to bounce off the inside of the skull. It does not involve penetration or a fracture of the bone of the skull.

Closed-captioned technology translates dialogue from a spoken language to a printed form (captions) that is then inserted at the bottom of a television or movie screen.

Cochlea is a snail-shaped bony structure that houses the actual organ of hearing.

Cochlear implant is an electronic device that is surgically implanted under the skin behind the ear and contains a magnet that couples to a magnet in a sound transmitter that is worn externally.

Cognitive taxonomies are ordered lists of cognitive skills or activities that can be used to differentiate expectations for students.

Compacting the curriculum involves first testing students to identify the content they have already mastered and then teaching them only the concepts that they have not yet mastered.

Complex communication needs mean students have difficulties producing speech that can impact communication and social development.

Computer-assisted instruction (CAI) refers to the use of computer technology to deliver instruction.

Conceptually Accurate Signed English (CASE) is a sign system used in the United States that involves signing concepts rather than the literal English translation.

Concomitant refers to two or more conditions (in this case, disabilities) occurring at the same time.

Conduct disorder consists of a persistent pattern of antisocial behavior that significantly interferes with others' rights or with schools and communities' behavioral expectations.

Conductive hearing loss occurs when there is damage to the outer or middle ear. This kind of loss can usually be corrected.

Congenital refers to an impairment that is present from birth or from the time very near birth; visual impairment occurs at birth or, in the case of blindness, before visual memories have been established.

Congenital deafness is a hearing loss that is present at birth.

Congenital disorder is a disorder that occurs at or before birth.

Congenital hearing loss is present upon birth, likely occurring either in utero or during birth.

Cooperative learning refers to instructional strategies in which small groups of students focus on a common learning task or activity.

Criterion-referenced assessments refer to measures of student performance compared to an existing or predetermined standard.

Cultural deficit theory blames the failure of students from culturally and linguistically diverse backgrounds on the disadvantages that they experienced within their own cultures.

Cultural difference theories also called cultural mismatch theories, contend that failure of students from culturally and linguistically diverse backgrounds in school cannot be attributed solely to their lack of assimilation into European culture.

Cultural reproduction theory holds that "racial and class inequity are reproduced over time through institutional and individual actions and decisions that maintain the status quo at the expense of less privileged groups."

Curriculum extension refers to efforts to expand the breadth and depth of the coverage of a given topic.

Curriculum-based measurement (CBM) involves direct assessment of a student's skills in the content of the curriculum that is being taught.

Cytomegalovirus (CMV) is a virus that is common and that is retained by the body once a person is infected. Most people have no symptoms from the virus or minor symptoms, but it can result in birth irregularities for the fetus/infant.

Deaf is a term used to describe a hearing loss greater than 70 to 90 decibels that results in severe oral speech and language delay or that prevents a person from understanding spoken language through hearing.

Deaf community is a group of individuals who are deaf; share a culture, attitudes, and a set of beliefs; and use American Sign Language to communicate.

Deaf-blindness refers to concomitant hearing and visual impairments, the combination of which causes such severe communication and other developmental and educational needs that they cannot be accommodated in special education programs solely for students with deafness or students with blindness.

Decibel (dB) is the unit used to express how loud sound is.

Deficit thinking refers to the idea that students from minority or underrepresented groups, such as students of color or students

who are immigrants, do not have what it takes to be successful in school due to some aspect of their culture.

Developmental disability refers to a condition that emerges during the developmental period, typically described as from birth to 18 years of age.

Dialect is a regional variation of a language, as when someone speaks English using terms or pronunciations common only in that region.

Differentiated instruction involves using different strategies such as flexible student instructional grouping, learning stations and learning centers, and two educators in the same classroom.

Discrete trial teaching is based on the three-term contingency outlined by applied behavior analysis: the discriminative stimulus, the response, and the reinforcer or consequence.

Distortions are modifications of the production of a phoneme in a word.

Domains of family quality of life include emotional well-being, parenting, family interaction, physical/material well-being, and disability-related support.

Due process hearing is a "mini-trial" before an impartial hearing officer at which educators and parents, usually represented by lawyers, present evidence upon which the hearing officer makes a decision.

Duration is the length of time any speech sound requires.

Dyskinetic cerebral palsy involves impairments in muscle tone affecting the whole body and changing throughout the day and week.

Dyslexia refers to the condition of having severe difficulty in learning to read.

Early hearing, detection, and intervention (EHDI) programs facilitate hearing screening of babies in the hospital, diagnoses of hearing loss by a pediatric audiologist, and getting intervention from trained professionals as soon as possible.

Early intervention (EI) is intervention that occurs within the first three years of life, focused on all areas of development, but especially speech and language for children with hearing loss.

Echolalia means repetitive speech and involves the repetition of words and phrases that the person hears.

Educational advocate is an adult appointed by the state education agency to represent the interests of children whose parental ties have been severed in educational decision making, such as IEP meetings.

Educational interpreter is a person who interprets spoken information into signed information, during school or school-related activities with students who are deaf.

Embedded instruction refers to instructional trials that are inserted (or embedded) into naturally occurring activities during the instructional day.

Encephalitis refers to inflammation of the brain.

Enrichment programs (including all-school enrichment) involve implementing practices that benefit students who are gifted (differentiation, creativity instruction, etc.) with all students in the school.

Epilepsy is a neural condition characterized by recurrent and unprovoked seizures.

Errorless learning refers to a procedure that presents the discriminative stimuli and arranges the delivery of prompts in a learning situation in such a way as to ensure that the student gives only correct responses.

Etiology describes the cause or origin of a medical condition.

Eugenics refers to procedures to improve the human race by encouraging the birth of children with allegedly "good" hereditary qualities and discouraging or preventing the birth of those with allegedly "undesirable" hereditary qualities.

Eustachian tube is the structure that extends from the throat into the middle ear cavity; its primary purpose is to equalize the air pressure on the eardrum when a person swallows or yawns.

Event recording involves an observer recording every occurrence of a behavior during an observation period instead of using the yes/no recording per interval that is characteristic of time sampling.

Exclusionary standard refers to embedding particular exemptions within a definition. For example, in the IDEA definition of learning disabilities, learning disabilities do not include learning problems that primarily result from visual impairment; hearing loss; mental retardation; emotional disturbance; or environmental, cultural, or economic disadvantages.

Expanded core curriculum describes the areas of instruction in which students with visual impairments need additional instruction because of the impact of their visual impairment on incidental learning. It includes compensatory skills, orientation and mobility, social interaction skills, independent living skills, recreation and leisure skills, career education, use of assistive technology, visual efficiency skills, and self-determination.

Expressive language disorder is characterized by difficulty in formulating ideas and information.

Externalizing behaviors are behavior disorders comprising aggressive, acting-out, and noncompliant behaviors.

Family means two or more people who regard themselves to be a family and who carry out the functions that families typically perform.

Family engagement refers to developing a trusting partnership between families and educators in which they share responsibility for student achievement and school improvement.

Family quality of life refers to the extent to which the family's needs are met, family members enjoy their life together, and family members have the chance to do the things that are important to them.

Family-professional partnerships are relationships in which families and professionals collaborate, capitalizing on each other's judgments and expertise in order to increase the benefits of education for students, families, and professionals.

Field observation involves observing and recording, in a longhand, anecdotal format, what a student is doing.

Field of vision (visual field) is the entire area of which an individual is visually aware when the person is directing her gaze straight ahead, typically 160 degrees.

Fingerspelling uses a hand representation for all twenty-six letters of the alphabet.

Fluency is the rate and rhythm of speaking.

FM/DM system is a system that allows a student to hear a person's voice (such as the teacher's voice) without the ambient noise of the environment (like the classroom). The speaker wears or uses a microphone which transmits the voice directly to the student's hearing device wirelessly.

Formative assessment involves frequent assessments of student progress to check for student understanding and learning and inform instruction.

Frequency is the pitch of a sound.

Functional behavioral assessment (FBA) is a process used to determine a specific relationship between a student's behaviors and the circumstances that triggered those behaviors, especially those that impede a student's ability to learn.

Functional disorders are those with no identifiable organic or neurological cause.

Functional vision assessment (FVA) is an evaluation of how an individual uses his vision to perform tasks. It results in a description of what an individual with a visual impairment does with his available vision, not an acuity measurement.

Functionally blind describes individuals who can use their available vision to some limited degree but acquire information about the environment primarily through their auditory and tactile senses.

General education curriculum refers to the curriculum used by nondisabled students.

Generalization refers to the ability to transfer knowledge or behavior learned for doing one task to another task and to make that transfer across different settings or environments.

Generalized anxiety disorder consists of excessive, overwhelming worry not caused by any recent experience.

Generalized seizures involve both cerebral hemispheres. An alteration of consciousness is a primary characteristic, and the seizure affects both sides of the body.

Genetic deficit theories typically support the notion that nonwhite people are genetically deficient when compared to white people.

Goal attainment scaling is a process that enables teachers to compare goals and to quantify student goal attainment.

Hard of hearing is a term used for individuals who have hearing loss of 25 to 70 decibels in the better ear, who benefit from amplification, and who communicate primarily through spoken language.

Hearing aids are small devices worn on or in the ear that make sounds louder, especially speech sounds. Hearing aids are worn by people with hearing loss of all ages.

Herpes virus is a virus leading to symptoms that range from cold sores, to genital lesions, to encephalitis; it causes disabilities in early infancy.

Hertz (Hz) is the unit used to express the frequency of sound and is measured in terms of the number of cycles that vibrating sound molecules complete per second.

Hyperactivity refers to behaviors associated with frequent movement, difficulty concentrating, and talking excessively.

Hyperbilirubinemia results from an excess accumulation of bilirubin in the blood, which can result in jaundice, a yellowing of the complexion and the whites of the eyes.

Hypernasality is when air is allowed to pass through the nasal cavity on sounds other than /m/, /n/, and /ng/.

Hyponasality occurs because air cannot pass through the nose and comes through the mouth instead.

Hypoxia is the lack of oxygen.

Impulsivity refers to behaviors such as difficulty awaiting one's turn, interrupting or intruding on others, and blurting out answers before questions have been completed.

Incidence refers to the rate of newly diagnosed cases of a condition in a specified time period (month, year, etc.).

Incidental learning occurs when an individual learns about a process or concept primarily through observation and without others knowingly providing instruction.

Inclusionary standard refers to embedding certain criteria within a definition so as to clearly state the conditions that the definition covers. For example, in the IDEA definition of learning disabilities, perceptual disabilities, brain injury, minimal brain dysfunction, dyslexia, and developmental aphasia are included conditions.

Incus is one of the small bones in the middle ear. It is sometimes called the *anvil* because of its shape.

Individualized education program (IEP) is a written plan for serving students with disabilities ages three through twenty-one.

Individualized family services plan (IFSP) is a written plan for providing services to infants and toddlers, ages zero to three, and their families.

Intensity (loudness or softness) is based on the perception of the listener and is determined by the air pressure coming from the lungs through the vocal folds.

Internalizing behaviors are behavior disorders comprising social withdrawal, depression, anxiety, obsessions, and compulsions.

Intracranial hemorrhage is a neurological complication of extremely premature infants in which the immature blood vessels bleed into the brain.

Keyword strategies teach students to link a keyword to a new word or concept to help them remember the new material.

Language is a structured, shared, rule-governed symbolic system for communicating.

Language disorder is difficulty in receiving, understanding, and formulating ideas and information.

Learning media assessment (LMA) is an evaluation of students who have visual impairments to determine the learning medium in which they function most efficiently as well as to identify those media in which additional instruction may be necessary.

Learning medium is the term used to describe the format(s) of reading and literacy materials available to individuals who have visual impairments and may include braille, print, large print, audiotapes, and access technology.

Learning strategies help students with learning disabilities to learn independently and to generalize, or transfer, their skills and behaviors to new situations.

Least restrictive environment (LRE) is an IDEA principle that requires that students with disabilities be educated to the maximum extent appropriate with students who do not have a disability and that they be removed from regular education settings only when the nature or severity of their disability cannot be addressed with the use of supplementary aids and services.

Legal blindness is a term that refers to individuals whose central visual acuity, when measured in both eyes and when they are wearing corrective lenses, is 20/200 or whose visual field is no more than 20 degrees.

Letter strategies employ acronyms or a string of letters to remember a list of words or concepts.

Life space analysis is a process in which teachers collect two kinds of data: (1) baseline data about how well a student functions in certain community settings and (2) information about the student's current environments and prospective environments for community-based instruction.

Long-term memory involves storing information permanently for later recall.

Loop systems involve closed-circuit wiring that sends FM signals from an audio system directly to an electronic coil in a student's hearing aid. The receiver picks up the signals, much as a remote-control device sends infrared signals to a television.

Low vision is experienced by individuals with a visual impairment who can use their vision as a primary channel for learning.

Low vision specialist is an individual, usually an optometrist, who has specialized in the measurement of the basic visual skills of individuals with low vision and who is knowledgeable about and prescribes glasses and other assistive devices that facilitate visual functioning in people whose vision is impaired.

Malleus is a small bone in the middle ear. It is sometimes called the *hammer* because of its shape.

Manual approach involves teaching the use of sign language for communication.

Mastery assessment is a process in which teachers collect data using frequent assessments or probes based upon rubrics or objectives that measure student mastery of content in lessons or units.

Mean refers to an average.

Mediation is a process in which the educators and parents submit their dispute to an independent, disinterested, and trained person who attempts to identify common ground and to make that common ground the basis for the resolution of a dispute.

Meningocele refers to the condition in which the covering of the spinal cord, but not the cord itself, protrudes through the opening created by a defect in the spine. This condition usually does not cause a person to experience mobility impairments.

Mixed cerebral palsy combines spastic muscle tone and the involuntary movements of athetoid cerebral palsy.

Mixed hearing loss is a type of hearing loss that is caused by both conductive and sensorineural damage.

Mnemonic is a device such as a rhyme, formula, or acronym that is used to aid memory.

Mood disorder involves an extreme deviation in either a depressed or an elevated direction or sometimes in both directions at different times.

Morpheme is the smallest meaningful unit of speech.

Morphology is the system that governs the structure of words.

Multidimensional model of intelligence considers multiple domains of intelligence as contrasted to only intellectual ability or academic achievement.

Multimodal treatments involves multiple interventions or treatments across modes or types of therapies.

Myelomeningocele refers to a condition in which the protrusion or sac contains not only the spinal cord's covering but also a portion of the spinal cord or nerve roots. This condition results in varying degrees of leg weakness, inability to control bowels or bladder, and a variety of physical problems such as dislocated hips or club feet.

Neural tube defects refer to birth defects that impact the brain, spine, or spinal cord (all part of the neural system).

Neuroimaging provides noninvasive detailed pictures of various parts of the brain that are helpful in determining the presence of a disability.

Nondiscriminatory evaluation is an IDEA principle that requires schools to determine what each student's disability is and how it relates to the student's education. The evaluation must be carried out in a culturally responsive way.

Norm group is a comparison group usually representing an average standard of achievement or development for a specific age group or grade level.

Norm-referenced assessments refer to measures that are standardized with a large sample and scores from which are compared to scores from the large sample, typically reporting a percentile ranking.

Obsessive-compulsive disorder are obsessions manifesting as repetitive, persistent, and intrusive impulses, images, or thoughts (i.e., repetitive thoughts about death or illness) and/or compulsions manifesting as repetitive, stereotypical behaviors (i.e., hand washing or counting).

Omissions occur when a child leaves a phoneme out of a word.

Open head injury refers to a brain injury in which the wound penetrates the scalp and skull.

Oppositional defiant disorder causes a pattern of negativistic, hostile, disobedient, and defiant behaviors.

Oral motor exam is examination of the appearance, strength, and range of motion of the lips, tongue, palate, teeth, and jaw.

Oral/aural format emphasizes the use of amplified sound to develop oral language.

Organ of Corti refers to the organ of hearing.

Organic disorders are those caused by an identifiable problem in the neuromuscular mechanism of the person.

Orientation and mobility (O&M) is a term used to describe the two components of travel: orientation (knowing where you are and where you want to go) and mobility (the safe, efficient, graceful movement between two locations). For students with visual impairments, instruction in O&M often is necessary.

Otitis media is an infection in the middle ear that can result in conductive hearing loss.

Otologist is a physician who specializes in diseases of the ear.

Oval window is the membrane that separates the middle from the inner ear.

Panic disorder involves overwhelming panic attacks resulting in rapid heartbeat, dizziness, and/or other physical symptoms.

Paraprofessionals are school staff included under the IDEA term supplementary aids and services who provide support to teachers and instructional supports to students.

Part B refers to the section of IDEA that addresses the social education of students who range from three through twenty-one years of age.

Part C represents the section of IDEA that addresses the needs of infants and toddlers ranging in age from birth through age two.

Partial participation rejects an all-or-none approach under which students either function independently in a given environment or not at all. Instead, it asserts that students with severe and multiple disabilities can participate, even if only partially, and indeed can often learn and complete a task if it is adapted to their strengths.

Partial seizures cause the student to lose consciousness and often to fall to the ground and have sudden, involuntary contractions of groups of muscles.

Peer tutoring involves pairing students one on one so that students who have already developed certain skills can help teach those and other skills to less advanced students and also help those students practice the skills they have already mastered.

Pegword strategy helps students remember numbered or ordered information by linking words that rhyme with numbers.

Perinatal refers, generally, to time periods immediately preceding, during, and immediately after birth.

Pervasive developmental disorders include five discrete disorders that are part of the autism spectrum, including autistic disorder, Rhett's disorder, childhood disintegrative disorder, Asperger syndrome, and pervasive developmental disorder not otherwise specified.

Phobia consists of the unrealistic, overwhelming fear of an object or situation.

Phonemes are individual speech sounds and how they are produced, depending on their placement in a syllable or word.

Phonological processing refers to the ability to process written and oral information by using the sound system of language.

Phonology is the use of sounds to make meaningful syllables and words.

Pidgin Sign English (PSE) is a sign system used in the United States and employs a basic American Sign Language vocabulary in English word order.

Pitch is affected by the tension and size of the vocal folds, the health of the larynx, and the location of the larynx.

Portfolio-based assessment is a technique for assembling exemplars of a student's work, such as homework, in-class tests, artwork, journal writing, and other evidence of the student's strengths and needs.

Positive behavior support is a proactive, data-based approach to ensuring that students acquire needed skills and environmental supports.

Positive interdependence refers to creating situations within cooperative learning groups where students have to work together to succeed.

Post-traumatic stress disorder refers to flashbacks and other recurrent symptoms following exposure to an extremely distressing and dangerous event such as witnessing violence or a hurricane.

Postnatal refers to the time period after birth.

Pragmatics refers to the use of communication in context.

Pre-referral interventions involve the delivery of more intense instruction, instruction for a longer duration, or different types of instruction provided to a student who is having difficulty to address the student's difficulty before "referring" a student for evaluation for eligibility for special education services.

Prelinguistic milieu teaching (PMT) is an effective language-acquisition instructional strategy based on the principle that children will learn if their instruction matches their interests and abilities.

Prenatal means occurring before birth; during the mother's pregnancy.

Prevalence refers to the total number or percentage of people with a given condition in the population at a given time.

Procedural due process is the principle of IDEA that seeks to make the schools and parents accountable to each other through a system of checks and balances.

Prodigy is a person who is gifted to the point of being unmistakably extraordinary.

Receptive language disorder is characterized by difficulty in receiving or understanding information.

Repetitive behavior involves obsessions, tics, and perseveration.

Resolution session (dispute resolution session) is a meeting involving the student's educators and parents in which they attempt to identify and find solutions for any disagreements about the student's education.

Resonance is determined by the way in which the tone coming from the vocal folds is modified by the spaces of the throat, mouth, and nose.

Risk ratios compare the proportion of a specific racial/ethnic group receiving special education services to the proportion among the total combined other racial/ethnic groups receiving special education.

Rubella is a viral infection, also called German measles, that causes a mild fever and skin rash. If a woman in the first three months of her pregnancy gets this disease, it can lead to severe birth defects in her child.

Savant syndrome is a condition in which individuals typically display extraordinary abilities in areas such as calendar calculating, musical ability, mathematical skills, memorization, and mechanical abilities.

Schizophrenia is characterized by psychotic periods resulting in hallucinations, delusions, inability to experience pleasure, and loss of contact with reality.

Schoolwide enrichment model (SEM) promotes challenging, high-end learning across a range of school types, levels, and demographic differences by creating services that can be integrated across the general curriculum to assist all students, not just students who are gifted.

Schoolwide positive behavior support (SWPBS) is a systems-level and evidence-based method for improving valued social and learning outcomes for all students.

Screening refers to the use of measures of a condition (such as visual impairment, hearing impairment, etc.) in the absence of symptoms of the condition. Screening usually involves the entire population of interest (e.g., all students in a school).

Seeing Essential English, Signing Exact English (SEE2) is a sign system used in the United States that borrows signs from American Sign Language and then adds signs that correspond to English morphemes.

Seizures are temporary neurological abnormalities that result from unregulated electrical discharges in the brain, much like an electrical storm.

Self-advocacy refers to advocating on one's own behalf or on the behalf of others with whom one shares common concerns.

Self-care skills refer to daily living skills pertaining to the care of oneself, including skills like eating, dressing, and going to the bathroom.

Self-determination refers to acting volitionally (that is, based upon conscious choice) to make or cause things to happen in one's life.

Self-injurious behavior involves engaging in behavior that might potentially injure oneself, such as striking oneself, cutting oneself, biting oneself, and head banging.

Self-instruction strategies involve teaching students to use their own verbal or other communication skills to direct their own learning.

Self-modeling strategies involve students observing themselves, typically through a video, performing a behavior, to learn how to perform a behavior and to evaluate the impact of an already performed behavior.

Self-monitoring strategies enable students to learn to collect data on their progress toward educational goals. They can do this through various formats, such as by charting their progress on a sheet of graph paper or completing a checklist.

Self-scheduling strategies involve the self-regulation of one's schedule, rather than relying on someone else to regulate the activities of the day.

Semantics refers to the meaning of what is expressed.

Sensorineural hearing loss occurs when there is damage to the inner ear or auditory nerve.

Separation anxiety disorder is excessive and intense fear associated with separating from home, family, and others with whom a child has a close attachment.

Service learning is a method for students to develop newly acquired skills by active participation and structured reflection in organized opportunities to meet community needs.

Shaken baby syndrome refers to a brain injury resulting from a situation in which a caregiver has shaken a child violently, often because the caregiver is frustrated by the child's crying.

Short-term memory is the mental ability to recall information that has been stored for a few seconds to a few hours.

Sign language uses combinations of hand movements to convey words and concepts rather than individual letters.

Simultaneous Communication, Total Communication, or Signed Exact English are systems of communicating that use fingerspelling and signs in English word order.

Slate and stylus is a tool used by people who are blind to write short notes to themselves. It consists of a slate, a hinged metal template, and a stylus (a small awl) that is used to punch the dots of a message in braille on a piece of paper inserted in the slate.

Social anxiety disorder entails experiencing intense fear and discomfort in having social interactions with others, along with worry about being negatively judged and feeling embarrassed.

Social interaction theories emphasize that communication skills are learned through social interactions.

Social stories are written by educators, parents, or students and describe social situations, social cues, and appropriate responses to those cues.

Sound-field amplification system enables the teacher to transmit her voice by using a lavaliere microphone and ceiling- or wall-mounted speakers.

Spastic cerebral palsy involves tightness in one or more muscle groups.

Specially designed instruction refers to adaptations of the content, methodology, or delivery of instruction to address a student's unique needs and ensure that the student can participate and make progress in the general curriculum.

Specific language impairment describes a language disorder with no identifiable cause in a person with apparently normal development in all other areas.

Specific learning disability means a disorder in one or more of the basic psychological processes involved in understanding or using spoken or written language.

Speech is the oral expression of language. The disorder may manifest itself in an imperfect ability to listen, think, speak, read, write, spell, or describe mathematical calculations.

Speech disorder refers to difficulty in producing sounds as well as disorders of voice quality (for example, a hoarse voice) or fluency of speech, often referred to as stuttering.

Speech reader is someone who is able to interpret words by watching the speaker's lips and facial movements without hearing the speaker's voice.

Spina bifida is a condition in which the person's vertebral arches (the connective tissue between one vertebra and another) are not completely closed; the person's spine is split—thus, spina (spine) bifida (split). Spina bifida is the most common form of neural tube defect.

Spina bifida occulta refers to a condition in which the spinal cord or its covering do not protrude and only a small portion of the vertebra, usually in the lower spine, is missing. This is the mildest and most common form of spina bifida.

Standard deviation is a way to determine how much a particular score differs from the mean (average).

Standards-based reform is a process that identifies the academic content (reading, mathematics) that students must master, the standards for the students' achievement of content proficiency, a general assessment of student progress in meeting the general curriculum and standards, and information from the assessments to improve teaching and learning and to demonstrate that the schools are indeed accountable to the students, their families, and the public.

Stapes is one of the small bones in the middle ear. It is sometimes called the *stirrup* because of its shape.

Student achievement standards define the levels of achievement that students must meet to demonstrate their proficiency in the subjects.

Student-directed learning strategies teach students with and without disabilities to modify and regulate their own learning.

Students with the most significant cognitive disabilities are students who cannot participate in regular state assessments, even with accommodations, and thus are eligible to participate in the alternate assessments based on alternate academic

achievement standards (AA-AAAS). ESSA—the Every Student Succeeds Act—limits the percentage of students who can take the AA-AAAS to 1 percent of the total student population.

Substitutions occur when a person substitutes one sound for another, as when a child substitutes /d/ for the voiced /th/ ("doze" for "those"), /t/ for /k/ ("tat" for "cat"), or /w/ for /r/ ("wabbit" for "rabbit").

Summative assessment refers to the use of testing to assess educational outcomes and to compare student performance with a predetermined standard so as to evaluate student performance.

Supplementary aids and services are aids, services, and other supports provided in general education classes or other education-related settings to enable children with disabilities to be educated with nondisabled children to the maximum extent appropriate.

Supports are resources and strategies that enhance functioning in everyday environments and that promote the personal well-being, development, education, and interests of a person.

Syndrome is a collection of two or more features that result from a single cause.

Syntax provides rules for putting together a series of words to form sentences.

Syphilis is a sexually transmitted disease that can cause an intrauterine infection in a pregnant woman and result in severe birth defects in her child.

System for augmenting language (SAL) focuses on augmented input of language.

T-Charts are charts that are laid out in the form of a capital letter *T*; they allow teachers to track two aspects of a behavior together.

Teletherapy is an educational intervention using a webcam and microphone; typically used with families who are not able to be seen in person by an early interventionist or educator. Professionals can coach parents via live, streaming video and learn how to work with their child at home using strategies for enhancing listening and language development.

Temperament refers to behavioral tendencies that are biologically based.

Theory of mind is an explanation of the delayed social development that suggests that individuals with autism do not understand that their own beliefs, desires, and intentions may differ from those of others.

Time sampling involves an observer who is recording the occurrence or nonoccurrence of specific behaviors during short, predetermined intervals.

Tonic-clonic seizures affect a student's motor control area of the brain, as well as sensory, behavioral, and cognitive areas.

Tonic-clonic seizures can either occur in only one region of the brain or spread to other brain hemispheres.

Topographical classification system correlates the specific body location of a movement impairment with the location of the brain damage.

Totally blind describes those individuals who do not receive meaningful input through the visual sense.

Toxoplasmosis is an infectious disease caused by a microorganism that can cause severe fetal malformations.

Trauma- and stressor-related disorder is a new category in DSM-5 that deals with incapacitating symptoms following exposure to a dangerous or traumatic event.

Traumatic brain injury (TBI) is caused by an external physical force, resulting in impaired functioning in one or more areas. Educational performance is adversely affected. The injury may be open or closed.

Tunnel vision occurs when an individual's visual field is reduced significantly so that only a small area of central visual acuity remains. The affected individual has the impression of looking through a tunnel or tube and is unaware of objects to the left, right, top, or bottom.

Twice-exceptional refers to students who are gifted and talented but who also experience a disability, such as a learning disability or ADHD.

Tympanography is not a hearing test but a test of how well the middle ear is functioning and how well the eardrum can move.

Unilateral is hearing loss in one ear only.

Universal design for learning (UDL) is the application of principles to the design of curricular and instructional materials to provide students across a wide range of abilities and from a variety of backgrounds with access to academic content.

Vestibular mechanism controls balance, helps a body maintain its equilibrium, and is sensitive to both motion and gravity.

Visual disability (including blindness) is an impairment in vision that, even with correction, adversely affects a child's educational performance. The term includes both partial sight and blindness.

Working memory refers to how students process information in order to remember it.

Wraparound refers to a philosophy of care that includes a definable planning process involving the child and family that results in a unique set of community services and natural supports individualized for that child and family to achieve a positive set of outcomes.

Zero reject is an IDEA principle that requires schools to enroll all students who have disabilities.

References

Chapter 1

American Association for Employment in Education. (2008). *Educator supply and demand in the United States*. Columbus, OH: Author.

Board of Education of the Hendrick Hudson Central School District v. Rowley, 458 U.S. 176 (1982).

Donne, J. (1986). Devotions upon emergent occasions. In M. H. Abrams (Ed.), *The Norton anthology of English literature* (pp. 1107–1108). New York: Norton.

Evans, K., & Vaandering, D. (2016). *The little book of restorative justice in education: Fostering responsibility, healing, and hope in schools*. New York, NY: Good Books.

Hussar, W. J., & Bailey, T. M. (2013). *Projections of education statistics to 2019 (NCES 2011-017)*. U.S. Department of Education, National Center for Education Statistics. Washington, DC: U.S. Government Printing Office.

Mish, F .C. (Ed.) (1990). *Webster's Ninth New Collegiate Dictionary*. Springfield, MA: Merriam-Webster, Inc.

Snyder, T. D., de Brey, C., & Dillow, S. A. (2016). *Digest of education statistics 2015 (NCES 2016-014)*. Washington, DC: National Center for Education Statistics, Institute of Education Sciences, U.S. Department of Education.

Turnbull, H. R. (1976). Families in crises. In T. Tjossem (Ed.), *Intervention strategies for high risk infants and young children* (pp. 765–769). Baltimore, MD: University Park Press.

Turnbull, H. R., Stowe, M. J., & Huerta, N. E. (2007). *Free appropriate public education: The law and children with disabilities* (7th ed.). Denver, CO: Love Publishing.

Turnbull, R. (2011). *The exceptional life of Jay Turnbull: Disability and dignity in America, 1967–2009*. Amherst, MA: White Poppy Press.

U.S. Department of Education. (2018). *39th annual report to Congress on the implementation of the Individuals with Disabilities Education Act, Parts B and C. 2017*. Washington, DC: Author.

Wehmeyer, M. L. (2009). Eulogy at Jay Turnbull's memorial service.

Wehmeyer, M. L., & Patton, J. R. (2017). *The Praeger international handbook of special education*. Santa Barbara, CA: ABC-Clio, LLC.

Chapter 2

Allday, R. A., Duhon, G. J., Blackburn-Ellis, S., & Van Dycke, J. L. (2011). The biasing effects of labels on direct observation by preservice teachers. *Teacher Education and Special Education, 34*(1), 52–58.

Balfanz, R., Byrnes, V., & Fox, J. (2015). Sent home and put off track: The antecedents, disproportionalities, and consequences of being suspended in the 9th grade. In B. J. Losen (Ed.), *Closing the school discipline gap: Equitable remedies for excessive exclusion* (pp. 17–30). New York, NY: Teachers College, Columbia University.

Boyes-Watson, C., & Pranis, K. (2015). *Circle forward: Building a restorative school community*. St. Paul, MN: Living Justice Press.

Brueggemann, B. (2014). Disability studies/disability culture. In M. L. Wehmeyer (Ed.), *The Oxford handbook of positive psychology and disability* (pp. 279–298). New York, NY: Oxford University Press.

Centers for Disease Control and Prevention. (2017). *Lesbian, gay, bisexual, and transgender health*. Retrieved from https://www.cdc.gov/lgbthealth/youth.htm/

Ciramicoli, A. P., & Ketcham, K. (2000). *The power of empathy: A practical guide to creating intimacy, self-understanding, and lasting love in your life*. London, England: Penguin Publishing Group.

Crenshaw, K. (1989). Demarginalizing the intersection of race and sex: A Black feminist critique of antidiscrimination doctrine. *University of Chicago Legal Forum*, 139–168 .

Devine, P. G., Forscher, P. S., Austin, A. J. & Cox, W. T. L. (2012). Long-term reduction in implicit race bias: A prejudice habit-breaking intervention. *Journal of Experimental Social Psychology, 48*, 1267–1278.

Dunn, D. S., & Andrews, E. E. (2015). Person-first and identity-first language: Developing psychologists' cultural competence using disability language. *American Psychologist, 70*(3), 255–264.

Evans, K., & Vaandering, D. (2016). *The little book of restorative justice in education: Fostering responsibility, healing, and hope in schools*. New York, NY: Good Books.

Fleischer, D., & Zames, S. (2011). *The disability rights movement: From charity to confrontation*. Philadelphia, PA: Temple University.

Forscher, P. S., Lai, C. K., Axt, J., Ebersole, C. R., Herman, M., Devine, P. G., & Nosek, B. A. (2017, October 5). *A meta-analysis of change in implicit bias*. Retrieved from osf.io/awz2p

Gay, G. (2013). Teaching to and through cultural diversity. *Curriculum Inquiry, 43*(1), 50–70.

Gay, Lesbian, and Straight Education Network (GLSEN) (2016). *Educational exclusion: Drop out, push out, and school-to-prison pipeline among LGBTQ youth*. New York, NY: GLSEN.

Gilliam, W. S., Maupin, A. N., Reyes, C. R., Accavitti, M., & Shic, F. (2016). *A research study report: Do early educators' implicit biases regarding sex and race relate to behavior expectations and recommendations of preschool expulsions and suspensions?* New Haven, CT: Yale Child Study Center.

Gold, M. E., & Richards, H. (2012). To label or not to label: The special education question for African Americans. *Educational Foundations*, Winter–Spring, 143–156.

Greenwald, A. C., & Nosek, B. A. (2001). Health of the Implicit Association Test at age 3. *Experimental Psychology, 48*(2), 85–92.

Gregory, A., & Clawson, K. (2016). The potential of restorative approaches to discipline for narrowing racial and gender disparities. In R. J. Skiba, K. Mediratta, & M. K. Rauch (Eds.), *Equality in school discipline: Research and practice to reduce disparities* (pp. 153–170). New York, NY: Springer Nature.

Gregory, A., Clawson, K., Davis, A., & Gerewitz, J. (2016). The promise of restorative practices to transform teacher-student relationships and achieve equity in school discipline. *Journal of Educational and Psychological Consultation, 26*(4), 325–353.

Institute of Disability. (2016). *2016 Annual disabilities statistics compendium*. Retrieved from https://disabilitycompendium.org/

Kirk, S. A. (1984). Introspection and prophecy. In B. Blatt & R. J. Morris (eds.), *Perspectives in special education: Personal orientations* (pp. 25–55). Glenview, IL: Scott Foresman.

Lipscomb, S., Haimson, J., Liu, A. Y., Burghardt, J., Johnson, D. R., & Thurlow, M. L. (2017). Preparing for life after high school: The characteristics and experiences of youth in special education. *Findings from the National Longitudinal Transition Study 2012. Volume 1: Comparisons with other youth: Full report (NCEE 2017-4016)*. Washington, DC: U.S. Department of Education, Institute of Education Sciences, National Center for Education Evaluation and Regional Assistance.

Losen, D. J., Ee, J., Hodson, C., & Martinez, T. E. (2015). Disturbing inequities: Exploring the relationship between racial disparities in special education identification and discipline. In B. J. Losen (Ed.), *Closing the school discipline gap: Equitable remedies for excessive exclusion* (pp. 107–117). New York, NY: Teachers College, Columbia University.

Merriam-Webster's Collegiate Dictionary. (2003). (11th ed.). Springfield, MA: Merriam-Webster.

Mills v. Washington, DC, Board of Education. (1972). 348 F. Supp. 866.

National Assessment of Educational Progress (2017). *National Indian Education Study 2015*. Retrieved from https://nces.ed.gov/pubsearch/pubsinfo.asp?pubid=2017161/

National Center for Education Statistics, U.S. Department of Education. (2016). *Student reports of bullying: Results from the 2015 School Crime Supplement to the National Crime Victimization Survey.* Retrieved from https://nces.ed.gov/pubs201s/2017015.pdf/

National Center for Education Statistics, U.S. Department of Education. (2017). *The condition of education 2017 (2017-144). English language learners in public schools.* Retrieved from nces.ed.gov/programs/coe/indicator_cqf.asp/

National Center for Education Statistics, U.S. Department of Education. (2017a). *Children and youth with disabilities.* Retrieved from https://nces.ed.gov/programs/coe/indicator_cgg.asp/

National Center for Education Statistics, U.S. Department of Education. (2017b). *The condition of education 2017.* Retrieved from https://nces.ed.gov/pubs2017/2017144.pdf/

National Clearinghouse for Educational Statistics (2017c). *Status and trends in the education of racial and ethnic groups: Indicator 7: English language learners.* Retrieved from https://nces.ed.gov/programs/raceindicators/indicator_rbc.asp/.

National Organization on Disability. (2010). *National Organization on Disability/Harris Survey of Americans with Disabilities.* Washington, DC: Author.

Okonofua, J. A., & Eberhardt, J. L. (2015). Two strikes: Race and the disciplining of young students. *Psychological Science, 26*(5), 617–624.

Pennsylvania Association for Retarded Children (PARC) v. Commonwealth of Pennsylvania. (1971, 1972). 334 F. Supp. 1257, 343 F. Supp. 279.

Riestenberg, N. (2012). *Circle in the square: Building community and repairing harm in school.* St. Paul, MN: Living Justice Press.

Rose, C. A., Monda-Amaya, L. E., & Eselage, D. L. (2011). Bullying perpetration and victimization in special education: A review of the literature. *Remedial and Special Education, 32*(2), 114–130.

Shollenberger, T. L. (2015). Racial disparities in school suspension and subsequent outcomes: Evidence from the national longitudinal survey of youth. In B. J. Losen (Ed.), *Closing the school discipline gap: Equitable remedies for excessive exclusion* (pp. 31–43). New York, NY: Teachers College, Columbia University.

Thiederman, S. (2015). *3 keys to defeating unconscious bias: Watch, think, act.* San Diego, CA: Cross-Cultural Communications.

Turnbull, H. R., Stowe, M. J., & Huerta, N. E. (2007). *Free appropriate public education: The law and children with disabilities* (7th ed.). Denver, CO: Love Publishing Co.

Turnbull, A. P., Fialka, J., Kyzar, K., Kemp, P., Aldersey, H., & Lindeman, D. (2013). *Empathetic communication.* Topeka, KS: Kansas Infant-Toddler Services, Department of Health and Environment.

Turnbull, H. R., Shogren, K. A., & Turnbull, A. P. (2011). Evolution of the parent movement: Past, present, and future. In J. M. Kauffman & D. P. Hallahan (Eds.), *Handbook of special education* (pp. 639–653). New York, NY: Routledge.

U.S. Department of Education. (2010). *29th annual report to Congress on the implementation of the Individuals with Disabilities Education Act, 2007* (Vol.1). Washington, DC: Author.

U.S. Department of Education. (2011). *Digest of educational statistics:* Retrieved from U.S. Department of Education, 2017.

U.S. Department of Education. (2016). *Student reports of bullying: Results from the 2015 School Crime Supplement to the National Crime Victimization Survey.* Retrieved from https://nces.ed.gov/pubs201s/2017015.pdf/.

U.S. Department of Education Office for Civil Rights. (2014). *Civil rights data collection data snapshot: School discipline.* Retrieved from https://ocrdata.ed.gov/downloads/crdc-school-discipline-snapshot.pdf/

U.S. Department of Education, National Center for Educational Statistics. (2017). *The condition of education 2017.* Retrieved from https://nces.ed.gov/pubs2017/2017144.pdf

U.S. Department of Education (2018a). U.S. Department of Education. (2018a). *39th annual report to Congress on the implementation of the Individuals with Disabilities Education Act, Parts B and C. 2017.* Washington, DC: Author.

U.S. Department of Education, National Center for Education Statistics. (2018b). *Children and youth with disabilities.* Retrieved from https://nces.ed.gov/programs/coe/indicator_cgg.asp/.

U.S. Department of Education Office for Civil Rights. (2016). *Protecting the civil rights of students in the juvenile justice system.* Retrieved from https://www2.ed.gov/about/offices/list/ocr/docs/2013-14-juvenile-justice.pdf/

van Swet, J., Wichers-Bots, J., & Brown, K. (2011). Solution-focused assessment: Rethinking labels to support inclusive education. *International Journal of Inclusive Education, 15*(9), 909–923.

Vohs, J. R. (1993). On belonging: A place to stand, a gift to give. In A. P. Turnbull, J. M. Patterson, S. K. Behr, D. L. Murphy, J. G. Marquis, & M. J. Blue-Banning (Eds.), *Cognitive coping, families, and disability* (pp. 51–66). Baltimore: Brookes.

Wachtel, T. (2016). *Defining restorative.* Retrieved from https://www.iirp.edu/pdf/Defining-Restorative.pdf/

Wilson, M. C., & Scior, K. (2014). Attitudes towards individuals with disabilities as measured by the Implicit Association Test: A literature review. *Research in Developmental Disabilities, 35,* 284–321.

Zablocki, M., & Krezmien, M. P. (2012). Drop-out predictors among students with high-incidence disabilities: A national longitudinal and transitional study 2 analysis. *Journal of Disability Policy Studies, 24*(1), 53–64.

Zehr, H. (2002). *The little book of restorative justice.* Intercourse, PA: Good Books.

Zehr, H. (2015). *The little book of restorative justice: Revised and updated.* Intercourse, PA: Good Books.

Chapter 3

Bembenutty, H. (2011). The first word: Homework's theory, research, and practice. *Journal of Advanced Academics, 22*(2), 185–192.

Blackwell, W. H., & Rossetti, Z. S. (2014). The development of individualized education programs: Where have we been and where should we go now? *SAGE Open,* 1–15. doi: 10.1177/2158244014530411

Blue-Banning, M. J., Summers, J. A., Frankland, H. C., Nelson, L. L., & Beegle, G. (2004). Dimensions of family and professional partnerships: Constructive guidelines for collaboration. *Exceptional Children, 70*(2), 167–184.

Bryk, A. S., & Schneider, B. (2002). *Trust in schools: A core resource for improvement.* New York: Russell Sage Foundation.

Burke, M. (2015). Developing collaborative family-school partnerships: A literature review of parent training and information centers in the United States. *Centre for Advancement in Inclusive and Special Education (CAISE),* Faculty Education, The University of Hong Kong.

Burke, M. M., & Hodapp, R. M. (2014). Relating stress of mothers of children with developmental disabilities to family-school partnerships. *Intellectual and Developmental Disabilities, 52,* 13–23.

Burke, M. M., & Hodapp, R. M. (2016). The nature, correlates, and conditions of parental advocacy in special education. *Exceptionality, 24*(3), 137–150. doi: 10.1080/09362835.2015.1064412

CADRE. (2008). *Part B—Three year annual report summaries for written complaints, mediations and due process.* Eugene, OR: Author. Retrieved January 20, 2007, from http://www.directionservice.org/cadre/statecomprpts.cfm

Carr, N. S. (2013). Increasing the effectiveness of homework for all learners in the inclusive classroom. *School Community Journal, 23*(1), 169–182.

Carroll, D. W. (2013). *Families of children with developmental disabilities.* Washington, DC: American Psychological Association.

Chiu, C., Kyzar, K., Zuna, N., Turnbull, A., Summers, J. A., & Gomez, V. A. (2013). Family quality of life. In M. L. Wehmeyer (Ed.), *The Oxford handbook of positive psychology and disability* (pp. 365–392). New York, NY: Oxford University Press.

Cooper, H., Robinson, J. C., & Patall, E. A. (2006). Does homework improve academic achievement? A synthesis of research, 1987–2003. *Review of Educational Research, 76*(1), 1–62.

Eskow, K. G., Summers, J. A., Chasson, G. S., & Mitchell, R. (2018). The association between family-teacher partnership satisfaction and outcomes of academic progress and quality of life for children/youth with autism. *Journal of Policy and Practice in Intellectual Disabilities, 15*(1), 16–25.

Family Voices. (2016). Family-to-Family Health Information Centers data report: Helping families of children and youth with special health care needs and the professionals who service them. Retrieved from http://www.familyvoices.org/admin/work_data/files/DataFactSheet_03-04-2010_NationalHighlights.pdf

Federal Register. (1981, January 19). Washington, DC: U.S. Government Printing Office.

Goldman, S. E., & Burke, M. M. (2015). The effectiveness of interventions to increase parent involvement in special education: A systematic literature review and meta-analysis. *Exceptionality, 25*(2), 97–15.

Goldstein, S., & Turnbull, A. P. (1982). The use of two strategies to increase parent participation in IEP conferences. *Exceptional Children, 48,* 360–361.

Government Accountability Office. (2014, August). *Special education: Improved performance measures could enhance oversight of dispute resolution.* Retrieved from http://www.gao.gov/products/GAO-14-390

Hampshire, P. K., Butera, G. D., & Hourcade, J. J. (2014). Homework plans: A tool for promoting independence. *TEACHING Exceptional Children, 46*(6), 158–168.

Harry, B., Klingner, J., & Hart, J. (2005). African American families under fire: Ethnographic views of family strengths. *Remedial and Special Education, 26*(2), 101–112.

Hoffman, L., Marquis, J. G., Poston, D. J., Summers, J. A., & Turnbull, A. P. (2006). Assessing family outcomes: Psychometric evaluation of the Beach Center Family Quality of Life Scale. *Journal of Marriage and Family, 68,* 1069–1083.

Hoy, W. (2012). School characteristics that make a difference for the achievement of all students: A 40-year odyssey. *Journal of Educational Administrator, 50*(1), 76–97.

Huang, D., & Cho, J. (2009). Academic enrichment in high-functioning homework afterschool programs. *Journal of Research in Childhood Education, 23,* 382–392.

Kyzar, K., Brady, S., Summers, J. A., & Turnbull, A. (in press). Family quality of life and partnership for families of students with deaf-blindness. *Remedial and Special Education.* https://doi-org.www2.lib.ku.edu/10.1177/0741932518781946

Kyzar, K. B., Brady, S., Summers, J. A., Haines, S. H., & Turnbull, A. P. (2015). Services and supports, partnership, and Family Quality of Life: Focus on deaf-blindness. *Exceptional Children, 83*(1), 77–91.

Langberg, J. M., Epstein, J. N., Becker, S. P., Girio-Herrera, E., & Vaughn, A. J. (2012). Evaluation of the Homework, Organization, and Planning Skills (HOPS) intervention for middle school students with attention deficit hyperactivity disorder as implemented by school mental health providers. *School Psychology Review, 41,* 342–364.

Lipscomb, S., Haimson, J., Liu, A. Y., Burghardt, J., Johnson, D. R., & Thurlow, M. L. (2017). Preparing for life after high school: The characteristics and experiences of youth in special education. Findings from the National Longitudinal Transition Study 2012. Volume 2: Comparisons across disability groups: Full report (NCEE 2017-4018). Washington, DC: U.S. Department of Education, Institute of Education Sciences, National Center for Education Evaluation and Regional Assistance.

Mandic, C. G., Rudd, R., Hehir, T., & Acevedo-Garcia, D. (2012). Readability of special education procedural safeguards. *The Journal of Special Education, 45,* 195–203.

McGee, C. (2012). Parent to parent: Giftedness with a twist. *PHP, 1*(5), 12–13.

Merriam-Webster's Collegiate Dictionary. (2003). (11th ed.). Springfield, MA: Merriam-Webster.

Merriman, D., Codding, R. S., Tryon, G. S., & Minami, T. (2016). The effects of group coaching on the homework problems experienced by secondary students with and without disabilities. *Psychology in the Schools, 53,* 457–470.

Mish, F .C. (Ed.) (1990). *Webster's Ninth New Collegiate Dictionary.* Springfield, MA: Merriam-Webster, Inc.

Mueller, T. G., & Carranza, F. (2011). An examination of special education due process hearings. *Journal of Disability Policy Studies, 22*(3), 131–139.

Mueller, T. G., & Vick, A. M. (2017). An investigation of facilitated individualized education program meeting practice: Promising procedures that foster family-professional collaboration. *Teacher Education and Special Education,* 1–15. doi: 10.1177/0888406417739677

National Association for Gifted Children. (2015). *2014–2015 State of the states in gifted education: Policy and practice data.* Retrieved from http://www.nagc.org/sites/default/files/key%20reports/2014-2015%20State%20of%20the%20States%20%28final%29.pdf

National Parent Technical Assistance Center. (2013). *Parent centers helping families: Outcome data 2012–2013.* Minneapolis, MN: Parent Technical Assistance Center Network.

Newman, L. (2005). *Family involvement in the educational development of youth with disabilities: A special topic report of findings from the National Longitudinal Transition Study-2 (NLTS-2).* Menlo Park, CA: SRI International.

Santelli, B., Markey, U., Johnson, A., Turnbull, R., & Turnbull, A. (2001). The evolution of an unlikely partnership between researcher and culturally diverse families: Lessons learned. *TASH Newsletter,* March/April.

SEDL. (2013). *Partners in education: A dual capacity-building framework for family-school partnerships.* Retrieved from https://www2.ed.gov/documents/family-community/partners-education.pdf

Shilling, V., Morris, C., Thompson-Coon, J., Ukoumunne, O., Rogers, M. A., & Logan, S. (2013). Peer support for parents of children with chronic disabling conditions: A systematic review of quantitative and qualitative studies. *Developmental Medicine & Child Neurology, 55,* 602–609.

Singer, G. H. S. (2006). Meta-analysis of comparative studies of depression in mothers of children with and without developmental disabilities. *American Journal on Mental Retardation, 111*(3), 155–169.

Singer, G. H. S., Marquis, J., Powers, L. K., Blanchard, L., DiVenere, N., Santelli, B., . . . Sharp, M. (1999). A multi-site evaluation of Parent to Parent programs for parents of children with disabilities. *Journal of Early Intervention, 22*(3), 217–219.

Stockwall, N. (2017). Designing homework to mediate executive functioning deficits in students with disabilities. *Intervention in School and Clinic, 53*(1), 3–11.

Summers, J. A., Poston, D. J., Turnbull, A. P., Marquis, J. G., Hoffman, L., Mannan, H., & Wang, M. (2005). Conceptualizing and measuring family quality of life. *Journal of Intellectual Disability Research, 49,* 777–783.

Turnbull, A. P., Turnbull, H. R., Erwin, E., Soodak, L., & Shogren, K. (2015). *Families, professionals, and exceptionality: Positive outcomes through partnerships and trust* (7th ed.). Boston, MA: Merrill/Prentice Hall.

U.S. Census Bureau. (2010). Current population survey (CPS)—definitions and explanations. Retrieved from http://www.census.gov/population/www/cps/cpsdef.html

U.S. Department of Education. (2017). Questions and answers (Q&A) on *U.S. Supreme Court Case Decision Endrew F. v. Douglas County School District Re-1.* Retrieved from https://sites.ed.gov/idea/questions-and-answers-qa-on-u-s-supreme-court-case-decision-endrew-f-v-douglas-county-school-district-re-1/

U.S. Department of Health and Human Services and U.S. Department of Education. (2016). *Policy statement on family engagement: From the early years to the early grades.* Retrieved from https://www2.ed.gov/about/inits/ed/earlylearning/files/policy-statement-on-family-engagement.pdf

Van Voorhis, F. L. (2011). Adding families to the homework equation: A longitudinal study of mathematics achievement. *Education and Urban Society, 43*(3), 313–338.

Vatterott, C. (2010). Five hallmarks of good homework. *Educational Leadership, 68*(1), 10–15.

Wagner, M., Newman, L., Cameto, R., Javitz, H., & Valdes, K. (2012). A national picture of parent and youth participation in IEP and transition planning meetings. *Journal of Disability Policy Studies*, 23(3), 140–155.

Wang, M., & Singer, G. H. S. (2016). *Supporting families of children with developmental disabilities: Evidence-based and emerging practices*. New York, NY: Oxford University Press.

White, S. E. (2013). Special education complaints filed by parents of students with autism spectrum disorders in the midwestern United States. *Focus on Autism and Other Developmental Disabilities*, 1–8. doi: 10.1177/1088357613478830

Williams, H. (1975). *Congressional Record*, June 15, p. 19489.

Chapter 4

Benner, G. J., Beaudoin, K., Mooney, P., Uhing, B. M., & Pierce, C. D. (2008). Convergent validity study of the BERS-2 Teacher Rating Scale and the Achenbach Teacher's Report Form: A replication and extension. *Journal of Child and Family Studies*, 17, 427–436.

Brown, L., Udvari-Solner, A., Frattura-Kampschroer, E., Davis, L., Ahlgren, C., Van Daventer, P., & Jorgensen, J. (1991). Integrated work: A rejection of segregated enclaves and mobile work crews. In L. H. Meyer, C. A. Peck, & L. Brown (Eds.), *Critical issues in the lives of people with severe disabilities* (pp. 219–228). Baltimore, MD: Brookes.

Buckley, J. A., Ryser, G., Reid, R., & Epstein, M. H. (2006). Confirmatory factor analysis of the behavioral and emotional rating scale-2 (BERS-2) parent and youth rating scales. *Journal of Child and Family Studies*, 15, 27–38.

Cole, C. M., Waldron, N., & Maid, M. (2004). Academic progress of students across inclusive and traditional settings. *Mental Retardation*, 42, 136–144.

Cosier, M., Causton-Theoharis, J., & Theoharis, G. (2013). Does access matter? Time in general education and achievement for students with disabilities. *Remedial and Special Education*, 34, 323–332.

De Graf, G., van Hove, G., & Haveman, M. (2017). More academics in regular schools? The effect of regular versus special school placement on academic skills in Dutch primary school students with Down syndrome. *Journal of Intellectual Disability Research*, 57, 21–38.

Drummond, T. (1994). *The Student Risk Screening Scale*. Grants Pass, OR: Josephine County Mental Health Program.

Endrew F. v. Douglas County School District RE-1, 580 U.S. _____ (2017).

Epstein, M. H. (2004). *Behavioral and Emotional Rating Scale (BERS-2): A strength-based approach to assessment* (2nd ed.). Austin, TX: Pro-Ed.

Giancreco, M. F., Cloninger, C. J., & Iverson, V. S. (2011). *Choosing outcomes and accommodations for children: A guide to educational planning for students with disabilities* (3rd Ed.). Baltimore, MD: Paul H. Brookes.

Hyatt, K. J., & Filler, J. (2011). LRE re-examined: Misinterpretations and unintended consequences. *International Journal of Inclusive Education*, 15, 1031–1045.

Jackson, L., Ryndak, D., & Wehmeyer, M. (2010). The dynamic relationship between context, curriculum, and student learning: A case for inclusive education as a research-based practice. *Research and Practice in Severe Disabilities*, 34, 175–195.

Jenkins, J., Schulze, M., Marti, A., & Harbaugh, A. G. (2017). Curriculum-based measurement of reading growth: Weekly versus intermittent progress monitoring. *Exceptional Children*, 84, 42–54.

Kauffman, J. M., Nelson, C. M., Simpson, R. L., & Ward, D. M. (2017). Contemporary issues. In J. M. Kauffman, D. P. Hallahan, & P. C. Pullen (Eds.), *Handbook of Special Education* (2nd Ed.) (pp. 16–28). New York, NY: Routledge.

Khetani, M. A., Cohn, E., Orsmond, G., Law, M., & Coster, W. (2013). Parent perspectives of participation in home and community life when receiving Part C early intervention services. *Topics in Early Childhood Special Education*, 32, 234–245.

Lane, K. L., Menzies, H. M., Oakes, W. P., & Kalberg, J. R. (2012). *Systematic screenings of behavior to support instruction: From preschool to high school*. New York, NY: Guilford Press.

Lane, K. L., Oakes, W. P., Ennis, R. P., Cox, M. L., Schatschneider, C., & Lambert, W. (2013). Additional evidence for the reliability and validity of the Student Risk Screening Scale at the high school level: A replication and extension. *Journal of Emotional and Behavioral Disorders*, 21, 97–115.

Lindstrom, J. H., & Sayeski, K. (2013). Identifying best practices in a shifting landscape: Making sense of RTI in the context of SLD identification. *Exceptionality*, 21, 5–18.

Madigan, K., Cross, R. W., Smolkowski, K., & Strycker, L. A. (2016). Association between schoolwide positive behavioural interventions and supports and academic achievement: A 9-year evaluation. *Educational Research and Evaluation*, 22, 402–421.

Perzigian, A. B., Afacan, K., Justin, W., & Wilkerson, K. L. (2017). Characteristics of students in traditional versus alternative high schools: A cross-sectional analysis of enrollment in one urban district. *Education and Urban Society*, 49, 676–700.

Quirk, C., Ryndak, D., & Taub, D. (2017). Research and evidence-based practices to promote membership and learning in general education for students with extensive support needs. *Inclusion*, 5, 94–109.

Rashid, T., & Asghar, H. M. (2016). Technology use, self-directed learning, student engagement and academic performance: Examining the interrelations. *Computers in Human Behavior*, 63, 604–612.

Reschly, A. L., Busch, T. W., Betts, J., Deno, S. L., & Long, J. D. (2009). Curriculum-based measurement oral reading as an indicator of reading achievement: A meta-analysis of the correlational evidence. *Journal of School Psychology*, 47, 427–469.

Rojewski, J. W., Lee, H., & Gregg, N. (2013). Causal effects of inclusion on postsecondary education outcomes of individuals with high-incidence disabilities. *Journal of Disability Policy Studies*, 25, 210–219.

Ryndak, D., Hughes, C., Alper, S., & McDonnell, J. (2012). Documenting impact of educational contexts on long-term outcomes for students with significant disabilities. *Education and Training in Autism and Developmental Disabilities*, 47, 127–138.

Ryndak, D., Taub, D., Jorgensen, C. M., Gonsier-Gerdin, J., Arndt, K., Sauer, J., . . . Allcock, H. (2014). Policy and the impact on placement, involvement, and progress in general education: Critical issues that require rectification. *Research and Practice for Persons with Severe Disabilities*, 39, 65–74.

Sailor, W., McCart, A. B., & Choi, J. H. (2018). Reconceptualizing inclusive education through multi-tiered system of support. *Inclusion*, 6, 2–18.

Sauer, J., & Jorgensen, C. M. (2016). Still caught in the continuum: A critical analysis of least restrictive environment and its effect on placement of students with intellectual disability. *Inclusion*, 4, 56–74.

Schalock, R., Borthwick-Duffy, S., Bradley, V., Buntinx, W., Coulter, D., Craig, E., . . . Yeager, M. (2010). *Intellectual disability: Definition, classification, and systems of support* (11th Ed.). Washington, DC: American Association on Intellectual and Developmental Disabilities.

Sharkey, J. D., You, S., Morrison, G. M., & Griffiths, A. J. (2009). Behavioral and Emotional Rating Scale-2 parent report: Exploring a Spanish version with at-risk students. *Behavioral Disorders*, 35, 53–65.

Tasse, M. J., Luckasson, R., & Schalock, R. L. (2016). The relation between intellectual functioning and adaptive behavior in the diagnosis of intellectual disability. *Intellectual and Developmental Disabilities*, 54, 381–390.

Taylor, S. (1988). Caught in the continuum: A critical analysis of the principle of least restrictive environment. *Journal of the Association for Persons with Severe Handicaps*, 13(1), 41–53.

U.S. Department of Education (2018). *39th annual report to Congress on the implementation of the Individuals with Disabilities Education Act, 2017*. Washington, DC: U.S. Department of Education, Office of Special Education and Rehabilitation Services, Office of Special Education Programs.

Vaughn, A. J., & Hoza, B. (2013). The incremental utility of behavioral rating scales and a structured diagnostic interview in the assessment of attention-deficit/hyperactivity disorder. *Journal of Emotional and Behavioral Disorders*, 21, 227–239.

Wehmeyer, M. L., & Shogren, K. A. (2017). Access to the general education curriculum for students with significant cognitive disabilities. In J. M. Kauffman & D. P. Hallahan (Eds.), *Handbook of special education* (pp. 662–674). New York, NY: Routledge.

Wehmeyer, M. L., Shogren, K. A., Kurth, J. A., Morningstar, M. E., Kozleski, E. B., Agran, M., . . . Ryndak, D. L. (2016). Including students with extensive and pervasive support needs. In J. P Bakken & F. Obiakor (Eds.), *Advances in special education* (Vol. 31): *General and special education inclusion in an age of change: Impact on students with disabilities* (pp. 129–155). London, UK: Emerald Group Publishing.

Wexler, J., Reed, D. K., Pyle, N., Mitchell, M., & Barton, E. E. (2015). A synthesis of peer-mediated academic interventions for secondary struggling learners. *Journal of Learning Disabilities, 48*, 451–470.

Chapter 5

Abbott, M., Beecher, C., Petersen, S., Greenwood, C. R., & Atwater, J. (2017). A team approach to data-driven decision-making literacy instruction in preschool classrooms: Child assessment and intervention through classroom team self-reflection. *Young Exceptional Children, 20*, 117–132.

Algozzine, B., Horner, R. H., Todd, A. W., Newton, J. S., Algozzine, K., & Cusumano, D. (2015). Measuring the process and outcomes of team problem solving. *Journal of Psychoeducational Assessment, 34*, 211–229. doi:10.1177/0734282915592535

American Educational Research Association. (2009). Ensuring early literacy success. *Research Points, 6*, 1–4.

Arden, S. V., Gandhi, A. G., Zumeta Edmonds, R., & Danielson, L. (2017).Toward more effective tiered systems: Lessons from national implementation efforts. *Exceptional Children, 83*, 269–280. doi:10.1177/0014402917693565

Bohanon, H., Fenning, P., Carney, K. L., Minnis-Kim, M. J., Anderson-Harriss, S., Mortoz, K. B., . . . Pigott, T. D. (2006). Schoolwide application of positive behavior support in an urban high school: A case study. *Journal of Positive Behavior Interventions, 8*, 131–145. doi:http://dx.doi.org/10.1177/10983007060080030201

Carr, E. G., Dunlap, G., Horner, R. H., Koegel, R. L., Turnbull, A. P., Sailor, W., . . . Fox, L. (2002). Positive behavior support: Evolution of an applied science. *Journal of Positive Behavior Interventions, 4*, 4–16, 20.

Carr, E. G., Horner, R. H., Turnbull, A. P., Marquis, J., Magito-McLaughlin, D., McAtee, M. L., . . . Doolabh, A. (1999). *Positive behavior support for people with developmental disabilities: A research synthesis.* Washington, DC: American Association on Mental Retardation.

Cheney, D., Flower, A., & Templeton, T. (2008). Applying response to intervention metrics in the social domain for students at risk of developing emotional or behavioral disorders. *The Journal of Special Education, 42*, 108–126. doi:10.1177/0022466907313349

Choi, J. H., Meisenheimer, J. M., McCart, A. B., & Sailor, W. (2017). Improving learning for all students through equity-based inclusive reform practices: Effectiveness of a fully integrated schoolwide model on student reading and math achievement. *Remedial and Special Education, 38*, 28–41. doi:10.1177/0741932516644054

Clarke, B., Doabler, C., Smolkowski, K., Kurtz Nelson, E., Fien, H., Baker, S. K., & Kosty, D. (2016). Testing the immediate and long-term efficacy of a tier 2 kindergarten mathematics intervention. *Journal of Research on Educational Effectiveness, 9*, 607–634. doi:10.1080/19345747.2015.1116034

Crone, D. A., Carlson, S. E., Haack, M. K., Kennedy, P. C., Baker, S. K., & Fien, H. (2016). Data-based decision-making teams in middle school: Observations and implications from the middle school intervention project. *Assessment for Effective Intervention, 41*, 79–93.

Cuticelli, M., Collier-Meek, M., & Coyne, M. (2016). Increasing the quality of tier 1 reading instruction: Using performance feedback to increase opportunities to respond during implementation of a core reading program. *Psychology in the Schools, 53*, 89–105. doi:doi:10.1002/pits.21884

Deno, S. L. (2016). Data-based decision-making. In S. R. Jimerson, M. K. Burns, & A. M. VanDerHeyden (Eds.), *Handbook of response to intervention: The science and practice of multi-tiered systems of support* (2nd ed., pp. 9–18). New York, NY: Springer.

Doabler, C. T., Clarke, B., Kosty, D. B., Kurtz-Nelson, E., Fien, H., Smolkowski, K., & Baker, S. K. (2016). Testing the efficacy of a tier 2 mathematics intervention: A conceptual replication study. *Exceptional Children, 83*, 92–110. doi:10.1177/0014402916660084

Drake, J., & Malloy, J. (2015). A practice guide to implementing RENEW in high schools. Retrieved from https://iod.unh.edu/sites/default/files/renew_implementation_in_high_schools_rdq_practice_guide_0.pdf

Eagle, J. W., Dowd-Eagle, S. E., Snyder, A., & Holtzman, E. G. (2015). Implementing a Multi-Tiered System of Support (MTSS): Collaboration between school psychologists and administrators to promote systems-level change. *Journal of Educational and Psychological Consultation, 25*, 160–177. doi:10.1080/10474412.2014.929960

Filter, K. J., Sytsma, M. R., & McIntosh, K. (2016). A brief measure of staff commitment to implement school-wide positive behavioral interventions and supports. *Assessment for Effective Intervention, 42*, 18–31. doi:10.1177/1534508416642212

Foorman, B. R., & Wanzek, J. (2016). Classroom reading instruction for all students. In S. R. Jimerson, M. K. Burns, & A. M. VanDerHeyden (Eds.), *Handbook of response to intervention: The science and practice of multi-tiered systems of support* (2nd ed., pp. 235–252). New York, NY: Springer.

Freeman, J., Simonsen, B., McCoach, D. B., Sugai, G., Lombardi, A., & Horner, R. (2015). Relationship between school-wide positive behavior interventions and supports and academic, attendance, and behavior outcomes in high schools. *Journal of Positive Behavior Interventions, 18*, 41–51. doi:10.1177/1098300715580992

Fuchs, D., & Fuchs, L. S. (2017). Critique of the national evaluation of response to intervention: A case for simpler frameworks. *Exceptional Children, 83*, 255–268. doi:10.1177/0014402917693580

Fuchs, L. S., Fuchs, D., & Malone, A. S. (2016). Multilevel response-to-intervention prevention systems: Mathematics intervention at Tier 2. In S. R. Jimerson, M. K. Burns, & A. M. VanDerHeyden (Eds.), *Handbook of response to intervention: The science and practice of multi-tiered systems of support* (2nd ed., pp. 809–328). New York, NY: Springer.

Fuchs, L. S., Fuchs, D., & Malone, A. S. (2018). The taxonomy of intervention intensity. *TEACHING Exceptional Children, 50*, 194–202. doi:10.1177/0040059918758166

Fuchs, L. S., Powell, S. R., Schumacher, R. F., Seethaler, P. M., & Fuchs, D. (2017). *Pirate Math Secondary Prevention: Word-problem solving intervention at second grade.* Nashville, TN: Vanderbilt University.

Gage, N. A., Leite, W., Childs, K., & Kincaid, D. (2017). Average treatment effect of school-wide positive behavioral interventions and supports on school-level academic achievement in Florida. *Journal of Positive Behavior Interventions, 19*, 158–167. doi:http://dx.doi.org/10.1177/1098300717693556

Garbacz, S. A., McIntosh, K., Eagle, J. W., Dowd-Eagle, S. E., Hirano, K. A., & Ruppert, T. (2016). Family engagement within schoolwide positive behavioral interventions and supports. *Preventing School Failure: Alternative Education for Children and Youth, 60*, 60–69. doi:10.1080/1045988X.2014.976809

Gersten, R., Beckmann, S., Clarke, B., Foegen, A., Marsh, L., Star, J. R., & Witzel, B. (2009). *Assisting students struggling with mathematics: Response to Intervention (RtI) for elementary and middle schools (NCEE 2009-4060).* Washington, DC: National Center for Education Evaluation and Regional Assistance, Institute of Education Sciences, U.S. Department of Education.

Gersten, R., Compton, D., Connor, C. M., Dimino, J., Santoro, L., Linan-Thompson, S., & Tilly, W. D. (2008). *Assisting students struggling with reading: Response to Intervention and multi-tier intervention for reading in the primary grades. A practice guide. (NCEE 2009-4045).* Washington, DC: National Center for Education Evaluation and Regional Assistance, Institute of Education Sciences, U.S. Department of Education.

Gersten, R., Jayanthi, M., & Dimino, J. (2017). Too much, too soon? Unanswered questions from national response to intervention evaluation. *Exceptional Children, 83*, 244–254. doi:10.1177/0014402917692847

Good, R. H., Kaminski, R. A., Shinn, M., Bratten, J., Shinn, M., Laimon, D., Smith, S., . . . Flindt, N. (2004). *Technical adequacy and decision making utility of DIBELS (Technical Report No. 7)*. Eugene, OR: University of Oregon.

Greenber, M. T., Domitrovich, C. E., Weissberg, R. P., & Durlak, J. A. (2017). Social and emotional learning as a public health approach to education. *The Future of Children, 27*, 13–32.

Hawken, L. S., & Breen, K. (2017). *Check-In, Check-Out* (2nd ed.). New York, NY: Guilford Press.

Horner, R. H., Kincaid, D., Sugai, G., Lewis, T., Eber, L., Barrett, S., . . . Johnson, N. (2013). Scaling up school-wide positive behavioral interventions and supports: Experiences of seven states with documented success. *Journal of Positive Behavior Interventions, 16*, 197–208. doi:10.1177/1098300713503685

Horner, R. H., & Sugai, G. (2015). School-wide PBIS: An example of applied behavior analysis implemented at a scale of social importance. *Behavior Analysis in Practice, 8*, 80–85. doi:10.1007/s40617-015-0045-4

Hudson, T. M., & McKenzie, R. G. (2016). Evaluating the use of RTI to identify SLD: A survey of state policy, procedures, data collection, and administrator perceptions. *Contemporary School Psychology, 20*, 31–45. doi:10.1007/s40688-015-0081-7

Jimerson, S. R., Burns, M. K., & VanDerHeyden, A. M. (Eds.). (2016). *Handbook of response to intervention: The science and practice of multi-tiered systems of support* (2nd ed.). New York, NY: Springer.

Jitendra, A., & Dupuis, D. N. (2016). The role of tier 1 mathematics instruction and elementary and middle schools: Promoting mathematics success. In S. R. Jimerson, M. K. Burns, & A. M. VanDerHeyden (Eds.), *Handbook of response to intervention: The science and practice of multi-tiered systems of support* (2nd ed., pp. 215–233). New York, NY: Springer.

Johnsen, S. K., Parker, S. L., & Farah, Y. N. (2015). Providing services for students with gifts and talents within a response-to-intervention framework. *TEACHING Exceptional Children, 47*, 226–233. doi:10.1177/0040059915569358

Klinger, J. K., Vaughn, S., & Boardman, A. (2015). *Teaching reading comprehension to students with learning difficulties* (2nd ed.). New York, NY: Guilford Press.

Lane, K. L., Kalberg, J. R., & Menzies, H. M. (2009). *Developing schoolwide programs to prevent and manage problem behaviors: A step-by-step approach*. New York, NY: Guilford Press.

Lane, K. L., Menzies, H. M., Ennis, R. P., & Oakes, W. P. (2015). *Supporting behavior for school success: A step-by-step guide to key strategies*. New York, NY: Guilford Press.

Lane, K. L., Menzies, H. M., Oakes, W. P., & Kalberg, J. R. (2012). *A comprehensive, integrated three-tier model to meet students' academic, behavioral, and social needs*. Washington, DC: American Psychological Association.

Lane, K. L., Oakes, W. P., Cantwell, E. D., & Royer, D. J. (2016). *Building and installing comprehensive, integrated, three-tiered (Ci3T) models of prevention: A practical guide to supporting school success*. Phoenix, AZ: KOI Education.

Lane, K. L., Oakes, W. P., Cantwell, E. D., Schatschneider, C., Menzies, H., Crittenden, M., & Messenger, M. (2016). Student Risk Screening Scale for Internalizing and Externalizing Behaviors: Preliminary cut scores to support data-informed decision making in middle and high schools. *Behavioral Disorders, 42*, 271–284. doi:10.17988/bd-16-115.1

Lane, K. L., Oakes, W. P., Jenkins, A., Menzies, H. M., & Kalberg, J. R. (2014). A team-based process for designing Comprehensive, Integrated, Three-Tiered (CI3T) Models of Prevention: How does my school-site leadership team design a CI3T model? *Preventing School Failure, 58*, 129–142. doi:10.1080/1045988X.2014.893976

Lane, K. L., Oakes, W. P., Lusk, M. E., Cantwell, E. D., & Schatschneider, C. (in press). Screening for intensive intervention needs at the secondary level: Directions for the future. *Journal of Emotional and Behavioral Disorders*. doi:10.1177/1063426615618624

Lewis, T. J., McIntosh, K., Simonsen, B., Mitchell, B. S., & Hatton, H. L. (2017). Schoolwide systems of positive behavior support: Implications for students at risk and with emotional/behavioral disorders. *AERA Open, 3*(2), 1–11. doi:10.1177/2332858417711428

Lewis, T. J., Mitchell, B. S., Bruntmeyer, D. T., & Sugai, G. (2016). School-wide positive behavior support and response to intervention: System similarities, distinctions, and research to date at the universal level of support. In S. R. Jimerson, M. K. Burns, & A. M. VanDerHeyden (Eds.), *Handbook of response to intervention: The science and practice of multi-tiered systems of support* (2nd ed., pp. 703–717). New York, NY: Springer.

Malloy, J. M., Bohanon, H., & Francoeur, K. (2018). Positive behavioral interventions and supports in high schools: A case study from New Hampshire. *Journal of Educational and Psychological Consultation*, 1–29. doi: 10.1080/10474412.2017.1385398

May, S., Ard, W., Todd, A., Horner, R., Glasgow, A., Sugai, G., . . . & Sprague, J. (2000). *School-Wide Information System (SWIS)*. Eugene, OR: University of Oregon, Educational and Community Supports.

McCart, A., Sailor, W., Bezdek, J., & Satter, A. (2014). A framework for inclusive educational delivery systems. *Inclusion, 2*, 252–264.

McIntosh, K., Chard, D. J., Boland, J. B., & Horner, R. H. (2006). Demonstration of combined efforts in school-wide academic and behavioral systems and incidence of reading and behavior challenges in early elementary grades. *Journal of Positive Behavior Interventions, 8*, 146–154. doi:10.1177/10983007060080030301

McIntosh, K., & Goodman, S. (2016). *Integrated multi-tiered systems of support: Blending RTI and PBIS*. New York, NY: Guilford Press.

McIntosh, K., Kelm, J. L., & Canizal Delabra, A. (2016). In search of how principals change: A qualitative study of events that help and hinder administrator support for school-wide PBIS. *Journal of Positive Behavior Interventions, 18*, 100–110. doi:http://dx.doi.org/10.1177/1098300715599960

Miciak, J., Fletcher, J. M., & Stuebing, K. K. (2016). Accuracy and validity of methods for identifying learning disaiblities in a response-to-intervention service delivery framework. In S. R. Jimerson, M. K. Burns, & A. M. VanDerHeyden (Eds.), *Handbook of response to intervention: The science and practice of multi-tiered systems of support* (2nd ed., pp. 421–440). New York, NY: Springer.

Miciak, J., Roberts, G., Taylor, W. P., Solis, M., Ahmed, Y., Vaughn, S., & Fletcher, J. M. (2018). The effects of one versus two years of intensive reading intervention implemented with late elementary struggling readers. *Learning Disabilities Research & Practice, 33*(1), 24–36. doi:doi:10.1111/ldrp.12159

Mitchell, B. S., Bruhn, A. L., & Lewis, T. J. (2016). Essential features of Tier 2 and 3 school-wide positive behavioral supports. In S. R. Jimerson, M. K. Burns, & A. M. VanDerHeyden (Eds.), *Handbook of response to intervention: The science and practice of multi-tiered systems of support* (2nd ed., pp. 539–562). New York, NY: Springer.

National Association for Gifted Children & the Council of State Directors of Programs for the Gifted. (2015). *2014–2015 state of the states in gifted education: National policy and practice data*. Washington, DC: Author.

National Center on Response to Intervention. (2010). *Essential Components of RTI: A Closer Look at Response to Intervention*. Washington, DC: U.S. Department of Education, Office of Special Education Programs, National Center on Response to Intervention.

Nese, R. N. T., & McIntosh, K. (2016). Do school-wide positive behavioral interventions and supports, not exclusionary discipline practices. In B. G. Cook, M. Tankersley, & T. J. Landrum (Eds.), *Instructional practices with and without empirical validity* (pp. 175–196, Chapter viii, 219 pages): Bingley, United Kingdom: Emerald Group Publishing.

Newton, J. S., Horner, R. H., Todd, A. W., Algozzine, B., & Algozzine, K. M. (2012). A pilot study of a problem-solving model for team decision making. *Education and Treatment of Children, 35*, 25–49.

Newton, J. S., Todd, A. W., Algozzine, K. M., Horner, R. H., & Algozzine, B. (2009). *Team-initiated problem solving training manual*. Eugene, OR: Educational and Community Supports, University of Oregon.

O'Neill, R. E., Albin, R. W., Storey, K., Horner, R. H., & Sprague, J. R. (2015). *Functional assessment and program development for problem behavior: A practical handbook* (3rd ed.). Stamford, CT: CENGAGE Learning.

Oakes, W. P., Lane, K. L., Cantwell, E. D., & Royer, D. J. (2017). Systematic screening for behavior in k-12 settings as regular school practice: Practical considerations and recommendations. *Journal of Applied School Psychology, 33,* 369–393.

Pearson Education. (2008). *AIMSWeb*. San Antonio, TX: Author.

Riffel, L. A., & Mitchiner, M. (2015). *Positive behavior support at the secondary "targeted group" level: Yellow zone strategies.* Thousand Oaks, CA: Corwin Press.

Riley-Tillman, T. C., & Johnson, A. H. (2017). Current advances and future directions in behavior assessment. *Assessment for Effective Intervention, 42,* 77–80. doi:http://dx.doi.org/10.1177/1534508416666068

Shogren, K. A., Wehmeyer, M. L., Lane, K. L., & Quirk, C. (2017). Multi-tiered systems of supports. In M. L. Wehmeyer & K. A. Shogren (Eds.), *Handbook of research-based practices for educating students with intellectual disability* (pp. 185–198). New York, NY: Routledge.

Solari, E. J., Denton, C. A., & Haring, C. (2017). How to reach first-grade struggling readers: An integrated instructional approach. *TEACHING Exceptional Children, 49,* 149–159. doi:10.1177/0040059916673296

Spear-Swerling, L. (in press) Structured literacy and typical literacy practices: Understanding differences to create instructional opportunities. *TEACHING Exceptional Children.* doi:10.1177/0040059917750160

Stormont, M. A., Thompson, A. M., Herman, K. C., & Reinke, W. M. (2016). The social and emotional dimensions of a single item overall school readiness screener and its relation to academic outcomes. *Assessment for Effective Intervention, 42,* 67–76. doi:10.1177/1534508416652070

Sugai, G., & Horner, R. (2010). Schoolwide positive behavior supports: Establishing a continuum of evidence-based practices. *Journal of Evidence-Based Practices for Schools, 11,* 62–83.

Sugai, G., Horner, R. H., Dunlap, G. Hieneman, M., Lewis, T. J., Nelson, C. M., . . . Wilcox, B. (2000). Applying positive behavioral support and functional behavioral assessment in schools. *Journal of Positive Behavioral Interventions, 2,* 131–143.

Swanson, E., Stevens, E. A., Scammacca, N. K., Capin, P., Stewart, A. A., & Austin, C. R. (2017). The impact of tier 1 reading instruction on reading outcomes for students in Grades 4–12: A meta-analysis. *Reading and Writing, 30,* 1639–1665. doi:10.1007/s11145-017-9743-3

Taylor, R. D., Oberle, E., Durlak, J. A., & Weissberg, R. P. (2017). Promoting positive youth development through school-based social and emotional learning interventions: A meta-analysis of follow-up effects. *Child Development, 88,* 1156–1171. doi:doi:10.1111/cdev.12864

Tobin, T. J., Lewis-Palmer, T., & Sugai, G. (2002). School-wide and individualized effective behavior support: An explanation and an example. *The Behavior Analyst Today, 3,* 51–75. doi:10.1037/h0099960

Todd, A. W., Horner, R. H., Newton, J. S., Algozzine, R. F., Algozzine, K. M., & Frank, J. L. (2011). Effects of team-initiated problem solving on decision making by schoolwide behavior support teams. *Journal of Applied School Psychology, 27,* 42–59.

Vaughn, S., & Roberts, G. (2007). Secondary interventions in reading: Providing additional instruction for students at risk. *TEACHING Exceptional Children, 39,* 40–46.

Vaughn, S., Wanzek, J., Murray, C. S., & Roberts, G. (2012). *Intensive interventions for students struggling in reading and mathematics: A practice guide.* Portsmouth, NH: RMC Research Corporation, Center on Instruction.

Vaughn Gross Center for Reading and Language Arts at The University of Texas at Austin. (2005). *Implementing the 3-tier reading model: Reducing reading difficulties for kindergarten through third grade students* (2nd ed.). Austin, TX: Author.

Vincent, C. G., Randall, C., Cartledge, G., Tobin, T. J., & Swain-Bradway, J. (2011). Toward a conceptual integration of cultural responsiveness and schoolwide positive behavior support. *Journal of Positive Behavior Interventions, 13,* 219–229. doi:10.1177/1098300711399765

Wanzek, J., Vaughn, S., Scammacca, N., Gatlin, B., Walker, M. A., & Capin, P. (2016). Meta-analyses of the effects of Tier 2 type reading interventions in grades K-3. *Educational Psychology Review, 28,* 551–576. doi:10.1007/s10648-015-9321-7

Wanzek, J., Vaughn, S., Scammacca, N. K., Metz, K., Murray, C. S., Roberts, G., & Danielson, L. (2013). Extensive reading interventions for students with reading difficulties after grade 3. *Review of Educational Research, 83,* 163–195. doi:10.3102/0034654313477212

Wexler, J., Vaughn, S., & Swanson, E. (2016). *Resources for improving low literacy levels in adolescents.* Austin, TX: The Meadows Center for Preventing Educational Risk.

Zirkel, P. A. (2017). RTI and other approaches to SLD identification under the IDEA: A legal update. *Learning Disaiblity Quarterly, 40,* 165–173.

Chapter 6

Alberto, P. A., & Troutman, A. C. (2013). *Applied behavior analysis for Teachers* (9th ed.). Upper Saddle River, NJ: Pearson.

Alper, S., & Raharinirina, S. (2006). Assistive technology for individuals with disabilities: A review and synthesis of the literature. *Journal of Special Education Technology, 21,* 47–64.

Archer, A. L., & Hughes, C. A. (2011). *Explicit instruction: Effective and efficient teaching.* New York, NY: Guilford Press.

Biggs, E. E., & Carter, E. W. (2017). Supporting the social lives of students with intellectual disability. In M. L. Wehmeyer & K. A. Shogren (Eds.), *Handbook of research-based practices for educating students with intellectual disability* (pp. 255–273). New York, NY: Routledge.

Bishop, C. D., Snyder, P., & Crow, R. (2015). Impact of video self-monitoring with graduated training on implementation of embedded instruction learning trials. *Topics in Early Childhood Special Education, 35,* 170–182.

Bouck, E. C. (2016). A national snapshot of assistive technology for students with disabilities. *Journal of Special Education Technology, 31,* 4–13. doi:10.1177/0162643416633330

Bouck, E. C., & Flanagan, S. M. (2016). Exploring assistive technology and post-school outcomes for students with severe disabilities. *Disability and Rehabilitation: Assistive Technology, 11,* 645–652. doi:10.3109/17483107.2015.1029537

Brock, M. E., Biggs, E. E., Carter, E. W., Cattey, G. N., & Raley, K. S. (2016). Implementation and generalization of peer support arrangements for students with severe disabilities in inclusive classrooms. *The Journal of Special Education, 49,* 221–232. doi:http://dx.doi.org/10.1177/0022466915594368

Brock, M. E., & Huber, H. B. (2017). Are peer support arrangements an evidence-based practice? A systematic review. *The Journal of Special Education, 51,* 150–163. doi:10.1177/0022466917708184

Carter, E. W., Cushing, L. S., Clark, N. M., & Kennedy, C. H. (2005). Effects of peer support interventions on students' access to the general curriculum and social interactions. *Research and Practice for Persons with Severe Disabilities, 30,* 15–25.

Carter, E. W., Sisco, L. G., Chung, Y.-C., & Stanton-Chapman, T. L. (2010). Peer interactions of students with intellectual disabilities and/or autism: A map of the intervention literature. *Research and Practice for Persons with Severe Disabilities, 35,* 63–79. doi:10.2511/rpsd.35.3-4.63

CAST. (2018). Universal Design for Learning Guidelines version 2.2. Retrieved from http://udlguidelines.cast.org

Ciullo, S., Falcomata, T., & Vaughn, S. (2015). Teaching social studies to upper elementary students with learning disabilities: Graphic organizers and explicit instruction. *Learning Disability Quarterly, 38,* 15–26. doi:10.1177/0731948713516767

Clarke, B., Doabler, C., Smolkowski, K., Kurtz Nelson, E., Fien, H., Baker, S. K., & Kosty, D. (2016). Testing the immediate and long-term efficacy of a tier 2 kindergarten mathematics intervention. *Journal of Research on Educational Effectiveness, 9,* 607–634. doi:10.1080/19345747.2015.1116034

Doabler, C. T., Clarke, B., Kosty, D. B., Kurtz-Nelson, E., Fien, H., Smolkowski, K., & Baker, S. K. (2016). Testing the efficacy of a tier 2 mathematics intervention: A conceptual replication study. *Exceptional Children, 83,* 92–110. doi:10.1177/0014402916660084

Filderman, M. J., & Toste, J. R. (2018). Decisions, decisions, decisions: Using data to make instructional decisions for struggling readers. *TEACHING Exceptional Children, 50,* 130–140. doi:10.1177/0040059917740701

Flowers, C., Test, D. W., Povenmire-Kirk, T. C., Diegelmann, K. M., Bunch-Crump, K. R., Kemp-Inman, A., & Goodnight, C. I. (2018). A demonstration model of interagency collaboration for students with disabilities: A multilevel approach. *The Journal of Special Education, 51*, 211–221.

Friend, M., & Cook, L. (2010). *Interactions: Collaboration skills for school professionals* (6th ed.). Columbus, OH: Merrill.

Friend, M., Cook, L., Hurley-Chamberlain, D., & Shamberger, C. (2010). Co-teaching: An illustration of the complexity of collaboration in special education. *Journal of Educational and Psychological Consultation, 20*, 9–27. doi:10.1080/10474410903535380

Fuchs, D., Fuchs, L. S., Mathes, P. G., & Simmons, D. C. (1997). Peer-Assisted Learning Strategies: Making classrooms more responsive to diversity. *American Educational Research Journal, 34*, 174–206. doi:10.3102/00028312034001174

Gebhardt, M., Schwab, S., Krammer, M., & Gegenfurtner, A. (2015). General and special education teachers' perceptions of teamwork in inclusive classrooms at elementary and secondary schools. *Journal for Educational Research, 7*, 129–146.

Hall, T. E., Meyer, A., & Rose, D. (2012). *Universal design for learning in the classroom: Practical applications*. New York, NY: Guilford Press.

Hamilton, L., Halverson, R., Jackson, S., Mandinach, E., Supovitz, J., & Wayman, J. (2009). *Using student achievement data to support instructional decision making (NCEE 2009-4067)*. Washington, DC: National Center for Education Evaluation and Regional Assistance, Institute of Education Sciences, U.S. Department of Education.

Jimenez, B. A., & Kamei, A. (2015). Embedded instruction: An evaluation of evidence to inform inclusive practice. *Inclusion, 3*, 132–144. doi:10.1352/2326-6988-3.3.132

Knight, V. F., Wood, C. L., Spooner, F., Browder, D. M., & O'Brien, C. P. (2015). An exploratory study using science etexts with students with autism spectrum disorder. *Focus on Autism and Other Developmental Disabilities, 30*, 86–99.

Leach, D. (2016). Using high-probability instructional sequences and explicit instruction to teach multiplication facts. *Intervention in School and Clinic, 52*, 102–107. doi:10.1177/1053451216636062

Lippman, P. C. (2010). *Evidence-based design of elementary and secondary schools: A responsive approach to creating learning environments*. Hoboken, NJ: Wiley.

Lowrey, A. K., Hollingshead, A., & Howery, K. (2017). A closer look: Examining teachers' language around UDL, inclusive classrooms, and intellectual disability. *Intellectual and Developmental Disabilities, 55*, 15–24.

McDonnell, J., Jameson, M. J., Riesen, T., & Polychronis, S. (2014). Embedded instruction in inclusive settings. In D. Browder & F. Spooner (Eds.), *More language arts, math, and science for students with severe disabilities* (pp. 19–25). Baltimore, MD: Brookes.

McDonnell, J., Johnson, J. W., & McQuivey, C. (2008). *Embedded instruction for students with developmental disabilities in general education classes*. Alexandria, VA: Council for Exceptional Children.

McDonnell, J., Johnson, J. W., Polychronis, S. C., & Riesen, T. (2002). The effects of embedded instruction on students with moderate disabilities enrolled in general education classes. *Education and Training in Autism and Developmental Disabilities, 37*, 363–277.

McDonnell, J., Johnson, J., Polychronis, S., Riesen, T., Kercher, K., & Jameson, M. (2006). Comparison of one-to-one embedded instruction in general education classes with small group instruction in special education classes. *Education and Training in Developmental Disabilities, 41*, 125–138.

McLeskey, J., Barringer, M.-D., Billingsley, B., Brownell, M., Jackson, D., Kennedy, M., . . . Ziegler, D. (2017). *High-leverage practices in special education*. Arlington, VA: Council for Exceptional Children & CEEDAR Center.

Morningstar, M. E., Lombardi, A., Fowler, C. H., & Test, D. W. (2017). A college and career readiness framework for secondary students with disabilities. *Career Development and Transition for Exceptional Individuals, 40*, 79–91.

Nelson, L. L. (2014). *Design and deliver: Planning and teaching using universal design for learning*. Baltimore, MD: Brookes.

Nelson, L. L., & Johnson, M. D. (2017). The role of technology in implementing universal design for learning. In M. L. Wehmeyer & K. A. Shogren (Eds.), *Handbook of research-based practices for educating students with intellectual disability* (pp. 255–273). New York, NY: Routledge.

Okolo, C. M., & Diedrich, J. (2014). Twenty-five years later: How is technology used in education of students with disabilities? Results of a statewide study. *Journal of Special Education Technology, 29*, 1–20.

Pancsofar, N., & Petroff, J. G. (2016). Teachers' experiences with co-teaching as a model for inclusive education. *International Journal of Inclusive Education, 20*, 1043–1053.

Papay, C., Unger, D. D., Williams-Diehm, K., & Mitchell, V. (2015). Begin with the end in mind: Infusing transition planning and instruction into elementary classrooms. *TEACHING Exceptional Children, 47*, 310–318.

Polychronis, S. C., McDonnell, J., Johnson, J. W., Riesen, T., & Jameson, M. (2004). A comparison of two trial distribution schedules in embedded instruction. *Focus on Autism and Other Developmental Disabilities, 19*, 140–151. doi:10.1177/10883576040190030201

Pratt, S. M., Imbody, S. M., Wolf, L. D., & Patterson, A. L. (2017). Co-planning in co-teaching: A practical solution. *Intervention in School and Clinic, 52*, 243–249.

Quinn, B. S., Behrmann, M., Mastropieri, M., Bausch, M. E., Ault, M. J., & Chung, Y. (2009). Who is using assistive technology in schools? *Journal of Special Education Technology, 24*, 1–13.

Ralabate, P. K., & Nelson, L. L. (2017). *Culturally responsive design for English learners: The UDL approach*. Boston, MA: CAST Professional Publishing.

Riccomini, P. J., Morano, S., & Hughes, C. A. (2017). Big ideas in special education: Specially designed instruction, high-leverage practices, explicit instruction, and intensive instruction. *TEACHING Exceptional Children, 50*, 20–27.

Roux, C., Dion, E., Barrette, A., Dupéré, V., & Fuchs, D. (2015). Efficacy of an intervention to enhance reading comprehension of students with high-functioning autism spectrum disorder. *Remedial and Special Education, 36*, 131–142. doi:10.1177/0741932514533998

Ruppar, A. L., Afacan, K., Yang, Y.-L., & Pickett, K. J. (2017). Embedded shared reading to increase literacy in an inclusive English/language arts class: Preliminary efficacy and ecological validity. *Education and Training in Autism and Developmental Disabilities, 52*, 51–63.

Salend, S. J., & Whittaker, C. R. (2017). UDL: A blueprint for learning success. *Educational Leadership, 74*, 59–63.

Salisbury, C., Woods, J., Snyder, P., Moddelmog, K., Mawdsley, H., Romano, M., & Windsor, K. (2018). Caregiver and provider experiences with coaching and embedded intervention. *Topics in Early Childhood Special Education, 38*, 17–29.

Santoro, L. E., Baker, S. K., Flen, H., Smith, J. L. M., & Chard, D. J. (2016). Using read-alouds to help struggling readers access and comprehend complex informational text. *TEACHING Exceptional Children, 48*, 282–292.

Schaefer, J. M., Cannella-Malone, H. I., & Carter, E. W. (2016). The place of peers in peer-mediated interventions for students with intellectual disability. *Remedial and Special Education, 37*, 345–356. doi:10.1177/0741932516629220

Scruggs, T. E., & Mastropieri, M. A. (2017). Making inclusion work with co-teaching. *TEACHING Exceptional Children, 49*, 284–293.

Shepley, C., Lane, J. D., Ayres, K., & Douglas, K. H. (2017). Assistive and instructional technology:Understanding the differences to enhance programming and teaching. *Young Exceptional Children, 20*, 86–98. doi:10.1177/1096250615603436

Smith, J. L. M., Sáez, L., & Doabler, C. T. (2018). Using explicit and systematic instruction to support working memory. *TEACHING Exceptional Children, 50*(4), 250–257. doi:10.1177/0040059918758151

Taub, D. A., McCord, J. A., & Ryndak, D. L. (2017). Opportunities to learn for students with extensive support needs: A context of research-supported practices for all in general education classes. *The Journal of Special Education, 51*, 127–137. doi:10.1177/0022466917696263

Thompson, J. R., Hughes, C., Walker, V., & DeSpain, S. N. (2017). Measuring support needs and supports planning. In M. L.

Wehmeyer & K. A. Shogren (Eds.), *Handbook of research-based practices for educating students with intellectual disability* (pp. 79–101). New York, NY: Routledge.

Thompson, J. R., Shogren, K. A., & Wehmeyer, M. L. (2017). Supports and support needs in strengths-based models of intellectual disability. In M. L. Wehmeyer & K. A. Shogren (Eds.), *Handbook of research-based practices for educating students with intellectual disability* (pp. 31–49). New York, NY: Routledge.

Villa, R. A., & Thousand, J. S. (2016). *Leading an inclusive school: Access and success for ALL students.* Alexandria, VA: ASCD.

Wilson, G. L. (2016). *Co-planning for co-teaching: Time-saving routines that work in inclusive classrooms (ASCD Arias).* Alexandria, VA: ASCD.

Woods, D. M., Geller, L. K., & Basaraba, D. (2018). Number sense on the number line. *Intervention in School and Clinic, 53*(4), 229–236. doi:10.1177/1053451217712971

Yell, M. L., & Bateman, D. F. (2017). *Endrew F. v. Douglas County School District* (2017): FAPE and the U.S. Supreme Court. *TEACHING Exceptional Children, 50,* 7–15.

Chapter 7

Adlof, S., Catts, H., & Lee, J. (2010). Kindergarten predictors of second versus eighth grade reading comprehension impairments. *Journal of Learning Disabilities, 43*(4), 332–345.

Ashkenazi, S., Black, J. M., Abrams, D. A., Hoeft, F., & Menon, V. (2013). Neurobiological underpinnings of math and reading learning disabilities. *Journal of Learning Disabilities, 46*(6), 1–21.

Astrom, R. L., Wadsworth, S. J., Olson, R. K., Willcutt, E. G., & DeFries, J. C. (2012). Genetic and environmental etiologies of reading difficulties: DeFries-Fulker analysis of reading performance data from twin pairs and their non-twin siblings. *Learning and Individual Differences, 22,* 365–369.

Christopher, M. E., Hulslander, J., Byrne, B., Samuelsson, S., Keenan, J. M., Pennington, B., . . . Olson, R. K. (2013). Modeling the etiology of individual differences in early reading development: Evidence for strong genetic influences. *Scientific Studies of Reading,* 1–19.

Codding, R. S. & Martin, R. (2016). Tier 3: Intensive mathematics intervention strategies. In S. R. Jimerson, M. K. Burns, & A. M. VanDerHeyden (Eds.), *Handbook of response to intervention: The science and practice of multi-tiered systems of support* (2nd ed., pp. 375–388). New York, NY: Springer.

Compton, D. L., Fuchs, L. S., Fuchs, D., Lambert, W., & Hamlett, C. (2012). The cognitive and academic profiles of reading and mathematics learning disabilities. *Journal of Learning Disabilities, 45*(1), 79–95.

Cortiella, C. & Horowitz, S. H. (2014). *The state of learning disabilities:* Facts, trends and emerging issues. New York, NY: National Center for Learning Disabilities.

De La Paz (2001). STOP and DARE: A persuasive writing strategy. *Intervention in School and Clinic, 36,* 234–243.

De La Paz, S., & Graham, S. (1997a). Strategy instruction in planning: Effects on the writing performance and behavior of students with learning difficulties. *Exceptional Children, 63,* 167–181.

De La Paz, S., & Graham, S. (1997b). Effects of dictation and advanced planning instruction on the composing of students with writing and learning problems. *Journal of Educational Psychology, 89,* 203–222.

Fletcher, J. M., & Vaughn, S. (2009). Response to intervention: Preventing and remediating academic difficulties. *Child Development Perspectives, 3*(1), 30–37.

Fuchs, G., & Fuchs, L. (2007). A model for implementing responsiveness to intervention. *TEACHING Exceptional Children, 38*(5), 14–20.

Geary, D. C. (2013). Learning disabilities in mathematics: Recent advances. In H. L. Swanson, K. R. Harris, & S. Graham (Eds.), *Handbook of learning disabilities* (2nd ed., pp. 186–213). New York, NY: Guilford Press.

Gillingham, A., & Stillman, B. W. (1997). *The Gillingham Manual: Remedial training for students with specific disability in reading, spelling, and penmanship.* Cambridge, MA: Educators Publishing Service, Inc.

Graham, S., & Harris, K. R. (2005). *Writing better: Effective strategies for teaching students with learning disabilities.* Baltimore, MD: Brookes.

Graham, S., Harris, K. R., & McKeown, D. (2013). The writing of students with learning disabilities, meta-analysis of Self-Regulated Strategy Development writing intervention studies, and future directions: Redux. In H. L. Swanson, K. R. Harris, & S. Graham (Eds.), *Handbook of learning disabilities* (2nd ed., pp. 405–438). New York: Guilford Press.

Harris, K. R., Graham, S., Mason, L. H., & Friedlander, B. (2008). *Powerful writing strategies for students.* Baltimore, MD: Brookes.

Hosp, J. L., Huddle, S., Ford, J. W., & Hensley, K. (2016). Learning disabilities/special education. In S. R. Jimerson, M. K. Burns, & A. M. VanDerHeyden (Eds.), *Handbook of response to intervention: The science and practice of multi-tiered systems of support* (2nd ed., pp. 43–58). New York, NY: Springer.

Judge, S. L., & Watson, S. M. R. (2011). Longitudinal outcomes for mathematics achievement for students with learning disabilities. *The Journal of Educational Research, 104,* 147–157.

Maki, K. E., Floyd, R. G., & Roberson, T. (2015, January 12). State Learning Disability Eligibility Criteria: A comprehensive review. *School Psychology Quarterly.* Advance online publication. http://dx.doi.org/10.1037/spq0000109

McLeskey, J., & Waldron, N. L. (2011). Educational programs for elementary students with learning disabilities: Can they be both effective and inclusive? *Learning Disabilities Practice, 26*(1), 48–57.

Mercer, C. D., Mercer, A., & Pullen, P. C. (2011). *Teaching students with learning disabilities* (7th ed.). Upper Saddle River, NJ: Pearson.

Morris, D. (2011). Interventions to develop phonological and orthographic systems. In A. McGill-Franzen & R. L. Allington (Eds.), *Handbook of reading disability research* (pp. 279–288). New York, NY: Routledge.

National Center for Educational Statistics (2017). *Children and youth with disabilities.* Retrieved from https://nces.ed.gov/programs/coe/indicator_cgg.asp/

Nelson, J. M., & Harwood, H. R. (2011). A meta-analysis of parent and teacher reports of depression among students with learning disabilities: Evidence for the importance of multi-informant assessment. *Psychology in the Schools, 48*(4), 371–384.

Pullen, P. C., Lane, H. B., Ashworth, K. E., & Lovelace, S. P. (2017). Specific learning disabilities. In J. M. Kauffman, D. P. Hallahan, & P. C. Pullen (Eds.), *Handbook of special education* (2nd ed., pp. 286–299). New York, NY: Routledge.

Reed, G. (2016). *Dyslexia: A practitioner's handbook* (5th ed.). West Sussex, United Kingdom: Wiley Blackwell.

Ritchey, K. D., & Goeke, J. L. (2006). Orton-Gillingham and Orton-Gillingham-based reading instruction: A review of the literature. *The Journal of Special Education, 40,* 171–183.

Snowling, M. J., & Hulme, C. (2008). Reading and other specific learning disabilities. In M. Rutter, D. V. M. Bishop, D. S. Pine, S. Scott, J. Stevenson, E. Taylor, & A. Thapar (Eds.), *Rutter's child and adolescent psychiatry* (5th ed., pp. 802–819). Malden, MA: Blackwell Publishing.

Swanson, H. L. (2016). Working memory and strategy instruction in children with learning disabilities. In R. Schiff & R. M. Joshi (Eds.), *Interventions in learning disabilities: A handbook on systematic training programs for individuals with learning disabilities* (pp. 227–242). Basel, Switzerland: Springer.

Tremblay, P. (2013). Comparative outcomes of two instructional models for students with learning disabilities: Inclusion with co-teaching and solo-taught special education. *Journal of Research in Special Education Needs, 13*(4), 251–258.

Wagner, R. K., & Torgesen, J. K. (2009). Using the comprehensive test of phonological processing (CTOPP) to assess reading-related phonological processes. In J. A. Naglieri & S. Goldstein (Eds.), *Practitioner's guide to assessing intelligence and achievement* (pp. 367–387). Hoboken, NJ: Wiley.

Wagner, R. K., Torgesen, J., Rashotte, C., & Pearson, N. A. (2013). *Comprehensive test of phonological processing, second edition (C20PP-2).* Retrieved from http://www.pearsonassessments.com/HAIWEB/Cultures/en-us/Productdetail.htm?Pid=CTOPP2

Chapter 8

American Speech-Language-Hearing Association (ASHA). (2007a). Accents and dialects. Retrieved from http://www.asha.org/about/leadership-projects/multicultural/issues/ad.htm

American Speech-Language-Hearing Association (ASHA). (2007b). *Childhood apraxia of speech*. Retrieved from www.asha.org/policy

American Speech-Language-Hearing Association (ASHA). (2010). *Roles and responsibilities of speech-language pathologists in schools*. Retrieved from http://www.asha.org/policy

American Speech-Language-Hearing Association (ASHA). (n.d.). *Inclusive practices for speech language pathologists*. Retrieved from http://education.wm.edu/centers/ttac/documents/packets/inclusivepracticesforspeech.pdf

American Speech-Language Hearing Association (ASHA). (n.d.). *School-Based Service Delivery in Speech-Language Pathology*. Retreived from https://www.asha.org/SLP/schools/School-Based-Service-Delivery-in-Speech-Language-Pathology/#settings

Apel, K., & Swank, L. K. (1999). Second chances: Improving decoding skills in the older student. *Language, Speech, and Hearing Services in Schools, 30*, 231–242.

Battle, D. (2012). *Communication disorders in multicultural populations* (4th ed.). Boston, MA: Butterworth-Heinemann.

Beukelman, D. R., & Mirenda, P. A. (2013). *Augmentative and alternative communication: Supporting children and adults with complex communication needs* (4th ed.). Baltimore, MD: Brookes.

Blackstone, S. (2006, September). The effects of modeling aided AAC. *Augmentative Communication News, 18*(3), 7–11.

Blackstone, S., Hunt-Berg, M., Nygard, J., & Schultz, J. (2004). *Social networks: A communication inventory for individuals with complex communication needs and their communication partners*. Verona, WI: Attainment.

Bloom, L., & Lahey, M. (1978). *Language development and language disorders*. New York, NY: Wiley.

Brandel, J., & Loeb, D. (2011). Program intensity and service delivery models in the schools: SLP survey results. *Language, Speech, and Hearing Services in Schools, 42*, 461–490.

Bunce, B., & Watkins, R. (1995). Language intervention in a preschool classroom: Implementing a language-focused curriculum. In M. Rice & K. Wilcox (Eds.), *Building a language-focused curriculum for the preschool classroom Vol. I. A foundation for lifelong communication*. Baltimore, MD: Brookes.

Capp, M. J. (2017) The effectiveness of universal design for learning: a meta-analysis of literature between 2013 and 2016, *International Journal of Inclusive Education, 21*(8), 791–807, DOI: 10.1080/13603116.2017.1325074

Caruso, A., & Strand, E. (1999). *Clinical management of motor speech disorders in children*. New York, NY: Thieme.

Chomsky, N. (1957). *Syntactic structures*. The Hague, the Netherlands: Mouton.

Cirrin, F., Schooling, T., Nelson, N., Diehl, S., Flynn, P., Staskowski, M., Torrey, T., & Adamczyke (2010). Evidence-based systematic review: Effects of different service delivery models on communication outcomes for elementary school-age children. *Language, Speech, and Hearing Services in Schools, 41*(3), 233–264.

Clapsaddle, K., & Palafox, P. (2013, August). Make it work: Steps to save our sanity: We've all heard the benefits of moving services into the classroom. But how, practically, do we do it? *The ASHA Leader, 18*, 26–27.

Cunningham, P. M., & Allington, R. L. (2010). *Classrooms that work: They can all read and write* (4th ed.). Boston, MA: Pearson Education.

Downing, J. E. (2005). *Teaching communication skills to students with severe disabilities* (2nd ed.). Baltimore, MD: Brookes.

Elder, P. S., & Goossens, C. (1994). *Engineering training environments for interactive augmentative communication: Strategies for adolescents and adults who are moderately severely developmentally delayed*. Birmingham, AL: Southeast Augmentative Communication Conference Publications.

Foley, B., & Staples, A. (2000, August). *Literature-based language intervention for students who use AAC*. Paper presented at the International Society for Augmentative and Alternative Communication Convention, Washington, DC.

Gillam, R., & Gillam, S. (2015). An introduction to the discipline of communication sciences and disorders. In R. Gillam, T. Marquardt, & F. Martin (3rd ed.), *Communication sciences and disorders: From science to clinical practice* (3rd ed., pp. 3–25). Sudbury, MA: Jones & Bartlett

Gillon, G. T. (2007). Phonological awareness—Implications for children with expressive phonological impairment. In B. W. Hodson (Ed.), *Evaluating and enhancing children's phonological systems—Research and theory to practice* (pp. 123–141). Greenville, SC: Thinking Publications.

Goossens, C., Crain, S., & Elder, P. (1992). *Engineering the preschool environment for interactive, symbolic communication*. Birmingham, AL: Southeast Augmentative Communication Conference Publications.

Haynes, W., & Pindzola, R. (2012). *Diagnosis and evaluation in speech pathology* (8th ed.). Boston, MA: Pearson Education.

Hoff, E. (2009). *Language development* (4th ed.). Belmont, CA: Wadsworth/Thompson Learning.

Howell, K. W., & Nolet, V. (2009). *Curriculum-based evaluation teaching and decision making* (3rd ed.). Belmont, CA: Wadsworth/Thompson Learning.

Hulit, L. M., Howard, M. R., & Fahey, K. R. (2014). *Born to talk: An introduction to speech and language development* (6th ed.). Boston, MA: Pearson.

Justice, L., & Redle, E. (2014). *Communication sciences and disorders: A clinical evidence-based approach* (3rd ed.). Boston, MA: Pearson.

Kuder, J. S. (2008). *Teaching students with language and communication disabilities* (3rd ed.). Boston, MA: Pearson Education.

Kumin, L. (2001). *Classroom language skills for children with Down syndrome: A guide for parents and teachers*. Bethesda, MD: Woodbine House.

Lombardino, L. J., Riccio, C. A., Hynd, G. W., & Pinheiro, S. B. (1997). Linguistic deficits in children with reading disabilities. *American Journal of Speech-Language Pathology, 6*, 71–78.

Losardo, A., & Notari-Syverson, A. (2011). *Alternative approaches to assessing young children*. Baltimore, MD: Brookes.

Lowden, K., Hall, S., Elliot, D., & Lewin, J. (2011). *Employers' perceptions of the employability skills of new graduates research commissioned by the Edge Foundation*. London University of Glasgow SCRE Centre and Edge Foundation.

McCormick, L., & Loeb, D. (2003). Characteristics of students with language and communication difficulties. In L. McCormick, D. Loeb & D. Schiefelbusch (Eds.), *Supporting children with communication difficulties in inclusive settings: School-based language intervention* (2nd ed., pp. 71–112). Boston, MA: Allyn & Bacon.

McGinty, A. S., & Justice, L. M. (2006). Classroom-based versus pull-out speech-language intervention: A review of the experimental evidence. EBP Briefs, 1(1), 1–25. i. EBP Briefs. A publication of AGS Publishing, now part of Pearson Assessments.

McFarland, J., Hussar, B., de Brey, C., Snyder, T., Wang, X., Wilkinson-Flicker, S., . . . Hinz, S. (2017). The Condition of Education 2017. Washington, DC: National Center for Education Statistics Retrieved from https://nces.ed.gov/pubsearch/pubsinfo.asp?pubid=2017144.

Mullen, R., & Schooling, T. (2010). The National Outcomes Measurement System for pediatric speech-language Pathology. *Language, Speech, and Hearing Services in Schools, 41*(1), 44–60.

Myles, B., & Simpson, R. (2003). *Asperger syndrome: A guide for educators and parents* (2nd ed.). Austin, TX: Pro-Ed.

National Institutes of Health. (2011). *Rett syndrome*. Retrieved from http://www.ncbi.nlm.nih.gov/pubmedhealth/PMH0002503

Nelson, N., & Van Meter, A. (2004). *The writing lab approach to language instruction and intervention*. Baltimore, MD: Brookes.

National Institute on Deafness and Other Communication Disorders (2016). Quick Statistics About Voice, Speech, Language. Retrieved September 18, 2018, from https://www.nidcd.nih.gov/health/statistics/quick-statistics-voice-speech-language

Owens, R. (2012). *Language development: An introduction* (8th ed.). Boston, MA: Allyn & Bacon.

Palilis, B. (2010, April). The path to inclusion: Online exclusive. *The ASHA Leader*. Retrieved from http://www.asha.org.publications/leader/2010/100427/path-inclusion.htm

Paradis, J., Genesee, F., & Crago, M. (2011). *Dual language development and disorders: A handbook on bilingualism and second language learning*. Baltimore, MD: Brookes.

Porter, G., & Burkhart, L. (2010). *Pragmatic organization dynamic displays communication books: Designing and implementing PODD communication books*. Victoria, Australia: Cerebral Palsy Education Centre.

Rice, M. L., & Wilcox, K. (1995). *Building a language-focused curriculum for the preschool classroom: Vol. I. A foundation for lifelong communication*. Baltimore, MD: Brookes.

Romski, M. A., & Sevcik, R. A. (1988). Augmentative communication system acquisition and use: A model for teaching and assessing progress. *National Student Speech Language Hearing Association Journal, 16*, 61–74.

Romski, M. A., & Sevcik, R. A. (1992). Developing augmented language in children with severe mental retardation. In S. F. Warren & J. Reichle (Eds.), *Communication and language intervention series: Vol. 1. Causes and effects in communication and language intervention* (pp. 113–130). Baltimore. MD: Brookes.

Romski, M. A., & Sevcik, R. A. (1996). *Breaking the speech barrier: Language development through augmented means*. Baltimore, MD: Brookes.

Romski, M. A., & Sevcik, R. A. (2003). Augmented input. In J. Light, D. Beukelman, & J. Reichle (Eds.), *Communicative competence for individuals who use AAC: From research to effective practice*. Baltimore, MD: Brookes.

Romski, M. A., Sevcik, R. A., & Forrest, S. (2001). Assistive technology and augmentative communication in inclusive early childhood programs. In M. J. Guralnick (Ed.), *Early childhood inclusion: Focus on change* (pp. 465–479). Baltimore, MD: Brookes.

Roseberry-McKibbin, C., & O'Hanlon, L. (2005). Nonbiased assessment of English language learners: A tutorial. *Communication Disorders Quarterly, 26*(3), 178–185.

Sturm, J., & Rankin-Erickson, J. (2002). Effects of hand-drawn and computer-generated concept mapping on the expository writing of middle school students with learning disabilities. *Learning Disabilities Research and Practices, 17*(2), 124–139.

U.S. Department of Education, National Center for Education Statistics. (2016). *Digest of Education Statistics, 2015* (NCES 2016-014), Chapter 2. Retrieved September 19, 2018 from https://nces.ed.gov/fastfacts/display.asp?id=59.

Verdolini, K. (2000). Voice disorders. In J. Tomblin, H. Morris, & D. Spriestersbach (Eds.), *Diagnosis in speech-language pathology* (2nd ed., pp. 233–280). San Diego, CA: Singular.

Chapter 9

American Psychiatric Association. (2013). *Diagnostic and statistical manual of mental disorders* (5th ed.). Washington, DC: Author.

Buckley, J. A., Ryser, G., Reid, R., & Epstein, M. H. (2006). Confirmatory factor analysis of the behavioral and emotional rating scale-2 (BERS-2) parent and youth rating scales. *Journal of Child and Family Studies, 15*(1), 27–38.

Centers for Disease Control and Prevention (CDC). (2016). *About the CDC-Kaiser ACE Study*. Retrieved from https://www.cdc.gov/violenceprevention/acestudy/about.html/

Ehrensaft, M. K., & Cohen, P. (2012). Contribution of family violence to the intergenerational transmission of externalizing behavior. *Prevention Science, 13*, 370–383.

Epstein, M. H. (2004). *Behavioral and Emotional Rating Scale (BERS-2): A strength-based approach to assessment* (2nd ed.). Austin, TX: Pro-Ed.

Epstein, M. H., Cullinan, D., Ryser, G., & Pearson, N. (2002). Development of a scale to assess emotional disturbance. *Behavioral Disorders, 28*(1), 5–22.

Flick, G. L. (2011). *Understanding and managing emotional and behavioral disorders in the classroom*. Upper Saddle River, NJ: Merrill/Pearson.

Forness, S. R., Freeman, S. F. N., Paparella, T., Kauffman, J. M., & Walker, H. M. (2012). Special education implications of point and cumulative prevalence for children with emotional or behavioral disorders. *Journal of Emotional and Behavioral Disorders, 20*(1), 4–18.

Gable, R. A., Tonelson, S. W., Sheth, M., Wilson, C., & Park, K. L. (2012). Importance, usage, and preparedness to implement evidence-based practices for students with emotional disabilities: A comparison of knowledge and skills of special education and general education teachers. *Education and Treatment of Children, 35*(4), 499–519.

Goodman, S. H., Rouse, M. H., Connell, A. M., Broth, M. R., Hall, C. M., & Heyward, D. (2011). Maternal depression and child psychopathology: A meta-analytic review. *Clinical Child and Family Psychology Review, 14*, 1–27.

Higa-McMillan, C. K., Francis, S. E., & Chorpita, B. F. (2014). Anxiety disorders. In E. J. Mash & R. A. Barkley (Eds.), *Child psychopathology* (3rd ed., pp. 345–428). New York, NY: Guilford Press.

Kabat-Zinn, J. (1994). *Wherever you go, there you are: Mindfulness meditation in everyday living*. New York, NY: Hyperion.

Kamphaus, R. W., & Mays, K. L. (2011). Assessment of internalizing behavioral deficits. In M. A. Bray & T. J. Kehle (Eds.), *The Oxford handbook of school psychology* (pp. 312–333). New York, NY: Oxford University Press.

Kann, L., McManus, T., Harris, W. A., Shanklin, S. L., Flint, K. H., Hawkins, J., . . . Zaza, S. (2016). Youth risk behavior surveillance—United States, 2015. *MMWR Surveillance Summaries, 65*(6).

Kimonis, E. R., Frick, P. J., & McMahon, R. J. (2014). Conduct and oppositional defiant disorders. In E. J. Mash & R. A. Barkley (Eds.), *Child psychopathology* (3rd ed., pp. 145–179). New York, NY: Guilford Press.

Kuniyoshi, J., & McClellan, J. M. (2014). Early-onset schizophrenia. In E. J. Mash & R. A. Barkley (Eds.), *Child psychopathology* (3rd ed., pp. 573–592). New York, NY: Guilford Press.

Lamb, G. D. (2011). Test review. *Journal of Psychoeducational Awareness, 29*(5), 479–483.

Landrum, T. J. (2017). Emotional and behavioral disorders. In J. M. Kauffman, D. P. Hallahan, & P. C. Pullen (Eds.), *Handbook of special education* (2nd ed., pp. 312–324). New York, NY: Routledge.

Lane, K. L., Barton-Arwood, S. M., Nelson, J. R., & Wehby, J. (2008). Academic performance of students with emotional and behavioral disorders served in a self-contained setting. *Journal of Behavioral Education, 17*, 43–62.

Linehan, M. M. (1993). *Skills training manual for treating borderline personality disorder*. New York, NY: Guilford Press.

Lipscomb, S., Haimson, J., Liu, A. Y., Burghardt, J., Johnson, D. R., & Thurlow, M. L. (2017). Preparing for life after high school: The characteristics and experiences of youth in special education. Findings from the National Longitudinal Transition Study 2012. Volume 2: Comparisons across disability groups: Full report (NCEE 2017-4018). Washington, DC: U.S. Department of Education, Institute of Education Sciences, National Center for Education Evaluation and Regional Assistance.

Losen, D. J., Ee, J., Hodson, C., & Martinez, T. E. (2015). Disturbing in equalities: Exploring the relationship between racial disparities in special education identification and discipline. In B. J. Losen (Ed.), *Closing the school discipline gap: Equitable remedies for excessive exclusion* (pp. 107–117). New York, NY: Teachers College Columbia University.

Mazza, J. J., Dexter-Mazza, E. T., Miller, A. L., Rathus, J. H., & Murphy, H. E. (2016). *DBT® skills in schools: Skills training for emotional problem-solving for adolescents (DBT STEPS-A)*. New York, NY: Guilford Press.

McClowry, S. G., Rodriguez, E. T., Tamis-LeMonda, C. S., Spellmann, M., Carlson, A., & Snow, D. L. (2013). Teacher/student interactions and classroom behavior: The role of student temperament and gender. *Journal of Research in Childhood Education, 27*(3), 283–301.

Menting, A. T. A., de Castro, B. O., & Matthys, W. (2013). Effectiveness of the Incredible Years parent training to modify disruptive and prosocial child behavior: A meta-analytic review. *Clinical Psychology Review, 33*, 901–913.

Merikangas, K. R., He, J., Burstein, M., Swendsen, J., Avenevoli, S., Case, B., . . . Olfson, M. (2011). Service utilization for lifetime mental disorders in U.S. adolescents: Results of the national comorbidity survey-adolescent supplement (NCS-A). *Journal of the American Academy of Child & Adolescent Psychiatry, 50*(1), 32–45.

Miller, A. L., Rathus, J. H., Linehan, M. M. (2007). *Dialectical behavior therapy with suicidal adolescents.* New York, NY: Guilford Press.

Miner, J. L., & Clarke-Stewart, K. A. (2008). Trajectories of externalizing behavior from age 2 to age 9: Relations with gender, temperament, ethnicity, parenting, and rater. *Developmental Psychology, 44*(3), 771–786.

Munkvold, L. H., Lundervold, A. J., & Manger, T. (2011). Oppositional defiant disorder—gender differences in co-occurring symptoms of mental health problems in a general population of children. *Journal of Abnormal Child Psychology, 39*(4), 577–587.

Nabors, L. (2016). *Medical and mental health during childhood: Psychosocial perspective and positive outcomes.* Basel, Switzerland: Springer.

U.S. Department of Education (n.d.). Supporting youth with disabilities in juvenile correction centers. Retrieved from https://sites.ed.gov/osers/2017/05/supporting-youth-with-disabilities-in-juvenile-corrections/

Prather-Jones, B. (2011). "Some people aren't cut out for it": The role of personality factors in the careers of teachers of students with EBD. *Remedial and Special Education, 32*(3), 179–191.

Ranney, M. L., Walton, M., Whiteside, L., Epstein-Ngo, Q., Patton, R., Chermack, S., . . . Cunningham, R. M. (2013). Correlates of depressive symptoms among at-risk youth presenting to the emergency department. *General Hospital Psychiatry.* Retrieved from http://dx.doi.org/10.1016/j.genhosppsych.2013.1005.1007

Rathus, J. H., & Miller, A. L. (2002). Dialectical behavior therapy adapted for suicidal adolescents. *Suicide and Life-Threatening Behavior, 32*, 146–157.

Rechtschaffen, D. (2016). *The mindful education workbook: Lessons for teaching mindfulness to students.* New York, NY: W. W. Norton & Company.

Rechtschaffen, D. J. (2014). *The way of mindful education: Cultivating well-being in teachers and students.* New York, NY: W. W. Norton & Company.

Reiss, F. (2013). Socioeconomic inequalities and mental health problems in children and adolescents: A systematic review. *Social Science & Medicine, 90*, 24–31.

Rice, E. H., Merves, E., & Srsic, A. (2008). Perceptions of gender differences in the expression of emotional and behavioral disabilities. *Education and Treatment of Children, 31*(4), 549–565.

Robb, A. (2013). Behavioral and psychiatric disorders in children with disabilities. In M. L. Batshaw, N. J. Roizen, & G. R. Lotrecchiano (Eds.), *Children with disabilities* (7th ed., pp. 523–543). Baltimore, MD: Brookes.

Scharfstein, L., Alfano, C., Beidel, D., & Wong, N. (2011). Children with generalized anxiety disorder do not have peer problems, just fewer friends. *Child Psychiatry and Human Development, 42*, 712–723.

Schoenfeld, N. A., & Janney, D. M. (2008). Identification and treatment of anxiety in students with emotional or behavioral disorders: A review of the literature. *Education and Treatment of Children, 31*(4), 583–610.

Sharkey, J. D., You, S., Morrison, G. M., & Griffiths, A. J. (2009). Behavioral and Emotional Rating Scale-2 Parent Report: Exploring a Spanish Version with At-Risk Students. *Behavioral Disorders, 35*(1), 53–65.

Singh, N. N., Lancioni, G. E., Hwang, Y. S., Chan, J., Shogren, K. A., & Wehmeyer, M. L. (2017). Mindfulness: An application of positive psychology in intellectual and developmental disabilities. In K. A. Shogren, M. L. Wehmeyer, & N. N. Singh (Eds.), *Handbook of positive psychology in intellectual and developmental disabilities.* New York, NY: Springer Series on Child and Family Studies.

Stoutjesdijk, R., Scholte, E. M., & Swaab, H. (2012). Special needs characteristics of children with emotional and behavioral disorders that affect inclusion in regular education. *Journal of Emotional and Behavioral Disorders, 20*(2), 92–104.

Stringaris, A., Maughan, B., & Goodman, R. (2010). What's in a disruptive disorder? Temperamental antecedents of oppositional defiant disorder: Findings from the Avon longitudinal study.

Journal of the American Academy of Child & Adolescent Psychiatry, 49(5), 474–483.

Thapar, A., Collishaw, S., Pine, D. S., & Thapar, A. K. (2012). Depression in adolescence. *Lancet, 379*, 1056–1067.

Thompson, K. C., & Morris, R. J. (2016). *Juvenile delinquency and disability.* Berlin, Germany: Springer.

U.S. Department of Education. (2016). *38th annual report to Congress on the implementation of the Individuals with Disabilities Education Act, 2016.* Washington, DC: Author.

U.S. Department of Education. (2017). Questions and answers (Q&A) on *U.S. Supreme Court Case Decision Endrew F. v. Douglas Country School District Re-1.* Retrieved from: https://sites.ed.gov/idea/questions-and-answers-qa-on-u-s-supreme-court-case-decision-endrew-f-v-douglas-county-school-district-re-1/

U.S. Department of Education. (2018). *39th annual report to Congress on the implementation of the Individuals with Disabilities Education Act, 2017.* Washington, DC: Author.

U.S. Department of Veteran Affairs. (n.d.). *PTSD: PTSD Center.* Retrieved from https://www.ptsd.va.gov/professional/treatment/children/ptsd_in_children_and_adolescents_overview_for_professionals.asp/

Velders, F. P., Dieleman, G., Henrichs, J., Jaddoe, V. W. V., Hofman, A., Verhulst, F. C., . . . Tiemeier, H. (2011). Prenatal and postnatal psychological symptoms of parents and family functioning: The impact on child emotional and behavioural problems. *European Child and Adolescent Psychiatry, 20*, 341–350.

Volpe, R. J., & Chafouleas, S. M. (2011). Assessment of externalizing behavioral deficits. In M. A. Bray & T. J. Kehle (Eds.), *The Oxford handbook of school psychology* (pp. 284–311). New York, NY: Oxford University Press.

Wagner, M., Kutash, K., Duchnowski, A. J., Epstein, M. H., & Sumi, W. C. (2005). The children and youth we serve: A national picture of the characteristics of students with emotional disturbances receiving special education. *Journal of Emotional and Behavioral Disorders, 13*(2), 79–96.

Wagner, M. (2014). Longitudinal outcomes and post-high school status of students with emotional or behavioral disorders. In H. M. Walker & F. M. Gresham (Eds.), *Handbook of evidence-based practices for emotional and behavioral disorders: Applications in schools* (pp. 86–103). New York, NY: The Guilford Press.

Waters, L., Barsky, A., Ridd, A., & Allen, K. (2015). Contemplative education: A systematic, evidence-based review of the effect of meditation interventions in schools. *Educational Psychology Review, 27*, 103–134.

Webster-Stratton, C., Rinaldi, J., & Reid, J. M. (2011). Long-term outcomes of Incredible Years parenting program: Predictors of adolescent adjustment. *Child and Adolescent Mental Health, 16*(1), 38–46.

Yeh, M., Forness, S. R., Ho, J., McCabe, K., & Hough, R. L. (2004). Parental etiological explanations and disproportionate racial/ethnic representation in special education services for youths with emotional disturbance. *Behavioral Disorders, 29*(4), 348–358.

Yoshikawa, H., Aber, J. L., & Beardslee, W. R. (2012). The effects of poverty on the mental, emotional, and behavioral health of children and youth: Implications for prevention. *American Psychologist, 67*(4), 272–284.

Chapter 10

American Academy of Child and Adolescent Psychiatry (AACAP) and American Psychiatric Association (APA). (2013). *ADHD: Parents medication guide.* https://www.psychiatry.org/patients-families/adhd/what-is-adhd/

American Psychiatric Association. (2013). *Diagnostic and statistical manual of mental disorders* (5th ed.). Arlington, VA: Author.

Barkley, R. (2016). *Managing ADHD in school: The best evidence-based methods for teachers.* Eau Claire, WI: PESI Publishing & Media.

Barkley, R. A. (2015). Psychological assessment of children with ADHD. In R. A. Barkley (Ed.), *Attention-deficit hyperactivity disorder: A handbook for diagnosis and treatment* (4th ed., pp. 455–474). New York, NY: Guilford Press.

Brown, T. E. (2013). *A new understanding of ADHD in children and adults: Executive function impairments*. New York, NY: Routledge.

Bussing, R., Mason, D. M., Bell, L., Porter, P., & Garvan, C. (2010). Adolescent outcomes of childhood attention-deficit/hyperactivity disorder in a diverse community sample. *Journal of the American Academy of Child & Adolescent Psychiatry, 49*(6), 595–605.

Bussing, R., Porter, P., Zima, B. T., Mason, D. M., Garvan, C., & Reid, R. (2012). Academic outcome trajectories of students with ADHD: Does exceptional education status matter? *Journal of Emotional and Behavioral Disorders, 20*(3), 131–143.

Cortese, S. (2012). The neurobiology and genetics of attention-deficit/hyperactivity disorder (ADHD): What every clinician should know. *European Journal of Paediatric Neurology, 16*, 422–433.

Demaray, M. K., Elting, J., & Schaefer, K. (2003). Assessment of attention-deficit/hyperactivity disorder (AD/HD): A comparative evaluation of five commonly used, published rating scales. *Psychology in the Schools, 40*(4), 341–361.

Denckla, M. B., Barquero, L. A., Lindstrom, E. R., Benedict, S. L., Wilson, L. M., & Cutting, L. E. (2013). Attention-deficit/hyperactivity disorder, executive function, and reading comprehension. In H. L. Swanson, K. R. Harris, & S. Graham (Eds.), *Handbook of learning disabilities* (2nd ed., pp. 155–168). New York: Guilford Press.

Evans, S. W., Langberg, J. M., Egan, T., & Molitor, S. J. (2014). Middle school-based and high school-based interventions for adolescents with ADHD. *Child and Adolescent Psychiatric Clinics of North America, 23*(4), 699–715.

Freitag, C. M., Hänig, S., Schneider, A., Seitz, C., Palmason, H., Retz, W., & Meyer, J. (2012). Biological and psychosocial risk factors influence symptom severity and psychiatric comorbidity in children with ADHD. *Journal of Neural Transmission, 119*(1), 81–94.

Glanzman, M. M., & Sell, N. (2013). Attention deficits and hyperactivity. In M. L. Batshaw, N. J. Roizen, & G. R. Lotrecchiano (Eds.), *Children with disabilities* (7th ed., pp. 369–402). Baltimore. MD: Brookes.

Katusic, M. Z., Voigt, R. G., Colligan, R. C., Weaver, A. L., Homan, K. J., & Barbaresi, W. J. (2011). Attention-deficit hyperactivity disorder in children with high intelligence quotient: Results from a population-based study. *Journal of Developmental and Behavioral Pediatrics, 32*(2), 103–109.

Langberg, J. M., Epstein, J. N., Becker, S. P., Girio-Herrera, E., & Vaughn, A. J. (2012). Evaluation of the Homework, Organization, and Planning Skills (HOPS) intervention for middle school students with attention deficit hyperactivity disorder as implemented by school mental health providers. *School Psychology Review, 41*, 342–364.

Langberg, J. M., Dvorsky, M. R., Molitor, S. I., Bourchtein, E., Eddy, L. D., Smith, Z. R., . . . Eadeh, H. M. (2018). Overcoming the research-to-practice gap: A randomized trial with two brief homework and organization interventions for students with ADHD as implemented by school mental health providers. *Journal of Consulting and Clinical Psychology, 86*(1), 39–55.

Langner, I., Garbe, E., Banaschewski, T., & Mikolajczyk, R. T. (2013). Twin and sibling studies using health insurance data: The example of attention deficit/hyperactivity disorder. *Heritability Research in Routine Health Care Data, 8*(4).

Mikami, A. Y., Griggs, M. S., Lerner, M. D., Emeh, C. C., Reuland, M. M., Jack, A., & Anthony, M. R. (2013). A randomized trial of a classroom intervention to increase peers' social inclusion of children with attention-deficit/hyperactivity disorder. *Journal of Consulting and Clinical Psychology, 81*(1), 100–111.

Morgan, P. L., Staff, J., Hillemeier, M. M., Farkas, G., & Maczuga, S. (2013). Racial and ethnic disparities in ADHD diagnosis from kindergarten to eighth grade. *Pediatrics*. doi:10.1542/peds.2012-2390

National Center for Health Statistics. (2017). *Attention deficit hyperactivity disorder (ADHD)*. www.cdc.gov.nzhs/fastats/adhd.htm/

Nigg, J. T., & Barkley, R. A. (2014). Attention-deficit/hyperactivity disorder. In E. J. Mash & R. A. Barkley (Eds.), *Child psychopathology* (3rd ed., pp. 75–144). New York, NY: Guilford Press.

Office for Civil Rights. (2016). *Students with ADHD and Section 504: A resource guide*. https://www2.ed.gov/about/offices/list/ocr/docs/dcl-know-rights-201607-504.pdf/

Pfiffner, L. J. & DuPaul, G. J. (2015). Treatment of ADHD in school settings. In R. A. Barkley (Ed.), *Attention-deficit hyperactivity disorder: A handbook for diagnosis and treatment* (4th ed., pp. 596–629). New York, NY: Guilford Press.

Roberts, W., Milich, R., & Barkley, R. A. (2015). Primary symptoms, diagnostic criteria, subtyping, and prevalence of ADHD. In R. A. Barkley (Ed.), *Attention-deficit hyperactivity disorder: A handbook for diagnosis and treatment* (4th ed., pp. 51–80). New York, NY: Guilford Press.

Rooney, K. J. (2017). Attention-deficit/hyperactivity disorder. In J. M. Kauffman, D. P. Hallahan, & P. C. Pullen (Eds.), *Handbook of special education* (2nd ed., pp. 300–311). New York, NY: Routledge.

Sjöwall, D., Roth, L., Lindqvist, S., & Thorell, L. B. (2013). Multiple deficits in ADHD: Executive dysfunction, delay aversion, reaction time variability, and emotional deficits. *Journal of Child Psychology and Psychiatry, 54*(6), 619–627.

Thapar, A., Cooper, M., Eyre, O., & Langley, K. (2013). Practitioner review: What have we learnt about the causes of ADHD? *Journal of Child Psychology and Psychiatry, 54*(1), 3–16.

Thompson, D. (2017). Kids with ADHD make 6.1M doctor visits a year: CDC. *HealthDay Reporter*. http://www.healthday.com/

U.S. Department of Education. (2016). *Thirty-eighth annual report to Congress on the implementation of the Individuals with Disabilities Act, 2013*. Washington, DC: Author.

Visser, S. N., Danielson, M. L., Bitsko, R. H., Holbrook, J. R., Kogan, M. D., Ghandour, R., M., . . . Blumberg, S. J. (2014). Trends in the parent-report of health care provider-diagnosed and medicated attention-deficit/hyperactivity disorder: United States, 2003, 2011. *Journal of the American Academy of Child & Adolescent Psychiatry, 53*(1), 34–46.

Zelazo, P. D., Blair, C. B., & Willoughby, M. T. (2016). *Executive function: Implications for education* (NCER 2017-2000). Washington, DC: National Center for Education Research, Institute of Education Sciences, U.S. Department of Education. This report is available on the Institute website at http://ies.edu.gov/

Chapter 11

Carter, E. W., Brock, M. E., & Trainor, A. A. (2014). Transition assessment and planning for youth with severe intellectual and developmental disabilities. *Journal of Special Education, 47*, 245–255.

Copeland, S. R., & Keefe, E. B. (2017). Teaching reading and literacy skills to students with intellectual disability. In M. L. Wehmeyer & K. A. Shogren (Eds.), *Handbook of research-based practices for educating students with intellectual disability* (pp. 320–342). New York, NY: Routledge.

Dekker, M. C., Ziermans, T. B., & Swaab, H. (2016). The impact of behavioural executive functioning and intelligence on math abilities in children with intellectual disabilities. *Journal of Intellectual Disability Research, 60*, 1086–1096.

Erickson, A. G., Clark, G. M., & Patton, J. R. (2013). *Informal assessment for transition planning* (2nd ed.). Austin, TX: PRO-ED.

Esbensen, A. J., & MacLean, W. E. (2017). Down syndrome. In M. L. Wehmeyer, I. Brown, M. Percy, K. Shogren, & W. L. A. Fung (Eds.), *A comprehensive guide to intellectual and developmental disabilities* (2nd ed., pp. 195–208). Baltimore, MD: Paul H. Brookes.

Graves, S. L., & Ye, F. F. (2017). Are special education labels accurate for black children? Racial differences in academic trajectories of youth diagnosed with specific learning and intellectual disabilities. *Journal of Black Psychology, 43*, 192–213.

Grigal, M., & Hart, D. (2010). *Think College! Postsecondary education options for students within intellectual disabilities*. Baltimore, MD: Brookes.

Heinrich, S., Knight, V., Collins, B. C., & Spriggs, A. D. (2016). Embedded simultaneous prompting procedure to teach STEM content to high school students with moderate disabilities in an inclusive setting. *Education and Training in Autism and Developmental Disabilities, 51*, 41–54.

Hudson, M. E., Browder, D. M., & Wood, L. A. (2013). Review of experimental research on academic learning by students with moderate and severe intellectual disability in general education. *Research and Practice for Persons with Severe Disabilities, 38,* 17–29.

Jimenez, B. A., & Staples, K. (2015). Access to the Common Core State Standards in mathematics through early numeracy skill building for students with significant intellectual disability. *Education and Training in Intellectual and Developmental Disabiltiies, 50,* 17–30.

Jimenez, B. A., Browder, D. M., Spooner, F., & Dibiase, W. (2012). Inclusive inquiry science using peer-mediated embedded instruction for students with moderate intellectual disability. *Exceptional Children, 78,* 301–317.

Karam, S. M., Barros, A. J. D., Matijasevich, A., dos Santos, I. S., Anselmi, L., Barros, F., . . . Black, M. M. (2016). Intellectual disability in a birth cohort: Prevalence, etiology, and determinants at the age of 4 years. *Public Health Genomics, 19,* 290–297.

Kim, R., & Dymond, S. K. (2010). Special education teachers' perceptions of benefits, barriers, and components of community-based vocational instruction. *Intellectual and Developmental Disabilities, 48*(5), 313–329.

Kurth, J., Marks, S., & Bartz, J. (2017). Educating students in inclusive classrooms. In M. L. Wehmeyer & K. A. Shogren (Eds.), *Handbook of research-based practices for educating students with intellectual disability* (pp. 274–295). New York, NY: Routledge.

McClain, C., Kodituwakku, E. L., & Kodituwakku, P. W. (2017). Fetal alcohol spectrum disorder, Part 1. In M. L. Wehmeyer, I. Brown, M. Percy, K. Shogren, & W. L. A. Fung (Eds.), *A comprehensive guide to intellectual and developmental disabilities* (2nd ed., pp. 243–255). Baltimore, MD: Paul H. Brookes.

McDonnell, J., Johnson, J. W., & McQuivey, C. (2008). *Embedded instruction for students with developmental disabilities in general education classes.* Reston, VA: Council for Exceptional Children.

McKenzie, K., Milton, M., Smith, G., & Ouellette-Kuntz, H. (2016). Systematic review of the prevalence and incidence of intellectual disabilities: Current trends and issues. *Current Developmental Disorders Reports, 3,* 104–115.

Patton, J. R., & Clark, G. M. (2013). *Transition Planning Inventory* (2nd edition) (TPI-2). Austin, TX: PRO-ED.

Percy, A., Brown, M., & Fung, W. L. A. (2017). Factors causing or contributing to intellectual and developmental disabilities. In M. L. Wehmeyer, I. Brown, M. Percy, K. Shogren, & W. L. A. Fung (Eds.), *A comprehensive guide to intellectual and developmental disabilities* (2nd ed., pp. 175–194). Baltimore, MD: Paul H. Brookes.

Percy, A., Machalek, K., Brown, M., Pasquali, P. E., & Fung, W. L. A. (2017). The first 1,000 days of fetal and infant development. In M. L. Wehmeyer, I. Brown, M. Percy, K. Shogren, & W. L. A. Fung (Eds.), *A comprehensive guide to intellectual and developmental disabilities* (2nd ed., pp. 475–494). Baltimore, MD: Paul H. Brookes.

Rehfeldt, J. D., Clark, G. M., & Lee, S. W. (2012). The effects of using the transition planning inventory and a structured IEP process as a transition planning intervention on IEP meeting outcomes. *Remedial and Special Education, 33*(1), 48–58.

Schalock, R., Borthwick-Duffy, S., Bradley, V., Buntinx, W., Coulter, D., Craig, E., . . . Yeager, M. (2010). *Intellectual disability: Definition, classification, and systems of support* (11th ed.). Washington, DC: American Association on Intellectual and Developmental Disabilities.

Shapiro, B. K., & Batshaw, M. L. (2013). Developmental delay and intellectual disability. In M. L. Batshaw, N. J. Roizen, & G. R. Lotrecchiano (Eds.), *Children with disabilities* (7th ed., pp. 291–306). Baltimore, MD: Brookes.

Shogren, K., Palmer, S., Wehmeyer, M. L., Williams-Diehm, K., & Little, T. (2012). Effect of intervention with the *Self-Determined Learning Model of Instruction* on access and goal attainment. *Remedial and Special Education, 33*(5), 320–330.

Shogren, K. A., Toste, J., Mahal, S., & Wehmeyer, M. L. (2017). Intrinsic motivation. In K. A. Shogren, M. L. Wehmeyer, & N. Singh (Eds.), *Handbook of positive psychology in intellectual and developmental disabilities* (pp. 285–295). New York, NY: Springer.

Shogren, K. A., Wehmeyer, M. L., Burke, K. M., & Palmer, S. B. (2017). *The Self-Determination Learning Model of Instruction: Teacher's Guide.* Lawrence, KS: Kansas University Center on Developmental Disabilities.

Shogren, K. A., Wehmeyer, M. L., Palmer, S. B., Rifenbark, G., & Little, T. (2015). Relationships between self-determination and postschool outcomes for youth with disabilities. *Journal of Special Education, 48*(4), 256–267.

Tassé, M. J. (2017). Adaptive behavior. In K. A. Shogren, M. L. Wehmeyer, & N. Singh (Eds.), *Handbook of positive psychology in intellectual and developmental disabilities* (pp. 201–215). New York, NY: Springer.

Tassé, M. J., Schalock, R. L., Thissen, D., Balboni, G., Bersani, H., Borthwick-Duffy, S., . . . Navas, P. (2016). Development and standardization of the Diagnostic Adaptive Behavior Scale: Application of response theory to the assessment of adaptive behavior. *American Journal on Intellectual and Developmental Disabilities, 121,* 79–94.

Thompson, J. R., Wehmeyer, M. L., Shogren, K. A., & Seo, H. J. (2017). The supports paradigm and intellectual and developmental disabilities. In K. A. Shogren, M. L. Wehmeyer, & N. N. Singh (Eds.), *Handbook of positive psychology in intellectual and developmental disabilities: Translating research into practice* (pp. 23–35). New York, NY: Springer.

U.S. Department of Education (2018). *39th Annual Report to Congress on the Implementation of the Individuals with Disabilities Education Act, 2017.* Washington, DC: U.S. Department of Education, Office of Special Education and Rehabilitation Services, Office of Special Education Programs.

Vicari, S., Costanzo, F., & Menghini, D. (2016). Memory and learning in intellectual disability. In R. M. Hodapp & D. J. Fidler (Eds.), *International Review of Research in Developmental Disabilities* (Vol. 50, pp. 119–148).

Wehmeyer, M. L., & Shogren, K. A. (2018). Self-determination and hope. In M. W. Gallagher & S. J. Lopez (Eds.), *The Oxford handbook of hope* (pp. 59–68). Oxford, UK: Oxford University Press.

Wehmeyer, M. L., Shogren, K., Palmer, S., Williams-Diehm, K., Little, T., & Boulton, A. (2012). The impact of the *Self-Determined Learning Model of Instruction* on student self-determination. *Exceptional Children, 78*(2), 135–153.

Williams-Diehm, K., & Palmer, S. P. (2017). High-quality educational programs for students with intellectual disability in elementary school. In M. L. Wehmeyer & K. A. Shogren (Eds.), *Handbook of research-based practices for educating students with intellectual disability* (pp. 383–405). New York, NY: Routledge.

Wood, L., Browder, D. M., & Flynn, L. (2015). Teaching students with intellectual disability to use a self-questioning strategy to comprehend social studies text for an inclusive setting. *Research and Practice for Persons with Severe Disabilities, 40,* 275–293.

Zhang, D., Katsiyannis, A., Ju, S., & Roberts, E. (2014). Minority representation in special education: 5-year trends. *Journal of Child and Family Studies, 23,* 118–127.

Chapter 12

Allen, R., & Smith, B. J. (2016). *Expelling expulsion: Using the Pyramid Model to prevent suspensions, expulsions, and disciplinary inequities in early childhood programs.* Tampa, FL: Florida Center for Inclusive Communities and University of South Florida.

Allen, R., & Steed, E. A. (2016). Culturally responsive Pyramid Model practices: Program-wide positive behavior support for young children. *Topics in Early Childhood Special Education, 36,* 165–175.

American Psychiatric Association. (2013). *Diagnostic and statistical manual of mental disorders* (5th ed.). Washington, DC: Author.

Anagnostou, E., Jones, N., Huerta, M., Halladay, A. K., Wang, P., Scahill, L., . . . Dawson, G. (2015). Measuring social communication behaviors as a treatment endpoint in individuals with autism spectrum disorder. *Autism, 19,* 622–632.

Bazzano, A., Zeldin, A., Schuster, E., Barrett, C., & Lehrer, D. (2012). Vaccine-related beliefs and practices of parents of children with autism spectrum disorders. *American Journal of Intellectual and Developmental Disabilities, 117,* 233–242.

Bettelheim, B. (1967). *The empty fortress: Infantile autism and the birth of the self.* London: Collier-Macmillan.

Boucher, J. (2012). Research review: Structural language in autistic spectrum disorder—Characteristics and causes. *Journal of Child Psychology and Psychiatry, 53*, 219–233.

Boyd, B. A., McDonough, S. G., & Bodfish, J. W. (2012). Evidence-based behavioral interventions for repetitive behaviors in autism. *Journal of Autism and Developmental Disabilities, 42*, 1236–1248.

Buxbaum, J. D., & Hof, P. R. (2013). *The neuroscience of autism spectrum disorders*. Oxford, UK: Elsevier.

Centers for Disease Control and Prevention (2016). *Community report from the autism and developmental disabilities monitoring (ADDM) network*. Atlanta, GA: Author.

Chandler, L. K., & Dahlquist, C. M. (2014). *Functional assessment: Strategies to prevent and remediate challenging behaviors in school settings* (4th ed.). Upper Saddle River, NJ: Pearson.

Chou, Y., Wehmeyer, M. L., Palmer, S., & Lee, J. H. (2017). Comparisons of self-determination among students with autism, intellectual disability, and learning disabilities: A multivariate analysis. *Focus on Autism and Other Developmental Disabilities, 32*, 124–132.

Christensen, D. L., Baio, J., Bruan, K. V. N., Bilder, D., Charles, J., Constantino, J. N., . . . Yeargin-Allsopp, M. (2016). Prevalence and characteristics of autism spectrum disorder among children aged 8 years—Autism and Developmental Disabilities Monitoring Network, 11 Sites, United States, 2012. *Morbidity and Mortality Weekly Report, 65*(3), 1–23.

DaWalt, L. S., Usher, L. V., Greenberg, J. S., & Mailick, M. R. (2017). Friendships and social participation as markers of quality of life of adolescents and adults with fragile X syndrome and autism. *Autism.* http://journals.sagepub.com/doi/10.1177/1362361317709202

DeStefano, F., Price, C. S., & Weintraub, E. S. (2013). Increasing exposure to antibody-stimulating proteins and polysaccharides in vaccines is not associated with risk of autism. *The Journal of Pediatrics, 163*, 561–567.

Dunlap, G., & Fox, L. (2015). *The Pyramid Model: PBS in early childhood programs and its relation to school-wide PBS*. Tampa, FL: Florida Center for Inclusive Communities and University of South Florida.

Dunlap, G., Smith, B. J., Fox, L., & Blase, K. (2014). Road map to statewide implementation of the Pyramid model. *Roadmap to Effective Intervention Practices #6*. Tampa, FL: University of South Florida, Technical Assistance Center on Social Emotional Intervention for Young Children.

Dunlap, G., Strain, P., & Fox, L. (2012). Positive behavior support and young people with autism: Strategies of prevention and intervention. In B. Kelly & D. F. Perkins (Eds.), *Handbook of implementation science for psychology in education* (pp. 247–263). New York, NY: Cambridge University Press.

Gann, C. J., & Umbreit, J. (2017). Video self-modeling was effective in promoting social initiations with young children with developmental disabilities. *Evidence-Based Communication Assessment and Intervention, 11*, 135–140.

Ganz, J. B., Earles-Vollrath, T. L., & Cook, K. E. (2011). Video modeling: A visually based intervention for children with autism spectrum disorder. *TEACHING Exceptional Children, 43*(6), 8–19.

Gray, C. (2013). Social stories™. In N. Grove (Ed.), *Using storytelling to support children and adults with special needs: Transforming lives through telling tales* (pp. 95–101). New York, NY: Routledge.

Ha, S., Sohn, I.-J., Kim, N., Sim, H. J., & Cheon, K.-A. (2015). Characteristics of brains in autism spectrum disorder: Structure, function, and connectivity across the lifespan. *Experimental Neurobiology, 24*, 273–284.

Hazlett, H. C., Gu, H., Munsell, B. C., Kim, S. K., Styner, M., Wolff, J. J., . . . Piven, J. (2017). Early brain development in infants at high risk for autism spectrum disorder. *Nature, 542*, 348–351.

Hemmeter, M. L., Snyder, P. A., Fox, L., & Algina, J. (2016). Evaluating the implementation of the Pyramid Model for Promoting Social-Emotional Competence in early childhood classrooms. *Topics in Early Childhood Special Education, 36*, 133–146.

Herringshaw, A. J., Ammons, C. J., DeRamus, T. P., & Kana, R. J. (2016). Hemispheric differences in language processing in autism spectrum disorders: A meta-analysis of neuroimaging studies. *Autism Research, 9*, 1046–1057.

Hill, A. P., Zuckerman, K. E., Hagen, A. D., Kriz, D. J., Duvall, S. W. van Senten, J., . . . Fombonne, E. (2014). Aggressive behavior problems in children with autism spectrum disorders: Prevalence and correlates in a large clinical sample. *Research in Autism Spectrum Disorders, 8*, 1121–1133.

Hyman, S. L., & Levy, S. E. (2013). Autism spectrum disorders. In M. L. Batshaw, N. J. Roizen, & G. R. Lotrecchiano (Eds.), *Children with disabilities* (7th ed., pp. 345–368). Baltimore, MD: Brookes.

Jain, A., Marshall, J., Buikema, A., Bancroft, T., Kelly, J. P., & Newschaffer, C. J. (2015). Autism occurrence by MMR vaccine status among US children with older siblings with and without autism. *Journal of the American Medical Association, 313*, 1534–1540.

Joseph, L., Thurm, A., Farmer, C., & Shumway, S. (2013). Repetitive behavior and restricted interests in young children with autism: Comparisons with controls and stability over 2 years. *Autism Research, 6*, 584–595.

Just, M. A., Keller, T. A., Malave, V. L., Kana, R. K., & Varma, S. (2012). Autism as a neural systems disorder: A theory of frontal-posterior underconnectivity. *Neuroscience and Biobehavioral Reviews, 36*, 1292–1313.

Kim, S. H., & Lord, C. (2012). New Autism Diagnostic Interview–Revised algorithms for toddlers and young preschoolers from 12 to 47 months of age. *Journal of Autism & Developmental Disorders, 42*, 82–93.

Kirby, A. V., Boyd, B. A., Williams, K. L., Faldowski, R. A., & Baranek, G. T. (2017). Sensory and repetitive behaviors among children with autism spectrum disorder at home. *Autism, 2*, 142–154.

Lauritsen, M. B. (2013). Autism spectrum disorders. *European Child and Adolescent Psychiatry, 22*, 37–42.

LeCouteur, A., Lord, C., & Rutter, M. (2003). *Autism Diagnostic Interview-Revised* (ADI-R). Western Psychological Services.

Lidstone, J., Uljarevic, M., Sullivan, J., Rodgers, J., McConachie, H., Freeston, M., . . . Leekam, S. (2014). Relations among restricted and repetitive behaviors, anxiety and sensory features in children with autism spectrum disorders. *Research in Autism Spectrum Disorders, 8*, 82–92.

Loomes, R., Hull, L., Mandy, W. P. L. (2017). What is the male-to-female ratio in autism spectrum disorder? A systematic review and meta-analysis. *Journal of the Academy of Child & Adolescent Psychiatry, 56*, 466–474.

Lord, C., & Jones, R. M. (2012). Annual research review: Re-thinking the classification of autism spectrum disorders. *Journal of Child Psychology and Psychiatry, 53*, 490–509.

Martin, J., Marshall, L., Maxson, L., & Jerman, M. (2016). *Self-directed IEP: Teacher's manual* (3rd ed.). Norman, OK: Zarrow Center for Learning Enrichment.

Mason, R. A., Davis, H. S., Ayres, K. M., Davis, J. L., & Mason, B. A. (2016). Video self-modeling for individuals with disabilities: A best-evidence, single case meta-analysis. *Journal of Developmental and Physical Disabilities, 28*, 623–642.

Mazurek, M. O., Kanne, S. M., & Wodka, E. L. (2013). Physical aggression in children and adolescents with autism spectrum disorders. *Research in Autism Spectrum Disorders, 7*, 455–465.

McCleery, J. P., Elliott, N. A., Sampanis, D. S., & Stefanidou, C. A. (2013). Motor development and motor resonance difficulties in autism: Relevance to early intervention for language and communication skills. *Frontiers in Integrative Neuroscience, 7*(30), 1–20.

Mehling, M. H., & Tasse, M .J. (2016). Severity of autism spectrum disorders: Current conceptualization, and transition to DSM-5. *Journal of Autism and Developmental Disorders, 46*, 2000–2016.

Minshawi, N. F., Hurwitz, S., Fodstad, J. C., Biebl, S., Morriss, D. H., & McDougle, C. J. (2014). The association between self-injurious behaviors and autism spectrum disorders. *Psychology Research and Behavior Management, 7*, 125–136.

Moskowitz, L. J., Walsh, C. E., & Durand, V. M. (2016). Assessment and intervention for self-injurious behavior using positive behavior support. In S. M. Edelson & J. B. Johnson (Eds.), *Understanding and treating self-injurious behavior in autism: A multi-disciplinary perspective* (pp. 151–185). London, UK: Jessica Kingsley Publishers.

Myles, B. S., Trautma, M. L., & Schelvan, R. L. (2013). *The hidden curriculum for understanding unstated rules in social situations for adolescents and young adults* (2nd ed.). Shawnee, KS: AAPC Publishing.

Nikopoulos, C. K., & Panagiotopoulou, I.-E. (2015). Video self-modeling for reducing vocal stereotypy in children with autism spectrum disorder. *European Journal of Behavior Analysis, 16*, 322–337.

O'Donnell, S., Deitz, J., Kartin, D., Nalty, T., & Dawson, G. (2012). Sensory processing, problem behavior, adaptive behavior, and cognition in preschool children with autism spectrum disorders. *The American Journal of Occupational Therapy, 66*(5), 586–594.

Orsmond, G. I., Shattuck, P. T., Cooper, B. P., Sterzing, P. R., & Anderson, K. A. (2013). Social participation among young adults with an autism spectrum disorder. *Journal of Autism and Developmental Disabilities, 43*, 2710–2719.

Perry, A., Koudys, J., Dunlap, G., & Black, A. (2017). Autism spectrum disorder. In M. L. Wehmeyer, I. Brown, M. Percy, K. A. Shogren, & W. L. A. Fung (Eds.), *A comprehensive guide to intellectual and developmental disabilities* (2nd ed., pp. 219–230). Baltimore, MD: Paul H. Brookes.

Qi, C. H., Barton, E. E., Collier, M., Lin, Y.-L., & Montoya, C. (2018). A systematic review of effects of social stories interventions for individuals with autism spectrum disorder. *Focus on Autism and Other Developmental Disabilities, 33*, 25–34.

Ramaswami, G., & Geschwind, D. H. (2018). Genetics of autism spectrum disorder. In D. H. Geschwind, H. L. Paulson, & C. Klein (Eds.), *Handbook of clinical neurology* (Vol. 147, pp. 321–329). Oxford, UK: Elsevier Science.

Ray-Subramanian, C. E., & Weismer, S. E. (2012). Receptive and expressive language as predictors of restricted and repetitive behaviors in young children with autism spectrum disorders. *Journal of Autism & Developmental Disorders, 42*, 2113–2120.

Reed, F. D. D., Hirst, J. M., & Hyman, S. R. (2012). Assessment and treatment of stereotypic behavior in children with autism and other developmental disabilities: A thirty year review. *Research in Autism Spectrum Disorders, 6*, 422–430.

Robledo, J., Donnellan, A. M., & Strandt-Conroy, K. (2012). An exploration of sensory and movement differences from the perspective of individuals with autism. *Frontiers in Integrative Neuroscience, 6*(107), 1–13.

Ryan, J. B., Hughes, E. M., Katsiyannis, A., McDaniel, M., & Sprinkle, C. (2011). Research-based educational practices for students with autism spectrum disorders. *TEACHING Exceptional Children, 43*(3), 56–64.

Schatz, R. B., Peterson, R. K., & Bellini, S. (2016). The use of video self-modeling to increase on-task behavior in children with high-functioning autism. *Journal of Applied School Psychology, 32*, 234–253.

Tager-Flusberg, H., & Kasari, C. (2013). Minimally verbal school-aged children with autism spectrum disorder: The neglected end of the spectrum. *Autism Research, 6*, 468–478.

Tick, B., Bolton, P., Happe, F., Rutter, M., & Rijsdijk, F. (2015). Heritability of autism spectrum disorders: A meta-analysis of twin studies. *Journal of Child Psychology and Psychiatry and Allied Disciplines, 57*, 585–595.

Timimi, S., & McCabe, B. (2016). Autism screening and diagnostic tools. In Runswick-Cole, K., Mallett, R., & Timimi, S. (Eds.), *Re-thinking autism: Diagnosis, identity and equality* (pp. 159–184). London: Jessica Kingsley Publishers.

Travers, J. C., Tincani, M., & Krezmien, M. P. (2013). A multiyear national profile of racial disparity in autism identification. *The Journal of Special Education, 47*, 41–49.

Treffert, D. A. (2014). Savant syndrome: Realities, myths and misconceptions. *Journal of Autism and Developmental Disorders, 44*, 564–571.

Uphold, N. M., Douglas, K. H., & Loseke, D. L. (2016). Effects of using an iPod app to manage recreation tasks. *Career Development and Transition for Exceptional Individuals, 39*, 88–98.

U.S. Department of Education (2018). *39th Annual Report to Congress on the Implementation of the Individuals with Disabilities Education Act, 2017.* Washington, DC: U.S. Department of Education, Office of Special Education and Rehabilitation Services, Office of Special Education Programs.

Watkins, L., Kuhn, M., Ledbetter-Cho, K., Gevarter, C., & O'Reilly, M. (2017). Evidence-based social communication interventions for children with autism spectrum disorder. *The Indian Journal of Pediatrics, 84*, 68–75.

Wehmeyer, M. L., & Shogren, K. A. (2016). Self-determination and choice. In N. N. Singh (Ed.), *Handbook of evidence-based practices in intellectual and developmental disabilities* (pp. 561–584). New York, NY: Springer.

Wehmeyer, M. L., Shogren, K. A., Little, T. D., & Lopez, S. J. (2017). *Development of self-determination through the life-course.* New York, NY: Springer.

Whyatt, C., & Craig, C. (2013). Sensory-motor problems in autism. *Frontiers in Integrative Neuroscience, 7*(51), 1–12.

Woolfenden, S., Sarkozy, V., Ridley, G., & Williams, K. (2012). A systematic review of the diagnostic stability of Autism Spectrum Disorder. *Research in Autism Spectrum Disorders, 6*, 345–354.

Xu, G., Strathearn, L., Liu, B., & Bao, W. (2018). Prevalence of autism spectrum disorder among US children and adolescents, 2014–2016. *Journal of the American Medical Association, 319*, 81–82.

Zander, E., Willfors, C., Berggren, S., Coco, C., Holm, A., Jifalt, I., . . . Bolte, S. (2017). The interrater reliability of the Autism Diagnostic Interview-Revised (ADI-R) in clinical settings. *Psychopathology, 50*, 219–227.

Chapter 13

Anderson, V., Catroppa, C., Godfrey, C., & Rosenfeld, J. V. (2012). Intellectual ability 10 years after traumatic brain injury in infancy and childhood: What predicts outcome? *Journal of Neurotrauma, 29*, 143–153.

Bedell, G. M., Wade, S. L., Turkstra, L. S., Haarbauer-Krupa, J., & King, J. A. (2017). Informing design of an app-based coaching intervention to promote social participation of teenagers with traumatic brain injury. *Developmental Neurorehabilitation, 20*, 408–417.

Biggs, E. E., Carter, E. W., & Gustafson, J. (2017). Efficacy of peer support arrangements to increase peer interaction and AAC use. *American Journal on Intellectual and Developmental Disabilities, 122*, 25–48.

Boeing, M., Barton, B., Zinsmeister, P., Brouwers, L., Trudel, T. M., Elias, E., & Weider, K. (2010). TBI-ROC Part Six: Lifelong Living after TBI. *Exceptional Parent, 40*(10), 32–37.

Brock, M. E., Biggs, E. E., Carter, E. W., Cattey, G. N., & Raley, K. S. (2016). Implementation and generalization of peer support arrangements for students with severe disabilities in inclusive classrooms. *The Journal of Special Education, 49*, 221–232.

Brock, M. E., & Carter, E. W. (2016). Efficacy of teachers training paraprofessionals to implement peer support arrangements. *Exceptional Children, 82*, 354–371.

Brock, M. E., & Carter, E. W. (2017). A meta-analysis of educator training to improve implementation of interventions for students with disabilities. *Remedial and Special Education, 38*, 131–144.

Brown, F., McDonnell, J. J., & Snell, M. E. (2015). *Instruction of students with severe disabilities* (8th ed.). Upper Saddle River, NJ: Merrill/Prentice Hall.

Brunner, M., Hemsley, B., Togher, L., & Palmer, S. (2017). Technology and its role in rehabilitation for people with cognitive-communication disability following a traumatic brain injury (TBI). *Brain Injury, 31*, 1028–1043.

Carter, E., O'Rourke, L., Sisco, L. G., & Pelsue, D. (2009). Knowledge, responsibilities, and training needs of paraprofessionals in elementary and secondary schools. *Remedial and Special Education, 30*, 344–359. doi:10.1177/0741932508324399

Claes, C., Van Hove, G., Vandevelde, S., van Loon, J., & Schalock, R. L. (2010). Person-centered planning: Analysis of research and effectiveness. *Intellectual and Developmental Disabilities, 48*, 432–453.

Collins, B. (2012). *Systematic instruction for students with moderate and severe disabilities.* Baltimore, MD: Paul H. Brookes.

Davies, D. K., Stock, S. E., King, L. R., Brown, R. B., Wehmeyer, M. L., & Shogren, K. A. (2015). An interface to support independent use of Facebook by people with intellectual disability. *Intellectual and Developmental Disabilities, 53*, 30–41.

Diegelmann, K. M., & Test, D. W. (2018). Effects of a self-monitoring checklist as a component of the Self-Directed IEP. *Education and Training in Autism and Developmental Disabilities, 53*, 73–83.

Douglas, S. N., Kammes, R., Nordquist, E., & D'Agostino, S. (2018). A pilot study to teach siblings to support children with complex communication needs. *Communication Disorders Quarterly, 39*, 346–355.

Downing, J. E. (2011). Teaching communication skills. In M. E. Snell & F. Brown (Eds.), *Instruction of students with severe disabilities* (7th ed., pp. 461–491). Upper Saddle River, NJ: Pearson.

Dymond, S. K., Butler, A. M., Hopkins, S. L., & Patton, K. A. (2018). Curriculum and context: Trends in interventions with transition-age students with severe disabilities. *The Journal of Special Education.* First published online: April 23, 2018, https://doi.org/10.1177/0022466918768776.

Faul, M., Xu, L., Wald, M. M., & Coronado, V. G. (2010). *Traumatic brain injury in the United States: Emergency department visits, hospitalizations and deaths 2002–2006.* Atlanta, GA: Centers for Disease Control and Prevention, National Center for Injury Prevention and Control.

Fuchs, L. S., & Fuchs, D. (n.d.). *What is scientifically-based research on progress monitoring?* Washington, DC: American Institute for Research National Center on Progress Monitoring. Accessed at https://files.eric.ed.gov/fulltext/ED502460.pdf on June 19, 2018.

Ganesalingam, K., Yeates, K. O., Taylor, H. G., Walz, N. C., Stancin, T., & Wade, S. (2011). Executive functions and social competence in young children 6 months following traumatic brain injury. *Neuropsychology, 25*(4), 466–476.

Giangreco, M. F., & Suter, J. C. (2015). Precarious or purposeful? Proactively building inclusive special education service delivery on solid ground. *Inclusion, 3*, 112–131.

Giangreco, M. F., Suter, J. C., & Hurley, S. M. (2013). Revisiting personnel utilization in inclusion-oriented schools. *Journal of Special Education, 47*(2), 121–132.

Gioia, G. A., Glang, A. E., Hooper, S. R., & Brown, B. E. (2016). Building statewide infrastructure for the academic support of students with mild traumatic brain injury. *Journal of Head Trauma Rehabilitation, 31*, 397–406.

Hagner, D., Kurtz, A., Cloutier, H., Arakelian, C., Brucker, D. L., & May, J. (2012). Outcomes of a family-centered transition process for students with autism spectrum disorders. *Focus on Autism and Other Developmental Disabilities, 27*, 42–50.

Inge, K. J., Graham, C. W., Erickson, D., Sima, A., West, M., & Cimera, R. E. (2016). Improving the employment outcomes of individuals with traumatic brain injuries: The effectiveness of knowledge translation strategies to impact the use of evidence-based practices by vocational rehabilitation counselors. *Journal of Vocational Rehabilitation, 45*, 107–115.

Jamieson, M., Cullen, B., McGee-Lennon, M., Brewster, S., & Evans, J. J. (2014). The efficacy of cognitive prosthetic technology for people with memory impairments: A systematic review and meta-analysis. *Neuropsychological Rehabilitation, 24*(3-4), 419–444.

Karver, C. L., Wade, S. L., Cassedy, A., Taylor, H. G., Stancin, T., Yeates, K. O., & Walz, N. C. (2012). Age at injury and long-term behavior problems after traumatic brain injury in young children. *Rehabilitation Psychology, 57*(3), 256–265.

Katz, T., & Barol, J. (2017). Building a village: Tapping into untapped resources. *Journal of Vocational Rehabilitation, 46*, 301–303.

Kelley, K. R., & Buchanan, S. K. (2017). College to career ready: Innovative practices that lead to integrated employment. *Journal of Vocational Rehabilitation, 46*, 327–332.

Kent-Walsh, J., Murza, K. A., Malani, M. D., & Binger, C. (2015). Effects of communication partner instruction on the communication of individuals using AAC: A meta-analysis. *Augmentative and Alternative Communication, 31*, 271–284.

Kyzar, K. B., Brady, S., Summers, J. A., & Turnbull, A. P. (in press). Family quality of life and partnership for families of students with deaf-blindness. *Remedial and Special Education.*

Kyzar, K. B., Brady, S. E., Summers, J. A., Haines, S. J., & Turnbull, A. P. (2016). Services and supports, partnership, and family quality of life. *Exceptional Children, 83*, 77–91.

Lajiness-O'Neill, R., Erdodi, L. A., & Lichtenstein, J. D. (2017). Traumatic brain injury. In J. M. Kauffman, D. P. Hallahan, & P. C. Pullen (Eds.), *Handbook of special education* (pp. 262–276). New York, NY: Routledge.

Livingstone-Lee, S. A., Skelton, R. W., & Livingston, N. (2014). Transit apps for people with brain injury and other cognitive disabilities: The state of the art. *Assistive Technology, 26*, 209–218.

Lopes, N. R. L., Eisenstein, E., & Williams, L. C. A. (2013). Abusive head trauma in children: A literature review. *Jornal de pediatria, 89*(5), 426–433.

MacKay, W., & Percy, M. (2017). Introduction to the nervous system. In M. L. Wehmeyer, I. Brown, M. Percy, K. A. Shogren, & W. L. A. Fung (Eds.), *A comprehensive guide to intellectual and developmental disabilities* (pp. 149–163). Baltimore, MD: Brookes.

Mazzotti, V. L., Kelley, K. R., & Coco, C. M. (2015). Effects of Self-Directed Summary of Performance on postsecondary education students' participation in person-centered planning meetings. *The Journal of Special Education, 48*, 243–255.

Mazzotti, V. L., Rowe, D. A., Sinclair, J., Poppen, M., Woods, W. E., & Shearer, M. L. (2016). Predictors of post-school success: A systematic review of NLTS2 secondary analyses. *Career Development and Transition for Exceptional Individuals, 39*, 196–215.

McCauley, S. R., Wide, E. A., Anderson, V. A., Bedell, G., Beers, S. R., Campbell, T. F., . . . Yeates, K. T. (2012). Recommendation for the use of common outcome measures in pediatric traumatic brain injury research. *Journal of Neurotrauma, 29*, 678–705.

Morningstar, M. E., Kurth, J. A., & Johnson, P. E. (2017). Examining national trends in educational placements for students with significant disabilities. *Remedial and Special Education, 38*, 3–12.

Mount, B., & Zwernik, K. (1988). *It's never too early, It's never too late: A booklet about personal futures planning for persons with developmental disabilities, their families and friends, case managers, service providers, and advocates.* St. Paul, MN: Metropolitan Council.

National Center on Deaf-Blindness. (2017). The 2016 national child count of children and youth who are deaf-blind. Retrieved from http://cb4cb5aa6990be188aff-8017fda59b77ece717432423a4f3b bdf.r43.cf1.rackcdn.com/2016-National-Deaf-Blind-Child-Count-Report-PDF-FINAL.pdf

Nittrouer, C. L., Shogren, K. A., & Pickens, J. (2016). A collaborative process to develop goals and self-management interventions to support young adults with disabilities in the workplace. *Rehabilitation Research, Policy, and Education, 30*, 110–128.

O'Brien, J., Pearpoint, J., & Kahn, L. (2010). *The PATH & MAPS handbook.* Toronto: Inclusion Press.

Orelove, F. P., Sobsey, D., & Gilles, D. L. (2016). *Educating children with multiple disabilities: A collaborative approach* (5th ed.). Baltimore, MD: Brookes.

Parker, A. T., Davidson, R., & Banda, D. R. (2007). Emerging evidence from single-subject research in the field of deaf-blindness. *Journal of Visual Impairment & Blindness, 101*(11), 690–700.

Percy, M., Brown, I., & Fung, W. L. A. (2017). Factors causing or contributing to intellectual and developmental disabilities. In M. L. Wehmeyer, I. Brown, M. Percy, K. A. Shogren, & W. L. A. Fung (Eds.), *A comprehensive guide to intellectual and developmental disabilities* (pp. 175–194). Baltimore, MD: Brookes.

Percy, M., Lewkis, S. Z., Thompson, M. D., Brown, I., Barbouth, D., & Armstrong, F. D. (2017). Introduction to genetics, genomics, and epigenetics, and intellectual and developmental disabilities. In M. L. Wehmeyer, I. Brown, M. Percy, K. A. Shogren, & W. L. A. Fung (Eds.), *A comprehensive guide to intellectual and developmental disabilities* (pp. 127–147). Baltimore, MD: Brookes.

Pierpoint, J., O'Brien, J., & Forest, M. (1995). *PATH: A workbook for planning positive possible futures* (2nd ed.). Toronto, Ontario: Inclusion Press.

Quirk, C., Ryndak, D. L., & Taub, D. (2017). Research and evidence-based practices to promote membership and learning in general education for students with extensive support needs. *Inclusion, 5*, 94–109.

Recla, M., Bardoni, A., Galbiati, S., Pastore, V., Dominici, C., Tavano, A., . . . Strazzer, S. (2013). Cognitive and adaptive functioning after severe TBI in school-aged children. *Brain Injury*, 27(7-8), 862–871.

Rosema, S., Crowe, L., & Anderson, V. (2012). Social function in children and adolescents after traumatic brain injury: A systematic review 1989–2011. *Journal of Neurotrauma*, 29, 1277–1291.

Rumrill, P., Elias, E., Hendricks, D. J., Jacobs, K., Leopold, A., Nardone, A., . . . McMahon, B. T. (2016). Promoting cognitive support technology use and employment success among postsecondary students with traumatic brain injuries. *Journal of Vocational Rehabilitation*, 45, 53–61.

Schaefer, J. M., & Andzik, N. R. (2016). Switch on the learning: Teaching students with significant disabilities to use switches. *TEACHING Exceptional Children*, 48, 204–212.

Schuh, M., Hagner, D., Dillon, A., & Dixon, B. (2016). Policy change through parent and consumer leadership education. *Journal of Disability Policy Studies*, 27, 234–242.

Schwartz, A. A., Holburn, S. C., & Jacobson, J. W. (2000). Defining person-centeredness: Results of two consensus methods. *Education and Training in Mental Retardation and Developmental Disabilities*, 35, 235–249.

Shogren, K. A., Wehmeyer, M. L., Davies, D., Stock, S., & Palmer, S. B. (2013). Cognitive support technologies for adolescents with disabilities: Impact on educator perceptions of capacity and opportunity for self-determination. *Journal of Human Development, Disability, and Social Change*, 21, 67–79.

Sinopoli, K. J., & Dennis, M. (2012). Inhibitory control after traumatic brain injury in children. *International Journal of Developmental Neuroscience*, 30, 207–215.

Smull, M., & Burke Harrison, S. (1992). *Supporting people with severe reputations in the community*. Arlington, VA: NASMRPD.

Stock, S. E., Davies, D. K., & Gillespie, T. (2013). The State of the Field in Applied Cognitive Technologies. *Inclusion*, 1(2), 103–120.

Tassé, M. J., Luckasson, R., & Schalock, R. L. (2016). The relation between intellectual functioning and adaptive behavior in the diagnosis of intellectual disability. *Intellectual and Developmental Disabilities*, 54, 381–390.

Therrien, M. C. S., Light, J., & Pope, L. (2016). Systematic review of the effects of interventions to promote peer interactions for children who use aided AAC. *Augmentative and Alternative Communication*, 32, 81–93.

Thompson, J. R., Hughes, C., Walker, V. L., & DeSpain, S. N. (2017). Measuring support needs and supports planning. In M. L. Wehmeyer & K. A. Shogren (Eds.), *Handbook of research-based practices for educating students with intellectual disability* (pp. 79–101). New York, NY: Routledge.

Thompson, J. R., Shogren, K. A., & Wehmeyer, M. L. (2017). Supports and support needs in strengths-based models of intellectual disability. In M. L. Wehmeyer & K. A. Shogren (Eds.), *Handbook of research-based practices for educating students with intellectual disability* (pp. 31–49). New York, NY: Routledge.

Thompson, J. R., Wehmeyer, M. L., Hughes, C., Shogren, K. A., Little, T. D., Copeland, S. R., . . . Tassé, M. J. (2016). *Supports Intensity Scale–Children's Version*. Washington, DC: American Association on Intellectual and Developmental Disabilities.

Trovato, M. K., & Schultz, S. C. (2013). Traumatic brain injury. In M. L. Batshaw, N. J. Roizen, & G. R. Lotrecchiano (Eds.), *Children with disabilities* (7th ed., pp. 473–486). Baltimore, MD: Brookes.

Turnbull, A. P., Blue-Banning, M. J., Anderson, E. L., Turnbull, H. R., Seaton, K. A., & Dinas, P. A. (1996). Enhancing self-determination through group action planning. In D. J. Sands & M. L. Wehmeyer (Eds.), *Self-determination across the lifespan: Independence and choice for people with disabilities* (pp. 237–256). Baltimore, MD: Paul H. Brookes.

U.S. Department of Education. (2013). Digest of education statistics, Children and youth with disabilities. Retrieved from http://nces.ed.gov/programs/digest/d13/tables/dt13_204.50.asp

U.S. Department of Education (2018). *39th Annual Report to Congress on the Implementation of the Individuals with Disabilities Education Act, 2017*. Washington, DC: U.S. Department of Education, Office of Special Education and Rehabilitation Services, Office of Special Education Programs.

U.S. Department of Health and Human Services, Centers for Disease Control and Prevention. (2013). *How many people have TBI?* Retrieved from http://www.cdc.gov/traumaticbraininjury/statistics.html

Vu, J. A., Babikian, T., & Asarnow, R. F. (2011). Academic and language outcomes in children after traumatic brain injury: A meta-analysis. *Exceptional Children*, 77(3), 263–281.

Wells, J. C., & Sheehey, P. H. (2012). Person-centered planning: Strategies to encourage participation and facilitate communication. *TEACHING Exceptional Children*, 44, 32–39.

Westling, D. L., & Fox, L. (2009). *Teaching students with severe disabilities* (4th ed.). Columbus, OH: Pearson.

Wong, D., Sinclair, K., Seabrook, E., McKay, A., & Ponsford, J. (2017). Smartphones as assistive technology following traumatic brain injury: A preliminary study of what helps and what hinders. *Disability and Rehabilitation: An International, Multidisciplinary Journal*, 39, 2387–2394. doi:http://dx.doi.org/10.1080/09638288.2016.1226434

Zabala, J. S. (2005). Ready, SETT, go! Getting started with the SETT framework. *Closing the Gap*, 23(6), 1–4.

Zatta, M., & McGinnity, B. (2016). An overview of transition planning for students who are deafblind. *American Annals of the Deaf*, 161, 474–485.

Chapter 14

Alarcón, G., & Valentín, A. (2012). *Introduction to epilepsy*. Cambridge, UK: Cambridge University Press.

Allen, S. E., Limdi, N., Westrick, A. C., Ver Hoef, L. W., Szaflarski, J. P., & Knowlton, R. C. (2018). Racial disparities in temporal lobe epilepsy. *Epilepsy Research*, 140, 56–60.

Atta, C. A. M., Fiest, K. M., Frolkis, A. D., Jette, N., Pringsheim, T., St. Germaine-Smith, C., . . . Metcalfe, A. (2016). Global birth prevalence of spina bifida by folic acid fortification status: A systematic review and meta-analysis. *American Journal of Public Health*, 106, 24–34.

Blumenthal, M. N. (2012). Genetic, epigenetic, and environmental factors in asthma and allergy. *Annals of Allergy, Asthma & Immunology*, 108, 69–73.

Boonen, H., & Petry, K. (2011). How do children with chronic or long-term illness perceive their school re-entry after a period of homebound instruction? *Child, Care, Health, and Development*, 38(4), 490–496.

Burnham, W. M. (2017). Epilepsy. In M. L. Wehmeyer, I. Brown, M. Percy, K. A. Shogren, & W. L. A. Fung (Eds.), *A comprehensive guide to intellectual and developmental disabilities* (2nd ed., pp. 313–321). Baltimore. MD: Paul H. Brookes.

Centers for Disease Control and Prevention. (2017). Most recent asthma data. www.cdc.gov/asthma/most_recent_data.htm/

Christensen, D., Braun, K. V. N., Doernberg, N. S., Maenner, M. J., Arneson, C. L., Durkin, M. S., . . . Yeargin-Allsopp, M. (2014). Prevalence of cerebral palsy, co-occurring autism spectrum disorders, and motor functioning—Autism and Developmental Disabilities Monitoring Network, USA. *Developmental Medicine and Child Neurology*, 56, 59–65.

Council on School Health. (2013). Role of the school physician. *Pediatrics*, 131, 178–182.

Crawford, D. (2011). Understanding childhood asthma and the development of the respiratory tract. *Nursing Children and Young People*, 23(7), 25–36.

Durkin, M. S., Maenner, M. J., Benedict, R. E., Braun, K. V. N., Christensen, D., Kirby, R. S., . . . Yeargin-Allsopp, M. (2015). The role of socio-economic status and perinatal factors in racial disparities in the risk of cerebral palsy. *Developmental Medicine and Child Neurology* 58, 809–813.

Engel, J. J. (2013). *Seizures and epilepsy* (2nd ed.). Oxford, UK: Oxford University Press.

Fehlings, D., & Hunt, C. (2017). Cerebral palsy. In M. L. Wehmeyer, I. Brown, M. Percy, K. A. Shogren, & W. L. A. Fung (Eds.),

A comprehensive guide to intellectual and developmental disabilities (2nd ed., pp. 263–271). Baltimore, MD: Paul H. Brookes.

Gibson, E. J., Santelli, J. S., Minguez, M., Lord, A., & Schuyler, A. C. (2013). Measuring school health center impact on access to and quality of primary care. *Journal of Adolescent Health, 11*, 1–7.

Hilton, C. L., Goloff, S. E., Altaras, O., & Josman, N. (2013). Review of instrument development and testing studies for children and youth. *The American Journal of Occupational Therapy, 67*(3), 30–54.

Hodge, S. R., Lieberman, L. J., & Murata, N. M. (2012). *Essentials in teaching adapted physical education: Diversity, culture, and inclusion.* New York, NY: Holcomb Hathaway Publishers.

Hoon, Jr., A. H., & Tolley, F. (2013). Cerebral palsy. In M. L. Batshaw, N. J. Roizen, & G. R. Lotrecchiano (Eds.), *Children with disabilities* (7th ed., pp. 423–450). Baltimore, MD: Brookes.

Hustad, K. C., Allison, K. M., Sakash, A., McFadd, E., Broman, A. T., & Rathouz, P. J. (2017). Longitudinal development of communication in children with cerebral palsy between 24 and 53 months: Predicting speech outcomes. *Developmental Neurorehabilitation, 6*, 323–330.

Hwang, J. L., & Davies, P. L. (2009). Rasch analysis of the school function assessment provides additional evidence for the internal validity of the activity performance scales. *The American Journal of Occupational Therapy, 63*(3), 369–373.

Johnson, D. W., & Johnson, R. T. (1991). *Cooperation and competition: Theory and research.* Edina, MN: Interaction.

Johnson, D., Johnson, R., & Holubec, E. (2008). *Cooperation in the classroom* (8th ed.). Boston, MA: Allyn & Bacon.

Jolliffe, W. (2016). *Learning to learn together: Cooperation, theory, and practice.* New York, NY: Routledge.

Keet, C. A., McCormack, M. C., Pollack, C. E., Peng, R. D., McGowan, E., & Matsui, E. C. (2015). Neighborhood poverty, urban residence, race/ethnicity, and asthma: Rethinking the inner-city asthma epidemic. *The Journal of Allergy and Clinical Immunology, 135*, 655–662.

Keeton, V., Soleimanpour, S., & Brindis, C. D. (2012). School-based health centers in an era of health care reform: Building on history. *Current Problems in Pediatric and Adolescent Health Care, 42*, 132–156.

Li, S., Ding, D., & Wu, J. (2013). Definitions and epidemiology of epilepsy. In S. D. Shorvon, R. Guerrini, M. Cook, & S. D. Lhatoo (Eds.), *Oxford textbook of epilepsy and epileptic seizures* (pp. 51–60). Oxford, UK: Oxford University Press.

Liptak, G. S. (2013). Neural tube defects. In M. L. Batshaw, N. J. Roizen, & G. R. Lotrecchiano (Eds.), *Children with disabilities* (7th ed., pp. 451–472). Baltimore, MD: Brookes.

McIntyre, S., Taitz, D., Keogh, J., Goldsmith, S., Badawi, N., & Blair, E. (2012). A systematic review of risk factors for cerebral palsy in children born at term in developed countries. *Developmental Medicine & Child Neurology, 55*, 499–508.

Nabors, L. A. (2016). *Medical and mental health during childhood.* New York, NY: Springer.

Pauly, M., & Cremer, R. (2013). Levels of mobility in children and adolescents with spina bifida: Clinical parameters predicting mobility and maintenance of these skills. *European Journal of Paediatric Neurology, 23*, 110–114.

Peny-Dahlstrand, M., Krumlinde-Sundholm, L., & Gosman-Hedstrom, G. (2013). Patterns of participation in school-related activities and settings in children with spina bifida. *Disability and Rehabilitation, 35*, 1821–1827.

Rabinovich, R. V., Patel, N. V., Gates, P. E., & Otsuka, N. Y. (2015). The relationship between the School Function Assessment (SFA) and the gross motor function classification system in ambulatory patients with cerebral palsy. *Bulletin of the NYU Hospital for Joint Diseases, 73*, 204–209.

Romeo, D. M., Sini, F., Brogna, C., Albamonte, E., Ricci, D., & Mercuri, E. (2016). Sex differences in cerebral palsy on neuromotor outcome: A critical review. *Developmental Medicine and Child Neurology, 57*, 835–843.

Ruijsbroek, A., Wijga, A. H., Gehring, U., Kerkhof, M., & Droomers, M. (2015). School performance: A matter of health or socio-economic background? Findings from the PIAMA Birth Cohort Study. *PLoS ONE, 10*, e0134780. https://doi.org/10.1371/journal.pone.0134780

School-based Health Alliance. (2013). 2010–2011 *Census Report of School-Based Health Centers.* http://www.sbh4all.org/site/c .ckLQKbOVLkK6E/b.8778055/k.F9F5/20102011_Census_Report.htm

Sheehey, P. H., Wells, J. C., & Rowe, M. (2017). Effects of self-monitoring on math competency of an elementary student with cerebral palsy in an inclusive classroom. *Preventing School Failure: Alternative Education for Children and Youth, 61*, 211–219.

Sheen, B. (2011). *Diseases & disorders: Asthma.* Farmington Hills, MI: Lucent Books.

Shields, N., Synnot, A. J., & Barr, M. (2012). Perceived barriers and facilitators to physical activity for children with disability: A systematic review. *Journal of Sports Medicine, 46*, 989–997.

Shorvon, S., Perucca, E., & Engel, J. (2015). *The treatment of epilepsy* (4th ed.). Oxford, UK: Wiley Blackwell.

Trivedi, M., Fung, V., Kharbanda, E. O., Larkin, E. K., Butler, M. G., Horan, K., . . . Wu, A. C. (2018). Racial disparities in family-provider interactions for pediatric asthma care. *Journal of Asthma, 55*, 424–429.

U.S. Department of Education (2018). *39th Annual Report to Congress on the Implementation of the Individuals with Disabilities Education Act, 2017.* Washington, DC: U.S. Department of Education, Office of Special Education and Rehabilitation Services, Office of Special Education Programs.

U.S. Preventative Services Task Force (2017). Folic acid supplementation for the prevention of neural tube defects: U.S. Preventative Services Task Force recommendation statement. *Journal of the American Medical Association, 317*, 183–189.

van Ool, J. S., Snoeijen-Schouwenaars, F. M., Schelhaas, H. J., Tan, I. Y., Aldenkamp, A. P., & Hendriksen, J. G. M. (2016). A systematic review of neuropsychiatric comorbidities in patients with both epilepsy and intellectual disability. *Epilepsy & Behavior, 60*, 130–137.

von Mutius, E., & Hartert, T. (2013). Pulmonary and critical care updates. *American Journal of Respiratory and Critical Care Medicine, 188*(2), 150–156.

Wang, Y., Liu, G., Canfield, M. A., Mai, C. T., Gilboa, S. M., Meyer, R. E., . . . Kirby, R. S. (2015). Racial/ethnic differences in survival of United States children with birth defects: A population-based study. *The Journal of Pediatrics, 166*, 819–826.

Wiener, J. S., Suson, K. D., Castillo, J., Routh, J., Tanaka, S., Liu, T., . . . Joseph, D. (2017). Bowel management and continence in adults with spina bifida: Results from the National Spina Bifida Patient Registry 2009-15. *Journal of Pediatric Rehabilitation Medicine, 10*, 335–343.

Williams, J., Mai, C. T., Mulinare, J., Isenburg, J., Flood, T. I., Ethen, M., . . . Kirby, R. S. (2015). Updated estimates of neural tube defects prevented by mandatory folic acid fortification—United States, 1995–2011. *Morbidity and Mortality Weekly Report, 64*(1), 1–5.

Wilson, C., Rapp, K. I., Jack, L., Hayes, S., Post, R., & Malveaux, F. (2015). Asthma risk profiles of children participating in asthma education and management program. *American Journal of Health Education, 46*, 13–23.

Wo, S. W., Ong, L. C., Low, W. Y., & Lai, P. S. M. (2017). The impact of epilepsy on academic achievement in children with normal intelligence and without major comorbidities: A systematic review. *Epilepsy Research, 136*, 35–45.

Zelleke, T. G., Depositaro-Cabacar, D. F. T., & Gaillard, W. D. (2013). Epilepsy. In M. L. Batshaw, N. J. Roizen, & G. R. Lotrecchiano (Eds.), *Children with disabilities* (7th ed., pp. 487–506). Baltimore, MD: Brookes.

Chapter 15

American Speech-Hearing-Language Association (n.d.). Causes of hearing loss in children, https://www.asha.org/public/hearing/Causes-of-Hearing-Loss-in-Children/

Behl, D. D., Blaiser, K., Cook, G., Barrett, T., Callow-Heusser, C., Brooks, B. M., & White, K. R. (2017). A multisite study evaluating the benefits of early intervention via telepractice. *Infants & Young Children, 30*(2), 147–161.

Bonvillian, J. D., Orlansky, M. D., & Novack, L. L. (1983). Developmental milestones: Sign language acquisition and motor development. *Child Development*, 1435–1445.

Centers for Disease Control and Prevention (2010). Identifying infants with hearing loss—United States, 1999–2007. *MMWR Morbidity and Mortality Weekly Report, 59*(8), 220–223.

DeCasper, A. J., & Spence, M. J. (1986). Prenatal maternal speech influences newborns' perception of speech sounds. *Infant Behavior and Development, 9*(2), 133–150.

Eimas, P. D., Siqueland, E. R., Jusczyk, P., & Vigorito, J. (1971). Speech perception in infants. *Science, 171*(3968), 303–306.

Gallaudet Research Institute (December 2005). *Regional and National Summary Report of Data from the 2004–2005 Annual Survey of Deaf and Hard of Hearing Children and Youth.* Washington, DC: Gallaudet Research Institute, Gallaudet University.

Geers, A. E., & Hayes, H. (2011). Reading, writing, and phonological processing skills of adolescents with 10 or more years of cochlear implant experience. *Ear and Hearing, 32*(1), 49S.

Geers, A. E., Mitchell, C. M., Warner-Czyz, A., Wang, N. Y., Eisenberg, L. S., & CDaCI Investigative Team. (2017). Early sign language exposure and cochlear implantation benefits. *Pediatrics, 140*(1), e20163489.

Hart, B., & Risley, T. R. (1995). *Meaningful differences in the everyday experience of young American children.* Baltimore, MD: Paul H Brookes Publishing.

Karpicke, J. D., Blunt, J. R., Smith, M. A., & Karpicke, S. S. (2014). Retrieval-based learning: The need for guided retrieval in elementary school children. *Journal of Applied Research in Memory and Cognition, 3*, 198–206.

Lederberg, A. R., Schick, B., & Spencer, P. E. (2013). Language and literacy development of deaf and hard-of-hearing children: Successes and challenges. *Developmental Psychology, 49*(1), 15–30.

Miller, E. M., Lederberg, A. R., & Easterbrooks, S. R. (2013). Phonological awareness: Explicit instruction for young deaf and hard-of-hearing children. *Journal of Deaf Studies and Deaf Education, 18*(2), 206–227.

Mitchell, R. E., & Karchmer, M. A. (2004). Chasing the mythical ten percent: Parental hearing status of deaf and hard of hearing students in the United States. *Sign Language Studies 4*(2), 138–163.

Moog, J. S., & Biedenstein, J. J. (1998). Teacher Assessment of Spoken Language: TASL. Moog Center for Deaf Education.

Moog, J. S., & Geers, A. E. (2010). Early educational placement and later language outcomes for children with cochlear implants. *Otology & Neurotology, 31*(8), 1315–1319.

Moores, D. F. (2010). The history of language and communication issues in deaf education. *The Oxford Handbook of Deaf Studies, Language, and Education, 2*, 17–30.

National Center for Hearing Assessment and Management (2018). State EHDI information, http://www.infanthearing.org/states_home/

Niparko, J. K., Tobey, E. A., Thal, D. J., Eisenberg, L. S., Wang, N. Y., Quittner, A. L., & CDaCI Investigative Team. (2010). Spoken language development in children following cochlear implantation. *JAMA, 303*(15), 1498–1506.

Perfetti, C. A., & Sandak, R. (2000). Reading optimally builds on spoken language: Implications for deaf readers. *Journal of Deaf Studies and Deaf Education, 5*(1), 32–50.

Stanberry, K. (n.d.): Finding out if your child is eligible for special education, https://www.understood.org/en/school-learning/special-services/special-education-basics/finding-out-if-your-child-is-eligible-for-special-education

Suskind, D. L., Graf, E., Leffel, K. R., Hernandez, M. W., Suskind, E., Webber, R., & Nevins, M. E. (2016). Project ASPIRE: Spoken language intervention curriculum for parents of low-socioeconomic status and their deaf and hard-of-hearing children. *Otology & Neurotology, 37*(2), e110–e117.

Stanovich, K. E. (2009). Matthew effects in reading: Some consequences of individual differences in the acquisition of literacy. *Journal of Education, 189*(1–2), 23–55.

Svirsky, M. A., Robbins, A. M., Kirk, K. I., Pisoni, D. B., & Miyamoto, R. T. (2000). Language development in profoundly deaf children with cochlear implants. *Psychological Science, 11*(2), 153–158.

Traxler, C. B. (2000). The Stanford Achievement Test: National norming and performance standards for deaf and hard-of-hearing students. *Journal of Deaf Studies and Deaf Education, 5*(4), 337–348.

Trezek, B. J., Wang, Y., Woods, D. G., Gampp, T. L., & Paul, P. V. (2007). Using visual phonics to supplement beginning reading instruction for students who are deaf or hard of hearing. *Journal of Deaf Studies and Deaf Education, 12*(3), 373–384.

U.S. Department of Education, EDFacts Data Warehouse (EDW): "IDEA Part B Child Count and Educational Environments Collection," (2016–17). Data extracted as of July 12, 2017, from file specifications 002 and 089.

Yoshinaga-Itano, C., Sedey, A. L., Wiggin, M., & Chung, W. (2017). Early hearing detection and vocabulary of children with hearing loss. *Pediatrics*, e20162964.

Chapter 16

Allman, C. B., & Lewis, S. (2017). *ECC essentials: Teaching the expanded core curriculum to students with visual impairments.* New York, NY: AFB Press.

Barclay, L. A. (2003). Preparation for assessment. In S. A. Goodman & S. H. Wittenstein (Eds.), *Collaborative assessment: Working with students who are blind or visually impaired, including those with additional disabilities* (pp. 37–70). New York, NY: AFB Press.

Conroy, P. W. (2005). English language learners with visual impairments: Strategies to enhance learning. *RE:view, 37*(3), 101–108.

Corn, A. L., & Lusk, K. E. (2010). Perspectives on low vision. In A. L. Corn & J. N. Erin (Eds.), *Foundations of low vision: Clinical and functional perspectives* (2nd ed., pp. 3–34). New York, NY: AFB Press.

Crudden, A. (2012). Transition to employment for students with visual impairments: Components for success. *Journal of Visual Impairment & Blindness, 106*(7), 389–399.

Emerson, R. W., Holbrook, M. C., & D'Andrea, F. M. (2009). Acquisition of literacy skills by young children who are blind: Results from the ABC braille study. *Journal of Visual Impairment & Blindness, 103*(10), 610–624.

Erin, J. N., & Levinson, S. (2007). Assessments: Identifying your child's needs. In S. LaVenture (Ed.), *A parents' guide to special education for children with visual impairments* (pp. 61–89). New York, NY: AFB Press.

Erin, J. N., & Topor, I. (2010). Functional vision assessment of children with low vision, including those with multiple disabilities. In A. L. Corn & J. N. Erin (Eds.), *Foundations of low vision: Clinical and functional perspectives* (2nd ed., pp. 339–399). New York, NY: AFB Press.

Ferrell, K. A. (2011) *Reach out and teach: Helping your child who is visually impaired learn and grow.* New York, NY: AFB Press.

Gallagher, B. A. M., Hart, P. M., O'Brien, C. Stevenson, M. R., & Jackson, A. M. (2011). Mobility and access to transport issues as experienced by people with vision impairment living in urban and rural Ireland, *Disability and Rehabilitation, 33*(12), 979–988.

Garber, M., & Huebner, K. M. (2017). Visual impairment: Terminology, demographics, society. In M. C. Holbrook, T. McCarthy, & C. Kamei-Hannan (Eds.), *Foundations of education (3rd ed.): Volume I: History and theory of teaching children and youths with visual impairments* (pp. 50–72). New York, NY: AFB Press.

Hatlen, P. H., & Curry, S. A. (1987). In support of specialized programs for blind and visually impaired children: The impact of vision loss on learning. *Journal of Visual Impairment & Blindness, 81*(1), 7–13.

Holbrook, M. C., & Rosenblum, L. P. (2017). Planning instruction in unique skills. In M. C. Holbrook, C. Kamei-Hannan, T. McCarthy (Eds.), *Foundations of education (3rd ed.): Volume II: Instructional strategies for teaching children and youths with visual impairments* (pp. 203–230). New York, NY: AFB Press.

Holbrook, M. C., Wright, D., & Presley, I. (2017). Specialized assessments. In M. C. Holbrook, C. Kamei-Hannan, T. McCarthy (Eds.), *Foundations of education (3rd ed.): Volume II: Instructional strategies for teaching children and youths with visual impairments* (pp. 108–164). New York, NY: AFB Press.

Hupp, G. S. (2003). *Cognitive differences between congenitally and adventitiously blind individuals* (Doctoral dissertation, University of North Texas). Retrieved from http://digital.library.unt.edu/ark:/67531/metadc4318/m2/1/high_res_d/dissertation.pdf

Kelly, S. (2011). The use of assistive technology by high school students with visual impairments: A second look at the problem. *Journal of Visual Impairment & Blindness, 105*(4), 235–239.

Koenig, A. J., & Farrenkopf, C. (1997). Essential experiences to undergird the early development of literacy. *Journal of Visual Impairment and Blindness, 91*(1), 14–24.

Koenig, A. J., & Holbrook, M. C. (1993). *Learning media assessment of students with visual impairments: A resource guide for teachers.* Austin, TX: Texas School for the Blind and Visually Impaired.

Lee, H., & Ponchillia, S. V. (2010). Low vision rehabilitation training for working-age adults. In A. L. Corn & J. N. Erin (Eds.), *Foundations of low vision: Clinical and functional perspectives* (2nd ed., pp. 760–792). New York, NY: AFB Press.

Lewis, S., & Allman, C. B. (2014a). Instruction and assessment: General principles and strategies. In C. B. Allman & S. Lewis (Eds.), *ECC essentials: Teaching the expanded core curriculum to students with visual impairments* (pp. 31–58). New York, NY: AFB Press.

Lewis, S., & Allman, C. B. (2014b). Learning, development, and children with visual impairments: The evolution of skills. In C. B. Allman & S. Lewis (Eds.), *ECC essentials: Teaching the expanded core curriculum to students with visual impairments* (pp. 3–14). New York, NY: AFB Press.

Liefert, F. (2003). Introduction to visual impairment. In S. A. Goodman & S. H. Wittenstein (Eds.), *Collaborative assessment: Working with students who are blind or visually impaired, including those with additional disabilities* (pp. 1–22). New York, NY: AFB Press.

Lowenfeld, B. (1973). Psychological considerations. In B. Lowenfeld (Ed.), *The visually handicapped child in school* (pp. 27–60). New York, NY: Day.

Lueck, A. H. (2004). Comprehensive low vision care. In A. H. Lueck (Ed.), *Functional vision: A practitioner's guide to evaluation and intervention* (pp. 3–24). Alexandria, VA: Association for Education and Rehabilitation of the Blind and Visually Impaired.

Lussenhop, K., & Corn, A. L. (2002). Comparative studies of the reading performance of students with low vision. *RE:view, 34*(2), 57–69.

Milian, M. (1997). Teaching braille reading and writing to students who speak English as a second language. In D. P. Wormsley & F. M. D'Andrea (Eds.), *Instructional strategies for braille literacy* (pp. 189–230). New York, NY: AFB Press.

Pogrund, R. L. (2002). Refocus: Setting the stage for working with young children who are blind or visually impaired. In R. L. Pogrund & D. L. Fazzi (Eds.), *Early focus: Working with young children who are blind or visually impaired and their families* (2nd ed., pp. 1–15). New York, NY: AFB Press.

Sacks, S. Z. (2006). Theoretical perspectives on the early years of social development. In S. Z. Sacks & K. E. Wolffe (Eds.), *Teaching social skills to students with visual impairments: From theory to practice* (pp. 51–80). New York, NY: AFB Press.

Sacks, S. Z., Lueck, A. H., Corn, A. L., & Erin, J. N. (2011). *Supporting the social and emotional needs of students with low vision to promote academic and social success.* Position paper of the Division on Visual Impairments, Council for Exceptional Children. Arlington, VA: Council for Exceptional Children.

Sacks, S. Z., & Page, B. (2017). Social skills. In M. C. Holbrook, C. Kamei-Hannan, T. McCarthy (Eds.), *Foundations of education (3rd ed.): Volume II: Instructional strategies for teaching children and youths with visual impairments* (pp. 753–803). New York, NY: AFB Press.

Social Security Act, 42 U.S.C. 1382c § 1614 (1936).

Swenson, A. M. (2016). *Beginning with braille: Firsthand experiences with a balanced approach to literacy* (2nd ed.). New York, NY: AFB Press.

Topor, I., & Rosenblum, L. P. (2013). English language learners: Experiences of teachers of students with visual impairments who work with this population. *Journal of Visual Impairment & Blindness, 107*(2), 79–91.

U.S. Department of Education. (2017). *IDEA Section 618 Data Products: Static Tables.* Retrieved March 14, 201, from https://www2.ed.gov/programs/osepidea/618-data/static-tables/index.html

Wall, R. S., & Corn, A. L. (2004). Students with visual impairments in Texas: Description and extrapolation of data. *Journal of Visual Impairment & Blindness, 98*(6), 351–356.

Wilkinson, M. E. (2010). Clinical low vision services. In A. L. Corn & J. N. Erin (Eds.), *Foundations of low vision: Clinical and functional perspectives* (2nd ed., pp. 238–295). New York, NY: AFB Press.

Wilton, A. P., & MacCuspie, P. A. (2017). Self-determination. In M. C. Holbrook, C. Kamei-Hannan, T. McCarthy (Eds.), *Foundations of education (3rd ed.): Volume II: Instructional strategies for teaching children and youths with visual impairments* (pp. 875–913). New York, NY: AFB Press.

Chapter 17

Baldwin, L., Omdal, S. N., & Pereles, D. (2015). Beyond stereotypes: Understanding, recognizing, and working with twice-exceptional learners. *TEACHING Exceptional Children, 47,* 216–225.

Betts, G. T., & Carey, R. J. (2010). *Response to intervention and the autonomous learner model: A complete approach to the gifted and talented.* Greeley, CO: ALPS Publishing.

Betts, G., Carey, R., & Kapushion, B. (2016). *Autonomous Learner Model resource book.* Waco, TX: Prufrock Press.

Betts, G., Kapushion, B., & Carey, R. J. (2016). The Autonomous Learner Model: Supporting the development of problem finders, creative problem solvings, and producers of knowledge to successfully navigate the 21st century. D. Ambrose & R. J. Sternberg (Eds.), *Giftedness and talent in the 21st century: Adapting to the turbulence of globalization* (pp. 201–220). Boston, MA: Sense Publishers.

Callahan, C. M., & Hertberg-Davis, H. L. (2017). *Fundamentals of gifted education: Considering multiple perspectives.* New York. NY: Routledge.

Coleman, M. R., & Roberts, J. L. (2015). Defining twice exceptional "2e." *Gifted Child Today, 38,* 204–205.

Firmender, J. M., Reis, S. M., & Sweeny, S. M. (2013). Reading comprehension and fluency levels ranges across diverse classrooms: The need for differentiated reading instruction and content. *Gifted Child Quarterly, 57,* 3–14.

Ford, D. Y. (2014). Segregation and the underrepresentation of blacks and Hispanics in gifted education: Social inequality and deficit paradigms. *Roeper Review, 36,* 143–154.

Ford, D. Y. (2015). Recruiting and retaining Black and Hispanic students in gifted education: Equality versus equity schools. *Gifted Child Today, 38,* 187–191.

Ford, D. Y. & King Jr., R. A. (2014). No blacks allowed: Segregated gifted education in the context of Brown v. Board of Education. *The Journal of Negro Education, 83,* 300–310.

Fultz, M., Lara-Alecio, R., Irby, B. J., & Tong, F. (2013). The Hispanic Bilingual Gifted Screening Instrument: A validation study. *National Forum of Multicultural Issues Journal, 10,* 1–26.

Gardner, H. (1983). *Frames of mind: The theory of multiple intelligences.* New York, NY: Basic Books.

Gardner, H. (2011). *Frames of mind: The theory of multiple intelligences* (3rd ed.). New York, NY: Basic Books.

Garn, A. C., Matthews, M. S., & Jolly, J. L. (2010). Parental influences on the academic motivation of gifted students: A self-determination theory perspective. *Gifted Child Quarterly, 54*(4), 263–272.

Housand, A., Housand, B., & Renzulli, J. (2016). *Using the Schoolwide Enrichment Model with technology.* Waco, TX: Prufrock Press.

Kalbfleisch, M. L., & Gillmarten, C. (2013). Left brain vs. right brain: Findings on visual spatial capacities and the functional neurology of giftedness. *Roeper Review, 35*(4), 265–275.

Kaufman, J. C., Plucker, J. A., & Russell, C. M. (2012). Identifying and assessing creativity as a component of giftedness. *Journal of Psychoeducational Assessment, 30*(1), 60–73.

Kerr, B., & McKay, R. (2013). Searching for tomorrow's innovators: Profiling creative adolescents. *Creativity Research Journal, 25,* 21–32.

Kettler, T., & Bower, J. (2017). Measuring creative capacity in gifted students: Comparing teacher ratings and student products. *Gifted Child Quarterly, 61*, 290–299.

Lee, S. Y., & Olszewski-Kubilius, P. (2012). Leadership development and gifted students. *Encyclopedia of adolescence* (pp. 1557–1565). New York, NY: Springer.

Maker, C. J. (1993). Creativity, intelligence and problem solving: A definition and design for cross-cultural research and measurement related to giftedness. *Gifted Education International, 9*, 68–77.

Maker, C. J., Zimmerman, R., Gomez-Arizaga, M. P., Pease, R., & Burke, E. M. (2015). Developing real-life problem solving: Integrating the DISCOVER problem matrix, problem based learning, and thinking actively in a social context. In H. Vidergor & C. R. Harris (Eds.), *Applied practice for educators of gifted and able learners* (pp. 131–168). New York, NY: Springer.

Matthews, M. S. (2017). Utilizing non-test assessments in identifying gifted and talented learners. In C. M. Callahan & H. L. Hertberg-Davis (Eds.), *Fundamentals in gifted education: Considering multiple perspectives* (pp. 135–146). New York, NY: Routledge.

McClain, M. C., & Pfeiffer, S. (2012). Identification of gifted students in the United States today: A look at state definitions, policies, and practices. *Journal of Applied School Psychology, 28*, 59–88.

Miller, A. L., & Neumeister, K. L. S. (2017). The influence of personality, parenting styles, and perfectionism on performance goal orientation in high ability students. *Journal of Advanced Academics, 28*, 313–344.

National Association for Gifted Children (2015). *State of the states in gifted education: Policy and practice data*. Washington, DC: Author.

Pablico, J., Diack, M., & Lawson, A. (2017). Differentiated instruction in the high school science classroom: Qualitative and quantitative analyses. *International Journal of Learning, Teaching and Educational Research, 16*, 30–54.

Pfeiffer, S. I. (2012). *Serving the gifted: Evidence-based clinical and psychoeducational practice*. New York, NY: Routledge.

Prast, E. J., Weijer-Bergsma, E. V., Kroesbergen, E. H., & Van Luit, J. E. H. (2018). Differentiated instruction in primary mathematics: Effects of teacher professional development on student achievement. *Learning and Instruction, 54*, 22–34.

Renzulli, J. S., & D'Souza, S. (2014). Intelligences outside the normal curve: Co-cognitive factors that contribute to the creation of social capital and leadership skills in young people. In J. A. Plucker & C. M. Callahan (Eds.), *Critical issues and practices in gifted education: What the research says* (2nd ed., pp. 343–362). Waco, TX: Prufrock Press.

Renzulli, J. S., & Reis, S. M. (2010). A technology-based application of the schoolwide enrichment model and high-end learning theory. In L. Shavinina (Ed.), *International handbook on giftedness* (pp. 1203–1224). New York, NY: Springer.

Rimm, S. B., Siegle, D. B., & Davis, G. A. (2017). *Education of the gifted and talented* (7th ed.). Columbus, OH: Pearson.

Ritchotte, J. A., Suhr, D., Alfurayh, N. F., & Graefe, A. K. (2016). An exploration of the psychosocial characteristics of high achieving students and identified gifted students: Implications for practice. *Journal of Advanced Academics, 27*, 23–38.

Robertson, S. G., Pfeiffer, S. I., & Taylor, N. (2011). Serving the gifted: A national survey of school psychologists. *Psychology in the Schools, 48*, 786–799.

Ruthsatz, J., Ruthsatz, K., & Stephens, K. R. (2014). Putting practice into perspective: Child prodigies as evidence of innate talent. *Intelligence, 45*, 60–65.

Sarouphim, K. M. (2009). The use of a performance assessment for identifying gifted Lebanese students: Is DISCOVER effective? *Journal for the Education of the Gifted, 33*(2), 275–295.

Sarouphim, K. M., & Maker, C. J. (2010). Ethnic and gender differences in identifying gifted students: A multi-cultural analysis. *International Education, 39*, 42–56, 76–77.

Singer, F. M., Sheffield, L. J., Freiman, V., & Brandl, M. (2016). *Research on and activities for mathematically gifted students*. New York, NY: Springer.

Smith, B. W., Dempsey, A. G., Jackson, S. E., Olenchak, F. R., & Gaa, J. (2012). Cyberbullying among gifted children. *Gifted Education International, 28*, 112–126.

Smutny, J. F., Walker, S. Y., & Honeck, I. E. (2015). *Teaching gifted children in today's preschool and primary classrooms: Identifying, nurturing, and challenging children ages 4–9*. Minneapolis, MN: Free Spirit Publishing.

Snyder, T. D., de Brey, C., & Dillow, S. A. (2016). *Digest of education statistics 2015* (51st ed.). Washington, DC: National Center for Education Statistics, Institute of Education Sciences, U.S. Department of Education.

Sternberg, R. J., Jarvin, L., & Grigorenko, E. L. (2015). Teaching for wisdom, intelligence, creativity, and success.

Tomlinson, C. A. (2017). *How to differentiate instruction in academically diverse classrooms* (3rd ed.). Alexandria, VA: ASCD.

U.S. Department of Education (2016). *2013–2014 civil rights data collection: A first look*. Washington, DC: U.S. Department of Education, Office for Civil Rights. Accessed on 2-18-18 at https://www2.ed.gov/about/offices/list/ocr/docs/2013-14-first-look.pdf.

Valiandes, S. (2015). Evaluating the impact of differentiated instruction on literacy and reading in mixed ability classrooms: Quality and equity dimensions of education effectiveness. *Studies in Educational Evaluation, 45*, 17–26.

VanTassel-Baska, J. (2000). Theory and research on curriculum development for the gifted. In K. A. Heller, F. J. Monks, R. J. Sternberg, & R. F. Subotnik (Eds.), *International handbook of giftedness and talent* (pp. 345–367). Amsterdam, the Netherlands: Elsevier.

Weeks, M., Wild, T. C., Ploubidis, G. B., Naicker, K., Cairney, J., North, C. R., & Colman, I. (2014). Childhood cognitive ability and its relationship with anxiety and depression. *Journal of Affective Disorders, 152–154*, 139–145.

Yarbrough, N. D. (2016). Assessment of creative thinking across cultures using the Torrence Tests of Creative Thinking (TTCT): Translation and validity issues. *Creativity Research Journal, 28*, 154–164.

Yoon, C. H. (2017). A validation of the Torrence Tests of Creative Thinking with a sample of Korean elementary school students. *Thinking Skills and Creativity, 26*, 38–50.

Name Index

Subject Index